GENDER

IDEAS, INTERACTIONS, INSTITUTIONS

SECOND EDITION

SOCIOLOGY TITLES

from

W. W. NORTON

The Contexts Reader, THIRD EDITION, edited by Syed Ali and Philip N. Cohen

Code of the Street by Elijah Anderson

The Cosmopolitan Canopy by Elijah Anderson

Social Problems, THIRD EDITION, by Joel Best

The Art and Science of Social Research by Deborah Carr, Elizabeth Heger Boyle, Benjamin Cornwell, Shelley Correll, Robert Crosnoe, Jeremy Freese, and Mary C. Waters

The Family: Diversity, Inequality, and Social Change, SECOND EDITION, by Philip N. Cohen

You May Ask Yourself: An Introduction to Thinking like a Sociologist, FIFTH EDITION, by Dalton Conley

Race in America by Matthew Desmond and Mustafa Emirbayer

The Real World: An Introduction to Sociology, SIXTH EDITION, by Kerry Ferris and Jill Stein

Essentials of Sociology, SEVENTH EDITION, by Anthony Giddens, Mitchell Duneier, Richard P. Appelbaum, and Deborah Carr

Introduction to Sociology, ELEVENTH EDITION, by Anthony Giddens, Mitchell Duneier, Richard P. Appelbaum, and Deborah Carr

Mix It Up: Popular Culture, Mass Media, and Society, SECOND EDITION, by David Grazian

Give Methods a Chance by Kyle Green and Sarah Esther Lageson

Readings for Sociology, EIGHTH EDITION, edited by Garth Massey

Families as They Really Are, SECOND EDITION, edited by Barbara J. Risman and Virginia E. Rutter

Uneasy Peace: The Great Crime Decline, the Renewal of City Life, and the Next War on Violence by Patrick Sharkey

Sex Matters: The Sexuality and Society Reader, FIFTH EDITION, edited by Mindy Stombler, Dawn M. Baunach, Wendy O. Simonds, Elroi J. Windsor, and Elisabeth O. Burgess

American Hookup: The New Culture of Sex on Campus by Lisa Wade

Cultural Sociology: An Introductory Reader edited by Matt Wray

American Society: How It Really Works, SECOND EDITION, by Erik Olin Wright and Joel Rogers

To learn more about Norton Sociology, please visit wwnorton.com/soc

GENDER

SECOND EDITION

LISA WADE

Occidental College

MYRA MARX FERREE

University of Wisconsin–Madison

W. W. NORTON & COMPANY, INC.

New York · London

W. W. Norton & Company has been independent since its founding in 1923, when William Warder Norton and Mary D. Herter Norton first published lectures delivered at the People's Institute, the adult education division of New York City's Cooper Union. The firm soon expanded its program beyond the Institute, publishing books by celebrated academics from America and abroad. By midcentury, the two major pillars of Norton's publishing program—trade books and college texts—were firmly established. In the 1950s, the Norton family transferred control of the company to its employees, and today—with a staff of four hundred and a comparable number of trade, college, and professional titles published each year—W. W. Norton & Company stands as the largest and oldest publishing house owned wholly by its employees.

Editor: Sasha Levitt
Assistant Editor: Erika Nakagawa
Project Editors: Taylere Peterson and Diane Cipollone
Managing Editor, College: Marian Johnson
Managing Editor, College Digital Media: Kim Yi
Senior Production Manager: Ashley Horna
Media Editor: Eileen Connell
Associate Media Editor: Ariel Eaton
Media Editorial Assistant: Samuel Tang
Marketing Director, Sociology: Julia Hall
Design Director: Jillian Burr
Director of College Permissions: Megan Schindel
Permissions Specialist: Bethany Salminen
Photo Editor: Travis Carr
Composition: Achorn International, Inc.
Manufacturing: Maple Press

Permission to use copyrighted material is included in the Credits, which begins on page 485.

Library of Congress Cataloging-in-Publication Data

Names: Wade, Lisa (Professor), author. | Ferree, Myra Marx, author.
Title: Gender / Lisa Wade, Occidental College, Myra Marx Ferree, University of Wisconsin, Madison.
Description: Second Edition. | New York : W. W. Norton & Company, [2018] | Revised edition of the authors' Gender : ideas, interactions, institutions, [2015] | Includes bibliographical references and index.
Identifiers: LCCN 2018039801 | ISBN 9780393667967 (pbk.)
Subjects: LCSH: Sex role. | Sex differences. | Feminist theory.
Classification: LCC HQ1075 .W33 2018 | DDC 305.3—dc23 LC record available at https://lccn .loc.gov/2018039801

ISBN: 978-0-393-66796-7 (pbk.)

W. W. Norton & Company, Inc., 500 Fifth Avenue, New York, N.Y. 10110
www.wwnorton.com
W. W. Norton & Company Ltd., 15 Carlisle Street, London W1D 3BS
    4 5 6 7 8 9 0

ABOUT THE AUTHORS

LISA WADE is an associate professor of sociology at Occidental College in Los Angeles, where she does research at the intersection of gender, sexuality, culture, and the body. She earned an MA in human sexuality from New York University and an MS and PhD in sociology from the University of Wisconsin–Madison. She is the author of over three dozen research papers, book chapters, and educational essays. Her newest book, *American Hookup: The New Culture of Sex on Campus*, is the definitive account of contemporary collegiate sexual culture. Aiming to reach audiences outside of academia, Dr. Wade appears frequently in print, radio, and television news and opinion outlets. You can learn more about her at lisa-wade.com or follow her on Twitter (@lisawade) or Facebook (/lisawadephd).

MYRA MARX FERREE is the Alice H. Cook Professor of Sociology at the University of Wisconsin–Madison. She is the author of *Varieties of Feminism: German Gender Politics in Global Perspective* (2012), co-author of *Shaping Abortion Discourse* (2002) and *Controversy and Coalition* (2000), and co-editor of *Gender, Violence and Human Security* (2013), *Global Feminism* (2006), and *Revisioning Gender* (1998) as well as numerous articles and book chapters. Dr. Ferree is the recipient of various prizes for contributions to gender studies, including the Jessie Bernard Award and Victoria Schuck Award. She continues to do research on global gender politics.

CONTENTS

PREFACE

Writing a textbook is a challenge even for folks with lots of teaching experience in the subject matter. We would never have dared take on this project without Karl Bakeman's initial encouragement. His confidence in our vision was inspiring and kept us going until the project could be placed into the very capable hands of Sasha Levitt, who ushered the first edition to completion with her meticulous reading, thoughtful suggestions, and words of encouragement. Sasha has since become an invaluable part of the revision process, with a perfect mix of stewardship, cheerleading, and collaborative fact-checking. She has kept us on target conceptually as well as chronologically, challenged us to think hard about the points that first-edition readers had raised, and yet kept the revision process smoothly moving forward to meet our deadlines. Without her firm hand on the tiller, our occasional excursions into the weeds might have swamped the revision with unnecessary changes, but her attention to updating sources kept us cheerful with the new evidence we landed. The revision might have ballooned with the new material we identified, but her editorial eye has kept us in our word limits without sacrificing anything important. Sasha has become a true partner in the difficult process of adding the new without losing the old, and we could not have pulled it off without her.

Of course, Karl and Sasha are but the top of the mountain of support that Norton has offered from beginning to end. The many hands behind the scenes include project editor Diane Cipollone for keeping us on schedule and collating our changes, production manager Ashley Horna for turning a manuscript into the pages you hold now, assistant editors Erika Nakagawa and Thea Goodrich for their logistical help in preparing that manuscript, designer Jillian Burr for her keen graphic eye, and our copyeditor, Katharine Ings, for crossing our t's and dotting our i's. The many images that enrich this book are thanks to photo editors Travis Carr and Stephanie Romeo and photo researchers Elyse Rieder and Rona Tuccillo. We are also grateful to have discovered Leland Bobbé, the artist whose half-drag portraits fascinated us. Selecting just one for the first edition was a collaborative process aided by the further creative work of Jillian Burr and Debra Morton Hoyt. Selecting a second was equally exciting and challenging. We're grateful for the result: striking covers that we hope catch the eye and spark conversation.

We would also like to thank the reviewers who commented on drafts of the book and its revision in various stages: Rachel Allison, Shayna Asher-Shapiro, Phyllis L. Baker, Kristen Barber, Miriam Barcus, Shira Barlas, Sarah Becker, Dana Berkowitz, Emily Birnbaum, Natalie Boero, Catherine Bolzendahl, Valerie Chepp, Nancy Dess, Lisa Dilks, Mischa DiBattiste, Erica Dixon, Mary Donaghy, Julia Eriksen, Angela Frederick, Jessica Greenebaum, Nona Gronert, Lee Harrington, Sarah Hayford, Penelope Herideen, Melanie Hughes, Miho Iwata, Rachel Kaplan, Madeline Kiefer, Rachel Kraus, Carrie Lacy, Thomas J. Linneman, Caitlin Maher, Gul Aldikacti Marshall, Janice McCabe, Karyn McKinney, Carly Mee, Beth Mintz, Joya Misra, Beth Montemurro, Christine Mowery, Stephanie Nawyn, Madeleine Pape, Lisa Pellerin, Megan Reid, Gwen Sharp, Mimi Schippers, Emily Fitzgibbons Shafer, Kazuko Suzuki, Jaita Talukdar, Rachel Terman, Mieke Beth Thomeer, Kristen Williams, and Kersti Alice Yllo, as well as the students at Babson College, Occidental College, Nevada State College, and the University of Wisconsin-Madison who agreed to be test subjects. Our gratitude goes also to the users of the first edition who offered us valuable feedback on what they enjoyed and what they found missing, either directly or through Norton. We've tried to take up their suggestions by not merely squeezing in occasional new material but by rethinking the perspectives and priorities that might have left such concerns on the cutting room floor the first time around. We hope the balance we have struck is satisfying but are always open to further criticism and suggestions.

Most of all, we are happy to discover that we could collaborate in being creative over the long term of this project, contributing different talents at different times, and jumping the inevitable hurdles without tripping each other up. In fact, we were each other's toughest critic and warmest supporter. Once upon a time, Lisa was Myra's student, but in finding ways to communicate our interest and enthusiasm to students, we became a team. In the course of the revision, we came to appreciate each other's strengths more than ever and rejoice in the collegial relationship we had in making the revision happen. We hope you enjoy reading this book as much as we enjoyed making it.

Lisa Wade
Myra Marx Ferree

GENDER

IDEAS, INTERACTIONS, INSTITUTIONS

SECOND EDITION

A MAN IN HEELS IS RIDICULOUS.

—CHRISTIAN LOUBOUTIN

Introduction

Among the most vicious and effective killers who have ever lived were the men of the Persian army. In the late 1500s, under the reign of Abbas I, these soldiers defeated the Uzbeks and the Ottomans and reconquered provinces lost to India and Portugal, earning the admiration of all of Europe. Their most lethal advantage was the high heel.[1] Being on horseback, heels kept their feet in the stirrups when they rose up to shoot their muskets. It gave them deadly aim. The first high-heeled shoe, it turns out, was a weapon of war.

Enthralled by the military men's prowess, European male aristocrats began wearing high heels in their daily lives of leisure, using the shoe to borrow some of the Persian army's masculine mystique. In a way, they were like today's basketball fans wearing Air Jordans. The aristocrats weren't any better on the battlefield than your average Bulls fan is on the court, but the shoes symbolically linked them to the soldiers' extraordinary achievements. The shoes invoked a distinctly *manly* power related to victory in battle, just as the basketball shoes link the contemporary wearer to Michael Jordan's amazing athleticism.

As with most fashions, there was trickle down. Soon men of all classes were donning high heels, stumbling around the cobblestone streets of Europe feeling pretty suave. And then women decided

Shah Abbas I, who ruled Persia between 1588 and 1629, shows off not only his scimitar, but also his high heels.

they wanted a piece of the action, too. In the 1630s, masculine fashions were "in" for ladies. They cut their hair, added military decorations to the shoulders of their dresses, and smoked pipes. For women, high heels were nothing short of masculine mimicry.

These early fashionistas irked the aristocrats who first borrowed the style. The whole point of nobility, after all, was to be *above* everyone else. In response, the elites started wearing higher and higher heels. France's King Louis XIV even decreed that no one was allowed to wear heels higher than his.[2] In the New World, the Massachusetts colony passed a law saying that any woman caught wearing heels would incur the same penalty as a witch.[3]

But the masses persisted. And so the aristocrats shifted strategies: They dropped high heels altogether. It was the Enlightenment now, and there was an accompanying shift toward logic and reason. Adopting the philosophy that it was intelligence—not heel height—that bestowed superiority, aristocrats donned flats and began mocking people who wore high heels, suggesting that wearing such impractical shoes was the height of stupidity.

Ever since, the shoe has remained mostly out of fashion for men—cowboys excluded, of course, and disco notwithstanding—but it's continued to tweak the toes of women in every possible situation, from weddings to the workplace. No longer at risk of being burned at the stake, women are allowed to wear high heels, now fully associated with femaleness in the American imagination. Some women even feel pressure to do so, particularly if they are trying to look pretty or professional. And there remains the sense that the right pair brings a touch of class.

The attempts by aristocrats to keep high heels to themselves are part of a phenomenon that sociologists call **distinction**, a word used to describe efforts to distinguish one's own group from others. In this historical example, we see elite men working hard to make a simultaneously class- and gender-based distinction. If the aristocrats had had their way, only rich men would have ever worn high heels. Today high heels continue to serve as a marker of gender distinction. With few exceptions, only women (and people impersonating women) wear high heels.

Distinction is a main theme of this book. The word *gender* only exists because we distinguish between people in this particular way. If we didn't care about distinguishing men from women, the whole concept would be utterly unnecessary. We don't, after all, tend to have words for physical differences that don't have meaning to us. For example, we don't make a big deal out of the fact that some people have the gene that allows them to curl their tongue and some people don't. There's no concept of *tongue aptitude* that refers to the separation of people into the curly tongued and the flat tongued. Why would we need such a thing? The vast majority of us just don't care. Likewise, the ability to focus one's eyes on a close or distant object isn't used to signify status and being right-handed is no longer considered better than being left-handed.

Gender, then, is about distinction. Like tongue aptitude, vision, and handedness, it is a biological reality. We are a species that reproduces sexually. We come, roughly, in two body types: a female one built to gestate new life and a male one made to mix up the genes of the species. The word **sex** is used to refer to these physical differences in primary sexual characteristics (the presence of organs directly involved in reproduction) and secondary sexual characteristics (such as patterns of hair growth, the amount of breast tissue, and distribution of body fat). We usually use the words

Louis XIV, king of France from 1643 to 1715, gives himself a boost with big hair and high heels.

male and **female** to refer to sex, but we can also use **male-bodied** and **female-bodied** to specify that sex refers to the body and may not extend to how a person feels or acts. And, as we'll see, not every body fits neatly into one category or the other.

Unlike tongue aptitude, vision, and handedness, we make the biology of sex socially significant. When we differentiate between men and women, for example, we also invoke blue and pink baby blankets, suits and dresses, *Maxim* and *Cosmopolitan* magazines, and action movies and chick flicks. These are all examples of the world divided up into the **masculine** and the **feminine**, into things we associate with men and women. The word **gender** refers to the symbolism of masculinity and femininity that we connect to being male-bodied or female-bodied.

Symbols matter because they indicate what bodily differences mean in practice. They force us to try to fit our bodies into constraints that "pinch" both physically and symbolically, as high heels do. They prompt us to invent

One of these people is not like the others. We perform gendered distinctions like the one shown here every day, often simply out of habit.

ways around bodily limitations, as eyeglasses do. They are part of our collective imaginations and, accordingly, the stuff out of which we create human reality. Gender symbolism shapes not just our identities and the ideas in our heads, but workplaces, families, and schools, and our options for navigating through them.

This is where distinction comes in. Much of what we believe about men and women—even much of what we imagine is strictly biological—is not naturally occurring difference that emerges from our male and female bodies. Instead, it's an outcome of active efforts to produce and maintain difference: a sea of people working together every day to make men masculine and women feminine, and signify the relative importance of masculinity and femininity in every domain.

Commonly held ideas, and the behaviors that both uphold and challenge them, are part of **culture**: a group's shared beliefs and the practices and material things that reflect them. Human lives are wrapped in this cultural meaning, like the powerful masculinity once ascribed to high heels. So gender isn't merely biological; it's cultural. It's the result of a great deal of human effort guided by shared cultural ideas.

Why would people put so much effort into maintaining this illusion of distinction?

Imagine those aristocratic tantrums: pampered, wig-wearing, face-powdered men stomping their high-heeled feet in frustration with the lowly copycats. *How dare the masses blur the line between us*, they may have cried. Today it might sound silly, ridiculous even, to care about who does and doesn't wear high heels. But at the time it was a very serious matter. Successful efforts at distinction ensured that these elite men really *seemed* different and, more importantly, *better than* women and other types of men. This was at the very core of the aristocracy: the idea that some people truly are superior and, by virtue of their superiority, entitled to hoard wealth and monopolize power. They had no superpowers with which to claim superiority, no actual proof that God wanted things that way, no biological trait that gave them an obvious advantage. What *did* they have to distinguish themselves? They had high heels.

Without high heels, or other symbols of superiority, aristocrats couldn't make a claim to the right to rule. Without difference, in other words, there could be no hierarchy. This is still true today. If one wants to argue that Group A is superior to Group B, there must be distinguishable groups. We can't think more highly of one type of person than another unless we have at least two types. Distinction, then, must be maintained if we are going to value certain types of people more than others, allowing them to demand more power, attract more prestige, and claim the right to extreme wealth.

Wealth and power continue to be hoarded and monopolized. These inequalities continue to be justified—made to seem normal and natural—by producing differences that make group membership seem meaningful and inequality inevitable or right. We all engage in actions designed to align ourselves with some people and differentiate ourselves from others. Thus we see the persistence of social classes, racial and ethnic categories, the urban-rural divide, gay and straight identities, liberal and conservative parties, and various Christian and Muslim sects, among other distinctions. These categories aren't all bad; they give us a sense of belonging and bring joy and pleasure into our lives. But they also serve as classifications by which societies unevenly distribute power and privilege.

Gender is no different in this regard. There is a story to tell about both difference and hierarchy and it involves both pleasure and pain. We'll wait a bit before we seriously tackle the problem of gender inequality, spending several chapters learning just how enjoyable studying gender can be. There'll be funny parts and fascinating parts. You'll meet figure skaters and football players, fish and flight attendants and, yes, feminists, too. Eventually we'll get to the part that makes you want to throw the book across the room. We won't take it personally. For now, let's pick up right where we started, with distinction.

Ideas

Most of us use the phrase "opposite sexes" when describing the categories of male and female. It's a telling phrase. There are other ways to express this relationship. It was once common, for example, to use the phrase "the fairer sex" or "the second sex" to describe women. We could simply say "the *other* sex," a more neutral phrase. Or, even, "*an* other sex," which leaves open the possibility of more than two. Today, though, people usually describe men and women as *opposites*.

Seventeenth-century Europeans—the same ones fighting over high heels—didn't believe in "opposite" sexes; they didn't even believe in *two* sexes.[2] They believed men and women were better and worse versions of the same sex, with identical reproductive organs that were just arranged differently: Men's genitals were pushed out of the body, while women's remained inside. As Figure 2.1 shows, they saw the vagina as simply a penis that hadn't emerged from the body; the womb as a scrotum in the belly; the ovaries just internal testes. As the lyrics to one early song put it: "Women are but men turned outside in."[3]

Seventeenth-century anatomists were wrong, of course. We're not the same sex. The uterus and fallopian tubes of the female body come from an embryonic structure that is dissolved during male fetal development. Conversely, men's internal sexual and

FIGURE 2.1 | 17TH CENTURY ILLUSTRATION OF THE VAGINA AND UTERUS

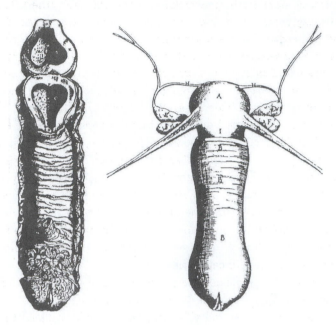

This anatomical illustration from 1611 of the interior of a vagina (left) and the exterior of a vagina and uterus (right) shows the Renaissance idea of female genitalia—an internal phallus.

reproductive plumbing has no corollary inside most women. The penis is not a protruding vagina, nor the vagina a shy penis.

But the idea that we are opposite sexes is not completely right either. The penis and scrotum *do* have something in common with female anatomy. The same tissue that becomes the scrotum in males becomes the outer labia in females; the penis and the clitoris are formed of the same erectile tissue and clustered nerve endings; and testes and ovaries are both gonads that make germ cells (sperm and eggs), one just a modified version of the other. If you're curious what it feels like to have the genitals of the other sex—and who hasn't wondered?—the truth is you probably already have a pretty good idea just by having genitals yourself. Our bodies are all human, developing from the same blob of tissue, modified to enable sexual reproduction. So while it's not perfectly correct to say there's only one sex, neither is it perfectly correct to say we're opposites.

Nevertheless, *opposite* is the word we use, and it has strong implications: that whatever one sex is, the other simply is not. Today most people in most Western countries are familiar with this idea, referred to in sociology as the gender binary. The word *binary* refers to a system with two and only two separate and distinct parts, like binary code (the 1s and 0s used in computing) or a binary star system (in which two stars orbit each other). So the term **gender binary** refers to the idea that there are only two types of people—male-bodied people who are masculine and female-bodied people who are feminine—and those types are fundamentally different and contrasting.

Because we tend to think in terms of a gender binary, we routinely speak about men as if they're all the same and likewise for women. The nervous parent might warn his thirteen-year-old daughter, for example, "boys only want one thing," while the Valentine's Day commercial insists all women love chocolate. In fact, most of us embrace gender categories in daily life and talk about "men" and "women" as if membership in one of these categories says a great deal about a person. We might say "I'm such a girl!" when we confess we're addicted to strawberry lip balm, or repeat the refrain "boys will be boys" when observing the antics of a young male cousin. If we're feeling hurt, we might even comfort ourselves by saying "all men suck" or "women are crazy." All these phrases rely on the idea that the terms *men* and *women* refer to meaningful categories.

We often talk this way but, when push comes to shove, we'll admit that we don't necessarily believe in such rigid gender stereotypes, especially when they're applied to us. When asked, most people will say they sort of do . . . and sort of don't . . . conform to the relevant stereotype. Maybe we're a woman who adores romantic comedies but is also first in line for the next superhero movie. Or maybe we're a man who enjoys a hot bath after a rugby game. This sort of mixing and matching of interests is typical. Accordingly, a large number of us don't believe we, *personally*, conform to a stereotype. And, in fact, when we stop and think about it, many and perhaps most of the people we know well don't fit into the stereotypes either. This leads us to the first of many probing questions we will attempt to answer throughout this book:

> **Q+A** **If we don't learn the idea of the gender binary by observing the people around us, where does the idea come from?**

This chapter will show that people who grow up in most contemporary Western societies learn to use a set of beliefs about gender as a scaffold for understanding the world. If we are well socialized, we will put people and things into masculine and feminine categories and subcategories out of habit and largely without thinking. We apply the binary to human bodies, believing men and women to have different and nonoverlapping anatomies and physiologies. We also apply it to objects, places, activities, talents, and ideas.

We become so skilled at layering ideas about gender onto the world that we have a hard time seeing it for what it really is. We don't notice when gender stereotypes don't make sense. Even more, we tend to see and remember things consistent with gender stereotypes, while forgetting or misremembering things inconsistent with those stereotypes. In other words, gender is a logic that we are talented at manipulating, but it is manipulating us, too.

Don't feel bad about it. Essentially all societies notice and interpret sex-related differences in our bodies, so we are no different in that sense. In fact, we'll explore some of the other ways that people have thought about gender in a later section. Before we do, though, let's take a closer look at our own unusual ideas about gender—the gender binary—and review the biology of sex.

THE BINARY AND OUR BODIES

At thirteen years old, Georgiann Davis's parents brought her to the doctor with abdominal pain.[4] After extensive examination and testing, she was told she had "underdeveloped ovaries" with a high chance of becoming cancerous. Her parents consented to surgery to remove them. Six years later she requested her medical records in the routine process of acquiring a new doctor, only to learn she'd never had ovaries at all. The doctors had lied: In fact, she'd had testes.

Georgiann was diagnosed with what physicians now call androgen insensitivity syndrome.[5] At fertilization, a Y sperm combined with an X egg, putting her on the biological path to becoming male. But her cells lacked the ability to detect the hormones that typically masculinize a body. So, even though she had XY chromosomes and testes that produced testosterone and other androgens, her testes remained in her abdomen as if they were ovaries, and the development of her external genitalia followed the female body plan.

People with androgen insensitivity syndrome are **intersex**, born with a reproductive or sexual anatomy that doesn't fit the typical definitions of female or male. People who are intersex remind us that while we tend to take for granted that everyone is unambiguously male or female, the path to such a straightforward body involves many complicated steps. Step one is conception. If a sperm with an X chromosome meets an egg, the fertilization kicks off the development of a female; if the sperm contains a Y chromosome, it kicks off the development of a male. Since all eggs have an X chromosome, men typically have an XY chromosomal profile and women have an XX. This, however, is just the beginning of a complex process involving at least eight steps, as shown in Table 2.1.

If the fertilized egg is XY, we should expect to see the development of testes. Setting this process in motion involves not just a Y chromosome but also several genes on the X chromosome and dozens of other genes located on yet other chro-

TABLE 2.1 | STEPS TOWARD BECOMING A "MAN" OR A "WOMAN" IN THE UNITED STATES

Step	Male Path	Female Path
chromosomes	XY	XX
gonads	testes	ovaries
hormones	androgens/estrogens	estrogens/androgens
external genitalia	penis, scrotum	clitoris, labia
internal genitalia	seminal vesicles, prostate, epididymis, vas deferens	vagina, uterus, fallopian tubes
secondary sex characteristics	pubic hair, deep voice, Adam's apple	pubic hair, breasts, menstruation
gender identity	male-identified	female-identified
gender expression	masculine	feminine

mosomes.[6] If this situation occurs and the testes begin making their particular cocktail of androgens and estrogens, then internal and external genitalia typical of males will develop. At puberty, the boy will grow pubic hair in a different pattern than his female counterparts and experience a deepening of his voice. He will probably have less breast tissue than the average female-bodied person.

Without the intervention of a Y chromosome, a fertilized egg will follow a female development path. The fetus will develop ovaries and internal and external genitalia typical of females. At puberty, the brain will instruct the ovaries to produce a different cocktail of androgens and estrogens that stimulate feminine patterns of body fat, an upside-down triangle of pubic hair, breasts, and a menstrual cycle.

Becoming a "man" or "woman" in the United States today, though, involves more than just physical development. It is considered normal for a male-bodied person, for example, to identify as male, feel good about one's identity as a man, and behave in masculine ways. This is his **gender identity**, a sense of oneself as male or female. Most of us also learn to communicate our gender identity through our appearance, dress, and behavior. This is our **gender expression**.

Most of us assume that one's body, gender identity, and gender expression will all line up but, as Georgiann's case illustrates, sometimes they don't. Dozens of conditions can result in a body that isn't clearly male or female, or one that doesn't match the identity or expression of the person who inhabits it. In fact, it is estimated that at least one out of every hundred people is intersex and more than one in ten report feeling as masculine as they do feminine, or more gender atypical than typical.[7]

The 10 Percent

People with intersex bodies are living proof that not everyone fits into a gender binary that allows only for opposite sexes. We all almost certainly know at least one intersex person—and we likely don't know who they are. Like Georgiann, sometimes even the people with the intersex condition don't know they are intersex. While some people are diagnosed as intersex at birth, other times it's discovered later in life; sometimes a person never learns of it at all.

Some intersex conditions are chromosomal. While most humans have XX or XY sex chromosomes, others are XXY, XXXY, XXX, XYY, or X. These conditions are caused by an anomaly in the cell division with which our bodies make egg and sperm. Sometimes sex chromosomes "stick" to each other and resist dividing with the rest of our chromosomes. Through this process, a person can make a sperm or egg with no chromosomes or two chromosomes instead of just one. In other cases, variations in development can produce male-bodied individuals with XX chromosomes (in which a gene on the Y chromosome critical for the development of testes has crossed over onto an X) and female-bodied individuals with XY chromosomes (in which that same gene was damaged or deleted).

A person can carry XXY chromosomes, for example, if a sperm carrying an X and a Y merges with an egg with an X.[8] A person born with three X chromosomes (after an XX egg merges with an X sperm) has what is called triple X syndrome.[9] Some women are born with only one chromosome, which occurs when an X egg or sperm merges with an egg or sperm without a sex chromosome.[10] Because the Y chromosome has so few genes, men can't be born with only a Y; an X is essential to life.

With the exception of being born with a lone Y, none of these conditions is fatal and both children and adults with these conditions tend to blend in with XY and XX people relatively easily. Most have gender identities that match the appearance of their perceived sex. Most XXX women will never even know they have a chromosomal condition at all because they typically don't exhibit any symptoms (other than being slightly tall). People with XXY chromosomes are often especially tall and have broader hips and less body hair than men who are XY. Women with only one X are somewhat more recognizable; they tend to be a bit short and have distinctive features. People with these chromosomal conditions are sometimes (but not always) infertile and sometimes (but don't always) face specific health problems.

Intersex conditions can also be caused by hormones. Sometimes a fetus has a hyperactive adrenal gland that produces masculinizing hormones. If the fetus is XX, then the baby will be born with an enlarged clitoris that resembles a small-to-medium-sized penis. Most babies born with this condition identify as female when they grow older and are perfectly healthy, as it is not a medical problem to have a slightly large clitoris. Georgiann's condition is also a hormone-based departure from the path to unambiguous male and female bodies; it is caused by an inability of cells to recognize androgens released by the testes both before and after birth. All of these outcomes occur in nature and reflect varieties of human development.

The gender binary, however, leaves no room for variety, so sometimes intersex children still undergo surgery in order to bring their bodies into line with social expectations, even when surgery is medically unnecessary.[11] Upon adulthood, many of these children have questioned the necessity of these procedures, noting the pain and suffering that accompanies any surgery, the frequent loss of physical function, the inability of infants or small children to give consent, and the mis-assignment of children to the "wrong" side of the binary. The work of intersex activists—those who, like Georgiann, have been trying to draw attention to the problems with medically unnecessary surgery before the age of consent—has influenced many doctors to delay surgery until people with intersex bodies can make informed decisions, but surgeries on infants have not ended. Discomfort with bodies that deviate from the gender binary continues to motivate some physicians and parents to choose medically unnecessary surgery for infants and children.

Another example of a group whose gender markers sometimes don't conform to the gender binary are, in many parts of the Western world today, called **transgender**. Also referred to simply as *trans*, the term refers to a diverse group of people who experience some form of **gender dysphoria**, a discomfort with the relationship between their bodies' assigned sex and their gender identity, or otherwise reject the gender binary.

In the United States, trans-identified people have recently gained much greater visibility. Laverne Cox, for example, star of the television show *Orange Is the New Black*, appeared on the cover of *Time* magazine and was named Woman of the Year by *Glamour* magazine in 2014. Olympic decathlon gold medalist Caitlyn Jenner announced her transition on the cover of *Vanity Fair* in 2015. Jazz Jennings, a transgender teenager, was given a reality show on TLC that same year. And in 2017, Danica Roem became the first openly trans person elected to a state legislature; she defeated the incumbent, a man who had introduced a bill that would have restricted trans rights.

The term *trans* includes people who undergo a full surgical transition, but also people who do not.

Danica Roem is a singer in a death metal band and the first openly trans person to be elected and serve in a U.S. state legislature.

Thomas Beatie was female-bodied at birth but chose to live his adult life as a man. Because he opted not to undergo a hysterectomy, he was able to give birth to three children.

Some want nothing more than to be as male or female as possible. To this end, some trans people take hormones to masculinize or feminize their bodies, have gender-confirmation surgeries to remake their bodies into ones with which they feel more comfortable, and live as the other sex. Others do only some or none of these things. Thomas Beatie, for example, made headlines when he became pregnant with the first of what would be three children. Thomas was born female but began to identify as a boy during childhood. He underwent some surgical transformation at age twenty-three but chose not to undergo a hysterectomy, preserving his ability to get pregnant and bear children.

Some trans people, then, identify as men or women, others identify as trans men or trans women, and still others identify as **nonbinary**, outside of or between the binary between male and female (also described as **genderqueer**). This includes people who identify as **gender fluid**, without a fixed gender identity. In light of these new terms, the word **cisgender** is increasingly used to refer to male- and female-bodied people who comfortably identify and express themselves as men and women, respectively.

While some trans, genderqueer, gender-fluid, and nonbinary people prefer to be referred to by the pronouns he/him and she/her, others prefer gender-neutral pronouns like the singular they/them or an alternative gender-neutral singular like ze/zir. Sometimes people choose a gender identity and stick with it; other times they evolve. Increasingly, social organizations are responding to these preferences. Facebook now offers dozens of gender-identity labels as well as a freeform field. It also allows people to choose up to ten identities and decide which friends see which, allowing users to control how they present themselves to different audiences. Dating sites, including Grindr, Tinder, and OkCupid, now allow people to identify as nonbinary. Nods to nonbinary identities, gender fluidity, and simple nonconformity are happening throughout American society. The makeup company CoverGirl, for example, hired James Charles to be its first male-identified ambassador and Calvin Klein released a fragrance it describes as "gender free."

A brand's willingness to hire James Charles—CoverGirl's first CoverBoy—indicates growing support of genderqueer performances.

These new ideas, shifting policies, and corporate decisions are increasingly inclusive of the estimated 10 percent (or more) of the human population who don't—or don't want to—fit into a rigid gender binary. And it's becoming clearer, as we learn more about both biology and identity, that there is no obvious way we could place them into the binary anyway. How would we decide where people with intersex bodies go? To qualify as male or female, does a person's body have to match *every* gender criterion, from chromosomes to hormones to genitals to identity? If so, what do we call the estimated 76 million people on earth who can't claim a "perfectly" male or "perfectly" female body? Would it be better to pick just one criterion as *the* determinant of sex? Which one? Should genitals trump chromosomes? Or are chromosomes more "fundamental"?

Moreover, who cares? If bodies function but don't fit into the gender binary, is that a problem? Who gets to decide? And where do we draw the line? How many millimeters separate a child with a small penis at birth and a child diagnosed as intersex? And if someone's body *does* fit all the criteria but their identity and expression diverge, why not give them tools that allow them to better fit their bodies to their gender identity, just as we provide eyeglasses or allow surgery for people with limited vision? How much body manipulation is "good" and how much is "bad"? And who gets to decide what to demand or allow?

Questions abound. And the truth is, we can't answer them satisfactorily. We can't because we're trying to impose a false binary on reality. Human bodies just don't come in the neat packages a gender binary assumes. Not even, in fact, when we consider the 90 percent of the population who seem like they do.

The Other 90 Percent

Remember, the gender binary doesn't just allow for only two sexes, it also makes the much stronger claim that we are "opposite sexes." The idea of "oppositeness" makes blurring the boundaries between masculinity and femininity "queer" and encourages cisgender men and women to maximize apparent difference in their gender expression, making the gender binary appear more real than it is. This is necessary because male and female bodies are not in a biological binary at all. They are far more alike than different. Even for physical characteristics on which there is a clear gender difference, we see a great deal of overlap.

Height is a great example. The average man is five and a half inches taller than the average woman.[12] So men are taller than women, right? Well, not really. The *average* man is taller than the *average* woman, but because both men and women come in a range of heights, some women are taller than many men, and many men are taller than some women. This is not a *binary* difference, one that posits that all men are taller than all women; it's an *average* difference, a measure of tendency, not absolutes (Figure 2.2).

We see this type of overlap in all sex-related traits. There are hairy women and men who can't grow a mustache; men with breasts and women with flat chests;

FIGURE 2.2 | THE RANGE AND OVERLAP IN HEIGHT AMONG AMERICAN MEN AND WOMEN

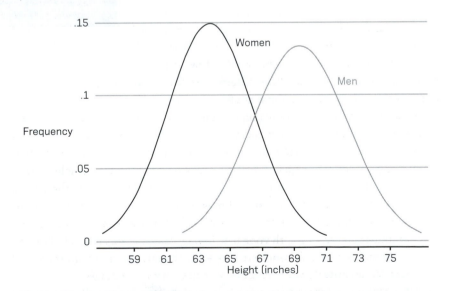

Source: Cheryl D. Fryar, Qiuping Gu, and Cynthia L. Ogden, "Anthropometric reference data for children and adults: United States, 2007–2010," National Center for Health Statistics, *Vital and Health Statistics* 1, no. 252 (October 2012).

women with strong bodies and broad shoulders and slender men who lift weights with little result. Even our reproductive abilities aren't perfectly binary. There are women who can't bear children, including all women who live past menopause. The truth is that our physical traits—height, hairiness, shape, strength, agility, flexibility, and bone structure—overlap far more than they diverge and vary widely over the course of our lives.

We *believe* in a gender binary, though, so the vast majority of cisgender people work hard to try to minimize this overlap, pressing our bodies into ideal male or female shapes. This is true even of the people we consider to be the most naturally perfect. Supermodel Adriana Lima, for example, once revealed the incredible routine she uses to prepare her body for the Victoria's Secret catwalk.[13] Already genetically blessed with a culturally ideal female body, she nonetheless has to train, restrict, and prepare. For months before the show she works out every day with a personal trainer. For the three weeks before, she works out twice a day. A nutritionist gives her protein shakes, vitamins, and supplements to help her body cope with the workout schedule. She drinks a gallon of water a day. For the final nine days before the show, she consumes only protein shakes. Two days before the show, she begins drinking water at a normal rate; for the final twelve hours, she drinks no water at all.

Victoria's Secret model Adriana Lima struts her stuff on the runway, displaying a body bestowed to her by nature and painstakingly sculpted by personal trainers and dietitians.

While this is an extreme example, consider how much time, energy, and money nonsupermodels spend trying to get their bodies to conform to our beliefs about gender. Women choose to eat salad, for example, when they'd rather have a burger and fries, while men are encouraged to make a spectacle of overeating. Gyms are effectively gender segregated, with most men at the weight machines trying to build muscles and most women on the exercise machines trying to lose weight. Women try to tone their bodies by building lean but not overly noticeable muscles with yoga and Pilates; men drink protein shakes and try to bulk up. Gender differences in size and strength aren't very pronounced naturally, but we sure do work hard to make them appear that way.

Similarly, many women take pains to keep their faces, legs, and armpits free of hair if there is any chance of it being spotted, sometimes shaving their entire pubic area, too. Men's body hair, in contrast, is seen as naturally masculine; they have the option to let it all hang out. By shaving, women preserve the binary idea that women don't have body hair and men do.

We gender the hair on our heads, too. Long hair and certain short styles signify femininity. Cropped hair is more masculine. Women bleach their hair blonde, sometimes platinum blonde, a hair color that is natural almost exclusively to children. Men almost never choose this color. When women go gray, they often cover it for fear of looking old. On men, in contrast, gray hair is often described as a sexy "salt-and-pepper" look.

People also tend to wear clothes that preserve the illusion of the gender binary. This starts when we're children, partly because clothes for kids are designed to emphasize gender difference.[14] Color-coding is one way we do it, with reds, grays, blacks, and dark blues for boys, and pinks, purples, turquoises, pale blues, and whites for girls. Beyond the gendered superhero/princess divide, boys' clothes are also decorated with trucks, trains, and airplanes; girls' with sparkly stars, hearts, and flowers. Even the animals decorating children's clothes are gendered, with lions and dinosaurs for boys, and kittens and bunnies for girls. Girls' clothes are tighter and cut to emphasize curves that they don't yet have—shirts for girls, for example, sometimes cinch at the waist or include lower necklines—whereas boys' clothes, even in the exact same sizes, are looser, boxier, and show off less skin. Clothes for boys are even made with stronger fabrics and more robust stitching than those of girls, on the assumption, perhaps, that boys will be active in their clothes and girls will not.

As adults, these trends in color, cut, and quality continue. Meanwhile, many women wear padded or push-up bras to lift and enhance their breasts and wear low-cut tops that emphasize and display cleavage (which men aren't supposed to have). High heels create an artificially arched spine that pushes out the breasts and buttocks. Form-fitting clothes reveal women's curves, while less form-fitting or even baggy clothes on men make their bodies appear more linear and squared off. Fitted clothes also help women appear small, while baggier clothes make men seem larger. Trying on clothes designed for the other sex is a quick and easy way to test how much they contribute to our masculine and feminine appearances.

When diet, exercise, and dress don't shape our bodies into so-called opposite ideal forms, some men and women resort to chemicals and cosmetic surgeries. Men are more likely than women to take steroids to increase their muscle mass or get bicep, tricep, chin, and calf implants that make their bodies appear more muscular and formidable. Women are more likely to take diet pills. Some undergo liposuction. If they don't think they're curvy enough, some women choose to get buttock implants or have a breast augmentation. Conversely, breast *reduction* surgeries are one of the most common plastic surgeries performed on boys and men, who are often horrified by the slightest suggestion of a "breast." The surgery is now the second most common cosmetic procedure for boys under eighteen (exceeding breast augmentation for girls of the same age) and the third most common procedure for men of all ages.[15]

In addition to working on the shape of their bodies, people learn different ways of moving their bodies that help tell a story of big, muscular men and small, delicate women. Masculine movements tend to take up space, whereas feminine movements minimize the space women inhabit. A masculine walk is wide, with the arms held slightly away from the body and the elbows pointed out. A feminine walk, in contrast, involves placing one foot in front of the other, swinging the arms in front of the body, and tucking the elbows for a narrower stride. A masculine seated position is spread out, disparagingly referred to as "manspreading." A man might open his shoulders and put his arms out to either side and spread his legs or rest an ankle on a knee, creating a wide lap. Women, in contrast, are taught to contain their bodies when seated. Women often sit with their legs crossed at the knees or the ankles, with their hands in their lap, and their shoulders turned gently in.

The sheer power we have over our bodies is illustrated by **drag queens** and **drag kings**, conventionally gendered men and women who dress up and behave like members of the other sex, usually for fun or pay. Some make a hobby, or even a career, of perfecting gender display, manipulating their bodies to signify either masculinity or femininity at will.

Drag queens and kings are excellent examples of how physical characteristics can be manipulated, but we all do drag in the sense that we use our bodies to display an artificially rigid gender binary. None of the tools used by drag queens to make their bodies look feminine is unfamiliar to a culturally competent woman. Makeup, fitted clothes, high heels, jewelry, and carefully styled hair are everyday tools of femininity. The queen may wear heavier makeup, higher heels, and more ostentatious jewelry than the average woman, but it's not really different, just exaggerated.

Surgery to correct the "ambiguous" genitals of intersex children and gender-affirmation surgery are both ways people respond to a gender binary that makes their bodies problematic; working out, dieting, and push-up bras are other ways. The cumulative effect of this collective everyday drag show is a set of people who act and look like "women" and a set who act and look like "men." If male and female bodies *were* naturally "opposite," as the binary suggests, we wouldn't feel compelled to work so hard to make them appear that way. Instead, much of the difference we see doesn't emanate from our bodies themselves but rather is the result of how we adorn, manipulate, use, and alter our bodies—including through surgery and drugs.

In sum, the logic behind the gender binary—that people come in two strongly distinct types—doesn't account for people whose biological markers aren't clearly in the male or female category, those whose identity or expression doesn't match their biology, or those who are actively working to force their bodies into a binary

W A R P A I N T

BY COCO LAYNE

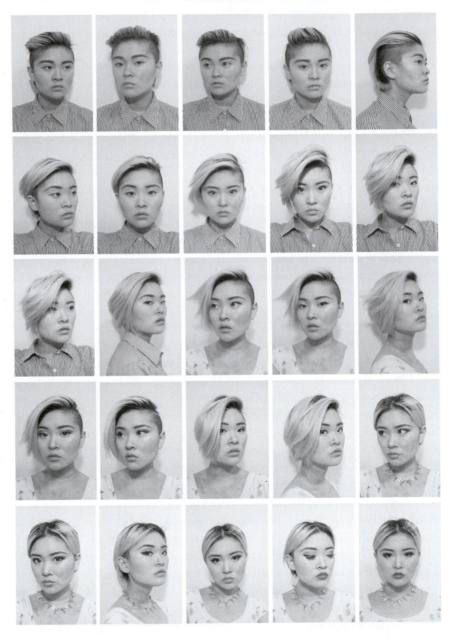

In her "Warpaint" project, artist Coco Layne shows how she transitions from appearing male to appearing female by way of her hairstyle, makeup, and clothes.

that doesn't exist in nature. Without this effort at distinction, some people would still be what our culture considers masculine or feminine, since some of our bodies do naturally conform to those types, but we wouldn't look *as* different as we do.

We do this work, though, or are forced to resist it, because we live in a society that believes in the gender binary. Not all societies do. In the next section, we'll take a quick tour through a few examples of societies that think about gender in significantly different ways. It reveals that the gender binary is just one way of thinking about the bodies with which we're born. Gender may be universal, that is, but how we think about it is not.

GENDER IDEOLOGIES

The gender binary, like the one-sex vision of the seventeenth-century anatomists, is an **ideology**, a set of ideas widely shared by members of a society that guides identities, behaviors, and institutions. **Gender ideologies** are widely shared beliefs about how men and women are and should be. The gender binary presumes that one's biological sex, gender identity, and gender expression all "line up"—that is, that we are all either male-man-masculine or female-woman-feminine. When we look around the world and backward through history, however, we don't see a universal gender ideology. Instead, we discover a dizzying array of different gender ideologies, ones that reveal that the gender binary is just one of many ways of thinking about gender.

To begin, some societies acknowledge three, four, or even five genders. When Europeans began colonizing what would become the United States in the late 1400s, more than one hundred American Indian tribes, for example, recognized people who were simultaneously masculine and feminine.[16] These individuals dressed and behaved like the other sex, but they weren't considered male or female. They were third and fourth genders, described collectively today as *two-spirit*. Charlie Ballard, a two-spirit who lives in Oakland and is a descendant of the Anishinaabe, Sac, and Fox tribes, explains that a "[t]wo-spirit is a whole person that embodies feminine and masculine traits."[17] The Navajo also have a fifth, gender-fluid category for a person whose gender is constantly changing, a *nádleehì*: sometimes a man, sometimes a woman, and sometimes a two-spirit. If a person is a nádleehì, no one is surprised by these changes, which can occur monthly, daily, hourly, or even by the minute.

In Hawaii, individuals who mainlanders might describe as two-spirit are called *māhū*. Kaumakaiwa Kanaka'ole, a Native Hawaiian recording artist who identifies as māhū, describes it as "the expression of the third self."[18] In the Cook Islands, similarly identified people are called *akava'ine*. In Tonga, they use the

Two hijras prepare to dance during a transgender conference in New Delhi.

word *fakaleiti*. And in Samoa they say *fa'afafine*, which translates to "in the manner of a woman."[19]

In Oaxaca, Mexico, feminine-acting male-bodied people identify as *muxe*; in
Brazil, *travesti*; and in India and Bangladesh, *hijra*, a third sex that is recognized
by both governments and used in official documents.[20] Unlike two-spirits and
the third genders of Polynesia, who adopt the everyday behaviors and typical
appearance of the other sex, hijras, muxes, and travestis perform a different and
sometimes exaggerated femininity. Laxmi Narayan Tripathi, who uses the pronoun "she," is a hijra who lives in Maharashtra, India. She explains her hijra
identity this way:

> *Being called gay or a man really upsets me. . . . A hijra is [someone who has transi-*
> *tioned from] male to female, but we don't consider ourselves female because cul-*
> *turally we belong to a completely different section of society. . . . They say it's the*
> *soul which is hijra. We feel we are neither man nor woman, but we enjoy femininity.*
> *I enjoy womanhood, but I am not a woman.*[21]

A muxe interviewed for the documentary *Beyond Gender*, who uses the pronoun
"they," had something similar to say about identity: "There are men, women, and
muxes," they said. "I am so comfortable being in between two. I myself represent

duality of two things because I have the strength of a male and the sensitivity of a female."[22] Another interviewee explained that they thought that generally people were fearful of the spaces in between masculinity and femininity, but that "being a muxe allows you to defeat that fear so that you can be your own self."[23]

Both hijras and muxes represent a third gender distinct from gay men and from each other. They reveal that there is no universal, or natural, set of gender identities. Gender identities are specific to cultures and places, such that how a person comes to identify depends on where and when they grow up. "I don't think that anywhere else it could be the exact same," says a muxe in Oaxaca, "because clearly the Istmo region is a thing of its own with a history of years and years. It's not a recent thing and this is what makes it unique. Obviously you cannot export it or replicate it."[24] Caitlyn Jenner, Laverne Cox, or Danica Roem may not have identified as trans if they had grown up somewhere else or at another point in history. This isn't to say that their experience here and now isn't authentic, only to suggest that how we interpret our feelings about our bodies will vary depending on the cultural resources we have for thinking about gender.

Genders other than man and woman are part of traditions all over the world: Pakistan, Thailand, Indonesia, Italy, Kenya, Tanzania, the Philippines, Nepal, Oman, Benin, Myanmar, Madagascar, Siberia, New Zealand, Australia, Peru, Ethiopia, Egypt, the Congo, and likely more.[25] Each of these cultures differs in how it conceptualizes the categories it recognizes and what role nonbinary people play. Sometimes they are expected to "prove" their membership by changing their bodies. Travestis, for example, are expected to feminize their bodies and hijras traditionally must show impotence. Other times the only requirement is community acknowledgment, as is the case for two-spirits.

In other words, genitals don't always determine one's gender. This is the case for the Gerai in West Borneo. The anthropologist Christine Helliwell spent time living with this group of subsistence farmers, immersing herself in the Dayak culture. They were studying her, too, and she discovered that her gender was uncertain to them for some time. This was, she said,

> despite the fact that people [knew] both that I had breasts (this was obvious when the sarong that I wore clung to my body while I bathed in the river) and that I had a vulva rather than a penis and testicles (this was obvious from my trips to defecate or urinate in the small stream used for that purpose, when literally dozens of people would line the banks to observe whether I performed these functions differently from them).[26]

From her Western point of view, breasts and a vulva counted as strong evidence she was female, but not to the Gerai. "Yes, I saw that you had a vulva," said a member of the community when she inquired, "but I thought that Western men might be different."

For the Dayak, being a man or woman is not tied to genitals. It is tied to expertise. A "woman" is a person who knows how to distinguish types of rice, store them correctly, and choose among them for different uses. As Helliwell learned more about rice and gained practice in preparing and cooking it, she became "more and more of a woman" in their eyes. Still, for many, her gender remained at least a little ambiguous because she "never achieved anything approaching the level of knowledge concerning rice-seed selection held by even a girl child in Gerai."

The Dayak are not unique in divorcing gender from genitals. The Hau in New Guinea do, too. They see masculinity and femininity as parts of the character that grow and fade with age and experience. For the Hau, children become male or female at puberty and then, over the life course, men lose masculinity with every son they father and women gain masculinity with each son they bear, until elders are again genderless. In pre-1900s Japan, in the years after puberty but before boys became full-fledged adults, they could occupy the status of another age-constrained gender: *wakashu*, a highly desirable third gender permitted to have sex with both men and women.[27]

Among the Lovedu in Zambia, gender is assigned neither by genitals nor age but by status.[28] A high-ranking woman "counts" as a man. She might marry a young woman and be the socially recognized "father" to their children (who are biologically fathered by the young woman's socially endorsed lover). A similar system has been documented among the Nnobi in Nigeria.[29]

In the Netherlands, children are taught that men and women are different but overlapping categories.[30] The Dutch do not teach children that men have "male" hormones and women have "female" hormones, as we typically, and wrongly, do in the United States. Instead, they teach them that all people have a mix of so-called male and female hormones, just in different proportions, which is true.[31] Further, they also emphasize that hormone levels vary among men and among women (not just between them) and that these levels rise and fall in response to different situations and as people of both sexes age.

Sometimes the biological quirks of a community shape its gender ideology. In an isolated village in the Dominican Republic, it became common for girls to become boys at puberty. A rare genetic condition called 5-alpha-reductase deficiency became concentrated in the community. The condition made genetically male children appear to be female until puberty, at which time what had been thought to be a clitoris grew into a penis and their testes suddenly descended from their abdomen. These children would then simply adopt male identities and live as men the rest of their lives. The villagers experienced this as a completely routine event, calling such boys *guevedoces*, or "eggs at twelve." A similar phenomenon happens among the Simbari in Papua New Guinea. They name the girls who grow up to be men *kwolu-aatmwol*, or "female thing transforming into male thing."

Mehran Rafaat, a six-year-old bacha posh in Afghanistan, poses cheekily with her twin sisters. After puberty, she will stop playing the part of a boy and be considered a girl again.

In some places, strict social rules lead to the acceptance of temporary or permanent sex-switching. In Afghanistan, girls are not allowed to obtain an extensive education, appear in public without a male chaperone, or work outside the home.[32] These restrictions are typically discussed as a burden for girls and women, but they can also be a burden on families. Daughters can only go out in public if they are chaperoned by a brother. Having a brother gives girls freedom and parents more flexibility; they can send their children on errands, to school, or on social visits without their supervision. Since boys can also work outside the home, sons can be a source of extra income. Families without sons can't do any of these things, so some simply pick a daughter to be a boy. They cut her hair, change her name, and put her in boy's clothes. This type of child is called a *bacha posh*, or "dressed up as a boy." One father of a bacha posh explains:

> It's a privilege for me, that she is in boys' clothing. . . . It's a help for me, with the shopping. And she can go in and out of the house without a problem.

Sex-switched children are accepted in Afghanistan. In fact, the phenomenon is common enough that most people are unsurprised when a biological girl suddenly becomes a social boy. Relatives, friends, and acquaintances accept and participate in the illusion. Later, when the child reaches puberty, she becomes

Haki is one of the remaining "sworn virgins" of Albania. Born female, Haki has lived her entire adult life as a man.

female again. Meanwhile, the family might choose a younger sibling to take over her role.

Unlike a bacha posh in Afghanistan, girls in Albania can live as boys *and* grow up to be socially recognized men.[33] To do so, girls have to publicly promise they'll remain virgins. The role of the *virgjinesha*, or "sworn virgins," emerged in the early 1400s when war left a dearth of men in many communities. Since only men had certain rights—to buy land, for example, or pass down wealth—all families needed either a biological man or someone who could stand in for one. Many girls would take the oath after their father or brother died. A similar identity emerged in the African Dahomey Kingdom in the 1700s; when the male population was decimated by war, women were allowed to become warriors, but only if they promised to remain childless.[34]

"It was my decision as well as the family's," explained Nadire Xhixha, who became a virgjinesha at thirteen years old when the only boy among her eight siblings tragically died. Speaking of her young adulthood, she said: "I lived freely, like all men back then. I smoked, I drank rakia [fruit brandy] and did many other things that were characteristic of men at the time." Xhixha lived the rest of her life as a man: "I've never done women's domestic chores such as cleaning and cooking. I lived in the village and worked alongside men. I worked hard. I worked like a man and lived like one."[35] Xhixha is one of a dwindling group of sworn virgins who still live in Albania today. As women are granted more rights, fewer girls feel the need to adopt a male identity for themselves or their families.[36]

How many genders are there? Is gender flexible? Can it change over the life course? Is it harmful to adopt a different gender identity for strictly practical reasons? Does it have anything at all to do with genitals? The answers to all these questions make sense only in concrete and specific times and places. Our sexed bodies are real, but gender ideologies can vary considerably, leading us to interpret our bodies, and our feelings about them, in many different ways. Might we have identified differently if we had grown up with different opportunities or faced different demands?

The ideology that dominates in the West—the gender binary—is somewhat unusual in requiring all bodies to fit into two and only two categories. It demands that certain traits and talents align with our bodies throughout our entire lifetime, to the exclusion of aspects of one's personality or other factors such as age, status, or expertise. We impose this binary on our bodies, as we've discussed, but also, as we'll talk about next, everything else.

THE BINARY AND EVERYTHING ELSE

Gender is a **social construct**, an arbitrary but influential shared interpretation of reality.[37] Social constructs are the consequence of **social construction**, the process by which we layer objects with ideas, fold concepts into one another, and build connections between them. The metaphor of "construction" draws attention to the fact that we are *making* something. This construction is "social" because, to be influential in society, the meaning ascribed to something must be shared.

Consider the word *hippo* as an example. The word doesn't look or sound anything like an actual hippopotamus, but English speakers have agreed that this particular assortment of lines and curves means a giant, gregarious, aquatic artiodactyl with stumpy legs and thick skin. And, likewise, when I say "hip" plus "oh," you know what I mean because we've given that order of those sounds that meaning.

Language is just an elaborate series of social constructs, but so is much of our daily lives. Most of us, in fact, start off every morning with a social construct: breakfast. In the United States, people sometimes call breakfast the "most important meal of the day." In parts of Eastern Europe, like Poland and Hungary, they double down on this idea, enjoying a traditional "second breakfast" (as do the Hobbits of Middle Earth). During the Middle Ages in Europe, though, they skipped breakfast altogether. The influential thirteenth-century Dominican priest Thomas Aquinas called breakfast *praepropere*, roughly translated as "the sin of eating too soon." It was allowed only for children, the elderly, the weak, and hard laborers.[38]

Whether one eats in the morning, and how often, is a social construct; so is what one eats. In the United States, it's traditional to eat either bacon and eggs or something sweet like cereal or pancakes, but breakfast varies around the world. In Korea, a traditional breakfast includes a savory broth-based soup with vegetables, something most Americans would recognize as lunch. In Japan, breakfast is often a rice stir-fry with dried fish in soy sauce. In Istanbul, it includes a healthy serving of olives. In Iceland, a slurp of cod liver oil. In Egypt, fava beans and a tomato-cucumber salad.[39] The variation in traditions reveals that "breakfast food" is a social construct.

We gender sweet and savory foods as feminine and masculine, respectively, too. Women can and do eat bacon and eggs for breakfast, but shoveling in a good, hearty portion of salty, fatty protein is a manly way to eat breakfast. And while men often have a sweet tooth, a waffle drenched in syrup-covered strawberries with a dollop of whip cream is a meal more easily associated with women. This gendering of breakfast food is an example of the social construction of gender.

The Social Construction of Gender

In the process of socially constructing the world, we often layer objects, characteristics, behaviors, activities, and ideas with notions of masculinity or femininity. Sociologists use *gender* as a verb when talking about the *process* by which something becomes coded as masculine or feminine. So we will sometimes say something is "gendered" or that we "gender" or are "gendering" things.

We gender just about everything. Ask yourself: Who, stereotypically, is a sports fan? Who do we expect to play rugby? Soccer? How much opportunity do women have to play American football? Men are allowed to figure skate, but are male figure skaters "masculine"? Are women basketball players feminine? Who cheers for whom?

Who, stereotypically, drinks Diet Coke? Coke Zero? Monster energy drinks? At dinner, who do we expect will order a steak? A salad? Who do we think is more likely to become a vegetarian? At a bar who, stereotypically, orders beer? A cosmopolitan? Whiskey? White wine?

Who, stereotypically, plays the drums? The flute? Who DJs? Who dances? Who sings? Which teenagers, typically, babysit? And which mow lawns? Who do you expect to major in computer science, engineering, physics? How about nursing or elementary education? After college, who, stereotypically, becomes a therapist? A CEO? For those who do not go to college, who do we expect will become a construction worker? A receptionist?

Even animals are divided by gender. In children's books, mice and rabbits are usually made to be female, but wolves and bears are made to be male. Are men, in their heart of hearts, allowed to love unicorns? Are women expected to have a pet snake?

Dogs, physics, energy drinks, and bacon and eggs. All these things are associated with masculinity, thrown together in a senseless pile. Whiskey and lawn-mowing share little in common, except that we associate them with men. Likewise with femininity. Nothing connects Diet Coke, ice skating, and being a therapist except the cultural prescriptions tying them all to women. Our social constructs, then, the collection of things we lump together as masculine or feminine, don't rely on logical connections between and among them. Instead, they are a jumble of unrelated ideas.

Not only are these things mostly unrelated, they're often contradictory. Consider how women are believed to be naturally inclined to do the most selfless job in the world (raising children) at the same time they're stereotyped as vain and overly concerned with trivial, superficial things (like fashion and makeup). If the latter is true, do women really make good parents? Likewise, men are believed to be especially capable of running a company, but they are also stereotyped as dopes who can't be counted on to remember to run the dishwasher. Are they focused and competent or not?

The gender binary also causes us to falsely *dis*connect masculine ideas from feminine ones, making it harder to form connections between these ideas. For example, even though we are taught that women have small hands and good coordination, making them ideal for needlework and sewing, we rarely notice that such characteristics would also make them excellent surgeons. The ways in which sewing and surgery are alike tends to escape our notice because they've been socially connected to femininity and masculinity, respectively, which we culturally expect to be opposites. Likewise, because we imagine men to be rational and women emotional, we think that the opposite of rational is emotional. In fact, rationality and emotion are linked.[40] When people suffer brain trauma that interferes with their ability to feel emotions, their decision-making powers are inhibited because emotion is a key part of careful decision-making, not its antithesis. Our association of emotion with women and rationality with men, however, falsely presents them as opposites.

Seeing Gender

We've grown up learning to see gender in the world and, sometimes frustratingly, we see it whether we like it or not. Metaphorically, this is because we wear **gender binary glasses**—a pair of lenses that separates everything we see into masculine and feminine categories. We acquire prescriptions for our gender binary glasses as we learn the ways of our culture. As we grow up, our prescriptions get tweaked as ideas about gender change around us. Some of us may even have weaker prescriptions than others. We all, however, own a pair.

If we belong to multiple subcultures, as most of us do, we may even have several different pairs of glasses. Sometimes we'll disagree about gendered meanings because someone else sees things a bit differently. A guy who grew up in Taos, New Mexico, with a father who sells healing crystals may have a different idea about what counts as masculine than his college roommate whose dad is the football coach. But when they argue, they will likely still argue about what is and isn't within the category of masculine. In other words, they may have different prescriptions, but they are both wearing glasses.

Our glasses help us see the world the way most other people around us do, but they also help us preserve the binary itself. We actively *use* our glasses, in other words, to gender the world around us. We need to do this because reality doesn't conform to a simple pink and blue vision of the world. Faced with these contradictions, our glasses encourage us to engage in progressive **gender binary subdivision**, the practice by which we divide and re-divide by gender again and again, adding finer and finer *degrees* of masculinity and femininity to the world. In one study, for example, boys showed little interest in My Little Pony toys until a researcher painted one black, gave it a mohawk, and added spiky teeth.[41] You can make a unicorn masculine after all.

We can do this progressive subdivision with just about anything. Dogs are masculine, for example (as opposed to the feminized cat), but poodles are feminine. Among poodles, though, the large standard poodle is a more masculine sort, while the teensy toy poodle is more feminine. Similarly, most people agree that cooking dinner is considered a feminine task, unless dinner involves grilling steak in the backyard or is done for pay at a restaurant. Housework is feminized and yard work is masculinized, unless we're talking about flower gardening, a subcategory of yard work associated with women.

The process of subdivision makes gender a complex cultural system rather than a single, rigid division of the world into masculine and feminine. In fact, subdivision is necessary for the whole idea of the gender binary to survive. Any time a challenge arises, like the poodle, we can protect the binary by dismissing deviations from it with reference back to the binary itself. If the guitar is a masculine instrument, how do we explain the pretty girl singing a love song while gently strumming a guitar cradled in her lap? We subdivide the guitar into electric (more masculine) and acoustic (more feminine) and further subdivide playing styles such that gentle strumming is feminized, and louder, more aggressive playing is seen as more appropriate for a man.

Likewise, if emotion is coded female, then what is anger? The masculinization of anger is a result of subdividing emotions in order to preserve the idea that women are more sensitive than men. Somehow our belief that men are prone to anger coexists with our belief that they rationally control their emotions. We don't resolve the contradiction by admitting the stereotype is false. Instead, we resolve it by subdividing emotions into masculine and feminine types. Because of the gender binary, men can be angry without being labeled "emotional."

Subdivision allows us to dismiss the toy poodle, pretty strummer, and emotional man as exceptions and not question the rule. In this way, we can maintain the illusion that the gender binary occurs naturally. Divisions of gender also make the gender binary appear to be timeless, even as cultures are constantly changing and the rules are being rewritten. When women began wearing pants in the mid-1900s, for example, their choice of attire was viewed as breaking the rule that men wore pants and women wore skirts. In the 1940s, the actress Katharine Hepburn was more than a little scandalous in slacks. By the 1960s, tight jeans and hip-hugging slacks further feminized pants, subdividing that category of clothing to reaffirm the binary. Today the binary persists despite women's ubiquitous adoption of pants. It just looks a little different: Men wear "men's pants" and women wear "women's pants." Progressive subdivision, then, makes the gender binary endlessly flexible, able to accommodate whatever challenges and changes emerge over time.

Thanks to our gender binary glasses, gender becomes part of how our brain learns to organize the world. Cells in our brains that process and transmit information make literal connections so some ideas are associated with other ideas in our minds. This phenomenon, called **associative memory**, is a very useful human adaptation. It's how we learned to think "big mouth, sharp teeth" and then "danger!" It's why we couldn't separate the idea "red" from "stop" even if we tried. (Both associations today can save our lives.) Associative memory latches onto gender, too, so when we grow up with a gender binary, our brain forms clusters of ideas revolving around the concepts of masculinity and femininity. Our brains, in other words, encode the gender binary.

Researchers can tap into our subconscious brain organization with the Implicit Association Test (IAT).[42] The IAT measures subconscious beliefs by comparing how quickly we can make connections between items. We are faster to connect two associated items than nonassociated items. In one study, gender-stereotyped words like *mechanic* and *secretary* were flashed on a computer screen, followed by a male or female name.[43] The viewer's task was to identify the name as male or female as quickly as possible. Results showed that, on average, it takes longer for a person to identify a name as male if it was preceded by a feminized word like *secretary* than with a masculinized word like *mechanic*. Viewers have to cognitively "shift gears." Many studies have confirmed this experiment, showing that we unconsciously associate feminine things with one another and masculine things with one another. (You can take the IAT yourself online at www.implicit.harvard.edu/.)

Another term for such embedded associations is **stereotypes**: fixed, over-simplified, and distorted ideas about categories of people. People who explicitly endorse gender stereotypes tend to show the strongest unconscious associations, but even those of us who refute stereotypes test "positive" for them on the IAT. Stereotypes are a natural way for human brains to work and it may be impossible to rid ourselves of them. Knowing them simply means that we're well socialized to a particular culture. We can be aware of how they distort our perception of reality and try to counter our brains' automatic stereotyping, but only if we have attention to spare.[44]

When our ability to think about resisting gender stereotypes is inhibited (when we are distracted or asked to respond quickly), essentially all of us revert to stereotypical thinking. For instance, when asked to perform the challenging task of recalling a series of random words, study respondents often use the gender binary as a scaffold on which to structure their recollections. In one such study, people were offered a set of masculine, feminine, and neutral words like *wrestling, yogurt, bubble bath, ant, pickup truck, shirt, water, steak*, and *flower.* When asked to recall the words later, respondents would cluster the words by gender, saying *wrestling, pickup truck*, and *steak* in a row, then *yogurt, bubble bath*, and *flower.*[45] Sometimes they would even add gendered words that weren't on the original list, adding *beer*, perhaps, or *perfume* because they fit so nicely with the concepts of steak and flower. Somehow, they just seemed to belong.

Socially trained brains help us get along with others whose brains are similarly trained. In other words, our gender binary glasses give us **cultural competence**, a familiarity and facility with how the members of a society typically think and behave. It's how we know *most people* think unicorns are supposed to appeal only to girls, even if we personally believe that the love of unicorns should know no bounds. This knowledge is important. In order to interact with others in a meaningful way, we need a shared understanding of the world. How do we communicate the idea of hippo, after all, if we're the only person around who thinks it's pronounced "washing machine"?

Whether out of conviction, mere habit, or the desire to see the world in the same way as people around us, we routinely apply a gender binary to characteristics, activities, objects, and people. This isn't reality; it's ideology. Our culture posits a gender binary, and we apply that binary to our world by peering at it through gender binary glasses. And those glasses, it turns out, bring the world into false focus.

Blurred Vision and Blind Spots

Our gender binary glasses enable us to perceive the world the way the people around us do, but they also often distort our vision.[46] Our lenses warp reality, causing us to dismiss, forget, and misremember the exceptions to the rule we encounter daily. Without this distortion, this constant *in*attention to deviations from the binary, the gender binary would appear patently false. It's preserved not because it's real, then, but because we learn to ignore or un-see evidence that falsifies it.

In a classic study, for example, five- and six-year-olds were shown both stereotype-consistent pictures (e.g., a boy playing with a train) and stereotype-inconsistent pictures (e.g., a boy cooking on a stove).[47] One week later, asked to recall what they had seen, children had more difficulty remembering the stereotype-inconsistent pictures than the stereotype-consistent ones. They also sometimes reversed the sex of the person in the picture (e.g., they remembered a *girl* cooking) or changed the activity (e.g., they remembered a boy *fixing* a stove). Many later studies have confirmed that children are more likely to forget an experience that deviates from stereotypes—skateboarding girls or belly-dancing boys—than one that fits in.[48]

This is true of adults, too. Stereotype-consistent experiences are more likely to be remembered and remembered correctly than stereotype-inconsistent ones.[49] We pay less attention to stereotype-inconsistent information and are quicker to forget it. When it is ambiguous as to whether what we are observing is stereotype-consistent or stereotype-inconsistent, we tend to assume the former, strengthening our preconceived notions. We may assume, for example, that a man who shoves a woman is attacking her, while a woman who shoves a man is defending herself, using gender stereotypes to interpret the encounter. Further, when we actively seek information, we tend to seek that which affirms our beliefs, not that which challenges them. Whenever stereotypes are activated, those stereotypes influence our attention, thinking, and memory, and they do so in their own favor.

Stereotypes are so powerful, in fact, that they are a source of false memories. In one study, people were asked to watch a dramatized account of a bicycle theft.[50] The actors playing the thieves varied. In some videos, the criminal was a masculine man, in others a feminine man, a feminine woman, or a masculine woman. Study subjects could remember more about the theft if the criminal conformed to gender stereotypes. This is because, just as with the words *yogurt*, *bubble bath*, and *flower*, it is easier to remember a set of ideas if they conform to a preexisting schema (in this case, criminal behavior = masculine = men). The authors write, "When eyewitnesses are exposed to a theft, gender schemas will enhance recall," but only if the criminal followed gender expectations and conventions.[51]

This phenomenon applies even to memories we would think would be impervious to such effects. In one surprising study, French high school students were asked to fill out a quick survey about whether men or women were better at math and art.[52] Reminded of the gender stereotypes, they were then asked to report their own scores on a national standardized test they'd taken two years prior. Amazingly, women underestimated their own performance on the math portion of the test and overestimated their performance on the art portion. Men misremembered in the opposite direction.

In these ways, and in many others, our gender binary glasses distort what we see. They often bring things into false focus and affect our cognition and memory. When we see counterevidence, it tends not to enter into our daily interpretation of the world. We may soon misremember it as having confirmed our preexisting beliefs. And our brain has been trained to direct us to make gender-stereotypical associations even if we are consciously prepared to say those stereotypes are wrong.

Revisiting the Question

 If we don't learn the idea of the gender binary by observing the people around us, where does the idea come from?

Everywhere!

Humans socially construct their worlds and gender is one way we do so. We use a gender binary to understand things, ideas, objects, activities, places, and more. We even apply the binary rule to our bodies, often treating gender-nonconforming bodies as in need of being fixed and putting responsibility on them for the misfit between their experience of gender and our cultural norm rather than on the gender binary itself. Many other cultures offer more space between and outside of male and female gender categories. This has been changing in the United States, as all cultures change. Still, despite growing awareness of nonbinary bodies, most Americans are still uncomfortable with the more than 10 percent of people who challenge their placement on the binary.

The gender binary also continues to press the remaining 90 percent to embody the gender binary much more closely than they naturally do. Meanwhile, everybody tends to underperceive variation in gender identity and expression. We apply a binary gender ideology to the world and what we end up seeing and remembering is false on many fronts. We assume our culture's arbitrary connections are the only way that the binary can be organized, erase nonbinary alternatives in our and other cultures, and subdivide our gender categories to draw attention away from the ways the binary doesn't work. This leads us to forget that gender stereotypes fail to describe most people we know well, including ourselves, and fail to notice that masculinity and femininity are jumbled and often contradictory categories. Our gender binary glasses distort our cognition, influencing what we see, as well as if and how we remember it.

Next . . .

The idea that gender is socially constructed likely bumps up against things we hear about blue and pink brains, the male sex drive, or female empathy, all seemingly irrefutable biological differences between men and women. With this in mind, we'll tackle this question next:

 The gender binary might be an ideology, but there are real differences between men and women, right?

This question is so much harder to answer than you might think.

FOR FURTHER READING

Fausto-Sterling, Anne. "The Five Sexes: Why Male and Female Are Not Enough."
    The Sciences (March/April 1993): 20–24.

Lorber, Judith. *Paradoxes of Gender.* New Haven: Yale University Press, 1994.

Martin, Carol, and Diane Ruble. "Children's Search for Gender Cues." *Current Direc-
    tions in Psychological Science* 13, no. 2 (2004): 67–70.

Paoletti, Jo. *Pink and Blue: Telling the Boys from the Girls in America.* Bloomington:
    Indiana University Press, 2012.

Ridgeway, Cecilia L. *Framed by Gender: How Gender Inequality Persists in the Mod-
    ern World.* New York: Oxford University Press, 2011.

Risman, Barbara. *Where Will the Millennials Take Us: A New Generation Wrestles
    with the Gender Structure.* New York: Oxford University Press, 2018.

Rupp, Leila. "Toward a Global History of Same-Sex Sexuality." *Journal of the His-
    tory of Sexuality* 10, no. 2 (2001): 287–302.

MEN ARE FROM NORTH DAKOTA,
WOMEN ARE FROM SOUTH DAKOTA.

—KATHRYN DINDIA[1]

3

Bodies

In a part of the ocean so deep that no light can reach it, an anglerfish hunts. She attracts prey with a glowing lure that springs from her forehead and looks suspiciously like something other creatures would like to eat. No matter if they are bigger than she, as she can swallow prey up to twice her body size.

She pays no attention to her male counterpart, who is tiny in comparison. Females can grow over three feet long, but males are never longer than a few centimeters. He, in contrast, needs her desperately. Born without a lure, a male anglerfish can't catch prey and, without a stomach, he couldn't digest it if he did. A male's only chance at survival is finding a female before he dies of starvation. If he's so lucky, he'll latch onto her with his mouth, initiating a chemical reaction that slowly dissolves his face into her body. Eventually he will lose all his organs and his entire body will waste away, except his testicles. A healthy female anglerfish will carry many pairs of testicles on her body, all that is left of the males who found their fate with her.

This is high **sexual dimorphism**. The phrase refers to typical differences in body type and behavior between males and females of a species. Across the range of species on Earth, some are highly sexually dimorphic and some are less so. The high end includes the green spoonworm (the male lives its entire adult life inside the

In some species, males and females appear very different from each other; in other species less so. Elephant seals, lions, and anglerfish are all species that are more sexually dimorphic than humans.

female's digestive tract); peacocks (males carry a resplendent half-moon of a tail with which to dazzle relatively drab females); and elephant seals (males outweigh females by about 4,600 pounds).

Other species have much lower sexual dimorphism. The male and female Fischer's lovebird, for example, look so much alike that even ornithologists (professional bird-folk) can't tell by looking. They have identical plumage, near-identical behavior, and their genitals are inside their bodies. Very experienced bird handlers might be able to tell based on feeling the width of a bird's pelvis (the females' are wider to allow egg-laying), but most people have to resort to genetic testing to know for sure.

Considering the range of sexual dimorphism among animals helps us put human sex difference in perspective. Given some of the extremes, we should be rather impressed by how obviously similar we are. If humans were as dimorphic by size as elephant seals, for example, the average man would tower six feet above the average woman. If we were as sexually dimorphic as the blanket octopus, the human man would be no bigger than a walnut. Human men don't have appendages that human women do not have (beyond the genitals, of course), like the horns of the Alaskan moose or the rhinoceros beetle, the mane of the lion, the poisonous claw of the platypus, or the bulging cheek flaps or bulbous nose of the orangutan and the proboscis monkey, respectively. Nor do human males come in pretty colors like the male species of many birds. If we were like Northern cardinals, men would be bright red with a black mask around their eyes and throat and women would look more or less as they do now.

Male and female humans are not exactly the same but, as Dorothy Sayers once said: "Women are more like men than anything else in the world."[2] Yet, we're more clearly male and female than your average pair of lovebirds. That's why we posed the question we did at the end of the last chapter:

 The gender binary might be an ideology, but there are real differences between men and women, right?

Most Americans believe that men and women are "basically different" in many ways and that biology explains much of this difference.[3] This chapter reviews the research on sex differences and similarities with the aim of understanding whether and how men and women are basically and biologically different. Are we different? How different are we? And is biology why? Prepare to be confused. These questions are much more difficult to answer than you might think. The answers involve a model of the relationship between biology and society that is far more complex than even scientists once imagined.

RESEARCH ON SEX DIFFERENCES AND SIMILARITIES

From a practical perspective, getting a clear understanding of how men and women are alike and different is a real challenge. As you'll see, whether we find differences, what causes those differences, and how large they are varies over time and across cultures; bodily differences respond to psychological manipulation and practice and training. They're also sensitive to how we design studies and define measurements. We would have to amass a lot of evidence and consider all the possible influences in order to determine which differences we find consistently and which we don't. And that's just what a team of psychologists led by Ethan Zell did.

Zell and his colleagues combined over 20,000 individual studies with a combined sample size of more than 12 million people.[4] It included over 21,000 measures of 386 traits: data on differences between men and women in thoughts, feelings, behaviors, intellectual abilities, communication styles and skills, personality traits, measures of happiness and well-being, physical abilities, and more.

TABLE 3.1 | THE SIZE OF OBSERVED SEX DIFFERENCES

Size of the Difference	% of Variables in Each Category
Negligible to Nonexistent	39%
Small	46%
Medium	12%
Large	2%
Very Large	1%

They separated the variables into ones for which there appeared to be negligible to no difference between men and women, and those for which there was evidence for small, medium, large, or very large differences. Table 3.1 shows the results: 39 percent of possible differences were negligible to nonexistent, 46 percent were small, 12 percent were medium, 2 percent were large, and 1 percent were very large.

The average difference between men and women—on all traits included in the study—fell into the small category, illustrated by the bell curve in Figure 3.1. The graph represents levels of self-esteem (from low on the left to high on the right) and the height of the curve represents the number of people who reported each level. Few people have very low self-esteem (far left) or very high self-esteem (far right). While Zell and his colleagues' analysis offered good evidence for a statistically significant difference between men and women, it's not a large one.

Other variables that fell into the categories of small to negligible to non-existent difference included reading comprehension and abstract reasoning; talkativeness, likelihood of self-disclosing to friends and strangers, tendency to interrupt others, and assertiveness of speech; willingness to help others; negotiation style, approach to leadership, and degree of impulsiveness; symptoms of depression, coping strategies, life satisfaction, and happiness; vertical jumping ability, overall activity levels, balance, and flexibility; willingness to delay gratification and attitudes about cheating; likelihood of wanting a career that makes money, offers security, is challenging, and brings prestige; and some measures of sexual attitudes and experiences (e.g., disapproval of extramarital sex, levels of sexual arousal, and sexual satisfaction).

FIGURE 3.1 | AN ILLUSTRATION OF A "SMALL" DIFFERENCE BETWEEN MEN AND WOMEN

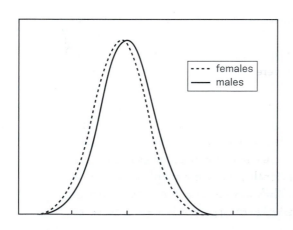

Medium-sized differences included physical aggression and visual-spatial abilities (turning a two- or three-dimensional object around in one's head), while the largest sex differences were for some measures of physical ability, especially throwing (because these differences are related to size, they are particularly pronounced after puberty). Large differences were also found in some measures of sexuality: frequency of masturbation and approval of casual sex.[5] Two traits show especially strong sexual dimorphism: sexual identity (most men identify as male and most women identify as female) and sexual object choice (most men are sexually interested in women and most women in men). Are these, then, the "real differences" our opening question asked about?

It depends on how you define "real."

DEFINING DIFFERENCE

When we wonder about the real differences between men and women, it's helpful to consider what kind of evidence we would need to conclude that we've discovered them. Is it enough just to be able to measure differences, like Zell and his colleagues did? Is it important that those differences be stable? That is, should the characteristics we're measuring be relatively unchanged across an individual's life? Or, even more, true throughout human history? To count as real, do they need to be found in all or most societies? Would finding a biological cause of the difference make it seem *more* real? And if we do find a biological cause, does it count as real only if it resists cultural influences like education and training? The following sections explore these questions by considering different definitions of the word "real."

Definition 1: Sex differences are real if we can measure them

Zell and his colleagues noted differences on 61 percent of characteristics. These are real in that the studies they included in their summary really observed them in real life. They are **observed differences**: findings from surveys, experiments, and other types of studies that detect differences between men and women. Is this what we mean by "real"?

Maybe not. There are lots of reasons why differences might be observed, and we might consider some of those observations to be more indicative of an underlying truth than others. For example, people sometimes act differently if they're being observed. Women smile more often than men, and men are more likely to engage in heroic helping behavior than women, but only if they know they're being watched.[6] Men are just as likely as women to offer emotional support to friends on social media via a private message, but less likely to do so publicly.[7] When people think they're alone or acting without an audience, sex differences can fade or disappear.

People also lie. Men typically report higher rates of masturbation than women, but when scientists do studies in which they increase the motivation to be honest (by, say, hooking up a man to a fake lie detector) and decrease their motivation to lie (by ensuring that the answers are anonymous), the frequency with which men report masturbating drops to the same level as women's. We see similar patterns in reported number of sexual partners and age at first intercourse.

In other cases, psychologists have discovered that they can manipulate study results quite easily. If you remind study subjects of a stereotype right before the test, in a trick called **priming**, test scores will reflect that stereotype. For example, if women are asked to identify themselves by their gender immediately before a test of empathy, the ability to understand and sympathize with others' feelings, they will do better than those who didn't answer a gender question.[8] Because women as well as men tend to associate empathy with women, priming women to think of themselves as women encourages them to focus on these capacities and may motivate them to try to do better. For men, reminding them that they're male lowers their scores.

You can also depress women's scores on empathy tests simply by asking them to imagine themselves as men for a few moments before they begin the experiment. In one study, women were asked to write a fictional story about a day in the life of a person named Paul.[9] Half were asked to write in the first person ("I") and the other half were asked to write in the third person ("he"). Women who wrote in the first person did better on the empathy test than their male counterparts, but women who had imagined themselves to be men did just as badly as the male study subjects.

Does this mean that women have an ability to be empathetic that men don't have, but only if they're motivated to be so? Nope. Men can be motivated to score higher on tests of empathy, too. You can do this by tricking them into thinking that the task they're performing is one that men are stereotypically good at (perhaps telling them that you're measuring leadership ability) or by offering a social or financial reward for doing well.[10] Similarly, men (presumably heterosexual ones) will do better on tests of empathy if they're told that women really like sensitive guys.[11]

Observed differences may also be quite obviously the result of social and cultural conditions. We might observe that women are more likely to carry a purse and have long hair and men are more likely to carry a wallet and wear their hair short. That's real, but these are simply **learned differences**, ones that are a result of how we're raised (for example, religion or parenting) or our sociocultural environment (like education or media consumption). We know, for example, that parents tend to see their sons as big, strong, and active and their daughters as little, pretty, and cute, then treat them accordingly.[12] Girl babies are more likely to be talked to; boy babies more likely to be handled. Accordingly, girls may develop quicker and stronger language skills than boys, while boys might outpace girls on motor skills. Is that what we're getting at when we're asking the question about real differences? Probably not. Some differences are simply a result of how we're treated.

The differences Zell and his colleagues observed, then, are real in that we really observed them, but they don't necessarily stand up when we poke and prod at them. Some are quite obviously just norms for men and women, unrelated to anything but culture. Others can shift, reverse, and disappear when we manipulate the conditions of the data collection. Perhaps what we need is a definition that carries more heft and stands up under such examination.

Definition 2: Sex differences are real if they are observed in all or most contemporary and historical cultures

Questions like the one this chapter is exploring—regarding the "real" differences between men and women—imply that we're interested in universal human truths, ones that are true around the world and throughout history. If we could find such a difference, we would have a compelling reason to think it was real. The majority of research on sex differences, however—in fact, the majority of research on behavioral differences of all kinds—uses subjects only from societies that are Western, educated, industrialized, rich, and democratic, five words that add up to the acronym WEIRD.[13]

And it turns out these samples really are weird: only 12 percent of the world's population lives in such a country and the people who do have been shown to be quite unusual compared to everyone else. When we do research that compares across cultures (over time and across countries and subcultures within a country), we discover that our weird samples have resulted in unusual findings, ones that don't stand up when we do research elsewhere.[14]

Let's take math ability as an example.

In 1992 the toy company Mattel released a talking Barbie doll that said, among other things, "Math class is tough!" Many people still believe that girls and women struggle in mathematics more than boys and men.[15] At the time Barbie was making her confession, it was true. Disparities in skill emerged in high school, with boys scoring slightly higher than girls on the math portion of the SAT, the standardized test for college admissions.[16] In the intervening twenty years, however, the gap has narrowed as girls have started to take math classes at the same rate as boys. This equivalence in test results suggests that the difference in performance in the 1990s had more to do with training and practice than gender.[17]

If we look at mathematical abilities across developed nations, girls do about as well as boys in about half the countries.[18] In the other half, boys outperform girls. In a few outlier countries, such as Iceland, girls outshine boys significantly. So, whether men or women appear to be better at math depends on what country you're looking at. Still, boys do better than girls more often than girls do better than boys, so maybe that's evidence that boys are slightly better than girls at math on average.

If you look a bit closer at the data, though, you'll also discover that this is true only if you compare boys to the girls in their own country. Math ability varies so widely across societies that sometimes girls who do worse than boys in their own country do significantly better than boys in other countries. For instance, though Japanese girls do less well than Japanese boys, they generally outperform American boys by a considerable margin.[19]

How we measure math ability also matters. Even if men and women are equally capable on average, men are more likely to be math geniuses.[20] Boys outnumber girls in the top 1 percent of math ability. Among twelve- to fourteen-year-olds, math prodigies are more likely to be male at a ratio of 3:1. So that's impressive. But, less impressively, boys are also more likely than girls to struggle with math.[21] Boys are more likely than girls to get nearly all the answers on a math test right, but they're also more likely to get nearly all the answers wrong. So when boys do better, they are usually also doing worse.

But, this, of course, also varies by country, over time, and across subgroups. Even among those whose math scores are in the top 1 percent, boys outperform girls among only some parts of the U.S. population. White male students outperform white female students at this high level of ability, but among Asians in the United States, girls outperform boys. Looking cross-culturally, girls also dominate the top 1 percent in Iceland, Thailand, and the United Kingdom. Boys, then, do not always outnumber girls when we look at the highest-scoring students. And in the United States, as girls and women have closed the gap between the average ability of males and females, they've also been closing the gap at the highest levels of mathematical ability.[22] We mentioned earlier that today boys outnumber girls at the genius level 3:1; in the 1980s, the ratio was 13:1.[23] That's quite a remarkable catch-up.

In any case, performance on the standardized tests used to evaluate ability doesn't predict who will get the highest grades in math classes. Girls in U.S. high schools and colleges get higher grades in math than boys.[24] While only a few decades ago most math majors were men, today they're about 50 percent female. Six times as many women get PhDs in mathematics today as they did in 1976.[25] And neither high scores on the SAT nor high grades predict who will opt for math-related careers. Many high-scoring girls don't go into these careers, and many poorly scoring boys do.

So, are men better at math than women? In part, it depends on how we test for math aptitude. If you go by standardized tests, sometimes boys outperform girls, but if you go by grades, girls outperform boys. If you test for genius-level math ability, boys in some populations outperform girls, but if you test for average level, girls and boys come out about even. And lastly, if you look at the most poorly performing students, girls come off looking much more capable than boys. But none of these generalizations about difference is consistent among groups in any given country, across countries, or even over time in a single population.

In fact, the best predictor of whether boys or girls do better in math is *belief*. Sex differences in math ability are lowest in countries whose citizens are least likely to believe that men are better at it.[26] There is a strong correlation between sex differences in math ability and the level of gender inequality in a country (Figure 3.2).[27] The differences diminish, and then disappear, as men and women

FIGURE 3.2 | GENDER GAP IN MATH ACROSS COUNTRIES

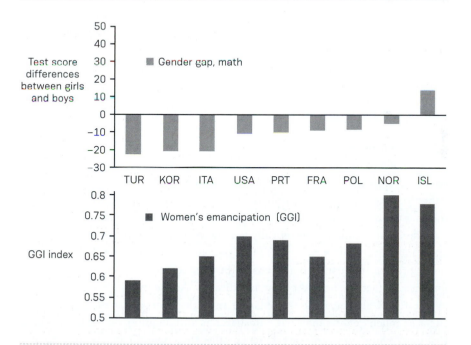

Note: With the exception of PRT (Portugal) and Iceland (ISL), the countries are abbreviated as their first three letters.
Source: Guiso Luigi, Fernando Monte, Paola Sapienza, and Luigi Zingales. "Culture, Gender, and Math." *Science* 320, no. 5880 (2009): 1164–65.

become more equal. It's all about practice. When girls are required and encouraged to take the same classes as boys and have the opportunity to go into math-based careers, we see the lowest sex difference on tests of math aptitude. All this suggests that the sex difference in math performance has more to do with training, practice, and opportunity than gender.[28]

This complex story about math ability is just one example of the way that observed sex differences often vary over time and across cultures. It isn't true of every observed sex difference. For example, female advantage in reading and male advantage in mental rotation (the ability to imagine an object rotating in your mind) do seem to be cross-culturally consistent, but the magnitude of the advantage varies considerably.[29] Men's greater interest in thrill- and adventure-seeking compared to women has remained constant since 1978, but the size of the difference has shrunk.[30]

When observed sex differences show variation over time and across cultures, it suggests that they are not inevitable and universal. When we see less variation, assuming they are "real" is more plausible. When sex differences resist cultural influence, it might be a hint that they are not just related to gendered stereotypes and opportunities, but may be part of being biologically human. That's our next definition.

Definition 3: Sex differences are real if they are biological

Biological differences include ones caused by our genes, hormones, and our brains. Let's review what scientists know about our bodies and how they do, don't, or might contribute to sex difference and similarity.

GENES Our **genes** are a set of instructions for building and maintaining our bodies. Each of us has a unique set of genes, our **genotype**, and an observable set of physical and behavioral traits, our **phenotype**. By our current working definition, the differences described by Zell and his colleagues are biological if they are phenotypes expressing differences shaped by our genes.

Individuals defined as genetically female carry XX chromosomes and genetically male individuals carry XY. Most people assume that the Y, by virtue of being present in most men and absent in most women, is a source of sex differences. In fact, it's not.[31] At least, not directly. As the image on the next page shows, the X chromosome is far larger than the Y chromosome and has ten times as much genetic material.[32] Research is still ongoing, but so far it seems that the Y chromosome doesn't do much other than give XY fetuses functioning testes and facilitate male fertility. Weirdly, it also causes hairy ears.[33] That's it.

Once the Y chromosome has set a body on the path to being male, though, other genetic consequences follow. Some genes are expressed only if they are in a male or female body, such as the genes that allow a woman to breastfeed. The expression of others is influenced by their hormonal environment. The baldness gene, for instance, thins hair on the head only in the presence of high levels of testosterone, so most women who carry the gene don't show signs of baldness. Curiously, the same gene that produces high voices in women also gives men low voices.

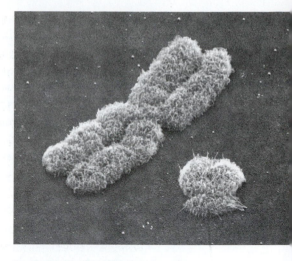

Despite its mighty reputation, the Y chromosome contains substantially less genetic material than the X chromosome.

The fact that most women have two X chromosomes and most men have only one seems to be a greater source of sex differences than the presence or absence of the Y. Human beings need only one X chromosome (that's why men can exist with only one of them) and so women's two Xs are redundant. The female body responds by using only one at a time. Which one they use, though, is random. In some cells the X chromosome they received from their father is active and, in others, the one they received from their mother.[34] This means that XX women can put a more diverse set of genes to work than can XY men. Twice as much. And that has some interesting effects.

Men's single X chromosome, for example, is why they are more susceptible to recessive traits, ones that won't be expressed in the presence of a gene for a dominant trait. If a trait carried on the X chromosome is recessive, men are more likely to show that trait, since they need to inherit only one gene to express the trait, whereas women need to inherit it on both their Xs. The inability to see the difference between red and green is an example. Men are fifteen times more likely than women to be red-green colorblind. If their single X has the gene for colorblindness, the cells in their eyes won't be able to detect the difference. No backup. Women, on the other hand, have to inherit two copies of the gene to be functionally colorblind. If they inherit only one gene for colorblindness, then some of the cells of their eyes will be colorblind and the other half won't be. So, such a woman will see the color differences better than the average colorblind man (though not quite as clearly as if she didn't have the gene at all).

Genetic influences like these contribute to some average physical differences between men and women. They also determine whether we develop ovaries or testes. This then sets most of us on hormonal paths to have male or female bodies, which influences physical outcomes like throwing ability. But the sex chromosomes themselves—despite being one of the biological differences between the categories male and female—don't seem to cause all that many differences of interest.

Most people, when inquiring about "real" sex differences, aren't thinking about breastfeeding, colorblindness, and hairy ears. They're thinking about the things that Zell and his colleagues measured: personality traits, emotional states, cognitive abilities, and physical potential. Most of those things, though, don't have sex-specific genetic causes. At least, not ones that we've discovered. To consider biological contributors to these other characteristics, we have to consider the influence of hormones and brain function.

HORMONES Our **hormones** are messengers in a chemical communication system. Released by glands or cells in one part of the body, hormones carry instructions to the rest of it. They trigger masculinization and feminization in utero and at puberty. They regulate basic physiological processes, like hunger and the reproductive cycle. And they influence our moods: feelings of happiness, confidence, and contentment. They are part of what inspires us to have sex, get into (or run away from) fights, and settle down and raise a baby.

Importantly, it's a mistake to use binary language and say that men have "male hormones" and women have "female hormones." All human hormones circulate in both men's and women's bodies, but some of them do so in different proportions. Men tend to have higher levels of androgens and women higher levels of estrogens. It's also wrong to say that androgens are "masculinizing" and estrogens are "feminizing." Estrogen sometimes has the same effects in females that testosterone has in males. During fetal development, for example, it is estrogen, not testosterone, that produces the changes in the male brain that differentiate men from women. Just as we are not "opposite sexes," our hormones are far from opposite in their chemical structure, presence, or function.

Still, differing levels of these hormones might contribute to sex differences. Testosterone usually gets the most attention. In fact, testosterone is strongly related to sex drive in both women and men and may be related weakly to physical aggression in men.[35] Since most men have more free testosterone than most women, this fact might partially explain why men are, on average, more aggressive than women and report higher sex drives (though social explanations for these likely play a role, too).[36]

Testosterone levels also correlate with visual-spatial ability, such as mental rotation.[37] Very high and very low levels of testosterone are correlated with poor visual-spatial ability, so high-testosterone women and low-testosterone men do best on visual-spatial tests because they both fall into the middle range. As men's and women's hormones fluctuate, their performance on tests fluctuates as well; women score better right before ovulation (when their testosterone levels are highest) and men score better in the spring (when their levels are lowest).

There is good evidence, too, that the hormone cycles that regulate women's menstrual cycles correspond to mild changes in mood, sexual interest, and partner choice,[38] but we see no changes across the menstrual cycle in women's memory, creativity, problem-solving ability, or athletic, intellectual, or academic performance.[39] Men experience hormone fluctuations as well, on both daily and seasonal cycles (testosterone is higher in the morning than other times of day, and in the fall compared to other times of year for men in the Western Hemisphere). Interestingly, studies of mood fluctuations in men find that they are just as emotionally "unstable" as women.[40] In other words, men get "hormonal" sometimes, too.

The relationship between hormone level and observed difference isn't straightforward, though. Men's bodies respond similarly to wide variations in testosterone levels (between 20 percent and 200 percent of normal). In contrast, women have been shown to be more sensitive to lower levels of testosterone, so women exposed to small amounts of extra testosterone tend to respond similarly to men exposed to large amounts.[41] That might explain why men and women don't show greater differences in sexual desire.

The differences that correlate with hormone levels are also quite small. Hormone fluctuations that regulate mood, for example, are a relatively minor force in determining our state of mind compared to, say, whether it's Monday morning or Friday afternoon.[42] And, in any case, none of these differences has been shown to have an impact on a person's ability to be successful at work. Average differences in mental rotation ability, for instance, don't affect whether men or women are capable of working in jobs like engineering or architecture.[43]

In sum, we find differing levels of androgens and estrogens in men's and women's bodies and those hormones have been linked to a limited number of observed differences: levels of aggressiveness, sex drive, and visual-spatial ability, as well as when (but not whether) we experience changes in mood. All the effects are small, with the possible exception of sex drive.

These may be good candidates for the "real" differences we're after. And hormones may also indirectly produce sex differences by influencing the development of our brains.

BRAINS The fetal brain develops in a sex-specific hormonal environment and there is research suggesting that sex differences are a consequence.[44] Scientists have documented average sex differences, for example, in brain anatomy (the size and shape of its parts), composition (characteristics of the tissue), and function (rate of blood flow, metabolism of glucose, and neurotransmitter levels).[45] Women have smaller brains on average (mostly explained by their overall smaller size), and men and women have different ratios of gray matter to white matter in some regions.[46] None of these differences is particularly pronounced and all are average differences with significant overlap (like the bell curve illustrating sex differences in self-esteem in Figure 3.1).

When we look at all the differences at once, though, we discover that female-like structures in a single brain often coexist with male-like structures. One study, for example, examined 625 brains, measuring the ten regions with the strongest evidence for sexual dimorphism.[47] Only 2.4 percent of the brains were internally consistent: all male-like or all female-like. This means that 97.6 percent of us are "gender nonconforming" in our brains and more than half of brains show substantial overlap.[48] What scientists have found, then, is that there are average differences between men and women in some structures and functions of the brain, but that tells us little about what any given person's brain will look like.

To complicate things further, studies tying these differences to traits or abilities remain largely elusive.[49] In other words, we don't know what the differences found in some parts of the brain actually *do*. Since it's unethical to expose developing fetuses to varying levels of hormones merely out of curiosity, directly testing what the effects might be in humans is difficult. One theory is that some of these physiological differences may actually be functioning to compensate for others, producing similarity from difference.[50] That is, our bodies may be evolved to enable sexual difference for the purposes of reproduction, but also compensate for any maladaptive differences that arise as a consequence of the tricky task of building male- and female-bodied people. So, counterintuitively, some differences might cause sameness. That's not the kind of "real" difference we're after either.

We do know that girls who are exposed to unusually high levels of androgens during fetal development are more likely than other girls to prefer "boy" toys and choose boys as playmates; they display more aggression and less empathy; and they're more likely to identify as nonheterosexual and express dissatisfaction with being a girl or woman.[51] But there's no reason to expect these girls' brains to be any more sex-typed than your average person's. Hormones likely have some influence on fetal brain formation, but the outcomes are far from straightforward.

Other research also suggests that gender identity and sexual orientation are determined in part by hormonally caused brain differences, though the evidence is not especially clear or strong.[52] The genitals develop earlier in pregnancy than the brain, so it's possible that the hormonal environment of the developing brain could be different from that of the developing genitals, creating discrepancies between the two. This might explain why some people experience same-sex desire or gender dysphoria, which is the feeling that one's biological sex and gender identity don't match. Research evaluating whether queer-identified women's or trans men's brains share traits with heterosexual, cisgendered men's brains, and queer-identified men's and trans women's brains share traits with heterosexual, cisgendered women's brains, is going on now—again, findings are suggestive but not especially clear or strong. Most neurologists believe that hormonal influence on the brain during fetal development plays a role, but only a small one.

We are able to observe differences between male and female bodies by looking at genes, hormones, and brains. These are biological, to be sure. But are they real? Some biological features are mutable, responsive to efforts to shift or dis-

FIGURE 3.3 | EXAMPLE OF A MENTAL ROTATION TASK

(a)   (b)

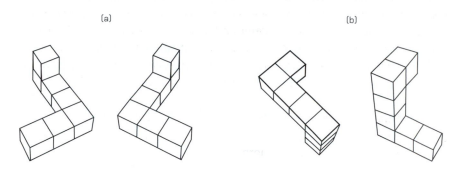

Mental rotation tasks like this one measure how easily and accurately you can determine whether two figures are identical except for their orientation. Assembling jigsaw puzzles is one use of this skill.

rupt them. Because we have bodies, *everything* about us is fundamentally biological, but biology isn't always destiny and biological traits aren't always fixed. If biologically based differences can be decreased in size, erased, or reversed quite easily, do they still count as real?

Consider mental rotation, our very best candidate for a large biological cognitive sex difference (Figure 3.3). It turns out that mental rotation can be taught, quickly and easily.[53] One study found that assigning women to a semester of *Tetris* (a simple video game that involves rotating and fitting various geometric shapes into one another) almost closed the preexisting gap between men's and women's scores.[54] In another study, just ten hours of video game play reduced the gap to statistical insignificance.[55] In a third study, five and a half hours of video game play erased the sex difference.[56] And in a fourth experiment, just two minutes of practice before the test did the same.[57]

It turns out that whatever natural ability an individual has for mental rotation, both men and women can improve with a little bit of practice.[58] Indeed, the difference between the scores of people with training and people without training is larger than the difference between men and women.[59]

While this finding doesn't rule out an inborn biological advantage for boys, neuroscientist Lise Eliot argues that ultimately, sex difference in mental rotation ability is probably the result of the fact that we don't teach mental rotation in school (so no one learns it there), and boys have a greater likelihood of learning it elsewhere (playing with building toys, spending lots of time with video games, and being involved in sports).[60] This theory gets added support from evidence that the sex difference we see in children from middle- and high-income backgrounds is not seen in children from low-income backgrounds, where boys don't have as much access to video games and building toys.[61]

Even the most robust cognitive sex difference we've ever measured is mutable, minimizable, and even erasable by instruction and practice, undone with just a few minutes of *Minecraft*.[62] As two prominent cognitive scientists explained, "Simply put, your brain is what you do with it."[63] In fact, lots of observed differences respond to intervention (and we will discuss more examples in the next section). For now, let's consider one final definition of real—the most strict of all.

Definition 4: Sex differences are real if they are biological and immutable

Perhaps a sex difference could count as real if it were observed, had a known biological cause, and could not easily be overcome by social interventions like training and priming. Sex differences in size and, by extension, throwing ability and some other physical differences would qualify. Gender identity and sexual orientation may be good candidates. And there are others, to be certain. Possibly different levels of sexual desire, aggression, empathy, and thrill-seeking. And, of course, there are the hairy ears.

But the majority of the sex differences documented by Zell and his colleagues probably would not qualify under this definition. This is a good time to remember the anglerfish. We're sexually dimorphic in that we reproduce sexually, and the process of making us reproductively male and female appears to lead to some other average differences. But on the spectrum of high-to-low sexual dimorphism, we're on the low side. We're of a similar size and weight, we have (almost) all the same appendages, we have the same desires, traits, and physical and cognitive abilities, even if there are some average differences here and there. Why do we think we *should* be able to establish a whole host of large, immutable biological differences between men and women, beyond the very necessary physical differences required for sexual reproduction, in the first place? We're quite clearly not "opposites."

But . . . why not? Why *aren't* we more different?

Well, that's another kind of question altogether.

SIMILARITIES BETWEEN THE SEXES

If it seems odd to ask about the similarities between men and women instead of the differences, it's because it is. What we call "science" today began to emerge during the Enlightenment in the 1700s. It would come to challenge religion as the arbiter of what was true and right. At the time, most men believed that it was obvious that women were an inferior category of human and they set about using science to prove it. Since distinction is a necessary precondition for hierarchy, a science of sex differences emerged.

When scientists posed their research questions, then, they almost exclusively posed variants of the one with which we began this chapter: "What are the real differences between men and women?" And they have been asking versions of this question for over 300 years. They've measured, weighed, poked, prodded, imaged, and assayed men's and women's bodies to find proof of the gender binary. It's a wonder, really, that they haven't found more definitive and more consequential differences.

It took a very long time before anyone thought to wonder whether there were any *other* questions to ask. Like what explains our similarities. To close out this chapter, then, let's explore some of the theories for why human males and females are so much alike. We'll explore three: biosocial interactions, intersectionality, and evolution.

The Natural Power of Human Culture

One of the things that makes humans stand out from all other animals is the extent to which we wrap ourselves in culture. We live on the same planet as all other earthly beings; we encounter the same trees and look at the same sky. But we live, simultaneously, in our collective imaginations, in a world that we invent, one with things that don't exist in nature: corporations, economies, wedding vows, holidays.

By virtue of being cultural, we're also diverse. Take any two human societies 3,000 miles apart and you'll find countless differences in their cultural practices and ideas. As a species, in fact, our ways of life are not just more varied than those of any other primate on earth; they are more varied than those of every other primate *combined*.[64] That is why reality shows like *Wife Swap*—in which two women from two very different backgrounds swap families for the purpose of producing mayhem—can run for seven seasons. Commenting on this, psychologist Cordelia Fine observed: "Other animals are fascinating, to be sure. Many are highly flexible and adaptable. But there just aren't that many ways to *be* a female baboon."[65]

This diversity is not merely cultural, though; it's *natural*. That is, it's our biology that makes it possible for us to be culturally different from one another. Understanding this is important because it helps us avoid the discredited and fruitless argument referred to as **the nature/nurture debate**. The "nature" side is premised on the idea that men and women are *born* different, and the "nurture" side presupposes that we *become* different through socialization alone. Both sides are wrong.

Scholars from all disciplines now overwhelmingly reject **naturalism**, the idea that biology affects our behavior independently of our environment. Likewise, we reject **culturalism**, the idea that we are "blank slates" that become who we are purely through learning and socialization. This should make sense. Any given sex difference can't be purely a result of "nurture" (a culturalist assumption) because it is only through our bodies that we encounter our social world. Nor can it be purely "nature" (a naturalist assumption) because our bodies don't exist in a vacuum. We begin interacting with the environment from the moment we are conceived, and all our biological functions evolved in the context of that interaction.

Instead, to understand humanity we have to consider **biocultural interaction**: how our bodies respond to our cultural environment and vice versa (Figure 3.4).[66] To describe our species with only nature or culture is like describing a rectangle with reference to only its length or width. Without both pieces of information, there *is* no rectangle.[67] Likewise, without both biology and culture, it's impossible to understand what it is to be human. The evidence for this is so overwhelming that scientists now agree that it makes no sense to talk about "human nature," except insofar as "the social *is* the natural."[68]

Perhaps the most obvious example of biocultural interaction involves physical characteristics like flexibility, strength, and speed. Within biological limits, our bodies react to use by developing the capacities we ask of them. We can get faster if we train, stronger if we lift, and more flexible if we stretch. In societies that ask people to develop these capacities, they will. And in ones that ask women and men to develop different capacities, men's and women's bodies will be more different than they would be otherwise.

FIGURE 3.4 | BIOCULTURAL INTERACTION

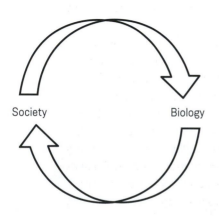

Consider marathons. Women in Western societies were discouraged from running for centuries and formally excluded from competing in marathons until the 1970s. In that time, men got much faster. When women were first allowed to compete, they were much slower than men, but they've gotten faster, too. In fact, they've gotten faster much more quickly than men ever did. Men collectively took approximately thirty years to shave thirty minutes off their best time; it took women only five.[69] Today the men's record is still faster than the women's record, but by less than ten minutes (Figure 3.5). What men and women are allowed and encouraged to do by culture shapes what their bodies are capable of doing.

FIGURE 3.5 | MARATHON WORLD RECORDS BY GENDER

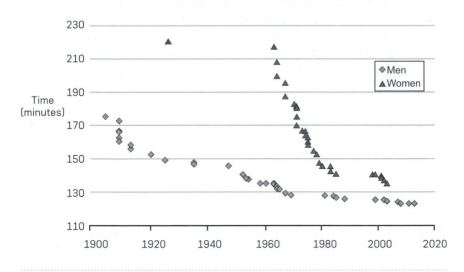

Source: International Association of Athletics Federations.

This is true of our brains, too.[70] Remember those kids playing *Tetris*? Consistent with what we know about brain plasticity, the change in ability manifests itself in our neuroanatomy. In one study, the brains of twelve- to fifteen-year-old girls were measured before and after a three-month period during which they played *Tetris* for an hour and a half each week.[71] At the end of the study, their brains were heavier and showed enhanced cortical thickness, with heightened blood flow to the area. Another study showed shifts in brain function.[72] Practice matters. Changes in the brain have been documented in response to a wide range of activities: juggling, dancing, singing, meditating, and even driving a taxi.[73] Of course they have. Our brain is a cultural organ, responding to our social environment.

Even our hormones and our genes are designed to respond to culture.[74] When we experience a culturally defined "win," for example, our bodies cooperate by using hormones to make us feel good about it.[75] Testosterone rises and falls in response to our interactions. If a man is anticipating a competition, his levels will rise. If he wins the contest, they'll go up further; if he loses, they'll go down.[76] This is true not only for sports, but for games like chess, too.[77] It also works if he's just sitting on the couch watching his favorite team.[78] If he does something he thinks is cool—like drive a sports car—his testosterone gets a bump; if he does it in front of other people, it jumps even higher.[79] In the immediate aftermath of the 2008 presidential election, for example, men who supported the losing candidate saw a drop in their testosterone levels; those who supported the winning candidate did not.[80] We think of behavior as being "testosterone fueled" when, in fact, it's also "testosterone fueling."[81]

Emerging evidence suggests that this is true in at least some ways for women, too. In one study, for example, women asked to exert power over others under experimental conditions found that doing so resulted in a rise in testosterone.[82] The authors suggest that gender differences in who is expected, allowed, and enabled to exert power may shape the average hormonal profiles of men and women. "A lifetime of gender socialization," they write, "could contribute to 'sex differences' in testosterone."

This phenomenon has society-wide implications. In men, forming a committed romantic relationship produces a decline in testosterone.[83] Having a baby can bring that testosterone level down even more.[84] A study of two communities in Tanzania found that such hormonal shifts can happen at the group level, too.[85] Hadza men were involved fathers, taking care of children alongside women. Datoga men did not parent, leaving the work to mothers. The difference in behavior was reflected in their testosterone levels: On average, Datoga men had higher levels than Hadza men.

Our genes also respond to the environment in a process called gene-environment interaction. Instead of dictating our phenotype in a simple, one-directional way, our genotype is flexible.[86] Each gene can express itself in many, sometimes thousands of, different ways. Our bodies adapt on the fly, smartly designing and redesigning themselves in response to the challenges of their environment. Even identical twins become genotypically different over time.[87]

Highly aggressive people, for example, often carry genes for aggression, but we have learned that having those genes does not, in itself, make a person violent. To express themselves in ways that facilitate violence, the genes need to be triggered by trauma.[88] Living in a happy home with loving parents decreases the likelihood that a person genetically predisposed to aggression will become aggressive. In contrast, poverty, a dysfunctional family life, and abuse all increase the chances that the genes for aggression will be "turned on" and lead to violent behavior. Genes matter: A person without a genetic predisposition for violence probably won't grow up to be violent, even if he or she suffers trauma.[89] But genes don't work in a vacuum. A person with the genetic predisposition may never become violent at all; it all depends on the quality of his or her life.

In some cultures, men are nurturing; in others, they are less so. In some environments, people genetically primed become aggressive; in others, they don't. Why? Because humans are not strictly evolved to be either nurturers or warriors. Instead, biology has given them the potential to be either, and more. Our brains, our bodies, the chemicals that circulate within them, and the genes that build them are all prepared to respond to our cultural environment. We have evolved to be flexible.

If fathers are actively involved with their children, their bodies respond in ways that help them be good dads.

So, in societies in which men and women are pressed into very different social roles, we might see the sexes developing quite different strengths and weaknesses. But these aren't necessarily "real." They're biological, to be sure, but they're embodied through a process of gender segregation and differential treatment. They are **deceptive differences**: ones that, by being observed, can make it seem as if men and women are more sexually dimorphic than they are across different times and cultures.[90]

Alternatively, in societies that put men and women onto the same path, they might look more alike than different. Our own society is probably somewhere in between. There are many ways in which we raise our girls and boys very similarly: they live in the same houses, have access to the same foods, go to the same types of schools, and so on. Then again, we dress them differently, buy them different toys, and encourage different activities, on average. Based on these facts, we should expect some differences (in sportiness, for example, or interest in dance), but also quite a lot of similarities (like the increasingly equal mastery of mathe-matics). If human bodies are designed to rise to the cultural occasion, embodying a gender binary is one way we do it, but challenging that gender binary is another. So sex similarity is as much a human biological possibility as sex difference.

Intersectionality: Putting Gender in Context

Another reason why men and women are so much alike is because they share so many other identities in common. Male-bodied and female-bodied people may be biologically designed to play different roles in reproduction at some point in their lives, but they are often the same race, class, nationality, religion, and more. Sometimes people live in societies that expect very different things from men and women. And while there are ways in which biology predisposed us to be different, the manifestation of such differences may be muted by the things men and women share: national, regional, and local cultures, for example, and the quality of their education, their diet and health, their occupations, their family structure, and social networks. And some male- and female-bodied people identify and express themselves as women or men, respectively, or trans, gender fluid, or nonbinary. Others belong to subcultures that otherwise encourage gender-nonconforming behavior, like some queer communities.[91]

Differences and similarities between women and men are filtered through these other life experiences. Men, for example, have 20 to 30 percent greater bone mass and strength than women, making women twice as likely to break a bone and four times as likely to be diagnosed with osteoporosis.[92] Genes and hormones contribute to this discrepancy, but an individual's bone health is also strongly affected by diet, leisure activities, and type of work.[93] Accordingly, among ultra-Orthodox Jewish adolescent boys, the gender pattern is reversed.[94] Boys in these communities are tasked with intensive study of religious documents from a young age, so they spend much less time exercising and more time indoors than other boys their age. As a result, their bones never grow as strong as those of their sisters, who have lighter study loads, do more physical chores, and get more sunlight. Both the biological and the cultural influence of gender on bone mass and strength, then, is mediated by the power of religion.

The idea that gender is not an isolated social fact about us but instead intersects with our other identities is called **intersectionality**.[95] We are not just males and females. A woman might be a white, middle-class, married woman who is religiously observant—once Catholic, now Evangelical Christian—and a parent of a two-year-old (with one on the way), who loves karaoke and votes Democratic. Or she might be an Eastern European immigrant to Milwaukee who moved to New Orleans, fell in love with jazz and bourbon, and plays rugby. Or perhaps a purposefully childfree bisexual Texan who works for the Girl Scouts, manages her epilepsy, collects Legos, and likes to spoil her quirky nephew.

We're going to talk a lot more about intersectionality later. For now, just notice that *all* the things that make us who we are shape our individual personality traits, emotional tendencies, cognitive abilities, and physical potential. When men and women share other identities and life experiences, those things

Sometimes men and women have more in common with each other than they do with others of their own sex.

bring the sexes together, producing even physical similarities as our complex bodies respond to shared cultural environments.

Evolution, Similarity, and Variation

Human males and females evolved to have different roles in reproduction: one sex carries, delivers, and nurses the babies, and the other contributes new genetic material. Given this, it is tempting to look to theories of evolution for straightforward accounts of "real" sex differences. And, in fact, it's common to hear people arguing that because we've evolved to have different roles in reproduction, we've also evolved to have different roles in *life*. This, however, doesn't stand up to the facts. There is overwhelming evidence for the process of human evolution, but not for the idea that men and women have evolved to be two very different kinds of humans, and especially not "opposite sexes."

To start, evolution-based thinking about humans often asserts that the so-called **nuclear family**—a mother and father with children who live together without extended kin—is natural. But this family form didn't exist until very recently. For most of our species' existence, humans lived together not in heterosexual pairs but **kin groups**, culturally variable collections of people considered family.

In **forager societies**—ones in which people migrate seasonally, following crops and game across the landscape—groups were relatively egalitarian. The responsibility for providing food fell on both men and women, and food was shared with everyone in the group.[96] Because everyone traveled together, evolution as a process would select for similarity in walking speeds. Similarly, both women's and men's bodies responded to their shared environment, whether a hot or a cold one, by adapting together to regulate body temperature by size and shape and color. Thus, some local groups evolved to be characteristically taller or shorter, heavier or lighter, darker or lighter.[97]

Instead of difference, then, there are good reasons we might have evolved similarities. Our ancestors lived together in common environments. They knew the same people, ate the same foods, traveled the same territory, shared the same beliefs, and raised the same kids. If it's evolutionarily adaptive for half the population to be good at something (making pottery, for example, or remembering where the bison graze), it could hardly be evolutionarily adaptive for the other half of the population to be bad at it.

It might even be deeply maladaptive. In a crisis, it could be fatal for a tribe to consist of two types of people who are incapable of taking on the work assigned to the other. Sudden shortages of male-bodied or female-bodied members in a group demanded that the other sex be able to cross the cultural divide. Think of the millions of single fathers across the world today. It simply doesn't make sense that men and women would evolve to have wildly different cognitive abilities, levels of physical strength, personality traits, or emotional dispositions. Being able to share responsibilities and substitute for one another is actually incredibly useful. Adaptive, even. There were (and are) strong evolutionary pressures toward sameness.

This is true even in terms of reproduction and childrearing. Children were born to women but raised by the larger group. Fatherhood was a social rather than a biological concept. First, we don't know how much early humans understood about what role men played in reproduction. And, second, because men had a genetic interest in all the group's children—any of whom could be defined as part of his lineage depending on the rules of the particular society—whose sperm were involved wasn't really relevant. As a result, women's sexuality was generally less tightly regulated than it has been in the past few hundred years. Without an interest in establishing paternity, there was also little need to control a fertile woman's sexual behavior.

Instead of being a strictly biological behavior, both men and women have always made sexual decisions in response to cultural rules.[98] Cultures, for example, sometimes assumed it was women rather than men who were more sexual; sometimes they expected fathers to initiate sons into homosexual relationships.[99] Overall, outside of the imperative to form nuclear families, there was more tolerance of homosexual behavior and more room for third genders (like the māhū of Hawaii, the muxe of Mexico, and the hijra of India discussed in the last chapter).[100] In fact, bi- and homosexual behavior may well have cemented alliances between people of the same sex, strengthening each of their positions in their groups and enhancing their access to reproductive sex (as it does among Bonobo chimps, our closest relative).[101] Tolerance of same-sex behavior also opened up possibilities for gender reassignments (like the Albanian sworn virgins) and female "husbands" (like among the Lovedu in Zambia).

The notion that men evolved to be promiscuous and avoid emotional entanglements with women is also a myth. The ability of men to "sow their seed" (to impregnate as many women as they can) is based on the idea that there was an endless field of fertile women to plow.[102] This was almost never the case. At any given time, the majority of women in a kin group were too young or too old to get pregnant; were already pregnant, with reduced fertility due to breastfeeding; or were infertile for unknown reasons. Even sex between two healthy fertile individuals only results in a pregnancy 3 percent of the time.[103] And, outside of monogamy, another guy's sperm might get to the egg first. Most men would have been lucky to sire twelve to sixteen children in their lifetime, not so many more than women's birthing nine to twelve. Instead of sowing seeds, a man's reproduction was probably maximized by having regular sex with a single woman or a few women with whom he was friendly.

Gender does appear to have mattered to most or all human groups throughout the history of our species, and we have almost certainly evolved to notice and care about the difference between males and females, but even this is not sufficient for producing evolved sex differences. Communities typically gendered their tasks, but *how* they were gendered varied. Bearing and nursing children was an exception, of course, because only (some) female-bodied people could do that. But in foraging societies, maternity would have been more of a life stage than a lifestyle. Hunting large animals often involved whole communities working together or groups of men of certain ages or statuses. Some forms of provision (gathering, farming, and hunting smaller animals) were more likely to be women's than men's work.[104] Still other tasks, like building houses, were sometimes considered feminine and sometimes masculine work according to the idiosyncrasies of cultural groups. Even after settled agriculture emerged, tasks and statuses were jumbled in multiple, cross-cutting hierarchies of value.[105] Our ancestors lived intersectional lives.

In other words, the social constructions of gender among early human groups were just as cross-culturally variable, historically changing, and ideologically jumbled as ours. None of this was consistent enough to account for an evolution into an "oppositeness" that spans the whole human species. Instead, current ideas about the "real" differences between men and women are based on what we see now in our WEIRD (Western, educated, industrial, rich, democratic) societies, which are really new ways of organizing gendered social life largely explained by the consolidation of power into large countries.[106]

To summarize, the idea that humans have evolved rigid and specific roles for individuals of each sex—that our different reproductive roles make for different life roles—doesn't do justice to the diversity of our ancestral environments, the power of our cultures, or our actual evolved biology. We have always had complex social lives (where gender was just one thing that mattered) and have always needed to cooperate and respond to unpredictable environments. All this means that, for humans, sexual dimorphism in nonreproductive capacities would not be particularly advantageous. We shouldn't be so surprised, then, to discover that research on sex differences has detected more overlap than the gender binary would predict. There may be ways in which we are different, and in some cultures those differences may be quite pronounced, but we also have the biological capacity to be quite alike.

Revisiting the Question

 The gender binary might be an ideology, but there are real differences between men and women, right?

Well, sure. But it's not nearly as simple as it sounds. As H. L. Mencken famously observed: "There is always an easy solution to every human problem—neat, plausible, and wrong."[107] It would be easy to say that the sex differences we observe are biological and immutable. It would be equally easy to say that they are cultural and easily undone. Neither is true.

Instead, both the sex differences and similarities we see are the result of a complex interplay between biology and society. These dynamic intersections are progressive (each moment we are someone slightly different from the moment before), contingent (what happens is dependent on what is happening both inside and around us), and probabilistic (making it more likely for some outcomes to occur and less likely for others, but never entirely determining the future). To paraphrase Edward O. Wilson, biology has us on a leash, but the leash is very, very long.[108]

If the biological flexibility enabled by that long leash is adaptive, allowing us—both as individuals and as a species—to respond to whatever environmental demands we encounter, then sex should be no exception. The gender binary that characterizes men and women as "opposite sexes" isn't reflected in the science and fails to do justice to what we know about human biology and history. Moreover, what differences we do find are also shaped by life experiences that are not centrally about gender.

For the remainder of this book, then, it's important not to fall back on explanations that offer simple answers. Biology matters, gender matters, society matters, and they all work together to make us the people we are. That's our true nature. We're an extraordinary species with a rich sociocultural life, one that men and women share, and our bodies have been designed for that flexibility.

Next . . .

OK, fine, so establishing that men and women are substantially different from one another isn't as easy as pop culture leads us to believe. But it still *seems* like men and women are different. They move differently, decorate themselves differently, choose different college majors and careers. If these differences aren't biological and immutable, then what are they? It's a good question:

 If men and women aren't naturally opposite, then why do they act so differently so much of the time?

It's time to put the "social" in social theory.

FOR FURTHER READING

Browning, Frank. *The Fate of Gender: Nature, Nurture and the Human Future*. New York: Bloomsbury Publishing, 2016.

Cherney, Isabelle D. "Mom, Let Me Play More Computer Games: They Improve My Mental Rotation Skills." *Sex Roles* 59 (2008): 776–86.

Fine, Cordelia. *Testosterone Rex: Myths of Sex, Science, and Society*. New York: W. W. Norton and Company, 2017.

Guiso, Luigi, Ferdinando Monte, Paola Sapienza, and Luigi Zingales, "Culture, Gender, and Math." *Science* 320, no. 5880 (May 30, 2008): 1164–65.

Jordan-Young, Rebecca. *Brain Storm: The Flaws in the Science of Sex Differences*. Cambridge: Harvard University Press, 2010.

Wade, Lisa. "The New Science of Sex Difference." *Sociology Compass* 7, no. 4 (2013): 278–93.

Zell, Ethan, Zlatan Krizan, and Sabrina Teeter. "Evaluating Gender Similarities and Differences Using Metasynthesis." *American Psychologist* 70, no. 1 (2015): 10–20.

YOU'RE BORN NAKED AND THE
REST IS DRAG.

—RUPAUL

4

Performances

In the last chapter, we reviewed what we know about the role of biology in contributing to the gender binary. After searching our genes, hormones, and brains for the source of our differences, we concluded that while men and women may not be biologically identical, we're not particularly dimorphic either. This may be because, while there are some biological forces pushing us apart, there are likely others—the potential evolutionary benefits of similarity, the responsiveness of our bodies to cultural influences, and the intersections of our identities, for instance—that bring us closer together.

We've also conceded that we do act in gendered ways much of the time, leading us to pose the question:

 Q+A

If men and women aren't naturally opposite, then why do they act so differently so much of the time?

Indeed, men and women do seem to be quite different in their choices about how to use their time and effort, often in ways that match stereotypical expectations. Women, for example, are 3.9 times as likely to major in education as men, while men are 4.3 times more likely to major in engineering.[1] Men prefer to play sports for exercise, while women are more likely to do Pilates, yoga, or dance.[2] Women are

When men and women hold hands, who leads and who follows? How do we learn to hold hands "right"? Gender becomes part of how we inhabit the world, sometimes in the subtlest of ways.

more likely than men to say that religion is "very important" to them and participate actively in religious activities.[3]

Even though we are rather similar, then, we often make divergent choices. These choices apply to an amazing range of activities and are both obvious and subtle. It's not just in careers and activities. We embody gender in little ways, too. It's in how we look at our fingernails, for example (with our hand held out and fingers splayed or with the palm turned toward us and the fingers curled in), how we hold a cigarette (between the thumb and forefinger or between two forefingers with the palm facing in), or how we hold hands with a partner of the other sex (men's palms are usually pointed backward and women's pointed forward such that her body is placed just slightly behind his as they walk). So, there are many differences between men and women in *practice*.

In this chapter, we explain such gendered social patterns as a consequence of social interaction, working on, through, and sometimes against individual biological or psychological predispositions. We argue that we learn complex sets of gendered expectations that tell us how to behave as men and women in varying situations. We sometimes act in gendered ways out of habit, but also come to understand that if we fail to do so, others may tease, hassle, or hurt us. We aren't simply socialized as children into gendered roles that we then automatically perform as adults. Instead, the process of acquiring a gendered sense of self is an active and ongoing one.

None of us, however, simply follows gendered expectations thoughtlessly. We become crafty manipulators. We make exceptions (for ourselves and others), and we apply very different standards depending on the situation and the person. In response, we each develop a way of managing gendered expectations that works for us as unique individuals—sometimes, even, as gender-nonconforming ones.

Sometimes it's easy to follow the rules and sometimes it's incredibly hard. Following rules creates cultural boundaries that are often painful for the people who are on the wrong side of them, by choice or circumstance. Sociologist Michael Kimmel says it beautifully:

> For some of us, becoming adult men and women in our society is a smooth and almost effortless drifting into behaviors and attitudes that feel as familiar to us as our skin. And for others of us, becoming masculine or feminine is an interminable torture, a nightmare in which we must brutally suppress some parts of ourselves to please others—or, simply, to survive. For most of us, though, the experience falls somewhere in between.[4]

The guy who hates football or has a gluten allergy to beer sometimes feels like an outsider. So, too, does the woman who wants to wear a tux to the prom or can't walk in heels. The man whose body is limber and powerful and who loves to dance to classical music may in fact train rigorously to be a ballet dancer, but he pursues these pleasures at the risk of critical assessments from others who question his gender or his sexuality. Likewise, women who are tall and strong and enjoy playing basketball sometimes find that the pleasures of their own bodies can come at a cost to their social life if others judge them to be "unfeminine."

Still, because it's easier to obey gender rules than break them—and life is challenging enough as it is—many of us behave in gendered ways most of the time. So, we contribute to those gendered patterns that we see around us, sustaining the illusion that the gender binary is natural and inevitable.

HOW TO DO GENDER

Sociologists use the phrase **doing gender** to describe the ways in which we actively obey and break gender rules. **Gender rules** are instructions for how to appear and behave as a man or a woman. They are, essentially, the social construct of gender restated in the form of an instruction. Such a rule was at the center of a story told by psychologist Sandra Bem about her four-year-old son, Jeremy, who decided to wear a clip in his hair to preschool one day. Bem recalls:

> *Several times that day, another little boy insisted that Jeremy must be a girl because "only girls wear barrettes." After repeatedly insisting that "wearing bar-rettes doesn't matter; being a boy means having a penis and testicles," Jeremy finally pulled down his pants to make his point more convincingly. The other boy was not impressed. He simply said, "Everybody has a penis; only girls wear barrettes."*[5]

Jeremy's schoolmate stated his objection in the form of a general rule. It wasn't that *he* didn't like it when boys wore barrettes, or that *Jeremy* specifically didn't look fetching in a barrette, it was that only girls and no boys under any circumstances should wear one. Jeremy's schoolmate articulated a rule for all boys that Jeremy had broken: *Only girls wear barrettes.*

You could likely brainstorm hundreds of such rules if you tried. They apply to every area of our lives, specifying how we should dress and decorate our bodies and homes, what hobbies and careers we should pursue, with whom we should socialize and how, and much more. Most of us do gender when we get ready in the morning; stand, sit, and walk; choose leisure activities; do our work; curate our personalities; and do routine activities like eating, bathing, driving, and even having sex.

Every day we do thousands of things that signal masculinity or femininity and we do them according to gender rules. When using social media, for example.[6] Women's choices tend to reflect the rules that they are supposed to be attractive, social, and sweet. They are more likely than men to try to make themselves appear beautiful or sexy in their pictures and to feature friends and family members. Women also post more pictures overall. Men, in contrast, appear to respond to gender rules that dictate they be active, independent, and anti-authority. Their profile pictures often include images of them playing sports, looking tough, and getting into trouble. While women are almost always looking into the camera, men will sometimes be looking away. Men are also more likely than women to be alone in their pictures or posing with expensive objects. There are gender differences in how men and women react to others online, too. Women are more likely to react and more likely to do so positively, with congratulations or encouragement. Men's reactions are more likely than women's to be argumentative, insulting, or ironic. These are, of course, only average differences, and the men and women you know may be different, but most people follow the rules much of the time.

Many of us learn a huge variety of gender rules implicitly, gradually absorbing them as we become increasingly acculturated into our families, communities, and societies. Some rules are relatively rigid (e.g., men do not wear eyeshadow), while others are more flexible and negotiable (if, in your part of the world, men do not have long hair or wear lipstick, how long is too long and does lip balm count?). You can also likely brainstorm rules that straightforwardly contradict one another, because the rules vary among cultures, change over time, and shift across contexts. We tend to become most aware of the rules when we are trying to master new ones; for example, we self-consciously "try on" adult gender attitudes and behaviors as we enter adolescence or when we choose a "look" and set of friends upon entering a new school.[7] At such transition times, our self-consciousness about gender conformity rises because we are aware that social acceptance can be at stake.

Cross-Cultural Variation in Gender Rules

Most gender rules are simple cultural agreements. For instance, grown men in the United States are supposed to physically touch each other only in very ritualized ways (like the back slap in the "man hug" or the butt slap in football for a job well done). In France and Argentina, however, men kiss on the cheek when they greet one another. In some Middle Eastern societies, men even hold hands.

Likewise, whereas skirts are strongly feminized in the United States, men wear kilts in Scotland and, in Arab countries, men wear a white robe called a

President George W. Bush welcomes Saudi Crown Prince Abdullah to his Texas ranch. Holding hands is not an accepted way for two adult men to touch in the United States but is a common practice in some Middle Eastern cultures.

thawb, often with a pink-and-white head covering. The color pink doesn't have feminine connotations in Arab countries the way it does in the West. And in Belgium, pink isn't for girls, nor is it gender neutral; it's for boys. Flowers are another icon of femininity in the West, but certain floral patterns on a kimono clearly signal masculinity in Japan.

What women and men *don't* wear is also dictated by gender rules. In the United States, it's against the rules for women to expose their breasts in public. We take this so seriously that whether women should be allowed to breastfeed in public is still a hot debate. This obsession with hiding women's nipples seems unduly conservative from a European standpoint; in some parts of Europe, it is perfectly acceptable for women to sunbathe topless. Americans might be surprised to hear that Europeans describe Americans as irrationally prudish. Many Americans, as well as Europeans, in turn, condemn the "veiling" practices associated with Islam. Like Europeans judging Americans for covering their breasts, Americans tend to think it is irrationally prudish for women to cover their heads. Only because the idiosyncrasies of our own culture tend to be invisible to us does it seem obvious that women should cover some parts of their bodies but not others.

It often isn't until we read about, travel to, or move to a different country, or otherwise very different cultural milieu, that we encounter rules that are noticeably unfamiliar to us, revealing our own rules as culturally specific. When we do, we become briefly aware of making choices, deciding either to follow or flout these local gender rules, before they again begin to seem "normal." For example, one study of Japanese women who went to work at multinational firms abroad found that carrying a briefcase or drinking beer with colleagues was initially alien to their idea of femininity. After becoming more comfortable in their new environment, however, many did not want to be assigned back to Japan, where this would not have been acceptable behavior for a woman.[8] We get practice at adapting to new gender rules throughout our lives because the gender rules we encounter are constantly undergoing both subtle and dramatic shifts.

Historical Variation in Gender Rules

While the rules for doing gender often feel timeless, they are, in fact, always changing. Consider the earring.[9] In the 1920s, only women of Italian and Spanish descent and sailors pierced their ears. For the women, it was an ethnic practice, similar to the small dot or *bindi* that Hindu women wear on their foreheads, while sailors wore them in the hope that a gold earring might serve as payment for a proper burial were they to sink, wash ashore, and be found by strangers. An American girl born in the 1930s wouldn't have pierced her ears, but she might have worn clip-on earrings. Clip-on earrings went out of style and pierced ears went mainstream in the 1960s.

In that decade, boys probably wouldn't have worn earrings of any kind. When their sisters and all her friends were getting their ears pierced, the only young men doing so were hippies and homosexuals. Twenty years later, during the '80s, male musicians and athletes popularized wearing earrings, but only in one ear. If a man decided to get an ear pierced, he would have gotten it in the left ear if he identified as heterosexual and the right ear if he were gay. A few decades after that, the side of the head would be irrelevant and the piercings would have signified nothing.

Whether and which ear is pierced is no longer culturally meaningful, but earring style remains so. Women are more likely to wear either elaborate or dainty earrings to signify femininity; men typically wear simple studs or small hoops. And now we pierce other things, too, and in gendered ways. Belly-button piercings are found almost exclusively on women, whereas men are more likely to stretch their earlobes with plugs or pierce their septum (that wall of tissue that separates the nostrils).

Gender rules change. They change across time, as the earring example illustrates, and also from context to context.

Michael B. Jordan, villain of the mega-hit superhero movie *Black Panther*, wearing his earrings. Or, to protect the gender binary, we might say "studs."

Contextual Variation in Gender Rules

Many of us take for granted the rules that guide our own gender display and easily adapt to cultural change. Our flexibility tends to mask the fact that the United States itself is a turbulent mixture of subcultures. Accordingly, doing gender, even in our daily lives, requires that we simultaneously know the rules of the cultural mainstream as well as those of the alternative cultures we visit. In other words, we need more than one pair of gender binary glasses.

Goths are a striking example. Amy Wilkins, a sociologist who studied a group of self-identified Goths in the Northeast, explains that they defy conventional gender expectations. Both women and men strive to attain a distinctive, even frightening appearance:

Goths tell the world and each other who they are by making their bodies freaky. Goth bodies are cloaked in black, pierced, tattooed, dyed, powdered white. The Goth style juxtaposes medieval romanticism with bondage wear; puffy velvet with

skin-tight PVC. Goths may sport dog collars and spikes, or fishnets and corsets—all
in somber colors: black or blood red.[10]

Goths cultivate a countercultural appearance, but they also go to work at places like banks and elementary schools. Some of them "do Goth" all the time, but most will adjust to more mainstream expectations when necessary, washing off the white powder when they're at work and leaving the dog collar at home.

Goths are an example of **cultural traveling**, moving from one cultural or subcultural context to another and sometimes back. Belinda did another kind of cultural traveling when she came out as a lesbian. As she joined a new community, she encountered people who policed her into a whole new set of subculture-specific gender rules:

Basically, within the lesbian community, I was completely made fun of. I used
to have people make fun of me for carrying a purse and looking "too girly" and,
"Oh, you're not really gay." Just those kinds of comments. So that was really hard
for me when I was coming out because I just wanted to be taken seriously, you
know? . . . So, my response to that [when I first came out] was to kind of change to
become less feminine, change my body posturing and the way that I dress and cut
off all my hair and that kind of stuff.[11]

Like Belinda, many of us have to adapt to new contexts and even adjust our look for different audiences. We all make cultural adjustments throughout our day and week. A guy driving home from a night at the sports bar with his buddies, during which he yelled at the TV, threw back beers, and pounded the table, will likely resort to a polite and professional manner the next morning at work. Both of these self-presentations are versions of masculinity. Likewise, a college student may comfort crying children at her job at a day care center, look to hook up at a party that night, and drag herself to class in sweats the next morning prepared to discuss the week's reading. In each context—the nurturer, the flirt, and the student—she does femininity differently.

The gender rules that apply to varying contexts can be quite nuanced. Knowing exactly what style and behavior rules are appropriate for a wedding (is it a day or night wedding?), a first date (is it coffee or dinner?), and a job interview (do you want to project creativity or reliability?) requires sophisticated calculations. Most of us make these cultural transitions rather easily, often flawlessly. And thank goodness. People who are incapable of "tuning" their behavior to the social context are at risk of coming off as psychologically disturbed or willfully deviant. The same glowing, silver gown that made an actress seem so glamorous on the red carpet at the Oscars would make her look drunk or deranged if she wore it at the grocery store the next morning.

In sum, we learn a set of gender rules that is specific to our societies. We also learn how that set of gender rules varies—from the funeral home to the class-

Attendees at a Gothic festival in Poland congregate, showing off their unique fashion. They likely tone down their appearance when in less Goth-tolerant settings.

room, from Savannah to San Francisco, and from age eight to eighty—and how to adjust to those changes. We don't get just one pair of gender binary glasses when we're kids; we get many pairs. And we're constantly getting new prescriptions as needed.

LEARNING THE RULES

Children begin to learn gender in infancy.[12] They can tell the difference between male and female voices by six months old and between men and women in photographs by nine months old. By the time they're one, they know to associate deep voices with men and high voices with women. By two and a half, most children know what sex they are and are "reaching out to social norms," trying to learn the rules.[13] By three years old, they tend to prefer play partners of their own sex and think more positively about their own group compared to the other.

Parents sometimes have to make hard decisions about how much to encourage their children to embrace or reject gendered expectations.[14] Some are adamant that gendered behavior is biological and see gender nonconformity as a sign that something is terribly wrong. Others feel equally strongly that gendered behavior is purely social and unnecessarily constraining and are as quick to push their children away from stereotypical behavior as other parents are to encourage it. Most parents are somewhere in between and, for reasons we'll explore later, are more comfortable with their girls' gender nonconformity than their boys'.

Children grow up in households, then, with varying levels of gender conformity and adherence to gendered divisions of labor. Sometimes taking out the trash is a dad's job, sometimes it isn't, and sometimes there's no dad. All children, then, learn the gender rules followed in their homes, but they also have to contend with an outside world that generally affirms gender difference. Most toy stores still sell "boy toys" and "girl toys," categorized in binary ways and coded with gendered messages about which sex is smart, caring, pretty, and tough.[15] Teachers sometimes separate school activities and games into boys versus girls; community and school sports are usually sex segregated, such that girls and boys rarely play alongside or against each other.[16] More often than not, children's television and books tell gender-stereotypical stories.[17] By the age of five, kids have absorbed a great deal of complex and even contradictory information about gender.[18] These are a child's first pairs of gender binary glasses.

Once children have gender binary glasses, they often begin to act in ways that reflect them, especially if their parents or peers reward or display gender-stereotypical behavior.[19] Children orient themselves to toys they believe are gender appropriate and begin to make assumptions about other people based on their gender. In preschool, they use gender as a criterion for whom to befriend and play with. They actively engage with the gender binary, sometimes even inventing gendered beliefs based on their observations, like one four-year-old who announced confidently to his parents on the way home from an Italian restaurant: "Men eat pizza and women don't."[20]

Developmentally, gender rules are absorbed just like all the other rules kids are busy learning, like how to cross the street safely, what's fair between siblings, and how to behave in a classroom. Growing up is all about learning rules, and kids themselves can be pretty rigid about doing things "right." This rigidity peaks around age six, which is exactly when many parents throw their hands up and give their sons toy guns and their daughters Barbie dolls. Though this rigidity is often used as evidence that gender is biological, psychologists have shown that it is largely because children aren't yet capable of absorbing and negotiating the rules in their full complexity.[21] Childhood rigidity is a learning phase more than proof of biological predispositions.[22]

As children learn that gender norms are not quite so strict, they become much more flexible about their own and others' conformity to gender expectations. They also actively resist these expectations and, as the story about Jeremy's barrette suggests, they teach each other the rules they (think they) know. Children, then, are participants in their own and others' socialization. They, like us, are negotiating gender rules from the get-go and setting up consequences for both one another and the adults around them. Sociologist Emily Kane, for example, describes giving into her preschool boy's desire for a set of trading cards glamorizing images of violent combat.[23] She preferred not to encourage her five-year-old to identify with this version of masculinity, but when her husband found him quietly crying after school because he was excluded from playing with his friends—"*all* the boys had these cards," he explained—she relented.[24] It was a choice between allowing her child to have a toy that she did not like and a son's loneliness and alienation. She bought the cards.

As we grow up, our ability to do gender in ways others will accept is not so rigid as to require a specific set of trading cards. Especially if we're exposed to children and adults who resist gender rules, we begin to see more flexible possibilities for ourselves.[25] We also learn to navigate gender rules in more sophisticated ways. Most of us become more tolerant of ambiguity and contradictions. But we continue to reach out to gender norms, continually learning and adjusting to new sets of gender rules that we encounter as we interact with new people, new places, and a changing social terrain.

Learning the rules, then, is a lifelong process that we actively negotiate. This means that a model of socialization in which genderless children are taught a gender role in their childhood, one that they then carry out over the rest of their lives, is wrong. This assumes that children are victims of their environment, infected with rigid versions of masculinity or femininity, never to recover fully. This is the model of socialization that assumes giving boys trucks or girls Barbie dolls is "injecting" children with a "virus" of sex-typed dualism that they will carry in them forever.

This "injection" idea of socialization fails on three fronts. First, it suggests that socialization is somehow finished by the time we're adults. Second, it leaves no room for the possibility that we actively consider and resist gender rules, something that Jeremy was doing even in preschool. Third, because the model fails to acknowledge that people resist and change gender rules, it can't explain cultural changes, such as the ones that made pierced ears acceptable at different times for women and men.

Accordingly, sociologists prefer a **learning model of socialization** that suggests that socialization is a lifelong process of learning and relearning gendered expectations as well as how to negotiate them. We don't *get* socialized once and for all but are constantly *being* socialized. This gives us credit for being *smart* members of our culture. We aren't cultural dupes; we are cultural *experts* who consciously and strategically adapt our behavior to changes in our social environments. We do this in negotiation with others, learning to manage conflict along the way, though usually without resorting to dropping our pants like Jeremy. We may get Barbie dolls but use them in unexpected ways, digging holes with their pointed toes or throwing their heads around like balls. Boys who are encouraged to play with trucks rarely grow up to be truck drivers. We are presented with symbols of gender from our childhood onward, but how we use the meanings our culture intends them to convey is partly up to us.

WHY WE FOLLOW THE RULES

Like the contents of the gender binary, then, the rules only *seem* simple and stable over time. Instead, they are complicated, constantly shifting, and even contradictory. We learn them, better understanding their intricacies as we grow older. And we follow them, more or less, much of the time. We do so out of habit, for pleasure, and because of encouragement and punishment from others.

Habit

Sometimes we follow gender rules because they are part of our culture. We simply become habituated. We get used to walking and sitting in a certain way, own a wardrobe of already appropriately gendered clothes, and have experiences in rewarding gender-conforming activities.

All this repeated practice allows us to do gender without really thinking about it. Psychologists call such frequently repeated behaviors "overlearned"; they are learned not only by our minds but by our bodies—like riding a bike or typing on a keyboard—so we no longer need to think about them.[26] Men's shirts, for example, are typically made so that the buttons are along the right and the button holes along the left; women's shirts are typically made the opposite way. When was the last time you had to stop and think about the relative location of the buttons and button holes on your clothes while getting dressed? Your hands just automatically go to the right places. Such overlearned knowledge often becomes especially noticeable when someone transitions from identifying and displaying masculinity to femininity, or vice versa.

Once we have overlearned a rule, we don't experience it as oppressive but as natural, however arbitrary it may be. Accordingly, it's often *easy* to follow gender rules, especially ones that are fundamental in our culture; we mostly do so unconsciously. American men don't often deliberate, for instance, about whether to pee sitting down or standing up. We potty train boys in the sitting position, but then make active efforts to train them to pee standing up such that, as men, the position is something they mostly take for granted as normal. On the flip side, it never occurs to most American women to pee standing up, even though, with parental training and practice, the majority could probably do so with little mess (or, at least, no more mess than that frequently left behind by men). In some parts of the world, such as Ghana or China, women do stand up to pee, whereas men in Germany and Japan often do not.

Many of the gender rules that we follow, then, are simply a matter of habit, overlearned and often nonconscious.

Pleasure

More than simply being habitual, following gender rules can be quite pleasurable. For a man who has overlearned conventional American masculinity, it is rewarding to enact that masculinity at a sports bar with the guys. He knows the script, the beer tastes great, and his team might win. The same is true for enacting those aspects of femininity that are overlearned. Many women, for instance, enjoy dressing up and looking nice in a specifically feminine way.

For just this reason, we may especially enjoy opportunities to do gender elaborately. You may relish formal events like quinceañeras, bar and bat mitzvahs, high school proms, and weddings. These events all call for strongly gendered displays: suits or tuxedos for men, dresses or gowns for women. It can be fun to pamper yourself at the salon, bring flowers to your date, and open doors or have them opened for you. It feels great to know that you look especially beautiful in your dress or unusually dashing in your tux. Success is intrinsically rewarding, and that is no less true when the success comes from performing gender in ways that other people admire.

Some of the pleasure of doing gender can come from doing gender in defiant ways. Evan Urquhart, for example, a self-identified "butch lesbian woman," initially started wearing men's clothes because she wanted to attract women who liked women; in the queer circles in which she lived, wearing men's clothes—breaking mainstream gender rules, that is, but following subcultural ones—was one way for her to communicate a lesbian identity.[27] She was surprised to discover, though, that wearing men's clothes wasn't just effective at attracting the attention of the kind of women she liked; it also *felt* good:

> *I realized almost immediately that I was feeling far more comfortable and confident and that I liked the way I looked in the mirror for the first time in my life. Other people who knew me said I looked more natural, more like my clothing fit my personality. It felt a bit like I'd been wearing an uncomfortable, ill-fitting costume all my life.*

Doing masculinity was pleasurable for Evan, and so she adopted the style. Since she was part of a subculture with a set of alternative gender rules that enabled her presentation, she was able to do gender in that way and enjoy it.

There's nothing new about drag: Even in 1915, people found it fun. This group of women is enjoying a night on the town donning suits, drinking beer, smoking cigars, and playing pool.

Observation

Sometimes we follow the rules simply because we're being observed. Consider the act of farting, a great example of a behavior that is sensitive to context. In a study of 172 college students, over half of heterosexual women, but only a quarter of the heterosexual men, reported being anxious about the possibility that someone might overhear their flatulence.[28] For men, a good fart can be a source of pride. "Because if it's strong," said one, "it's more manly." Almost a quarter of heterosexual men said they sometimes farted in front of people on purpose; only 7 percent of heterosexual women said the same. Nonheterosexual men, interestingly, were the least comfortable with others' awareness of their flatulence, and nonheterosexual women sat squarely between heterosexual men and women.

Of course, the nature of the audience matters, too. If observation changes what we do, then who is doing the observing is part of why. A study of women's

public eating—dining in restaurants with a companion—found that women dining with male companions took smaller bites and ate more slowly than women
dining with other women.[29] They were also more likely to sit still, maintain good
posture, and use their napkins more delicately. The author of the study, sociology major Kate Handley, explained:

> When their companion was a man, women used their napkins more precisely and
> frequently than when their companion was another woman. In some cases, the
> woman would fold her napkin into fourths before using it so that she could press
> the straight edge of the napkin to the corners of her mouth. Other times, the woman
> would wrap the napkin around her finger to create a point, then dab it across her
> mouth or use the point to press into the corners of her mouth. Women who used their
> napkins precisely also tended to use them quite frequently.
>
> In contrast, women dining with a female companion generally used their nap-
> kins more loosely and sparingly. These women did not carefully designate a specific
> area of the napkin to use, and instead bunched up a portion of it in one hand and
> rubbed the napkin across their mouths indiscriminately.

Both the farting and the eating examples reveal that gender isn't necessarily a
part of who we are but rather something we perform when others are listening
or watching. Sometimes those others, moreover, aren't simply passive observers
but people who actively encourage or punish us.

Policing

Sometimes we follow the rules because breaking them can attract negative attention. Let's revisit the story of Jeremy and his barrette. Jeremy's indignant schoolmate felt confident that he was entitled to enforce the unwritten rule that boys
don't wear barrettes. Despite Jeremy's protestations, his schoolmate remained
insistent, pushing Jeremy to defend his decision to wear one. Sociologists use
the term **gender policing** to describe responses to the violation of gender rules
aimed at promoting conformity.

When we are policed, we are being taught that negative consequences will
follow if we fail to learn the rules and follow them, at least when someone is
watching. Gender policing happens every day. It comes from our friends, our
love interests, our parents, bosses, and mentors. It's part of our daily lives. Some
of it can be brutal and painful (especially for people who don't fit in binary
boxes), but much of it is friendly and humorous or takes the form of teasing.
Consider these stories from our students:

- As James came in from a Saturday night with friends, his father warned,
  "Get to bed. We're going to the woods tomorrow." "Nah, Dad," the son

replied. "I can't." His dad began to tease him, saying: "What? You too good to go hunting with your dad now?"

- Chandra goes to her economics class wearing sweats, a ponytail, and no makeup. A guy with whom she's been flirting all semester says to her, humorously, "Aw! What's with the sweats?! I thought you liked me!"
- Sun, waiting in line to use a single-stall bathroom, sees that the men's bathroom is open and starts toward it. As she walks in, her friend says, "You're not going to use the *men's* bathroom, are you!?"

In each of these stories, a person breaks a gender rule and is then subjected to a demand for them to give an **account**, an explanation for why the person broke the rule that works to excuse his or her behavior. In the first example, James's disinterest in going to the woods with his dad broke a common rule in rural working-class communities: *Men should want to hunt.* When Chandra's guy friend used her appearance to suggest she wasn't interested in him, he affirmed the rule: *Women should dress up for men they want to impress.* Sun's friend expressed surprise that Sun would dare to use a restroom labeled "Men." The rule is clear: *Use the appropriate gender-designated bathroom.*

A raised eyebrow, a derisive laugh, or a comment like "Are you sure you want to do that?" are what sociologists think of as **accountability**, an obligation to explain why we don't follow social rules that other people think we should know and obey. We are reminded of our accountability to gender rules when people raise an eyebrow at our behavior, quiz us on our decision-making, or offer mild disapproval. Being held to account is a gentle way to induce conformity. It is easier to avoid awkward questions and others' approval is rewarding. Over time, accountability can make big differences in our lives. Asking women to account for their ambition, for example, may undermine their willingness to develop or indulge it, while calling men to account for being insufficiently ambitious will steer them toward seizing challenges and showing off their successes.

Mildly negative reactions to gender nonconformity, though, and the threat of being unpopular, are reasonably tolerable prices to pay for the freedom to be ourselves. What is less easily tolerated are demands for an account that are intended to shame us and push us back in line. This more aggressive response to breaking gender rules is captured in the term policing, a response to the violation of gender rules that is aimed at exacting conformity. When women are called "dyke," "bitch," or "cunt," they are often being policed for being strong or assertive, characteristics that a binary lens sees as masculine and unacceptable for women. Conversely, when men are called "pussy" or "girl," they are often being accused of not being strong or assertive, and in the logic of the gender binary, that means not masculine. The accusation that a woman is being "bossy" or the put-down phrase "nice guys finish last" applied to a man who isn't sufficiently aggressive are ways that both women and men do gender policing.

Because of policing, the risks of nonconformity go beyond just being judged, though that can be bad enough. We can lose our friends, lovers, or the support of our parents. We may be fired or passed over for jobs or promotions because our gender display doesn't please clients or coworkers. Gender policing can also be emotionally and physically brutal. The FBI reported 1,363 victims of hate crimes against sexual minorities, trans, and gender-nonconforming people in 2016.[30] Sexual minorities break the rule that *men should have sex with women and women should have sex with men*. Trans and gender-nonconforming people break the rule that *people's gender identity and performance should match their apparent biological sex*. Sometimes the consequences for breaking these gender rules is living with other people's discomfort; sometimes it's violence.

Because the rules themselves vary situationally, so does the nature of our accountability and our risk of being policed. It is certainly dangerous to be queer in some contexts, but it can be quite fun at Halloween or at gay-friendly bars. Middle school boys who study hard may be teased for being "fags," but if they adopt a tough-guy performance to avoid taunting, they may be policed by their teachers and parents for trying to look and act "hard," especially if they are not white. Female athletes may be told by their coach to be more aggressive on the field but policed by their parents or peers if they don't show a more "ladylike" gender performance off it. We, like Jeremy, are policed into multiple and even contradictory gender displays by people with various, often clashing agendas.

Some of us may also be more heavily or lightly policed than others. In contexts where there is a high tolerance for both gender nonconformity and sexual minorities, identifying as nonheterosexual can be a blanket excuse, getting people out of following lots of rules, even those that have nothing to do with signaling sexual attraction. In contexts where there is low tolerance, though, sexual minorities may feel that their safety depends on hyper-conforming. Cisgendered men and women, especially if their bodies naturally fit into gendered expectations (like short, thin women and tall, strong men) may face fewer demands for accountability than people who identify as trans or whose bodies don't give as strong cues about being female or male. A less obviously male or female person may threaten others' sense of right and wrong, making them feel entitled to push that person to "prove" who they are by adorning themselves in the signs of masculinity or femininity, like gendered jewelry, clothes, shoes, and hairstyles.[31]

Both policing and the milder calls for gender accountability are more influential if they come from someone we care for (like your girlfriend or boyfriend) or who has power over us (such as your boss). We also hold ourselves accountable, kindly and cruelly. We watch TV and read fashion blogs or lifestyle magazines to learn how, and how not, to dress. We read the sports section to make sure we can talk about who won the big game last night and how. We stand in front of the mirror and inspect our faces, scrutinize our bodies for too much or not enough hair, and hope for bumps and bulges in gender-appropriate places. We anticipate not just questions, but consequences, if we fail to meet gender standards.

We inspect our behavior no less than our bodies: Were we too loud or forward? Too meek or agreeable? Sometimes we call ourselves ugly names or feel shame or disgust. We punish our bodies with overexercise or starvation. We police our words and our tone of voice, watching to ensure that we don't sound too opinionated (if we're women) or too emotional (if we're men). We may force ourselves to major in engineering when we really prefer English literature because we know we'll later be judged by the size of our paycheck; or we may choose to stay single because our friends will never let us hear the end of it if we let them know we're gay; or we may not tell a guy that we like him because we fear being seen as "desperate."

We even recruit others to help keep us accountable. We ask each other to evaluate our bodies, our clothes, and our interactions with others. When women get ready for a party together, they frequently ask one another to assess their outfits, looking for a second opinion as to whether they are wearing just the right clothes. Many women try to follow this tricky rule: *Women should dress sexy but not slutty.* "You can wear a short skirt or a low-cut top," we hear, "but not both." There may be nothing malicious in this; it is simply women trying to help their friends follow the rules that they know apply to them.

We also use media, often unconsciously, to advertise and test gender rules with our friends and family. When we get together to watch the Oscars and snark at the outfits or take pleasure in laughing at a man's failure on some reality TV show, we are telling each other what makes a person likable, look good, or deserve respect. Often, our evaluations are gendered. Through these routines, we learn what our friends think is ugly, slutty, sloppy, gay, bitchy, weak, and gross and, accordingly, how we should and shouldn't dress and act around them. Collective reactions to celebrity fashions and personalities, then, can serve to clarify and affirm rules, giving us resources to avoid being policed.

And, of course, we participate in policing others directly. We create consequences for those who break the rules. We kindly ask for accounts when we want to warn our friends and family members that they are at risk of being policed by someone less benevolent than we are. If we are deeply disconcerted by seeing a rule we care about broken, we may give in to the temptation to be mean-spirited or cruel in policing even those we call friends. We may even feel a sense of injustice or unfairness if the rules we follow—sometimes at a sacrifice—are broken by others who can do so without apparent consequences.

Between accountability, the social demand for an explanation, and policing, we collectively ensure that our choices about whether and how to follow gender rules have real social consequences. Some are mild and some are severe, but they all shape the distribution of rewards and punishments. Facing this, we have three choices: follow the rules, break the rules and face the consequences, or figure out how to persuade others to let us break the rules.

HOW TO BREAK THE RULES

Breaking gender rules is routine. Sometimes we break the rules because it is impossible to follow them, no matter how badly we would like to. The mother undergoing chemotherapy, for example, may not be able to care for her husband and children the way she feels she should. The aging man may not be able to perform sexually the way men are told they must. Likewise, the guy who is five foot two simply can't be taller than most women.

Other times, rules are downright contradictory, like the one that says that men should be able to drink a lot of alcohol but also remain in control. Or maybe we're part of a subculture that requires breaking gender rules endorsed by the mainstream, like the female rancher whose daily life involves getting poop on her shoes. Sometimes we don't have the resources to follow a rule, like the man who can't afford to treat women on dates. At times we break a particular rule because we have concluded that following it is personally undesirable or socially wrong, like people who identify as nonbinary and mix and match forms of gender expression.

Although policing is about using social pressure to make noncompliance costly, not every deviation from a gender rule results in negative consequences for the rule breaker. Remember the three stories discussed earlier in this chapter? In each case, it turns out, the rule breaker got away with breaking the rule. Each avoided any penalty by offering an acceptable account.

Let's revisit the stories, this time following them through to the end:

- As James came in from a Saturday night with friends, his father warned, "Get to bed. We're going to the woods tomorrow." "Nah, Dad," the son replied. "I can't." His dad began to tease him, saying: "What? You too good to go hunting with your dad now?" James just said, "No, football tryouts are next week and I was gonna run drills with Mike in the morning." "Go get 'em, son," said his father.
- Chandra goes to her economics class wearing sweats, a ponytail, and no makeup. A guy with whom she has been flirting all semester says to her, humorously, "Aw! What's with the sweats?! I thought you liked me!" And she smiles and replies, "Hey! I just came from the gym." He reassures her, "I figured. I was just kidding."
- Sun, waiting in line to use a single-stall bathroom, sees that the men's bathroom is open and starts toward it. As she walks in, her friend says,

"You're not going to use the *men's* bathroom, are you!?" Sun says, "I wouldn't, but I really have to go!" Her friend nods sympathetically.

As these stories illustrate, we can get away with breaking rules if we have a good excuse. When the characters above say, "Football tryouts are next week," "I just came from the gym," or "I really have to go," they are offering an account to justify why they are breaking the rule.

These accounts may or may not be true, but they offer a sufficient explanation to others that makes gender nonconformity *incidental* rather than *intentional*. That is, the rule breaking isn't interpreted as an attack on the rule itself but an unfortunate and unavoidable deviation. In this way, accounting does more than excuse one's behavior. By explaining why an exception should be made in their case, the speakers are affirming the rule itself. So James *really* is saying: "[Of course I would go hunting], it's just that football tryouts are next week." Chandra is saying: "I [would have dressed up for you, but I] just came from the gym." And Sun is saying, "I wouldn't [use the men's bathroom normally], but I really have to go!"

Importantly, these speakers didn't respond, "Actually I don't like hunting" or "Who says I have to dress up for you?" or "It's stupid that I can't use the men's bathroom!" Such responses reject the rule altogether. This is actually quite rare; people don't usually defy gender rules outright because confronting them head-on can cause conflict. Instead, if the rule breaker affirms the legitimacy of the rule, the one asking for an account is usually satisfied, and conflict is avoided.

Interestingly, such verbal affirmations of the rule often work just as well as a change in behavior; infractions are punished only when they aren't excused. That's why trans men are more likely to be victims of hate crimes than guys dressed up like women at Halloween. Halloween is an account. It is a way for men to say, "[I would never dress like a woman normally, but] it's Halloween!" A trans person has no such excuse. The Halloween reveler is an exception that proves the rule; being trans is an attack on the rule itself.

In addition to learning the rules in all their variety, then, part of gender socialization is learning what exceptions and accounts are acceptable in different social circles. Accounting is therefore a skill. Jeremy had not yet mastered the art of accounting. He wasn't sophisticated enough to negotiate his gender with his schoolmate and resorted instead to dropping his pants, a rather primitive way of proving he was a boy. Explicit conflict over gender rule breaking is typical of younger kids who have just begun to learn the rules and haven't yet mastered the act of explaining away violations. In contrast, adults tend to be quite good at offering accounts, though some of us are better at it than others.

But there is always the risk that our accounts will fail. Our student Jeff spoke of his failed account:

I told my guy friends I couldn't hang out with them because I was going to a movie with my girlfriend. They asked me what movie and I said, sheepishly, because I knew they were going to laugh at me: Sweet Home Alabama. *They laughed hysterically because I was going to see a "chick flick."*

Jeff broke a rule: *Guys don't watch chick flicks.* And his friends policed him by laughing. So Jeff offered an account, but it didn't work:

Even though I really did want to see the movie, I said: "Because [my girlfriend] wants to see it, and if she's not happy, then I'm not happy." This just made them laugh at me more. "You're totally whipped!" they cried.

Jeff's account failed to excuse his rule breaking (seeing a chick flick) because it broke another gender rule about heterosexual relationships: *Men don't submit to their girlfriends' desires.* While Jeff's account might have worked in an all-girl or mixed-gender group, his account wasn't accepted by this particular group of young, single men, who responded to his accounts with shaming and sanctioning. Despite his best efforts, his gender performance was policed.

We make strategic decisions as to when and how often to test the limits of our rule breaking. We may tend to overconform when we are in an unfamiliar setting but break lots of rules in a familiar setting, and we may even provide accounts on behalf of others when we know them or the setting well. "Janice is taking up the trumpet just like her big brother," we might comment. "I suppose the family can't afford another instrument." Or "John is being so quiet and self-effacing; he must be really nervous with his father in the room."

Higher social status usually provides greater immunity from others' policing. Those of us who think more quickly on our feet, are opinion leaders among our peers, or are exceptionally well liked or charismatic can get away with an amazing amount of rule breaking. You probably know someone who gets a pass on rules. And some people like to test the rules more than others, trying to see how much they can get away with. We all probably know someone like this, too, just as we know people who are extremely risk averse. All of us, though, break the rules at least a little bit. We sometimes make strategic gambles, breaking the rules in situations where we suspect we will have our accounts accepted or the stakes are low if they are not.

Like following the rules, breaking the rules can be fun, empowering, and rewarding. The risks of breaking a rule may be outweighed by the value of doing something you want or nudging the world toward a future society you'd like to see. When a woman wears sweats and a baggy T-shirt to class, she sends the message that she doesn't care what anyone else thinks, and that can be empowering. Wearing sweats and a baggy T-shirt, however, is only defiant in the context of a rule against doing so. So breaking rules doesn't mean you're "free" from

Thanks to her lovable personality, comedienne and talk show host Ellen DeGeneres gets a pass on strict gender rules. Her talk show continues to attract record numbers of audience members, even as she dons menswear, keeps her hair short, and appears with her wife.

them. It is as much a reaction to the rules as following them. Even the shape of rebellion, then, is determined by the gender binary and its dictates.

In sum, because we can't or don't want to follow gender rules, we break them quite frequently. We can do this fairly easily most of the time, so long as we offer a "good" excuse, one that affirms the rule that is being broken. All of this affirmation makes the rules seem legitimate and true. That is, we manage simultaneously to break and affirm the rules, making it seem like everyone buys into them, while still accommodating a wide range of both male and female behavior.

THE NO. 1 GENDER RULE

Gender rules vary across cultures, subcultures, and history; intersect with other identities; and vary in strength. But one rule transcends all identities and is true across cultures and subcultures and throughout recent history. That rule is *do gender*.[32] No matter how you do gender, if you want to be treated like an integrated member of society—a person whom others want to know, work with, play with, and love—doing gender in some recognizable way is compulsory. In the West, this generally means that you *must* identify as a man or a woman, not both, and not something else. And you *must* perform a culturally recognizable form of masculinity or femininity, especially if you could conceivably pass as the other sex and/or naturally look a little androgynous. Usually this performance is expected to match one's genitals. Even in places that are welcoming of trans men or women, people who identify as trans are usually expected to do a recognizable version of masculinity or femininity. And cultures with more than two genders also expect the members of third, fourth, and fifth gender categories to be recognizable as such.

If you do not do gender, you become **culturally unintelligible**. You will be so outside the symbolic meaning system that people will not know how to interact with you. This is the experience of one sociologist, Betsy Lucal, an androgynous-looking woman who doesn't do femininity. She writes:

Trans women like Caitlin Jenner can avoid some policing by following the gender rules that newly apply to them.

> *Using my credit cards sometimes is a challenge. Some clerks subtly indicate their disbelief, looking from the card to me and back at the card and checking my signature carefully. Others challenge my use of the card, asking whose it is or demanding identification. One cashier asked to see my driver's license and then asked me whether I was the son of the cardholder. Another clerk told me that my signature on the receipt "had better match" the one on the card.*[33]

What Lucal understands all too well is that if you really don't or can't do gender, it is a serious communicative crisis for everyone interacting with you. Consequently, most of us do gender at least a little—and usually more than a little. Doing gender preserves our membership in our cultural community and ensures that those around us treat us with a modicum of benevolence.

This need to be culturally intelligible is why we see gendered social patterns. We see them because everyone is doing gender. We may not do it all the time, we may not do it enthusiastically, and we may not do it in the same way. We may not even do it in accordance with our genitals, but we do it. And while we don't hesitate to provide accounts in order to break the weaker rules, the strong rules are followed by almost everyone, lest one face truly harmful and dangerous levels of policing. The strongest rule of all—the rule to do gender—has nearly 100 percent compliance.

Thus, while the contents of the gender binary are constantly shifting as we move across time and space, the binary itself persists. It persists in our minds (because we fashion our perception of the world to match it); it persists in our bodies (because we adorn and manipulate them to reflect it); and it persists in our society (because we perform it in interaction with others).

Revisiting the Question

If men and women aren't naturally opposite, then why do they act so differently so much of the time?

We see gendered patterns in society because we learn rules for gendered performances through lifelong processes of socialization. The gender rules themselves are incredibly complex, varying across time, cultures, subcultures, and even contexts. We adjust our gendered performances, often seamlessly and unconsciously, as we encounter different situations and audiences.

Sometimes we follow these rules because it is enjoyable to do gender well. Much of the time, however, we follow them out of habit. At other times, we quite consciously follow rules. We may do so because we feel accountable to ourselves and others. Or we may expect and want to avoid policing.

Being policed by others pushes us to comply with gender norms in order to avoid feeling humiliated, stupid, or excluded—or to avoid physical harm. And we police others, too, because it can give us the inverse feeling of satisfaction, superiority, and entitlement. Accounts are a way of deflecting the negative consequences of rule breaking. They are part of the ordinary give and take of social life, in which making ourselves understandable to others is how we participate in creating shared meanings.

Even rule breaking, though, has a way of affirming the binary and its rules. If we know the rules, we can offer a good excuse, one that assures the questioner that we are committed to the rules, just like he or she is, in all cases but this one. As long as most people, most of the time, can offer satisfactory accounts for rule breaking, such violations will not undermine our collective enforcement of the rules and the gender binary they uphold.

Accountability, accounting, and policing all function to produce and protect the gender binary in the face of bodies, personalities, interests, and inclinations that are diverse, regardless of the gender label we hang on ourselves. If we were naturally feminine or masculine in this binary way, there would be no need to police gender performances. Because the rules are complex, and even contradictory, we learn to do gender and account for rule breaking in many different ways. The fact that we can know, follow, and justify different sets of rules for different contexts is another indication that our gender is not simply a part of our biology over which we have no control.

Somewhere between reaching out to learn the rules, learning how to follow them flexibly, accounting for the many instances in which we break them, and seeking subcultures that share our sense of what rules were "made to be broken," we manage to develop a way of doing gender that more or less works for us, given our opportunities and constraints. We grow up into culturally adept, gendered adults and leave some of the rigidities of childhood behind.

Next . . .

Our strategy for managing gendered expectations, of course, is also shaped by other personal characteristics, such as our social class and residential location, race and ethnicity, immigration status, sexual orientation, age and attractiveness, and our physical abilities and disabilities. It is to this fact that we turn next, asking:

If gender is just one part of who we are, why isn't it crowded out by all the other things about us that are meaningful and consequential?

The answer will add many more layers of complexity to our theory of gender.

FOR FURTHER READING

Bridges, Tristan. "Doing Gender with Wallets and Purses," *Inequality by (Interior) Design* (blog), April 2, 2013, www.inequalitybyinteriordesign.wordpress.com/2013/04/02/doing-gender-with-wallets-and-purses/.

Jacques, Juliet. "What Sort of Woman Do I Want to Be?" *Guardian*, February 9, 2011.

Kane, Emily W. *The Gender Trap: Parenting and the Pitfalls of Raising Boys and Girls*. New York: New York University Press, 2012.

Lucal, Betsy. "What It Means to Be Gendered Me: Life on the Boundaries of a Dichotomous Gender System," *Gender & Society* 13, no. 6 (1999): 781–97.

Ridgeway, Cecilia L. *Framed by Gender: How Gender Inequality Persists in the Modern World*. New York: Oxford University Press, 2011.

West, Candace, and Don Zimmerman. "Doing Gender." *Gender & Society* 1, no. 2 (1987): 125–51.

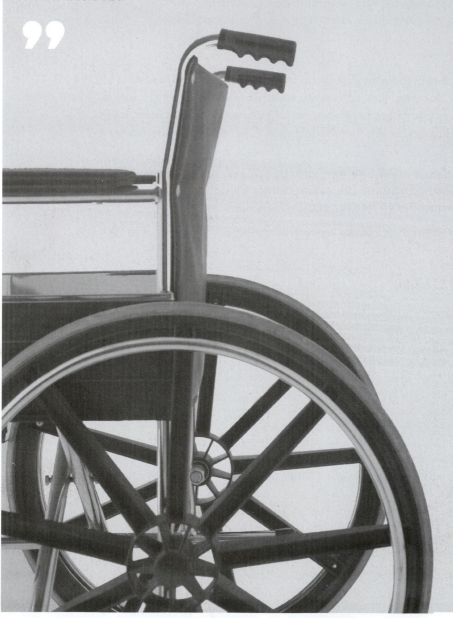

> **EVER SINCE I'VE BEEN IN A WHEELCHAIR, I'VE STOPPED GETTING CATCALLED.**
>
> —FEM KORSTEN[1]

5

Intersections

By now you've been introduced to the idea that gender isn't something we are, but something we do. Gender rules offer guidance on how to act, and we often follow them. People we interact with push us to follow gender rules, too. While we sometimes break them, we usually do so in ways that affirm the rule itself. As a result, gendered patterns emerge.

One might observe, however, that gender is just one of many things about us that make us who we are. Some of us fit easily into the gender binary, but many of us don't; some bodies bring admiration, other bodies bring pity or derision; some of us have lots of money to spend, others have less. Our gender, then, sits alongside many other socially salient facts about us. Accordingly, we asked:

Q+A   **If gender is just one part of who we are, why isn't it crowded out by all the other things about us that are meaningful and consequential?**

Other things don't crowd out gender because the other things about us are themselves gendered. Gender, in other words, *inflects* all our other identities, just as our other identities inflect our gender. Gender isn't more important than age, for example, nor is age more important than gender. Instead, there is *a gendered way to age*.

Age is what sociologists call a **social identity**, a culturally available and socially constructed category of people in which we place ourselves or are placed by others.[2] Many social identities carry substantial personal significance and interpersonal consequence. In the United States, these include sexual orientation, race, citizenship status, gender, class, age, religion, disability status, body size, whether we live in an urban or rural environment, and arguably more. These identities *matter*. We read other peoples' appearances, body language, accents, turns of phrase, and fashion choices for signs of these identities and tend to filter information about people through them.

Our social identities can be intensely felt and deeply meaningful, but we don't come to them in a vacuum. Through the process of distinction, our cultures invent them and give them meaning and value. Because they are social, some identities bring us **privilege**, unearned social and economic advantage based on our location in a social hierarchy; others do not. These identities—including gender—then interact to shape our lives in complex ways.

This is how it comes to be that there is a gendered way to age. Likewise, there is a gendered way to manage being rich or poor. Whatever our race, we experience it in gendered ways, too. Similarly, the experiences of being gay or straight, or an immigrant, native-born, or indigenous are all simultaneously gendered. All these things together make up our complex social identities, shaping the kinds of gender rules to which we are held accountable and our ability to both follow and break them.

This chapter explores how gender interacts with some of our other identities. It first reintroduces the idea of intersectionality—the term used to describe this phenomenon—then explores how some social identities carry expectations that require or inspire people to do gender differently. It would be impossible to do justice to *every* intersection of culturally relevant identities; there are thousands of such intersections. Instead, this chapter simply offers some models of how gender might intersect with other social positions. Be alert for other intersections and think about how gender intersects in sometimes surprising ways as identities combine to make us the unique individuals we are.

INTERSECTIONALITY

When asked to imagine a "man" or a "woman," most Americans don't at first envision a female coal miner, a native of Mexico, or a man in a turban. The mythical inhabitants of the gender binary—the prototypical man and woman who usually come to mind—fit into a rather narrow slice of reality. They are usually white, middle or upper class, heterosexual, able bodied, urban, Christian, and native-born American. In other words, the gender binary *normalizes* one kind of man and one kind of woman by setting aside other types of people. This is good for maintaining the binary because marginalizing certain populations as exceptions, like subdividing, keeps the story of gender difference simple, but it doesn't reflect real life.

In real life, we're not just male, female, trans, or nonbinary—we don't just have a gender—instead, we're multifaceted individuals with many identities. Accordingly, understanding how we do gender has to address that complexity.[3] We introduced this perspective in Chapter 3 as intersectionality, a term that refers to the fact that gender is not an isolated social fact about us but instead intersects with all the other distinctions between people made important by our society.

Do these folks look "normal"? If so, it's only because American culture centers white, middle-class heterosexuals, defining everyone else as outside the norm.

When we do gender, we are also expected to account for all these other identities. We do gender, for example, but also parenthood. When those two identities combine, we get motherhood and fatherhood, two intersectional identities that are policed very differently. How we follow or break the social rules related to motherhood and fatherhood is further shaped by what is possible given our income, marital status, and health as well as whether we are at risk of discrimination due to our race, sexual orientation, or religiosity (or lack thereof).

Juggling all these identities, we hope to build lives that are consistent with our values and goals, while adapting to the unique positions we occupy not just on—or off—the gender binary, but a much, much more *complicated* cultural map. If this sounds fraught with difficulty, it is—and much more so for some than others. Still, all of us try our best to manage the expectations, opportunities, and constraints we face. Finding a way of doing gender that works for us as unique individuals who are also shaped by other aspects of our identity and the material realities of our lives is called a **gender strategy.**[4]

Our varying strategies add up to many culturally recognizable masculine and feminine archetypes. There is the Girly Girl, who emphasizes her femininity most of the time; the Tomboy, who rejects many feminine characteristics; the Jock, whose identity revolves around sports; and the Dork, who prefers *World of Warcraft* to football. These recognizable stereotypes (no less socially constructed, of course, than "man" and "woman") guide us in carving out an identity that we like and can feel good about. From there, we try to "be ourselves," breaking the rules associated with the subcategories of masculinity and femininity in order to try to be recognized as not *just* a Party Girl, Farm Boy, or Science Geek.

The remainder of this chapter looks at how some of our personal characteristics and social identities shape our gender strategies, including our economic
class; the countries, states, and cities where we live; our race and ethnicity; our
immigrant status and whether our country's official language is our first language; our sexual orientation; and what our body looks like and can or can't do.
Remember that these aren't the only important social identities we carry, and
this chapter only scratches the surface of all the ways even this handful of identities intersects. It's simply an introduction to how this thing called *intersectionality* works.

ECONOMIC CLASS AND RESIDENCE

Many countries, including the United States, are characterized by significant
inequalities between the richest and poorest members of society. Middle- and
upper-class families tend to live in cities and suburbs surrounded by excellent
social services, educational opportunities, and employment options. In contrast,
many poor and working-class people live in modest suburban developments,
inner-city neighborhoods, or small communities in rural America, including on
land reserved for Native American nations, most of which have fewer resources
and opportunities than wealthy communities. These variables—economic class
and place of residence—intersect with each other and with gender, making certain gender strategies more available to some Americans than others.

Individuals with higher incomes and greater wealth have more resources
to shape their lives to match their ideals. Many men in high-pay, high-status
occupations, for instance—men who work as lawyers, doctors, and account
executives—often invest heavily in their career and identify strongly with their
job. A senior personnel manager named Bill, a participant in a study on workplace norms, revealed that his life was focused almost exclusively on work.[5] He
argued that no one in his line of work could get ahead without putting in at least
fifty or sixty hours per week. Emily, his wife, stayed home and took care of their
house and four children. Of his marriage, Bill said,

> *We made a bargain. If I was going to be as successful as we both wanted, I was
> going to have to spend tremendous amounts of time at it. Her end of the bargain
> was that she wouldn't go out to work. So I was able to take the good stuff and
> she did the hard work—the car pools, dinner, gymnastics lessons. . . . Emily left
> Oakmont College after two years when we got married. . . . I really had it made. I
> worked very long hours and Emily just managed things.*[6]

Earning more than enough money to support his family on one income, and
married to a woman whom he believes is happy to manage things at home, Bill's

gender strategy was to excel in the masculine pursuit of extraordinary career success. He was a Breadwinner.

Because Emily was married to a Breadwinner, she had the option of choosing a Family Focused strategy that allowed her to concentrate on raising children, being a good partner to her husband, and keeping a beautiful home. Some upper-class married women embrace this strategy; they welcome the opportunity to be out of the rat race and feel good about investing in their children's or husband's success. Others may feel pressure from their spouses or others to stay home. In either case, to be Family Focused is also to risk becoming financially dependent on their partner (for now) or their children (later).

Some affluent married women may reject this binary division of labor from the start and instead bargain with their husbands for a Co-Breadwinner strategy in which they nurture their own careers, too. Because they earn enough money between the two of them, Co-Breadwinners can have paid help take care of the housework and childcare that a Family Focused spouse would do. This was the strategy adopted by another family. Both lawyers, Seth and Jessica identified strongly with their jobs and could afford to hire a nanny, a housekeeper, a gardener, a driver, and a neighborhood boy to play with their son, allowing them to put in a combined 120 hours of work each week.

Our gender strategies are not only a reflection of our personalities but also the twists and turns of our lives.[7] Both women and men are more likely to adopt a Family Focused strategy when they encounter limited job opportunities, marry someone with a high-paying job, or discover, perhaps to their own surprise, that they prefer parenting. Men and women are more committed to careers when they discover that they enjoy and are good at them. In other words, the strategies that we plan for as teenagers and young adults often turn out to be maladaptive or otherwise unsatisfying, so we often end up being happy in places we never intended to go.

Our strategies, though, are never just a result of personality and chance; they are also contingent on our class status. Few families can afford to leave a spouse at home, like Bill did, or hire as much domestic help as Seth and Jessica did. Instead, most two-parent families need both incomes to make ends meet. If they have children, these families' options are limited to Breadwinner/Supportive Spouse or Super Mom/Super Dad. Supportive Spouses take a part-time or low-effort job that allows them to prioritize a partner's Breadwinner role, producing a one-and-a-half income compromise for the family. Super Moms (and sometimes Super Dads) take on the challenging task of working a full-time job, being a parent, and being responsible for housework and other family needs, including—if married—supporting their spouses' work. Most single mothers are pushed into the Super Mom strategy by default; they must do it all because there is no one else, they're unlikely to make enough money to hire outside help, and the workplace is unsympathetic and inflexible.[8]

Importantly, there are still a lot more Super Moms than Super Dads and many fewer female Breadwinners than male ones. This is in part because which strategy we choose is influenced not just by our preferences and resources but by how other people judge our choices in light of our gender. Men who focus on work are less likely to face policing than women, especially if the men are Breadwinners. In some instances, men can do minimal amounts of childcare and be considered model fathers. "I get more credit than she does," said one postal worker dad who made a point to be an involved parent.[9] "I just feel like I'm doing what any person should do," said another involved dad, shaking his head over how his wife's friends swooned over his participation.[10] Women, in contrast, are held to a higher standard and are more likely than men to be blamed if the house is messy or the kids are misbehaved. Men, for their part, are judged more harshly for failing to earn enough income.

Working-class men who want to be involved fathers may raise eyebrows if they opt to be a Stay-at-Home Dad; the Super Dad is a more socially acceptable strategy. A study of working-class emergency medical technicians, for example, showed that these men prioritized their families alongside their work.[11] As one explained: "[I]t's long hours at times, but honestly, I get four days off in a row with my kids. How many people get that much?"[12] Implicitly contrasting himself with the Breadwinner who can't take off much time from work, this Super Dad embraced active parenting as part of his gender strategy.

Working-class men try to carve out a masculinity that both feels good and is possible given their circumstances, sometimes actively contrasting their blue-collar masculinity with that of white-collar men whom they may disdain as "wimps" and "paper-push[ers]."[13] Construction workers sometimes adopt this gender strategy.[14] Their bosses may be Breadwinners, but because they also stay in air-conditioned trailers in front of computers all day, the workers can claim to be the "real men" doing the "real work" on site. They may "not know what fork is used for salad," like their bosses do, but they know "which drill bit is used for different forms of masonry under different and varying conditions," something their managers do not know.[15] With this logic, these Blue-Collar Guys can embrace a strategy that is available to them *and* feel good about themselves as men.

Similarly, women who grow up on farms or ranches may be accustomed to dressing and acting in ways consistent with the work they do to help their families.[16] In response, some of these women may embrace the Tough Gal strategy. Ester, for example, grew up on a farm and enjoyed the physical and often dirty work: "I helped my dad a lot on the farm, raising . . . livestock," she said.[17] "I really enjoyed driving the farm machinery! It just empowered me, driving a tractor or truck." Teresa, who grew up in a similarly rural town, said of her high school: "There were farm girls [who] might dress up for the prom, but they also could slaughter a hog."[18] Tough Gals may take pride in their ability to do things asso-

Working construction requires skill, strength, and a tolerance for risk, all things that may make these men feel good about themselves as men even if they aren't drawing paychecks as large as some.

ciated with boys and men, while also disdaining the Girly Girl as overly soft or dependent. Like Blue-Collar Guys, they may contrast their own femininity with that of different kinds of women in ways that make them feel good about who they are.

All these examples demonstrate that our gender strategies aren't simply products of our individual personalities and luck. They are also shaped by the constraints and opportunities afforded by our class status, the places where we grew up, and the norms of local subcultures. In the next section, we'll discuss how our gender identities also intersect with race.

RACE

Like our economic class and place of residence, race shapes our gender strategies and gender shapes our experience of race. Race—like gender—is a social construction and an important distinction in American life.[19] Some racial groups are denigrated, others valorized; all are subject to advantages and disadvantages related to their unique histories. In this section, we look at three examples: the experiences of gender for black, white, and Asian Americans.

African American Men and Women

The United States sustained a system of racialized slavery for over 200 years. This system of **racism**—social arrangements designed to systematically advantage one race over others—was justified, in part, by the argument that white elites weren't captors but caretakers. Proponents of enslavement argued that the complicated responsibilities of freedom were simply too much for black people's simple minds.[20] Black men were stereotyped as jolly buffoons who were helpless to take care of themselves, let alone anyone else. Like women and children, it was argued, black men needed a "master" to take care of them.

After emancipation in 1865, the stereotype of black men as weak and ineffectual was no longer useful to white supremacists. Much more useful was the idea that black men were aggressive, prone to criminality, and sexually dangerous. With this justification, the white population terrorized the black community in a vicious, violent, and often deadly campaign to keep black people "in their place."[21]

Beliefs about black people in the United States still reflect these strategic stereotypes designed to shore up white power. Black people are stereotyped as tougher and more athletic than white people, meaner and more aggressive, and prone to criminal behavior and sexual promiscuity.[22] These characteristics, notably, are also stereotypes of masculinity. Black men, then, are frequently stereotyped as *hyper*masculine: super aggressive (as athletes or criminals) and super sexual (as players, philanderers, and potential rapists). In other words, for black men, being black *intensifies* expectations based on their gender.[23]

This stereotyping starts when boys are children. Sociologist Ann Ferguson showed how teachers in the United States interpret the bad behavior of white and black boys differently.[24] White boys are seen as inherently innocent; they may misbehave, but it is not out of malice. Black boys, in contrast, are stereotyped as prone to criminality; their misbehavior is "stripped of any element of childish naïveté."[25] As a result, black boys are more likely than white boys to be suspended from school.[26]

As early as kindergarten, parents of black boys start teaching their sons how to manage other people's racist ideas.[27] If they want to be seen as "good," black boys have to perform an unusual degree of deference, to behave in ways considered "sissy" when performed by white boys. Even otherwise innocent behaviors may be read as suspicious if performed by a black child. A woman named Rebecca, for example, recalled trying to explain to her teenage nephew that a hoodie wasn't necessarily just a hoodie on his young, black body:

> *I tried to explain that to him because he didn't understand. He said, "I am just wearing my hoodie." [I said,] "But baby, I understand what you are doing, and*

there is nothing wrong with that, but if you walk through the neighborhood near my school, [people] see something different."[28]

It wasn't fair that he couldn't wear what his white peers could wear without the risk of attracting unwanted attention, Rebecca said, but it was reality.

This "enactment of docility" and hyperawareness of others' prejudice is simply preparation for adulthood.[29] Indeed, some adult black men report adopting strategies designed to manage the racist hypermasculine stereotypes that others attribute to them. Some take care never to raise their voice. Others make a point to dress professionally even in nonprofessional settings. Some report never jogging in white neighborhoods, lest it look like they're running away from or toward something or someone.[30] The journalist Brent Staples, a six-foot-two black man, describes whistling classical music when he walks on dark streets late at night. "Everybody seems to sense that a mugger wouldn't be warbling bright, sunny selections from Vivaldi's *Four Seasons*," he writes wryly.[31] The Gentle Black Man, and other strategies meant to defray mistrust based on one's skin color, is a way of doing masculinity that some black men use to avoid being stereotyped as a Dangerous Black Man.

This does more than just interrupt racist narratives; it's a survival strategy. Young black men, even teenagers and young boys, are twenty-one times more likely to die at the hands of police than their white counterparts, despite the fact that they are less likely than young white men to be engaged in criminal activity (Figure 5.1).[32] In the majority of cases, black men who die at the hands of police

FIGURE 5.1 | KILLED BY POLICE DURING ARREST, BY CIRCUMSTANCES

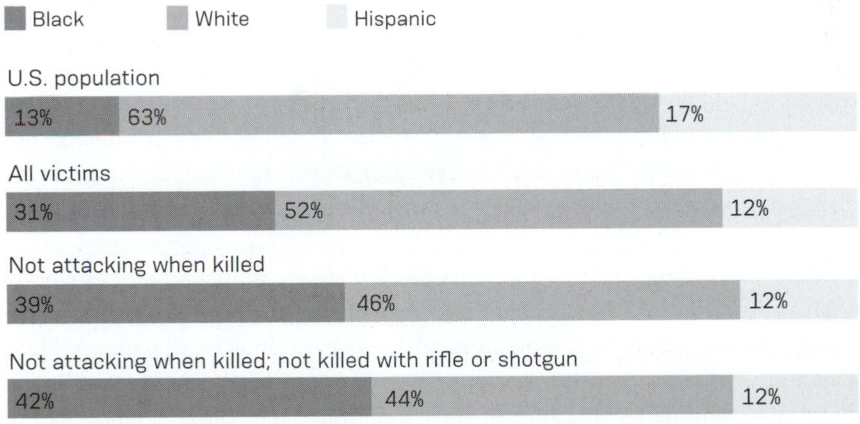

■ Black ■ White ■ Hispanic

U.S. population
13% | 63% | 17%

All victims
31% | 52% | 12%

Not attacking when killed
39% | 46% | 12%

Not attacking when killed; not killed with rifle or shotgun
42% | 44% | 12%

Source: 2012 Supplementary Homicide Report, FBI.

are unarmed and nonviolent. In fact, they are more likely to be unarmed and nonviolent than men of other races who die in this way, suggesting that in many cases the *only* thing threatening about a black man is the combination of his race and gender.[33] This is what motivated the creation of the hashtag #blacklivesmatter and inspired Colin Kaepernick and many of his fellow professional football players to kneel for the National Anthem before games.

It's not only black men who are imagined to be more masculine and more threatening than white people; black women are also attributed traits associated with masculinity. Like the stereotypes of black men, these stereotypes of black women are related to what white elites found useful.[34] Slave captors required both men and women to do hard labor and suffer harsh punishments, and enslaved women were sometimes forced into sex and required to produce children for their master. If black women had been stereotyped as physically frail, emotionally delicate, and sexually pure, as white women were, then none of this could be justified.[35] To protect both the institution of slavery and the ideology of gender, black women were stereotyped as more like black men than white women: masculine instead of feminine.

The stereotype that black women are unfeminine persists today, such that black women are frequently confronted with the perception that they are less feminine than white women, regardless of how they act.[36] That is, a black woman's race *interferes* with people's perception of her as feminine. Because of this, the Girly Girl strategy is harder for black women to pull off than the Tough Gal strategy. This is especially true if they appear more "African": have tightly curled hair, darker skin, broader noses, and fuller lips.

The contemporary notion of the Strong Black Woman—a black woman who can withstand any amount of disappointment, deprivation, and mistreatment—has its roots in this idea.[37] So does the notion of the Angry Black Woman, which includes the idea that black women are louder, pushier, and more demanding than other women.[38] Research on health care suggests that this stereotype leads physicians to take black women's pain and suffering less seriously.[39] When black mothers struggle to make ends meet when working poorly paid jobs, instead of being praised as Super Moms, they're often denigrated as "welfare queens": not just poor mothers but bad ones.[40] These same stereotypes are also part of why the sexual assault of white women is taken more seriously than that of black women.[41]

And, just like black boys and men, black girls are punished more severely than white girls by their teachers and are, as adults, more likely than white women to be killed in interactions with police.[42] Intersectionality scholar Kimberlé Williams Crenshaw has jumpstarted a campaign, represented by the hashtag #sayhername, that aims to draw attention to the police violence disproportionately faced by black women.[43]

People gather in Union Square in New York City to participate in a #sayhername vigil for black women and girls killed at the hands of the police. Drawing attention to the fact that black women also are being killed makes the media more accountable for the gendered way dangerous overpolicing is being depicted. (Photo source: Mia Fermindoza)

To counter stereotypical beliefs and the accompanying risks, many black women try to *overcompensate* by doing more femininity than they would otherwise.[44] In some cases, this may be because they know a performance of femininity will be rewarded, whereas failing to do it will be punished. The writer Hannah Eko, for example, a black woman who is frequently misgendered, observes that avoiding this requires her to do more femininity than similar-looking women with different skin tones:

> I'm supposed to go to frustrating lengths to "prove" I'm feminine and offset my blackness (keep my hair long, my voice soft, my clothes appropriately girly), while women who are white or lighter in appearance are given more latitude for experimentation.[45]

On white women, she notes, androgynous clothes and very short haircuts are seen as playfully "boyish"; on black women, they're intimidatingly "manly."

But there are costs to conforming to white standards of beauty. Because femininity is implicitly white, doing femininity can feel like doing whiteness. So some black women may feel that adopting a Girly Girl strategy is capitulating to or internalizing racism. "Our oppression has been so well done," said an

African American teenager named Nia, "we don't even see that our own values in terms of beauty are very skewed."[46] For her, resisting white standards of feminine beauty was "empowering."

Nia embraced a Black Is Beautiful strategy. Such a strategy might involve selecting African-inspired clothing styles and colors, wearing headwraps or hairstyles like braids or dreadlocks, and reframing characteristically black features as both feminine and beautiful. But because black femininity is policed differently than white femininity, these women likely pay costs—both interpersonal and professional—for this self-love, and contend with a higher likelihood of being mistreated or even abused by authority figures.

For black women, then, the Girly Girl, Tough Gal, and Black Is Beautiful strategies are always both gendered and raced. Each comes with both benefits and costs, sometimes deadly ones. Black women, though, are not the only people in America struggling with intersecting expectations. Asian Americans are, too.

Asian American Men and Women

Asian American men face a predicament precisely opposite that of African American men. While black men are stereotyped as hypermasculine, East Asian men are stereotyped as deficiently masculine. If black men and women are masculinized, Asian men and women are feminized.[47] Asians of both sexes are assumed to be smaller, lighter, and less muscular than whites. Asian women are stereotyped as quiet, deferential, and shy, while Asian men are often depicted as less masculine than other races: nerdy, not brawny; passive and reserved; even deficiently sexual.

These stereotypes don't come out of thin air but, like the stereotypes of African Americans, are rooted in history.[48] During the gold rush of the 1800s, the United States brought Chinese men as laborers, often against their will. Tens of thousands of men, living in all-male groups, had to learn how to perform domestic tasks for themselves. Later, when they were forced out of their jobs in farming, mining, manufacturing, and construction, they became servants or opened businesses offering domestic services to the wider population. By virtue of doing "women's work," East Asian men were feminized in the cultural imagination.

For Asian men, then, racial stereotypes interfere with their ability to conform to gender expectations. Some Asian men try to counter this stereotype by acting more aggressively than they otherwise would.[49] Gary, a Chinese American lawyer who describes himself as a "jockish type," explains: "Well, I think the stereotype is that Asian men are docile. . . . That is the reason I decided to be a trial attorney—to cut against that." Being a trial attorney requires Gary to fight on behalf of his clients, a behavior that is inconsistent with the Asian stereotype.

Gary's Assertive Asian gender strategy—being gregarious, dating frequently, excelling in athletics, and achieving in a job that requires him to be aggressive—has worked out well for him: He is a very successful lawyer. But it is also a daily battle. Most of his potential clients, he explains, have never encountered a Chinese American lawyer and worry that he won't be able to represent them well. "Do I have to overcome [the stereotype] every day?" Gary asks himself out loud. "Yes, I do." He has to prove to others, continually, that he is not passive in the courtroom.

Asian women are also racially feminized. In the mid-1800s, thousands of Chinese and Japanese women were brought to the United States against their will to work as sex slaves.[50] A trader might pay a starving family in China $40 for a daughter and then sell her to a brothel in San Francisco for $2,500. The large numbers of Asian prostitutes, alongside the Japanese geisha stereotype, *hyper*feminized Asian women as demure, passive, and sexually available.

The stereotype lives on as Asian women continue to face a hyperfeminization relative to white women, an intensification of gender expectations like that experienced by black men. Asian women are often expected to be passive and deferential and may receive unwelcome attention for these presumed traits.[51] Karen Eng, a Japanese American, describes the stereotypical Asian woman:

> *The fantasy Asian is intelligent yet pliable, mysterious yet ornamental. She's also perpetually prepubescent—ageless and petite, hairless, high-pitched, girly. . . . As I once overheard someone saying, she's "tuckable" under the arm.*[52]

This fantasy Asian girl appeals, particularly, to men who want a submissive girlfriend or wife, but Eng has no interest in being "tuckable." She doesn't want to be anyone's geisha or China doll, but some men assume that she will be: "No matter how many combinations of combat boots, 501s, and ratty Goodwill coats you wear," she says, "they still see a little Oriental flower."[53]

Eng doesn't adopt an Oriental Flower strategy because it conflicts with her self-concept. Instead, she uses an Assertive Asian strategy of her own. Lisa, an eighteen-year-old Korean American, has adopted this strategy, too:

> *I feel like I have to prove myself to everybody and maybe that's why I'm always vocal. I'm quite aware of that stereotype of Asian women all being taught to be submissive. . . . I don't want that to be labeled on me.*[54]

But while Gary can use his identity as a man to account for behavior inconsistent with the feminized Asian stereotype, Asian women can't account for their counterstereotypical behavior that way. Accordingly, some Asian women use different strategies for different audiences. Andrea, a twenty-three-year-old Vietnamese American, describes her strategy switching:

> *When I'm with my boyfriend and we're over at his family's house or at a church function, I tend to find myself being a little submissive. . . . But I know that when I get home, he and I have that understanding that I'm not a submissive person. I speak my own mind and he likes the fact that I'm strong.*[55]

Asian women and men, then, like black men and women, face challenges because of the way gender stereotypes intersect with beliefs about their race.

White American Men and Women

In contrast to African and Asian Americans, white Americans are racially *un*marked. The **unmarked category** is the social identity that is assumed for a role or context without qualification. Taxi drivers are assumed to be male and nurses female, which is why we still sometimes hear phrases like "female taxi driver" and "male nurse." Likewise, though same-sex marriage is legal, it's still largely assumed to be between a man and a woman unless it's marked as a "gay" marriage. Being unmarked means that it's likely that others see us as the norm in a specific role. In contrast, being marked is an acknowledgment that we're an outlier or deviation.

Unless marked with a modifier like Cuban or Native, then, Americans are generally assumed to be white (and Christian, middle class, heterosexual, etc.). "American" and "white American" are usually synonymous, which is why politicians can get away with saying things like "real Americans" or "working families" and most people understand they're contrasting white Americans to immigrants, people of color, Muslims, and people using stigmatized government benefits.

Because white Americans are unmarked—considered just "regular people" in the United States—they are also considered "normal." This includes being "normally gendered": whites are not seen as too masculine or too feminine, or not masculine or feminine enough, based on their race alone. Consequently, if they have the personality and resources for it, white men and women can rather easily adopt any of a range of gender strategies, including the most widely prized ones. In high school or college, a young woman who is born into the middle class with genes that give her light skin and a petite, thin body type can be an All-American Girl, while the young man who is sufficiently athletic, racially white, and class privileged can be an All-American Guy.

By virtue of being unmarked, white Americans also carry the stigma of being "regular," "plain," and "uninteresting." Whiteness is even sometimes used as a metaphor for normal or boring: Nonexperimental sex is "vanilla," clean-cut people are "white bread," and an unimportant untruth is a "white lie." This is another reason why the Family Focused, Supportive Spouse, and Breadwinner are implicitly white strategies: They are imagined to be the opposite of cool, exciting, or dangerous.

Accordingly, some middle-class white people try to distance themselves from the respectable but bland image that is bestowed on them by virtue of their race and class. The Goths discussed in Chapter 4 were doing just that. Most were white and middle class and "doing" freakiness was a way for them to "become a little cooler" and "differentiate themselves from the mainstream."[56] They enjoyed the disconcerting effect their appearance had on others. Unlike, say, black men, who are often perceived as threatening, white folks have to work hard to make other people uncomfortable.

White people don't always carry every possible privilege, though. When being white intersects with being poor and living in an urban neighborhood, these realities intersect with whiteness. Sociologist Amy Wilkins studied poor, urban white women who lived alongside and identified with their black and Puerto Rican neighbors.[57] These women adopted the "street" fashion, mannerisms, and language of their neighbors of color with whom they shared a class but not a racial background. This Tough Gal strategy offered white women freedom from the more restrictive gender rules for middle- and upper-class white women—they could be assertive, outspoken and openly sexual—but the strategy came at a cost. The women of color in their neighborhoods sometimes called them "wannabes" and described them as imposters. Summarizing, Wilkins writes,

> White girls who "don't know who they are." They're loud, annoying, always fighting, too proud of having sex. They wear the wrong clothes. They smoke the wrong cigarettes. They talk wrong, have the wrong attitudes, and have the wrong priorities. And they have the wrong boyfriends.[58]

By virtue of being white, these women had to try harder to enact the Tough Gal strategy, and the women of color around them recognized it as overdone and possibly even inappropriate. From the perspective of the poor white women who adopted this strategy, however, being a "wannabe" was one of their best options. Without class privilege, these young women didn't have the option to be an All-American Girl, so being a Tough Gal gave them "an inhabitable, if stereotyped and degraded, persona."[59]

These discussions of the options typically faced by white, black, and East Asian men and women are only a peek into how race, like economic class and place of residence, shapes opportunities for performing gender. People from Latin America and the Middle East as well as South Asians and Native Americans have their own particular challenges that are not captured by these examples. And an increasing proportion of all Americans are identifying as multiracial, which further complicates the strategic choices available. But intersectionality is about more than just race and class. We turn next to sexual orientation.

SEXUAL ORIENTATION

Contemporary Western societies are strongly **heteronormative**, designed on the assumption that everyone is heterosexual. Just as most tools are designed for right-handed people and most homes for the able-bodied, our society is designed primarily for heterosexuals. Accordingly, the unmarked sexual orientation is heterosexuality. The most commonly used marked categories are *gay*, *lesbian*, and *bisexual*; together, these groups are considered **sexual minorities**.

Unmarked individuals are generally presumed heterosexual unless there are culturally recognizable signs indicating otherwise. In the United States, some of these culturally recognizable signs are directly related to sexual orientation (for example, displaying a "gay" wedding photo at work), but many are instead related to gender expression: Effeminate men are read as gay while masculine women are often assumed to be lesbian. Indeed, some of us claim to have excellent "gaydar," or the ability to detect, radar-like, sexual minorities in our presence. What we are looking for is neither the presence nor the absence of sexual desire for people of the same sex, but rather gender deviance: "swishy" men and "manly" women. That is, we are looking for people who are breaking gender rules.

The American tendency to expect gay men to act feminine and lesbians to act masculine means that heterosexuals may be motivated to avoid gender-bending strategies. A heterosexual woman who performs "too much" masculinity may be suspected to be a lesbian. This may or may not bother her on principle, but she may consider the possibility that it will be interpreted as a signal that she's sexually uninterested in men. To attract men's sexual attention, she may feel she has to do a certain amount of femininity. Likewise, some heterosexual men may avoid feminine styles and interests for the same reason: it might send the wrong signals. Societies that conflate gender-bending with same-sex attraction create incentives for heterosexuals to conform to gender norms lest their identity be mistaken.

Facing these same constraints, but often with different motivations, sexual minorities do gender in a variety of ways depending in part on whether they want to "pass" as heterosexual. Many want to keep their sexual orientation a secret from at least some people because of **heterosexism**, individual and institutional bias against sexual minorities. Since our gaydar is tuned to detect gender deviance, gender conformity is an excellent way to hide in plain sight. Brandon, for example, a white gay man living in rural Colorado, explained how he tries to pass as heterosexual: "I try to live as straight a life as possible. Whether it's dressing, the car I drive, the area I'm in. When I fill up at a gas station, my greatest fear is to look at another guy the wrong way."[60]

Brandon feels compelled to hide his sexual orientation because of **compulsory heterosexuality**, the gender rule that men be attracted to women and women

Olympians Gus Kenworthy and Adam Rippon both identify as gay but have adopted very different gender strategies.

to men. In some cases, breaking this rule can attract vicious or violent policing, especially if one is gender nonconforming.[61] Even for sexual minorities living in places where being "out" isn't dangerous, though, following gender rules can be advantageous. Many people are more tolerant of sexual minorities who are gender conforming than those who are gender deviant. Asked how she would feel about having a lesbian roommate, for example, a college student expressed just this sentiment:

> If my roommate was a lesbian and she was more feminine, I think I would be more comfortable. . . . [If she was] like me—she looked girly—it wouldn't matter if she liked guys or girls. But if it was someone that was really boyish, I think it would be hard for me to feel comfortable.[62]

Likewise, a gay Latino man insisted: "I could never bring home someone that was the stereotype of a *joto* or *maricón*," using derogatory Spanish words for feminine-acting gay men. "He wouldn't fit in with the family."[63] People who are gay or lesbian, but not *queer*, are sometimes more accepted, both among sexual minorities and in the wider society.

Because sexual minorities face prejudice not based just on their sexual orientation but also their gender performance, some sexual minorities adopt a Not

Too Queer strategy. Some women do this because femininity suits them. Others do so because—as with black women—presenting a conventionally (white, heterosexual) feminine appearance brings rewards, while failing to do so brings costs. One tall, forty-one-year-old white lesbian copywriter named Rebecca, for example, explained that she uses makeup to mute her "difference" from heterosexual coworkers and clients: "I even try to take a little bit of that threat off, you know, by saying you don't have to worry about me being different."[64] Some gay men also adopt the Not Too Queer strategy.[65] This overall strategy of minimizing difference is also called **homonormativity**, a practice of obeying most gender rules with the noted exception of the one that says we must sexually desire and partner with someone of the other sex.

One challenge for women and men who adopt a Not Too Queer strategy is recognizability. In a heteronormative society, gender conformity may make same-sex sexual orientation invisible.[66] Gay men, lesbians, and bisexuals may want to be visible for multiple reasons: They may want to upset heteronormativity, find people to date or marry, or ward off unwanted attention from the other sex. With this in mind, they might adopt a Recognizably Butch or Queer strategy.[67] For women, this strategy might involve adopting more masculine clothes and mannerisms and avoiding makeup and long hair. One forty-year-old woman explained:

> I have a dyke look that I assume when I want to fit in more with lesbian social settings, and I think I've been more careful about keeping my haircut very crisp and clean so I can look more dyke-y when I want to.[68]

Doing gender in a way that communicates our sexual identity to both mainstream society and subcultures can be especially tricky for people who identify as bisexual. If gender nonconformity marks one as gay or lesbian, and conformity marks one as heterosexual, what is a person who is attracted to both or all sexes to do?

Race matters here, too. Sexual minorities of color often discover that queer spaces are also white spaces, while communities of color can be homophobic spaces, ones that are not just oriented toward heterosexuals but hostile toward sexual minorities.[69] Malachi, for example, a two-spirit-identified member of the Sturgeon Lake First Nation, explains how his people had lost sight of their third-gender tradition in the process of colonization, leading him to face homophobia at home. In a nearly Canadian city, he encountered more tolerance for his gender identity and sexual orientation but less for his race. In the urban gay community, he explained, "there still is all of the stereotypes and being discriminated for being aboriginal."[70]

The way that racial stereotypes are gendered affects how much femininity needs to be performed if lesbians and bisexual women want to be seen as less "different."[71] Because stereotypes about East Asians include the idea that they are more feminine than white people, Asian lesbians may not need to work as hard to seem "normal," but they may have a harder time being recognizably lesbian or bisexual. One Cambodian American lesbian explained that she felt she had to adopt a combination of Recognizably Butch and Assertive Asian to get people to see her as she is:

> I guess that's one reason why I'm so in your face and out about being a dyke. . . . I'm invisible as a lesbian because I look in [an Asian] cultural way—that is, where I have long hair, you know—and I despise that invisibility.[72]

For Asian lesbians, doing femininity makes them extra invisible.

Conversely, to be seen as feminine, black lesbians have to confront stereotypes applied to both black people and lesbians, both of which masculinize them.[73] Accordingly, they may face more pressure than either white or Asian women to perform femininity, since appearing heterosexual may be one of the few nonstigmatizing identities that they carry, especially if they are also working class or poor. In a study of black lesbian women in New York City, for example, those who adopted a Recognizably Butch strategy knew they were risking policing from the wider society, including their own African American community.[74] About half chose to dress in a more feminine way for this reason, though a fifth described choosing to dress somewhat masculine and the rest adopted a variety of gender-blending styles. Those who didn't adopt a masculine look risked being invisible as queer in the predominantly white lesbian feminist community. Notably, even black women who did adopt more masculine styles often went unnoticed by white lesbians, perhaps because the white women attributed whatever masculinity they did perceive to the black women's race.

In some parts of the West today, then, sexual minorities are embraced; in others, same-sex desire is still stigmatized; and whether we want to be out is also dependent on our particular personalities. Whatever the case, our gender performances are read as signs of our sexual identity. How all of this works, of course, can change, if one crosses a border and encounters a new set of cultural rules.

IMMIGRATION

When people move from one country to another, the gender strategies they employed in their place of origin may suddenly be impossible or undesirable. Immigrants may find themselves in an entirely different social class or a strange new living environment. They may be struggling to learn a new language and face **xenophobia**, institutional and individual bias against people seen as foreign.

Members of Trans Queer Pueblo, a group that advocates for the rights of LGBT undocumented immigrants, participate in the Phoenix Pride Parade. People of color who are also sexual minorities and immigrants face harsh policing across all their intersectional identities.

In some cases, they are suddenly a racial or ethnic minority and unfamiliar with the stereotypes others apply to them.

When sexual minorities migrate from one country to another, for example, they encounter new cultural rules about how to do gender that intersect with the recipient country's unique approach to sexual orientation. Americans tend to endorse group identities based on interests or membership in political, religious, and ethnic groups. Accordingly, many believe that people have a right to be "out" and recognized for one's sexual identity. In France, though, sexual orientation is supposed to be a marginal part of one's self concept, eclipsed by a generic Frenchness. What's important, one man explained, "is that you're French before anything and we don't care if you're anything else."[75] Wearing your identity on your sleeve is considered distasteful and making a big deal about coming out is seen as overly theatrical.

When Xavier moved to the United States, he welcomed the opportunity to adopt a gay identity. "I don't feel there is one way to be an American," he explained. "You can hyphenate your identity in the U.S. while you can't really in France." Danielle, who immigrated to France, enjoys her new country for just the opposite reason: "[I]n the U.S., people want to know your label immediately," she explained. She prefers things the French way.

Some immigrants have a harder time finding strategies that connect their gender identities, sexual desires, and national, racial, and ethnic backgrounds. A study of men who immigrated to London from sub-Saharan Africa found that many were happy to be living in a society that was more accepting of homosexuality, but they still resisted identifying as "gay."[76] The term implied a lifestyle they didn't embrace. One African immigrant explained:

> If I say gay, it comes with lots of associations and ideas in terms of how you live your life, what kind of culture you are into, what kind of music and kind of the whole construct around that label that most of us, even me, I don't associate myself with.[77]

This man was still trying to find a gender strategy that bridged the gap between his cultural background and the gender rules and gay culture he encountered in London.

Just as sexual minority immigrants may begin rethinking their identity, men and women who migrate as married couples may begin rethinking what it means to be a husband and wife. Doing so may mean adjusting to a new economic class; their skills and educational degrees may not translate into the same privileges in their new country, while smaller social networks and language barriers limit job choices.[78] Some immigrants adjust their ideas of masculinity and femininity accordingly.[79] Immigrant couples who once enjoyed the Breadwinner/Family Focused strategies may discover that their new circumstances require them to establish economic and domestic in- or inter-dependence.[80]

Wives who migrate without their husbands, for example, often face very low wages and little job protection but feel great pride in being able to help support their families back home.[81] Wives who stay home may discover that an absent husband similarly requires them to take on tasks previously ruled unsuitable for women. One woman, for example, who stayed in Mexico while her husband went to the United States, remarked on her responsibilities for taking care of both the feminine and masculine tasks of the home and joked: "Now I am a man and a woman!"[82]

Husbands who migrate without their wives may also develop skills that they were able to avoid learning in their home countries. A migrant to the United States named Marcelino, for example, explained how his circumstances required him to adjust his gender strategy:

> Back in Mexico, I didn't know how to prepare food, iron a shirt or wash my clothes. I only knew how to work, how to harvest. But ... [here] I learned how to do everything that a woman can do to keep a man comfortable. ... Necessity forced me to do things which I had previously ignored.[83]

While many men migrate in order to fulfill the masculine responsibility of bread-winning, in the process they may develop feminine skills to counterbalance the loss of female household support.

Married couples who migrate together must adjust their gender strategies as a couple. Some wives transition from Family Focused to Super Moms. A Mexican migrant to the United States, for example, explained: "I now have three jobs. I take care of the house and kids, I take care of my husband, and I clean hotel rooms. I work ten hours a day outside of the home and six hours in the home."[84] Like all Super Moms, migrant mothers struggle to keep up with the demands on their time, even if they enjoy their newfound opportunities and responsibilities.[85]

In response, some migrant women begin to change their ideas about what kind of woman they want to be and what kind of husband they prefer. Rosa, an interviewee from El Salvador, explained:

> *Maybe it's the lifestyle. Here [in the U.S.], the man and the woman, both have to work to be able to pay the rent, the food, the clothes, a lot of expenses. Probably that ... makes us, the women, a little freer in the United States.... In this country if you are courageous and have strength, you can get ahead by yourself, with or without [a husband].... I would say that's why here the woman doesn't follow the man more.*[86]

When women like Rosa embrace a new gender strategy in response to new cultural and economic realities, they often ask their husbands to embrace a new gender strategy, too, one more like the Super Dad. Ricardo talked about the adjustment:

> *Here we both work equally, we both work full-time.... If she is asked to stay at work late, I have to stay with the children.... In El Salvador it was different. I never touched a broom there [laughing].... Here, no. If she quits, we don't eat. It's equal.*[87]

Jacobo, from Guatemala, is enthusiastic about his wife working and has high hopes for her future:

> *There are many opportunities here [in the U.S.] and she is smart in business and she can learn English quickly.... It upsets me to find her at home all the time [babysitting], when she could be doing something better.*[88]

Not all migrants adopt sharing strategies. Some men, like Ricardo and Jacobo, respond positively to the change that comes with economic interdependence; other husbands resist. Likewise, some women pine for the days when they could be Family Focused or afford maids and nannies. Whatever choices migrants

make, however, are shaped by the differently gendered opportunities and constraints they encounter, as well as those related to their other identities.

Stories of immigration reveal how dependent our gender strategies are on
our social context. Travel from one geographical place to another creates both
new opportunities and new constraints, all of which interact with gender. There
are other kinds of traveling, too, which brings us to our final set of identities:
aging and disability. Both are a kind of travel: through time into an older body
or through accident or illness into a body that works quite differently.

ABILITY, AGE, AND ATTRACTIVENESS

Bodies are one of our most potent resources for doing gender. Our body's age,
abilities and disabilities, and degree of conformity to conventional standards
of attractiveness combine to shape what gender strategies we can pull off.[89] To
begin, let's consider ability and disability.

The Gender of Disability

Thanks to **ableism**, individual and institutional bias against people with differently abled bodies, disabled people are often at a disadvantage when interacting
with other people and making their way in their society. In addition to contend-
ing with ableism, disabled men and women also face specific challenges when
attempting to do gender.

When asked to describe what it means to be a man, Jerry—a sixteen-year-old
wheelchair user with juvenile rheumatoid arthritis—emphasized self-reliance.
A man, he explained, is "fairly self-sufficient in that you can sort of handle just
about any situation in that you can help other people and that you don't need
a lot of help."[90] For Jerry, growing up meant struggling to live up to his idea of
manliness:

> *If I ever have to ask someone for help, it really makes me feel like less of a man. I
> don't like asking for help at all. You know, like even if I could use some, I'll usually
> not ask just because I can't, I just hate asking.*

Not only did Jerry himself feel like less of a man as a result of his disability, but
his female peers similarly didn't seem to see him as a "guy." "I might be a 'really
nice person' [to them]," he said, "but not like a guy per se. I think to some extent
that you're sort of genderless to them."[91]

Like Jerry, most disabled men have to accept not only an inability to be
self-sufficient but also the inability to live up to other masculine ideals, like the

ability to be physically assertive and sexually successful. If a disabled man has the resources to live alone and pay for renovations, technologies, and human assistance—that is, if he is quite wealthy or commands a very high salary—he may be able to retain much of the illusion of self-sufficiency he enjoyed before he was injured. Damon, for example, a quadriplegic who requires twenty-four-hour personal care, was able to feel independent because he could afford to be so. Explaining, he emphasized that he has help, but *he* is in charge, "directing" both people and activities:

> *I direct all of my activities around my home where people have to help me to maintain my apartment, my transportation, which I own, and direction in where I go. I direct people how to get there, and I tell them what my needs will be when I am going and coming, and when to get where I am going. . . . I don't see any reason why [I can't] get my life on just as I was having it before.*[92]

For Damon and some other disabled men, regaining independence is an Able-Disabled strategy that preserves a sense of masculinity. It may even enhance it, given that men with disabilities must overcome great obstacles to have what other men may take for granted.

Not all men, however, have Damon's resources. A study of young black and Latino men from impoverished inner cities found that adapting to degrees of paralysis due to spinal cord injuries left them feeling like "half a man."[93] They pointed to the inability to enact the same highly physical masculine Tough Guy strategy that their neighborhoods encouraged and they had once enjoyed. "No longer could the men walk with a swagger and stand tall in a way that emanated power; no longer could the men have sex anywhere at any time; no longer could the men physically fight a potential threat."[94]

In the absence of money, disabled men may opt to adopt an Emphatically Hetero strategy designed to remind others that they retain a distinctly masculine sexuality.[95] A man named Roger, for example, experienced problems with memory, speech, and motor control caused by brain injuries sustained in a car accident. To compensate, he embraced the sexual objectification of women, plastering his living space with images of "bikini-clad women lying on cars and motorbikes."[96] When the female sociologist who interviewed him entered his home, he immediately winked at her and asked her to do his dishes. His humor emphasized the fact that while he was disabled and she was not, he was still a man. Enacting a more youthful version of this strategy, a young man named Dag who was paralyzed at twenty-two used a programmed speaking device to whistle at women.[97] Dag's strategy, like Roger's, was a way to remind others that he was not just male but masculine.

Sports are another arena that offers disabled men the opportunity to assert their masculinity. Wheelchair rugby, originally called "murderball," is an aggres-

Wheelchair rugby allows disabled men to reclaim their masculinity by proving that they are just as assertive and competitive as they were before their injury.

sive and risky contact sport that enables players to prove their athletic prowess and fearlessness in the face of danger. The fact that they play through their particular physical limitation suggests an extraordinary degree of manliness, counteracting the loss of masculinity they experienced when they were injured.

If men's identities are troubled by an inability to be *assertive* with their bodies, women's identities are more often tied up with their ability to be physically *attractive*. Like able-bodied women, disabled women learn the cultural rule that it's important for women to be sexy at the same time that stereotypes of the disabled portray them as unsexy, even asexual.[98] Beth, a woman with multiple sclerosis, writes: "I am sure that other people see a wheelchair first, me second, and a woman third, if at all."[99] Disability rights activist Judy Heumann explains:

> You know, I use a wheelchair, and when I go down the street I do not get to be sexually harassed. I hear nondisabled women complaining about it, but I don't ever get treated as a sexual object.[100]

Some women respond to this degendering and desexualization by trying to conform to gendered expectations as much as possible. Harilyn was one of these women. She writes:

> I was determined to prove I was a "normal" woman. I deliberately sought the most handsome man to parade around.... I became pregnant out of wedlock at

seventeen, which was extremely affirming for me. One of my proud moments was parading around the supermarket with my belly sticking out for all to see that I was indeed a woman, and that my body worked like a normal woman's body.[101]

Occupying a position in "no woman's land" can inspire women to hyper-conform, as Harilyn did, but it can also give them permission to resist cultural definitions of femininity.[102] Some disabled women find that their injury or illness gives them the insight and permission they need to escape from rigid standards of beauty. As one disabled woman with some difficulty with motor control explained: "If I tried to put on mascara, I'd put my eye out, you know; I could never physically do it."[103] For her, being unable to enact the Girly Girl strategy has been liberating:

It's meant that I'm dealing with having a better balance in life as a person, not just as a person with a disability. So I think that we're able to be who we are as women 'cause we don't fit the stereotype maybe.[104]

Class also plays a role. Siv had adopted a Family Focused strategy before an accident left her paralyzed from the chest down with only some arm movement.[105] Fortunately for her, this didn't disrupt her gender strategy very much; with her husband's income and her disability check helping to pay for help around the house—a housekeeper and nurse—she was able to continue on as the emotional center of her family. Siv "came out with her femininity intact."[106]

Disability interacts with masculinity and femininity, as well as other things about us, making the transition to a life with a disability different for men and women. Age is another life transition, one that we all face, and one that intersects with attractiveness in gendered ways.

Age and Attractiveness

Society has strict age-related rules that pressure us to "act our age."[107] So, as we grow older, our ability to "pull off" different gender strategies changes. Sociologist Cheryl Laz explores the language we use to discuss the ways in which age limits our behavior:

"Act your age. You're a big kid now," we say to children to encourage independence (or obedience). "Act your age. Stop being so childish," we say to other adults when we think they are being irresponsible. "Act your age; you're not as young as you used to be," we say to an old person pursuing "youthful" activities.[108]

Staying up all night at clubs is typically seen as fun-loving for young adults; among forty-somethings, a sign perhaps that someone is failing to "settle down."

Becoming a parent is believed to be a blessing at thirty, a curse at thirteen. Learning to snowboard seems typical for a twenty-eight-year-old but risky for a fifty-eight-year-old. Just as there are gender rules, then, there are age rules. These rules press us to "do" our age by doing things that are judged as neither "too immature" nor "too old" for the number of candles on our birthday cake.

These age-related rules are gendered. Socially, men and women age at different rates and in different ways. Playing with dolls may be tolerated in a two-year-old boy who isn't expected to know the rules, but worrisome in a twelve-year-old boy who, by then, is seen as breaking a rule that he is supposed to want to obey. Girls, in contrast, can play with dolls throughout childhood and even collect them in adulthood with little to no need to account for that interest.

People learn early on that age matters for how they do gender. Consider Anna-Clara, Fanny, and Angelica, three eleven-year-olds already well versed in these rules. Anna-Clara explains:

> Frankly it's ridiculous to wear thong [underwear] at our age. Eighth, ninth grade, that's when girls start to be mature enough for it. When you are, like, in the fifth grade, it looks ridiculous if you walk around with thongs.[109]

Anna-Clara's friends, Fanny and Angelica, may admire high heels, but they believe they're not yet ready for them. Angelica recalls: "I saw these beige boots, which I thought were nice. But I wouldn't buy them. They had rather high heels." Fanny concurred, remarking that she'd be more than happy to police Angelica if she were to break this rule: "If Angelica wears such shoes, I tell her that they're adults' shoes."

These eleven-year-olds will eventually age into thongs and high heels—their brothers will not, at least not without paying pretty severe consequences—but they will also age back out again. This is because, in addition to age-related gender rules, aging limits and changes our options for how to do gender in more physical ways. As we age, our appearance and physiology may no longer support certain strategies (like high-impact athleticism and long days in fashionable shoes); our bodies become increasingly disabled by injury, illness, and time; our age is interpreted by others as ugliness; and we come to face **ageism**, an institutionalized preference for the young and the cultural association of aging with decreased social value.[110]

Because more emphasis is placed on women's physical attractiveness than men's, however, women lose more esteem as they age.[111] For women, writer Susan Sontag explains, beauty is tightly tied to youth: "Only one standard of female beauty is sanctioned: the girl."[112] In other words, for women, preserving youthfulness and preserving attractiveness are one and the same. For men, she argues, there are two standards of beauty: the boy and the man. This allows men to transition to a different attractiveness as they age, one not available to women. She writes:

> *The beauty of a boy resembles the beauty of a girl. In both sexes it is a fragile kind of beauty and flourishes naturally only in the early part of the life-cycle. Happily, men are able to accept themselves under another standard of good looks—heavier, rougher, more thickly built. A man does not grieve when he loses the smooth, unlined, hairless skin of a boy. For he has only exchanged one form of attractiveness for another: the darker skin of a man's face, roughened by daily shaving, showing the marks of emotion and the normal lines of age. There is no equivalent of this second standard for women. The single standard of beauty for women dictates that they must go on having clear skin. Every wrinkle, every line, every gray hair, is a defeat.*[113]

Once a woman's youthful beauty fades, she will be expected to adopt a strategy of invisibility. The asexual and maternal Grandma, perhaps. Duncan Kennedy, who studied fashion-advice TV shows, explains:

> *Old women . . . are expected to accept the conventional social assessment that they are sexually unattractive, and dress so as to minimize their sexuality. If they dress sexily . . . [they] are likely to be interpreted as rebels or eccentrics or "desperate," and sanctioned accordingly.*[114]

Women have to get the timing just right. If they adopt this strategy too early, they'll be accused of "letting themselves go." If they wait too long, they'll fail to "age gracefully." The term *cougar* reveals this kind of policing, implying that older women who are interested in sex with younger men are predatory animals.

We see such bias, for example, in the evaluation of the "realness" of marriages between men and women when one is an American citizen and the other is attempting to immigrate. In a study of an advice forum for people attempting to get their partners to the United States, concerns about what marriages are fraudulent are both gendered and aged.[115] When the American partner is a woman who is older than her male partner, observers tend to assume that the younger man is exploiting her. On the assumption that no young man would genuinely choose to be with a woman who is "past her prime," observers raise a "red flag" on the relationship. "Sorry to be blunt," said one such observer to a woman seeking advice, "but you sound desperate. You see it as love. He sees it as his ticket to America."

In contrast, when an American man is seeking immigration papers for a substantially younger woman, his behavior is regarded as "rational" instead of desperate—a logical choice for a well-resourced man who desires a sexually available and grateful domestic helper. This is the case even when he explicitly uses an agency that matches U.S. men with women seeking such a "ticket" into the country. A healthy relationship is assumed to involve his money and her attractiveness, so in these gendered calculations an older man and young woman look right together. Determining whether a couple is attempting to defraud the U.S. government, then, is a gendered process related to beliefs about what kind of age-discrepant relationships are "normal" and "believable."

Aging is gendered, but it's also intersectional, and it takes more of a toll on some groups than others. Class-privileged All-American Boys may grow up to be Breadwinners and, then, Distinguished Gentlemen, replacing the admiration they enjoyed for their looks and physical fitness with the admiration that comes with building a successful career and becoming a valued leader. An aging body may be harder on a Blue-Collar Guy who relies on his body's ability to do the demanding job on which his sense of masculinity rests. As his physical abilities fade, he may come to rely on his ability to demand respect as a family Patriarch.

Wealthier women can look younger longer with excellent nutrition, good medical care, expensive beauty products, well-made and well-fitting clothes, gym memberships, personal trainers, and even cosmetic procedures. Some older women with high lev-

In her eighties, Supreme Court Justice Ruth Bader Ginsburg is known for wearing a "super diva" T-shirt during workouts. She is one of a small number of women who has been able to combine authority and attractiveness to become a widely admired Grande Dame.

els of cultural recognition participate actively in public life as Grande Dames. Ruth Bader Ginsburg, Jane Fonda, and Oprah Winfrey are proud older women who get respect, but not everyone has the resources or profile required to do so. And, no matter how many resources a woman has, her aging appearance will likely be judged and penalized more harshly than a man's.

Aging can be worse for working-class women like service workers and home care workers who, like working-class men, also work in physically demanding jobs. Sometimes their work trades directly on their attractiveness. Waitresses and receptionists, for example, may see their employability slip or their raises and tips decline as they age, without having the class privilege that enables them to replace looks with occupational success. It's a cruel reality: Because beauty is expensive, working-class women, on average, lose their looks more quickly than more class-privileged women, at the same time that losing their looks carries greater costs.

Moreover, women who live in unsafe urban environments, who have few opportunities for exercise and few amenities for doing so, may be more likely to be obese in middle age and to have age-related diseases like high blood pressure and diabetes.[116] The passing years take a greater toll on the poor and people of color than others. New research now shows that the persistent experience of discrimination over a lifetime does harm to the body, aging both men and women more quickly and contributing to illness.[117] Attractiveness and ability intersect, influenced by our other identities and circumstances, shaping our gender strategies throughout our lives.

Revisiting the Question

If gender is just one part of who we are, why isn't it crowded out by all the other things about us that are meaningful and consequential?

Gender isn't crowded out by other characteristics because it doesn't compete with those things, it colludes with them. Gender intersects with our other socially salient identities, inflecting them with gendered meaning, and every social position allows for different combinations of distinctions that carry costs and rewards. As we carve out a masculine or feminine identity, we develop strategies designed to manage all these expectations, constraints, and opportunities.

Some gender strategies are more realistic for us than others. Our individual characteristics, the organization of our societies, distinctions of value in our culture, and economic resources available to us all affect what we can pull off personally. Where we fall in this complex landscape of inequalities shapes the consequences for deviation from and conformity to gender rules. In simple words, we don't all have the same choices for doing gender.

Given our lot in life, most of us try to adopt a gender strategy that maximizes our own well-being and life chances. We often try to claim widely admired identities and distance ourselves from stigmatizing ones, but we don't all have the same resources to do so. So we often choose the least stigmatizing identity we can, like the "wannabes"; reject the rules, like those who insist that Black Is Beautiful; or try to negotiate with what is valued, like Blue-Collar Guys. We also experiment with multiple strategies across different situations, like the women who oscillate between Oriental Flower and Assertive Asian, or we use positive elements of masculinity or femininity to push away stigma, like the Able-Disabled and the Not Too Queer. We accept that others may accuse us of de-emphasizing parts of ourselves, like the black woman who attempts All-American Girl or the working-class man who is a Super Dad. We know we can't be everything to everyone, but we walk the tightrope of social disapproval across the complicated set of distinctions as best we can.

Next . . .

We are diverse individuals, with identities that go far beyond just gender, who use our free will and cultural competence to manage others' expectations of us. This is much easier for some of us than others, and some of us have much better options. Yet, we see a pattern in how men and women respond to these challenges: Men tend to find the gender binary, the science that attempts to uphold it, and the social rules that enforce it, less objectionable than women and people of other genders. And men have a much weaker tradition of protesting the way things are and asking for change. This seems like a good time to pose the question:

If both men and women are constrained by a binary gender system, why is it that more women than men find this system unfair?

This question brings us to the part of the book where we directly tackle the issue of inequality.

FOR FURTHER READING

Anzaldúa, Gloria. "La Conciencia de la Mestiza." *Borderlands/La Frontera: The New Mestiza*. San Francisco: Spinsters/Aunt Lute, 1987.

Collins, Patricia Hill. *Black Feminist Thought: Knowledge, Consciousness, and the Politics of Empowerment*, 2nd Ed. New York: Routledge, 1999.

Collins, Patricia Hill and Sirma Bilge. *Intersectionality*. Malden, MA: Polity, 2016.

Crenshaw, Kimberlé W. "Mapping the Margins: Intersectionality, Identity Politics, and Violence against Women of Color." *Stanford Law Review* 43, no. 6 (1991): 1241–99.

Espiritu, Yen Le. *Asian American Women and Men: Labor, Laws and Love*. Lanham, MD: Rowman and Littlefield, 2008.

Gerschick, Thomas J. "Toward a Theory of Disability and Gender." *Signs* 25, no. 4 (2000): 1264.

Hoang, Kimberly. "Transnational Gender Vertigo." *Contexts* 12, no. 2 (2013): 22–26.

Moore, Mignon R. *Invisible Families: Gay Identities, Relationships, and Motherhood among Black Women*. Berkeley: University of California Press, 2011.

Sontag, Susan. "The Double Standard of Aging." *The Saturday Review*, September 23, 1972, 29–38.

Wilkins, Amy. *Wannabes, Goths, and Christians: The Boundaries of Sex, Style, and Status*. Chicago: University of Chicago Press, 2008.

WHAT A PIECE OF WORK IS MAN!

—WILLIAM SHAKESPEARE

6

Inequality:

MEN AND MASCULINITIES

For a study of men's experience reading lifestyle magazines, a young man named Reid was asked to reflect on the impact gender rules had on him: the rules that a man should be emotionally and physically strong, at the top of his game professionally, and sexually successful with women. In response, Reid said that aligning those expectations with his real self was a type of work: "[R]econciling the expectations that other people in my life may have of what a man should be," he said, was something he had to actively do.[1] Finding a gender strategy that felt "right" to him didn't come entirely naturally. He didn't find the work especially onerous— "It's pretty easy for me," he explained—but he acknowledged that it wasn't so easy for others.

The last chapter discussed how living in a gendered society requires men and women to develop culturally recognizable gender strategies. This chapter explores, in more detail, what that looks like for men, arguing that a rigid gender binary system that requires us to do gender in specific ways is not optimal for either men or women. Men don't always experience this as a burden but, as Reid's comments suggest, it's still work.

This chapter also considers why men haven't been on the forefront of the movement to challenge the gender binary. The political activism aimed at changing gender relations has been called "feminism" and the "women's movement" because it has been primarily led and supported by women. Even today it is women, more than men, who object to the way their lives are gendered.[2] This leads us to our question:

 Q+A **If both men and women are constrained by a binary gender system, why is it more women than men find this system unfair?**

This chapter resolves this question by looking at how the costs and rewards of doing gender are distributed unequally. While men and women both need to do gender in order to be seen as fully functional members of society, we do not do gender in symmetrical ways, and the consequences of our gender performances are not the same. This is because the gender binary is *hierar-chical*. It places men above women, values masculinity above femininity, and routinely brings men and women together into relationships in which women are positioned as helpers to men.

This is bad for both men and women, but in different ways. For men more than women, it narrows the range of life experiences that seem acceptable and right. For women more than men, it results in reduced social status, lower financial rewards, and an expectation that men's needs and interests should take priority. Gender inequality, then, isn't just about preferring men over women. It involves a far more complex calculus. Let's begin with an example.

THE GENDER OF CHEERLEADING

At its inception in the mid-1800s, cheerleading was an all-male sport. Characterized by gymnastics, stunts, and crowd leadership, it was considered equivalent in prestige to that flagship of American masculinity: football. As the editors of the *Nation* saw it in 1911:

> The reputation of having been a valiant "cheer-leader" is one of the most valuable things a boy can take away from college. As a title to promotion in professional or public life, it ranks hardly second to that of having been a quarterback.[3]

Indeed, cheerleading helped launch the political careers of three U.S. presidents: Dwight D. Eisenhower, Franklin Roosevelt, and Ronald Reagan were cheerleaders.[4] Actor Jimmy Stewart was head cheerleader at Princeton. Republicans Rick Perry, Tom DeLay, and Mitt Romney all led cheers for their schools' teams.

Being a cheerleader was a "great responsibility" and a "high honor."[5] Comparing cheerleaders to Pericles of ancient Athens—statesman, orator, and military

The men of the Yale University cheerleading team stand proud in 1927.

general—the *New York Times* in 1924 described Stanford University's all-male cheerleaders as "lithe, white-sweatered and flannel-trousered youth" projecting "mingled force and grace" and a "locomotive cheer."[6] As late as 1927, cheerleading manuals still referred to the reader exclusively as a "man," "chap," or "fellow.[7]

Women were first given the opportunity to join squads when large numbers of young men were deployed to fight World War I, leaving open spots that women were happy to fill. The entrance of women into the activity, though, was considered unnatural and even inappropriate. Argued one opponent in 1938:

> *[Women cheerleaders] frequently became too masculine for their own good. We find the development of loud, raucous voices . . . and the consequent development of slang and profanity by their necessary association with [male] squad members.*[8]

Cheerleading was too masculine for women.

When the men returned from the war, there was an effort to push women back out of cheerleading. Some schools even banned female cheerleaders. In 1939, Gamma Sigma, the national college cheerleaders' fraternity, refused to include female cheerleaders or recognize squads that did. "Every year there is a campaign to take them in," said the fraternity's president, "but every year we keep them out."[9] Ultimately, of course, the effort to preserve cheer as an exclusively male activity was unsuccessful. With a second mass deployment of men during World War II, women cheerleaders were here to stay.

By the 1960s and 1970s, cheerleaders were primarily female and the activity became less about leadership and more about support and sexiness.

But that wasn't the end of the story. Instead of changing how we thought about women, the presence of women in cheer changed how people thought about cheering. Because women were stereotyped as cute instead of "valiant," cheerleading's association with women led to its trivialization. By the 1950s, the ideal cheerleader was no longer a man with leadership skills; it was someone with "manners, cheerfulness, and good disposition." In response, boys pretty much turned away from cheerleading altogether. By the early 1960s, men with megaphones had been replaced by perky girls with pom-poms:

> *Cheerleading in the sixties consisted of cutesy chants, big smiles and revealing uniforms. There were no gymnastic tumbling runs. No complicated stunting. Never any injuries. About the most athletic thing sixties cheerleaders did was a cartwheel followed by the splits.*[10]

In the span of a hundred years, cheerleading evolved from a respected pursuit to a silly show on the sidelines. As it became more female, its value and prestige declined. By 1974, those same Stanford cheerleaders were described as "simple creatures" who needed only two things: "blondeness, congenital or acquired, and a compulsively cute, nonstop bottom."[11]

We've seen similar changes repeatedly in recent American society: in leisure activities like cheer, but also in occupations like "secretary," and in literature and the arts. We may even be seeing such changes right now, as women are increasingly entering college majors like biology or careers like law. The "demotion" of an arena of life as it undergoes a "sex change" is common. Understanding these demotions requires exploring the relationship between gender and power.

GENDERED POWER

Patriarchy: Then and Now

America and many European societies were patriarchies well into the 1800s and, in some cases, the 1900s. The literal meaning of the word **patriarchy** is "the rule of the father." It refers to the control of female and younger male family members by select adult men, or patriarchs.

In fully patriarchal societies, only patriarchs have rights. Women have no right to their own bodies and no right to the children they bear. Men decide where the family lives and whom their children marry. If a woman works outside the home, she does so only with the permission of the head of household (a father, brother, or husband), and her earnings are given directly to him. A patriarch may have social and legal permission to punish his wife or wives and his children physically, brutally if he chooses. He is "the king of his castle," so his word is law at home.

Meanwhile, because men alone have legal and civil rights, only men are entitled to act freely in the outside world, where they may—or may not—choose to represent the interests of their wives and children. In societies like these, women cannot vote, serve on juries, use birth control, work after marriage, keep their own wages, attain a divorce, have custody of their children, enlist in the military, own property, hold political office, or sue for discrimination, among many other restrictions.

Life really was like this for a long time, but as democracies replaced monarchies, the relationship among citizens changed, first among men with wealth and then among wider classes of men. Democratic states offered a new political bargain that gave rights to an ever-increasing range of men. Patriarchy was slowly replaced by a **democratic brotherhood**, the distribution of citizenship rights to certain classes of men. Each newly incorporated class of men—sometimes represented by political parties, unions, or fraternal associations like Elks and Knights of Columbus—often tried to keep the next class of men out. But slowly, as poor men, men of color, immigrants, and indigenous men fought for the rights of citizenship offered to elite men in these early democracies, the brotherhood grew.

Women had to fight, too. Only gradually, in struggle after struggle, did they see victories, earning one hard-fought right at a time.[12] These struggles have changed both laws and customs so that today most Western countries are based upon **formal gender equality**—the requirement that laws treat men and women as equal citizens. Incredibly, though the idea is rather new and was once considered absurd, equal rights for women has come to be seen as common sense. Most people in most countries today, that is, see both classic patriarchy and its modified form in democratic brotherhoods as deeply and unacceptably unfair.

However, even as patriarchy has steadily declined as a principle of law, its underlying way of *thinking* about gender still persists. First, even though people no longer need to be male to count as full citizens, men continue to be conceived of as the generic human, with women as deviant from the norm. Men, in other words, are the unmarked human. This becomes clear when we consider how political concerns are separated into *political issues* and *women's issues*; the bathroom symbol for *men's* is the same one used for *person* on "walk" signs and elsewhere; classes on gender are often assumed to be primarily about women, as if only women are gendered; and cartoon animals, in the absence of cues like hair bows or long eyelashes, are assumed to be male.[13] Men's identity as men is often invisible, even to themselves, while women's identity as women is usually centrally important. All too often, in other words, men are people and women are women.

Some argue that *man* stands in for *human*, so the stick figure in pants, for example, really does reflect all of us. But that's not how our brains work. Studies show that the words *he*, *his*, and *man*, when used generically to refer to individuals or the human race, tend to conjure up images of men, not men and women together.[14] The words *human*, *individual*, and *person* work the same way.[15] Women are all too often excluded from the terms in practice, even if they're in the definition. One sign we still live in a modified patriarchy, then, is the persistent centering of men as normal or neutral and the marginalizing of women as a modified, nonneutral type of person.

We see this in media, too, where men's characters and stories predominate (Figure 6.1). A study of the top-grossing 200 nonanimated films in 2015, for example, found that only 17 percent were headlined by women without a male co-lead.[16] Male characters received almost twice as much screen time as women and had more than twice as many lines. Half of the movies that have won Best Picture since 1929 fail to pass the Bechdel Test, a check as to whether a movie has even a single scene in which two named female characters talk to one another about something other than a man.[17] We see similar dynamics in comics, primetime television commercials, video games, children's books, and cartoons.[18] Girls and women don't take center stage in American media as often as boys and men, reflecting the general belief that women can identify with men (because men are people), but men can't identify with women (because women are women).

FIGURE 6.1 | PROPORTION OF WORDS SPOKEN BY MEN VS. WOMEN IN BEST PICTURE–WINNING FILMS*

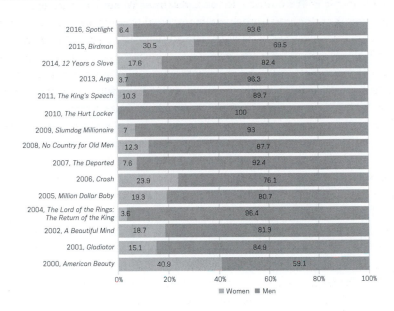

*All female and male characters who speak more than one hundred words.
Source: Data from Hanah Anderson, "The Pudding," https://pudding.cool/2017/03/film-dialogue.

Second, patriarchal thinking persists in the continued equation of power with masculinity.[19] In both classic patriarchies and democratic brotherhoods, the right of an individual to act in the world authoritatively was contingent on being male. To have power was to be a man. In other words, power itself was gendered. In contemporary American English, masculinity and femininity are still used as synonyms for power and powerlessness, respectively. According to thesaurus.com, synonyms for the word *power* include *male, manful, manlike, manly,* and *masculine,* while synonyms for *weakness* include *effeminate, effete, emasculate,* and *womanly.*[20] Likewise, the word *femininity* is said to be synonymous with the terms *docility, delicacy,* and *softness,* whereas the word *masculine* is taken as synonymous with the terms *courageous, hardy, muscular, potent, robust, strong,* and *vigorous.*[21]

These synonyms reveal that gender is a metaphor for power.[22] To be seen as less masculine is to be seen as less powerful, even feminine. Conversely, to be powerful is to invoke the aura of masculinity. If we want to tell someone to stop being weak and grasp power, we tell them to *man up.* If we want to communicate that a person, idea, or institution is strong, we often do so with gendered language: powerful cars are "testosterone-charged," aggressive rock music is

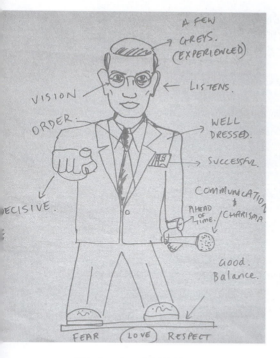

This drawing of an ideal leader assumes a male body and masculine demeanor are essential.

"cock rock," and to find one's courage is to "strap on a pair."

In the media, just as men are overrepresented, they are more likely than women to be portrayed as aggressive, brave, and physically strong.[23] An analysis of 34,476 comic book characters, for example, found that male superheroes were more likely than female ones to have super strength, stamina, and invulnerability.[24] In contrast, female superheroines specialized in mental instead of physical powers, like empathy, precognition, or seduction. Even among superhumans, then, masculinity is closely tied to strength and invulnerability, with feminine powers more mental and manipulative.

Most societies today are a far cry from classic patriarchies, where fathers were little kings, or democratic brotherhoods, where men closed ranks to exclude all women. But neither is patriarchy wholly gone. Instead, American and many other societies are contradictions: characterized by both some degree of formal gender equality and the persistence of patriarchal ideas. We call these modern societies **modified patriarchies**, societies in which women have been granted formal gender equality but where the patriarchal conflation of power with men and masculinity remains a central part of daily life.

Most of us live in societies, then, that are widely, even if unofficially, characterized by patriarchal relations. Specifically, three relations of inequality shape the hierarchical nature of contemporary gender dynamics: sexism, androcentrism, and subordination.

Relations of Inequality

Sexism is the favoring of male-bodied over female-bodied people, both ideologically and in practice. It's the best word to describe valuing male over female children, the belief that women are naturally weaker than men, or the conviction that men are better suited for public office.[25] Evidence of sexism is ubiquitous. In a recent study, for example, 127 professors of biology, chemistry, and physics were asked to evaluate the application materials of a fictional person seeking a laboratory manager position.[26] Half the professors received a résumé with a female name; the other half received the exact same résumé with a male name. On average, compared to male applicants, females were rated as less competent, less hirable, and deserving of less mentorship and a lower salary. Both male and female professors showed this bias.

Psychologist Janet Swim and colleagues reviewed 123 similar experimental studies asking subjects to evaluate writing, artwork, behavior, job applications, and biographies attributed to fictional men or women.[27] The aggregated study results show that, holding everything else constant, women are evaluated less positively than men. The same résumé, piece of art, or life's work is seen as less impressive if the evaluator thinks it was created by a woman instead of a man. Our legacy of patriarchal gender relations tilts people's preferences toward men, putting a thumb on the scale in favor of male-bodied people.

If sexism is sex-based prejudice, then **androcentrism** is gender-based prejudice: the granting of higher status, respect, value, reward, and power to whatever is seen as masculine compared to what is seen as feminine. Androcentrism is different from sexism because it doesn't reward people with male bodies over people with female ones; instead, rewards accrue to *anyone* who can do masculinity. Androcentrism means what is valued in men (masculinity) tends to be valued in everyone, but what is valued in women (femininity) tends to be valued only in women. This is why women wear pants, but men don't wear skirts; why women become surgeons, but men have largely abandoned pediatrics; and why women have pushed their way into soccer and ski jumping, but men are leaving synchronized swimming and softball to the ladies. It's why girls who are boyish are affectionately called tomboys, but boys who act girlish are derisively called sissies.

The pattern is clear, for example, with first names.[28] Once a traditionally male name starts being given to girls, the rate at which parents give it to boys starts to decline. The name Leslie, for example, was almost exclusively for boys until the 1940s.[29] As it rose in popularity for girls in the 1970s, it fell in popularity for boys. A selection of names that have undergone a similar "sex change" are listed in Table 6.1. Such changes are always from male to female. The very fact that parents may give their daughters traditionally male names is evidence that a touch of perceived masculinity is considered good or advantageous for girls, but femininity does not do the same for boys.

In a third relation of power, men and women are brought together into hierarchical relationships. The placing of women into positions that make them subservient to or dependent on men is called **subordination**. Nursing, for instance, is not just feminine and female, it also puts nurses into a subordinate relationship with doctors.[30] Doctors tell nurses what to do; nurses "help" doctors do their job. The same is true for the gendered relationships between managers and their assistants, dentists and dental hygienists, and lawyers and paralegals.[31] These

TABLE 6.1 | U.S. NAMES GIVEN PRIMARILY TO GIRLS THAT WERE ONCE GIVEN EXCLUSIVELY TO BOYS

Addison	Bailey	Hadley	Lindsay	Monroe	Shelby
Allison	Beverly	Haven	Madison	Paris	Stevie
Ashley	Blair	Kelsey	McKenzie	Peyton	Sydney
Aubrey	Cassidy	Kennedy	McKinley	Presley	Taylor
Avery	Dana	Lauren	Meredith	Reagan	Whitney

Source: https://nametrends.net/.

occupational roles are gendered. In the United States, women represent 90 percent of registered nurses, 91 percent of receptionists, 95 percent of administrative assistants, 95 percent of dental hygienists, and 86 percent of paralegals.[32] Some men become receptionists and paralegals, of course, but this doesn't change the underlying understanding that it's "women's work." Likewise, women become managers and dentists, but typically the support they receive from subordinates is still provided by women.

Because the subordination of women to men is seen as normal, we sometimes even see it between men and women in otherwise equal positions.[33] Sociologist Patricia Yancey Martin, who spent years observing interactions in Fortune 500 companies, recounted many ways in which women were expected to help or support male colleagues as if they were an assistant.[34] In one case, two vice presidents stood talking in a hallway as a phone rang, unanswered. After a few rings, the man asked the woman why she wasn't answering the phone. In fact, this was no more her job than his, but because she was a woman, it just seemed to make sense that she do it. Even when they have the same job title, women are more likely than men to be asked, or silently expected, to make the coffee, plan parties, take notes, order food, and clean up after meetings, as well as attend to clients or colleagues having emotional breakdowns. Notably, none of this work brings any rewards or accolades for women. It is just expected of them.

When roles are gendered, then, they often place a woman in a position subordinate to a man, helping him (and cheering him on) as he does the high-profile, exciting, well-rewarded work. The supporting role is a distinctly feminine one, and it brings men and women—and masculine and feminine activities—into a distinctly close yet unmistakably hierarchical relationship. And as we just saw, this sometimes happens even when men and women are otherwise equal.

We do not live in a world that simply insists upon gender distinction. We live in one that imbues men, masculine people, and masculinized activities with more visibility, status, value, and power than women, feminine people, and feminized activities. This is what makes gender about power, not just difference. These asymmetries in the gender binary—and the relations between men and women that emerge—make doing gender a *different* challenge for men and women. For the remainder of this chapter, we'll talk about how men negotiate the hierarchical gender binary.

GENDER FOR MEN

Doing Masculinity, Avoiding Femininity

Sociologist Emily Kane was interested in how the hierarchical gender binary influenced parents' interactions with their kids, so she set out to interview parents about their children's gender-conforming and nonconforming behavior.[35] She found that parents of boys expressed near universal distress over boys' interest in the "icons of femininity."[36] Kane explains:

> Parents of sons reported negative responses to their sons' wearing pink or frilly clothing; wearing skirts, dresses, or tights; and playing dress up in any kind of feminine attire. Nail polish elicited concern from a number of parents, too, as they reported young sons wanting to have their fingernails or toenails polished. Dance, especially ballet, and Barbie dolls were also among the traditionally female activities often noted negatively by parents of sons.[37]

Parents' negative reaction to boys' "feminine sides" reflects androcentrism and the stigmatizing nature of femininity for men. They took for granted that feminine interests and behaviors were inappropriate and were confused when their boys acted this way. It suggested something was *wrong*. "Is he going to grow up to be gay? Trans? Does he have a bad relationship with his father? Is his mother too overbearing? What is going on!?" The behavior demanded explanation. Kane found that even parents who were tolerant of gender deviance themselves often sought to protect their sons from social disapproval by discouraging their adoption of femininity in public.

Kane's research was conducted in the early 2000s, so it best describes the childhood environment of today's young adults. While newer data, from 2017, shows that about 68 percent of Americans believe that it's a "good thing" for parents to encourage children to explore the toys and activities typically associated with the other gender, a gender difference remains: 76 percent of people think this is a good idea for girls, while 64 percent think it's a good idea for boys.[38] Younger people and women are more supportive of cross-gender play than older people and men, but no matter how you slice the data, people tend to feel more comfortable when girls do it than boys.

Because of these lessons, boys tend to grow up learning to avoid femininity. A whole host of slurs reflect this imperative: like *sissy* or *soft*, used to suggest that a boy is not boy enough, and *cuck* or *pussy-whipped*, applied to men who are perceived to be overly deferential to women. Likewise, insults like *girl* and *woman* literally use a female identity to disparage boys and men. Other common slurs reference women or femininity, like *bitch* and *douche*. All these terms reflect a sexist and androcentric world, telling both boys and girls, in no uncertain terms, that being feminine makes you a girl and being a girl is worse than being a boy or man.

The slurs related to homosexuality—*fag, homo, gay*—send the same message. Being gay is actually incidental.[39] Any man or boy who is perceived to be feminine attracts these slurs. In fact, studies have shown that boys and men often actively avoid calling *known* homosexuals by these terms, even when they otherwise liberally pepper their language with them. In one study of college athletes, "everything was fag this and fag that," but after some of their teammates revealed their sexual orientation, the athletes stopped using it in reference to the gay players.[40] "They say, 'this is gay,' and 'that's gay,'" one gay athlete explained, "but they don't mean it like that."[41] In other words, they don't mean "gay" as in *gay*; they mean "gay" as in *feminine*. Accusations of homosexuality are forms of gender policing. This is true, also, of slurs like *cocksucker* and the phrase *suck my dick*; each denigrates someone who sexually services a man—male or female—and thereby inhabits the feminine side of the binary.

The chorus of slurs stigmatizing men who perform femininity sends a consistent message, a rule designed to guide all men's behavior: *Guys, whatever you do, avoid acting like a girl.* In at least some parts of their lives, then, men face enormous pressure to avoid doing anything associated with women. And, indeed, 69 percent of young men say that they feel at least some pressure to be ready to throw a punch if provoked, 61 percent say they feel pressure to have a lot of sexual partners, and 57 percent say they feel pressure to talk about women in a hypersexual way.[42]

These same young men, though, are less likely than men of previous generations to see themselves as "very masculine." Only 24 percent describe themselves that way and, even among older men, only about third do so.[43] Since many men don't naturally feel this way, being sufficiently masculine and avoiding femininity can require constant vigilance, extending to the most trivial of things—even what men are allowed to drink. In an online slideshow with the title "Drinks Men Should Never Order," the list of drinks men are compelled to avoid includes anything blended or slushy; Jell-O shots or anything "neon"; white zinfandel; drinks with "an obscene amount of garnish"; anything with whipped cream; anything that ends with "tini" (except an "honest" martini); malt beverages (unless they are "40s"); anything with Diet Coke; cosmopolitans (they're "downright girly"); wine coolers; anything that comes with an umbrella; anything fruity (including fuzzy navels, Bacardi breezes, mai tais, screwdrivers, margaritas, daiquiris, and Alabama slammers); all mixed drinks (seriously, all of them); and anything with a straw.[44] A similar slideshow (there are dozens) concludes with the insistence that, above all else, a guy can't have anything "she's having" on the assumption that anything a woman drinks is immediately off-limits for men.

Because of androcentrism, *anything* a woman does can become off-limits for men. One result is **male flight**, a phenomenon in which men abandon feminizing arenas of life. This is what happened with cheerleading as well as to many classic boys' names. As we've hinted, the same happens in professional occupations.[45] A study of veterinary school applications, for example, found that for every 1 percent increase in the proportion of women in the student body, 1.7 fewer men applied.[46] One more woman was a greater deterrent than $1,000 in extra tuition. Male flight exacerbates the trend toward feminization initiated by women's entrance, quickly ramping up the pace at which a given domain seems inappropriate for men. And like we saw with cheerleading, once an activity or occupation becomes feminized, its value is diminished.

Men will even flee quite valuable arenas to avoid femininity. Consider education. Women are now outperforming men at all levels of schooling. They are more likely to be identified as "gifted and talented" in elementary school, half as likely to be held back a year in middle school, and less likely to drop out of high school.[47] They get higher grades in high school and take more advanced classes.[48] In fact, there is no longer any level of higher education in which men dominate. Women earn 61 percent of associate's degrees, 57 percent of bachelor's degrees, and 60 percent of master's degrees. They even earn 52 percent of PhDs.[49]

As girls and women have come to excel in school, boys and men have increasingly associated education with femininity. Thinking studiousness is for girls, they don't study or, if they do, they may hide their hard work.[50] Underachievement is seen as cool for men, especially if they pretend not to care. Accordingly, men have become less interested in educational achievement than women, especially if they've strongly internalized the rules of masculinity.[51] Will men abandon education because women are getting too good at it? What else will they let go once schooling, "honest" martinis, and "James" have gone to the girls? And why are men doing this to themselves?

Hegemonic Masculinity

Hegemony is a sociological concept used to help us understand the persistence of social inequality. It refers to a state of collective consent to inequality secured by the idea that it's inevitable, natural, or desirable. An idea is hegemonic only when it is widely endorsed by both those who benefit from the social

Quarterback Tom Brady represents the hegemonic man, one who, by virtue of seeming to live up to masculine expectations, affirms the idea that men are superior to women.

conditions it supports as well as those who do not. Hegemony, then, means widespread consent to relations of systematic social disadvantage.

The phrase **hegemonic masculinity** refers to a type of masculine performance, idealized by men and women alike, that functions to justify and naturalize gender inequality, assuring widespread consent to the social disadvantage of most women and some men.[52] The practice of hegemonic masculinity creates the "real man" in our collective imagination who theoretically embodies all the most positive traits on the masculine side of the gender binary. He has the athlete's speed and strength, the CEO's income, the politician's power, the Hollywood heartthrob's charm, the family man's loyalty, the construction worker's manual skills, the frat boy's tolerance for alcohol, and the playboy's virility.

We then attribute these individual traits to the category "man." All men, simply by virtue of being men, can make a claim to all of them, even if they aren't able to achieve the impossible goal of being all those things. A married father who loves only his wife, for example, may nod approvingly at the playboy and say, "*We men* love to chase women."

Meanwhile, the playboy, who is a struggling musician, can point to the politician and say, "*We men* are in control," while the politician points to the frat boy and says, "*We men* like to party hard." That frat boy may be getting solid Cs, but he can point to the doctor and say, "*We men* are ambitious," while the doctor, who may never have punched anyone in his life, can cheer on the professional boxer and say, "*We men* know how to fight." The boxer, who voluntarily submits to getting hit in the face, can point to the scientist and say, "*We men* are logical." You get the idea. Just by membership in the category, all men get to identify with the characteristics we attribute to men in general. In this way, men benefit from the hegemony of masculinity. They can lay a socially valid claim to advantage by virtue of the traits attributed to their sex.

Interestingly, not all the traits believed to be typical of men are good. In fact, many are negative.[53] Television commercials often show men as bumbling parents, perpetual adolescents, and sex-crazed losers. They drink too much and fight too easily. Because masculinity is hegemonic, though, men's bad behaviors are either excused, with the typical "boys will be boys" account, or used to allow them to avoid subordination in "helping" roles.

One negative stereotype, for example, is that men are dirty. If so, who can blame them if they don't help keep the house clean? "I have a very high threshold for squalor," one man said, comparing himself to his wife. "If my partner could bear the filth past the point that I get triggered to clean I believe the situation [would] lean more in her favor."[54] "It is not that it is women's work," said another, "women . . . are [just] far more particular about cleanliness than men."[55] Aw shucks, these guys are saying, the women around me just happen to have higher standards of cleanliness, so I guess they will have to do the grunt work.

Similarly, the stereotype that men are bad with kids is used to excuse dads from having to take care of them, the stereotype that men are competitive gives them a pass for being uncomfortable if their wives make more money, and the stereotype that they're "naturally" aggressive gives them permission to lose their temper. "I stepped on toes," said a businessman about being confrontational at work, but insisted: "If you want to play it safe . . . you don't get a hell of a lot done."[56] "It don't matter how much a man loves his wife and kids," said another man about the stereotype that men are sexually insatiable, "he's gonna keep on chasing other women."[57]

Such accounts are called **exculpatory chauvinism**, a phenomenon in which negative characteristics ascribed to men are offered as acceptable justifications of men's dominance over women.[58] *Exculpatory* means "to free someone from blame," while the word *chauvinism* refers, in this context, to bias in favor of men. Exculpatory chauvinism, then, refers to the tendency to absolve men of responsibility for performances that embody negative male stereotypes, while simultaneously offering social rewards for such behavior, such as free time from family life, success at work, and a license to enjoy dominating others.

Men, in this logic, aren't all good and they're certainly not necessarily *better* than women; they're just *better suited* to lead, score, decide, and defend. Exculpatory chauvinism doesn't say that men are superior human beings, just that they're "designed for dominance."[59] So, for men to be seen as rightly in charge, it's not necessary for male stereotypes to be positive; men need only to position these stereotypes in such a way as to reap the rewards of the most highly valued parts of life.

Importantly, however, the benefits of masculinity are not awarded equally to all men. Some men are able to enact more of the features of hegemonic masculinity. And some are able to get away with more "bad" behavior than others. Hegemonic masculinity helps men, but it also hurts them, and it does so unequally.

The Measure of Men

Failures to embody hegemonic masculinity can cause some men to be seen (or even see themselves) as lesser men. These judgments establish and reflect a

hierarchy of masculinity, a rough ranking of men from most to least masculine, with the assumption that more is always better. Along the hierarchy we find multiple **masculinities** that vary in their distance from the hegemonic ideal, the nature of the deviation, and in their intersections with other identities. The plural of the word refers to the fact that men do masculinity differently given their social positions, intersectional identities, and the highly variable contexts of each interaction. They do so, though, not without consequence, but in ways that advantage and disadvantage them.

Because hegemonic masculinity draws on values associated with the privileged ends of *all* hierarchies in a society, not just the gender hierarchy, the ability to embody this ideal is greater for a man in Western societies who is well educated, tall, affluent, white, heterosexual, able-bodied, fit, Christian, and native-born. Accordingly, men who are subordinated in other hierarchies are vulnerable to being judged as failing to embody hegemonic masculinity and as rightly belonging lower on this hierarchy. This is why Asian men are often imagined to be not manly enough, and why disabled and aging men sometimes feel like they're losing their masculinity; society defines "real men" as something they're not. Black and white working-class men are often portrayed as particularly strong with hard-working bodies, but black men are seen as lacking the economic power that "real" hegemonic masculinity implies and white working-class men's masculinity is deemed compensatory and imbalanced: tough to the point of brutishness and, thus, unintelligent and prone to violence.

Men who are physically weak, emotional, uncool, or who break important gender rules are all vulnerable to being defined as lesser men. Boys and men report that having a chubby or fat body is read as weakness, while lean bodies with large muscles communicate confidence, power, and mental strength.[60] Beginning in earnest in the 1980s, the mass media in the United States have held male bodies up to greater scrutiny, often idealizing hard-bodied, bulging physiques that are unattainable for most men.[61] As a result, negative body image is increasing among men and boys, and is especially noticeable among sexual minority men.[62]

Even men who are blessed with the physical bodies, cultural identities, social circumstances, and personalities that allow them to perform hegemonic masculinity most easily will never be able to rest assured that they are "real" men. Men's ability to meet these standards is limited by the inherent contradictions of the ideal. Consequently, men's social status is always at risk, no matter how privileged they seem. All men fail sooner or later. They will fail, first, because the hegemonic man is an impossible fiction: a jumble of idealized, contradictory elements. A person can't be both a perfect husband and a playboy, a team player and an aggressive egotist, or hard bodied and hard drinking. No single man will ever be able to approximate the full scope of hegemonic masculinity.

Meanwhile, as contexts change, the masculinities men are expected to per-form often shift around them, making for social traps into which men can fall. For example, considering the rules of "guy talk," Evan put it this way:

> *There is . . . your kind of dodgy uncle who takes you to the pub or you're out with the boys and that [locker room talk is] just a normal common talk. . . . So you're under pressure to express masculinity at the pub, but then once everyone's around, you're expected to invert that, that's where the conflict is. And then there's corpo-rate pressure and societal pressure basically to suppress it, but there is this kind of masculine pressure to exaggerate it.*[63]

Evan is aware that a crass sort of guy talk is demanded in some contexts and punished in others. While he has agency to choose what types of masculinity to do and knows the rules about when and where to deploy each type, he is also sensitive to the constant possibility that he might misjudge a situation and do the wrong masculinity at the wrong time.

At an even more basic level, men will fail to live up to hegemonic masculin-ity because hegemonic masculinity claims that its performers never lose. Yet, no one can win all the time. A man's masculinity is potentially undermined by competitive losses, disability, or age. All men will at times, or eventually, find themselves lacking in some way, leading every man "to view himself—during moments at least—as unworthy, incomplete, and inferior."[64] As Michael Kaufman, a scholar of masculinities, explained:

> *Whatever power might be associated with dominant masculinities, they also can be the source of enormous pain. Because the images are, ultimately, childhood pictures of omnipotence, they are impossible to obtain. Surface appearances aside, no man is completely able to live up to these ideas and images.*[65]

But many men try. They try to "stay in control," "conquer," and "call the shots"; they try to "tough it out, provide, and achieve" and, in the meantime, they have to repress the things about them that conflict with hegemonic masculinity.[66] They have to try not to feel, need, or desire the things they're not supposed to feel, need, or desire. To do otherwise is to face to **emasculation**, a loss of masculinity.

"Fragile" Masculinity

Men's calculated and even exaggerated avoidance of femininity is described in pop culture as a type of fragility. As sociologist Gwen Sharp explains it, it's as if "masculinity is so fragile that apparently even the slightest brush with the feminine destroys it."[67] Sensitive to emasculation, men are more likely than women to respond to gender cues on products, avoiding those that signal femininity.[68] As a result, some companies design products intended to soothe and reassure men of their manliness. Often this is subtle, but sometimes it's not. Products like "Brogurt" (yogurt for men), "Brogamats" (yoga mats for men), "mandles" (candles for men), and "Kleenex for men" are tongue-in-cheek. Or are they? They certainly work to reassure men that their dabbling in femininity won't diminish their manliness. And when we spy the sleek, dark gray line of Dove Men Care personal grooming products, or others like it, we're seeing the same phenomenon.

Fragile masculinity is premised on the notion of **precarious masculinity**, the idea that manhood is more difficult to earn and easier to lose than womanhood.[69] A woman is something one *is*, while a man is something one *does*, meaning that womanhood is bestowed at birth, but manhood is attained and sustained through action. Testing this idea, psychologist Jennifer Bosson led a study in which subjects were asked to finish the sentences "A real man . . ." and "A real woman . . ."[70] The results revealed that men usually completed the first sentence with an action (for example, "A real man works hard") and the latter with a trait ("A real woman is honest"). Women just *are* women, but men have to prove they're men every day.

In the face of a threat, the precariousness of masculinity can lead to **compensatory masculinity**, acts undertaken to reassert one's manliness in the face of a threat. In a subsequent study, Bosson randomly assigned male college students to either braid ropes or braid hair. After five minutes of braiding, the men were told that they could choose their next activity: hitting a punching bag or doing a puzzle.[71] The men who braided hair were twice as likely to choose boxing as the men who braided rope. Braiding hair, in other words, was emasculating enough that these men sought out an activity that allowed them to reestablish a sufficient level of masculinity.

Other scholars doing similar studies get the same results. Men whose masculinity is threatened do more pushups, consume more energy drinks, and report an increased likelihood of buying an SUV.[72] They are more likely to exhibit homophobia, endorse male superiority, excuse violence and sexual assault, and want their country to go to war.[73] Researchers have also found that because expressing care for the health of the earth is considered feminine, men litter more than women, recycle less, eat less sustainably, and use more energy.[74] Some men even go so far as to avoid ecofriendly branded colors. The future of life on our planet, in other words, is in the hands of men who are made nervous by the color green.

Importantly, it's not necessarily women who men are nervous around. Much of the policing of men is done by men themselves. In a set of interviews with college students, men talked about the importance of seeming masculine in front of their male friends. Chauncey described putting his "man face" on.[75] Jason reported that he only listened to R&B music when he was alone. Kumar would do "stupid hook-up things . . . just to kind of prove yourself."[76] Chet talked about the difficulty he had being open with even his closest friends: "If a guy starts opening up to another guy, he will joke around like, 'You look like you are ready to make out with me.' . . . I have done it."[77] Men must do masculinity in order to avoid policing, much of which comes from other men.

Classic patriarchies and democratic brotherhoods were always as much about relations among men as they were about relations between women and men; modified patriarchal relations still are. Hegemonic masculinity doesn't simply position men above women, it arranges men in a hierarchy all their own, one that takes into account all of men's intersectional identities. This hierarchy grants men the privilege of looking down on women, but it also positions them such that other men may be looking down on them. To be a man in America is to be arrayed in a hierarchy according to how well one does masculinity and threatened, constantly, with the possibility of failure and slippage.

Because many men are toward the bottom of this hierarchy, or were once or will be, it's simply not true to say that all men always have more power than all women. Being male is an advantage, yes, and being a *masculine* male is a greater advantage, for sure. But men who can't or won't do masculinity, or whose masculinity is stigmatized, will find themselves near the bottom of the masculine hierarchy. Women with other kinds of privilege—like race or class privilege—may enjoy greater overall social esteem.

Because gender is not the only game in town, men's disadvantages can significantly outweigh their gender advantage. White women have more wealth and live in better neighborhoods than black men (and black women) do, for example, and can mobilize racial power to continue to exclude them. Moreover, because of **colorism**, a racist preference for light over dark skin, a light-skinned Latina woman may have more social power than a dark-skinned Latino man. Because we are also arranged in a class hierarchy, a male gardener likely has significantly less esteem and opportunity than the rich woman whose flowers he cultivates; because of disability stigma, an able-bodied woman may be taken more seriously than a man with a spinal cord injury; because of religious prejudice, a Christian woman may pass through airports with more ease than a Muslim man. It's important to remember that some women have significantly more power, resources, and status than some men, even if men, on average, have more than women. As Kaufman explains: "Within each group, men usually have privileges and power relative to the women in that group, but in society as a whole, things are not always so straightforward."[78]

As a result of the expectation that men live up to an impossible ideal, the uneven way in which masculine power is distributed, and the pressure men face to be someone they're not, many individual men do not *feel* particularly powerful at all. Many feel downright powerless in many areas of their lives: at work, in their relationships, and in relation to other men on whose judgment their status in the hierarchy of masculinity depends. Men, it turns out, often feel a disconnect between who they are and the power "men" are said to have. There is a good reason for this, but it is not, as some like to argue, because we no longer live in a society characterized by gender inequality. Instead, hegemonic masculinity affirms men's power over other men as well as men's power over women.

For men, then, there are also costs to pay. And because gendered hierarchies are strongly and even violently policed, both conformity and resistance can be dangerous.

The Danger of Masculinity

Extreme conformity to the more aggressive rules of masculinity, or **hypermasculinity**, is glorified in many corners of our culture.[79] We particularly idealize

The movie poster for *300: Rise of the Empire* glamorizes hypermasculine violence.

it in some music genres (such as rap and heavy metal) and in action movies and video games that glamorize male violence and erase its real-life consequences. We also see hypermasculine performances by some athletes (especially in highly masculinized sports like football and hockey). These performances naturalize male violence, aggression, and anger. Moreover, because hegemonic masculinity assumes one can never be too masculine, men's violence can be justified by saying that they're protecting or defending someone or something good (see, for example, the good guy with a gun in countless Hollywood movies every year).

Despite the prevalence of hypermasculinity, men are *not* naturally violent. Instead, men must be trained to resist the sensation of empathy and encouraged to enter dangerous situations enthusiastically.[80] We see hypermasculinity nurtured in some fraternities, occupations, military units, police squads, neighborhoods, gangs, and prisons. Men in these situations may avoid demonstrating feminized qualities like empathy, nurturance, kindness, and conflict avoidance in favor of exaggerated performances of verbal and physical aggression. Almost no man does hypermasculinity all the time, but sometimes a man's mother, girlfriend, or wife is the only person who ever sees him without his hypermasculine mask.

Suppression of empathy often starts somewhere around middle school. To be close friends, men need to be willing to confess their insecurities, be kind to each other, and sometimes sacrifice their own self-interest—a description of friendship that men themselves articulate and say they want. This, though, is incompatible with the rules of masculinity that define bonds among men as based on competition and expressed in aggressive acts. So as boys grow up to be men, they learn to resist the impulse to connect nonhierarchically with other men.[81]

Psychologist Niobe Way interviewed boys about their friendships in each year of high school. She found that younger boys spoke eloquently about their love for their male friends but, at about age fifteen, this began to change. One boy, for example, said this as a freshman:

> [My best friend and I] love each other . . . that's it . . . you have this thing that is deep, so deep, it's within you, you can't explain it. It's just a thing that you know that person is that person. . . . I guess in life, sometimes two people can really, really understand each other and really have a trust, respect and love for each other.[82]

By his senior year, he had changed his mind:

> [My friend and I] we mostly joke around. It's not like really anything serious or whatever. . . . I don't talk to nobody about serious stuff. . . . I don't talk to nobody. I don't share my feelings really. Not that kind of person or whatever. . . . It's just something that I don't do.

In part because of the rules of masculinity, adult, white heterosexual men have fewer friends than women and other men.[83] Since friendship strongly correlates with physical and mental health, this is one way in which closely following the rules of masculinity is bad for men.[84] There are many others.

HARM TO THE SELF Taking masculinity to an extreme makes men dangerous to others, but it also threatens to make men dangerous to themselves. Men are significantly more likely than women to disregard their own safety. They are more likely than women to break seat belt laws, drive dangerously, smoke cigarettes, take sexual risks, and abuse drugs and alcohol; they make up 75 percent of those arrested for drunken driving and 82 percent of those arrested for public drunkenness.[85] They are almost three times more likely to die in a car accident.[86] They go into dangerous jobs and may resist safety rules, accounting for 93 percent of occupational deaths.[87] Among teens who help their families

Professional bodybuilder Ronnie Coleman breathes pure oxygen immediately after competing in Mr. Olympia. Organizers make oxygen available backstage because contestants are frequently lightheaded after their performance.

with farm work, boys are less likely than girls to use protective gear and take safety precautions.[88]

Some argue that being male is the strongest predictor of whether a person will take risks with their health.[89] Men are less likely than women to undergo health screenings, get regular exercise, see a doctor if they feel sick, and treat existing illnesses and injuries.[90] The association of lotion and body care with women leads men to dismiss the importance of sunscreen. It should then come as no surprise that men are two to three times more likely than women to be diagnosed with skin cancer.[91]

Likewise, high school and college athletes accept competitive demands that they exercise so hard that they overheat and collapse on the field, while body builders can die from the damage done to their bodies with steroids and diuretics. The image above shows Ronnie Coleman breathing through an oxygen mask, immediately after walking off the stage at the Mr. Olympia competition. He would take first place. Photographer Zed Nelson explains that oxygen is frequently administered to contestants: "The strain of intense dieting, dehydration, and muscle-flexing places high levels of strain on the heart and lungs, rendering many contestants dizzy, light-headed, and weak."[92]

Sociologists Douglas Schrock and Michael Schwalbe summarize the research on men and self-harm:

As with crime, much of this health-damaging behavior may be symbolic, intended to signify capacities to control one's own life, to be invulnerable and needless of help, and to be fearless and hence not easily intimidated by others. The effort to signify a masculine self ... can be toxic.[93]

In fact, men are more likely than women to avoid seeking help for depression and are three and a half times more likely than women to commit suicide.[94]

HARMING OTHERS Men are also more likely than women to commit violent acts against others. This is partly a result of men's anti-empathy training, and possibly also a form of compensatory masculinity. Men account for 88 percent of those charged with murder and nonnegligent manslaughter, 77 percent of those charged with aggravated assault, 70 percent of those charged with family violence, 78 percent of those charged with arson, 86 percent of those charged with robbery, and 91 percent of those charged with unlawful carrying of weapons (Table 6.2).[95]

Though men enact the overwhelming majority of violence, the gendered nature of violence often remains invisible because we tend to accept that men

TABLE 6.2 | ARRESTS BY SEX, 2016

Offense charged	Percent male
Murder and nonnegligent manslaughter	88
Rape	97
Robbery	86
Aggravated assault	77
Burglary	81
Arson	78
Larceny-theft	58
Motor vehicle theft	78
Fraud	62
Embezzlement	51
Vandalism	78
Weapons; carrying, possessing, etc.	91
Drug abuse violations	77
Driving under the influence	75

Source: Federal Bureau of Investigation, "Crime in the U.S., 2016." Retrieved from https://ucr.fbi.gov/crime-in-the-u.s/2016/crime-in-the-u.s.-2016.

are naturally this way. Though this may slowly be changing, the fact that it is men who commit most violence is taken as ordinary and unremarkable. So, the fact that gang violence, suicide bombings, serial killings are also all overwhelmingly perpetrated by men seems normal, as does the fact that, of the 216 mass shootings in the United States since 1996, only five were committed by a woman acting alone.[96]

Men are also more likely to join violent hate groups, those organized around hatred toward and the enactment of violence against others: white supremacist and neo-Nazi groups, for example, and Islamist jihadist collectives.[97] Women join these groups, too, but they are a minority and are less likely than male members to engage actively in physical fights, train for violent conflict, or enact terrorist plots. Research on what attracts men to these groups reveals that many are not particularly drawn to the hateful ideology so much as the promise of a connection to especially masculine men who affirm their own manliness.

Young boys are often targeted as recruits. Many, like those who engage in other violent behavior, are on the bottom end of the masculine hierarchy, bullied and made to feel small and weak. Hate groups promise them "an alternate route to proving manhood."[98] Tore Bjørgo, for example, a former skinhead from Sweden, described the appeal of the hate group this way:

> When I was 14, I had been bullied a lot by classmates and others. By coincidence, I got to know an older guy who was a skinhead. He was really cool, so I decided to become a skinhead myself, cutting off my hair, and donning a black Bomber jacket and Doc Martens boots. The next morning, I turned up at school in my new outfit. In the gate, I met one of my worst tormentors. When he saw me, he was stunned, pressing his back against the wall, with fear shining out of his eyes. I was stunned as well—by the powerful effect my new image had on him and others. Being that intimidating—boy, that was a great feeling![99]

The attraction of hate groups can't be explained by masculinity alone, but we can't explain the appeal without it either.

Hegemonic masculinity—this single standard of esteem for men—makes the position of even the most advantaged men perilous. Meanwhile, it sometimes presses them to put themselves or others in danger, or actively do harm even to those whom they profess to care about, whether these are their "brothers" in a fraternity or an army unit or a romantic partner. This is what is called **toxic masculinity**, strategic enactments of masculinities that are harmful to both the men who enact them and the people around them. While the hegemonic ideal is not the same as the toxic versions that are drawn from it, some men's efforts to live up to it can be harmful.[100]

So why don't parents, boys, and men just say no to hegemonic masculinity?

Bargaining with Patriarchy

Instead of repudiating hegemonic masculinity and the harm it can do, many men embrace strategies that allow them to benefit from being men, even if it simultaneously gives other men status over them. In other words, being *girly* places one at the bottom of the male hierarchy, and that's bad, but being *a girl* would be even worse. Accordingly, many men, even those who populate the bottom rungs of this hierarchy, will defend hegemonic masculinity, and many parents who want their boys to have as much status as possible when they grow up will do so, too.

This is called a **patriarchal bargain**—a deal in which an individual or group accepts or even legitimates some of the costs of patriarchy in exchange for receiving some of its rewards.[101] Both men and women make patriarchal bargains. When men do so, they accept some degree of subordination on the hierarchy of masculinity in exchange for the right to claim a higher status than women and some other men.

Few men make these bargains out of a simple desire to exert power over others. Instead, they make them because status translates into resources that raise their quality of life and protect them from stigma and physical harm. Esteem from others—and the intimacies, connections, and jobs into which it translates—offers people autonomy, safety, and life satisfaction. Men make patriarchal bargains because they want to maximize their happiness, not necessarily because they desire to dominate other men and women. They may be encouraged to do this from the time they're little by parents who want them to succeed, understanding that raising a boy who refuses to play by patriarchy's rules opens him up to criticism and limits his options in life.

Patriarchal bargains, then, are about figuring out how to thrive in a patriarchal society. For men, fundamentally, they're about investing at least a little in their identity as a man—the kind of person patriarchy has historically privileged—and finding pleasure, or safety, in distancing oneself from women, femininity, and feminine men. This includes not only doing masculinity and avoiding femininity, but putting men first and women second: seeing other men as more valuable, important, and authoritative people in general (while making exceptions for specific women like mothers, sisters, daughters, and wives).

We start making patriarchal bargains as children. Sociologist Michael Messner described a moment during his boyhood when he made such a bargain. He sensed early on being a boy and not a girl was important and that being a boyish boy was important, too. It was easy to figure out that sports were a "proving ground for masculinity" and that excelling would bring approval. Attracting this esteem, however, also meant enforcing the hierarchy as he ascended it. In particular, he recounts teasing and bullying a nonathletic boy. This, he explains, was "a moment of engagement with hegemonic masculinity" where he acquiesced to patriarchy, agreeing to uphold a masculine hierarchy that empowered him but disempowered others.[102]

All along the hierarchy of masculinity, men make patriarchal bargains. Men often rise to the top of the hierarchy exactly by doing so and, once they're there, their privileged status depends on enforcing it. At the highest levels of large, powerful corporations, for example—where 80 percent of the leadership is male and 72 percent is both white and male—high-status men often close their networks and hoard information and opportunities.[103] One way they do so is by forming cliques—or "old boys' clubs"—that women and less privileged men have a hard time breaking into.

In the study of interactions of Fortune 500 companies discussed earlier, for example, male employees often socialized, but only among themselves.[104] Women weren't invited to these bonding sessions and, if they invited themselves, tended to feel unwelcome. Men of color often felt the same. Masculinity can be mobilized to create pleasurable bonds among men, but that bonding is also exclusionary, leaving out specific kinds of others in order to protect the masculine hierarchy.

Because patriarchal bargains involve valuing other men more than women, sometimes men forget that women are part of their audience at all. Jokes that sexually objectify or demean women, for example, are sometimes told in front of women because the men telling them are trying to impress their male colleagues or friends. What women think of these jokes isn't part of their calculation, because their performance of masculinity really isn't for them. In one workplace incident, for example, a man brought a pair of women's underwear to a board meeting and pretended to discover them in his pocket. The men in the meeting laughed uproariously; the women did not.[105] The men were surprised at their female colleagues' objection to the hijinks, claiming it was only to be "funny." They had made a patriarchal bargain long ago, one that focused their attention on other men who, not incidentally, were also usually the ones who held the keys to raises and promotions. They were unpracticed at considering how a woman might respond to such a joke because considering women's responses wasn't something they routinely did.

Men lower on the masculine hierarchy also make patriarchal bargains. Gay men, for example, have a choice: They can choose to emphasize their masculinity so as to maximize the power that comes with being men or align themselves with women against the gender binary. Sometimes they do the former. In one case, a group of gay male students formed a college fraternity.[106] Though they had two relevant identities—they were *gay* and they were *men*—they allowed heterosexual *men* to be members of the fraternity, but not *gay* women. In this way, they sought to highlight the more socially valuable identity. The brothers only welcomed women as "little sisters," the (ostensibly heterosexual) women who play a supportive role in Greek life. One brother explained:

I would prefer straight women because the lesbians would try and take over. A straight woman might enjoy being a little sister and attending functions and hanging out, while a lesbian would consider the role subordinate and get tired of it quickly, trying to dominate and manipulate the program. Basically, a straight woman might understand the role while a lesbian would not.... I see their role as supportive and basically helping out.[107]

As this quote illustrates, these gay men welcomed women into their fraternity, but only as subordinates. Meanwhile, they were enthusiastic about making alliances with men of all sexual orientations.

Nerds, dorks, and geeks form a trifecta of subordinated masculinities marginalized by some combination of social awkwardness, lack of athleticism, and a penchant for video and role-playing games. These men often know they're near the bottom of the hegemonic hierarchy of masculinity, but rather than reject hegemonic masculinity, they embrace their position in exchange for the right to exclude, subordinate, and sexually objectify women.[108] This practice exploded into public awareness in 2014 with the controversy now known as #gamergate. Male gamers mobilized as defenders of their male-dominated world, targeting a group of women who were publicly questioning the sexism prevalent in video games.[109]

Fans in Tokyo line up to play the new *Grand Theft Auto* video game. The game's advertising prominently features a buxom blonde in a bikini.

This bonding among men crosses racial and class lines, as illustrated by the career of white rapper Eminem. Throughout his career, Eminem has aligned himself with black people, both musically and politically, at the same time that he has embraced misogyny and homophobia.[110] In his ninth album, released in 2017, he critically refers to President Donald J. Trump's support of Confederate monuments and associates him with Nazis and white supremacists. On other tracks, though, he raps graphically about women's body parts, alternating compliments with gendered insults and sexual demands. On still another track, he takes the perspective of a serial killer who targets young, beautiful women. In calling for Trump's impeachment and criticizing his policies for their impact on people of color, Eminem claims a position on the political left, but his politics do not extend to support of women, nor to black men who are gay. Eminem has made a patriarchal bargain.

Paradoxically, it may be the men who benefit the least from hegemonic masculinity (including poor men, black men, nerds, and gay men) and the men who benefit the most (like the leadership at Fortune 500 companies) who defend it most aggressively.[111] Men at the bottom of the hierarchy are trying to hold onto what little privilege they have, while men at the top are invested in resisting any change to the hierarchy on which they are so comfortably perched. All men, however, are pressed to bargain with patriarchy, one way or another, in an effort to squeeze some benefit from the gender binary and its attendant hierarchy. When they do so, they affirm hegemonic masculinity rather than attack it, aiming to improve their position, not tear the whole thing down. At the very least, this protects them from the negative consequences of challenging the system.

CAN MASCULINITY BE GOOD?

In America today, some men are actively trying to find new ways of being men, ways that don't hold up patriarchy, reward hypermasculinity, or oppress women or other men. They are acting to distance themselves from sexist, androcentric, subordinating, and toxic forms of masculinity. In doing so, they're asking whether it's possible to identify as a man and do masculinity in a way that is good for them and for others.

These men are inventing and adopting what are called **hybrid masculinities**, versions of masculinity that selectively incorporate symbols, performances, and identities that society associates with women or low-status men.[112] These men may mix aspects of femininity into their personalities, "queer" their lifestyles, resist the impulse to climb the masculine hierarchy, and refrain from making choices that advantage them at the expense of others. Hybrid masculinities are interesting because they potentially undermine the importance of gender distinction, give femininity value, de-gender hierarchical relationships, and deconstruct the hierarchy of masculinity.[113]

Hybrid masculinities, then, could be an exciting step toward a more gender-equal society. Unfortunately, while there is considerable academic study left to do and much more everyday experimentation left to try, the existing research doesn't yet support the idea that men who adopt hybrid masculinities are doing so in ways that substantially undermine gender inequality. Instead, they do more to obscure it: feminizing or queering styles of expression but failing to do much to challenge men's hold on powerful positions.[114]

An example, to start: For over a decade, and on four continents, an anti-rape campaign that used the slogan "My Strength Is Not for Hurting" aimed to teach young men not to sexually exploit others.[115] The goal was admirable, but in emphasizing men's strength and their responsibility to protect women, the campaign reinforced the idea that women are weak and in need of protection, as opposed to the idea, for instance, that women have rights to their own bodies that deserve to be respected. The campaign tried to persuade men to be chivalrous instead of exploitative, but it didn't challenge the underlying unequal relationship between men and women.

Scholars argue that these hybrid masculinities aren't living up to their potential for several reasons. First, some hybrid masculinities are largely symbolic. A corporate boss, for example, may heartily endorse the formation of a support group for his female employees but resist investing resources into understanding their problems or helping them succeed. A married man may identify as gender egalitarian and supportive of feminism but neglect to do his fair share of the housework and childcare. Or a heterosexual man may condemn homophobia and befriend gay men but vote for politicians who are anti-gay because they promise to keep his taxes low. Supporting women, identifying as gender egalitarian, and embracing sexual minorities help move our societies toward greater equality, but more concrete changes—shifts in our laws, how we spend money, and how we organize families—are needed to realize it.

Second, men who adopt hybrid masculinities sometimes ask for "extra credit" for being "good" men. The faith-based pro-family organization "Promise Keepers," for example, a nearly thirty-year-old movement that operates on three continents, is based on the idea that men should be good caretakers of their family, but also naturalizes men's role as the head of the household.[116] Like the "Strength" campaign, the "Keepers" movement encourages men to adopt a hybrid masculinity that incorporates a feminine ethic of care, but it also positions men's power over women as inevitable. In the anti-rape campaign, it's inevitable because men's ability to overpower women is unquestioned (in fact, fighting back stops an attempted rape 82 percent of the time).[117] In the "Keepers" case, men's control of women is guaranteed by divine decree. God says so. The implication is that a woman should be grateful to be married to a man who doesn't exploit his (rightful) power over her.

The final problem we find with hybrid masculinities is the tendency for men who adopt them to use them to claim status. When men claim to be "good men," they are often also claiming to be "better" than men they identify as "bad," and those men are usually ones who are already on the lower end of the masculine and other hierarchies. In this case, differentiating between "good" and "bad" men just becomes another way to affirm, not break down, hegemonic masculinity and the hierarchy of men.

One study, for example, examined the ideals adopted by rich young men attending a therapeutic boarding school: a rehabilitation-focused school serving high school–age boys who had developed drug and alcohol problems, with tuitions ranging between $4,500 and $9,500 a month.[118] Most boys initially resisted the idea that they needed to be open about their personal pain, share their emotions, and develop expressive communication styles. As they adjusted to their new school's expectations, however, they reframed these typically feminized traits as characteristic of a secure and healthy masculinity, contrasting themselves with boys and men whose masculinity was still fragile, compensatory, or toxic.

This translated into a sense of entitlement to the class privilege that they would have upon graduation. School administrators taught them to lead off-site Alcoholics Anonymous meetings and sponsor community members, thus putting teenagers in charge of men of all ages, from varied backgrounds, with substantially more experience with both addiction and recovery. Nonetheless, the school encouraged the young men to see themselves as "leaders" of these "lesser" men, thanks to their enlightened masculinities. This further prepared them to go on to lead as privileged adults. "My dad and I used to have major trust issues," said one of the boys:

> [He] used to threaten to kick me out, take me out of the will, all that. Now that we've worked through our issues and actually talk and trust each other with things, he's talking about putting me in charge of one of the divisions of his company after I get a degree.[119]

As this quote shows, these young men may have redefined their masculinity, but they have used that redefinition to justify stepping right into their position at the top of the masculine hierarchy. Moreover, by adopting a hybrid masculinity, they now thought that they weren't just *lucky* to have dads who could launch their careers, but genuinely *deserving* of that advantage by virtue of being better men.

Men who adopt hybrid masculinities often see themselves as the "good guys," but they still value the fact that they're *guys*. Continuing to embrace an idealized masculinity that they believe differentiates them in important ways from women, they remain invested in gender distinction and seem to resist giving up the substantive advantages being male affords them.[120] In this way, hybrid masculinities are just another patriarchal bargain, a way for men to distance themselves from recognizably sexist, androcentric, and subordinating attitudes and behaviors, but in ways that still give them benefits over women and other men.

So, *can* masculinity be good?

We don't know. Gender scholars—including many, many men—have spent a lot of time trying to answer that question.[121]

The trouble is that we live in a modified patriarchy, a culture in which masculinity has been used to symbolize and represent superiority over women and lesser men for more than four thousand years. Masculinity *is* power; it's always been power. Power is part of the definition—masculinity is synonymous with measures of strength, dominance, and high status—and its meaning is gained in the context of a gender binary. So its very existence is dependent on a contrast with a femininity that is weak, subordinate, and low status.

If we somehow excised from masculinity the dominating, toxic, and compensatory behaviors, alongside all the other bad things like being afraid to express emotions, then what is left is a series of *wonderful* traits: duty, honor, hard work, sacrifice, leadership, and the like. And that's lovely. But for these to be traits of men, we must also say that women are not these things. And is that true? Is that fair? Are women not dutiful, honorable, and hard working? Do they not sacrifice? Can they not lead? The truth is that "good men" aren't good *men*, they're good *people* and they share good traits with women, who are good people, too.

Can masculinity be good? We don't know. We know that *men* can be good. But whether they need masculinity to do it is an open question.

We also need to ask: Is masculinity good for men? On that we have stronger data. Masculinity is one of the things that make men feel good about themselves, but it's also a substantial form of oppression. In many ways, it hurts men. It hurts some men a lot. It hurts men who disinvest in masculinity and pay the price as well as many of those who embrace it. After all, it is some men's belief that they *should* somehow be better than women and other men—that they are failures if they're not—that is the cause of much of their sadness, self-loathing, and silent suffering.

Revisiting the Question

If both men and women are constrained by a binary gender system, why is it more women than men find this system unfair?

There are good reasons for men to find the system unfair. Because gender rules make femininity only for women, men must avoid performing it. Their daily lives and social interactions with both men and women are constrained by this imperative. As a result, men may repress those parts of themselves that don't reflect hegemonic masculinity and emphasize those that do, sticking only to man-approved masculinity, at least in public or around certain kinds of people.

It's no surprise, then, that men sometimes find the rules of masculinity to be strict, arbitrary, and even painful. Many men, though, follow gender rules and press others to do so, too, because upholding the hierarchical gender binary means preserving the privileges that come with maleness. This means often rough policing of the boundaries of masculinity. This can make masculinity dangerous, creating circumstances in which men are pushed to make dangerous choices, exposed to violence, or incited to harm others.

Under these conditions, men make strategic choices. Sometimes, they have to choose between following the rules or being seen as a failure; at other times masculine privilege may feel like the only kind of advantage they have. Men also may think that the costs of getting too close to femininity are too high. Accordingly, most men make patriarchal bargains in at least parts of their lives.

Still, no amount of bargaining protects them from the fear of emasculation. Wherever they fall in the hierarchy, all men have to live with some fear of losing the traction they've gained and sliding down to join those on whose disadvantage their advantage depends. Ironically, men who may have the most to gain by rejecting the gender binary—those who fail to approximate the hegemonic ideal, live miserably under its rules, or are victimized by others for their rule breaking—are often the ones who are the most defensive about it because their grip on it is most fragile. They defend hegemonic masculinity because at the very least it guarantees them superiority over somebody: women.

This helps explain why so few men actively challenge the gender binary, but we have yet to tackle why so many women do. To answer our question fully, we need to understand women's experiences.

FOR FURTHER READING

Bridges, Tristan, and C. J. Pascoe. "Hybrid Masculinities: New Directions in the Sociology of Men and Masculinities." *Sociology Compass* 8, no. 3 (2014): 246–58.

Connell, Raewyn W. *Masculinities*, Second Edition. Berkeley: University of California Press, 2005.

Edwards, Keith, and Susan Jones. "'Putting My Man Face On': A Grounded Theory of College Men's Gender Identity Development." *Journal of College Student Development* 50, no. 2 (2009): 210–28.

Johnson, Alan. "Can a Man Be a Human Being?" *Unraveling the Knot* (blog), September 2, 2015. https://agjohnson.wordpress.com/2015/09/02/can-a-man-be-a-human-being/.

Kimmel, Michael. *Healing from Hate: How Young Men Get Into—and Out of—Violent Extremism*. Berkeley: University of California Press, 2018.

Pugh, Allison. "Men at Work." *Aeon*, December 4, 2015. https://aeon.co/essays/what-does-it-mean-to-be-a-man-in-the-age-of-austerity.

Way, Niobe. *Deep Secrets*. Cambridge: Harvard University Press, 2011.

> **SOME OF US ARE BECOMING THE MEN WE WANTED TO MARRY.**
> —GLORIA STEINEM

Inequality:

WOMEN AND FEMININITIES

The last chapter focused on how gendered power shapes men's experiences. This chapter discusses women's lives. It argues that, on the one hand, women have a lot more freedom than men to enjoy both masculine- and feminine-coded parts of life, a freedom that offers women many exciting opportunities and simple pleasures. On the other hand, because doing femininity is at least somewhat compulsory, and we live in an androcentric society, women also have to adopt gender performances that harm them as individuals and produce group disadvantage. After reviewing the realities facing women, the chapter concludes with an overview of the big picture. But first, the chapter starts the way the last one did: with cheerleading.

CHEERLEADING TODAY

As you now know, in the 1800s male cheerleaders were respected for their ability to lead a crowd. Women joined teams during World War II, eventually prompting men to abandon the activity. By the 1960s, cheerleading teams were essentially all female and served simply to support male athletes. No longer equivalent to being a quarterback, cheerleading was now a cute sideshow to the main event.

Cheerleaders at a University of Nevada, Las Vegas, basketball game blend feminine grace, peppy enthusiasm, and impressive athleticism.

It wouldn't stay this way. Eventually, cheerleading would be remasculinized—by women. By the 1990s, cheer involved intense athleticism. Gymnastics were back and stunts became increasingly difficult and dangerous. An entire industry was built around cheer competition.[1] Between 1990 and 2012, injuries among cheerleaders would increase almost twofold; concussions almost tripled.[2]

Today, men are slowly returning to cheerleading. Recruitment aimed at men again appeals to their masculinity, emphasizing physical strength and, this time, access to women. "Want strong muscles? Want to toss girls? Our Cheer Team needs stunt men!!" encouraged a recruitment poster at a university.[3] "In cheerleading," echoed a football player–turned-cheerleader, "you get to be around all these beautiful women."[4]

Despite these changes, cheer retains feminine dimensions. Female cheerleaders wear sexy outfits that offer their bodies as spectacles for others to enjoy. A cheerleader's primary job still is to root for football and basketball teams. That is, it remains largely a "feminine auxiliary to sport," not the serious main event.[5] Cheer also retains a performative aspect that seems unsuited to men. Sociologists Laura Grindstaff and Emily West, who did research on cheerleaders, explain:

> *Appearing before a crowd requires that cheerleaders be enthusiastic, energetic, and entertaining. This is accomplished not just through dancing, tumbling, or eye-catching stunts, but also through the bubbly, peppy, performance of*

"spirit."... It includes smiling, "facials" (exaggerated facial expressions), being in constant motion, jumping, and executing dynamic arm, hand, and head motions—all considered feminine terrain.[6]

As one male cheerleader said, somewhat embarrassedly, "a game face for a cheer-leader is a big smile," not exactly the threatening grimace or strained expression associated with the competitiveness or exertion believed to characterize "real" sports.[7]

Most people still associate cheerleading with femininity and, as a result, continue to take it less seriously than other physical activities. As a result, despite the high-impact athleticism that now characterizes many squads, less than half of U.S. high school athletic associations define high school cheerleading as a sport and neither the U.S. Department of Education nor the National Collegiate Athletic Association (NCAA) categorizes it as one.[8] Instead, cheerleading is frequently labeled an "activity," akin to the chess club. Accordingly, cheerleading remains unregulated by organizations responsible for ensuring the safety of athletes, leading to higher rates of injury among cheerleaders than among American football players.[9] Among all types of high school and college sports, cheerleading accounts for a whopping 66 percent of injuries to female athletes with the potential to result in permanent disability.[10]

Cheerleading is somehow simultaneously masculine and feminine, hard-core and cute, athletic and aesthetic, admired and belittled. It also sexualizes femininity, making women's ability to appeal to assumed-heterosexual men centrally important, even if they're pulling off impressive physical feats at the same time. It is, in other words, very much like what being a woman can feel like today. Unlike men, who are encouraged to avoid femininity and do masculinity, women are strongly encouraged to embrace *both*.

GENDER FOR WOMEN

In many ways, the daily lives of women are much less constrained than those of men. Unlike men, who face policing when they do gender in ways that are associated with the other sex, women's performances of masculinity are often regarded positively, such that women today are doing almost everything men do. People are starting to notice that girls are pretty great. In fact, in a dramatic change from the past, American parents may no longer prefer having sons to having daughters.[11]

Emily Kane, the sociologist who documented parents' nervousness about their sons' performances of femininity, for example, found that parents weren't at all troubled by their girls' gender-nonconforming behavior.[12] In fact, they were downright tickled if their daughters wanted to wear a dinosaur backpack, collect

Many people admire women who enter masculine occupations, not only because they are defying stereotypes but because, by virtue of being associated with men, such occupations are more esteemed than feminine ones.

bugs in the backyard, or dress up like a superhero. They favorably described their daughters as "rough and tumble" and "competitive athletically," even endorsing their girls' interest in icons of masculinity like trucks and tools.[13] And while they felt a need to uncover a reason for their sons' preference for girly things, their daughters' interest in masculine things needed no such explanation. Since masculine activities are highly valued, it made perfect sense that girls would be drawn to them and parents would be proud.

Adult women benefit from this greatly. Women now have the freedom to enjoy the complex flavors of scotch, the rigorous training of law school or the military, the risks and rewards of casual sex, and the thrill of learning to fly an airplane or compete in extreme sports. They can become construction workers or architects and feel the deep satisfaction of watching one's work materialize; they can become surgeons or CEOs and choose to take responsibility for human life and corporate profits. In fact, in 2016 the very last occupation off-limits to women in the United States—combat positions in the military—was officially opened.[14]

These developments are all rightly interpreted as signs that women have gained much equality with men, a state of affairs most Americans endorse. Measured by the scope of gender rules, then, the life options of women in contemporary Western societies are undoubtedly more open than men's. It's a good time to be a woman. But there's a catch.

The Importance of Balance

While women are allowed and even encouraged to do masculinity, a woman who performs *too much* masculinity attracts the same policing as a man who does even *a little* femininity. Women who perform too much masculinity violate the gender binary and break the number one gender rule, the rule that one has to identify as male or female and perform gender in a way that's consistent with their identity. In other words, if women want to do masculinity, they have to balance it with femininity.

Women who do this, who carefully walk a line between masculinity and femininity, are the new female ideal. Only 32 percent of Americans say that people look up to "womanly women" (compared to 53 percent who say that they look up to "manly men").[15] Not surprisingly, then, only 19 percent of young adult women today describe themselves as "very feminine," compared to about a third of Gen Xers and Boomers and the majority of those in the generation before.[16] While men still resist describing themselves as "nurturing" and "sensitive," women are about as likely or even more likely than men to describe themselves as "physically strong," "assertive," and "intelligent."[17] The model woman, the one all women are supposed to try to be these days, is *not* the perfect picture of femininity; she is both feminine and masculine.

Reflecting this change in the ideal woman, media coverage often fawns over women who do both masculinity and femininity gracefully. Christmas Abbott, for example, is a CrossFit competitor, nationally ranked weightlifter, and the first woman to serve in a NASCAR pit. Media profiles of Abbott highlight her achievements in these masculine-coded arenas, but they often also balance their glowing accounts with references to her femininity. At CNN, for example, the narrator concludes with the reassurance that Abbott "refuses to leave her femininity behind" and "remains a woman in every sense." Onscreen, Abbott explains:

> The ongoing joke is, if I'm not in tennis shoes, I'm in pumps. And I love wearing dresses and curling my hair. But that doesn't mean that I don't like to get dirty. You know, I like to work. I like to be physical in my work. And I think that it's been overlooked that women can do both.[18]

Abbott asserts that doing "both" is an "overlooked" possibility for women, but in fact, it's a widely endorsed ideal. Elsewhere, a profile of Abbott in *Cosmopolitan* emphasizes that she "doesn't have to choose between being strong and beautiful."[19] She replies: "You can be a gym rat and turn around and be a hot little minx." At the tattoo-focused *Inked* magazine, where she is profiled and photographed naked, it is remarked that her tattoos include everything from butterflies to pistols and a figure holding both a flower and a sword.[20] The message,

Presenting oneself as a sex object is one way for women who do masculinity, like CrossFit competitor and weightlifter Christmas Abbott, to balance their gender performance.

she explains, is "Be nice to everybody but always be ready to protect yourself." Now *that's* balance.

What people find so impressive about Abbott is not simply the fact that she excels in masculine areas like NASCAR and weightlifting. Instead, it's in her balance of both masculinity and femininity: She's strong *and* beautiful, in sneakers *and* heels, in dresses *and* dirty. And the beauty, heels, and dresses aren't incidental; they're a critical part of her self-presentation.

As Abbott illustrates, women have the opportunity to do masculinity and earn the esteem that comes with valued traits and activities. But there are limits to how much appropriation of masculinity will be tolerated by others. Being intelligent, ambitious, outspoken, and sporty is great, but being properly feminine is essential. In this way, doing femininity can be understood as an account for breaking the rule that requires women to leave the guy stuff to guys. It's a way of saying: "I know it looks like I'm encroaching on men's territory but be assured I know my place as a woman." When women acquiesce to the requirement that they perform femininity, it is a way of letting the men around them know that *they know* that they're still first and foremost female. Presenting themselves as objects for the heterosexual male sexual imagination, as Abbott does, is one very effective way to do this.

The requirement that women balance masculine interests, traits, and activities with conventional femininity is called the **feminine apologetic**. The term points to how a woman's performance of femininity can be a way to soothe others' concerns about her appropriation of masculinity. Abbott "gets away with" being masculine by also performing a conventional feminine sexual attractiveness. She, like other women in the West today, is allowed to do "anything she wants to do," as long as she also sends clear signals that she wants men's approval. This is the lesson Barbie teaches us so well: Barbie can do anything—she can be a doctor, an astronaut, an athlete, or a presidential candidate—but the important thing is that she look good while doing it. Barbie's relentless takeover of so many masculine arenas would be quite a bit more threatening if she wasn't doing a bang-up job of performing femininity, too.

Like Christmas Abbott, the character of Wonder Woman, played by Gal Gadot in the 2017 feature film, is both sexy and strong. A male love interest affirms that she's still feminine enough to fall in love.

Abbott has an advantage in this regard. She was born blond into a society that privileges whiteness, with features considered conventionally pretty. It's easier for her to do the feminine apologetic than it is for women who aren't at ease with or granted as much femininity to start. A woman named Zoe, for example, who identifies as a black lesbian, invokes Barbie when explaining the difficulty she had identifying with the femininities she saw represented around her: "I never felt like a girl," she said. "There weren't even black people on TV when I was growing up. The white people were Barbie, and I am not Barbie."[21]

Zoe couldn't identify with Barbie and didn't want to be an All-American Girl, so figuring out a balance between masculinity and femininity that others would approve of was more challenging for her. Women who are ascribed masculinity by American culture—like queer and black women—may not have as many options for mixing in masculinity. Instead, they may be forced to perform a feminine apologetic regardless of whether they deliberately mix masculinity into their personas.

For black women, this is often a question of hair.[22] Femininity is implicitly white, so light-colored, long, straight, or gently wavy hair is associated with femininity. Accordingly, black women with curly or kinky dark hair have to decide whether to leave it natural, wear wigs, or try to force it to resemble a white aesthetic. Many high-profile black women do the latter, including women as

Regardless of their personal preferences, both Beyoncé and Solange Knowles must make strategic decisions about what to do with their hair, knowing that others will evaluate them based on their choices.

powerful as Michelle Obama and Beyoncé. Others choose to stay natural, like Beyoncé's sister, Solange Knowles. Sometimes they do so because it fits with their identity and politics. This was certainly true for Jenny, an African American woman. She explains her decision to wear hers in dreadlocks:

> *I consider myself in a constant state of protest about the realities of cultural alienation, cultural marginalization, cultural invisibility, discrimination, injustice, all of that. And I feel that my hairstyle has always allowed me, since I started wearing it in a natural, to voice that nonverbally.*[23]

While black women can choose to wear their hair in ways that reflect their own personal values and aesthetics, they must also contend with the way others respond to them. As Jenny knows very well, on black women in America, hairstyles aren't personal, they're political. Black women's hair has been the subject of decades of lawsuits.[24] Natural hairstyles like twists and braids were not allowed for women in the military until 2014.[25] In 2016, a U.S. federal court held that it's legal for an employer to fire a person for their hairstyle; in the case at hand, a woman who wore her hair in dreadlocks.[26] By forgoing the natural, black women can offer a feminine apologetic, and possibly a race apologetic, too, one that can help them succeed in white-dominated spaces. Making their hair look less "black" is a way of saying: "I'm not *that* kind of black woman." The kind, that is, that doesn't know her place.

Referencing this kind of policing in the voiceover for a Nike commercial, the tennis champion Serena Williams, herself African American, states matter-of-factly, "I've never been the right kind of woman. Oversized and overconfident. Too mean if I don't smile. Too black for my tennis whites. Too motivated for motherhood."[27] The visuals show her, victorious on the tennis court, with natural hair, and the narration takes a turn: "But I am proving, time and time again," she says, "there's no wrong way to be a woman."

Serena is indisputably one of the greatest athletes—of any gender—of all time. If anyone is proof that women can do and be anything, she is it. But her claim that there is no wrong way to be a woman is aspirational. We're not there yet.

Right Balances and Wrong Ones

Women do sometimes refuse or fail to perform enough conventional femininity to effectively soothe the concerns of the people around them. In practice, then, there are wrong ways to be a woman. We call them **pariah femininities**: ways of being a woman that, by virtue of directly challenging male dominance, are widely and aggressively policed.[28] Women who perform pariah femininities are ones who don't defer to men (*bitches, ballbusters, cunts,* and *nags*), who don't seem to care if men find them attractive (*dykes* and *hags*), who have or withhold sex without concern for whether men approve (*sluts, whores, teases,* and *prudes*), or who do not form households with men (*shrews, spinsters,* and *old maids*).

Such women don't balance, they *defy.* They refuse to perform a femininity that compliments hegemonic masculinity. Or, they simply cannot do conventional femininity. They have too little money, the wrong mix of identities, or the wrong bodies: ones that are overweight, disabled, old, or otherwise not amenable to a sexualized gaze.

These femininities are described as *pariah* because they are stigmatizing to the women who adopt or are ascribed them. To do them is to risk rejection, verbal attack, violence, and even ostracism. Choosing these identities can be exhilarating, because defiance is a thrill, but doing so puts women at risk of attracting the familiar slurs, and worse.

The punishments for women who embody pariah femininities reveal that women are afforded the opportunity to balance masculinity and femininity, but not exactly as they like and not in any proportion they please. Women must do *enough* femininity and the *right kind* of femininity, given their subcultural environment and mix of identities. A woman working on a construction site, for example, might talk dirty and wear coveralls like her male colleagues but also need to prove her femininity by regularly going on dates with men. An out lesbian working as an aggressive prosecutor at a law firm may be expected to wear a pencil skirt, heels, and colorful blouse to court. A woman from a conservative religious background may be allowed to pursue a high-powered career, so long as her family knows that she plans to quit her job as soon as she marries. What mix of femininity and masculinity women choose to perform depends on their particular intersection of identities and context, but one thing is for sure: if you're a woman, your gender presentation needs to be balanced just right.

Because a central feature of socially constructed womanhood is attractiveness to presumed heterosexual men, that aspect of femininity—being conventionally sexually attractive—is often a nonnegotiable part of striking the right balance. Some behaviors cross an invisible line. Half of high school girls play sports, for example, and a quarter pursue careers in science, technology, or math, but only 5 percent of women let their armpit hair grow.[29] Studies show that a majority of college students identify women with armpit hair as radically feminist, overly aggressive in their gender politics, and possibly man-hating.[30] Women whose choices signal a rejection of the sexualized definition of femininity are perceived as especially threatening.

In sum, the requirement that women do femininity, combined with the more recent option also to do masculinity, gives women a great deal more behavioral freedom than men have today. Women can adopt a wider range of interests, activities, and behaviors, while men are mostly constrained by the imperative to avoid femininity. Women, of course, also face constraints related to their gender performance, but women's constraint is of a different sort than men's: She can do (almost) anything she likes, so long as she also acts to affirm the hierarchical gender binary on which men's privilege and power depend. That means doing sufficient levels of a certain kind of femininity, particularly the imperative to make herself attractive to heterosexual men.

The constraints women face, though, extend further. Not only are they required to do specific amounts and kinds of difference *from* men, they are required to do inferiority *to* men. Because femininity is, by definition, disempowering.

Doing More, Winning Less

Recall that we live in a modified patriarchy, one that associates power with men and masculinity and powerlessness with women and femininity. Whatever personality traits, styles, activities, and spheres of life are deemed feminine, then, are going to be subject to the three relations of gender inequality: sexism, androcentrism, and subordination.

SEXISM Because of enduring sexism, a woman's mere femaleness is always a possible source of prejudice. As we discussed in the last chapter, this means that whatever women do, they have to do it better than men if they want to be evaluated as equally good. One well-documented case of such prejudice is the orchestral audition.[31] Beginning in the 1970s, some orchestras switched to "blind" auditions. The hiring committee would sit in the theater and see only a large blind or screen. The musician would walk forward from the back of the stage, sit behind the screen, play, and leave. They would be heard but not seen. The hope was that the process would result in the committee hiring the best musician, without regard to sex, race, or any other prejudicial factor.

At first, there was no change in the proportion of women hired, suggesting that sexism was not to blame for the low numbers of women in orchestras. But then someone noticed a sound: footsteps. When a woman walked across the stage, the click-clack of her high heels, compared to the clop-clop of men's flats, was giving her away. When they required all musicians to take off their shoes before they walked across the stage, the likelihood that a woman would advance to the final rounds rose by about 50 percent.

For better or worse, life isn't a barefooted, blind audition. In most circumstances, all other things being equal, a woman can be as good as a man—as smart, creative, talented, hard-working, strong, devoted, diligent, or accomplished—and she'll be evaluated as less than. Even when she does more, when she outperforms her male counterparts, she's likely to win less.

ANDROCENTRISM Women must also contend with androcentrism. Because femininity is disparaged relative to masculinity, the gender rules that require a feminine apologetic also require women to perform a devalued identity.[32] Many traits associated with femininity are quite actively disparaged in our societies. Some of us think that focusing on the feminized task of raising children makes women boring or unambitious. We look down on mom-related activities—like scrapbooking, recipe swapping, and attending PTA meetings—or make fun of "mom jeans" and "mom hair." On the flip side, women who are obsessed with fashion are "shallow." If they wear skimpy clothes, they're "insecure." And if they get cosmetic surgery, they're "desperate." Meanwhile, if a woman can't manage both to mother and conform to a culturally determined definition of sexual attractiveness, she fails doubly.

Sometimes androcentric disparagement of people who do femininity is shrouded in what sounds like a compliment. Sociologists call this **benevolent sexism**: the attribution of positive traits to women that, nonetheless, justify women's subordination to men.[33] We may put women on pedestals and revere them on the assumption that they're supportive, loving, patient, and kind, but this reverence is a double-edged sword. Women's ability to love others, in this narrative, is beautiful, but it's also an emotional weakness that threatens their ability to compete and dominate in work, sports, or politics. Being nice doesn't win games, promotions, or elections.

Likewise, conventionally feminine women are admired for their graceful and small bodies, but it's also believed that these bodies leave them incapable of strenuous physical tasks and vulnerable to attack. This leaves them in need of assistance and protection from stronger, more physically powerful people (that is, men). Benevolent sexism, by making women more dependent on men by virtue of the positive characteristics attributed to femininity, ultimately positions women as inferior. In this way, it is the inverse of exculpatory chauvinism. While the latter uses negative stereotypes about masculinity to justify men's dominance, the former uses positive stereotypes about women to justify their subordination.

Androcentrism is why we can't speak of a hegemonic femininity the way we speak of a hegemonic masculinity. Recall that the hegemonic man represents all the traits we value in an ideal *person*. That's why both men and women are encouraged to emulate him. There is no hegemonic femininity because feminine traits and activities are seen as desirable only for women. There are idealized femininities, certainly, that women can strive to attain, but feminine traits and activities are not *universally* desirable. No version of femininity is seen as good for everyone, male and female alike.

SUBORDINATION Finally, because power is gendered, the requirement to do femininity is also the requirement to do subordination. The areas in which women are seen as naturally superior to men, for example, are often self-sacrificial. Women, it is believed, are better suited than men to forgo their leisure time, educations, and career aspirations in order to help others. The icons of femininity—mother, wife, nurse, secretary, teacher—are supportive, not leading roles, and ones that leave women less intellectually developed, accomplished, and impressive than men.

Someone doing femininity well smiles at others sweetly, keeps her voice melodic, and asks questions instead of making declarations. A conventionally feminine person lets others take care of her: open her door, order her meal, and pay her tab. A feminine sexuality is one that waits and responds, never acts or initiates. A feminine body is small and contained; "[m]assiveness, power, or abundance in a woman's body is met with distaste."[34] Subordination is about never bothering others with one's own discomfort or concerns.

Sociologist Dana Berkowitz's research on Botox, for example, a toxin injected into the face to smooth wrinkles, found that it specifically reduces women's ability to project *negative* emotions that might cause discomfort in others: scowls of disapproval, grimaces of distaste, furrowed brows of worry, and tight eyebrows of anger. It even erases what is known as "resting bitch face," ensuring that women always look pleasant.[35] Botox, then, enables women to do femininity better by ensuring that no one around them is able to read their faces for unladylike thoughts.

Women can feel the need to do this even in extreme circumstances.[36] A study of white, middle-class Midwestern American mothers revealed that many of them tried to be nice even in the midst of giving birth. They showed interest in others, tried to be gracious, and avoided raising their voices or making demands, preferring to try to "give birth like a girl." If they failed, they apologized, to their husbands, the staff, and anyone they might have bothered. One of these mothers, Valerie, recalled her experience:

> I remember between contractions here, I could hear the other people in the next room, and I remember thinking—'cause I was very loud at this point—and I remember thinking I felt bad because I was being so loud and this poor woman [giving birth] in the next room must be thinking awful thoughts about me.[37]

In the next room, it turned out, the other woman giving birth was worried about Valerie. She sent in a note later, via the nurse, letting Valerie know that she hoped her labor went well.

Being considerate of others in the middle of giving birth is very nice indeed, but it may come at the cost of one's own well-being. It's hard work to try to be lovely while undergoing one of the most demanding and painful experiences of any human's life. And withholding information or not standing up for oneself under such circumstances can be dangerous. Understanding that there are costs to being unladylike, though, some women "discipline themselves from the inside out."[38] They put others first, even when it is difficult or dangerous to do so. That is the very definition of subordination.

All of this is, truly, about power. To do femininity is to do deference and to do deference is to do femininity, so much so that even computerized assistants, like Siri and Alexa, default to female.[39] More broadly, the bodily styles, facial expressions, and demeanors we associate with femininity are all associated with deference. Whatever the power hierarchy, the performance of femininity overlaps with the performances of those who are interacting with people with power over them: job applicants with their interviewers, enlisted soldiers with their superiors, and students in the offices of their professors. Femininity, the philosopher Sandra Lee Bartky writes, is "a language of subordination."[40] We know this because we see it used to indicate subordinate status in other contexts:

In groups of men, those with higher status typically assume looser and more relaxed postures; the boss lounges comfortably behind the desk while the applicant sits tense and rigid on the edge of his seat. Higher-status individuals may touch their subordinates more than they themselves get touched; they initiate more eye contact and are smiled at by their inferiors more than they are observed to smile in return. What is announced in the comportment of superiors is confidence and ease.[41]

Likewise, speech forms associated with women—hedging ("I'd kind of" and "It seems like"), hyper-politeness ("I'd really appreciate it if" and "If you don't mind"), and questions in response to questions (like answering "When would you like to eat dinner?" with "Around seven o'clock?")—are actually typical not just of women, but of all people in weak positions relative to others.[42]

When women refuse to do subordination—when they don't keep their voices down, offer a pleasant countenance for men, or defer to male authority—they stray into pariah territory. And that makes them a target of **hostile sexism**, the use of harassment, threats, and violence to enforce women's subservience to men. Hostile sexism relies on patriarchal gender relations, since the anger some men feel toward women is rooted in a sense of entitlement to having women in the roles of carers, helpers, sex partners, or admirers. When women don't subordinate themselves to men, then, it can feel to some men like an assault on their rights. This can lead some men to feel a sense of **aggrieved entitlement**, anger that something men rightfully own or deserve is being unjustly taken or withheld from them.[43]

Compared to such hostile sexism, it's easy to interpret benevolent sexism as expressing a female-friendly gender order, but that's not how it works. They are two sides of the same coin: Benevolent sexism rewards women's subservience with men's approval, protection, and support (sometimes called "chivalry"), but if women fall or jump from their pedestal, hostile sexism takes its place. Protection and support are revoked in favor of verbal or physical assault. Benevolent sexism is Plan A; hostile sexism is Plan B. Reflecting this, societies usually either have low rates of hostile and benevolent sexism or high rates; the two types of sexism rise and fall together.[44]

Take street harassment as an example, remarks some men make in public to women they don't know. Often these oscillate between niceties and sexualized hostility. Compliments can quickly turn into insults and threats if they are not met with the response the men think they deserve: a feminine apologetic in the form of a smile, a "thank you," or another polite response. Women who ignore or reject men's compliments are often subjected to a vicious onslaught of insults or threats. Likewise, in intimate relationships, attention and flattery can quickly turn toward control and coercion.[45] And women who become the targets of such hostility are often blamed for it on the assumption that they could have, and should have, offered a feminine apologetic to appease their partners.

Benevolent sexism isn't a kindness, then, it's a trap. If both the risk and protection are at the hands of men—that is, if *men* are the problem and *gentlemen* are the solution—then women are always positioned such that they need men in order to be safe. Moreover, it's difficult to know which men are threats and which are protectors. Should a woman accept this man's offer to walk her home? Who is more dangerous to her: the man in the alley or the man she's suddenly alone with on the street at night? The latter she thinks of as a friend but, then again, three-quarters of women who are sexually victimized are assaulted by someone they know.[46] What to do? This is the type of difficult calculation women make routinely as part of their strategic practice of femininity.

In this sense, hostile sexism is a measure of the cracks in the system. If women never challenged male authority—and if sexual minority men, gender-nonconforming men, and trans men and women never behaved in ways that undermined the gender binary—there would be less need to reassert patriarchy by force. In fact, it is sometimes the lowest-status men, desperately holding onto the bottom rungs of the masculine hierarchy, who are most threatened by disruptions to

Cartoonist B. Deutsch illustrates what it feels like to be sandwiched between both hostile and benevolent sexism.

gender distinction and hierarchy. In a study of gamer behavior, for example, it wasn't all men but rather the men with the lowest scores who most aggressively attacked women players.[47] This suggests that sexually charged taunts, insults, pranks, and violence are about gender policing: putting "uppity" women back "in their place" so as to preserve the gender binary and the illusion of male superiority.

Women, then, have more freedom than men to do gender as they like. They can do both masculinity *and* femininity. However, the combination means women are required to adopt features and behaviors that are actively disparaged, indicate weakness, or naturalize service to others. And, if they don't want to do these things, there is a carrot and a stick—a benevolent and a hostile sexism—that may change their minds. With these three strikes against them, women struggle to attain the power, prestige, and personal accomplishment that are the currency of masculine arenas. And, whether or not they strike a balance that pleases others, both doing—and not doing—femininity can be dangerous.

When Being a Woman Gets Dangerous

HARM FROM OTHERS In 2014, at the University of California, Santa Barbara, a college student named Elliot Rodger murdered three Asian men before setting out to get revenge on women. In his video manifesto, he proclaimed:

> *I am going to enter the hottest sorority house at UCSB and I will slaughter every single spoiled, stuck-up, blond slut I see inside there. All those girls I've desired so much. They have all rejected me and looked down on me as an inferior man if I ever made a sexual advance toward them.*[48]

When all was said and done, he'd injured thirteen and murdered six. Then he killed himself.

Rodger felt that he was positioned unfairly low in the masculine hierarchy. Mixed Chinese-British ancestry, he considered himself superior to Asian men by virtue of being half-white. He was especially infuriated when black and Asian men, who he considered lesser, "won" the "prizes" to which he believed he was entitled, specifically socially desirable women (white, blonde, and attractive).

Rodger did not believe, deep down, that women had the right to deny him their bodies. He felt *entitled* to sex with these women. His desire to kill them, in other words, was motivated by the belief that they were not obeying the rules of femininity, which included subordinating themselves to his sexual needs. His mass shooting was an act of gender policing and an example of hostile sexism rooted in aggrieved entitlement.

When aggrieved entitlement leads to murder, the crime can be described as a misogynistic murder. **Misogyny** refers to men's fear and hatred of women with power. And **misogynistic murder** is the killing of women by men who are motivated to punish women for (attempting to) exercise that power. Such murders are disturbingly common. In 1989, Marc Lepine murdered fourteen women in a killing spree in Montreal, during which he repeatedly screamed, "I want women!" and "I hate feminists!" In 1996, Darrell David Rice murdered two women camping in Virginia, explaining that they "deserved to die because they were lesbian whores."[49] In 1998, a teacher and four female students, chosen because of their sex, were killed by Arkansas middle schoolers Mitchell Johnson and Andrew Golden. In 2006, Charles Roberts IV went to an Amish schoolhouse, separated the boys from the girls, and shot ten girls, killing five. In 2009, George Sodini, angry at being sexually "rejected" by women, walked into an aerobics class and sprayed bullets into the crowd of female strangers.[50] In 2010, Gerardo Regalado killed his wife and then shot six more women at a Florida restaurant, sparing the men. In 2016, Arcan Cetin, a man with a history of domestic violence and sexual harassment—who had once allegedly told a friend, "American girls hate me"—went to a makeup counter in a Macy's and killed four women and a man.[51] In 2018, at least two men would praise Elliot Rodger shortly before engaging in mass murder. One of them was Alek Minassian; he mowed down pedestrians in Toronto, killing ten, mere minutes after vowing on Facebook to "destroy" women who sexually rejected him. The other was Nikolas Cruz. Promising "Elliot Rodger will not be forgotten," Cruz walked into Stoneman Douglas High School in Parkland, Florida, with a semi-automatic weapon, killing three adults and fourteen teenagers.[52]

It is obvious that the victims of such mass killers are innocent of any blame, but the same inference is not always made when homicides and abuse are carried out by the partners, ex-partners, or would-be-partners of specific women. This is the kind of abuse and homicide we see daily. Approximately 25 percent of women have been victims of intimate partner violence, compared to 11 percent of men.[53] About 4.5 million women have had an intimate partner threaten them with a gun.[54] Acting on such threats, boyfriends and husbands commit 39 percent of all female homicides; in contrast, girlfriends and wives commit 3 percent of male homicides.[55] Twice as many women as men will be victims of sexual assault, and both men and women are substantially more likely to be assaulted by men than women.[56] Sometimes even mass shootings aren't impersonal: 54 percent involve the targeting of an intimate partner or family member.[57] A quarter of all casualties of mass shootings are children known to the shooter, primarily his own or his intimate partner's.

In the United States, sexual minorities and people who are gender nonconforming are sometimes attacked or killed because they violate gender rules; trans women and men who display femininity are most often targeted.[58] It is estimated that transgender women are more than four times more likely than other women to be killed; trans women of color are at particularly high risk.[59] Policing gender, in other words, can be truly violent. In 2017, sexual minority cis men and trans women accounted for 85 percent of those killed in gender- and sexual orientation–related hate crimes, reflecting the pattern of violence against not just those who deviate from the binary but those who adopt femininity when they do.[60]

Such murders, and other forms of hostile sexism, are not caused by women or gender nonconformity but by men's misogyny and homophobia.[61] They are caused by a mixture of hatred, anger, and fear. This is not a problem of individual men, and it certainly can't be chalked up to mental illness. This is a social problem. It's the persistence of patriarchal ideas—the idea that women and feminine people should subordinate themselves to men and masculinity—that fuels aggrieved entitlement and the violence that comes with it.

(MIS)MANAGING HARM When women set out to manage the violence they expect or experience from men, they sometimes engage in self-harm or victim blaming. Women often blame themselves for the violence they suffer and offer excuses for men. In one study, even the volunteers at a domestic violence shelter who insisted on principle that women were never to blame for their own assaults, were in practice quite likely to offer women's own behavior to explain what "set him off."[62]

On college campuses, women sometimes accuse sexual assault victims of being "naïve" or "stupid." "She somehow got like sexually assaulted," said one woman about an acquaintance who'd been victimized. "All I know is that kid [that raped her] was like bad news to start off with. So, I feel sorry for her but it wasn't much of a surprise for us. He's a shady character." By suggesting that she and her friends knew better than to hang out with the perpetrator, she suggests that information and social savviness can keep women safe.

For many women, imagining that the target "must have done something" wrong or stupid gives them a false sense of security. It also requires women to restrict their lives in the hope of staying safe, or at least safer: monitoring what one says online, for example, not being out alone after dark, and never getting too drunk. Being opinionated, out alone, or drunk does not warrant being attacked, but deciding that being these things is somehow "stupid" or reckless does increase the likelihood of self-blame should things go wrong. As Laurie Penny says about suggestions that her writing provokes internet trolls:

> What makes victim-blaming so insidious is that it isn't just about shifting the blame—it's about sending a message to anyone else who might be dumb enough to think they can do whatever that victim was doing and get away with it.[63]

Notably, dividing women into those who are and aren't smart enough to protect themselves from violence also undermines the solidarity necessary to fight to end it once and for all.

Many women find themselves in a double bind: If they are vulnerable and deferential, they are easy prey, but if they are self-protective and self-assertive, they are pariahs. This is, of course, only if they don't believe they are capable of protecting themselves in the first place. In the West, women's bodies are socially constructed as weaker and more fragile than men's—inherently vulnerable to and helpless in the face of men's violence—and women often internalize this idea.[64]

Even women who are born male-bodied often come to believe this. Interviews with trans women show that as individuals transition from male to female, most learn to embody a sense of physical vulnerability.[65] Trans women, like cis women, are more likely than cis men to be subject to sexually objectifying gazes and touched without permission. Meanwhile, adopting women's fashions—heels that shorten and unbalance their stride and skirts that restrict how they bend and sit—reduces the power and freedom women sense in their own bodies. They're also subject to all the stereotypes about the female body, including the idea that it is inherently vulnerable to men's stronger and more violent bodies. Despite being socialized as men and being, on average, taller and more muscular than cis women, trans women often come to feel similarly vulnerable. A trans woman named Rebecca, for example, said the following when asked if she walks alone at night:

> I just don't do it. I used to when I was a man. Yeah, I'd be anywhere I wanted to. I didn't fear anything but as a woman, yeah, I'm very cautious. . . . Because we are victims. We're the type of person that other people prey upon because we're the weaker sex, so to speak.[66]

Having internalized the idea that women are "victims" and the "weaker sex," Rebecca now acts accordingly. Between her sense of herself as vulnerable and the very real statistics on trans women's victimization, it's easy to see why.

Part of women's struggle to redefine femininity is overcoming an inability to imagine that they are loud, strong, angry, or dangerous. Self-defense instructors, for example, often teach women who assume, wrongly, that they are helpless to defend themselves against a man. In fact, maneuvers that take little strength—a thumb to the eye socket, a punch to the throat, an elbow to the nose, a quick kick to the knee cap, or a twist of the testicles—can often bring an attempted assault to an end.[67] Research has shown that hollering, fighting back, or fleeing reduces the likelihood of a completed rape by 81 percent, without increasing the severity of injuries sustained by victims.[68]

Women are powerful, but they often don't recognize, or they resist using, that power. This is a problem even in Sweden, one of the most gender-egalitarian countries in the world. To that end, kindergarten teachers in Sweden are now actively and effectively teaching girls how to yell.[69] Called a "compensatory gender strategy," the idea is to counter the gender-stereotypical socialization the kids are getting elsewhere. Boys, then, are being taught to give massages and girls are being told to "throw open the window and scream."

How individual girls and women manage risks of violence will vary, of course, but the collective challenge women face is in finding a way to fight back against misogyny. To the extent that conventional femininity offers only a choice between victim (helpless but protected by benevolent sexists) or pariah (powerful but punished by hostile ones), women will find it difficult to claim a strategy of self-assertion that is effective, feels good, and is tolerated by the people around them.

Bargaining with Patriarchy

Though women have choices about how to do femininity, and options for mixing in masculinity, they are still subject to rules and restrictions when it comes to their gender performances. Women, then, like men, make patriarchal bargains to maximize their autonomy, safety, and well-being in the face of sexism, androcentrism, and subordination. Whereas men are presented with essentially one kind of bargain, adopting hegemonic masculinity as much as they can or else accepting low status in the masculine hierarchy, women can choose among three types of bargains.

One bargain involves trading one's own attainment of power for the protection and support of a man. This bargain involves performing **emphasized femininity**, an exaggerated form of conventional femininity "oriented to accommodating the interests and desires of men."[70] With this strategy, a woman attempts to perfect a performance of femininity in exchange for the support of a man who will share his privilege with her. Stay-at-home moms, for example, have struck one such patriarchal bargain, making their family-focused strategy their side of a gendered economic deal. They provide feminized, unpaid work in the home for their husband and children. In return, their husbands share their income and benefits: providing a well-stocked kitchen, vacations, affordable health insurance, and a secure retirement.

Other women—disparagingly called "gold diggers"—offer their beauty and attentiveness to economically successful men. Aspiring models who work the high-end party circuit, for example, can get work as nonsexual partners for very wealthy men.[71] The women get designer clothes, gourmet meals, and luxury trips in exchange for performing a "strategic intimacy" that allows the men to feel attractive and important. Likewise, in high-end clubs in Vietnam, corporate men hire beautiful women to smooth their negotiations with male clients.[72] In some cases, a woman doing emphasized femininity may become a rich man's wife. In exchange for financial support, these women promise to keep their bodies taut, their clothes flattering, and their hair and faces attractive. The man has a lovely companion, then, to appreciate and display, either as a "trophy wife" or a temporary companion.

The family-focused wife and the lovely companion are making the same patriarchal bargain: doing a version of emphasized femininity in exchange for male support. In both cases, the woman's performance contributes to men's relative status, helps men succeed economically, and enhances men's quality of life. Women have traded the direct attainment of their *own* power for the indirect attainment of *his*. Neither raising kids nor being beautiful pays the rent, ensures women they won't be destitute when they're old, or makes their voices heard.

Thus, the position of those who perform emphasized femininity is always precarious; they can't control how much reward men offer and on what terms. They are dependent on men's ongoing willingness to support them, even as the things they have to offer decrease in value. Children grow up and leave the house, and beautiful faces and bodies face the march of time. It's a risky bargain for women: what upper-class men have to offer (money and status) are universally desirable goods and likely build over their lifetimes, whereas the bargaining position of women who are counting on their emphasized performance of femininity inevitably will weaken.

To this day, Marilyn Monroe remains an icon of emphasized femininity.

Being a doctor's wife is risky, so instead many women have decided that it is safer and more practical to become doctors themselves. Women with ambitions to enter male-dominated professions may make a patriarchal bargain that involves being "just one of the guys," a strategy sociologist Michael Kimmel refers to as **emphatic sameness**. In his study of the first women to integrate military schools, Kimmel found that some women tried to make the fact that they were female as invisible as possible.[73] Distancing themselves from other women, they tried to be "cadets" instead of "female cadets."

Many women do emphatic sameness, downplaying the feminine in themselves in exchange for the right to do quite a bit of masculinity. These women may declare majors associated with men and deride women who major in feminized subjects like literature or elementary education. They may make sports a central part of their lives and dismiss cheerleaders as not real athletes. They may choose not to have children and decide that mothers are not serious about

An emphasized sameness approach allows this woman to blend in with male recruits to the New York Police Department.

pursuing personal or professional accomplishments. By embracing androcentrism, they hope to avoid both benevolent and hostile sexism.

In fact, doing emphatic sameness is a way for some women to gain power as individuals in a society that values masculinity. The bargain has limits, though. First, this strategy is probably only possible in very specific kinds of masculinized contexts, those where men have agreed to tolerate the presence of women who are very successful in the performance of masculinity. Everyone at the military school Kimmel studied, for example, was doing masculinity. That's how everyone—male or female—fit in and succeeded. In such a context, the requirement that women balance masculinity with femininity may be relaxed.

Second, emphatic sameness is a limited individual bargain because it depends on the denigration of femininity in general. The majority of women who do emphatic sameness reject femininity but are still understood by others to be female. They may not be rewarded for their performance of femininity, but the expectation that they will reveal their intrinsic femininity at some point remains. If they are heterosexual, finding a sexual partner may demand being disavowed as a "pal." If they are not, being perceived as asexual may be the only way to avoid pariah status. In either case, their bargain backfires: they end up embodying the very thing they've agreed is valueless.

Moreover, this bargain reinforces the idea that women and girly stuff are trivial and worthless. So, the emphatic sameness bargain undermines attempts to empower women *as a group*, even if it allows individual women to have more power than they would otherwise. Notice that the most successful women (surgeons, judges, politicians) usually rely on a team of less advantaged women (housekeepers, nannies, nurses, secretaries). The surgeon may have achieved a level of prestige usually reserved for a man, but she does so on the backs of other women who do devalued, still-feminized work on her behalf.

Most women don't do either emphasized femininity or emphatic sameness consistently. In different contexts or times of their lives, they may strike different bargains. They alternate between masculinity and femininity in accordance with a patriarchal bargain called **gender equivocation**, using masculinity and femininity strategically when either is useful and culturally expected.

This was the case, for example, for a group of young women studied by sociologist Nikki Jones.[74] These women were all enrolled in a violence-intervention project located in a low-income, mostly African American neighborhood of Philadelphia. Living in high-violence neighborhoods, the women had developed strategies for both doing gender and staying safe. Like their male peers, they were willing to fight to protect their reputation. Despite this Tough Gal strategy, the women understood that in some contexts they were required to perform femininity and were rewarded for doing so.

Jones documents a young woman, Kiara, collecting signatures for a neighborhood petition. She approached strangers assertively to discuss the petition, strategically drawing on both feminine flirtation and masculine argumentation to get signatures. She would flirt with male acquaintances walking by, but then defiantly criticize the police as they passed the station. She was, when she needed to be, she said, "aggressive for the streets," but could also, when it was useful to her, be "pretty for the pictures."[75] When it came to her gender performance, Kiara equivocated, using whichever strategy provided the best bargain at the moment.

These patriarchal bargains—emphasized femininity, emphatic sameness, and gender equivocation—are not equally available to every female-bodied person. The women studied by Jones largely didn't have the option to choose emphasized femininity; their Tough Gal strategy acknowledged that knowing how to fight "like a man" was necessary to survive in their neighborhoods. Likewise, the ability to perform emphasized femininity to land a rich husband depends in part on a person's particular body and face. Not everyone is born with a conventionally attractive, physically able body that they can train to be slim and graceful. It helps to have some money to start with, too. Conversely, some women may not have the temperament to be a family-focused parent or the ambition or opportunity to pursue a demanding career. Most women aim to find a bargain that seems practical and potentially rewarding, even if not ideal. However, no matter what bargain women make, there is a cost to be paid.

It's called the **double bind**, a situation in which cultural expectations are contradictory, making success unattainable. Satisfying only one or the other expectation inevitably means failure, and it is impossible to do both. In the case of women in contemporary Western societies, the double bind refers to the idea that to be powerful is to fail as a woman and to succeed as a woman is to give up power.

Women can and do fall from grace in either direction. We see this phenomenon, for example, in sports. South African Olympian sprinter Caster Semenya is an example of a woman who was attacked for doing too little femininity, whereas tennis player Anna Kournikova is an example of an athlete who did too much. Semenya's physical body, surprisingly fast races, and refusal to do femininity both on and off the track led to an investigation of her biological sex that threatened her career. Under this pressure, she submitted to a public makeover—a last-ditch attempt at an apologetic.

In contrast, Kournikova's successful embodiment of femininity pushed her out of her tennis career and into modeling. Today she is frequently mocked as one of the worst professional athletes of all time; the fact that she was once ranked eighth in the world is eclipsed by her sex appeal. She still frequently graces the covers of men's magazines.

Backlash against female politicians also often reflects the double bind. Women candidates have some ability to gender equivocate on the campaign trail, but this bargain doesn't necessarily help them.[76] On the one hand, women are criticized for not being sufficiently feminine. In 2012, Geun-hye Park, then a candidate for president of South Korea, was criticized by her opponent for not having children. Her opponent's spokesman said that she "has no femininity" because she wasn't "agonizing over childbirth, childcare, education, and grocery prices."[77] Both Julia Gillard, former prime minister of Australia, and Angela Merkel, the current chancellor of Germany, have faced similar charges. Because these female leaders don't have children, critics said, "they've got no idea what life's about" and are not "real women."[78] Even women with children can find their emphasis on gender sameness—their toughness or status in masculinized positions—used against them. One need not approve of all of Nancy Pelosi's or Hillary Clinton's political positions to recognize the hostile sexism underlying the caricatures of them as emasculating shrews.

On the other hand, if female candidates do emphasized femininity, this tends to hurt them, too.[79] Consider the treatment of Sarah Palin, the Republican choice for vice president, during the 2008 presidential primaries. On the campaign, she emphasized her femininity with long hair, stylish clothes that hugged her body, and a cheerful demeanor. But because she performed femininity, Palin was seen as pretty but incompetent: a contrast to the masculinized image of a smart, strong, and effective politician.[80] Male commentators gushed over her attractiveness, saying that she was "by far the best-looking woman ever to rise to such heights" and "the first indisputably fertile female to dare to dance with the big

Caster Semenya's astonishingly fast times on the track and disinterest in performing gender while she raced prompted the International Association of Athletics to investigate her biological sex. Her makeover for *You* magazine (right) was an effort to assure others of her femininity.

dogs." But they also pejoratively called her "girlish," compared her to a "naughty librarian," and dubbed her "Caribou Barbie." A pundit for CNBC claimed that she was politically successful only because "men want to mate with her" and said that he (and other men) would vote for her because he wanted her "lying next to me in bed." It wasn't long before she became a joke to much of America, inspiring MILF memes and look-alike stripper contests in Las Vegas. While Palin certainly had her faults, her downfall was also distinctly gendered.

On a national stage, how can an ambitious woman strike a balance between masculinity and femininity that pleases everyone? If voters tolerate some kinds of balances but not others, and the balances they tolerate differ across regions; between the cities, suburbs, and countryside; up and down the class ladder; and along the political spectrum, among other divides, how can a woman ever escape the double bind?

Women, like men, make patriarchal bargains to maximize their autonomy and well-being. Men face substantially tighter restrictions than women, but the bargains available to them—while fewer than those available to women—offer greater rewards. Women enjoy more flexibility because there are more socially endorsed strategies for them to use, but no matter what bargain women seek to make, the outcomes are not in their favor.

THE BIG PICTURE

Gender inequality has been a part of Western culture for a very long time. Through all that time, people have been actively challenging the basis, logic, and fairness of patriarchal ideas and practices. Today, those people are called feminists.

Feminism, most simply, is the belief that all men and women should have equal rights and opportunities. The word was borrowed from the French in the late 1800s, when many women around the world were still the property of men by law. It has been used ever since to describe efforts to reduce women's disadvantage relative to men and free both men and women from harmful and oppressive gender stereotypes.

While feminism is principally concerned with gender inequality, intersectionality—differences among men and among women—has become central to the conversation. Especially since the 1970s, scholars and activists have been theorizing what it means to include all women in their mission.[81] Ultimately, it became clear that if one cared *strictly* about gender inequality, a feminist utopia was entirely compatible with other types of injustice. In this imaginary world, women would simply be equal to "their" men—ones of the same race, class, and so on. If those men were disadvantaged by other forms of injustice, then women would be, too. This was morally objectionable to most feminists because it charted a feminism for only rich, white, and otherwise privileged women. Many argued this was not feminism at all.

Today many feminists, arguably most, take as their target the **matrix of domination**, a structure in which multiple hierarchies intersect to create a pyramid of privilege, leaving on top only those people who are advantaged in every hierarchy.[82] As a result, when someone identifies themselves as feminist today, they often mean to say they're part of a network of activists targeting a wide range of injustices. Other social justice movements have pushed for this more inclusive feminism, arguing that it's important to consider not just one injustice at a time, but how they work on each other simultaneously to create bargains that are not merely patriarchal but also cement class, race, and sexuality as interacting systems of inequality. In this sense, intersectionality has been theorized as not just part of our identities or social locations, but as a call for social practices that challenge unjust systems of all kinds.[83]

In addition to embracing intersectional analysis, feminists have been on the forefront of theorizing masculinity and the way the gender binary might be harmful to men. Many men today identify as feminist or pro-feminist, and they have formed organizations aimed at fighting gender inequality and its harmful effects on both men and women.[84] In Canada, men founded the White Ribbon Campaign, an effort by men to end men's violence against women, now active in sixty countries.[85] The National Organization of Men against Sexism in the United States works toward gender equality on the belief that "men can live as happier and more fulfilled human beings by challenging the old-fashioned rules of masculinity that embody the assumption of male superiority."[86] And Men Can Stop Rape works to promote "healthy, nonviolent masculinity" and "cultures free from violence."[87] There are many more such organizations around the world.

Even in the very early years of feminism, people understood that it had the potential to change men's lives for the better as well as women's. The early feminist Floyd Dell, writing in 1917, argued: "Feminism will make it possible for the first time for men to be free." He believed feminism was the path to full humanity and the only hope for true love between men and women. Criticizing the elite marriages he saw around him, he wrote:

> When you have got a woman in a box and you pay rent on the box, her relationship to you insensibly changes character. . . . It is no longer a sharing of life together— it is a breaking of life apart. Half a life—cooking, clothes, and children; half a life—business, politics, and baseball. It doesn't make much difference which is the poorer half. Any half, when it comes to life, is very near to none at all.[88]

Dell would likely be impressed at the lives women are leading today, thanks to a real reduction in both legal and interpersonal forms of explicit sexism. But he'd be deeply troubled by the continued pressure men face to live half a life.

This pressure has, in fact, been getting worse, not better. Since the 1970s, both men and women have become increasingly androcentric.[89] Men are feeling more pressure than ever to conform to a narrowing range of acceptable masculinities. Even hybrid masculinities—those that mix femininity in—seem to uphold patriarchal relations. Our societies have yet to deliver on the promise to men that Dell envisioned.

As we've seen, contemporary gender relations are not ideal for women either. It will become increasingly clear in the coming chapters that women's bargains with patriarchy are limited in rewards. Mixing in more masculinity helped accelerate women's participation in the economy in the 1960s but the increases stalled out by the 1990s.[90] The percent of women in the workforce, for example, went up by 30 percentage points between 1962 and 1992 but has only risen a few percentage points since. The gap between women's pay and men's also narrowed substantially during these years but has been relatively stable since the mid-1990s.[91] Between 1971 and 1981, sex segregation in white-collar occupations declined precipitously, but since the mid-1980s it's been steady. The percent of PhD recipients who identify as female went up by about 20 percentage points in the ten years before 1981 but took another thirty years to move another 20.[92]

This state of affairs inspired scholars to argue that the United States and other similar Western countries are in the middle of a **stalled revolution**, a sweeping change in gender relations stuck halfway through.[93] Women have increasingly embraced opportunities in masculine arenas, but few men have moved toward feminine options. This new gender order hurts both men and women, but differently; men suffer more *as individuals*, while women are harmed more *as a group*.

Men are harmed as individuals because hegemonic masculinity pushes them to obey its imperatives. Androcentrism restricts men's lives, asking them to destroy or hide parts of themselves that don't fit the hegemonic model. As a result, they have narrower life options. Some men find this oppressive; others don't, not because it isn't repressive—there's no doubt that it is—but because there are worse things than being boxed into valued and rewarded roles in society. A lot of men aren't that upset, it turns out, by being told they shouldn't do something they learned to not want to do, concluding that it's OK to leave high heels, dirty diapers, and salads to women. Masculinity is oppression, in other words, dressed up as superiority, which isn't *so* bad, at least for those whose superior standing doesn't seem to be slipping away from them.

Our gender regime is bad, then, for men's mental and physical health as individuals, but collectively works out better for men on the whole. As a group, men benefit because hegemonic masculinity is socially and economically rewarded; it is the face of power, which they see as theirs. Men face less pressure to bother with things we've learned to belittle, to defer to others, or to sacrifice their own needs. In fact, because men are required to eschew femininity as much as possible, men are free to grab brazenly for power, act on self-interest, and mobilize support from other men for their success in ways that are actively disparaged for women. When the gender binary does exact costs from men, they are more likely to interpret this as individual failure than systematic outcomes of patriarchal legacies.

In contrast, as individuals, women benefit from the greater flexibility that modified patriarchy affords them but face more harm as a group by the costs that sexism, androcentrism, and subordination still impose collectively. All women, regardless of the bargains they strike as individuals, must contend with the risks of assault and the possibility of becoming a pariah. All their diverse strategies are fitted within the boundaries of gender inequality. Collective costs include benevolent or hostile sexism, being hamstrung by the double bind, dependency on men for safety and support, and the requirement to adopt devalued, subordinating, and sexualized gender performances.

All this limits women's ability to perform gender in ways that truly disrupt the system. Women as a group pay more of the costs of the hierarchical gender binary, then, measured by the economic vulnerability and physical danger they face; as such, women are more likely to name and resist the unfairness of these costs.

The revolution is yet unfinished, but the resistance is hard to miss.

Revisiting the Question

If both men and women are constrained by a binary gender system, why is it that more women than men find this system unfair?

The gender binary is a distinction, not just a difference; it's about hierarchy. The masculine side of the binary is presumed to be not just different but *better than* the feminine side. And most of us have internalized this idea, at least a little, learning to see men and masculine people as more valuable and impressive than women and feminine people.

As a result, girls and women are generally encouraged to mix a little masculinity into their personality and enter previously male-dominated leisure activities and occupations. Unlike men, for whom the other sex's territory is stigmatizing, for women, it can be quite appealing. It feels good to excel in arenas that others value. It brings status and reward, sometimes even from the people whose opinions matter most: men with good positions in the masculine hierarchy and control over most social rewards. Why wouldn't women want to embrace the opportunity to do a little masculinity, or even quite a lot? In fact, women's eagerness to incorporate masculinity and move into masculine arenas is proof of femininity's low value. In hindsight, one of the reasons women have been so keen to embrace masculinity is because it feels good to be seen as better than the women who do not. This is their patriarchal bargain.

Women who do just masculinity, though, or who don't perform the right kind of feminine apologetic, will not be rewarded. They will be policed, often and severely, and even women with flawless performances still may face abuse and be blamed for provoking it. Yet all women must do at least some femininity and, when they do, they'll be performing a devalued identity, one that seems rightfully subordinated. As individuals, women can resist these mechanisms of oppression by deftly doing masculinity and strategically appropriating masculine roles. Some women will do so spectacularly, rising to the corner offices of the biggest companies and powerful positions in our government. But women as a group will never be on an equal footing with men because men aren't required by virtue of their gender to perform powerlessness and deference.

This is why women, more so than men, have fought to dismantle patriarchy. It's also why the word "feminism," and not "masculinism," has come to represent the movement, though today it is as much about freeing individual men from repressive gender rules as it is about giving women the choices patriarchy denies them. Likewise, feminists are increasingly intersectional in insisting that liberating both men and women will involve challenging every axis of all our societies' intersecting oppressions: racism, colorism, ableism, heterosexism, class inequality, and prejudices based on religion, immigration status, cognitive difference, physical size, mental illness, and more. The real story about gender and power isn't a simple one about women's disadvantage, then, but a complicated one that reveals the costs that a hierarchical gender binary imposes on the vast majority of us, a system of unequal gender relations that is just one part of a wider matrix of domination. And feminism is what we call our efforts to undo it.

Next . . .

Thus far we've discussed the social construction of gender in our ideas, the policing of gendered performances in interaction, and patriarchal power relations. These are all very powerful forces. But what about free will, self-determination, and personal initiative? We're a free country, after all—isn't it still possible to reject the gender binary; ignore what other people say; refuse to accept or enact sexism, androcentrism, and subordination; and live a life free of all this gender stuff, even if that means paying some social costs? How about deciding to give up male privilege or to live with the low status of a social pariah? That line of inquiry leads us to our next chapter:

 When it comes down to it, regardless of social construction and social pressure, don't we live in a society in which it's possible to just be an individual?

It turns out, no.

FOR FURTHER READING

Friedman, Hilary Levey. "Soccer Isn't for Girly Girls? How Parents Pick the Sports their Daughters Play." *The Atlantic*, August 6, 2013.

Glick, Peter, and Susan Fiske. "An Ambivalent Alliance: Hostile and Benevolent Sexism as Complementary Justifications for Gender Inequality." *American Psychologist* 56, no. 2 (2001): 109–18.

Halberstam, Judith. "An Introduction to Female Masculinity: Masculinity without Men." In *Female Masculinity*. Durham: Duke University Press, 1998, 1–43.

Katz, Jackson. *The Macho Paradox: Why Some Men Hurt Women and How All Men Can Help*. Naperville, IL: Sourcebooks, Inc., 2006.

Mears, Ashley. *Pricing Beauty: The Making of a Fashion Model*. Berkeley: University of California Press, 2011.

Yancey Martin, Patricia. *Rape Work: Victims, Gender, and Emotions in Organization and Community Context*. New York: Routledge, 2005.

NOTHING IS POSSIBLE WITHOUT
PEOPLE, BUT NOTHING LASTS
WITHOUT INSTITUTIONS.

—JEAN MONNET[1]

8

Institutions

Thus far we've talked about the way that individuals look through gender binary glasses, internalize gender norms, and police their own and others' gender performances. We've also discussed how our ideas about men and women—and our expectations for our own and others' behavior—aren't just different; they're unequal. Finally, we've considered how people get away with breaking gender rules and form communities that support the gender rules they endorse. This makes it seem like, no matter how pervasive the gender binary lens and how strong the pressure to do gender, an individual *can* make the difficult decision to live a gender-neutral or gender-fluid life if he or she wants to. In other words:

Q+A   **When it comes down to it, regardless of social construction and social pressure, don't we live in a society in which it's possible to just be an individual?**

The answer to this question is, in fact, no. Gender is a set of ideas and something one does when interacting with other people, but it's also an organizing principle that permeates our social institutions. Because ideas about gender shape the environments in which we live, these ideas exert an influence on our lives independent of our own beliefs, personalities, and interactions. It's simply not true that if we reject the gender binary as individuals, and refuse to let others police us, we'll be free of gender. Gender—and gender inequality, too—is part of the fabric of our lives.

We'll start by introducing the idea of the institution, then discuss how institutions are gendered in ways that reproduce both difference and inequality.

THE ORGANIZATION OF DAILY LIFE

Most schools in the United States—from kindergarten to college—take a three-month break during the summer. Most kids enjoy the break without asking why, but there's a reason we do it this way. Not a natural reason, but a social one.

Before the late 1900s, urban schools met year-round while rural schools met for only six months, letting students off to help on their families' farms.[2] Urban schools eventually decided to break during the summer because that was when the wealthy liked to travel and also because, before the invention of air-conditioning, schools were oppressively hot and stuffy during those months. As education became more important and fewer kids were growing up on farms, rural schools increased the length of their abbreviated school year to match that of urban schools. Our precious summer vacation was born.

Summer vacation has a history, then, but today we mostly just accept that this is how things are done. It is now part of how Americans "do" school. In this sense, American education is an example of what sociologists call an **institution**, a persistent pattern of social interaction aimed at meeting a need of a society that can't easily be met by individuals alone.

The institution of education meets the needs of individuals to educate their own and others' kids. Giving the next generation the information and skills they'll need to be productive workers and responsible citizens is difficult or impossible for today's parents, who generally don't have the knowledge, the know-how, or the time to teach their kids themselves. In response, we take on education collectively, creating a systematic way to achieve the goal of an educated citizenry.

Carefully organized and controlled, the institution of education dictates the when, where, and how of teaching: the standards, curricula, and credentials students and teachers are held to; occasions for enacting them (like the first day of school, graduation, field trips, and snow days); and teachers' unions that negotiate with districts and states to determine pay. The institution of education

American high school students toss their caps to celebrate completing one stage of education as it is institutionalized in the United States.

involves organizations: primary and secondary schools, colleges, and universities as well as federal and state departments of education, private and charter schools, and companies (like those offering the SAT, ACT, and other tests, as well as test prep). There are also commonly accepted routines—parents helping with homework, organizing carpools, and holding fund-raising events—and spectacles like swim meets, senior prom, and graduation.

For the most part, all these organizations and routines are taken for granted as just what school is like. In this sense, much of how we achieve institutionalized tasks is simply normative. **Norms** are beliefs and practices that are well known, widely followed, and culturally approved (like back-to-school shopping trips). Conformity with institutionalized ways of doing things is also secured with formal **policies**, which are explicit and codified expectations, often with stated consequences for deviance (like rules related to attendance). Many policies elaborate on and reinforce norms, transforming common sense into regulations (like no cheating on tests); some policies explicitly are intended to override and change beliefs and practices that have become the norm (like texting in class). Some norms and policies are strongly enforced while others are enforced only weakly.

Because institutions are about *collectively* meeting the needs of individuals, they are very different from the social forces we've discussed so far. We can try to get cultural ideas we don't like out of our brains, surround ourselves with people who support our personal choices, and accept whatever consequences come with breaking social rules, but it is essentially impossible to avoid institutions. They impose themselves on our lives.

If you didn't have a stay-at-home parent or a parent who is a teacher, for example, your summer vacation was likely inconvenient or expensive for them. Child care during those months may have strained their budget while, depending on your age, leaving you at home to fend for yourself might have been criminal neglect. Yet the trouble it caused your parents didn't make the institution magically transform. Summer vacation is summer vacation. In this way, institutions affect our lives whether we like it or not. Our institutions are social inventions, but they are so pervasively and persistently part of our lives that they seem like concrete, unmovable, nonnegotiable facts of life.

We can't just be an individual, then, because we are part of a society that is replete with institutions. Education is but one example. We also have institutions designed to promote global peace and prosperity (involving, but not limited to, the United Nations, World Health Organization, and Doctors Without Borders); defend the country (the military, the Central Intelligence Agency, the Department of Homeland Security); keep citizens safe from violent crime (neighborhood watch programs, prisons, law enforcement, and the judiciary); enable transportation (airlines, public buses and trains, road construction, highway patrol, waterways); promote social welfare (food-stamp programs and Social Security, psychiatric institutions, child social services); raise the next generation (schools, camps, youth groups, and families); deliver and monitor health care (hospitals, insurance companies, the American Medical Association); promote the national economy (regulations on printing money, incorporating businesses, borrowing and lending, insuring property, discharging debt); entertain, inform, and make life meaningful (newspapers, organized religion, professional sports, art, the film industry); and shape the overall conditions of life and the future of our societies (advocacy organizations, labor unions, nonprofit groups, political parties, and legislative bodies).

These are all institutions. Together, they form the **social structure**: the entire set of interlocked institutions within which we live our lives. We call it a "structure" because institutions, in concert, create a relatively stable *scaffolding*. If we want to be a doctor, for instance, we know we have to go to college and then medical school. The path, or structure, already exists. We know we are expected to follow it and we trust that a medical degree will still be a requirement to begin a career in medicine when we finish our schooling eight or more years later. The stability of institutions, and the relationships between them, provide a framework that enables us to make rational decisions about our future. Structures are helpful because they help us know what we wish to accomplish, as well as how to do so.

Until quite recently, medical schools limited the number of women they allowed to enter degree programs in any given year.

And yet, the social structure is also a source of constraint. Sometimes climbing the scaffolding requires resources we don't have. If we can't afford the combination of tuition and eight years out of the workforce required to become a doctor, we probably won't become one. It wouldn't matter how much medical knowledge and experience we amassed, we'd still be criminals if we practiced without a license. Or we may not have access to the right scaffolding at the right time. In the 1960s and early 1970s, many medical schools did not accept women or they set a 5 to 10 percent cap on female admissions, so many women who were interested in medicine did not apply to medical school, thinking it unrealistic, or didn't get in if they did.

Institutions both enable and constrain our lives, but there is no opting out. We can condemn state and federal governments as incompetent and corrupt, become an anarchist, and stay home on voting day, but Congress is still going to pass legislation to which we will be held accountable. And if we break the law and get caught, we'll face legal penalties even if we personally object to the law. We could go "off the grid" to avoid capitalism, find an isolated spot in the wilderness, cut down trees, build a hut, and live off roots and berries. Then again, where did we get our ax? Will we bring a book on poisonous mushrooms? Even the hermit will buy a few things to get along and, in any case, he or she can't help but draw on knowledge acquired through institutions like schools, family, and the mass media.

We live in, through, and with institutions and, by shaping our opportunities, they shape our lives. These institutions, moreover, are gendered.

GENDERED INSTITUTIONS

A **gendered institution** is one in which gender is used as an organizing principle. In a gendered institution, men and women are channeled into different, and often differently valued, social spaces or activities and their choices have different and often unequal consequences.

Education, for example, isn't just an institution, it's a gendered institution. Education is gendered through both norms and policies. Policies like gendered honorifics for teachers ("Mr." and "Ms."), gender-specific dress codes, and gender-segregated classes, like separate sex education units for girls and boys, make gender an organizing principle of schooling. Meanwhile, informal norms further make gender part of the routine practice of school. There is no policy requiring that the girls populate the monkey bars and boys populate the sports fields at recess, for instance, but that may be how kids distribute themselves nonetheless.[3]

Many American elementary school playgrounds feature this kind of "geography of gender," but the importance of gender often fades once students return to the classroom, where students are rarely seated by gender but instead seated alphabetically or arranged in other ways conducive to an orderly classroom.[4] In education, as well as other institutions, the importance of gender varies.[5] Kindergarten play kitchens and AP math classes, for example, may be more gendered than nap time and Algebra I. **Gender salience**—the relevance of gender across contexts, activities, and spaces—rises and falls across the different parts of the institutional landscape.

Whether via policies or norms, gender is a persistent feature of elementary education, making it a gendered institution. When new students arrive, they are inserted into this already-existing system. The system is reproduced and enforced by a collection of others who assign esteem and stigma, or success and failure, according to how well new students follow or otherwise contend with the existing norms and policies. If you, an intrepid first grader, were to arrive at one of these schools, you would quickly learn when and how gender was important. You could then choose whether to conform or deviate, but you *would* contend with it one way or another.

Gendered institutions are interesting from a sociological point of view because they affirm and enforce both gender difference and inequality. In the next two sections we'll talk about why gendered institutions matter, starting with an intimate example: our plumbing.

THE INSTITUTIONALIZATION OF GENDER DIFFERENCE

A Room of Her Own

In developed countries, public sanitation is an institution, and thank goodness. It would be impossible for all individuals in a complex society to build and maintain a personal toilet in every location in which they might find themselves, so providing a safe and sanitary way to eliminate personal waste is a social task. Without sanitary institutions, our daily lives would include routine exposure to both the act and product of urination and defecation. We would, in other words, have to poop in public, smelling and stepping over other people's feces, exposed to the diseases that humans harbor in bodily fluids. In fact, 14 percent of the world's population does just that.[6]

Where you live, however, you likely benefit from a sewer system that quietly and invisibly transports human waste to treatment plants where it is variably burned, hauled off to landfills, given to farmers, and released back into the water supply. Above ground, sanitation policies ensure the provision of bathroom facilities in workplaces, schools, restaurants, department stores, government buildings, airports, and elsewhere. We typically find men's and women's rooms in these locations, requiring us to pick one or the other. This makes public sanitation a gendered institution.

The idea that men and women should have separate bathroom facilities emerged during the 1800s. During that era, women and men were first brought together as workers in factories. The idea of men and women working side by side on the factory floor threatened to upset cherished Victorian beliefs about the differences between them. One such belief was that women were more fragile than men and, therefore, less suited to working for pay. Reflecting this belief, the Department of Labor reported in 1913 that a "woman's body is unable to withstand strains, fatigues, and [de]privations as well as a man's."[7] As a solution, another study recommended the provision of "rest or emergency rooms" on the assumption that women were "likely to have sudden attacks of dizziness, fainting or other symptoms of illness."[8] *Restrooms*, a word you likely recognize, were small private rooms with a bed or chair available to women workers struck by some sudden feminine malady. The provision of restrooms reasserted women's fragility, easing the threat that their presence in the workplace posed to the Victorian gender ideology.

Women's restrooms served a second purpose, too. Employers placed them between the factory floor and the women's toilets so that women had to pass through them on their way to the bathroom. Whenever a woman went into the

Nurses rest in a women's "restroom."

restroom, then, men could pretend she was just going to *rest*; they could be in happy denial that women ever went in to *poop*. In other words, sex-segregated bathrooms, with the restroom as a buffer, allowed Victorian women to carefully conceal any sign of bodily functions and allowed men to pretend that women never used the bathroom at all.

The idea caught on. In 1887, Massachusetts enacted the first law mandating sex-segregated toilets.[9] By 1920, forty-three states had followed suit. Today, every state in the United States requires the provision of separate bathrooms for men and women in every public building and private business with a minimum amount of foot traffic.[10]

Gender and Bathrooms Today

Sex-segregation of toilet facilities has become a powerful norm, if an increasingly contested one. Even if we think it's silly, most of us use the "correct" bathroom in public if at all possible. To most of us, using the other gendered bathroom seems *wrong*. This is often true even when the bathrooms in question are stand-alone rooms with a single toilet and a door that locks. Accordingly, most of us have likely found ourselves waiting patiently in line to use the proper toilet while ones designated for the other sex sit empty.

Notably, if there *isn't* a single stick figure on the door, we'll use the same restroom as someone of the other sex without hesitation. This is true in many smaller businesses and workplaces with only one bathroom. It's also true on airplanes. The bathrooms at the back of the plane *could* be designated male- or female-only but, out of a concern that passengers get back to their seats as soon as possible, they aren't. Men and women also use the same bathrooms at home. Having men's and women's bathrooms in your house would be a novelty, a gag. Everyone knows it's completely unnecessary.

Just as in the Victorian era, then, today's sex-segregated bathrooms serve *social*, not biological functions. Most people don't think that women need a fainting couch within arm's reach, but different bathrooms continue to allow women to keep bodily functions we still define as "unladylike" away from men. Likewise, gender-specific bathrooms allow women to do body work that's supposed to remain invisible; when done in public, fixing one's hair, smoothing one's clothes, checking for blemishes, and reapplying lipstick all reveal to the viewer that appearing effortlessly feminine requires a lot of work and surveillance. Sex segregation of bathrooms gives women a sex-segregated space in which to do this. To a lesser extent, the same is true for men.

Providing different bathrooms for men and women also assumes that everyone needs to protect their private parts from the other sex, but not the same sex. In other words, the policy assumes everyone is heterosexual. That bathrooms are designed without same-sex desire in mind is obvious when we consider that bathrooms not only separate "men" from "women," but are actually designed with the expectation that male-bodied people will expose their penises to one another when urinating. This approach to bathrooms was obviously institutionalized before homosexuality became a part of popular consciousness.

And, of course, sex-segregated bathrooms uphold the gender binary itself. They don't allow for the possibility that some people don't identify as either male or female, are male but look female (or vice versa), appear altogether gender ambiguous, or are in the process of transitioning. Betsy Lucal, the gender-ambiguous sociologist we discussed earlier, described the challenge of using bathrooms in public places:

> Encounters in public rest rooms are an adventure. I have been told countless times that "This is the ladies' room." Other women say nothing to me, but their stares and conversations with others let me know what they think. I will hear them say, for example, "There was a man in there."[11]

In response, Lucal has to make efforts to try to reduce the chances that she'll be stared at, insulted, or even confronted by managers or police:

If I must use a public rest room, I try to make myself look as nonthreatening
as possible. I do not wear a hat, and I try to rearrange my clothing to make my
breasts more obvious. . . . While in the rest room, I never make eye contact, and I
get in and out as quickly as possible. Going in with a woman friend also is helpful;
her presence legitimizes my own. People are less likely to think I am entering a
space where I do not belong when I am with someone who looks like she does.[12]

Trans, genderqueer or fluid, and ambiguous-appearing individuals like Lucal can
be significantly inconvenienced by sex-segregated bathrooms, but the binary
approach to sanitation can cause everyone problems from time to time, like when
we really have to go and there's a long line for one bathroom but not the other, or
when we're trying to help a child or elderly person of the other sex use a public
toilet. Eliminating sex-segregated bathrooms, or requiring the provision of at
least some gender-neutral ones, is often described as a policy that would help
nonbinary people, but it would actually help cis people, too.

In the past few years, the politics of bathrooms have increasingly become a
topic of public debate. Currently, U.S. federal law makes it illegal for employers
to force trans employees to use the bathroom that corresponds to their sex at
birth and not their gender identity, but doesn't offer trans students the same
protection.[13] Nineteen states have passed laws protecting trans people's right
to use the bathroom of their choice in *any* public place.[14] Many airports, sports
arenas, and other large facilities have added "family bathrooms" or gender-
neutral "disabled" ones, which offer a way around the gender binary for trans
folks as well as for fathers with daughters and mothers with sons.

Other states, mostly in the South, have passed or considered bills restricting
bathroom rights, largely based on the claim that allowing trans people access to
women's bathrooms (but, notably, not men's) is dangerous. Opponents of Houston's failed anti-LGBT discrimination law, which included trans bathroom rights,
made the case like this:

Any man at any time could enter a woman's bathroom simply by claiming to be
a woman that day. No one is exempt. Even registered sex offenders could fol-
low women or young girls into the bathroom and if a business tried to stop them,
they'd be fined. Protect women's privacy. Prevent danger.

A supposed risk to cisgender women and girls, based on an assumption that all
penis-bearing humans are potentially dangerous, is a common justification for
anti-trans bathroom bills today.

Historically, the vulnerability of women and girls was also the argument
made against desegregating bathrooms by race. In the 1940s, the specter of race-
integrated bathrooms was used to argue against racial integration more gener-

ally.[15] Opponents of integration pointed out that it would mean the end of white-only bathrooms, falsely claiming that it would put white women in danger from diseases carried by black women. A few decades later, in the 1970s, it was the possibility of black *men* using white women's restrooms that helped sink the proposed equal rights constitutional amendment sought by feminists. So, when opponents of trans bathroom rights make references to women's safety, they are drawing on a long American tradition of portraying white women as vulnerable and white men, black men, and black women as dangerous. Today it is supposedly trans women who are the threat; the details have changed, but the strategy is the same.

The example of sex-segregated bathrooms shows how institutions can be gendered, as well as how the intersection of gender with other identities can be politicized. It also reveals how policies can enforce ideas about gender and be both introduced and changed when there is political and public will. And the politics around trans access to restrooms is a good reminder that institutional changes can often have effects well beyond the targeted constituency, giving everyone more flexibility in how they use the facilities.

Institutions, though, do more than make certain ideas about gender difference part of daily life, they also contribute to gender inequality. To understand this latter point better, let's turn to an institution many of us first encounter on the school playground: sports.

THE INSTITUTIONALIZATION OF GENDER INEQUALITY

How individuals experience sports varies tremendously. Some find it intimidating, some exhilarating; some shrink from the competition, others come alive under pressure. Some of us are blessed with strong and graceful bodies that bound, bend, and twist; others of us struggle to gain quickness, coordination, and endurance. We all have to work harder at this as we get older and our bodies become less spry.

Regardless of whether we like sports, they're part of an institution that shapes our experiences. Little Leagues and after-school programs are complex organizations that engage children in sports in prescribed ways. Once American children start school, they may be required to take physical education classes that teach certain sports and not others; schools are also sites where team play and competition are taught and encouraged. Our teams need someone with whom to have matches, bouts, or games, so other schools nearby also need to field teams for the same sports. The space and equipment requirements for various sports—tracks, courts, fields, balls, bats, mitts, and sticks—are provided by

The aerial view of a high school in Idaho is a testament to the infrastructure required to support the institutionalization of popular American sports.

schools and city and state parks departments and manufactured and sold by companies for profit.

Colleges and universities also allocate money, space, and time to athletics. They are driven not just by enjoyment but by the public exposure and potential alumni dollars that accrue to schools with successful or otherwise beloved teams. They have relationships with middle and high schools that funnel talented students into colleges offering scholarships. The mass media follow certain college sports, making games lucrative for colleges and networks alike. Companies, in turn, can count on televised or streamed sporting events to find audiences to which they can advertise their goods and services. Regulatory bodies, such as the NCAA, define the rewards that sports can offer to athletes and the standards of the competition.

In fact, the entire economy benefits from the institution of sport. In the United States, sales of sporting goods exceeded $87 billion in 2016.[16] Major League Baseball and the National Football League (the two most lucrative sports in the United States) earned $10 billion and $14 billion, respectively, in 2017.[17] The U.S. sports industry, put together, is worth nearly $500 billion. Individuals who profit—a list too vast to compile here, but one that includes not just owners, athletes, sports journalists, merchandisers, and marketing executives, but also cashiers, janitors, vendors, ticket takers, and owners and employees of nearby souvenir shops, hotels, bars, and restaurants—are all invested in the industry. Meanwhile, there is a vast infrastructure (stadiums, arenas, tracks) and media empire (an ever-multiplying number of ESPN channels along with at least seventeen other sports networks).

Sports are an impressive behemoth of institutionalization. And they are also strongly gendered, making them an institution that, despite having changed dramatically in the past several decades, continues to work to establish a hierarchy among men and demonstrate women's supposed inferiority.

Separating the Men from the Boys

One of the first recreational physical activities taken up by women was bicycling. It was the 1890s, and it changed women's lives.[18] Bicycles made women mobile. They allowed women to travel miles from their homes. Bicycles required lighter garments with fewer restrictions of movement, inspiring changes in the norms of women's dress. "Let me tell you what I think of bicycling," said the women's rights activist Susan B. Anthony. "I think it has done more to emancipate women than anything else in the world. I stand and rejoice every time I see a woman ride by on a wheel."[19] Bicycles gave women *freedom*.

People didn't like it.

Doctors warned that women were unfit for exertion and that bike riding would cause headaches, heart trouble, depression, insomnia, and exhaustion.[20] They told women that riding bikes was to risk getting "bicycle face," a possibly permanent clenching of the jaw and bulging of the eyes caused by strain. Bicycling caused women to be flushed, or pale, and grimacing, but weary. It should be reserved, the doctors insisted, for men.

Women didn't listen. They rode bikes and, in the next one hundred years, would progressively risk their faces and put their bodies to the test, integrating sport after sport. Today, millions of women play sports around the world. In fact, almost as many high school and college women play sports as do men.[21]

Despite the ordinariness of the female athlete today, though, sports are still considered masculine.[22] Sports are part of a boy's basic "manhood training."[23] They are "[t]he epitome of what a man's supposed to be."[24] Playing sports—and thinking, watching, and talking about sports—is "astonishingly important" for young men.[25] Not surprisingly, then, most boys get involved with sports at some level. Their first plush toy may be a soccer ball; their first T-shirt may feature a baseball and bat. A boy's first memories of bonding with his father may involve watching football on TV or playing T-ball in the backyard. Informal games in the neighborhood may transition into Little League and then participation on school-based teams.

Because sports are so strongly associated with masculinity, excelling in sports is one way for young boys to show they're "real boys" and, later, "real men."

Sports, though, don't simply offer boys and men an avenue through which to claim esteem; they place individual boys and men into the hierarchy of masculinity. Recall that sociologist Michael Messner described his decision to embrace sports as his first "engagement with hegemonic masculinity," a moment in which he accepted that he would have to belittle other men if he was to ascend the hierarchy.[26] Importantly, he notes that sports aren't just about individual accomplishment; they are also about competition: "It is being better than the other guys—*beating them*—that is the key to acceptance."[27] As Messner argues, sport "serves partly to socialize boys and young men to hierarchical, competitive, and aggressive values."[28] While some men excel, others fail. Picking teams may be one of the most formative experiences of hierarchy in kids' lives, one that can be traumatic for those boys picked last—or exhilarating for a girl chosen to be "one of the guys." In this sense, sports, especially the most masculinized sports, is one way that we affirm the value of masculinity for everyone.

Most men, of course, eventually focus their energies elsewhere. As men recognize that it's unlikely that they'll become professional athletes, many turn their attention to their educations, careers outside of athletics, or the daily rhythms of raising a family. But the institution of sport will likely continue to play a symbolic role in their lives. Some men trade the physical competition for a more passive consumption of televised sports and sports news. Men cheer for their respective teams on big flat-screen TVs, engaging in friendly trash-talking of opposing teams and their fans. They jostle for relative position by owning better paraphernalia, holding season tickets with better seats, knowing sports history and statistics more thoroughly and, of course, bragging when their team wins. It's a culture-wide, feel-good, male-bonding extravaganza, one that retains a competitive aspect as fans jostle for dominance. Men who aren't interested in sports suffer many of the same disadvantages as men who don't play well.

No matter that most men aren't especially impressive athletes themselves. Because they're men, even couch potatoes can point to the game and claim they share something important and meaningful with LeBron James, Aaron Rodgers, or Cristiano Ronaldo.[29] As one male fan said: "A woman can do the same job I can do—maybe even be my boss. But I'll be damned if she can go on the football field and take a hit!"[30] Of course, the vast majority of men couldn't "take a hit" either, but this is beside the point. Instead, sports like football serve as a *cultural* testament to the idea that, no matter what happens, men are men and women are women.

A Team of Her Own

Most Americans will agree that men are naturally better athletes by virtue of their size and strength. But the truth is that our culture has selected for sports that emphasize the few physical advantages men have over women, even going so far as to define physical activities in which women outperform men as not sports at all. In an alternative reality in which this didn't happen, we can imagine a different world of sports, one that worshipped and rewarded the physical skills in which the average woman excels more than the average man. The philosopher Jane English tried such a thought experiment. She pondered:

> Speed, size, and strength seem to be the essence of sports. Women are naturally inferior at "sports" so conceived. But if women had been the historically dominant sex, our concept of sport would no doubt have evolved differently. Competitions emphasizing flexibility, balance, strength, timing, and small size might dominate Sunday afternoon television and offer salaries in [the] six figures.[31]

Rhythmic gymnastics is exceptionally athletic and offers feats of strength and skill to admire, but it is not a prized and well-rewarded part of U.S. sports culture.

In English's thought experiment, basketball and football are replaced by gymnastics and horseback riding, with nonstop coverage of long-distance marksmanship and billions of dollars spent on dance competitions.

This is not our world. Instead, media coverage of sports keeps a raw, grimacing, bulging, powerful male body front and center in our culture.[32] It's no accident, argues Messner, that the most popular sports in America are also ones based on what he terms "the most extreme possibilities of the male body."[33] Using American football as an example, he explains:

> Football . . . is clearly a world apart from women. . . . In contrast to the bare and vulnerable bodies of the cheerleaders, the armored male bodies of the football players are elevated to mythical status, and as such, give testimony to the undeniable "fact" that there is at least one place where men are clearly superior to women.[34]

The bodies of these professional athletes serve as icons of masculine physical achievement. Their extraordinary feats of athleticism tell a story about men and male bodies. In this way, the symbolic link between the male spectator and the male athlete establishes men's supposed superiority over women.

On the assumption that women are lesser athletes than men, the institution of sport segregates women and men in almost all cases. There are some exceptions—equestrianism and synchronized swimming are sex integrated (though we see few men in the latter)—but, in general, sex segregation in sports is the rule. Almost all team sports feature sex-segregated teams, leagues, meets, and games that ensure men and women never compete with or against one another. Likewise, individual sports like long-distance running, swimming, and ski jumping usually do not put men and women in direct competition. They even rank records separately.

Both those on the political left and political right tend to think this is a good way to organize sports, given the assumption that men are stronger, faster, and bigger than women. If women played with or against men, it is argued, they'd get hurt; if they competed against men, they'd lose; and if they went out for the same team, they wouldn't get on. Accordingly, sex-segregated teams are supported by both conservatives who think women are more fragile than men and liberals who want women to have the same opportunities.

Sorting by sex, however, also organizes sports in ways that affirm cultural beliefs in gender difference and inequality. We will explore two different ways that sex segregation is used to affirm a hierarchical gender binary.

Different but Equal?

First, sorting allows us to require—with both policies and norms—that men and women play the same sports in different ways. Both women and men play hockey, for instance, but whereas men are allowed to "check" (body slam) one another, it is against the rules for women to do so and punishable with penalties. Likewise, tackle football is the province of "real men"; women (and "lesser men") are allowed to play "flag" (also sometimes called "powder puff") football. At the Olympics, female competitors in BMX, or bicycle motocross, ride a shorter course with less difficult obstacles than their male counterparts; so do the women who compete in slalom, downhill, and cross-country skiing.[35] In the case of baseball, women are sorted into a related but different game, softball, with its own equipment and rules. These differing policies—especially those that forbid women to be as physically aggressive or take on the same challenges—mean that women and men are required to do sports both differently and unequally, with women doing a lesser version. Whether women and girls *could* play or ride the way men and boys do remains an open question this way; the rules ensure that we'll never know.

The different aesthetic expectations for male and female athletes, sometimes encoded in judging guidelines, also create sports that reinforce beliefs about men's and women's talents and abilities. Writing about the feminine apologetic in figure skating, sociologist Abigail Feder keenly observed that one of a female skater's most useful talents is the ability to disguise the incredible athleticism required and, instead, make it look effortless.[36] Whereas male figure skaters have been valued for appearing powerful and aggressive on the ice, the judging norms for female figure skaters frown upon this. Instead of athleticism, an ability to look beautiful and graceful is valued in women. She is supposed to look serene and at rest, no matter that she is launching herself into the air at twenty miles an hour or rotating so quickly through a flying sit-spin that she might give herself a nosebleed.

Bodybuilding is on the flip side of the gender binary but has the same gendered expectations. Judges are instructed to evaluate men only on how muscular they are, but to judge women on both their muscle development and their femininity.[37] The International Federation of Bodybuilding and Fitness, the organization that sets the rules for judging competitions and serves as the gateway to the Mr. and Ms. Olympia competitions, slots women into divisions that limit accumulation of muscle mass: "bikini fitness," "fit model," and "wellness fitness" (some of which have parallel men's divisions and some of which do not).[38]

In these competitions, women can be penalized for being "too big." One judge confessed to a bodybuilder who had taken a disappointing eighth place:

In bodybuilding competitions, rules constrain women's muscular development, rewarding women who display sculpted but not overly muscled bodies. Long hair, heavy makeup, and sparkly bikinis act as a further feminine apologetic.

"As a bodybuilder you were the best, but in a *women's* bodybuilding competition I just felt that I couldn't vote for you."[39] In 2005, the federation officially requested that female bodybuilders reduce their muscle mass by 20 percent and in 2015, the federation ended the Ms. Olympia competition altogether.

The examples of figure skating and bodybuilding show that separating women and men allows us to require that even the most elite of athletic performances conform to gendered expectations. It's circular logic: The idea that men and women have fundamentally different physical abilities is used to institutionalize policies that ensure women and men don't participate in the same sports in the same way. And because they don't, we can easily go on believing that men and women have fundamentally different physical abilities.

Who Loses if Women Compete with Men?

A second way sex segregation in sports protects a belief in the hierarchical gender binary is by ensuring that men and women never compete against one another. But whom does this protect? On the assumption that women would always come in second to men, it might seem like sex segregation protects women, giving them a "chance." And maybe that's true for individual women. But if we zoom out, it becomes clear that it's men as a group, not women as a group, who benefit from sex-segregated sports.

Segregation allows the assumption that men outperform women to go untested. If we integrated sports, this would be put to the test, repeatedly. In those tests, if women always lost, women as a group would lose nothing; we already think they're inferior athletes. But if men lost, they would lose much more than the match; they would lose the presumption of male superiority.

This was Messner's argument. Reflecting on his own experience in elementary school, he wrote:

> The best athlete in my classes never got to play with us. She was a girl. Somehow we boys all knew that she was the fastest runner, could hit a baseball further than any of us, yet we never had to confront that reality directly. Our teachers, by enforcing strict sex segregation on the playground, protected our fragile male egos from the humiliation that presumably would result from losing to a girl.[40]

Many young boys and their parents intuit this. In 2011 a high school threatened to forfeit a junior varsity football game unless a girl on the opposing team sat out.[41] Mina Johnson, a five-foot-two-inch 172-pound linebacker, had "gain[ed] a reputation in the league as a standout junior varsity player"; she sacked a six-foot quarterback in her very first game. Nevertheless, not wanting to be the cause of a lost opportunity for her team, she agreed not to play. The opposing team still lost—60 to 0, in fact—but apparently that was less humiliating than losing to a girl.

In 2017, high school golfer Emily Nash competed alongside her male peers in the Central Massachusetts Division III Boys Tournament.[42] She was allowed to play as a member of the team because her school didn't have a girls' golf team. Because it was otherwise a boys-only tournament, however, her individual scores didn't count. So even though she had the best tournament-wide score, beating every other boy on every team, the first-place trophy went to the male runner-up. Still, by virtue of being able to play at all, the message came through loud and clear: *sometimes girls beat boys at their own game.*

What does sex segregation in sports do? It protects boys and men. As one mother of a boy wrestler put it: It's "unfair for girls to compete against boys. . . . [It puts boys] in a no-win situation. . . . If he wins, it's just a girl, and if he loses, his life is over."[43] It's important to be empathetic to the experiences of men in a world characterized by sexism and androcentrism, but unfair to boys? Hardly. It's extra humiliating to lose to a girl only because we've already decided that women *should* lose.

Still, we might object, doesn't segregating sports by sex give women an opportunity to play that they might otherwise not have? Not really. Gender is neither a necessary nor logical way to organize sports and make competitions fair.[44] Any justification for this criterion is based on using gender as an imprecise substitute for other, better variables: height, weight, or athletic ability.

Consider wrestling, the sport causing the mother quoted earlier such angst. Wrestling matches have traditionally been organized by weight class. People in the same weight class, considered equally paired, wrestle each other. The relevant characteristic here isn't gender at all; it's weight. So men and women of the same weight class should be considered good competitors. Using this logic, girls and women have been pressing coaches to allow them to wrestle and have been joining previously all-male high school wrestling teams since the 1990s. Today, there are thousands of female wrestlers on teams. In fact, in 2006 Michaela Hutchison from Alaska became the first girl to win a state high school mixed-sex wrestling championship.[45] She wasn't the last.

Basketball could also be organized according to size and skill instead of sex. Instead of sex-segregated teams, it might make more sense to separate teams into taller and shorter players. Tall women could play with tall men and shorter men and women could play together. Or, alternately, we could set up mixed-gender teams and then sort them into "fair play" leagues by average height and relative successes. Then agility, speed, and shooting skill could be more directly compared, with all teams competing for the players who have what they need.

The same logic applies to American football, where being big and heavy is an advantage in several positions. Women are almost entirely excluded from football on the logic that they're too small to play. But most men are also too

Proving that wrestling is not just for men, Sara Dosho of Japan and Aline Focken of Germany compete in a bronze-medal match.

small to play football. Having two or more teams organized by size would give everyone a chance to play: men, women, and other folks, too. It would reduce the incentives for teams to strive universally to get ever bigger and would also make hits less dangerous for those who enjoy the game but worry about the physical toll on the body and brain.

Or, if the issue is ability, why not divide up competition that way? Foot races are already organized according to qualifying times, so why is it necessary to further break it down by gender? If a woman *can* lift as much weight or run as fast as a man, why stop her from competing against him? If we desegregated sexed sports, the top ranks of many might be disproportionately populated by cis men, but they would also likely be disproportionately populated by the young, people with resources and leisure time, and other variables that predict talent and the ability to develop skills. We let the chips fall where they may. We could do the same with gender. Lindsey Vonn, for example, one of the most decorated skiers of all time, whose times very often best those of her male peers, has asked to be allowed to enter men's races. International racing officials have thus far said no.

She acknowledges that this will likely harm her chances of coming in first. "But," she has said, "I would like to at least have the opportunity to try."[46]

If we did this—if we organized sports by weight, height, skill, or qualifying times—women might be less likely than men to rise to the top of some sports, but it'd be much more difficult to claim that women are too small, weak, slow, or fragile to compete with men at all. There'd always be some women who would outperform even some of the best men, as there already are. If we allowed this fact to become clear, the belief that women are lesser athletes than men would be much more difficult to justify. Meanwhile, we'd open sports to everyone: men and women of all shapes and sizes, along with people who have historically been excluded from gender-binary sports almost entirely—trans men, trans women, and people who are known to be intersex.

We might even come to question whether the "top" leagues with competitors with the most extreme body types are actually the most interesting ones to watch. Football played without a premium on huge bodies or basketball played by teams of people with average heights might look more exciting than the leagues that are valued merely because they are "men's" and thus presumed to be "the best." Hockey fans often speak admiringly of the excellent stick work of the women's teams and, with more assists and fewer dunks, women's basketball showcases an impressive cooperation that better reflects the sport's roots. Some men might fit in better in these leagues, and more fans might turn to them, if only they were not disparaged by being classified as "women's."

Sex-integrated sports would also ensure that women got paid what they are worth. Segregated sports make it possible to justify paying female athletes less than male ones. The assumption is that women are inferior athletes and less interesting and impressive to watch, so fans don't support them and media companies don't feature them or put much effort or money into broadcasts. As a result, prize monies and salaries for male athletes far exceed those for female athletes. The *minimum* salary for players in the National Basketball Association, for example, is about $560,000 a season. In contrast, the *average* salary for the Women's National Basketball Association is less than 10 percent of that, at $50,000.[47] The highest-paid professional male basketball player earned over $34 million for the 2017–2018 season. The highest-paid female players made just over $100,000—less than one-fifth of the minimum salary for a male player. In 2017, only one woman made the *Forbes* list of the top one hundred highest-paid athletes: Serena Williams.[48]

These disparities in income are pervasive throughout the sports world, even once we account for gender differences in performances. Concluding a study of pay in professional golfing, professor of sport management Todd Crosset acknowledged that male golfers outperform female golfers on average, but these differences are, all things considered, very small.[49] Both sets of golfers are remarkably dedicated, skilled, and talented. To Crosset, the vast differences in prize money—regularly over $300 million for the men's Professional Golf Association Tour, compared to less than $70 million for the Ladies Professional Golf Association Tour—largely reflect the "social significance" of male versus female athletics, not their respective athleticism.[50] Sports fans, he explained, often argue that men's sports get more support and attention because male athletes are better. But, he countered:

> If it was truly skill that fans were going to see, how can we explain the lack of fan support for women's college teams that could easily handle boys' high school teams, which draw more fans. Quite simply, sports have more significance for men regardless of skill level.[51]

It's sexism that drives the unequal attention and rewards that accrue to male and female athletes; institutionalized sex segregation is the foundation on which unequal attention and rewards rest.

The policy and norms of sex segregating sports make sports an institutional arena in which beliefs in gender difference and inequality are routinely and ritualistically rehearsed. This is part of the institution of sport, one we can opt into or out of but can't ignore or overrule. If we want to be athletes, we have to play by these rules. If we're a girl and we want to play baseball, we're up against more than the discomfort that sometimes comes with breaking gender rules and the policing that follows; we're also confronted by the fact that there isn't a girls' baseball team at our school. Even if there *were* a girls' baseball team, though, who would we play? Girls' baseball teams haven't been institutionalized and, since it takes a community to field an entire league, changing this is very difficult.

We discuss the difficulty of changing institutionalized ways of doing things in the final section of this chapter.

INSTITUTIONAL INERTIA AND CHANGE

As individuals we may wish to change or ignore the institutions we confront, but this is far more difficult with institutions than it is with ideas or social interactions. Institutions are more resistant to change and more difficult to ignore because institutional patterns reflect widespread norms and are often encoded in formal policy. A return trip to the restroom offers a case study.

Sociologist Harvey Molotch was part of a failed effort to install a gender-neutral bathroom during the renovation of a space designed for the edgy New

York University Department of Social and Cultural Analysis.[52] While the department included trans faculty members who would clearly benefit from a gender-neutral bathroom and other faculty members were intrigued by the opportunity to push gender boundaries, they nevertheless ended up with conventional sex-segregated toilets. Why?

The first reason was related to inconvenience and expense. Contractors and designers are intimately familiar with the design requirements of sex-segregated bathrooms, making the installation of sex-integrated ones a new challenge. Sitting down to design a new kind of bathroom takes time and this is expensive. The administration was reluctant to draw out the process and spend extra money on a brand new restroom design. It was cheaper and faster to rely on the tried-and-true approach. Molotch wrote:

> Everyone "knows" what a building restroom should be like, that it will involve toilets and sinks, signs and separations, some spaces with urinals and some not.... To innovate means going back to the drawing boards, rethinking architectural opportunities and constraints, and checking continuously to make sure everyone is aware of the plan now being implemented. This is a hassle, one with financial implications and new potentials for error.... Working through details of restroom innovation was an extra, one that burdened an already crowded agenda.[53]

The second reason the initiative failed had to do with discomfort with the very idea. The NYC Department of Buildings requires all large new buildings to install sex-segregated facilities, so the university had to submit a petition for an exemption. The city turned them down. The university appealed, but lost. The building commissioner expressed "concerns about security and liability."[54]

This result suited many of the future inhabitants of the building just fine, it turned out. Not everyone actually liked the idea of gender-neutral restrooms. Some of the female faculty cited the belief that men were messy, a discomfort with potential for male nudity, and a fear of meeting strange men in close quarters during off-hours. Meanwhile, the non-faculty staff generally was not on board with radically rethinking gender. They weren't gender radicals; they just wanted to pee in peace. Molotch's hopes for change were crushed.

As this example shows, doing things differently can be challenging on multiple fronts. This isn't to say that institutions can't be changed, but changing them requires a *collective* shift in norms and routines. Sometimes this simply means a slow but steady disinvestment in the old ways, like when school and workplace dress codes began to allow girls and women to wear pants. Other times, institutions change in response to shifts in the broader social structure, like when women entered the workforce during World War II.

Sometimes change is a result of the collective work of activists and politicians. It was this kind of work that resulted in the passage of Title IX, an amendment to the Civil Rights Act of 1964, which states, "No person in the United States shall, on the basis of sex, be excluded from participation in, be denied the benefits of, or be subjected to discrimination under any education program or activity receiving Federal financial assistance."[55] Passed in 1972, Title IX meant that schools and colleges receiving federal funding could not legally give preference to men. Instead, they had to allocate their resources to men and women in proportion to their interest and enrollment.

Here is where sports come back in. The intention of Title IX was to change the norms that gave preference to men in all sorts of fields, from medical schools to sports teams. Because most schools and colleges have extensive athletics departments, sports were included among the resources that schools were required to dole out fairly. Eventually, even grudging and partial compliance with the requirements of Title IX dramatically increased the opportunity for women to play sports (Figure 8.1). In the forty-five years since the passage of Title IX, the number of female athletes climbed more than tenfold among high school girls and more than threefold among college women. Today, 42 percent of high school athletes and 44 percent of college athletes are female.[56]

The changes in the institution of sport are visible in baseball. When Kay Johnston wanted to play Little League in 1950, she cut off her braids, put on her

FIGURE 8.1 | PARTICIPATION IN NCAA CHAMPIONSHIP SPORTS

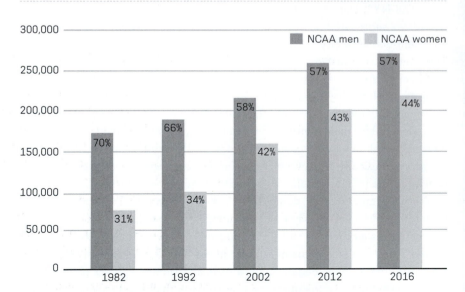

Source: NCAA, "45 Years of Title IX: The Status of Women in Intercollegiate Athletics," www.ncaa.org/sites/default/files/TitleIX45-295-FINAL_WEB.pdf.

Mo'ne Davis made the cover of *Sports Illustrated* for her Little League World Series shutout. Seen in the middle of what might be a 70 mph pitch, Davis is an example of what girls and women can do when they are given the opportunity.

brother's clothes, and signed up under the name "Tubby." She made the team, but when she was found out, the national organization instituted a formal policy forbidding girls from playing.[57] After Maria Pepe challenged this exclusion in 1972, the court decided in 1974 that antidiscrimination law demanded opportunities for girls to play Little League ball. Some of them have proved spectacularly good. Ten girls have played on boys' teams that made the Little League World Series, and Mo'ne Davis, a thirteen-year-old with a 70 mph fastball, pitched a shutout there in 2014.

Although most girls who play are still funneled into softball, athletes like Davis aren't taking no for an answer. And the people in charge of baseball are starting to notice. As a result, the idea of integrating baseball seems more possible than ever before. In 2016, another woman pitcher, Sarah Hudek, was awarded the first college baseball scholarship. In 2017, Major League Baseball invited one hundred girls to a "Trailblazer" weekend of competitive baseball, following up in 2018 with a "Breakthrough" series of invitational games to offer girls major league coaching and scouting.[58] Who knows what will happen next.

The remarkable increase in the number of women playing sports—from Little Leagues to the pros—reveals the power of institutions to shape the experience of individuals and change social ideas. New policies allowing women to play will shift norms, making the idea that women are biologically fated to lose to men seem less and less reasonable. Though we've got a long way to go, we've also come quite a long way from the Victorian idea that women are so weak they need a room to rest.

Institutions often resist change, but they are not unchangeable. When even a minority of people recognizes that institutionalized practices are cultural, not natural and inevitable, they open opportunities for themselves and others who want to do things differently. This isn't always easy, but it's always possible. And institutions never change unless people—like you—begin to question them. Taking chances and bucking expectations may not lead anywhere in your lifetime— both Kay "Tubby" Johnston and Maria Pepe were booted out of Little League— but, over time, a few rocks can become a landslide. In the moment, one never knows what small acts of defiance are making history, but one thing is for sure: history will be made.

Revisiting the Question

 When it comes down to it, regardless of social construction and social pressure, don't we live in a society in which it's possible to just be an individual?

When someone is so focused on the details that they miss the big picture, they are sometimes told they can't see the forest for the trees. Each tree is a unique individual well worth understanding, but together they form a landscape and an ecosystem that is equally important to understand. Thinking in terms of institutions reminds us to zoom out and look at the forest in which we live.

To understand gender, we need to examine the institutional structures and persistent patterns of interaction that are *our* landscape and ecosystem. Because these sometimes present men and women with different opportunities and obstacles, they produce gender difference and inequality regardless of the inclinations or attitudes of the people who move through them. It's not possible, then, to be just an individual. Some things simply resist our personal beliefs and desires about the way the world could or should be.

Once we recognize that some of the institutions central to our daily lives are strongly gendered, it becomes clear that, as sociologist Raewyn Connell once argued, there are "gender phenomena of major importance which simply cannot be grasped as properties of individuals."[59] Societies are bigger than the sum of their parts. Gender isn't just an individual phenomenon; it's an institutional one. These institutions present *real* opportunities and obstacles. Because institutions are designed to last, they prove hard to change. Policies will be stubbornly defended by those who benefit from them, and norms create habits and taken-for-granted expectations that are inherently sticky. Even when we can't just step out of line and change society to fit our own preferences, individuals working together absolutely can—and always have.

Next . . .

The end of this chapter marks the halfway point of this book. By now you have a strong understanding of how sociologists theorize gender as a set of ideas, a relationship between our bodies and our societies, a series of ongoing actions and interactions, and multiple interconnected institutions. Together they form the **gender order**, the social organization of gender relations in a society. The gender order is pervasive, expanding horizontally to affect all dimensions of a society and vertically to shape everything from the individual to the whole society. It intersects with other social hierarchies, establishing a matrix of domination that includes other inequalities, as well as gendered ones.

You've gained a set of theoretical tools to help you better understand what is going on around you and how your participation both affirms and disrupts gendered ideas, interactions, and institutions. The second half of this book takes a different approach. Using the theory you now know, it takes a closer look at some important parts of life: sexuality, family, the workplace, and politics. Before talking about where we are, however, it's helpful to talk about how we got here. The next chapter picks up where this one left off, with the process and politics of social change.

FOR FURTHER READING

Berger, Peter, and Thomas Luckmann. "Society as Objective Reality." In *The Social Construction of Reality: A Treatise on the Sociology of Knowledge*. Garden City, NY: Doubleday, 1966, 63–146.

Britton, Dana. "Gendered Organizational Logic: Policy and Practice in Men's and Women's Prisons." *Gender & Society* 11, no. 6 (1997): 796–818.

Cooky, Cheryl and Michael Messner. *No Slam Dunk: Gender, Sport, and the Unevenness of Social Change*. New Brunswick: Rutgers University Press, 2018.

Davis, Alexander K. "The Hidden Privilege in 'Potty Politics.'" *Contexts* 16, no. 3 (2017): 34–41.

Johnson, Allan. "Patriarchy, the System: An It, Not a He, a Them, or an Us." In *The Gender Knot: Unraveling Our Patriarchal Legacy*. Philadelphia: Temple University Press, 1997, 27–50.

McDonagh, Eileen, and Laura Pappano. *Playing with the Boys: Why Separate Is Not Equal in Sports*. New York: Oxford University Press, 2008.

THE ONLY LASTING TRUTH
IS CHANGE.

—OCTAVIA BUTLER

9

Change

We all know the scene. He gets down on one knee in a restaurant that is a tad above his price range. The ladies at the next table, spying him kneeling, clasp their hands to their chests and inhale. The room is suddenly hushed. All eyes turn toward the couple. Out pops the box. Her eyes widen; the bottom lashes moisten with the first sign of tears. He pushes out his arms, meaningfully pressing the box upward in her direction, imploring as he pulls back the velvety lid to reveal a glimmering dia . . . No, not a diamond. The ladies lean in. A thimble!

A small metal cap worn over the tip of one's finger to protect it from needle points was the engagement item of choice for early Americans.[1] It is just one of many items that have served as a symbol of a commitment to marry. Rings didn't become the standard sign of betrothal until the late 1800s and diamond rings only became standard later still, in the 1930s. Despite the hype about how "diamonds are forever," the diamond engagement ring is less than one hundred years old, with no guarantee of lasting into the next millennia.

Marriage is an institution, and a socially constructed one. Today we think about marriage as a source of love, care, and commitment, but it was and continues to also be governed by informal norms and formal laws that determine the rights and responsibilities of spouses. Marriage is also a gendered institution. It used to be much more so, with substantially fewer rights for women. Diamonds, it turns out, haven't always been a girl's best friend.

Marriage has changed and is changing still. The same can be said for the other institutions we address in this chapter: sexuality, family, and work. Like diamond rings, things that seem timeless are often recent and fragile inventions, including many of the things we take for granted as natural, normal, or inevitable today. This chapter offers a dynamic historical view of what often feel like static traditions. To begin, let's start with one undeniably transformative moment: the arrival of the Puritans on the rocky East Coast of the North American continent.

THE EVOLUTION OF SEX

The notion of the puritanical—zealous adherence to extraordinarily strict religious or moral rules—was named after the Puritans, and rightly so. They believed that sex should be restricted to intercourse in heterosexual marriage with the aim of reproduction. All nonmarital and nonreproductive sexual activities were forbidden, including pre- and extramarital sex, homosexual sex, masturbation, and oral or anal sex, even if married. Violations of the rules were punished by fines, whipping, public shaming, ostracism, or even death.

Women were thought to be especially vulnerable to sexual sin because they were believed to be more sexual than men. Men were socially constructed as stalwart, strong, stoic; women, in contrast, as unstable, indulgent, and emotional. The Puritans considered women to be a "weaker vessel" and, consequently, to have "less mastery over [their] passions."[2] In their reading of the Bible, Eve succumbed to the forbidden fruit not because she was curious, but because she couldn't restrain her desire. Men were supposedly more self-disciplined and concerned with more important things than sex.

The Puritans were downright scandalized by the sexual lives of North America's native residents.[3] They were organized into several hundred ethnolinguistic groups, so their practices and norms varied, but they were consistently more permissive than the Europeans. As we've previously discussed, many tribes accepted intercourse outside of committed relationships, both monogamy and polygamy were practiced, unions were formed and dissolved at will, and same-sex sex and gender nonconformity were accepted. Native Americans also often cared very little about whose child was whose. After the arrival of the French in the early 1600s, one Naskapi man was warned by a missionary that his failure to police his wife's sexual activity might result in her being impregnated by another man. He responded: "You French people love only your own children, but we all love all the children of our tribe."[4]

This Naskapi man could be rather nonchalant about both sexual behavior and parentage, in part because his tribe didn't subscribe to the idea of private property. His attitude is typical of **forager societies** that migrate seasonally, following crops and game across the landscape. Anthropologists and archaeologists have shown that both private property and patriarchy consistently emerge together as societies transition from foraging to settled **agrarian** societies, ones that cultivate domesticated crops.

Since for most of human history the only way to prove paternity was to control women, female sexual freedom is often curtailed when societies transition from forager to agrarian economies. Once communities put down roots, both literally and figuratively, there can be ownership of land. Once there is ownership of land, there can be the consolidation of wealth. Once wealth is consolidated, people become concerned with passing it down to heirs. And once people become concerned with passing down wealth, it becomes important to make sure wives don't become pregnant with other men's babies. The immigrants who came from Europe in the 1600s had already undergone this transition and, accordingly, they had very different ideas about the function of sex than the millions of American Indians who populated North America at the time.

PURITAN MORALITY ENFORCED.

Adherence to the Puritan moral code was often enforced by stringent punishments, such as being locked in stocks for the purpose of public humiliation.

Sex for Babies

Differences like those between American Indian tribes and the Puritan settlers are often described in cultural or religious terms, but there were concrete reasons, too, why the Puritans were so darn puritanical. The colonizers lived a fragile existence: Many people were dying from exposure, starvation, illness, and war. They were threatened with extinction, so reproduction was essential to the group's survival. This motivated the Puritans to channel their sex drive toward the one sexual activity that made babies: penile-vaginal intercourse. It was against the rules to do anything else and also against the rules to not do it. Having intercourse with your spouse was required; women who weren't getting pregnant were encouraged to divorce their husbands and marry new ones.[5]

Population concerns also led the Puritans to be quite forgiving when people broke the rules they held so dear. When there was survival in numbers, both ostracism and punishment by death harmed the community as well as the individual. So even though both men and women broke sexual rules routinely, the harsher penalties were rarely imposed. Instead, fines and public shaming served as a mechanism by which the Puritans could forgive sexual deviations. In other instances, settlers bent the rules for reasons related to the sex ratio. In the Chesapeake-area colonies, for example, men outnumbered women four to one.[6] Women were sparse, so even a "disgraced" woman could count on a man being happy to have her.

Like the rules that guide doing gender, the Puritans' sexual rules were designed to be broken, with exceptions made when it was for the colonists' greater good. They weren't so devoted to their moral principles, it turns out, that they weren't willing to break them for their own benefit. In addition to forgiving their own sins, including killing and raping Native peoples, they made it impossible for the African women and men they enslaved to follow their rules. Slaves were legally denied the right to marry, making nonmarital sex and childbearing inevitable.[7] In a cruel twist, white elites would claim that black "immorality" was "a natural inclination of the African race" in order to defend forced breeding and their rape of female slaves.[8] The colonists extolled godliness, but didn't extend to everyone the opportunity to be godly.

The colonists' sexual values and behaviors were shaped not by religion alone, but also by the rigors and culture of colonization and an economy based on the exploitation and dehumanization of Africans and Native peoples. Their belief in restricting sex to intercourse was compatible with their need to reproduce themselves. When it wasn't—when their population sustainability or economic viability was at stake—they were happy to look the other way, forgive misdeeds, or even make following the rules impossible. The Puritans surely earned their reputation, but beneath the strict rules were human beings who were fallible, rebellious, and brutally strategic.

Eventually the Puritans' approach to sexuality would fall victim to new and different institutional demands and opportunities: economic change, technological innovations, medical advances, and political upsets. One of those was the Industrial Revolution.

Sex for Love

Beginning in the 1700s and advancing through 1900, the Industrial Revolution first brought metal tools and steam-powered manufacturing, then factories, mechanization, and assembly lines. The need for labor drew many people out of small communities and into cities, where people were more densely packed and more anonymous.

This was a dramatic change. In pre-industrial agrarian societies, the majority of men and women both lived and worked at home, whether on their own farms or those of feudal lords. Together, moms, dads, daughters, and sons grew crops and tended orchards, fed and slaughtered pigs and chickens, milked cows and churned butter, pickled vegetables and salted meat, and made things like soap, candles, and clothes from scratch. Everyone needed to work together to make what they needed to survive. At this time, children were still a necessity. Babies quickly grew up to be helpers and then farmhands.

Industrialization undid all of this. First, it separated work from home. No longer sitting on fertile land, people increasingly had to leave the house to "go to work" in factories, mines, and shops that belonged to others. In return, they received money, their **wage**, with which they would go out and buy the things they once made. The process by which goods transition from something a family provided for itself into something bought with a wage is called **commodification**: the making of some-

In the era of tenement housing, large families in cramped quarters often necessitated the storage of toddlers in wire cages attached to the windows.

thing into a **commodity**, a thing that can be bought and sold.

The new industrial economy would dramatically change how people thought about reproduction. Though useful on farms, kids became a burden in cities, where lodging was expensive and overcrowded. This gave couples an incentive to have fewer children, and because industrial production had made condoms increasingly cheap and effective, they had the capacity to limit family size.[9] Marital fertility rates dropped dramatically between 1800 and 1900: from 6 or more children per woman to 3.5 in the United States, England, and Wales.[10]

In this context, a sexual ethic that restricted sex to efforts to make babies didn't make sense. People needed a new logic to guide sexual activity.[11] In response, over the course of the 1800s, Victorians slowly abandoned the idea that sex was only for reproduction, embracing the now familiar idea that sex could be an expression of love.[12] The Romantic Era had arrived.

The Victorians also introduced the **gendered love/sex binary**, a projection of the gender binary onto the ideas of love and sex, such that women are believed to be motivated by love and men by sex.[13] Dualistic thinking about the opposition of body and soul meant that if women were more romantic than men, they were also less carnal.[14] Reversing Puritan beliefs about women's voracious sexuality, the Victorians feminized love and masculinized sex.

Early feminists were among those who embraced these ideas. They advocated the idea that women took more naturally to both sexual moderation and romantic love. They thought they could convince their contemporaries that women were men's equals if they could persuade them that women were more spiritual. In an effort to attract and support female members, Protestant churches repeated these notions. As this idea spread throughout Victorian society, women were re-imagined as *naturally* chaste, innocent of the vulgar sexual desires felt by men, and motivated by love instead of lust.[15] Men, in contrast, were believed to be more deeply tied to their bodies, constantly torn between the carnal and the celestial. This is when the idea of "opposite sexes" really took hold, as did the **sexual double standard**, different rules for the sexual behavior of men and women.

The Victorians sustained the notion that women were free of sexual thoughts and men were dens of sexual depravity by giving men an outlet for their more perverse inclinations: prostitution. Early capitalism had worsened life for those at the very bottom.[16] Prostitution was a way for poor women to support themselves and their families. At the same time, it functioned to protect "the virgin of the wealthier classes and shield their married women from the grosser passions of their husbands."[17] By one estimate, London alone was home to 8,600 prostitutes in the mid-1800s. Manhattan had one prostitute for every sixty-four men, and there was one for every thirty-nine and twenty-six men in Savannah, Georgia, and Norfolk, Virginia, respectively.[18]

Just as Puritans had used the (impossible to avoid) sexual transgressions of enslaved Africans as proof of their inferiority, Victorian intellectuals would champion the purity of middle- and upper-class women and scorn the "uncivilized" sexual behavior of poor women.[19] Today we know this as the **good girl/ bad girl dichotomy**, the idea that women who behave themselves sexually are worthy of respect and women who don't are not.

At the time, all these ideas were radically new, and they would continue to evolve as American society entered the 1920s.

Sex for Pleasure

The 1920s was a period of economic prosperity, technological innovation, and artistic experimentation. Americans call this decade the Roaring Twenties; in France it is called the *Années Folles*, or the "Crazy Years."[20] This era saw the invention of "sexy," literally; the word was first recorded to mean "sexually attractive" in 1923.[21] The '20s were sexy because, unlike the countryside, the

The Charleston, a jaunty dance invented during the 1920s, allowed men and women to dance side by side as equals instead of together as a lead and follow.

city offered unsupervised mixed-sex mingling that lent itself easily to flirtation and romance.

Concentrations of people with money, free time, and the opportunity to socialize inspired the birth of mass entertainment. Amusement parks catered to flirtatious young people, "nickelodeons" showed newly invented moving pictures with larger-than-life seductions, and burlesque clubs kept the morality police at bay with pasties and G-strings. In Harlem and other centers of African American life, high-end clubs featuring black musicians attracted white patrons, encouraging racial integration and introducing them to a new form of music: jazz. Revelers danced the "hug me close" and the "hump-back rag" in dimly lit ballrooms where singers mastered the art of innuendo, singing "keep on churnin' till the butter come" and "it ain't the meat, it's the motion" (*not* songs about food). As historians John D'Emilio and Estelle Freedman wrote, "More and more of life, it seemed, was intent on keeping Americans in a state of constant sexual excitement."[22]

People in small communities, as well as in the upper classes, continued the Victorian tradition of "calling" in which young men were invited to the homes of young women for chaperoned visits. In cities, though, young working people invented "dating."[23] This wasn't dating as we know it today (an effort to find a romantic partner); it was a social strategy. In the interest of being seen and having fun, a successful dater would "go out" with a different person, preferably an attractive and well-regarded one, every night of the week.

Dating shifted the balance of power. Because it took place in the home, calling was an activity over which women had substantial control. Women decided who came over and when, how they socialized, and provided snacks or entertainments of their choice. As historian Beth Bailey writes, dating "moved courtship out of the home and into the man's sphere."[24] Whereas advice books during the Victorian era strongly discouraged men from calling without being invited, advice books on dating scolded women who would dare "usurp the right of boys to choose their own dates."[25]

Part of the reason men were accorded such an exclusive right involved the expense. Unlike calling, dating required that someone pay for the transportation, food, drink, and entertainment that the couple enjoyed. With no equal-pay laws protecting women's wages, working women could barely afford rent; entertainment was an impossible luxury.[26] This was the basis for **treating**, a practice through which a man funds a woman's night on the town. One government vice investigator, horrified by this new development, reported, "Most of the girls quite frankly admit making 'dates' with strange men. . . . These 'dates' are made with no thought on the part of the girl beyond getting the good time which she cannot afford herself."[27] The owners of establishments, hoping to keep the customers coming, worked hard to convince the public that "treating" was not tantamount to prostitution.

The inequitable responsibility for the cost of dating was not lost on men. Some were resentful of the fact that women now expected to go out on expensive dates. Men were nostalgic for the good old days of calling, which cost them nothing. For their part, women tried to make themselves, literally, worth it. This meant being an attractive and pleasing companion. Whereas for most of American history a plump and voluptuous body had been conflated with health and fertility, "reducing diets" suddenly became all the rage.[28]

Likewise, women began wearing makeup and nail polish, previously used only by sex workers. During the '20s an attractive face and body, as well as a certain degree of sexual accessibility, became more central to a woman's value. Claimed one ad:

> *The first duty of woman is to attract. It does not matter how clever or independent you may be, if you fail to influence the men you meet, consciously or unconsciously, you are not fulfilling your fundamental duty as a woman.*[29]

Cosmetics industry profits increased more than eightfold in just ten years, from $17 million in sales to $141 million.[30]

There were ways in which the '20s created new potential for gender equality, too. Women's growing freedom meant that men and women could mix socially

A lipstick advertisement from the 1930s emphasizes women's efforts to "fascinate" men while also stressing how "natural" rather than "theatrical" or "painted" she would appear.

and hold intimate conversations. Half of all women coming of age during the Roaring Twenties had premarital intercourse, and being a virgin at marriage was beginning to seem quaint. For middle-class men, this freedom meant that they could have sex with female peers instead of with poor women, women they enslaved, sex workers, and each other. These changes brought both men and women pleasure and paved the way for more gender-egalitarian relationships. Many young people were excited by this development and liked the idea of finding a partner who would be a "soul mate," someone who brought them joy and happiness.

Still, sex remained dangerous for women. With birth control information limited by law and still condemned by most churches, 28 percent of women became pregnant before marriage, up from 10 percent in 1850, a rise seen disproportionately among the urban working class.[31] Without a community in place to force men to "do the right thing," and with abortion newly illegal (in all states but one by 1910), women were more likely than those of earlier eras to have a child outside of marriage.[32] Since women were still paid wages much below men's, raising a child alone could lead to a lifetime of poverty, assuming the mother was not forced to hand over the child to an orphanage. In other words, while the 1920s was a time

The Roaring Twenties provided ample opportunity for working-class men and women to mingle and play out from under the watchful eyes of their parents.

of rising heterosexual opportunities, these opportunities came with huge costs to women.

The same was true for individuals who experimented with gender fluidity or experienced same-sex desire. Simply by virtue of crowding, cities made it possible for queer communities to emerge.[33] Meanwhile, the development of mass entertainment, and the sheer range of opportunities a large city could support, allowed sexual and romantic subcultures to thrive. As early as 1908 it was reported that "certain smart clubs [we]re well known for their homosexual atmosphere."[34] No longer tied as tightly to family farms on which biological reproduction—that is, heterosexuality—was a survival strategy, young people could consider putting their personal passions ahead of family responsibilities.[35]

The combination of industrialization, urbanization, the commercialization of leisure, and new freedoms for women all increased the ability of unmarried men and women to congregate without supervision. This freedom altered the environment in which sexuality was experienced, as well as the norms for sexual behavior. Eventually the lifestyle first enjoyed by working-class youth in cities would become "mainstream" and the expression of same-sex desire would become increasingly "normal." With the exception of a short-lived detour in the 1950s, the sexual attitudes and behaviors of young people have become increasingly permissive ever since.[36] Marital practices have changed just as dramatically.

THE EVOLUTION OF MARRIAGE

For thousands of years, marriage served economic and political functions unrelated to love, happiness, or personal fulfillment.[37] Prior to the Victorian era, love was considered a trivial basis for marriage and a bad reason to marry. There were much bigger concerns afoot: gaining money and resources, building alliances between families, organizing the division of labor, and producing legitimate male heirs. For the wealthy and, to some extent, the middle classes, marriage was important for maintaining and increasing the power of families. The concerns of the working classes were similar, if less grand: "Do I marry someone with fields near my fields?" "Will my prospective mate be approved by the neighbors and relatives on whom I depend?" "Would these in-laws be a help to our family or a hindrance?"[38] Marriages were typically arranged by older family members. They thought it foolish to leave something that important to the whims of young people.

These marriages were patriarchal in the original sense of the term. Men were heads of households and women were human property, equivalent to children, enslaved peoples, and servants. A woman was entered into a marriage by her father, who owned her until he "gave her away" at the wedding. We call these

patriarch/property marriages. The husband was the patriarch and his wife was his property.

This logic—that marriage is a form of property ownership—led to many laws that seem outrageous today. If an unmarried woman was raped, for instance, the main concern was the harm to her father's property. She became less valuable when she lost her virginity, so the rapist could make amends for the bad deed by marrying her. It was a "you break it, you buy it" rule. A wife who was believed to be infertile could be discarded, like a broken TV, as she was useless if she couldn't produce sons to pass on her husband's wealth, power, and legacy. If her husband died, she could be inherited like livestock. In many cultures, she was passed on to her husband's brother; the important thing was that her future children still carried her husband's last name.

Feminist activists of the 1800s and early 1900s fought to end patriarch/property marriages. One of the earliest feminist demands was for women to have the legal right to *own* property rather than *be* property. This right would eventually make many other rights possible: the right to vote and decide one's own citizenship; the right to work, keep one's own wages, and build financial credit; the right to have a voice in family decisions; and, if divorced, the right to ask for custody of one's children. All of these issues were part of early feminist struggles.

In response to feminist activism, as well as other forces, marriage would change. By the 1950s, on the heels of industrialization, a new kind of marriage would be institutionalized, the one that we typically and misleadingly call "traditional" today.

The Breadwinner/Housewife Marriage

Industrialization broke up the then-traditional family. As Americans were increasingly pulled into the workplace, husbands and fathers were replaced by employers. Capitalism valued cheap labor regardless of the costs to the family. Since the subordinate status of women and children made their labor especially cheap, capitalists were happy to employ them and pay them less. This drove men's wages down, leading them to fear the end of their authority over their wives and children. Now that even men had bosses, and economic survival depended on an entire family's income, a patriarch's role as head of household could be called into question. If he was no more valuable at work than she was, then gender would no longer organize day-to-day life and patriarchy would vanish.

Intellectuals of the time worried that capitalism would destroy the family completely, but instead of abandoning patriarchal marriage altogether—an option advocated by some at the time—men organized to modify and modernize patriarchy. They did so, in part, through unionization. Pushing back against capitalism, labor unions argued that working men had the right to be able to support

a "home and family" on their wages alone.[39] Through protests, strikes, and boy-
cotts, unions carved out a new way of life for adult white men. They instituted
laws meant to reduce competition among workers (restrictions on child labor and
legislation that barred women and men of color from well-paying jobs) and enable
men's wives to stay at home (child-rearing allowances and maternity leaves).

They eventually succeeded in institutionalizing a **family wage**: an income
paid to one male earner that was large enough to support a home, a wife, and
children. Built upon the family wage, a new kind of marriage emerged, the
breadwinner/housewife marriage: a separate but equal model of marriage
that defined men's and women's contributions as different but complementary.
Unlike patriarch/property marriage, breadwinner/housewife marriage did not
legally subordinate wives to husbands (that is, she was no longer his property),
but it did rigidly define roles: Women owed men domestic services (cleaning,
cooking, child care, and sex); in return, men were legally required to support
their wives financially. If either failed to play their part, they could sue for
breach of contract.

Some societies had stronger unions and, therefore, stronger breadwinner/
housewife policies than others. Europe went much further than the United States.
West Germany and the Netherlands, for example, paid women a wage for raising their children during the early months (and sometimes years), gave big tax
breaks to married couples with only one earner, and offered cash bonuses for
each child. Weaker "breadwinner policies" (in the United States) and stronger
ones (in much of Europe) made it more or less possible for men to support a
housewife, while pushing women out of the workforce with more or less force.

Policies put in place in the aftermath of World War II further changed how
Americans organized families. Most notably, during the '40s and '50s the U.S.
government collaborated with private investors to build suburbs and facilitate
homeownership. This was the birth of the "American dream." The G.I. Bill—
designed to reward soldiers and help them reintegrate into society—offered only
white male veterans college scholarships and cheap mortgages. Meanwhile,
the government funded the building of an interstate highway system that connected the cities to the countryside much more efficiently. This led to a boom
in housing developments, to which cities strung power lines and dug sewer
tunnels. These government investments transformed America into a land of
homeowners for the first time in history.

Home, though, was farther from work than ever and the growing distance
between the two cemented the idea of **separate spheres**, a masculinized
work world and a feminized home life. At work, male employees engaged in
production, the making of goods for sale. Since capitalism is a competitive system, factory owners pushed workers to be as efficient as possible. Men, then, were
pressed to become the kind of people capitalism found most useful: more interested in work than family and concerned with maximizing economic success.

After World War II, the U.S. government subsidized the building of the first suburbs, where normative ideas of the family came to be signified by a married man and woman with two to three fresh-faced, smiling children.

Living in such a world required that men master the qualities of competitiveness, aggression, and ruthlessness. "'It's a jungle out there,' says the stereotypical male provider when his wife and kids meet him at the door."[40]

Inside that door, he was supposed to find not just a house, but a home: a warm, comfortable space filled with people who cared for him. There would be his loving children, doting wife, and devoted dog. Under the glow of their admiration, he could recharge to fight another day. At home there was supposedly no production, only **reproduction**, the making and nurturing of human beings.

In creating this environment, women were expected to specialize in a particular kind of supportive and loving emotional work that society needed. The notion that women could and should wholeheartedly embrace this work is called the **cult of domesticity**.[41] It emerged as an idea during the Victorian era—at the same time that we feminized the idea of love—and spread downward through the social classes along with homeownership and the family wage. Together with the ideology of separate spheres, the cult of domesticity protected at least one part of life from the harsh capitalist values of rationality and cost-benefit analysis.

This was an entirely different kind of family. In the mixed-sex environments innovated in the 1920s and mainstreamed over the next several decades, men and women met and got to like one another. They married by choice and were expected to find comfort in their relationship. But becoming whole in the process of marriage meant joining the feminine and the masculine together into one household. Doing this required strict enforcement of gender roles, heterosexuality, and monogamy, leading to a short-lived and uneasy experiment: 1950s America.

THE FUNNY '50S

The icon of Rosie the Riveter signifies the work opportunities offered to women during World War II. In fact, women did enter many occupations previously dominated by men. After the war ended in 1945, however, they were subject to a countercampaign designed to push them back into the home. Marketers, columnists, scientists, public intellectuals, and the U.S. government all decried the undoing of the new breadwinner/housewife family, defending its gender-specific family roles as natural. This resulted in a concerted entrenchment of the nuclear family. As the historian Stephanie Coontz explains:

> At the end of the 1940s, all the trends characterizing the rest of the twentieth century suddenly reversed themselves. For the first time in more than one hundred years, the [average] age for marriage and motherhood fell, fertility increased, divorce rates declined, and women's degree of educational parity with men dropped sharply. In a period of less than ten years, the proportion of never-married persons declined by as much as it had during the entire previous half century.[42]

All of these trends would reverse within a few decades. Historically speaking, then, middle-class marriages in the 1950s were *weirdly* family oriented.

The era was unusually conservative in other ways, too. If city life in the 1920s was high energy, sexy, and fun, the 1950s was relatively prudish. The government passed decency standards for Hollywood movies, ensuring that sex was kept off the screen and bad things always happened to "bad" girls. In 1952, books and magazines with sexual content were banned. Comic books were considered especially corrupting. In an official report, Congress argued that comic books gave "short courses in . . . rape, cannibalism, carnage, necrophilia, sex, sadism, masochism, and virtually every other form of crime, degeneracy, bestiality, and horror."[43]

Likewise, the idea that women were uninterested in sexual pleasure made it inconceivable that women felt for women what men felt for them. No matter how close women were, or what they did together, no one imagined it to be *sexual*. Out from under any suspicion of lesbianism, women formed intimate and romantic relationships with each other. Correspondence between women during this time is full of language like the one found in this letter that Jeannie wrote to Sarah in 1864:

> *Dear darling Sarah! How I love you & how happy I have been! You are the joy of my life. . . . I cannot tell you how much happiness you gave me, nor how constantly it is all in my thoughts. . . . My darling how I long for the time when I shall see you. . . . Goodbye my dearest, dearest lover . . . A thousand kisses . . . I love you with my whole soul.*[44]

It sounded like friendship at the time. Maybe it was, but maybe not.

In the 1920s, college girls breathlessly described girls on whom they were **smashing**, a term they used to describe a same-sex crush.[45] These crushes weren't all platonic. In a survey of 1,200 female college graduates from the 1920s, 28 percent of women enrolled in single-sex schools reported that they had been in a sexual relationship with another woman, along with 20 percent of women at mixed-sex schools.[46] They would write letters to their mothers about it. No one thought it odd. Instead, it was believed to be a normal developmental phase. So long as young women eventually married men, sexual and romantic relationships with other girls were considered harmless.

Americans in the '50s felt quite differently, though, about intimate relationships between men.[47] In the United States, the idea of a homosexual *person*, as opposed to a person who engages in homosexual *practices*, was new. The Puritans were familiar with homosexual behavior, but it had never occurred to them that particular people were distinctively homosexual. In their view, all humans were brimming with the potential for sin. Variation in how likely a person was to have sex with someone of the same sex was considered a measure of how godly they were, not an innate preference for one sex or the other.[48] While Puritans who felt same-sex desire may have experienced guilt and shame, they would not have paused to wonder if they were different kinds of people than anyone else.

The idea that a person could be a homosexual didn't become a part of the collective consciousness until World War II. One out of every eight American males—almost every young, fit man between eighteen and twenty-six years old—served in the war.[49] As a result, unmarried people on both the front lines and the home front found themselves largely in the company of the same sex. Indulging in homoerotic encounters became easier and more tempting. Wrote one young man: "The war is a tragedy to my mind and soul . . . but to my physical being, it is a memorable experience."[50] World War II was so conducive to exploring same-sex attraction that it's been called "a nationwide 'coming out' experience."[51]

With this newly imagined possibility, some soldiers rejected conventional heterosexuality and, after the war, instead pursued a gay "lifestyle."[52] The first gay bars in the United States opened in the 1940s and the first gay advocacy

A housewife stops to feed her son while in the midst of ironing, as the Army–McCarthy hearings of 1954 play on television. The politics of the 1950s were aimed at rooting out "communist" ideas like child care and gender equality.

organization would be founded in 1951.[53] Notably, these new communities were mostly for men. Gay women would remain less visible to the public and each other, at least for a while. Women in same-sex relationships were still often read by others as "celibate" spinsters.[54] Alongside poor mothers, many of these pioneered the field of social work; they were allowed to take such a public role specifically because they had no husbands or children.

Growing awareness and more community among men who identified as gay invoked a backlash. Cities passed laws saying alcohol couldn't be sold to gays and lesbians and they outlawed same-sex dancing and cross-dressing.[55] In response to the so-called homosexual menace, the U.S. government sought to purge men who had sex with men from public jobs on the assumption that they were "by definition morally bankrupt and, as such, politically suspect."[56] Much of the private sector followed suit. We often discuss this as a time when the government was focused on identifying and expelling Communists, but it was more common for people to lose their jobs for suspicion of homosexuality. Senator Joe McCarthy, famous for these efforts, said that anyone who opposed him was "either a Communist or a cocksucker."[57] "Mannish" unmarried women were also often fired or forced to quit. Refusing to perform a feminine apologetic at work, they were suspected of gender deviance and considered a threat to "normal" families.

The politics of the 1950s were unique. They were unusually family focused, conformist, pro-censorship, and gender policing. We know from the Puritans, though, and from the burgeoning queer communities at the time, that communities don't always behave in ways that live up to mainstream values. What was happening behind the closed doors of so-called traditional marriage?

Sex and Marriage in the '50s

A young woman in the 1950s might have been seriously concerned about her marriage prospects. Hundreds of thousands of men had been killed in the war and tens of thousands of soldiers married foreign women while abroad.[58] *The New York Times* reported that 750,000 young women would likely never marry. The process of securing a husband, then, became serious business. So while it may have made sense to go out with a different guy each night in the 1920s, flitting from guy to guy didn't seem so smart when there weren't enough guys to go around. Accordingly, during the 1950s dating was being edged out by a new practice, **going steady**, an often short-lived, but still exclusive, public pairing off. Going steady was "social security"; it ensured that a girl would always have a date on important nights and lessened the chances that she would end up an "old maid."[59]

In the 1950s, the custom of going steady among teenagers guaranteed that girls would have companions to institutionally organized events, such as the senior prom, and facilitated both romantic and sexual experimentation.

Ironically, this interest in marriage accelerated premarital sexual experimentation in exactly the decade known most for its conservatism.[60] Compared to couples who might enjoy just one night together, couples that went steady were more likely to "neck" (kissing on the neck and mouth), "pet" (touching below the neck), or "go all the way." Adults objected to these new trends but couldn't stop them. Necking and petting, if not intercourse, were becoming expected parts of any youthful romantic relationship. According to one 1952 advice manual, if a girl "wishes to be a member of the dating group," then "mild sexual contact" is "one of the requirements."[61]

Despite the conservative overtones, the undercurrent of the 1950s—represented by the swinging hips of Elvis and the flamboyance of Little Richard—was a sexy one. Meanwhile, the new ubiquity of the automobile did for suburban youth of the '50s what living in cities had done for the working-class youth of the '20s: It provided the opportunity to socialize without parental supervision. Hence the invention of "parking," driving off to a remote location, pulling off the road, and necking, petting, or more in the backseat.

Emotionally intense relationships led to sex and the highest rate of teen pregnancy in American history. At its peak in 1957, one out of every ten women aged fifteen to nineteen gave birth.[62] But there was no teen pregnancy crisis. Instead of a rash of single teen mothers, the age of marriage dropped to a one-hundred-year low and babies born "premature" (healthy-weight babies that arrived less than nine months after the wedding) reached a one-hundred-year high. At the end of the Victorian era, the median age at first marriage was twenty-six for men, twenty-two for women, and rising. By 1950, it had dropped to twenty-three for men and twenty for women, and it would remain this way throughout the decade (Figure 9.1).[63]

Eventually it would be impossible to pretend that either the youth or the adults in the 1950s were sexual goody-goodies. The fable was dealt a heavy blow with the publication of sexologist Alfred Kinsey's elaborate and extensive reports on the sexual behavior of 18,000 men and women.[64] Published in 1948 and 1953, his books sold a quarter of a million copies. They roundly discredited the idea that it was only teenagers who were breaking the sexual

FIGURE 9.1 | MEDIAN AGE AT FIRST MARRIAGE, 1900–2017

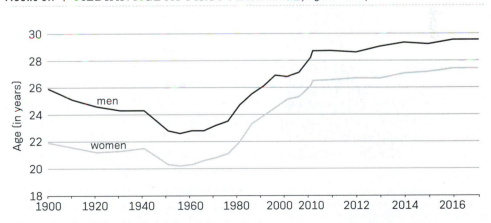

Source: U.S. Census Bureau, Current Population Survey, Annual Social and Economic Supplements, 2017 and earlier.

rules, revealing that premarital "petting" was nearly universal, 90 percent of men and 50 percent of women had premarital sex, 90 percent of men and 60 percent of women masturbated, and 50 percent of men and 25 percent of women had had extramarital sex. A third of men and 13 percent of women reported having homosexual sex, while a full 50 percent of men and 37 percent of women reported same-sex attraction. The cat was out of the bag.

If sex was hiding behind the happy innocence of poodle skirts and saddle shoes, unhappy marriages were disguised by the flower beds and fresh lawns of suburban homes. By 1963, the game was up. A book called *The Feminine Mystique* forever changed the way America thought of housewives. The title referred to a mythology—the idea that women were gleefully happy as wives and mothers—that strongly contrasted with reality. Written by feminist Betty Friedan, it documented widespread unhappiness among middle-class married women in the 1950s and 1960s. Writes Friedan:

> *Each suburban wife struggled with it alone. As she made the beds, shopped for groceries, matched slipcover material, ate peanut butter sandwiches with her children, chauffeured Cub Scouts and Brownies, lay beside her husband at night—she was afraid to ask even of herself the silent question—"Is this all?"*[65]

The book spent six weeks on *The New York Times* best seller list; its first printing sold 1.4 million copies.[66] Women wept with recognition, claiming that it was a "bolt of lightning," a "revelation," a "bombshell."[67] Friedan's book revealed the cracks in the breadwinner/housewife model, fault lines that would contribute to its demise.

STRAINED BY SEPARATE SPHERES While people were now marrying for love, the separate roles of breadwinner and housewife—with the husband working overtime and the wife busy with children and housework—drained the life out of the friendships that couples had built before marrying. The differences in their daily lives left them strangers to one another. Less than a third of spouses described their marriages as "happy" or "very happy."[68]

Stranded in the suburbs and with few other adults to talk to, privileged wives living the American dream often felt isolated, lonely, and bored. Many had earned college degrees and resented being pushed out of the workforce at the end of World War II.[69] Instead of finding housework and child care endlessly stimulating and enjoyable, many chafed under the expectation that they would find fulfillment this way.[70] Gleaming linoleum could only bring so much joy. Child care was tedious and tiring. They worried that their brains were wasting away while they did endless rounds of shopping, cooking, and cleaning. When *Redbook* asked readers to send letters about "Why Young Mothers Feel

Trapped," 24,000 women responded.[71] One 1950s housewife described her life as nothing but "booze, bowling, bridge, and boredom."[72]

There was, indeed, lots of drinking. Behind the flirty cocktails of the 1950s—the Pink Squirrel and the Singapore Sling—were women drinking just to get through the day. Drugs, too. Pharmaceutical companies developed "daytime sedatives for everyday" in response to housewives' complaints.[73] Unheard of in the mid-fifties, in 1958 doctors prescribed 462,000 pounds of tranquilizers; that number more than doubled the next year.[74] White middle-class women—the group most likely to be in a breadwinner/housewife marriage—were four times as likely to take them as any other type of person.[75] "Many suburban housewives were taking tranquilizers like cough drops," wrote Friedan.[76] The pills were known, colloquially, as "mother's little helpers."

Wives weren't the only ones unhappy, though. Marriage was essentially compulsory for men; often jobs and promotions depended on their ability to show that they were good family men. Bachelors were considered immature ("Why can't he settle down?") or deviant ("Is he a homosexual?"). Meanwhile, men were wary of women who saw them only as a "meal ticket," or felt overwhelmed by being the only person on whom their wives could rely for emotional support, not to mention adult conversation. A whole genre of humor emerged, designed to resonate with men's own sense of being trapped (hence the idea of the wife as a "ball and chain").

Tapping into this sentiment, Hugh Hefner launched *Playboy* magazine in 1953. Hefner changed ideas about masculinity.[77] Encouraging men to stay single and avoid commitment, he mainstreamed the notion of a man who didn't marry but was anything but gay. As the writer Barbara Ehrenreich explained, "The playboy didn't avoid marriage because he was a little bit 'queer,' but, on the contrary, because he was so ebulliently, even compulsively heterosexual."[78] Hefner introduced a new set of gender rules for men that rewarded men's resistance to marriage and monogamy, leading to the still-present myth that men must be dragged, kicking and screaming, to the altar.[79]

Both men and women, then, enjoyed fantasizing about a life without a spouse, kids, and a mortgage, but it was women who were truly vulnerable in marriage.

SEPARATE AND UNEQUAL While both men and women had their dissatisfactions, women carried virtually all the risks of a breadwinner/housewife marriage. These marriages weren't overtly patriarchal—just as the Victorian ladies had hoped, women were now seen as men's equals: different and complementary instead of better and worse—but women were still financially dependent on men. In classic androcentric fashion, the masculine sphere of work was evaluated as important and admirable, while the feminine sphere of the home was seen as somehow less so.

Hugh Hefner, the founder of *Playboy*, exemplifies a new ideal of masculinity that was becoming hegemonic in the supposedly staid 1950s.

The imbalance in the value attributed to work and home was literal. Men's work was *worth* something; they received a wage in exchange for it. In contrast, women were working in and around the home just as they'd been doing since agrarian times but getting less credit for it than ever. Capitalist rationality and the new golden rule—he who has the gold makes the rules—replaced explicit patriarchy. It wasn't his penis anymore that made him the "head of household"; it was his paycheck.

Prior to industrialization, women's labor—both the work of maintaining a household and the birthing and rearing of children—was understood to be *work*. After industrialization, however, with the separation of work from home, women's labor seemed to disappear; it was men who "went to work," while women just "stayed home." Because women's work was newly invisible, housewives seemed dependent on men, but not vice versa. Her dependence on his wage was obvious to everyone, but his dependence on her cooking, cleaning, shopping, and child care often was not.

To be fair, a housewife would be in big trouble if she lost her breadwinner, but a breadwinner needed his housewife, too. Without her, he had hungry, dirty, misbehaving children he couldn't leave alone, plus no clean clothes to wear, an empty belly, nothing in the fridge, and a filthy house. He either had to stay home himself or hire someone to replace his wife. Even a family wage wasn't designed to support a house, children, *and* a full-time, paid babysitter and housekeeper, though; it relied on him getting the domestic work for free. So, the degree to which wives supported husbands' breadwinning activities was swept under the rug, so to speak.

Middle- and upper-class women didn't just become unpaid and unrecognized housewives, they also gave up incomes of their own, the likelihood of having a successful career in the future, and the status that comes with doing work deemed important. All this was theoretically fine *if* the marriage lasted, her husband valued her contribution, and he consistently earned a good income. If the marriage fell apart—if the husband couldn't hold up his end of the bargain or traded her in for a younger, more attractive, or more submissive woman—wives could end up divorced and destitute, often with children. This was not an unlikely scenario; between a quarter and a third of marriages in the 1950s ended in divorce.

The government tried to protect "displaced homemakers," as they were called, by requiring alimony (monthly cash payments to ex-wives from their former husbands) and making divorce legally difficult (by requiring proof that a spouse had broken the marriage contract, for example), but marriage remained an intrinsically risky bet for women. Pretty soon the idea that they needed to secure their own future incomes and opportunities "just in case" carried quite a bit of weight.

Women looked to the workplace for answers.

GOING TO WORK

At the same time that the breadwinner/housewife model was emerging as the societal ideal, women were leaving the home to go to work. Even at its height, the 1950s version of the traditional marriage was more myth than reality. Due to legal discrimination, the family wage was elusive for most men of color and immigrant men. Black soldiers were excluded from the G.I. Bill that made the American dream a reality for white soldiers. They didn't get the college loans and mortgages that launched white families into the middle class and, even if they could afford to move into the suburbs without government help, most of these communities explicitly barred black people. As a result, many black families were left behind in cities that governments neglected. Even among native-born, white families, only a third could survive on a single wage. Poor women and women of color entered the wage economy from the beginning and stayed there.

Soon middle-class white women were joining them. Before 1940, more than 80 percent of women who married left the labor force on their wedding day and never came back.[80] In the next twenty years, the proportion of married women who worked doubled.[81] Most of these were "returning workers," mothers of somewhat older children who were willing to give up sewing their children's clothes

FIGURE 9.2 | COMPOSITION OF FEMALE LABOR FORCE BY
MARITAL STATUS, 1890–1980

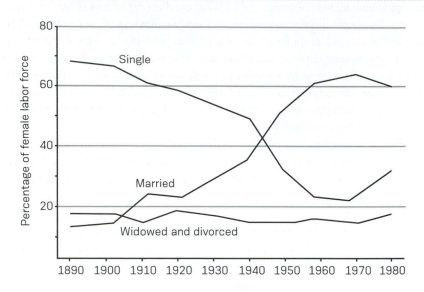

Source: Lynn Weiner, *From Working Girl to Working Mother: The Female Labor Force in the United States, 1820-1980*
(Chapel Hill: University of North Carolina Press, 1986).

and baking bread and cookies in exchange for the money to buy these products.
Buying rather than making was a sign of status, a boon to the economy, and
something the kids wanted because they now saw these products on TV.

These women filled the offices of the growing corporate class, often serving
as secretaries to white-collar men, whose managerial jobs were also becoming
more common.[82] Mirroring the breadwinner/housewife at home, "office wives"
filled an important role in the expanding economy. The newly visible "middle
class"—sitting between manual workers and corporate bosses—opened doors
for more and more women to work for pay. By the 1960s, when Betty Friedan
challenged the "feminine mystique," women were already deciding they wanted
a public as well as a domestic life.

The economy also needed more workers.[83] Between the loss of more than a
quarter million men in World War II and a low birthrate during the 1920s and
1930s, America had lost a substantial stock of the working population.[84] In order
to keep churning, the economy had to incorporate all kinds of women, not just
poor women (who had always worked) and young women (who often worked
between high school graduation and marriage).[85] To do so, rules that limited
women's working were often discarded.

Beginning in the late 1800s, for example, **marriage bans**—policies against employing married women—were common in banking, teaching, office work, and government jobs. A majority of U.S. school districts had bans against hiring married women, as did over half of all firms employing office workers.[86] Bans were expanded to manufacturing work during the 1930s in an effort to save jobs for men during the turmoil of the Great Depression. After the war, however, these bans began to seem harmful to the economy and bad for employers, who wanted all their options. By 1951, the percent of school districts that had a marriage ban had dropped from 87 to 18 percent, though pregnancy bans were often put in their place.

Even as marriage bans were being discarded by most industries, many other policies were more resistant to change. These included **protective legislation**, policies designed to protect women and children from exploitation by restricting their workplace participation. Beginning in the mid-1800s, almost every American state passed some protectionist laws.[87] These became national in the 1920s, and banned women from working long hours, doing night work, lifting even moderate weights, or taking dangerous jobs (though exceptions were made for jobs like waitressing, housekeeping, and nursing that were "for women" regardless of these demands).

Protectionist laws were rationalized on the belief that all women were or would be mothers, and that the state needed to protect their reproductive capacities.[88] While some feminists objected and resisted these laws, poorer women were glad to have them. Women who were more concerned with being able to get promotions or enter jobs that these laws kept out of reach were ready to see them go, along with the barriers that schools and employers created to keep women from getting degrees in law, medicine, and aviation.[89]

They recognized protective legislation as benevolent sexism; the laws used the language of protection to slot young women into largely dead-end jobs. The assumption that women were unsuited for certain kinds of work, or that they would quit or be fired upon pregnancy, was a disincentive to both women and employers in the 1950s and 1960s.[90] For women, extended schooling and training might make it more likely that they would marry a man with a promising career (get an "MRS degree," as it's jokingly called), but it was unlikely to have any payoff in the workplace. Employers were loath to put any time into on-the-job training for women on the assumption that they'd work five to seven years and then quit upon marriage and not come back. Training them for professions was pretty much out of the question. Instead, women were largely hired into jobs that offered them little or no chance of building skills or moving up a promotion ladder.

In 1964 this type of discrimination against women became illegal in the United States. In a last-ditch effort to ensure that a bill mandating equal treatment of African Americans would fail, Virginia Democrat Howard Smith added "sex" to the Civil Rights Act, thus including sex in the list of characteristics against which workplace discrimination would be illegal: race, color, religion, and national origin.[91] He thought the idea of equal treatment for men and women was so preposterous that it would surely kill the bill. Much to his chagrin and surprise, it passed anyway. Only in part an accident (there were women in Congress who worked to make Smith's joke a reality), the Civil Rights Act made it illegal to discriminate against women in the workplace.[92]

The enforcement of this law, however, was not automatic. Women had to fight to make it happen. The National Organization for Women, for example, stepped up to challenge the then-prevalent practice of segregating all job advertisements by sex category. They argued that advertising job opportunities with "help wanted—female" or "help wanted—male" was discriminatory. When the courts agreed, it meant that women were no longer just pulled into the labor force where employers wanted them but could at least try to choose their work-life plans for themselves.

As the economy grew and demographics changed through the 1950s and 1960s, married women and mothers of older children increasingly entered the workforce. As their numbers climbed but their opportunities were blocked, women's discontent grew—both with the current system of employment and with the breadwinner/housewife marriage as a system. By the end of the 1960s, quite a few women were angry about the mix of devaluation and restricted choices that they faced in trying to create a life strategy that would combine work and family.[93]

They set out to change that. By 1980, 51 percent of all women were employed, and married and single women were employed at equal rates. Even 40 percent of mothers with children under eighteen had at least a part-time job.[94]

WORK AND FAMILY TODAY

In 2003, James Dobson Jr., founder of Focus on the Family, wrote: "Unless we act quickly, the family as it has been known for 5,000 years will be gone."[95] The truth is, the patriarch/property marriage was already gone and the breadwinner/housewife marriage was fading fast. Even in the 1950s, the strength of the family wage on which the breadwinner/housewife model depended was waning. The economy was changing in ways that made marriage less essential. It was becoming increasingly easy for a man of means to buy a housewife's services in the market. Dinner could be eaten at restaurants; maids could clean his house and wash his laundry; and female companionship (both free and paid) was a cocktail lounge away. If many of the services of a housewife could be obtained in the marketplace, why should men marry at all?

For women, too, marriage was slowly becoming less essential. The Civil Rights Act, alongside later antidiscrimination laws, began to be enforced in the 1970s. The 1972 law against discrimination in schooling opened up a number of professional doors that had been firmly bolted. Women began to look at college degrees as more than just a good way to find a husband. They began streaming into professional education just as the United States was transitioning from an industrial economy founded on production to a **service and information economy**, one dependent on jobs focused on providing services for others (such as waiting tables, working in nail salons, or providing administrative assistance) or working with ideas (like engineers, computer programmers, and college professors).

If a woman could earn a wage herself, a state of financial dependence was less attractive. Since men created more housework than they contributed, even though she couldn't afford outside help, she had fewer chores to do without a husband around.[96] Given how risky marriage was for women, and its questionable benefits, holding out until she could find a husband with whom she could innovate a new model of marriage, or not marrying at all, seemed like a fine idea to some women.

Divorce laws changed, allowing both men and women to initiate proceedings without proving infidelity, physical abuse, or failure to provide economic support.[97] More women were deciding that an uncooperative husband—one who kept them from returning to school or work when the children were older or who failed to do his share of the housework—was something they could do without. Women themselves began some divorce proceedings, even though their living standards fell much more than men's did.[98]

Just like when gay-identified men began building lives outside of the breadwinner/housewife marriage, women's attempts to do so invoked a backlash. Phyllis Schlafly, a vocal anti-feminist campaigner of the 1970s, denounced such women as "runaway wives" and fought the emergence of new feminist social services like shelters for women fleeing domestic violence or hotlines offering support to rape victims.[99] The long-running "mommy wars" were stoked by the media, pitting mothers excited by new employment opportunities against those who feared that these new options for women would further devalue the work they did at home.[100]

Most women, though, wanted both: to achieve what came to be called "work-life balance." This was something, in fact, that almost all women wanted: poor women in bad working conditions were more likely to want better jobs than no job at all, while even women with great professional opportunities struggled with the responsibilities at home.[101] To strike a work-life balance, women needed more than nondiscrimination laws. They needed pro-family policies that acknowledged that some workers didn't have wives at home taking care of all their domestic needs. Pretty soon men would want and need this, too.

Balancing Work and Family

The breadwinner/housewife model of marriage makes even less sense now than it did in the 1950s. Both men and women are now increasingly educated and employed for longer periods of their lives. Age at first marriage and first birth has bounced back up. The expectation that women will leave the labor force permanently when they have their first child, let alone at marriage, has vanished, as has the idea that a man becomes a good father merely by dropping his paycheck on the table. Fathers who are engaged with their wives in the day-to-day work of parenting and mothers who work are the norm rather than the exception. If they need to, both men and women can do without marriage. And, if they do marry, they will need a model of marriage that fits with the more gender-egalitarian demands of the new economy.

In response, the breadwinner/housewife ideal has been replaced by an idealized **partnership marriage**, a model of marriage based on love and companionship between two equals who negotiate a division of labor unique to each couple. The law has cleared the way for such marriages. In response to over a century of feminist activism and demands, the marriage contract today is almost entirely gender neutral, providing the same rights and responsibilities to men and women. Both men and women are now responsible for paying alimony to a spouse who spent time out of the workforce to take care of the family. A male widower can now collect his wife's Social Security check instead of his own (in the 1950s, 1960s, and 1970s, only bereaved wives could do this). Men no longer have special rights to manage the family money. Nearly all states now confer equal standing to both spouses in issues of child custody.

Because partnership marriage involves a gender-neutral contract, married couples are free to organize their lives however they wish. And they do. Coontz writes:

> *Almost any separate way of organizing caregiving, childrearing, residential arrangements, sexual interactions, or interpersonal redistribution of resources has been tried by some society at some point in time. But the coexistence in one society of so many alternative ways of doing all of these different things—and the comparative legitimacy accorded to many of them—has never been seen before.*[102]

Today we see family-focused dual-earner couples (working part-time and taking turns caring for kids) and work-focused dual-earner couples (working overtime and hiring gardeners, maids, and nannies). We see male breadwinners married to housewives and, in small but growing numbers, female breadwinners married to househusbands, too. Gay couples adopt all these family forms as well. Grandparents are stepping back in to offer child care and income support in a way that had become rare in the 1950s nuclear family model of the suburbs.[103]

Increasingly, the idea of nonmonogamous, polyamorous unions of more than two people and open relationships in which couples negotiate extra-pair sex are part of the conversation about what relationships can look like.

Marriage no longer determines one's living arrangements. While it remains the norm that couples will live together once married, some don't. Some live in separate cities either by choice or circumstance while others live in the same town but choose to live apart, a phenomenon referred to as "living apart together."[104]

While marriage is still normative, it is not so surprising anymore when people reach their thirties, forties, or fifties without marrying.[105] Just half of U.S. adults today are married and about one in seven lives alone.[106] It's totally normal to be single, even as a "grown-up." While it may be preferable to some, marriage is no longer necessary for entrance to adulthood, nor is it a prerequisite for having a child. It is certainly no longer a job requirement. It's rarely used, at least explicitly, to cement political alliances or hoard wealth.

For these reasons, marriage itself is less necessary than it was in the past, so much so that we might ask whether it is still a major institution. Some people choose to live together without being married, others neither marry nor cohabit. Nearly half of Americans (44 percent) have lived with someone without being married.[107] Fully 41 percent of nonmarried people say they don't want to marry or are not sure.[108] Parenting now occurs in the absence of marriage. Today 40 percent of children are born to unmarried parents.[109] A majority of Americans (86 percent) say that a single parent and a child "count" as a family. Meanwhile, about one in five Americans is freely choosing not to have children.

Since the primary reason to marry in Western cultures today is still love, marriages are both more voluntary and less stable. As Stephanie Coontz explains, the "same things that made marriage become such a unique and treasured personal relationship during the last two hundred years, paved the way for it to become an optional and fragile one."[110] People divorce. When they do, they often take children with them, sometimes into new marriages, creating "blended families." A third of Americans have a step- or half-sibling and 13 percent are raising stepchildren.[111] The high rate of divorce does not signal a decline in the value of marriage. Instead, Americans engage in what sociologist Andrew Cherlin calls the "marriage-go-round": they both marry *and* divorce more frequently than people in other countries.

Since marriage is more about choice and pleasure than ever, it makes sense to some to reduce further the rules about who can marry whom.[112] In 1967 the United States Supreme Court struck down laws against interracial marriage and, in 2015, the Court made same-sex marriage legal in all fifty U.S. states. A majority of Americans believe that sexual minorities deserve the same rights as heterosexuals.[113] Citizens of many other countries agree: Same-sex marriage rights are now the law in Argentina, Australia, Belgium, Brazil, Canada, Columbia, Denmark, England and Wales, Finland, France, Germany, Greenland,

Since the Supreme Court made same-sex marriage legal in 2015, same-sex couples in many states have exercised their right to marry.

Iceland, Ireland, Luxembourg, Malta, the Netherlands, New Zealand, Norway, Portugal, Scotland, South Africa, Spain, Sweden, and Uruguay. These decisions are increasingly paving the way for trans men and women to be able to marry whomever they choose without scrutiny.

Despite the ascendance of this new partnership model, the degendering of marriage law, and the legalization of same-sex marriage, the breadwinner/housewife model still echoes through our personal lives and political debates. It competes with and sometimes lives quietly alongside the partnership model, producing the types of trouble that contradictions cause. Still, despite the trouble, and despite the clamor to return to the breadwinner/housewife model of marriage, partnership marriage is here … maybe not to stay, but for now.

CONCLUSION

When you hear people defend the idea of "traditional marriage," you would be smart to ask which one they mean. The patriarch/property model of marriage reigned supreme for thousands of years, while the breadwinner/housewife model was but a blip on the historical timeline. Today's marriage contract reflects a partnership model that facilitates personalization. The unprecedented diversity in family forms found in Western societies today reflects the choices we are now able to make.

The institution of marriage has changed not only because feminists insisted that it was unfair to women, but also because of shifts in the institutions with which marriage intersects: industrialization, the rise of cities and then suburbs, the demands of capitalism, global competition, technological innovation, and more. Political activism and changing socioeconomic relations have changed marriage as well as other institutions, warping and tweaking all of them separately and together.

All the other institutions we discussed in this chapter are also changing. Even sexual practices aren't simply driven by values or nature but reflect shifts in opportunity provided by technological, economic, political, and demographic change. Likewise, the workplace has evolved, pushing and pulling men and women into different kinds of work and changing and being changed by their relationships in the home. When we take the long view, we see tumultuous upheaval of social norms and institutions, making any natural and universal idea of gender relations—based on biology or religion or anything else—seem increasingly implausible.

Next . . .

In the next four chapters, we explore the on-the-ground realities that people face today. We start with sexuality. It is difficult to imagine, perhaps, that social forces shape this most intimate part of our personal selves. Desire for sexual and romantic connection is felt so deeply that it seems impervious to "outside" influences. We imagine you might ask, in a hopeful tone:

Gendered ideas, interactions, and institutions may affect almost every part of my life, but some things are personal and my sexuality is mine and mine alone. Isn't it?

Alas, dear reader, alas.

FOR FURTHER READING

Cancian, Francesca. "The Feminization of Love." *Signs* 11, no. 4 (1986): 692–709.

Coontz, Stephanie. "The World Historical Transformation of Marriage." *Journal of Marriage and Family* 66, no. 4 (2004): 974–979.

D'Emilio, John and Estelle Freedman, *Intimate Matters: A History of Sexuality in America*. Chicago: University of Chicago Press, 1997.

Ehrenreich, Barbara. *The Hearts of Men: American Dreams and the Flight from Commitment*. New York: Anchor Books, 1987.

Goldin, Claudia. "The Quiet Revolution that Transformed Women's Employment, Education, and Family." *The American Economic Review,* 96, no. 2 (2006): 1–21.

Hull, Kathleen, Ann Meier, and Timothy Ortyl. "The Changing Landscape of Love and Marriage." *Contexts* 9, no. 2 (2010): 32–37.

Katz, Jonathan. "The Invention of Heterosexuality." *Socialist Review* 20 (1990): 7–34.

Strasser, Susan. *Never Done: A History of American Housework*. New York: Macmillan, 2000.

SEX IS NOT A NATURAL ACT.

—LEONORE TIEFER[1]

10

Sexualities

Part of the "whole college experience," many students say, involves going to parties, getting drunk, meeting someone new, making out, and maybe having sex.[2] These are **hookups**, one-time nonromantic sexual encounters. As one student describes it: "There's this system that's like, you're gonna get drunk, randomly meet randoms, and just, like, whatever happens."[3] Scholars call this system **hookup culture**, a norm on many American residential colleges in which casual sexual contact is held up as ideal, encouraged with rules for interaction, and institutionalized in much of higher education. All told, 70 percent of students will hook up at least once before graduation.[4]

For *American Hookup: The New Culture of Sex on Campus*, your first author asked 101 students to share their experiences with hookup culture. And they did, submitting over a million words of gossip, theories, rants, celebrations, and stories. The resulting book, together with lots of other excellent research, has given scholars a pretty good idea of what sex looks like on campuses today.[5]

To begin, most students report being eager to experiment with their sexuality, at least a little. They also report feeling pressure to do college "right," which seems to require a casual attitude toward sex. Many students believe, or think that their peers believe, that college is a time to go wild and have fun. They may even believe that separating sex from emotions is what sexual liberation looks like.

For students who are enthusiastic about casual sex—up to 25 percent—this works out well.[6] Casual sex raises their self-esteem and lowers rates of anxiety and depression. Students who don't take well to hookup culture, though, often struggle. About a third abstain from hooking up altogether, leaving many feeling isolated from their peers. The remainder of students, just under half, participate with mixed feelings and mixed experiences.

There are reasons why casual sex has so captured college life. Understanding hookup culture's history helps us see that sexualities, though deeply personal, are also expressed in a context.[7] This chapter builds on the last, exploring how gendered ideas, interactions, and institutions shape our sexual experiences. It also considers who benefits most from the social organization of sexuality: the distribution of pleasure, violence, and power. Throughout, it will become clear that the answer to the following question is no:

Q+A   **Gendered ideas, interactions, and institutions may affect almost every part of my life, but some things are personal and my sexuality is mine and mine alone, isn't it?**

You probably suspected it. We've already encountered the sexual regimes of the Puritans, the romantic Victorians, the revelers of the 1920s, and the experimental teenagers of the 1950s. In all cases, sexual attitudes and behaviors were strongly influenced by the cities, circumstances, and societies in which these individuals lived. The same is true now. To understand how, we'll learn about the rebels of the sexual revolution, see what followed, take a closer look at sexuality today, and end somewhere that might be familiar.

SEX: THE NEAR HISTORY OF NOW

After World War II ended in 1945, birth rates increased in North America, Australia, New Zealand, and most European countries. In the United States, they rose from just over two children per woman to a high of nearly four.[8] By 1970 the number of eighteen- to twenty-four-year-olds had increased by over 50 percent.[9] We call this generation the "baby boomers."

Youth often push boundaries set by adults and the boomers were no exception. Members of this generation protested the intractable Vietnam War and fought for African Americans' civil rights. Violent attacks by American government authorities—both on the Vietnamese and on American anti-war and civil rights protesters—stirred a more general resistance to authority. Boomers' desire to find their own way rather than conform to dominant norms of sex and gender fed into the growth of the women's movement, gay liberation, and the sexual revolution.[10]

These movements reinforced permissive rather than punitive attitudes about sex, including rising approval of nonmarital sex and sex between teenagers.[11] The timing was perfect. The first birth control pill went on the market in 1960, and by 1965, it had been prescribed to six million women.[12] That year, the U.S. Supreme Court granted married people the unrestricted right to use birth control. It extended that same right to single people in 1972 and legalized abortion in the first and second trimesters in 1973. Suddenly men and women could have sex together for fun with substantially less fear of an unintended pregnancy or pregnancy-induced marriage.

Life was changing for sexual minorities and trans men and women, too. In the summer of 1969, a group of trans, gay, and nonbinary folks changed history when they revolted against police harassment in New York's Greenwich Village, kicking off several nights of protest that would be dubbed the "Stonewall Riots."[13] The Gay Liberation Front, one of the first gay rights organizations, was founded a week later. On the anniversary of the riots, the first gay pride parades were held in New York, Los Angeles, Chicago, and San Francisco.

By 1973 "homosexuality" would be removed from the American Psychiatric Association's list of mental disorders.[14] In 1977, San Francisco would elect the first openly gay person to public office. Inspired by "black is beautiful," "gay is good" became a rallying cry, and Americans began coming out in record numbers. Four years after Stonewall, there were almost 800 gay and lesbian organizations in the United States. Sexual minority men and women weren't just out of the closet, they were out and proud.

In the next decade, gay men's communities would be devastated by the HIV/AIDS epidemic.[15] In the United States, though not in other countries, HIV

If you *really* love him...

Rubbers – Every Time!

Facing a hostile federal government, gay men in the early HIV era organized their own safer sex campaigns. Love for each other, and for their community, was one basis on which they mainstreamed the use of "rubbers," or condoms.

affected gay men early, alongside injection drug users and other vulnerable populations. The first reports were in 1981. Within ten years, 8 to 10 million people were infected.[16] A diagnosis was a death sentence.

Because gay men were a disparaged population, politicians were slow to support research, prevention, and treatment. Gay men responded by protesting government inaction and exploitation by pharmaceutical companies. They also turned to their own communities, organizing the most effective safer sex campaign the world has ever seen. Way ahead of the medical community, light years ahead of heterosexuals, and unsupported by the federal government (which banned AIDS prevention materials that acknowledged homosexual sex), gay men became the first people in history to normalize condom use.

Out of fear of HIV, many children in the 1980s and 1990s received at least some comprehensive sex education, the kind that encourages abstinence but also teaches young people how to engage in sexual activity more safely. This education delayed the onset of intercourse and increased the chances of contraceptive use, without increasing the frequency of sex or number of acquired partners.[17] But there was swift backlash.[18] The federal government refused to offer funding for anything other than abstinence-only sex education, the kind that instructs students to refrain from sex until marriage and provides no practical information beyond strategies for saying no. Beginning in the mid-1990s, millions of federal dollars would be spent on these programs, which studies have shown to have no effect at all, not even on rates of abstinence.[19]

Just as comprehensive sex education was becoming more rare, the internet arrived, changing the media landscape. Among other things, the internet raised the level of competition between media producers exponentially. In 1955, the "Golden Age" of television, there were four channels. That's one for every 41.5 million Americans. By 1994, there was one for every 1.7 million Americans.[20] As of this writing, in addition to hundreds of cable channels, there are 170 million active webpages on the internet. That's one website for every 45 people on the planet.

With so much competition for attention, people making media content learned that more was more.[21] More fighting, more explosions, faster cars, scarier monsters, bloodier gore, cruder humor, and bigger and badder disasters. And more sex, too. So much sex that some have argued that media has become "pornified," with only a thin line between so-called pornographic and so-called non-pornographic media.[22] Most young people aren't receiving comprehensive sex education at school, but they're getting quite an education online.

Harkening back to the 1920s, when women had to be "sexy" to get treated to a night on the town, women's bodies have borne more of this pornification than men's. Women in media, particularly conventionally attractive and feminine white women, are often portrayed as sexual objects. **Sexual objectification** is the reduction of a person to his or her sex appeal. To be clear, it's not the same thing as finding someone's body desirable; it's attraction to a body in the *absence* of an acknowledgement of the internal life of the person desired. Both men and women are objectified in popular culture, and gay men more than heterosexual men, but women overall are objectified much more.[23]

Pornography itself has become more extreme, too. Today the pornography industry makes billions of dollars a year producing material that is substantially more exploitative and violent than in earlier eras, involving more physically punishing sex acts and degrading language.[24] At the same time as there is more pornography than ever, it is accessed more easily, and a record number of Americans agree that it is morally acceptable.[25] PornHub, one of the industry's largest websites, reported 28.5 billion visits in 2017; that's 81 million visitors a day.[26]

Why have so many young people embraced pornography? Maybe because they think that to disapprove of it would be to disapprove of sex itself. Despite the efforts of abstinence-only educators and against the wishes of many conservative-leaning Americans, the core tenets of the sexual revolution—that we should embrace and explore our sexualities—have become powerful ideas in the United States.

SEX AND "LIBERATION" TODAY

In the decades since the 1960s, the longstanding pressure to say no to sex has been replaced by a different pressure. Many young people in the United States, though by no means all, have come to feel that grasping their sexual freedom, enacting their sexual liberation, and empowering themselves require them to say yes.[27] Yes to learning about sexuality; to talking about it, brashly; to feeling comfortable seeing it, in all its explicitness; and to displaying one's body sexily. Yes to kink, also, and other marginalized forms of sexual expression and whatever activities promise pleasure or discovery. And yes to doing it casually, just for fun. To say no to any of these things, the logic goes—to be conservative about sex, take sex seriously, or simply be uninterested in sex—is to deprive oneself of freedom, liberation, and empowerment. Saying no is now considered old-fashioned, even regressive.

Consider that today many people believe that being a virgin is a liability after a certain age.[28] About a third of fifteen- to twenty-four-year-olds say that they feel pressure to be sexually active, and half of women and a third of men report losing their virginity before they're ready.[29] "I thought that only nerds, religious nuts, and momma's boys were untouched when they started college," asserted a white heterosexual woman (in reality, half of traditional-age students are virgins when they start college).[30] On college campuses, some young people choose to lose their virginity in a one-time hookup just so they can say they did.[31] Only about 5 percent of Americans are now virgins on their (first) wedding night.[32]

The conflation of sexual liberation with saying yes comes out of the intersection of the women's movement and the sexual revolution. Feminists at the time were fighting the Victorian ideas of separate spheres and opposite sexes. These were behind the gendered love/sex binary, that idea that women are primarily interested in love and men primarily in sex, and the sexual double standard, judging women harshly for their sexual behavior and lauding men for theirs. To dismantle these ideas, feminists needed to do two things: (1) undo the sexist idea that women didn't "belong" on the masculine side of the binary, which included the right to have and enjoy sex without criticism, and (2) undo the androcentric idea that things on the feminine side of the binary weren't valuable and good, which included a desire for love and commitment.

As we've seen, they got half of what they wanted. Women can now enter male-dominated arenas and embrace at least some masculine qualities and interests, including being sexual and having sex for sex's sake, like a stereotypical man. But the androcentric devaluation of femininity is stronger than ever, leading some to think that desiring love and commitment is sweet but a little pathetic. This was based on the idea that the cavalier approach to sex characterized as masculine was what a natural, freely expressed sexuality would look like, whereas a more careful approach to sex, especially one that emphasized the context of loving care, was overly cautious and even repressed. A feminine approach to sex, in other words, was framed as "repressed" and a masculine approach to sex as "free."[33] The very definition of sexual liberation came to be modeled on a male stereotype of sexuality.

Many women today take this definition for granted, leading them to believe that adopting a masculine approach to sex is a way of grasping their liberation and gaining equality with men. This is especially true among white, heterosexual women raised in middle- and upper-class families. One woman fitting this description explained her approach to sex: "I railed against the idea that women were needy, dependent, easily heartsick, easily made hysterical by men, attention-obsessed, and primarily fixated on finding romance," she said insistently.[34] "I did this by proving how very like a boy I could behave." She engaged in what she called "sexual tomboyery":

> I figured the best way for a girl to reject oppressive sexism would be to act in exact opposition of what our sexist society expects of a decent woman; to get exactly what she wants from men, whenever she wants it. In essence, objectify them back.

Many young women feel the same. And many young men accept this definition of liberation, too.

Granted, there are many good things about this. The imperative to say yes means greater tolerance for other peoples' choices. This opens up possibilities for new identities and practices, from pansexuality to roleplay.[35] Once considered a sin akin to bestiality, for example, oral sex is now widely accepted. We no longer fear that masturbation causes blindness. Over a third of women and almost half of men have engaged in anal sex. Nine out of ten Americans report that they would accept a lesbian, gay, or bisexual family member or friend. People of all sexual orientations are increasingly interested in exploring forms of consensual nonmonogamy like **polyamory** (the open practice and encouragement of long-term intimate relationships with more than one partner at a time) and **open relationships** (in which committed partners agree that each can have sexual encounters outside the relationship). On many other measures as well, Americans are not as puritanical as they once were.

The new imperative to say yes to sex, though, isn't merely a lifting of old rules, it's a new set. Real sexual freedom would be the right to have sex or not, however one likes, and for any reason, without social consequences. It's not really freedom if you *have* to say yes. In fact, it can feel quite oppressive for people who don't want to say yes, don't want to say yes right now, or don't want to say yes to just anything or anyone. Many people who identify as asexual, alongside immigrants from more conservative countries and people who hold tightly to their faith, do not feel free in this context at all.[36]

But a person doesn't have to be religious or conservative to feel pressured by these new sexual norms. After voluntarily turning down a hookup with a friend of a friend, for example, a student who considered herself quite radical worried that she was being a prude:

> I'm so embarrassed by that, and so I want to distance myself from it. I "know" that I should want to have sex all the time, and should take advantage of it when I get the chance; especially when it's a girl who's showing interest in me. But I didn't.... [P]ressure to be sexual was and has been SO CONSTANT for so long.... I feel as if by not voluntarily taking part in it, I am weird, abnormal, and a prude.[37]

Young people today often feel like having sex is more of an expectation than an opportunity.

Moreover, the sexual playground promised by this new set of rules is not necessarily equally fun for everyone. Even if we are more sexually free now than we have been in the past, freedom is not the same thing as equality. To what, exactly, are we saying yes? Like the women of the 1970s, today's young women want to say "yes to sex and no to sexism."[38] But that's easier said than done.

Similarly, coming out of the closet is now an unquestioned destination for anyone who has even an inkling of same-sex sexual desire. Accordingly, men and women with these desires often feel compelled to be "out," lest they be seen by others as repressed, cowardly, or ashamed. Recall, though, that the idea that homosexuality is an identity is rather new; both in the United States and elsewhere, the notion that homosexuality can be merely a behavior persists. In China, for instance, most men over the age of forty don't recognize a gay identity, even those who have frequent sexual liaisons with other men.[39] Younger Chinese men are more likely to adopt a Western-style gay identity, but they do not necessarily value coming out to everyone. Some Americans think similarly.[40] A national survey asked self-identified heterosexuals if they'd ever had a sexual encounter with someone of the same sex: Ten percent of women and 2 percent of men said they had.[41] Researchers studying sexually transmitted infections have found this to be frequent enough that they define the population as "men who have sex with men" (MSM) and "women who have sex with women" (WSW) rather than queer-identified.

Being out is considered psychologically healthy in many parts of the West today and many people proudly identify as a sexual minority. But some don't. Research on voluntarily closeted men and women shows that some people happily "decenter" their same-sex desires, opting not to act on them, without suffering from shame or a sense of repression.[42] To insist that everyone who feels such desire *must* identify as a sexual minority and live openly as such is no less coercive than insisting that people *may not* do these things. Being out is good and fine, but true freedom would mean embracing the choices people make, regardless of whether they match one's personal model of liberation.

The remainder of this chapter is dedicated to exploring the way that heterocentrism and gender inequality shape how we think about and engage in sexual activity. It will look at how we define sex, divide up desire, and array ourselves in a hierarchy of attractiveness. It will also discuss how we "do" sex and the relationship between our sexual scripts and sexual violence.

GENDERED SEXUALITIES

Sex Defined

Most Americans continue to assume, absent clear signs otherwise, that new people they meet are heterosexual and committed to **monogamy**, the open practice and encouragement of long-term intimate relationships with only one person. Accordingly, our institutions are still organized around the assumption that every sexual or romantic couple involves one man and one woman, as indicated by things like "his" and "hers" embroidered towels and wedding ring sets. This is especially obvious around Valentine's Day, when companies offer hotel rooms fit for a "king and queen," spa packages for "beauty and her beast," and romantic dinners for "Romeo and his Juliet."

Reflecting this hetero- and **mononormativity**—the normalizing of monogamy—the word "sex" is generally used to refer to one sexual activity in particular: penile-vaginal intercourse. Euphemisms like "home base" and "all the way" are widely understood to refer to that specific activity. It's the "it" in "Did you do it?" This is the **coital imperative**, the idea that any fully sexually active couple must be having penile-vaginal intercourse (also known as "coitus") and any fully completed sexual activity will include it.[43] When we ask young people directly what they think "counts" as sex, essentially 100 percent will say intercourse, but there's plenty of disagreement about everything else.[44]

"Mr." and "Mrs." decorative pillows and other his and her sets highlight how our institutions still assume that all sexual couples include a man and a woman.

Especially in certain circumstances, like virginity loss, the imperative has substantial power. Many young people don't think they've truly lost their virginity until a penis goes into a vagina, no matter how many genitals they've encountered or sexual acts they've performed.[45] This includes some gay men and lesbians. And though nonheterosexuals generally have more expansive definitions of sex, the penis is still often centered. About 90 percent think penile-anal intercourse counts as sex, for example, but there's more confusion about what counts as sex between women.[46]

By unnecessarily constraining sexual options, the coital imperative creates potential problems for men and women having sex together, too. When penile-vaginal intercourse is defined as "real sex," and everything else is just "foreplay," having penile-vaginal intercourse can feel compulsory. If intercourse is undesired, difficult, or impossible—when women experience pain when penetrated or when men struggle to maintain erections—the coital imperative defines their sexuality as dysfunctional.[47]

Since men reliably have orgasms during intercourse, but women do not, the coital imperative also prioritizes an activity that privileges his orgasm at the expense of hers.[48] So does the practice of women performing oral sex upon men sooner in a relationship than men perform it on women, as well as more often and with more intent to produce orgasm.[49] These two facts result in an **orgasm gap** in mixed-sex pairings, a phenomenon in which women report fewer orgasms than men. Women having sex with men enjoy, on average, only one orgasm for every three of their partners'.[50]

FIGURE 10.1 | PERCENTAGE OF WOMEN HAVING AN ORGASM IN FOUR SEXUAL CONTEXTS, BY OCCURRENCE OF SELECTED SEXUAL BEHAVIORS

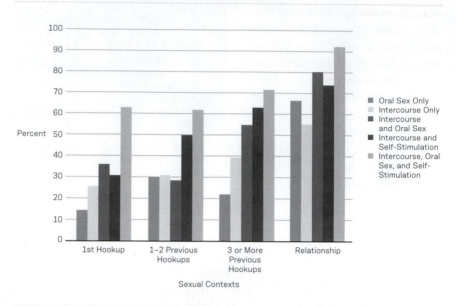

Note: Oral sex refers to receiving oral sex.
Source: E. A. Armstrong, P. England, and A. C. K. Fogarty, "Orgasm in College Hook-ups and Relationships," in *Families as They Really Are*, ed. Barbara Risman (New York: W. W. Norton and Company, 2009).

Myths about men's and women's bodies suggest that this gap is inevitable, with the female orgasm finicky and the male orgasm, if anything, too eager.[51] But this isn't the case. Some countries have larger orgasm gaps than others: the one in the United States, for example, is twice as large as the ones in Brazil and Japan.[52] When women have sex with women, they have two to three times as many orgasms as women who have sex with men.[53] As the far right column in Figure 10.1 shows, when college women are in relationships with men and a variety of forms of stimulation is used, they have orgasms 92 percent of the time.[54] And, when women are alone, their rate of orgasm is as high as 96 percent.[55] Even women who never have orgasms with male partners often do regularly when they masturbate.[56] Women could have just as many orgasms as men if participants decided to prioritize it.

We naturalize the orgasm gap, though, treating it as inevitable, because we tend to believe that women are genuinely less sexual than men.[57] But that isn't true either. Instead, we've divided up desire, taking from women the pleasure of lust and taking from men the pleasure of being lusted after.

Divided Desire

To be *sexy* is to be an object of desire for others; to be *sexual* is to have the capacity to experience sexual desire.[58] Most of us want to both feel sexual and be sexy but, thanks to the gendered love/sex binary, we learn to divide these phenomena by gender.[59] Men are sexual, we are told, and women are sexy. Men desire and women are desirable. Men want women. And what do women want? Women want to be wanted.

In sex education, for example, boys' sexuality is overtly linked with pleasure, if only because his orgasm is mentioned in the context of reproduction.[60] Girls are more likely to get warnings about pregnancy and sexual coercion. The clitoris, the organ responsible for female orgasm, is almost never mentioned. Parents, likewise, rarely discuss the pleasurable aspects of sex, especially with their daughters.[61] Teenage girls are taught to think of their sexuality as something that can "get them into trouble" and are more likely than teenage boys to associate sex with violence, disease, pregnancy, and "bad reputations."[62]

Real women and girls are seen through lenses formed by omnipresent sexually explicit images of women's bodies presented as desirable objects for the gaze of the presumptively heterosexual male consumer.

Media echoes this privileging of male desire. Much of it assumes a **heterosexual male gaze**, meaning that content is designed to appeal to a hypothetical heterosexual man.[63] Plotlines and visuals intended to incite men's desire draw our attention to men's **subjectivity**, their internal thoughts and feelings. This is an acknowledgment that they are sexual, which is good, but it's also a prescription. A particular kind of woman is consistently portrayed as sexually desirable, repetitively implying that she is the only proper object of their sexual attraction. In this way, men undergo a process of **sexual subjectification**: they are told what their internal thoughts and feelings should be. For men attracted to women, this prescription may limit their ability to recognize when they're attracted to women outside the very narrow ideal; for men attracted to men, it may limit their ability to recognize attraction at all.

For women, the heterosexual male gaze means being regularly exposed to idealized images of female bodies. As a result, many women internalize the idea that their value is heavily dependent on their ability to conform to a narrow and largely unattainable definition of attractiveness, whereas men's value is somewhat less so.[64] In one survey, people were three times as likely to say that women, compared to men, face "a lot of pressure" to be physically attractive.[65] Research on lesbians is mixed. Some hints that they may be protected because they are uninterested in male sexual attention, but other research suggests that the idealized images still take a toll.[66]

We see this outsized emphasis on women's versus men's attractiveness in data collected from online dating sites and apps. Data from OkCupid, for example, the third most popular platform, reveals that both men and women value attractiveness in each other, but men much more so (see Figure 10.2).[67] The most attractive men receive ten times the average number of messages; the most attractive women receive twenty-five times the average.

This asymmetric emphasis on women's appearance suggests that, at least in the abstract, women's value is less tied to who they are and what they do, and

FIGURE 10.2 | NUMBER OF MESSAGES RECEIVED VS. RECIPIENT'S ATTRACTIVENESS

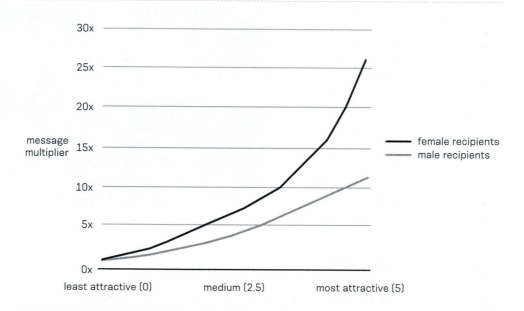

Source: Christian Rudder, "Your Looks and Your Inbox," *OkTrends* (blog), November 17, 2009. Retrieved from https://web.archive.org/web/20100725135317/http://blog.okcupid.com/index.php/your-looks-and-online-dating.

more tied to how they look. Understanding this, many women **self-objectify**, internalizing the idea that their physical attractiveness determines their worth. During sex, worrying about how they look may translate into a process called **spectating**, watching one's sexual performance from the outside.[68] Spectating women might try to stay in sexual positions they think are flattering, arrange their body to make themselves look thinner or curvier, try to keep their face looking pretty, and ensure they don't make embarrassing noises. They may even avoid orgasm because doing so means losing control of these things. Because of spectating, some women have "out-of-body sexual experiences" in which they don't focus much on how sex *feels*. And, sure enough, research has shown that the more a woman worries about how she looks, the less likely she'll experience sexual desire, pleasure, and orgasm.[69]

While heterosexual men are less likely to be sexually objectified, gay and bisexual men in same-sex encounters can be positioned as the objectifier, the objectified, or both. Standards of fitness and attractiveness among queer men, and in media content aimed at them, can be as unrealistic as those aimed at women. In response, sexual minority men report higher levels of self-objectification than heterosexual men and a sense of being under an objectifying gay male gaze.[70] One man interviewed about his experiences, for example, complained that sex often left him feeling "used" by men:

> You get tired of being used. . . . [I] was just nothing but this little receptacle. . . . It wasn't reciprocal. . . . I need to feel like some attention is to me and I'm not just this machine. . . . It makes me one dimensional. It just makes me an object.[71]

It may be that the objectifying gaze isn't so much heterosexual as it is masculine, reflecting a stereotypically male orientation toward sex that emphasizes "scoring" over connection and (as the black, lesbian, feminist writer Audre Lorde describes it) "sensation without feeling."[72]

The discomfort of being sexually objectified may also help explain why so many heterosexual men are uncomfortable among gay and bisexual men. Used to being the subject, suddenly they may be an object. Many women and queer men have grown accustomed to this feeling, whether they enjoy it or not. For the heterosexual man who has generally been spared an objectifying gaze, it might be quite disconcerting to suddenly be on the other side of such a one-sided relationship.

The Erotic Marketplace

Not everyone is considered worthy of an objectifying gaze. The phrase **erotic marketplace** refers to the ways in which people are organized and ordered according to their perceived sexual desirability. The term *market* is typically used to describe the abstract space in which goods and services are attributed economic value. In the erotic marketplace, some people have more erotic "capital" than others.[73] Data from OkCupid is useful here, too.

RACE, GENDER, AND SEXUALITY As the chapter on intersectionality showed, race is gendered.[74] Racism and colorism play a role in the erotic marketplace, then, as does the socially constructed gender of race. Racial stereotypes about black and Latino men—epitomized in the "black buck" and "Latin lover" archetypes—portray them as especially sexual and sexually skilled compared to white men.[75] This is a double-edged sword, and a sharp one. By virtue of these stereotypes, they may be desired as sexual partners—"I think when a white guy approaches you he just wants a trophy. That's how it always comes off," said one African American man about his experience in gay bars—but being fetishized doesn't necessarily feel good.[76] It's just another type of sexual objectification.

There's also the possibility that black and Latino men may be perceived as *too* masculine and, therefore, sexually dangerous. Representations of Latino men in media often portray them idling on the street, oozing a vaguely threatening sexuality, and harassing women who nervously walk by; the stereotype of black men as sexually dangerous to white women has its roots in the white supremacist need to demonize black men after the end of slavery.[77] Based on these notions, some potential partners may avoid black and Latino men.

Consequently, black and Latino men may police their own behavior, knowing that racism means that their acts will be judged more harshly than those of white men.[78] This kind of decision has been described as a **politics of respectability**, a form of resistance to negative racial stereotypes that involves being "good" and following conservative norms of appearance and behavior.[79] Because people of color are marked categories in the United States, anything they do may be read by others as reflecting not individual choice but group characteristics. Thus, they face an additional layer of concern when making sexual choices: the possibility of affirming harmful beliefs about their racial group. This includes a heightened risk of being prosecuted or suffering violence.

For Asian men, stereotypes based on race are straightforwardly negative. When asked to describe how Asian Americans were stereotyped, Michael, a Chinese American, responded that it "blends in with Asian-women-in-America stereotypes."[80] He elaborated: "Asian men are smooth. Expected to be submissive. Expected to be quiet and not speak up and express their feelings. And they're supposed to be small-dicked." Asian men are seen by some as unmasculine and, therefore, sexually deficient.[81] Research shows that even some Asian women may think so.[82] This led one man of Japanese and Mexican descent to say: "Even the Asian girls that I liked, they would always like White guys."[83]

We see these gendered racial patterns in the OkCupid data. In terms of compatibility, as measured by an algorithm, all races match with all other races

TABLE 10.1 | PERCENT CHANCE THAT A MAN IN EACH RACIAL GROUP WILL RECEIVE A RESPONSE FROM AN INQUIRY

Racial Group	Men Messaging Women	Men Messaging Men
White	29%	45%
Native American	28%	44%
Middle Eastern	26%	48%
Pacific Islander	25%	38%
Latino	23%	42%
Asian	22%	38%
Black	22%	35%
South Asian	21%	38%
Average	**28%**	**43%**

Source: Christian Rudder, "How Your Race Affects the Messages You Get," *OkTrends* (blog), October 5, 2009. Retrieved from https://web.archive.org/web/20111008215612/http://blog.okcupid.com/index.php/your-race-affects-whether -people-write-you-back/.

rather equally.[84] But all races aren't equally valued in the erotic marketplace. Table 10.1 lists how often men receive replies. In a society that centers and elevates whiteness, we would expect that white men would have an advantage, and they do. White men are more likely than men of any other race to get a response from women and the second most likely, after Middle Eastern men, to get a response from men. In both cases, Native American men follow close behind these men in popularity.

Conversely, black and Latino men are among the least likely to get a response from either women or men, with Latino men doing somewhat better among men messaging men. This suggests that the stereotype of hypermasculinity hurts more than helps black and Latino men in the erotic marketplace. Asian men, too, are among the groups that get the least frequent responses. In one study of online dating behavior, college-educated white women were actually more likely to respond to a white man without a college degree than an Asian man with one.[85]

Racism—both the kind that fetishizes and the kind that denigrates—also affects the desirability of women. Asian women, by virtue of being seen as extra-feminine, are viewed by some as more sexually malleable than white women; this may make them appealing to men who are looking for subservient partners. One white American man who prefers Asian women explained: "I'm kind of a soft guy. I really find [white] American women overly aggressive."[86] There is some evidence that this dynamic plays out among sexual minority men, too, with Asian men being seen as sexual partners who will play a feminized role.[87]

TABLE 10.2 | PERCENT CHANCE THAT A WOMAN IN EACH RACIAL GROUP WILL RECEIVE A RESPONSE FROM AN INQUIRY

Racial Group	Women Messaging Women	Women Messaging Men
Middle Eastern	50%	52%
Pacific Islander	46%	49%
Asian	44%	53%
Latina	43%	50%
South Asian	43%	63%
White	42%	51%
Native American	42%	49%
Black	34%	47%
Average	**42%**	**51%**

Source: Christian Rudder, "How Your Race Affects the Messages You Get" and "Same-Sex Data for Race vs. Reply Rates," *OkTrends* (blog). Retrieved from http://blog.okcupid.com/index.php/your-race-affects-whether-people-write-you-back/ and https://web.archive.org/web/20110116062331/http://blog.okcupid.com/index.php/same-sex-data-race-reply/.

Table 10.2 shows that Asian, Pacific Islander, South Asian, and Middle Eastern women do very well in the erotic market. These are the four groups most likely to receive a response from women messaging men, and three of the top four from women messaging women. In contrast, black women face a situation similar to that of Asian men. Racial stereotypes that masculinize African Americans relative to whites undermine a black woman's value in the erotic marketplace. Black women—whether they are college educated or not—are least likely to receive a response.[88] Latina women fall somewhere in between.

Actual dating and marriage patterns reflect what we see online.[89] White people are more likely to marry Latinos, Native Americans, or Asians than they are to marry black people. Perhaps the stereotype of the "feisty Latina" or "hot Latin lover" is less costly to Latinas and Latinos than the stereotype of the "angry black woman" or "scary black man" is to African Americans. Here the intersection of gender and race matters, too. White men are more likely to marry Asian than black women, and white women are more likely to marry black men than Asian men.[90] Reflecting colorism, lighter-skinned racial minorities are more likely to intermarry with whites than darker-skinned minorities.

Evidence further suggests that people are more comfortable experimenting with interracial relationships than they are committing to them.[91] When white teenagers date white peers, they introduce them to their parents 71 percent of the time, but nonwhite girlfriends or boyfriends get to meet parents only 57 percent of the time. Black teenagers are also reluctant to introduce their white boyfriends or girlfriends, though the difference is smaller. In general, the rate of interracial dating tends to decrease as levels of commitment increase. People are more likely to date partners of a different race than they are to live with them and they're even less likely to marry them. Sexual minorities of both sexes are more likely to date interracially, but race clearly still plays an erotic role.[92]

EROTICIZED INEQUALITY Gender also straightforwardly shapes ideas about how men and women should couple. Because of sexism, for example, couples in which the man appears to have more power than the woman seem most natural and desirable. Cultural norms dictate that men be taller, stronger, bigger, older, and more educated than their female partners, and have a higher-status job that brings in more income. It doesn't have to be a Cinderella story, but we've learned to feel attracted to a gentle asymmetry.

The data on age puts this in stark relief. Age is an imperfect measure of both attractiveness and accomplishment: personal maturity, career success, and financial security. As we've already seen, men seeking women put a premium on attractiveness (which for women is conflated with youth) and a younger woman's lesser accomplishment is no drawback (and may even be desirable). Men seeking women on OkCupid report that they'll consider dating women who are quite a lot younger, but only a bit older.[93] As they age, men's lower bracket stays low. The average thirty-year-old man, for instance, says he's interested in dating a woman as old as thirty-five and as young as twenty-two. A man at forty will date a woman as old as forty-five but as young as twenty-seven.

This is what men *say*, anyway. In practice, men mostly seek contact with the youngest women in their reported age bracket and women who fall *below* it.[94] Their willingness to date "down" suggests that they prefer or will accept a mate whose career is "behind" their own. The average woman, conversely, prefers to date a man who is her age or older. As women age, they will accept about five years on either side. In actual messaging, they tend to focus on men their own age. At some point in this skewed erotic market, the oldest and most accomplished women and the youngest and least accomplished men are boxed out.

For men, then, being bigger, stronger, and older, having advanced degrees, and enjoying a high-prestige, well-paid occupation are always advantages. For women, all these things carry both advantages and disadvantages. Gains may help her catch an accomplished man, but she might reasonably worry that too many gains could knock her out of the competition altogether. Meanwhile, her ability to attract men may decrease as she ages, while the men in her same age cohort become relatively *more* attractive. His achievements count more toward his attractiveness than hers do, and fading looks harm her more than him.

Many women understand this. In a study of newly admitted MBA students, respondents were asked to indicate their expected future salaries. Half were told that their peers would see their answers and half were told they'd be confidential. There were no differences in the salaries reported by men and women in the latter group, but single women who thought their peers would see their answers reported salary goals $18,000 lower than single women promised confidentiality.[95] They also reported lower ambitions, less interest in leadership, and less willingness to travel. Men and non-single women didn't show this difference. Concerned that seeming too ambitious or being too successful might make them unattractive to men, women sometimes moderate their career goals. They're not delusional if they do. Women who make more money than the men they're dating are less likely to get married and, if they are married, more likely to get divorced.[96]

Discrimination based on conformity to gender expectations isn't limited, of course, to mixed-sex matches. The very limited research on women seeking women suggests that they have a slight preference for feminine women.[97] A wider literature on men seeking men has found preferences for "straight-acting" men, reflecting the hegemony of masculinity and androcentric bias against femininity.[98] On Grindr and other apps, some men try to enhance their erotic capital by advertising their masculine qualities and concealing their feminine ones, a practice described as **mascing** (a portmanteau of "masculine" and "masking").[99]

Mascing may include expressing an interest in sports, emphasizing one's interest in the outdoors, or growing a hearty beard. It may even include identifying as heterosexual. "[T]here are a lot of guys out there that are like me," said one heterosexual-identified man who regularly sought out other men for sex.[100] Many of these men actually avoided gay-identified men, preferring other heterosexual-identified men or ones who identify as bisexual. One explained that he liked "straight guys" because "I identify with them more because that's kinda, like [how] I feel myself. And bi guys, the same way. We can talk about women [and watch] hetero porn."[101] It's probably not necessary for every stirring of one's loins to prompt an identity crisis, but prejudice against femininity—whether in oneself or in others—is still androcentrism, even when men who have sex with men are doing it.

While our individual preferences seem very personal, the data from OkCupid and other research into sexual preferences reveal that our aggregated choices conform to social hierarchies.[102] Gender and race hierarchies clearly shape our ideas about who is an appealing and appropriate sexual and romantic partner. And, as the next section will show, when two people are in the position of acting on their sexual attraction to one another, gendered dynamics persist.

Gendered Scripts

When sexual interactions unfold in real time, they are guided by information we've gleaned about what sex is, how it works, who does what, and what it means. This knowledge, or set of instructions, is called a **sexual script**, the social rules that guide sexual interaction.[103] Because of sexual scripts, people with a shared culture usually engage sexually in similar ways. Generally, sexual scripts assume sex occurs between two people. They kiss first (closed mouth), then have close body contact with more kissing (open mouth), and only then move to grabbing and squeezing. Once this all has occurred, the couple gets horizontal. Then there's more kissing and groping, including the touching of genitals through clothes. Clothes start coming off; usually tops before bottoms. If it's a mixed-sex couple, her clothes usually come off first (her shirt, his shirt, her pants, his pants, etc.); it's a toss-up if it's a same-sex couple, but their sexual interactions may be guided by differences in gender performance rather than their identity. The scripts of both mixed-sex and same-sex couples may still have a somewhat rigid ascending order of intimacy: fellatio before cunnilingus, oral before penile-vaginal, penile-vaginal before anal, and oral before anal, all depending on what body parts are involved.

We tend to be especially careful to follow sexual scripts when we are first becoming sexually active, or first becoming active with a new partner. Scripts are particularly helpful when we're concerned about doing sex "right." They create predictability and ease social interaction: *Did they kiss me back? Aha, now I have clearance to try for second base.* We police one another around these sexual rules. In some cases, they're even enforced with laws. The rule that French kissing comes before fondling, for instance, isn't just a guideline; someone who moves straight to second base could be charged with sexual battery, a legal term for unwanted but nonviolent sexual touching.

The sexual script is also gendered, featuring more masculine and more feminine roles. The masculine role in sex is an assertive one involving making the first move, touching first, pushing the interaction along, and removing a partner's clothes. The feminine role in sex is responsive. A feminine sexuality is one which waits, never acts or initiates. The feminine partner is put into sexual positions by the masculine partner. The masculine partner penetrates; the feminine partner is penetrated.

In practice, of course, people rarely behave in purely feminine and masculine ways, but men who have sex with women and women who have sex with men will probably recognize these dynamics. People who have sex with people of the same sex may recognize them, too, as masculinity and femininity are not features of male-bodied and female-bodied people, respectively, but can be "done" by anyone of any body and identity. Some gay and bisexual men may be in the habit of playing more of a responsive than assertive role in sex. And gay and bisexual women are quite obviously capable of playing an assertive role with one another, otherwise they would never have sex at all.

Because the script puts women in the position of enacting a feminine version of sexuality that is responsive to sexual activity but doesn't initiate it, women might not ask their male partners for orgasms or tell them how to give them one.[104] Because of the coital imperative and a gendered love/sex binary that prioritizes his sexualness and her sexiness, orgasmic equality would require quite a bit of reimagining of what is sexually possible. The script adds one more layer of difficulty, because now she doesn't just have to *feel* differently (not just sexy, but sexual), she has to *act* differently (not just receptive, but assertive). Likewise, men enacting a masculine version of sexuality have to do the same: see themselves as sexy, not just sexual; learn to prioritize her orgasm as well as their own; and find a way to be responsive in bed alongside being assertive. All of this is a lot to overcome, especially the first few times two people are in bed together.

The same masculine imperative to have sex, and the defining of reluctance as feminine, is also behind the **push-and-resist dynamic**, a situation in which it's normal for men to press sexual activity consistently in the direction of increasing sexual intimacy (whether he wants to or not) and for women to stop or slow down the accelerating intimacy when he's going "too far" (whether she wants to or not).[105] This interferes with people's ability to enjoy what they're experiencing. Men may be thinking about what they *aren't yet doing*. Women, in turn, can't get too swept away because they can't necessarily count on men to pace intimacy comfortably. They, for their part, are left thinking about what they *might do*. In neither case are men and women actually thinking about what they *are doing*, making it difficult for either partner to be in the moment, simply experiencing pleasure.

The push-and-resist dynamic also, predictably, contributes to sexual violence.

Sexual Violence

In the United States, one in three women and one in six men have experienced sexual violence; young people, the working class and poor, racial minorities, people with disabilities, people who are imprisoned, and gender-nonconforming people are at highest risk.[106] Men are the vast majority of perpetrators, representing 97 percent of people arrested for sexual assault.[107] These men often don't believe their behavior constitutes sexual assault, even when it matches legal definitions.[108] Men who rape are more likely than other men to have been sexually or physically abused themselves.[109]

THE POLITICS OF SEXUAL VIOLENCE That we even identify sexual assault as a crime and collect these statistics is rather new. Among the English who colonized the United States, women were property.[110] Men could do whatever they wanted with their property, including rape it. If you raped someone else's property, though, you damaged the goods. So rape was a crime, but it was a property crime; more like theft than assault. Enslaved people were also defined as property, so the men given legal right to own them could violate them with impunity.[111] The colonists denied Native American men property rights, so unless Native women were owned by or married to white men, raping them wasn't a crime at all.[112] Much of this was true until about 150 years ago.

Even then, things didn't change right away. Well into the 1970s, domestic violence, sexual harassment, and sexual assault went largely unregulated by the government. Violence between intimate partners was seen as part of men's legitimate right to "govern" their own homes. Sexual harassment was so normalized that there was no name for it.[113] And rape—especially when perpetrated by a friend or acquaintance—was often dismissed as an occupational hazard of being female. Until 2014, the United States government defined rape as a crime against women; raping men was not a crime, leaving male victims invisible and with no legal remedies.[114]

To change this, activists raised money, recruited volunteers, opened domestic violence shelters, and staffed rape crisis lines.[115] They redefined sexual violence as a crime, collected data to demonstrate its prevalence, and argued that state involvement was essential to protecting victims' rights.[116] Rates of rape began to decline.[117] In 1986, the Supreme Court criminalized sexual harassment. In 1993, marital rape became illegal in all fifty states. In 1994, Congress increased criminal penalties for sexual violence and began funding special sexual assault units in police departments. In 2013, this was extended to include protections for immigrant and Native American women.

These are impressive accomplishments, but there is a lot of work left to be done. It's still hard for victims to get justice. Commonly, they are unsure whether what happened to them was a crime or worry they won't be believed.[118] **Victim blaming**, identifying something done by victims as a cause of their victimization, is common, and many victims fear that they will face more trouble than the person who assaulted them.[119] Only one out of every three sexual assaults is reported to the police.[120] Of those that are reported, only 2 percent will lead to a conviction. In comparison, twice as many robberies are reported to police, with nearly three times as many convictions.

Even in best-case scenarios, convictions can be cold comfort. In 2015, Stanford swimmer Brock Turner was discovered behind a dumpster with his hands inside an unconscious woman. He was convicted, in part thanks to a medical exam and two eye witnesses, and was sentenced to six months in jail for assault with intent to rape and sexual penetration with a foreign object. Turner's father objected to any sentence at all, saying that it was a "steep price to pay for 20 minutes of action."

But it wasn't just his father who minimized Brock Turner's criminal behavior. The judge, too, expressed concern for Turner's future and stated that he didn't believe that Turner would be "a danger to others." Imagine being the victim in that courtroom. After being sexually assaulted, she submitted to a legal medical exam, reported to police, and suffered through a criminal trial, only to hear the judge say that he worried that prison time "would have a severe impact" on her assailant. It turns out Turner only served half his sentence anyway. Three months—a summer vacation's worth of punishment.

Rape myths frequently underlie the decisions and judgments of police officers, medical examiners, lawyers, judges, jurors, and the victims themselves, including the persistent belief that sexual crimes are falsely reported more often than other crimes (they're not).[121] For male victims, women of color, and anyone who carries socially stigmatized characteristics, it's even harder to get justice; police officers sometimes decide whether to investigate reports of sexual assault based on the victim's race, age, sexual orientation, or income level.[122] Men of color are more likely than white men to be put on trial and be convicted and, when they are, they receive harsher sentences.[123] Black men are three and a half times more likely to be wrongly convicted of sexual assault than white men, and especially likely to be wrongly convicted if the victim is a white woman.[124] Continuing, and increasingly intersectional, work on this issue is critical.[125]

RAPE AND CULTURE We have a long way to go before sexual violence becomes rare, but it could be. In fact, it's extraordinarily rare in some societies.[126] Instead of an inevitability, sexual violence is a cultural artifact. Some environments make it more likely than others. Environments that facilitate sexual assault—ones that justify, naturalize, and even glorify sexual pressure, coercion, and violence—are called **rape cultures**.

The idea that men are naturally sexually aggressive is part of rape culture, as is the idea that women are inherently vulnerable to men.[127] Vulvas and vaginas are socially constructed as passive and physically delicate (flower-like, easily crushed or bruised) or simply thought of as a vulnerable space (a "hole").[128] Penises, in contrast, are symbolically active and strong; they become "rock hard" and are used to "hammer" and "pound," while men's highly sensitive testicles are usually left out of this equation altogether.[129] All of this contributes to our tendency to believe that men can effectively use their penises as weapons, their bodies are otherwise invulnerable, and women are helpless to defend themselves. In cultures where rape is rare, the social construction of men's and women's body parts emphasizes the vulnerability of the penis and testicles (sensitive, floppy, fleshy structures exposed on the outside of the body), the power of the muscles surrounding the entrance to the vagina, and the mysterious depths into which penises must blindly go.[130]

Alongside this social construction of the body are media reflections of rape culture.[131] Routine in regular programming are images that glamorize scenes of sexual force, sex scenes in which women say no and then change their minds, and jokes that trivialize sexual assault, especially of men. Rape scenes in movies and on television are common plot twists or character devices and often are

This British police campaign that intends to reduce the incidence of rape does so by putting the onus of preventative action on the woman, as do campaigns on many U.S. college campuses.

purposefully designed to be sexually titillating to male viewers. Fictional perpetrators are disproportionately men of color and, since 9/11, Muslim.

When news media covers sex crimes, they often focus on the victim's behavior, reporting on whether she was drinking alcohol, flirting prior to the assault, wearing sexually provocative clothes, or making risky choices.[132] White women get more sympathetic coverage. Perpetrators who seem "respectable"—wealthy, white men, for instance—are most often given the benefit of the doubt. Not uncommonly, stories about rape are described as "sex scandals," as if they are equivalent to a story about a celebrity's kinky fetish.

Rape culture also encourages and can even compel men to enact the push-and-resist dynamic, sometimes aggressively. As a result, many people who have sex with men experience a range of sexual pressure, manipulation, coercion, and force throughout their lives. It starts in elementary school.[133] Much of this isn't criminal, just cruel and dehumanizing. Altogether it reveals what feminist writer Robert Jensen calls a "continuum of sexual intrusion."[134] Many sexualized interactions, as a result, end up being coercive and manipulative, even when not criminal.

Americans' confusion about this was on full display in 2017, when a story about a first date with the comedian Aziz Ansari was published.[135] According to his date, after a dinner over a bottle of wine, they went to his apartment and he quickly initiated sexual activity. Without ascertaining her comfort level or consent, Ansari undressed them both and began kissing and touching her breasts, pulling her hands toward his penis, and putting his fingers in her mouth and vagina. When she asked him to "slow down" or mentioned that she felt "forced," which she did repeatedly, he would stop momentarily and then start again. Nothing she said or did persuaded him to stop trying to push her into sexual activity.

The public reaction to this story, mixed between people who saw his behavior as exploitative and those who saw it as entirely routine, reveals considerable disagreement about how hard men are allowed to push, how much pushing women are expected to tolerate, and how hard women should have to try to get men to listen to them. The fact that many or even most women have multiple experiences like these is part of why the revelation of movie producer Harvey Weinstein's decades of abuse of women in the entertainment industry, alongside dozens of other men outed for similar behavior around the same time, snowballed into a hashtag. By saying #metoo, millions of women confirmed the sheer ubiquity of coercive behavior, from merely selfish to truly egregious.[136]

The preponderance of this push-and-resist dynamic doesn't make just for confusing and uncomfortable sexual interactions, it also gives camouflage to people who are intent on exploiting their peers, making aggressive sexual behavior seem normal or, at least, not so far from the norm. When men behave this way, it is often brushed aside as "boys will be boys." This is exculpatory chauvinism: giving men a pass for their exploitative, cruel, and otherwise thoughtless and dehumanizing behavior. The dynamic is also a catalyst for sexual assault.

We teach men, and even women, that being sexually aggressive is good, then expect them to parse the difference between pushy and criminal. It can be a thin line, and sometimes people cross it.

We see all of these dynamics, and more, on many college campuses today.

COLLEGE HOOKUP CULTURE

The prototypical American college party today is a drunken mix of elation and recklessness. "Things get out of hand," sociologist Thomas Vander Ven observes, "but in an entertaining sort of way."[137] Indeed, the party is euphoric in part because it's just a little dangerous. At its climax, it's a world apart—Vander Ven calls it "drunkworld"—a place where it's normal for people to "fall down, slur their words, break things, laugh uncontrollably, act crazy, flirt, hook up, get sick, pass out, fight, dance, sing, and get overly emotional."[138] Casual sex, by virtue of being slightly reckless but oh-so-exhilarating, fits right in.

This kind of party is most often associated with fraternities, and rightly so. Fraternity men invented this party in the 1800s and began sharing it with wider and wider circles of peers beginning in the 1920s.[139] At the time, and well into the 1970s, colleges acted like substitute parents, treating students like children by imposing curfews, censorship, and punishments for drinking and sexual activity.[140] The boomers successfully pushed back against these practices, and that's when things really got wild. The minimum drinking age was eighteen, so students could party pretty much as hard as they wanted, and they did.[141] By 1978, when the movie *Animal House* cemented the relationship among college, alcohol, and sex, it was routine to have all-out parties in residence halls. The alcohol industry took notice, spending millions of dollars in the 1980s to convince college students to drink.[142]

Then, in 1987, the balance of power on campus shifted. The federal government convinced all fifty states to raise their drinking age to twenty-one. Now students who wanted to party had a problem. Campus authorities were policing residence halls, bars and clubs required an ID, and most sororities weren't allowed to throw parties with alcohol. First-year students, especially, were unlikely to have upper-class friends living in private apartments and houses. On many college campuses, then, a fraternity house was the only place students knew to go to party like they thought they should. The men who belonged to fraternities wealthy enough to have private houses happily filled that void, claiming a role at the center of college life.[143] This gave a small group of students—ones who were disproportionately wealthy, white, and heterosexual, and almost exclusively men—a lot of power to shape their peers' social and sexual lives.

Thirty-eight fraternity members attempt to squeeze into a Volkswagen Bug in 1959. Shenanigans have been a part of fraternity life for more than 200 years.

This is the background to life on many residential college campuses today. The men of wealthy, historically white fraternities—or, on some campuses, men in other formal or informal fraternity-like brotherhoods—still have an oversized influence on the college party scene. Members of this segment of the male college population also tend to be especially enthusiastic about hooking up, so they throw parties that facilitate nonromantic one-time sexual encounters.[144] Worrisomely, fraternity men are also more likely, on average, to report rape-supportive attitudes and admit to having committed acts of sexual aggression.[145]

Students attend these parties for myriad reasons, but one reason is because the fraternity party has become *the* college party: the way all students are supposed to want to have fun.[146] The mass media reflects this, socializing young people into believing that college life is really as crazy as it looks on TV.[147] These sexy, raucous parties resonate, too, with the current definition of sexual liberation: saying yes instead of no and, for women, grasping one's "liberation" by acting like a stereotypical guy.

This is why hookup culture dominates most college campuses. It's not because everyone is doing it, and it's certainly not because everyone likes it. A third of students say that their intimate relationships on campus have been "traumatic" or "very difficult to handle."[148] Between two-thirds and three-quarters wish they had more opportunities to find a long-term romantic partner.[149] Instead, hookup culture dominates campuses because the students who *do* like it have a great deal of power, and the cultural messaging students receive—both about higher education generally and the relationship among sex, fun, and liberation—all conspire to make hookup culture seem "right." This suits some students better than others.

Who Hooks Up?

Most students overestimate how often their peers are hooking up, as well as how "far" they go and how much they enjoy it.[150] According to a survey of over 24,000 students at twenty-one different colleges and universities, the average number of hookups reported by seniors is eight.[151] A third of students won't hook up at all and 20 percent of seniors report that they have yet to lose their virginity. Only 14 percent of students hook up more than ten times in four years.[152] Almost half of first-time hookups include just kissing; fewer than a third include intercourse.[153]

Fraternity and sorority members hook up almost twice as much as everyone else, while students who are nonwhite, poor or working class, and nonheterosexual hook up with their peers less often than their counterparts.[154] For sexual minorities, for example, college parties are not always safe or friendly. Though girl-on-girl kissing is common, it's generally assumed to be for male attention. Some women use this activity to explore their attraction to other women, but others report only doing it if they're confident that the other woman is heterosexual.[155] These latter women are actually *more* homophobic than women who don't kiss other women at parties.[156] The irony is not lost on gay, bisexual, and questioning women, who often feel not only invisible but taunted by the practice. While gay and bisexual men report higher rates of hooking up than average, they generally don't find the hookup scene welcoming; they're more likely than any other group to go off campus to hook up.[157]

While black men hook up somewhat more than average, black women, Latino and Latina students, and Asian men and women are less likely than white students to hook up.[158] This is in part because when students of color hook up, they risk affirming harmful beliefs about their racial group, so some embrace a politics of respectability. Some may explicitly define hooking up as something typical of white students and choose to distance themselves from the behavior.[159] "We don't sleep around like white girls do," said a Filipina American expressing this view.[160] "If I started hooking up," said an African American man, "my friends would be saying I'm, like, 'acting white.'"[161] Some men of color further assume they can't get away with the same level of sexual aggressiveness as white men.[162] And they're probably not wrong. The erotic marketplace plays a role here, too, racializing desirability. Just like in the wider culture, black women and Asian men tend to rank low in the erotic hierarchy on campus, while Asian and white women and white men tend to rank high.

Research also suggests that class-privileged students hook up more often than other students.[163] Among women, this may be because peers are much quicker to ascribe the "slut" label to working-class women, even when they are less sexually active than their richer peers.[164] Working-class students may also be more focused on getting through school and may not think they can afford to focus on their social lives. One Latina and white woman observed:

> Some of these girls don't even go to class. It's like they just live here. They stay up until 4 in the morning. [I want to ask,] "Do you guys go to class? Like what's your deal? . . . You're paying a lot of money for this. . . . If you want to be here, then why aren't you trying harder?"[165]

Students from families with tight budgets are also likely to have a job outside of school and may live at home to save money. These students have less time to spend partying and less opportunity to do so. Sharing a small house with one's parents—often a car or bus ride from the party—isn't conducive to casual sex or heavy drinking.[166] Students who live at home, especially young women, are subject to surveillance from parents who may have rules against drinking, drug use, sexual activity, and staying out late. Lydia, for example, a Latina student who lived at home, imagined that dorm life was more autonomous: "They don't have parents worrying about when they get home or calling them. . . . They do as they please."[167]

Men and women hook up at similar rates, but women report higher rates of regret, distress, and lowered self-esteem.[168] The gendered love/sex binary introduced by the Victorians would suggest that this is because women are more interested in love than sex and men are more interested in sex than love. In fact, men are slightly more likely than women to say that they'd be interested in a committed relationship.[169] Women's greater dissatisfaction is probably not due to an aversion to casual sex not shared by men, but to their greater exposure to sexist and subordinating experiences.

Gendered Power

Exactly because of the gendered love/sex binary, it's assumed that men want casual sex and women don't, thus all women are presumed to be hooking up with the hope that a committed relationship will evolve. This logic tells men that every woman they hook up with wants a boyfriend, so they should act aloof after a hookup to ensure the women don't get the "wrong idea." Women, for their part, may act aloof, too. They understand that some people don't believe women are capable of being casual about sexual activity, so they go to extra lengths to prove they can be. Whether either of the partners actually *is* romantically interested in the other is beside the point; in hookup culture, revealing a desire for connection is pathetically feminine, and nobody wants to be that.[170]

A majority of college students do form romantic relationships, but these relationships tend to emerge out of a series of hookups, during which both students may act as if they're not interested in each other.[171] In the meantime, because women are stereotyped as less capable than men of controlling their emotions, men have more power in these interactions. Women may enthusiastically participate in hookup culture, then, expecting to experiment sexually with men who see them as equals, but they may discover that many men don't see them that way.

Deanna reflected on just such an experience for *American Hookup*. A guy she had previously been with pulled her aside to glumly tell her that he wasn't interested in a relationship. She told him she was fine with that (and she was), but he pressed on apologetically. "He more and more drastically emphasized asking if I was OK," she recounted, "as if he had somehow damaged me, seeming to expect a flood of tears."[172] His behavior was revealing. She thought they were *both* having fun, but he hadn't seen it that way. Reflecting on their encounters, she wrote:

> The stigma attached to women being the emotional creatures in the relationship and the men being the physical ones had never been so apparent to me. . . . He clearly thought that he was the one with the power to hurt and I was the one that was expected to cry with anguish.

Some men hooking up with women do not see or treat them as equals, and one in three men report respecting their female partners less after hooking up with them.[173] This is a good recipe for creating feelings of regret, distress, and lower self-esteem among the women who participate.

Notably, we only think that men are better at hooking up because hookup culture is premised on a stereotypically masculine version of sexuality, which is not the only way to experiment with or commit to multiple sexual partners. Consensually nonmonogamous practices, for example, are based on the idea that people can be loving toward multiple partners (in the case of polyamory) or committed to someone emotionally without sexual exclusivity (in the case of open relationships). In neither case does sexual nonexclusivity involve a denigration of commitment or connection, nor require being callous or cold in order stave off such things.

Hookup culture falsely conflates caring with committed, monogamous relationships because it's based on a gender binary: monogamous, caring sex with just one person (the supposedly feminine kind of sex) and nonmonogamous, casual sex with multiple partners (the supposedly masculine kind of sex).[174] If we collapse the gender binary, we can imagine many other possibilities, including sex that is casual and caring and nonmonogamous. What would a hookup culture that embraced the feminine look like?

Pleasure and Danger

Sexual pleasure is also unevenly distributed. In first-time hookups, women hooking up with men report 35 percent as many orgasms as their partners.[175] This is the same orgasm gap we see off campus: about one for every three. In this case, though, we know for sure that at least some college men are perfectly capable of giving women orgasms. The orgasm gap in hookup culture appears to be a measure of a couple's interest in each other, with concern for women's orgasms increasing as two people hook up together repeatedly and then enter a relationship. When men and women are in committed relationships with each other, the orgasm gap shrinks from 65 to 20 percentage points, with women having 80 percent as many orgasms as their boyfriends.

Both men and women are likely culprits. For their part, some men appear to value their girlfriends' pleasure, but not that of women with whom they only hook up. One male college student, for example, insisted that he always cared about "her" orgasm.[176] However, when asked if he meant "the general her or the specific," he replied, "Girlfriend her. In a hookup her, I don't give a shit." Other men take a similar approach:

> If it's just a random hookup, I don't think [her orgasm] matters as much to the guy. . . . But if you're with somebody for more than just that one night . . . I know I feel personally responsible. I think it's essential that she has an orgasm during sexual activity.[177]

To be fair, women often don't put their own pleasure first either: "I will do everything in my power to, like whoever I'm with, to get [him] off," said one woman about her priorities during a hookup.[178] Both men and women tend to believe that men are more entitled to orgasms. This is illustrated most strikingly by a bisexual student who realized, upon putting some thought into it, that he concentrated on giving his partner an orgasm when he hooked up with men, but getting one when he hooked up with women.[179]

If women experience less pleasure in hookup culture than men, they also face more danger. One in four senior women report being sexually assaulted in college, with 10 percent reporting that someone tried to physically force them to have sex; 5 percent reporting that someone tried but did not succeed; and 11 percent reporting that someone had sex with them while they were unconscious or otherwise incapacitated.[180]

Emma Sulkowicz, a visual arts student at Columbia, made national headlines when she began carrying her mattress around campus to dramatize the inaction of university officials after she reported being sexually assaulted by a fellow student.

Heterosexual women are not alone in being at high risk of victimization. They are joined by gay men and bisexual women, who are more likely than heterosexual women to report being assaulted, and bisexual men, who are almost as likely. Trans and nonbinary students almost certainly suffer high rates of sexual assault on campus, though we don't have good research on these populations yet.[181] Heterosexual men and lesbian women have the lowest rates, with 3 percent of both groups reporting rape by physical force and 3 and 5 percent reporting rape by incapacitation, respectively. These numbers are not trivial either. As with the national statistics, the vast majority of perpetrators of sexual assault are male, regardless of the sex, gender identity, or sexual orientation of the victim, with 8 percent of college men reporting behavior matching the definition of sexual assault.[182]

Rates are high on campus in part because hookup culture is a rape culture.[183] Its sexual scripts make coercive behaviors look and feel normal (plying people with alcohol or pulling them into secluded parts of a party), while making a feminized interest in and concern for one's partner off-script (including care about their pleasure and consent). This camouflages the behavior of students who are intent on raping their peers, but it also puts all students at risk of perpetrating rape. If students carelessly and assertively seek sex with strangers and acquaintances, and do so regularly under drunken conditions, with little concern for their sexual partners' well-being, then we might expect high rates of coercion.

And if men are put in the "push" role in the push-and-resist dynamic, then we might expect men in particular to be perpetrators. Serial perpetrators are a problem on college campuses, but a longitudinal study of rape perpetration found that four out of five college men who commit rape before graduating are not serial perpetrators.[184] They rape only once. It may not be the content of one's character but the context of hookup culture—the risk-loving parties, the pressure to "get" sex, and the normalization of aggressive sexual behavior—that leads some students to commit sexual crimes.

Rape culture also makes it difficult for campus activists fighting sexual violence to hold colleges accountable for effective prevention and fair adjudication, though much progress has been made on this front. In 2011, the Office for Civil Rights released a statement explaining that Title IX, a law that prohibits sex-based discrimination in education, requires colleges to be proactive in reducing rates of sexual violence.[185] Responding to this clarified mandate, students at hundreds of colleges submitted complaints to the Department of Education, arguing that their institutions were ignoring or mishandling sexual assault.[186] The results of the investigations prompted the Obama White House to develop a guide for reducing rates and responding to alleged assaults.[187] The Trump administration has since rescinded the 2011 statement, but not before student

Andrea Pino and Annie E. Clark sit against a wall documenting their efforts to organize student activists across the United States. Thanks to organizing like theirs, almost 500 colleges are or have been under investigation by the Office for Civil Rights for mishandling sexual violence.

activists raised a great deal of awareness and pushed many institutions to institute better and stronger policies.

What happens next will be up to students themselves. The victim of Brock
Turner, the Stanford student who served three months in jail on three counts of
felony sexual assault, bravely released the statement she made to the court on
the day of his sentencing. "Hopefully this will wake people up," she said, refer-
ring to his short sentence. "If anything, this is a reason for all of us to speak
even louder."[188]

Communities can come together to change norms. Bystander intervention
programs—ones that educate students about sexual assault and teach them how
to spot likely incidents and safely intervene—are effective in reducing rates of
sexual violence, so are programs that teach students to recognize sexually coercive behavior and practice assertive and aggressive responses.[189] A next step
may be thinking bigger, not only about the acute problem of sexual assault,
but the many problems in the wider sexual culture. Promoting a culture that
values feminine approaches to sexuality, gives equal importance to female
pleasure, embraces sexual minorities and gender-nonconforming students, and
addresses intersectional inequalities could be the way to make colleges safer
spaces for all students.

Revisiting the Question

 **Gendered ideas, interactions, and institutions may affect
almost every part of my life, but some things are personal
and my sexuality is mine and mine alone, isn't it?**

The women's movement, gay liberation, and the sexual revolution changed the
landscape of sexual opportunity for young Americans, but it would be wrong
to describe this cultural shift as a simple embrace of freedom. The movements
established a new set of rules for sexuality, including a new imperative to say
yes to sex. For women this presented a new set of problems. The coital imperative, gendered love/sex binary, sexual double standard, and sexual script continue to give men more power in interactions, create fertile ground for sexual
violence, and contribute to the orgasm gap between men and women, while privileging an objectifying male sexual gaze. Men, conversely, are prescribed a
narrow heterosexuality, policed if they step outside its boundaries, and put at
risk of engaging in criminal behavior.

If the playground is uncomfortable for some heterosexual men and unsafe
for many heterosexual women, then sexual minorities, nonbinary individuals,
and trans men and women are at even higher risk of rejection, mistreatment,
and violence. Troubled sexual dynamics play out among these populations as
well. No sexual encounters, regardless of the identities and body parts of the

people involved, are automatically devoid of gendered power, sexual objectification, sexual violence, or other forms of prejudice like racism.

Sex, no less than anything else about life, reflects our cultural values and is shaped by interactional norms and institutional forces. Though it can feel deeply personal, in many ways it's not. That means that efforts to bring about freer and more equal sexual opportunities will involve changing the context in which we make our sexual choices. Since college students (who are disproportionately white and class privileged) are often agents of social change for everyone, it will be fascinating to see how their work influences the sexual opportunities of the generations both ahead and behind them, as well as people who attend college later, commute to college, or don't go to college at all (who are disproportionately nonwhite, poor, and working class).

For young people who don't have a traditional college experience, as well as people well beyond their college years, hookup culture may be just something they read about in a book. The hookup script may have escaped hookup culture, somewhat inflecting everyone's dating experiences, but the wider American culture still very much valorizes love, romance, and monogamous marriage. While some college students are struggling with the dynamics of hookup culture, then, other people are attempting to follow dating scripts that more resemble the 1950s, navigating engagements and weddings and extended families, trying to keep love (and sex) alive in marriage, adjusting to aging and increasingly devalued bodies, and managing divorce, re-entering the dating pool, and possibly remarrying. Even most college students will ultimately turn away from casual sex, and rather soon—two-thirds are married by their thirtieth birthday— and they, too, will face new and different sexual and romantic challenges.[190] What are those marriages like?

Next . . .

Hookup culture may make relationships seem passé, but nearly two-thirds of college students will be married by their thirtieth birthday.[191] These marriages have more potential to be true partnerships than any in history. For the first time in thousands of years, marriage law prescribes to men and women the same rights and responsibilities. One source of oppression for women appears to have crumbled.

And yet, despite changes aimed at giving women equal footing, over the last thirty years women who marry men have become increasingly unhappy with their marriages. The data show that women today experience significantly less wedded bliss than men married to women, women married to women, and single women.[192] In fact, despite the cultural messages that insist that women crave marriage and children more than men do, research shows us that the happiest women are single and without children. This prompts us to ask:

If marriage is better for women than ever, why do women married to men report lower levels of happiness than men married to women, women married to women, and single women?

An answer awaits.

FOR FURTHER READING

Armstrong, Elizabeth. "Accounting for Women's Orgasm and Sexual Enjoyment in College Hookups and Relationships." *American Sociological Review* 77, no. 3 (2012): 435–62.

Armstrong, Elizabeth, Laura Hamilton, and Beth Sweeney. "Sexual Assault on Campus: A Multilevel, Integrative Approach to Party Rape." *Social Problems* 53 (2006): 483–99.

D'Emilio, John, and Estelle Freedman. *Intimate Matters: A History of Sexuality in America*. Chicago: University of Chicago Press, 1997.

Ghaziani, Amin. *Sex Cultures*. Cambridge, UK: Polity Press, 2017.

Harding, Kate. *Asking For It: The Alarming Rise of Rape Culture and What We Can Do About It*. Boston: De Capo Lifelong Books, 2015.

Wade, Lisa. *American Hookup: The New Culture of Sex on Campus*. New York: W. W. Norton and Company, 2017.

Ward, Jane. *Not Gay: Sex between Straight White Men*. New York: New York University Press, 2015.

“

OH, THIS WILL *REALLY* INTEREST MY *WIFE*.

—A HUSBAND[1]

”

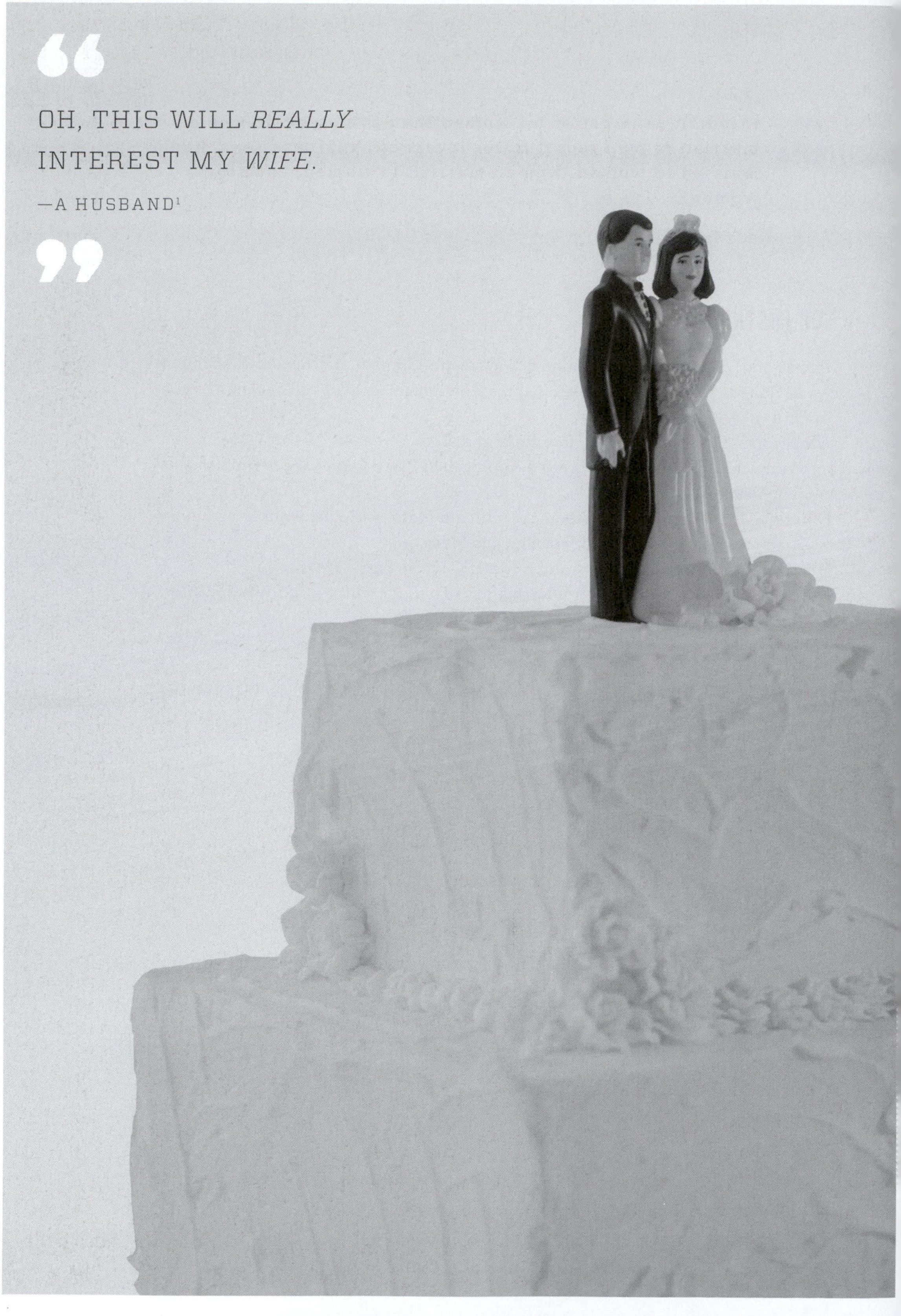

Families

Thanks to hundreds of years of legal reform and social change, individuals have substantially more freedom to arrange their relationships as they wish. This is what feminists have been fighting for and what many people want. Even marriage is no longer gendered by law, a change that also paved the way for same-sex marriage and helped give trans men and women the opportunity to partner without confronting gender-related hurdles.

Still, of all the folks who marry today, it is women in mixed-sex partnerships who have the most troubled relationship to marriage.[2] Counter to stereotypes, women are less eager than men to marry. Once married, wives are less happy than husbands. More than a third of men, but less than a quarter of women, think happiness comes more easily to married people than singles. Men are more likely to believe in the idea of a "soul mate"; women are more skeptical.

Women are as likely as men to have an affair that precedes a divorce and more likely to initiate a separation. This is in part because they're significantly less likely than men to think a child needs both a mother and a father. After divorce, women are happier than they were when married; for men, the opposite is true. Accordingly, divorced women are more likely than divorced men to say they'd prefer to never marry again.

Women in mixed-sex marriages are also less happy than women in same-sex marriages.[3] While these marriages are similar in most ways, men married to men, and especially women married to women, seem to have more satisfying unions than men and women who are married to each other. They argue less, are better at conflict resolution, and take disagreements less personally.

All this has prompted the question:

Q+A   **If marriage is better for women than ever, why do women married to men report lower levels of happiness than men married to women, women married to women, and single women?**

The reasons have to do with how people arrange their family lives, and these arrangements affect not just women married to men, but all kinds of partnerships. To understand these dynamics, this chapter explores the gendered nature of housework and childcare in culture and conversation, then looks at the surprising contrast between what people say they want and how they actually divide paid and unpaid work in practice. It will also review new and emerging family arrangements, as well as some oldies-but-goodies, with an emphasis on how gender intersects with other features of families.

Throughout, the chapter will show how woman bear disproportionate responsibility for devalued and unpaid categories of labor as a result of sexism, androcentrism, and subordination. This disadvantages women as a whole, exacerbates inequality among women, and places them at odds with one another. Unfortunately, while we think of families as places where love and care take center stage, they are also places in which both difference and inequality are reproduced.

GENDERED HOUSEWORK AND PARENTING

Today only 20 percent of all mothers are stay-at-home moms with a working husband.[4] In fact, nearly three-quarters of all moms, including almost two-thirds of moms with preschoolers, are in the workforce.[5] Accordingly, breadwinner/housewife marriages—today better described with the gender-neutral term *breadwinner/homemaker*—are outnumbered by both single-parent families and two-parent families in which both partners engage in paid work.

Families without a homemaker face a specific challenge: finding time to do the childcare, cleaning, feeding, and errand-running that housewives historically have done for breadwinner husbands. For single parents and families with two or more working parents, that work is described as the **second shift**, the work that greets us when we come home from paid work.[6] Groceries must be bought, dinner must be cooked, messes must be cleaned, chores must be supervised, cars must be gassed, homework must be reviewed, budgets must be balanced, and kids must be bathed and put to bed. That's a lot of work!

Working two jobs—one paid at work and one unpaid at home—can be exhausting. In fact, over half of married fathers and three-quarters of both married and single mothers say they have too little time for themselves; a third of dads and over 40 percent of married and single moms say they're always rushed.[7] These trends are true in most North American and Western European countries, but they are especially extreme in the United States among the middle and upper classes.[8]

Further, the second shift isn't gender-neutral terrain. Childcare and housework still carry the gendered meanings they did when breadwinner/housewife families were considered ideal.[9] And that's a problem. Conflict over household responsibilities is among the top reasons why between a third and half of all marriages will end in divorce and why becoming a parent is notoriously hard on both mixed- and same-sex couples.[10] The remainder of this section discusses why, reviewing the social construction of childcare and housework and the actual and ideal division of labor in families today.

Childcare and Housework in Culture

Individual mothers are the primary caregivers in only 20 percent of cultures and, in most of these, children are given considerably more independence than we tend to think is wise today.[11] Indeed, according to historian Peter Stearns, for most of American history children were seen as "sturdy innocents who would grow up well unless corrupted by adult example and who were capable of considerable self-correction."[12] In other words, so long as they didn't encounter a person who set out to harm them deliberately, children could be expected to look after themselves, learn about life, and become well-adjusted adults.

In the 1800s, some experts even argued that too much attention paid by mothers to their children was harmful. Women were given strict warnings not to overlove. John Watson, who wrote one of the best-selling child advice books of all time, cautioned that "mother love is a dangerous instrument":

> *An instrument which may inflict a never-healing wound, a wound which may make infancy unhappy, adolescence a nightmare, an instrument which may wreck your adult son or daughter's vocational future and their chances for marital happiness.*

As for affection, Watson advised: "Kiss them once on the forehead when they say goodnight. Shake hands with them in the morning." But only, he said, "if you must." Parents were advised against hugging, kissing, and letting a child sit in their lap.

Responding to the Watsons of the time, wealthy white Victorian wives embarked on a deliberate and self-interested effort to preserve their social standing.[13] Recall that the gendered work/home distinction was new, emerging with the rise of cities, and so was the idea that what women did at home wasn't work. Pressing back against the devaluation of their freshly separated sphere, and adjusting to men's disengagement from the home, these women claimed that mothering was an essential, delicate, and time-consuming enterprise. This was the birth of the **ideology of intensive motherhood**, the idea that (1) child-rearing should include "copious amounts of time, energy, and material resources"; (2) giving children these things takes priority over all other interests, desires, and demands; and (3) it should be mothers who do this work.[14]

Intensive mothering is still culturally dominant in the United States today among the middle and upper classes. It appeals today especially because it intersects with the economic insecurity of the past few decades. If getting ahead matters, then there's no time to waste; intensive mothering starts the minute, or even before, the child is born. Parents also worry that if they don't take steps to ensure otherwise, their children may fall below the parents' own class position. In an effort to protect their children against this, part of intensive mothering includes **concerted cultivation**, an active and organized effort to develop in children a wide range of skills and talents.[15] This is typically aimed at fostering high self-esteem, strong academic marks, a well-rounded set of capacities and interests, and confidence interacting with adults and navigating social institutions.

When children are small, intensive parenting means avoiding the use of playpens or other restraining devices in favor of close supervision. Meanwhile, concerted cultivation means providing constant interaction and stimulation; offering brain-stimulating toys and activities; and engaging in negotiation instead of instruction. For older children, the work includes maximizing children's educational achievement (volunteering at school, meeting with teachers, helping with homework); keeping a close eye on their grades (guaranteeing they get good marks through cajoling, threatening, or helping); and organizing educational trips and buying learning games (trips to zoos and children's museums, math- and science-based video games and apps). Finally, it means enrolling them in and ferrying them to and from school, after-school, and weekend activities (piano lessons, Little League, dance classes) and giving them at least some of the material goods they want but don't necessarily need (the "right" clothes and accessories).

Attachment parenting, or intensive motherhood, involves keeping one's child close at all times—perhaps even while checking email.

Not everyone has the time to be an intensive parent or the money to engage in concerted cultivation, but because these approaches are endorsed by upper- and upper-middle-class families, they tend to dominate conversations among mommy bloggers, parenting experts, child psychologists, and advice-book authors. Americans receive daily messages affirming the idea that it is women's respon- sibility to care for both the home and their children. Advertisements for home décor, cleaning supplies, and food for families almost exclusively feature or target female consumers.

Even when parenting guides, magazines, and newspaper articles don't make an explicit claim that mothers should be the primary parents, most assume they are.[16] "You've undoubtedly been smooching your baby and saying things like 'Give mommy a kiss!'" reads one parenting magazine, revealing that by "you" they mean the mother.[17] Parenting websites sometimes feature a "Dad Zone," indicating that the rest of the website is *really* for moms.[18] There's even a sneaky linguistic switcheroo that reveals that mothers are considered the primary parent and fathers the secondary one. While the male version of a term usu- ally comes before the female—for example, "men and women," "his and hers," and "boys and girls"—writing about parenting usually uses the phrase "mom and dad."

When books, magazines, and websites about parenting do address fathers, they often aim to convince men that being an active parent is fun, engaging, and important. Mothers don't receive these messages on the assumption that they're already wholly invested. To make parenting seem right for dads, marketers offer them shortcuts. Whereas commercials and advertisements for elaborate or healthy meal options typically feature moms, advertisements that feature dads are often for fast food, microwaveable meals, or pizza delivery.

If dads are not portrayed as reluctant parents, they're often portrayed as incompetent ones. Movies and television shows spanning decades, from *Mr. Mom* (1983) to *Who's the Boss?* (1984–1992) to *3 Men and a Baby* (1987) to *Married with Children* (1987–1997) to *The Simpsons* (1989–) to *Kindergarten Cop* (1990) to *Everybody Loves Raymond* (1996–2005) to *Family Guy* (1999–) to *Daddy Day Care* (2003) to *Grown Ups* (2010) to *Moms' Night Out* (2014), portray dads as bumbling and in over their head. Fathers alone with their children are often played to comic effect: He'll burn the toast, dress his daughter in summer clothes on a winter day, or mix darks with lights in the washer.[19] Exasperated women are often shown swooping in and relieving men of household duties on the understanding that it would be easier for them to just do it themselves.

The assumption that childcare is primarily for mothers shows up in advertisements for a variety of products.

The ABC comedy *Baby Daddy*, about a twentysomething who suddenly becomes a father after a one-night stand, uses the stereotype of fathers as incompetent caregivers to comedic effect.

Housework and Childcare in Practice

Exposed to these cultural messages, many people internalize the idea that housework and childcare are feminized activities. A study of men with male roommates, for example, found that many of them thought cleanliness was "girly."[20] Doing masculinity meant not caring whether the house was clean, or at least pretending not to care. "It's whatever," said Rick when asked about how he and his roommates keep the house clean. He insisted that he didn't even think about it. "It doesn't really matter. I mean, it's not like something I consider. It's not like I'm caring about it if it happens or not."[21]

Since caring about cleanliness is feminized and our society is androcentric, these men avoided doing household tasks if they could. Jeremy explained that when all the dishes were dirty, they'd eat out or order in rather than wash them. When these men did do housework, they had to come up with an account: some motivation *other* than a feminized desire for cleanliness. They would put off doing laundry until they had nothing left to wear or wait to clean the toilet until their moms were coming for a visit.

Of course, manliness, however it is socially constructed, is not a natural or universal trait in men. So, while some men were quite comfortable with this system, it frustrated other men who preferred cleanliness. "I'm not his wife," grumbled one cleanliness-inclined roommate. If he said nothing, he ended up either living with the mess or doing the majority of the housework himself. If he complained, he faced gender policing from his housemates.

Interviews with female partners of trans men also illustrate the feminization of domestic work.[22] In a study of these partnerships, women did the majority of the housework and the trans men's identity as men made this gendered division of labor seem natural. Often this arrangement was justified by the trans men's masculinity. "He's very forgetful and he doesn't take care of himself and he's messy and all this other stuff," said one interviewee named Lilia. "I feel like he's very specifically like a boy in this way."[23] That gendered division also made the men's female partners feel more feminine. Lilia continues: "I clean up on my own free will and try and take care of him.... It makes me feel very female."[24]

Studies of gay fathers suggest that childcare is feminized, too. Gay dads sometimes use language associated with women to describe their desire for children and their role as a caregiver. They talk about listening to their "biological clocks," having "maternal instincts," and being "housewives" and "soccer moms."[25] An excerpt from a conversation between Nico and Drew, for example, a couple with twin toddlers, shows just how much the "mother as true nurturer" idea pervades their thinking about parenting:

> *Nico: Since I don't work as often, I am more of the mom role. I am home more with them. I'm the one who takes them to the park during the week and I usually feed them and . . .*

> *Drew: Wait, I am just as much a mommy as you! Just because my job is more lucrative does not automatically make me the dad, and besides, we both feed them dinner, read to them, get them to bed and I always do the dishes so that you can relax.[26]*

Nico and Drew both used language that indicated that parenting is a woman's activity: the "mom role."

Even when men are actively parenting, the feminine social construction of childcare causes others to see it as the exception rather than the rule.[27] In a study of stay-at-home fathers, a dad named Lew explained that strangers are regularly inspired to comment on what they view as an odd sight—a man alone with kids:

> *When I go out with the kids, people always say, "Oh, so you're babysitting the kids today?" Or, "Oh, it's daddy's day," or "You must have the day off from work," or something like that. They assume that I work somewhere and this is just this random day that I happen to be with the kids, which really irritates me.[28]*

Other stay-at-home dads report similar experiences. One dad was confronted by a group of police officers after they received a report that a "suspicious" man was carrying a baby. In fact, he was walking through his own neighborhood with his own child.

Studies of male roommates, gay couples, women partnered with trans men, and single dads all reveal the feminization of housework and childcare. And, if we zoom out, we find that family life is, in fact, strongly gendered.[29] In America today, both men and women in mixed-sex relationships are working hard, spending about the same amount of time on paid and unpaid work combined, but the proportion of time men and women spend in paid and unpaid work differs in gender-stereotypical ways. On average, mothers spend twenty-five hours per week working for pay, while fathers spend nearly forty-three hours, an eighteen-hour difference; fathers spend about eighteen hours per week on the house and kids while mothers spend thirty-two, or fourteen more. To put it more simply, fathers do about two-thirds of the paid work and one-third of the unpaid work, and mothers do the inverse.[30] This disparity grows larger as relationships become more serious: from boyfriend/girlfriend to a couple that lives together, from cohabitation to marriage, and from married to married with kids.[31]

BREADWINNERS, HOMEMAKERS, AND SUPERSPOUSES As the averages suggest, the most common type of family is one that involves **specialization** (splitting unpaid and paid work so that each partner does more of one than the other) instead of **sharing** (doing more or less symmetrical amounts of paid and unpaid work). Some of these families resemble the idealized 1950s bread-winner/homemaker model. Advocates of this model are called **traditionalists**: they believe men should be responsible for earning income and women should be responsible for housework and childcare. Frank, for instance, explains: "I look at myself as pretty much a traditionalist. It's the way I am inside. I feel that the man should be the head of the house. He should have the final say."[32] Carmen, Frank's wife, agrees. She just wants to be "taken care of," she says.[33]

We see traditional breadwinner/homemaker marriages mostly at the highest and lowest family income levels.[34] Highly paid men who make the elusive "family wage" can afford for one parent to stay home. Among the wealthiest 5 percent of families, 42 percent include a stay-at-home parent. These families may rely on one earner voluntarily.

Over half of families with incomes in the bottom 20 percent of households also have a person who stays home full-time.[35] Instead of being voluntary, this is often the only choice for poorer families. In America the average cost of infant care is $9,589 a year, an amount that exceeds the average in-state college tuition.[36] On average, childcare for children four and under will absorb 64 percent of a full-time minimum-wage worker's earnings; in Massachusetts, where it's the most expensive, it absorbs nearly 90 percent of the income of that same worker.[37] If parents are low income, they may save money by leaving one or the other partner at home.

In one-earner families, whether high or low income, the full-time home-maker is usually a wife. Though there are twice as many stay-at-home dads as there were twenty years ago, they account for only 5 percent of committed stay-at-home parents.[38] Four out of five dads at home report that they're home only because they're unemployed, ill or disabled, in school, or retired. African American, Hispanic, and Asian men, and men with limited education, are more likely to stay home than white men and highly educated men.[39]

A modified version of the breadwinner/homemaker marriage is the bread-winner/*super*spouse marriage, one in which breadwinners focus on work and their spouse both works and takes care of the home. Advocates of this model are called **neo-traditionalists**: They believe that a woman should be able to work if she desires, but only if it doesn't interfere with her "real" duty to take care of her husband and children. Many neo-traditionalists are in "one-and-a-half" breadwinner marriages, where women's part-time employment is fitted around her primary obligation to be a homemaker. Sam, for example, a neo-traditionalist, explains that he would accept a working wife, but, "[i]f she wanted to work, I would assume it's her responsibility to drop the kids off at grandma's house or something. She's in charge of the kids. If she's gonna work, fine, but you still have responsibilities."[40] Unlike breadwinner/homemaker marriages, these families are usually economically secure but not wealthy: well-off enough to afford day care, but not secure enough to live on one salary alone.

Superspouses are, to put it bluntly, busy. By definition, they work full- or part-time and still take on the lion's share of the second shift: juggling work, the logistics of day care, and the needs of a spouse and children. The average employed mother spends sixty-three hours a week on paid and unpaid work.[41] She also has four fewer hours of leisure time than your average employed father and spends more time multitasking.[42]

Especially if they're women, superspouses also do the majority of the invisible work: the intellectual, mental, and emotional work of parenting and household maintenance. They do more of the learning and information processing (like researching pediatricians), more of the worrying (like wondering if their child is hitting developmental milestones), and more of the organizing and delegating (like deciding what to cook for dinner). As you can imagine, superspouses often wear themselves out and can feel like they're falling short in every part of life: as a parent, as a spouse, and as an employee.

When dads step in to do some of this work, it is often described as "giving mommy a break," "babysitting," and "pitching in."[43] Traditional and neo-traditional husbands can be good "helpers," but usually only if their partners actively give them tasks to do. Nina, for example, who is partnered with a trans man, describes her management of their household this way: "I remind him to

Superspouses like Claire Dunphy are a fixture of modern families. Men's involvement in family life often comes at the margins of their commitment to paid jobs, while women are expected to ensure that the fundamentals at home are taken care of, regardless of what jobs they hold.

do a lot, and am the planner and really sort of controlling about a lot of things. He is the one who is super flaky and forgetful. . . . So the dynamic is me trying to keep on the ball about things and him assuming that I'm going to take care of it."[44]

The constant organizing and delegating of superspouses may make it seem like they're in charge at home, and in a sense they are, but "the assumption of [largely] female responsibility [also] means that, on another level, [breadwinners] are in charge—because it is only with their permission and cooperation that women can relinquish their duties."[45] Getting breadwinners to help, in other words, can sometimes be a job all its own. Ruth, in a relationship with Cindy for nearly a decade, comments:

I have learned how to read Cindy for moods and I know when I can get her to do stuff and when I can't. It's sort of a subtle negotiation. I don't know if she realizes that I am scanning the moments waiting to ask her to clean out the fireplace or hose out the garage, but that's what I do. I sort of get in tune with the rhythm of her life now and it seems to work.[46]

Don had something similar to say about his same-sex partner, Gill:

> *I have to prod him; "bitch at him" is what he would say. I have found it difficult to figure out ways to bring up the condition of the house without creating too much of a fight. I sort of have learned that there are certain times to bring it up. I especially try to avoid bringing things up when he just gets home from work. I find he is more willing to help, or at least to hear it, later at night. Of course, he doesn't see any of this—it's annoying—nor does he recognize what an effort it is to get him to help.*[47]

Even if superspouses don't have to do it all, then, it's still up to them to keep track of what needs to be done, divvy up the work, and figure out how to cajole or entice their partners into helping.[48] This makes many superspouses into frantic taskmasters and can create ugly interpersonal dynamics. When they have to ask for help, superspouses often feel like "nags," while the breadwinner may feel "henpecked."

This isn't just exhausting and bad for happiness in marriage, though; it is objectively disempowering.

The Loss of Status and Security

Victorian women introduced the ideology of intensive motherhood as a way to resist the androcentric devaluation of the domestic sphere, but these efforts were not wholly successful. Housework and childcare are still low-status activities. When journalist Ann Crittenden had her first child, for example, she was a foreign correspondent for *Newsweek*, a financial reporter for *The New York Times*, and a Pulitzer Prize nominee. None of this seemed to matter, she said, when she became a mother. Whereas once she'd been "*The* Ann Crittenden" at fancy New York cocktail parties, now she was "just a mom." She wrote that she felt like she'd "shed status like the skin off a snake."[49] A woman she interviewed about this phenomenon explained how it felt to go from being a young professional to a young mother:

> *We are the very women who were successful in what the women's revolution was all about, which was to be able to get out there and be the equal of the guys. . . . And suddenly [you have a baby and] you're back in the female world. It's a shock. . . . Raising children is still part of a relatively low-status world. Everything was gone once I started to stay home. In my new job as a mother, I had no salary and no professional contacts. . . . No more dinners out. No work clothes. . . . It was as if everything were being taken away from me.*[50]

People sometimes say that a woman who stays at home "doesn't *do* anything." "Oh, so you don't work?" a homemaker might be asked, as she quickly mops the kitchen floor so she can have time to run by the dry cleaner before picking up her child from preschool, feeding him a snack, and finding something for him to do so she can begin preparing dinner for her spouse and ten-year-old. Even homemakers sometimes refer to their work as "*just* staying home"; doing nothing important, in other words.

When we have asked our students what their parents would think if they decided to have a child right after graduation and become a stay-at-home caregiver, both men and women often suggest that their parents would be disappointed, even aghast. Among other possible responses, students imagine their parents would ask, "What did we spend all that money on college for!?" or exclaim, "That would be a waste of your intelligence!" It's as if people think parenting requires zero knowledge and even less brain power.

No wonder many men aren't interested in doing it. In fact, many men express just these sentiments when asked how they would feel if *they* specialized in domestic labor. Josh, for instance, explains:

> I would never stay home. I have a friend who's like that, and I strongly disapprove. The father just stays home. I think it's wrong because his wife's out there working seven days a week, and he's doing nothing except staying home.[51]

Gay men often view housework similarly. Rich, for example, asked, "What about one's self-respect?" when he contemplated being a full-time homemaker. "I don't see how one could live with oneself by not doing *something* for a living."[52] Note how Josh and Rich's language—"doing nothing" vs. "doing something"—betrays their belief that feminized household labor isn't really anything at all.

In interpersonal relationships, those who specialize in domestic work sometimes feel as though their partners don't value their contribution to the household, and they might be right. In an interview, a husband let slip how little regard he had for the last twelve years of his wife Kuae's life, during which time she'd been a stay-at-home mom:

> Being the kind of person I am, Type A . . . always going after something, I wonder what I could have done, having twelve years to sort of think about what I want to do. I sometimes think, Wow, I could have been an astronaut in twelve years, or I could have been something different that I'd really enjoy. . . . What could I have been in twelve years of self-discovery?[53]

His comments reveal indirectly that he was wondering what Kuae had been doing, as if taking care of a home and three children took no time at all. To him, she had done nothing, effectively wasting those twelve years. For her part, Kuae was well aware that her husband devalued her work at home: "I think he has struggled with assigning value," she said stonily.

People who specialize in the unpaid labor of the household might also feel they have less of a voice in their relationships. One wife who quit her job to stay home with her children gave an example of how she'd lost bargaining power:

> It's funny now because he is the breadwinner so there have been … opportunities to relocate and get a better position and the money was better. You're just put in a position where you have to just follow. Before when we were both working we would talk it out. I'd say, "No, I want to stay here." And now you really can't.[54]

Stay-at-home fathers can feel similarly. About his wife, one explained,

> She's the one bringing home the money right now so I feel, in financial decisions, I feel a little, I don't want to use the word uncomfortable, but I mean a little bit more uncomfortable about, saying oh, we should spend, we should buy this or do this or that sort of thing. Yeah, I guess I'm a little self-conscious in a way that I'm not contributing to our financial means.[55]

We see these status and power differences in all kinds of couples where one person specializes in domestic work: among mixed-sex neo-traditionalists, gender-swapped mixed-sex couples, same-sex relationships, and even polyamorous relationships involving three or more people.[56] In losing status, homemakers often feel at least somewhat subordinated to their breadwinners. The vulnerability that comes with taking disproportionate responsibility for domestic work, though, isn't limited to status and interpersonal power. It's also economic.

THE MOMMY TAX Taking time out of the workforce to raise small children and then reentering it with less momentum means lost wages, benefits, and Social Security contributions. A college-educated American woman, for example, is likely to sacrifice nearly $2 million over the course of her lifetime for the pleasures of having children.[57] Mothers who take three years or more off incur, on average, a 37 percent decrease in income; mothers who take less than a year off see a drop of 11 percent.[58] It's wryly called the "mommy tax."[59]

These numbers reveal that one of the functions of marriage is still to transfer economic resources from men to women, or breadwinners to caregivers. As long as homemakers or superspouses remain married to breadwinners who are willing to share their income and wealth, this may not be very noticeable, but if the breadwinners rescind their support or the family-focused spouse chooses divorce, the economic vulnerability of the latter can become painfully obvious. This asymmetric focus, then, with caregivers spending more time with the house and children and breadwinners spending more time at work, may look fair on the face of it—they both put in approximately the same number of hours on their shared lives—but because we reward only one of those jobs with money, this asymmetry hurts caregivers (mostly women) more than breadwinners (mostly men) in the long run. In same-sex partnerships, it harms anyone who takes a feminized role.

Outsourcing Inequalities

One way to adjust this asymmetry is to hire help. Some neo-traditional families engage in extensive **domestic outsourcing**: paying nonfamily members to do family-related tasks. Such arrangements are especially common among highly educated, career-focused, professional-class couples working in fields like tech, medicine, law, or finance. If both parents want to remain on accelerated career tracks, most of these families will need to hire a substantial amount of outside help.

To a certain extent, some level of domestic outsourcing is now the rule for families. Nannies are outsourced childcare, for example, but so is in-home or institutional day care. We also outsource meals (eating in restaurants, getting take-out, ordering delivery, or buying prepared meals from the grocery store), work around the house (hiring housekeepers, gardeners, a "handyman" to fix things, a neighbor kid to shovel the sidewalk after it snows), chores and errands (accountants, tailors, dry cleaners, dog groomers, drivers, or mechanics), and

This photo features an example of the top of the care chain, in which the caregiving of middle- or upper-class children becomes the responsibility of poorer women, often women of color, whose own children receive less care as a result.

direct childcare and instruction (babysitters, of course, but also tutors, swimming instructors, and camp counselors).

Outsourcing is a way couples with class privilege can build and maintain egalitarian relationships, but it does nothing to undermine the devaluation of feminized work. Instead, it displaces the harm, pushing it off onto other, more disadvantaged women and deepening the inequality among them.[60] When families outsource childrearing and domestic work, the people they hire are almost always female and poorer than the family members who are buying their services: 95 percent of domestic workers are women, 54 percent are a racial or ethnic minority, 32 percent have less than a high school education, 46 percent are foreign born, and 35 percent are noncitizens.[61]

Domestic jobs are generally considered "bad jobs," ones with long hours, low pay, little flexibility, no security or chance for advancement, and few benefits. The average wage for a live-in nanny, for example, is $6.76 an hour.[62] Only as of 2013 were domestic workers legally entitled to pay at or above the minimum wage and to days off, overtime, and contributions to their Social Security accounts. The Supreme Court has also denied them the right to unionize.

Importantly, many of the women who perform housework and childcare for other people also have children of their own, and they usually are not allowed to bring them to work. Because their wages are low, they purchase the even lower-wage services of even poorer women. These women, in turn, leave their own children with family members or friends. Sociologist Rhacel Parreñas calls this a **care chain**, a series of nurturing relationships in which the care of children, the disabled, or the elderly is displaced onto increasingly disadvantaged paid or unpaid carers. She explains:

> An older daughter from a poor family in a third world country cares for her siblings (the first link in the chain) while her mother works as a nanny caring for the children of a nanny migrating to a first world country (the second link) who, in turn, cares for the child of a family in a rich country (the final link).[63]

Caring brings in decreasing financial returns as you go down the chain. A nanny working for a wealthy family in the United States might earn $400 a week. She, in turn, may pay a live-in domestic worker in her country of origin $40 a week. That worker may leave her children to be taken care of by their older sister or grandmother for free.

These care chains are not only economic; they displace love and its benefits by pushing it up the chain.[64] Nannies who are also parents find their love and attention displaced onto their employers' children.[65] They spend weekdays organizing and chaperoning character- and skill-building activities with the children they're paid to care for; on weekends and evenings they have to fit in their own errands, house cleaning, and other routine activities for their own families. A nanny may enjoy this time with her children but having to fit in all the work that's part of her own second shift will substantially cut down on quality time.

This displacement is especially extreme for migrants. Vicky, a thirty-four-year-old mother who left the Philippines to work for a family in Beverly Hills, explains how she misses her five children: "[It's] very depressing," she sighed. She finds solace in loving the child for whom she nannies: "In my absence from my children, the most I could do with my situation is give all my love to that child."

So the child in Beverly Hills benefits from Vicky's love as well as the love of his or her own parents. Vicky's time and attention are diverted from her own children, whom she can love only from afar. That absence is partially filled by attention from their lower-paid nanny in the Philippines, who likely has her own child or children in an even less secure arrangement, where they are deprived of a certain amount of love and attention from their own mother. In other words, the excess love that the child in Beverly Hills receives comes at the expense of other, less fortunate children.

Class-privileged women, and others married to breadwinners, can replace themselves. In making this patriarchal bargain, they may avoid (some of) the mommy tax and excel at work, thereby dodging the consequences that come with being "just" a mom or stay-at-home dad. That's nice, but it isn't "women's liberation," even when women do it, because it depends on *another woman* coming in to do that work. Outsourcing may help individual women and other family-focused spouses, but it doesn't lift up women as a group, nor does it undermine the devaluation of femininity or avoid perpetuating gendered forms of subordination.[66]

In sum, because of androcentrism, we devalue the feminized domestic sphere relative to the masculinized work sphere. Because of sexism, we feel comfortable expecting women to bear the brunt of this trivialized, unpaid, and sometimes disparaged activity. And an intersectional lens reveals that when the harm is displaced, it is often displaced onto women of color, poor women, and migrant women. In this way, mixed-sex partnerships are a systematic form of gender subordination not unlike the relationships between doctors and nurses or bosses and secretaries: They bring men and women into different and unequal relationships. The fact that this occurs through coupling instead of occupational choices doesn't mean it's not a form of inequality; it's just a particularly intimate one.

Is this what people really want? It turns out, mostly not. When the sociologist Kathleen Gerson asked eighteen- to thirty-four-year-olds how they would ideally divide homemaking and breadwinning in a mixed-sex relationship, only a minority said they wanted to do so by gender.[67] The majority—about 80 percent of women and 70 percent of men across all races, classes, and family backgrounds—said they preferred a relationship with "flexible gender boundaries."[68] Among people under thirty, almost no one idealizes strongly gendered divisions of labor anymore.[69] Most men and women today are neither traditionalists nor neo-traditionalists; they're **egalitarians**, preferring relationships in which both partners do their fair share of breadwinning, housekeeping, and childrearing.

This raises a question: If men and women want relationships in which they share paid and unpaid work about equally, why do studies find that both mixed- and same-sex couples specialize in practice? The answer, as you'll see in the next section, is that sharing is hard.

BARRIERS TO EQUAL SHARING

Both work and family are **greedy institutions**, ones that take up an incredible amount of time and energy.[70] High expectations for workers intersect with high expectations for parenting, making it difficult or impossible for people to be successful at work, feel good about how much time they spend at home, and attend to their personal well-being.[71] Often couples come to the conclusion that one or both partners need to spend less time at work and more time at home.

Institutional Barriers

Features of the economy make it difficult for both parents to share. Real sharing often means both spouses need to retreat into lower-paying, less demanding occupations or, alternatively, work part-time. Most families can't afford to have all their income be compromised by low wages or limited hours; they may, though, be able to afford one compromised income.

Even if a family could theoretically afford two compromised incomes, marriage and employment law can make this challenging. Most families access health insurance through a parent's employer, but this benefit typically accrues only to employees who work a forty-hour workweek. Families with no employer-provided insurance rely on the health care markets—colloquially called "Obamacare"—but these are substantially more expensive, especially for a family of three or more. If possible, the smartest financial choice for a family is to have at least one adult who can satisfy an entire family's health care needs through an employer. In other words, a breadwinner. Citizens of countries with nationalized health care don't face this problem, giving them more options for how to organize their families.

Among high-income earners, the Social Security tax further rewards breadwinner/homemaker families over those that share these duties; the income of a couple in which one earns $140,000 a year and the other earns nothing is taxed less than a couple in which both partners earn $70,000.[72] This is a tax incentive for specializing couples and a tax burden for sharing ones.

The scarcity of time also constrains families' options. The placement of homes, childcare centers, workplaces, and doctors' offices in different parts of town is an institutional barrier to sharing paid and unpaid work. Long commutes add to the workday, making it even more difficult for income earners to participate in home life. Commutes aren't inevitable but a consequence of zoning laws that separate residential and commercial districts. If we zoned differently, it might be easier for families to share housework.

When couples realize that specialization is necessary, often the smartest thing to do is rely on the career of the partner who has a higher salary and greater opportunity for advancement. But the workplace, as the next chapter will make clear, is no more gender-neutral than the family. In mixed-sex relationships, men typically earn more money than women, making it sensible for many families to choose to prioritize the man's career for purely economic reasons. But even when the woman is better paid, protecting the man's ego becomes a reason to defer to his job, and she is the one who makes amends with housework.[73]

If a child arrives, it may make sense, above and beyond any biological or ideological reasons, for the mother to take time off from work instead of the father. Many moms relish this opportunity and many dads are jealous. Still, there is a price to pay: Each month a woman stays out of the workforce is a month in which her partner is building a career. By the time she's ready to work full-time again, he's "ahead" of her. He may have gotten a promotion or a raise; in any case, his greater experience now makes him more employable.

Now it makes even *more* economic sense for the couple to prioritize his career instead of hers. Instead of deciding to let her take a turn—so she can prioritize work for a while and he can enjoy the pleasures of family life—she may get a part-time job or switch to a less demanding occupation. This may be the best option for the pair, but it also strengthens his advantage over her in the workplace and motivates continued specialization. The more a couple specializes, the more economic sense it makes to continue doing so.

As new mothers cut back on their work hours, new fathers ramp up at work.[74] As is clear in Figure 11.1, additional children accelerate this trend. As a result of their longer workdays, men often do less housework.[75] In response, wives often work even less, citing their husbands' hours and the new housework demands as a reason why.[76] Once a couple specializes, even if they imagine it is just a temporary concession to time pressures, there is a tendency for the disparity to grow and grow.

All of this helps explain, too, why three-quarters of same-sex couples also specialize.[77] Their divisions of labor are generally more equal than those of mixed-sex couples, come in more diverse forms, and follow logics other than gender difference, but they are subject to the same social forces pushing them toward specialization.[78] So, most same-sex couples specialize, especially once they have kids.

FIGURE 11.1 | AVERAGE NUMBER OF PAID WORK HOURS PER WEEK, BY NUMBER OF CHILDREN

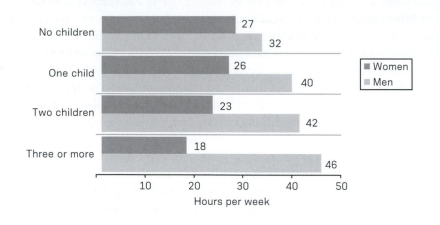

Source: Pew Research Center, "On Pay Gap, Millennial Women Near Parity—For Now," December 11, 2013, www.pewsocialtrends.org/2013/12/11/on-pay-gap-millenial-women-near-parity-for-now/.

"The truth is," said psychologist Abbie Goldberg, "same-sex couples wrestle with the same dynamics as heterosexuals. Things are humming along and then you have a baby or adopt a child, and all of a sudden there's an uncountable amount of work." Facing that uncountable amount of work, and state and workplace policies that reward specialization, same-sex couples make many of the same choices that mixed-sex couples do. Sarah, for example, a woman raising five children with her wife, explained: "For me, the choice to stay home seems easier than us both working and both stressing about who's going to do what. That just seems impossible."

Institutional forces make sharing difficult, pushing couples of all kinds toward specialization, especially once they have children. For mixed-sex relationships, there is further ideological pressure to make that specialization gendered.

Ideological Barriers

Recall that men were pressed into wage work during the Industrial Revolution and told to be good cogs in the profit-making capitalist machine: reliable workers who would put their companies before their families. In return, they were promised wives who would make their homes a caring refuge from work. Women, for their part, were sold the cult of domesticity, an ideology that sold dependency on men with the promise that women could avoid the dog-eat-dog world of work and be supported by adoring husbands. These ideas still have a strong purchase on American culture such that, when push comes to shove, many men have a hard time abandoning the breadwinner role and many women find themselves strongly drawn to the idea of being the warm center of family life.

When egalitarian men are asked about their "fallback plan," for example—what they would like to do if they discovered that sharing wasn't possible—70 percent choose a neo-traditional arrangement.[79] It turns out, if equal sharing proves too difficult, men overwhelmingly hope to convince their partners to de-prioritize their careers and focus on homemaking and raising children. Matthew exemplifies this plan:

> If I could have the ideal world, I'd like to have a partner who's making as much as I am—someone who's ambitious and likes to achieve. [But] if it can't be equal, I would be the breadwinner and be there for helping with homework at night.[80]

Most men value their role as workers too much—and perhaps homemaking too little—to imagine de-prioritizing their own career. "If somebody's gonna be the breadwinner," Jim said, "it's going to be me."[81]

Only a quarter of egalitarian women prefer neo-traditionalism as a fallback plan, but they may find themselves negotiating about how to divide labor with a husband who does. They may not like it, but they may also not be willing to let their *ideas* about marriage end their *actual* marriage. Simultaneously, they may find themselves the subject of a set of ideas about parenting that powerfully shapes their thinking about their role in the family.

Whatever their beliefs about marriage, many women, especially those in the middle and upper classes, ascribe to the ideology of intensive motherhood and aim, or wish, to put their children at the center of their lives. "For me," said one such mother, "I feel it is vital to be there for my children every day, to consistently tend to their needs, to grow their self-esteem, and to praise them when they're right, to guide them when they're not, and to be a loving, caring mom every minute of the day."[82]

Women who can't intensively mother will often either feel like they're failing at motherhood, or be judged by others as failing. Women who work full-time, migrate to another country to support their families, do their mothering from prison, or ascribe to a different model of motherhood, for example, are all often criticized or pitied for their failure to do mothering right. When women can, they often try their best to live up to this expectation. "I think that people don't look at you and say, 'oh, there's a good mother,'" said one such mother, "but they will look at people and say, 'oh, there's a bad mother.' Being a mother, I worry about what everyone else is going to think."[83]

In this sense, mothers face a double bind that fathers do not. On the one hand, their paid employment may be necessary for paying the bills, buying a house in a good school district, or saving for college tuition. On the other hand, intensive mothering is deemed crucial in giving their child "an edge." This escalating competition for maternal time has been called the "rug rat race."[84] Fear of falling behind drives many mothers to do as much as they can; and rich or poor, no amount is ever enough.

If they have the resources, many mothers will choose to disinvest in their careers, at least in the short term. If they have a husband, he likely agrees. Faced with these ideological and institutional pressures, many otherwise egalitarian women and men will choose a traditional or neo-traditional arrangement. This may satisfy many men. Recall that the majority of men choose neo-traditional family forms as their fallback plan, but only a quarter of women do the same. What do women overwhelmingly choose as their fallback plan? In that same study, they chose divorce.

GOING IT ALONE

As illustrated in Figure 11.2, faced with a husband who insists that they should be a homemaker or work part-time, almost three-quarters of women would rather divorce and raise their kids alone. Fifty-nine percent and 66 percent of women say that parenting and working, respectively, is "very important" or, even, "one of the most important things" in their lives.[85] Only 37 percent say the same about marriage.

What appears to be a happy convergence between men's and women's ideals—both are egalitarians—can turn into an intractable situation. When their ideals bump up against an institutional context that makes sharing difficult, and their fallback plans come to the fore, many couples feel betrayed and resentful. Some of these couples will divorce. And, when couples separate, custody is granted to the mother the majority of the time: 80 percent of custodial parents are mothers and almost half of all mothers will spend at least some time as a single parent.[86]

Other people simply won't end up with someone either to share or specialize with at all. About a third of adults—including both heterosexuals and sexual minorities—will spend their prime childbearing and rearing years without a spouse.[87] Many of these individuals will choose to have and raise children anyway.

Sociologists Kathryn Edin and Maria Kefalas, for example, spent five years getting to know 162 racially diverse low-income single mothers in Philadelphia.[88] Many of them had children while they were young and unmarried, some-

FIGURE 11.2 | MEN'S AND WOMEN'S FALLBACK PLANS

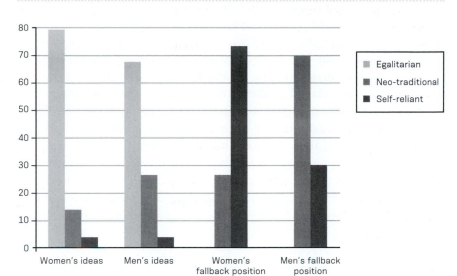

Source: Kathleen Gerson, *The Unfinished Revolution: Coming of Age in a New Era of Gender, Work, and Family* (New York: Oxford University Press, 2010), 129.

thing many Americans believe to be self-defeating. Why did these women make this choice? Why didn't they work hard in school, go to college, find a job and a husband, and *then* have children?

The answer to this question is counterintuitive. While the U.S. government has argued that the answer to unmarried mothers in poverty is to convince them to value marriage, these young women *already* value marriage very much. The marriages in their neighborhoods are all too often torn apart by poverty and men's imprisonment. With these relationships in mind, young women are hopeful yet skeptical about the possibility of finding someone with whom they can build a stable relationship. If they do find someone, they often wait five or ten years before marrying the man they're dating. They want to be as sure as possible that their partnership will last. In contrast, middle-class women tend to feel confident they can make a marriage work, so they wait only one or two years. It's exactly because low-income women take marriage so seriously, and understand its fragility, that they're less likely to marry before having a child.

And when young low-income women do get pregnant, they may have more reason to have the child than not. Middle- and upper-class women in high school see a child as interfering with their plans for college and a career. Poor youth don't often imagine that these things are on the horizon for them, and they may be right. So why should they wait? They consider an early pregnancy less than ideal, but something they can embrace. Moreover, children help make a difficult life feel meaningful.[89] Parenting is one of the few truly important and rewarding activities that isn't systematically made unavailable to them.

On the other end of the class spectrum, some middle- and upper-class women make the same choice at an older age.[90] As having a child "out of wedlock" has become less stigmatized, voluntary unmarried motherhood has increased. Between 1994 and 2014, the number of women who reached their mid-forties as never-married mothers tripled, and an increased proportion of these were women with postgraduate degrees like JDs, MDs, and PhDs.[91] Some of these women cohabitated instead of marrying and some had children before starting or completing their education, but others simply never found a partner with whom to have a child. As they age, these women may perceive their "biological clock" as offering them only a choice between "settling" for a husband they wouldn't freely choose (which some do) or having a child on their own.[92] Anna, a forty-year-old "single mother by choice," explains how she came to her decision:

> I really believe that children are made from two people that love each other and want to create a family. But if that is not an option, you just have to draw a way around really. Because if you are running out of time, you just have to see what option you have to have a child. And then have a father [later].[93]

When women today have the economic resources, access to technology, and enough social support to make a family without a husband, increasingly, they do.

Single parenting—whether after divorce or by choice—exposes the economic vulnerability that comes with responsibility for housework and childcare. Forty-three percent of single mothers live below the poverty line, compared to 24 percent of single fathers.[94] Nearly a third of families led by single mothers are food insecure, with 13 percent using food pantries; a third spend more than half their income on housing.[95]

Some of these single parents are poor because they aren't working. This is partly because it's just not possible to be at work and at home at the same time. Day care is a must. But, as we've already discussed, day care costs often exceed the earnings of a person working full-time, even more than full-time, if it pays near minimum wage. Or childcare leaves so little money left over that it's impossible to afford even an austere lifestyle. For some single parents, the math just doesn't add up.

Government subsidies for low-income single parents help some out of this bind, but these programs are woefully underfunded in the United States and don't reach a large proportion of the people in need. Even if they are able to access these programs, parents are only allowed to use them for two years, after which they are ineligible. Twenty American states have children on waiting lists for subsidized childcare. In the state with the longest waiting list, Texas, parents of 41,600 children are eligible, but the state has no money for them and nowhere to place them.[96] When single parents can't afford to work because of the cost of childcare and failing public services, it contributes to the short- and long-term financial fragility of caregivers.

Most single parents work full-time, though, and many of them are in poverty, too. Nearly three-quarters of single moms work for wages, but this doesn't guarantee financial security.[97] The U.S. federal minimum wage is $7.25 an hour. A full-time employee earning minimum wage who doesn't miss a single day of work for a year earns $290 a week before taxes; that's $15,080 a year. According to how the government measures poverty, that's enough to support a single adult but, for a single adult with a child, it's officially below the poverty line.[98] Consequently, 25 percent of single mothers and 15 percent of single fathers are **working poor**, individuals who work but still live in poverty.[99]

The economic costs and structural contradictions of single parenting apply to everyone, but women bear the brunt of the disadvantage. This is because women are more likely to specialize in domestic work, more likely to end up as single parents, and more likely to work in underpaid industries. As a result, we are seeing a **feminization of poverty**, a trend in which the poor are increasingly women and, of course, their children, too. Stunningly, becoming a mother has been identified as the single strongest predictor of bankruptcy in middle age and poverty in old age.[100]

Divorcees who are lucky enough to have a higher income, as well as the upper- and upper-middle-class women who choose to raise children on their own, may do fine financially. But doing so often means working demanding jobs that require them to engage in extensive domestic outsourcing. For high-income single mothers, this might mean hiring a nanny; for those with middle incomes, it might involve a twice-monthly housekeeper, day care, and lots of take-out dinners. In both cases, they're able to trade economic resources for goods and services that mothers have traditionally provided, at the risk of exacerbating inequality between women.

So far we've discussed how ideological and institutional forces press families to make often-gendered choices that align with a traditional or neo-traditional ideology. These forces typically reinscribe sexism, androcentrism, and subordination. Alternatively, couples try to create equity in their partnership by outsourcing, though this, in turn, reinscribes class, race, and migration-related inequalities. Not uncommonly, domestic arguments about how to divide paid and unpaid work end in divorce. Other individuals never find anyone to share or specialize with at all and choose single parenthood out of a sense of necessity. The financial struggles of single parents, especially when they're low income, signal the extent to which the system is still designed with breadwinner/housewives in mind. That is, it is still assuming and promoting women's dependence on men.

Perhaps that is why, in the past one hundred years, women in traditional household arrangements have been among the most unhappy.[101] Like the 1950s housewives who took tranquilizers to get through their days, today's stay-at-home mothers are decidedly less happy on average than moms who work. Even if they really *wanted* to be a stay-at-home wife, often they find being one less fulfilling or comfortable than they imagined. Likewise, neo-traditional households, with their overworked, "nagging" wives and entitled, "hen-pecked" husbands, are often embattled and unstable. Partly for this reason, these partnerships end in divorce more often than any other kind.[102]

What are our alternatives?

NEW, EMERGING, AND ERSTWHILE FAMILY FORMS

In this section, we review three alternative ways of arranging family life: engaging in dual-nurturing, deciding not to have children, and constructing non-nuclear families.

Dual-Nurturing

If one strategy for creating equity between two spouses is for both to orient themselves toward their careers, another is for both spouses to point their energies in the opposite direction. **Dual-nurturers** turn away from work and toward the home to focus together on the housework and childcare.[103] They make the second shift their priority. Pulling back on their career ambitions and financial goals enables couples truly to share.

Not everyone has the resources to adopt this strategy. In addition to needing to be able to tolerate lower incomes, institutional forces penalize dual-nurturers, making it expensive and increasing the family's tax burden. Adopting dual-nurturing, then, means making economic sacrifices. For some dual-nurturers, the opportunity arises because of the nature of their work: They may share farm labor, run a small business together out of their home, hold jobs with odd but complementary schedules like teachers and firefighters.[104] Some have jobs with high enough incomes that they can actually both work part-time or both forgo career investments that would cost them too much time. But dual-nurturers are generally only able to disinvest at work if they already have some financial advantage. A freelance editor and an accountant, for example, may each be able to work part-time but charge very high hourly rates for what work they do. Together, they might make enough money to pay their bills, while taking turns being home during the day with their children.

In making these choices, dual-nurturers can challenge the sexist idea that women should be held uniquely responsible for the undervalued work of housework and childcare, the one that so often translates into gendered subordination. Partly for this reason, dual-nurturers are among the happiest of mixed-sex couples.[105] The higher likelihood of sharing among same-sex couples is one theory for why they are happier on average than mixed-sex ones.[106]

Dual-nurturing, though, doesn't undermine the androcentric devaluation of childcare and housework. Instead, both partners simply have to live with it. The low status and economic risks faced by homemakers and superspouses, in other words, accrue to *both* members of a dual-nurturer couple. It takes a real ideological commitment by both partners, along with a substantial financial advantage, to make it work.

Even in these couples, though, the ideological commitment to the male breadwinner and female homemaker lingers. Sociologists generally consider duties shared if the division of labor is between 40/60 and 60/40. It turns out that half-and-half arrangements where men and women in mixed-sex relationships split paid and unpaid work exactly 50/50 are not the happiest of sharing agreements.[107] They're the second happiest. The happiest are ones in which there is a slightly asymmetrical division of labor tilted in the stereotypical direction: a woman who does 60 percent of the domestic work and a man who does 60 percent of the breadwinning. Gender-swapped relationships—in which the man does 60 percent of the homemaking and the woman does 60 percent of the breadwinning—are the least happy of the three (though they are still happier than breadwinner/homemaker and breadwinner/superspouse marriages). This suggests that people in mixed-sex partnerships are more comfortable with *almost* sharing than with sharing, and that when the script gets flipped, it can strain relationships.

Choosing Not to Have Children

Faced with the challenge of balancing work and family life, some adults choose not to have children at all. In 2016, the U.S. birthrate was the lowest on record in the last thirty years.[108] One out of seven Americans between the ages of forty and forty-four is without children.[109] While traditionally women with higher levels of education were most likely to eschew childbearing, women with less education are increasingly following suit.

The decision to go "childfree" is partly a response to the demands of the ideology of intensive mothering and concerted cultivation. Kay, a twenty-four-year-old accountant-in-training, explained why she didn't want to become a mother:

> *To be honest, the biggest thing that comes to mind is sacrifice. And it just seems sacrifice of your own personal identity and all of your own wishes or desires, you have to give those up for someone else. It just seems a terrible, terrible burden.*[110]

Especially for middle- and upper-class women and men, opting not to have children may be attractive because it offers them the opportunity to do other interesting things. This concept is still rather new for women. Highly effective birth control options and abortion became legal and accessible only during the late '60s and '70s, and only since then have women had the opportunity to excel in challenging, respected, and high-paying careers. For women who have access to these occupations, having children is no longer the only way to feel like they're doing something valuable with their lives.

In fact, while some child-raising arrangements make for happier couples than others, it is *not* having kids that might be associated with the greatest happiness.[111] It depends on how you measure it. Parents report a greater sense of purpose and meaning in life than nonparents. They are more *satisfied* with their lives, more assured that their life has purpose. Anthony, for example, gushed about the meaning having a child gave to his life: "You have this little person who desperately needs you, and nothing in the world is more important to you."[112]

In contrast, nonparents may be less fulfilled, but they are happier day-to-day. Parents, especially women, report more frequent negative emotions than nonparents, more distressing financial problems, lower-quality marital relationships, and higher levels of depression, distress, and anxiety. This is especially true when parents have young children but is also true long after the kids have left the house.[113] Samantha, for example, a thirty-four-year-old professional, decided that she wasn't interested in the daily demands of parenting: "the little baby voices, and the screaming, and the tantrums, and the constant questions."[114] She wanted to continue to excel in her career, travel, enjoy delicious meals, and bask in quiet afternoons. And she did.

By this measure, parents are less happy than nonparents across the globe.[115] In almost all kinds of countries—developing or developed, socialist or democratic, conservative or liberal—raising kids is associated with a decline in well-being. In most cases, the more children people have, the less happy they are.

There are two clear exceptions. One is when people live in societies that offer very little or no safety net to the old. In countries in which children keep their parents out of poverty, people with kids are happier than people without, but only after their kids are grown up. The other is when countries offer generous family-friendly policies: paid time off after the birth or adoption of a child, free or affordable day care, flexible work hours, and ample vacation time and sick leave.[116] The United States is neither so harsh to its elderly nor so generous to its parents. In fact, the happiness gap between parents and nonparents in the United States is the largest in the industrialized world.[117]

Some people realize this and choose not to have children because they believe they'll be happier if they do not. For women, this choice is especially fraught. The cult of domesticity impels women to become mothers, suggesting that it is women's nature and destiny to make homes for husbands and their children. Women who do not do this are turning away from this social construction of womanhood and refusing to take on a supportive role in family life. They may not be able to perform enough feminine apologetic to satisfy some people in their lives or even the bystanders in their social environments.

This means that women who don't have children, especially those who never marry, are a kind of feminine pariah. They are the shrews, spinsters, and old maids of fairy tales. In real life, they are objects of pity, criticism, and blame. Especially if they have children and leave them, even in safe and happy circumstances, they risk condemnation. More than bad mothers, such women may be called monsters. Pariah status ensures that they serve as cautionary tales, warning young women of what will happen to them if they don't fulfill their reproductive duty.

Extending Families

As we discussed several chapters ago, our ancestors lived mostly in kinship groups and depended on a wide circle of biologically related and unrelated adults for survival. And, in fact, kinship and kinship-like family structures persist in many cultures and are emergent in others. The Mosuo in China, for example, practice what in English is referred to as "walking marriage."[118] Mothers live with their mothers and grandmothers, who head the family. They may maintain a long-term, monogamous, and romantic relationship with the father(s) of their children, but the Mosuo consider this separate from motherhood and the childrearing home. Instead of living with the mothers of their children, fathers live with their own mothers. They may provide financial support and visit their children, but neither is considered necessary. The children's primary male role models are usually their uncles, who also live with the children's grandmother, perhaps forming walking marriages with women living in other extended family homes.

From the Mosuo point of view, separating romantic and sexual relationships from the bearing and raising of children is smart. It ensures that romantic whims and sexual urges don't disrupt the happiness, health, and home life of the child. Meanwhile, because the family of origin is never eclipsed by a procreative family, the Mosuo system reduces the likelihood that elders will be abandoned by their families when they need support in old age. And if a parent dies or disappears, there is a whole family available to care for the child.

Extended families—ones in which married couples live with aunts, uncles, grandmas, grandpas, and other relatives—most resemble the oldest human family form and have persisted across the world in different ways. Today it remains common in the Middle East, Central and South America, sub-Saharan Africa, and Asia.[119] Other societies have tried to develop modern kinship networks. On the Israeli kibbutz, children live in group homes and are tended to by professional caregivers.[120] Parents spend a few hours a day with their children, bonding and playing but leaving the routine care to the professionals. Particularly in Mediterranean and Eastern European countries, parents often select godparents strategically.[121] Godparents may be designated guardians in the case a child is orphaned, but they are even more likely to contribute to a child's education or employment; in turn, godchildren may owe caregiving or economic support responsibilities to elderly godparents. In the United States, too, extended family ties are crucial supports for overstretched parents.[122]

Among many African American residents of poor and low-income neighborhoods in the United States today, young mothers rely on **othermothers**, women in the neighborhood who act as substitute mothers out of inclination or kindness.[123] In turn, they are othermothers to other women's children. Fatherhood, as well, is often less closely connected to biology; men often act as **otherfathers**, taking an interest even in children who are not their own.[124] In these communities, both maternal and paternal attention comes from many different sources. Sometimes it takes a village—and the village rises up in response.

A professional caregiver gets five cute toddlers ready for lunch on this kibbutz in Western Galilee, Israel. Kibbutz life reflects the desire of Jewish immigrants to reconstruct labor and caregiving collectives in Israel after their actual extended families were killed in the Holocaust.

If low-income parents are forced to get creative out of economic need, sexual minorities have been forced to get creative due to biological and legal constraints. Especially before adoption and assisted-reproductive technologies were legally available to them, sexual minorities formed "families by choice."[125] Two men in a relationship may have recruited a close female friend to be the mother of their child or a lesbian couple may have asked a best male friend to donate sperm. These adults then sometimes collaborated as co-parents, with three or four adults collectively committed to building a family together. Even in mixed-sex couples, turning to open adoption or surrogacy often brings another biological parent into the mix of relations with children.

Moreover, because divorce and remarriage are so common, many families today are made up of not just mom and dad, dad and dad, or mom and mom, but mom, stepmom, dad, stepdad, and a whole host of nonbiologically related siblings, aunts, uncles, grandparents, and cousins. In these cases, many adults share responsibility and, in the case of shared custody, children often live in more than one household at a time.

Increasingly, families in Western societies are starting out with a mix of biological and chosen kin. An alternative to monogamy, **polyamory** is the open practice and encouragement of long-term intimate relationships with more than one partner at a time. Children born into these partnerships may have many adults on whom they can depend, who love and care for them as families did before the nuclear family became the norm in the West.[126] They may think it odd that other children don't have so many adults around. As one three-year-old growing up in a polyamorous family exclaimed incredulously after a playdate with a child growing up in a monogamous one, "Tasha only has two parents! Just two of them!"[127]

Many hands make light work, so polyamorous and other forms of extended families have the advantage of being able to share the burden of the second shift across more than one or two adults. It's easier to get the kids picked up from school, help with homework, and make dinner when there are three or four people to do it, or when one doesn't have to do it every night of the week. Moreover, income from several adults may give the family more economic stability and each individual greater flexibility, perhaps enabling many adults to work less (not a dual- but a triple- or quadruple-nurturer arrangement) or one or more adults to carry the burden of breadwinning and domestic work (combining breadwinner/breadwinner/homemaker/superspouse into one arrangement).

In these arrangements, of course, there is a high probability that the adults who take primary responsibility for housework and childcare will be women. And furthermore, there is no guarantee that those individuals won't suffer reduced status, interpersonal power, and economic security; institutional factors all but ensure that they will. Moreover, as much as such arrangements have the potential to ease the burden of the second shift by distributing it among many adults, there is also the potential of burdening just one family-focused adult with supporting multiple breadwinners. Bigger families do not necessarily translate into an absence of gender ideology, but they are one way that people are trying to manage balancing paid work and the second shift and may be a terrain on which gendered divisions of labor may be challenged.

Revisiting the Question

If marriage is better for women than ever, why do women married to men report lower levels of happiness than men married to women, women married to women, and single women?

Marriage contracts are no longer explicitly gendered, but gender continues to organize family life. Even before a couple decides to marry, they start deciding how to deal with patriarchal traditions embedded in our culture: whether to have a gender-neutral or -specific wedding, to keep their last names or share one (and whose name remains), and to have or adopt a child—or go childfree. These and other choices become reflected in how gender infuses housework and childcare, too.[128]

In contrast to actual divisions of labor, most men and women want to build egalitarian families in which both paid and unpaid work is shared. Even when both partners want this kind of balance, however, deep-seated ideological beliefs and coercive institutional forces often make sharing difficult. Facing those difficulties, happy couples can discover that their fallback plans diverge dramatically. Relationships don't always survive the negotiations that follow.

Meanwhile, the continued feminization of housework and childcare contributes to ongoing inequality. Doing domestic work translates into a loss of status, bargaining power, and financial security. This situation harms everyone who specializes in this work: homemakers, single parents, working parents married to neo-traditionalists, dual-nurturers who turn away from work, and poorly paid domestic workers. Overwhelmingly, these people are female.

Women are less happy than men in marriage, then, because it is an institution that systematically presses them into doing the low-status domestic work of our society. This, in turn, puts them in the position of having less interpersonal power and financial security than the people (mostly men) on whom they have to depend. Same-sex couples' decisions may not be based on biological sex, but they reflect androcentrism and gendered subordination if the domestic work is undervalued and the person who does it loses status and becomes dependent on their partner for economic support.

Alternative family forms—dual-nurturing, extending families, and childfree families—are intriguing. Each represents a different way of trying to balance paid and unpaid work. Ideological and institutional forces, however, combine to keep these arrangements in the minority in the West. Economic infeasibility and the power of policing make these choices difficult. And gender ideology can as easily warp these family forms as it does others, making developing truly egalitarian relationships elusive even in the process of innovation.

All of this is complicated—tremendously so—by that other greedy institution: work.

Next . . .

Since 1964 the federal government has strengthened gender equality in the workplace. Today women make up 47 percent of the workforce, and they can be found in every occupation.[129] Still, men reap more rewards at work. Women are less likely than men to be in well-paid, high-prestige jobs that are considered skilled and involve managing employees. Our question for the next chapter is:

If women now have equal rights in the workplace, why aren't they as successful as men at work?

Let's find out.

FOR FURTHER READING

Ball, Carlos. *The Right to Be Parents: LGBT Families and the Transformation of Parenthood.* New York: New York University Press, 2012.

Blackstone, Amy. "Doing Family without Having Kids." *Sociology Compass* 8, no. 1 (2014): 52–62.

Harrington, Brad, Fred Van Deusen, and Iyar Mazar. *The New Dad: Right at Home.* Boston: Boston College Center for Work and Family, 2012.

Hondagneu-Sotelo, Pierrette and Ernestine Avila. "'I'm Here, but I'm There': The Meanings of Latina Transnational Motherhood." *Gender & Society* 11, no. 5 (1997): 548–71.

MacDonald, Cameron. *Shadow Mothers: Nannies, Au Pairs, and the Micropolitics of Mothering.* Berkeley: University of California Press, 2010.

Moore, Mignon. *Invisible Families: Gay Identities, Relationships, and Motherhood among Black Women.* Berkeley, University of California Press, 2011.

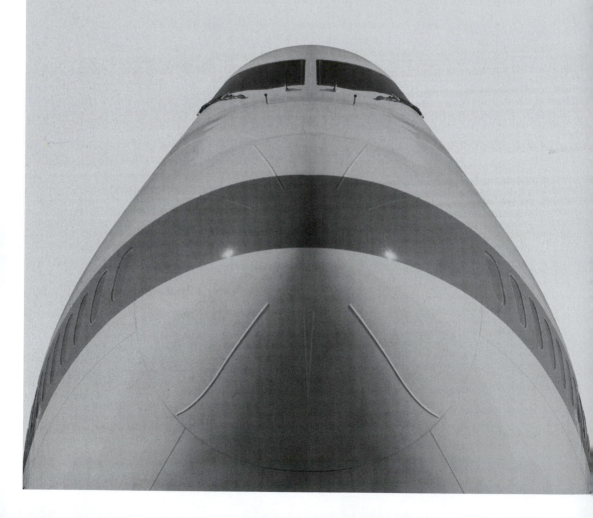

12

Work

Today's women are giving men a run for their money. Two-thirds say a high-paying job is important to them, compared with 56 percent of men.[2] And yet, in early 2018, the median weekly income for women with college degrees was $1,022; for comparable men, it was $1,353.[3] Even among the most high-achieving young people, men's pay outpaces women's. A study of Harvard grads, for example, found that men entering the finance industry were four times more likely than women to report a starting salary of more than $110,000.[4] Likewise, among Harvard grads going into technology and engineering jobs, 79 percent of men reported a salary of more than $90,000, compared with 44 percent of women. This gap in pay only gets wider over time: women in their early twenties earn $0.96 for every dollar earned by men, but by the time they're in their fifties and sixties, they're earning just $0.74.[5]

This difference in male and female earnings persists despite women's eagerness to earn and federal laws designed to guarantee equality, which led us to ask:

Q+A   **If women now have equal rights in the workplace, why aren't they as successful as men at work?**

I'm Cheryl. Fly me to the Sunshine States of America.

You think I'm just another pretty face? I'm not.

I'm a fresh attitude towards air travel to the States. A refreshingly honest definition of who we are, why we're special, and what we're doing to be even better.

Here's who we are: We're Cheryl (me), and Margie and Linda and Laura and Jo. And a lot of people behind the scenes, like Bob and Tom and Ron and Lee. (They're not just pretty faces either.)

And here's what we're doing (and why we're special): We're helping nice people (hopefully you) go to nice places in the Sunshine States of America, like Miami and other warm places in Florida and the Caribbean and Latin America, plus New Orleans and Houston and Los Angeles and San Francisco. We're helping nice people have fun en route, too: with movies* and stereo* and delicious meals, and just being left alone, if that's what you want.

The way we figure it: the more we like you, the more you'll like us. It's that simple.

So we're not just a bunch of people. We're an airline. And you can call us by our first name: National.

Fly Cheryl. Fly National Airlines.

For reservations call your travel agent or National Airlines, 81 Piccadilly, London, W.1. (01-629 8272).

*Movies and stereo by In-Flight Motion Pictures, Inc. Available at nominal charge.   National honours American Express, Barclaycard, Carte Blanche, Diners Club, UATP, our own card and cash.

This ad for National Airlines of London from the 1960s invites readers to "fly Cheryl."

This chapter gets up close and personal with occupations and earnings. Drawing on data from the U.S. Bureau of Labor Statistics, it explains how paid work is gendered in ways that affirm difference and entrench inequality. It considers how the U.S. economy is specifically structured to produce big winners and big losers, and how this model hurts people of all genders, but carries an extra punch for women. Some of the disadvantage, we'll see, is due to simple discrimination against women, but it also involves the tendency for jobs to be predominantly male or female, the different value attributed to men's and women's work, the challenge of being both a good parent and a good worker, and employers' beliefs about mothers and fathers.

So buckle up, put your seatbacks and tray tables in their full upright and locked position, and direct your attention to the flight attendant.

THE CHANGING WORKPLACE

"Next to being a Hollywood movie star, nothing was more glamorous," said a starry-eyed stewardess in 1945.[6] World War II was over and women were being pushed out of the workforce, but flight attendants were embarking on a new adventure. Only about 10 percent of Americans had ever flown and most were afraid to do so.[7] Stewardesses were certifiably adventurous. They took risks, saw the world, and rubbed elbows with the elite: their passengers. As historian Kathleen Barry contends: "Few women journeyed as regularly or as far from home, or came into contact with the rich and famous as often, as a typical stewardess did."[8]

Airlines hired women whom they believed represented ideal femininity. Chosen for their beauty and poise, and almost exclusively from among the white, educated, and slender, they were as much of an icon as Miss America.

The promise of a fresh-faced, kind, and accommodating stewardess was a staple of airline advertising. As one of America's sweethearts, she also appeared in commercials for products from soft drinks to cigarettes.

By the 1960s, airlines were in the "business of female spectacle," unabashedly selling women's attractiveness to customers.[9] Perhaps most famous was the National Airlines campaign in which stewardesses saucily invited passengers to "Fly Me."[10] Their advertising included the guarantee "We'll Fly You Like You've Never Been Flown Before." Feminists later replied, "Go Fly Yourself, National!"

The strategy of sexual objectification was industrywide: Continental stewardesses pledged, "We Really Move Our Tails for You"; Air Jamaica promised, "We Make You Feel Good All Over"; Air France replied, "Have You Ever Done It the French Way?"; Braniff Airlines asked their male passengers, "Does Your Wife Know You're Flying with Us?"; TWA offered flights with stewardesses of exotic nationalities; and Pacific Southwest Airlines riffed on their acronym, having flight attendants wear buttons that said "Pure, Sober, and Available."[11] Uniforms followed suit: mini-skirts, short shorts, and go-go boots.

In the 1960s and 1970s, airlines sexualized their stewardesses to attract a mostly male customer base. As part of this effort, Southwest Airlines flight attendants were required to wear hot pants and leather go-go boots.

Still, it wasn't all fun and hot pants. Standards of appearance were strict.[12] Disqualifications and dismissals were issued for big feet, chubby legs, poor posture, the wrong haircut, glasses, acne, short nails, imperfect teeth, not wearing makeup, or any supposed flaw the recruiters identified. They claimed their objections to broad noses, coarse hair, and full lips were race-neutral, but, of course, they were not.[13] When first hired in the 1970s after multiple court battles, African American flight attendants were expected to straighten their hair. A ban on "hook noses" was used to exclude Jewish women.

Women were required to wear girdles and submit to routine weigh-ins and measurement of their busts, waists, hips, and thighs. They were fired if they gained weight. "You run a $1.5 billion business," said a United Airlines official, "and it boils down to whether some chicks look good in their uniforms. If you have fat stewardesses, people aren't going to fly with you."[14] Airlines also terminated the employment of women who got married, became pregnant, or reached their early thirties. A manager once told a group of flight attendants: "If you haven't found a man to keep you by the time you're twenty-eight, then TWA won't want you either."[15]

Stewardesses also faced routine sexual harassment. Airlines marketed them as available sex partners and then instructed them that the customer was always right.[16] African American flight attendants faced their own unique version; some of the overwhelmingly white customers were hostile racists, but others would proposition them for a "black experience."[17]

Meanwhile, female flight attendants were among the most poorly paid employees in the airline industry. They were paid a third of what pilots earned and two-thirds the wages of the mostly male ground workers. They were also paid significantly less than the few male flight attendants; at Pan Am, for example, men earned 140 percent of a female flight attendant's salary. Men also enjoyed promotions, more responsibility, nicer accommodations on layovers, larger pensions, greater scheduling flexibility, and more sick leave. Plus, they didn't face weigh-ins, girdles, or forced retirements.

Then 1964 happened. Stewardesses filed a case against the airline industry on the first day the government began considering violations of the new Civil Rights Act.[18] Flight attendants would initiate one hundred lawsuits in eighteen months. Over the next sixty years, women across the occupational spectrum would follow suit, aiming to gain access to essentially all occupations. Companies no longer had the right to pay women less, deny them promotion, or otherwise discriminate based on gender. As companies faced potential lawsuits, their overtly discriminatory practices slowly eroded.

Yet, men—especially class-privileged white men—continue to have substantial advantages in the workplace today. Men are more likely to engage in paid work than women and work more hours per week and more weeks per year. They get better benefits (like health insurance, unemployment coverage, vacation and sick days, and retirement plans) and are more likely to get on-the-job training. They are more likely to have jobs considered "skilled" and to be in management. They unquestionably dominate the highest rungs of corporate ladders: 75 percent of executive and senior-level managers, 80 percent of board members, and 95 percent of the CEOs of Fortune 500 companies are men.[19] Men outnumber women so overwhelmingly that there are more CEOs named James than there are women CEOs.[20]

Perhaps the most succinct measure of men's advantage in the workplace is the **gender pay gap**, the difference between the incomes of the average man and woman who work full time. In 2017, the median earnings of American men working full time were $941 per week.[21] Comparably, full-time working women earned $770, or 82 percent of men's wages. To put it another way, among workers employed full time, women earned $0.82 for every dollar a man made.

As revealed in Figure 12.1, the gap has been steadily shrinking for nearly 200 years. Much of this is due to women's rising wages, but about a quarter of

FIGURE 12.1 | VARIATION IN WOMEN'S EARNINGS FOR EVERY DOLLAR OF MEN'S FOR FULL-TIME WORKERS

Comparison	Cents/Dollar	Comparison	Cents/Dollar
By state in the United States		*By education (United States)*	
California	$0.88	Less than high school	$0.77
Florida	$0.87	High school graduate	$0.78
New Jersey	$0.80	Some college or associate's degree	$0.77
Texas	$0.82	Bachelor's degree and higher	$0.75
Washington, D.C.	$0.88		
Wyoming	$0.72		
By country		*By race or ethnicity (United States)*	
Germany	$0.79	Black women, men	$0.93
Ireland	$0.86	Black women, white men	$0.68
Italy	$0.95	Asian women, men	$0.75
Poland	$0.93	Asian women, white men	$0.93
Sweden	$0.87	Hispanic women, men	$0.87
United Kingdom	$0.79	Hispanic women, white men	$0.62
		White women, men	$0.82
By year (United States)			
1820	$0.35	*By age (United States)*	
1890	$0.46	16–24	$0.95
1930	$0.56	25–34	$0.89
1960	$0.61	35–44	$0.83
1970	$0.60	45–54	$0.78
1990	$0.72	55–64	$0.74
2000	$0.74	65+	$0.76
2010	$0.81		

Sources: European Commission, "Gender Pay Gap Statistics," March 2018. Retrieved from http://ec.europa.eu/eurostat /statistics-explained/index.php/Gender_pay_gap_statistics#Gender_pay_gap_levels_vary_significantly_across_EU; Bureau of Labor Statistics, "Highlights of Women's Earnings in 2016," August 2017. Retrieved from www.bls.gov/opub /reports/womens-earnings/2016/home.htm; Bureau of Labor Statistics, "Labor Force Statistics from the Current Population Survey: Table 37: Median Weekly Earnings of Full-Time Wage and Salary Workers by Selected Characteristics," January 2018. Retrieved from www.bls.gov/cps/cpsaat37.htm.

the narrowing since 2000 represents declining wages for working-class men, which have fallen by almost 7 percent.[22] Women's wages have similarly been harmed by the overall economy, but women have also been increasing their education, shifting into better-paying jobs, and working more. Conversely, the things that used to protect men's wages, like labor unions and manufacturing jobs, have been on the decline.[23]

Women of all races make less money than their male counterparts, but the size of the gap differs. It's smaller among groups that have overall lower wages, mostly because racial minority men, with the exception of some Asian groups, earn especially low incomes. Notice that the gap varies both among American states and among different countries. Governments that keep most women out of the labor force typically show smaller wage gaps, since the women who do work full time are more educated and less representative of the population. This is why the wage gap in Italy, where women are less often employed, is so much smaller than in Sweden, where nearly all women are working. The wage gap also increases, if unevenly, across the life cycle.

Perhaps surprisingly, the gap is largest among men and women who earn professional degrees in fields such as law and medicine.[24] Mean earnings of women and men managers with MBAs, for example, are fairly close directly after graduation, but nine years later the gap has grown (from $15,000 to $150,000).[25] At the very top, the wage disparities just get bigger. Among mid-career MBAs in the top 10 percent of earners, men earn over $1 million and women earn less than half that.

All told, because of the gender wage gap, the average American woman will earn $439,958 less in her lifetime than the average man.[26] Compared to white non-Hispanic men, African American and Native American women will be out almost $900,000 and Latinas almost $1.1 million. This harms women's economic stability in old age directly (it helps to have an extra half-million or more upon retirement) and also indirectly (women's average Social Security retirement benefit is about 75 percent that of men's, mostly thanks to the wage gap).[27] Not only do women have less than men when they retire, they need more because they tend to live longer. As a result of these disparities, retired women are twice as likely as retired men to be living in poverty.[28]

This chapter explores the gendered forces behind this inequality: job segregation, gender discrimination, and the practice and ideology of parenting. It'll also look at how work experiences are shaped by class, race, gender, sexuality, and age. It concludes with some observations about the current economy and both men's and women's opportunities within it.

JOB SEGREGATION

A licensed pilot, Ellen Church could have been the first female commercial pilot when she was hired by Boeing in 1930, but the company didn't allow women in the cockpit.[29] So, she became the first female flight attendant instead. A different woman would be hired as a pilot a few years later, but she would be the exception that proved the rule.[30] It would be four decades before we would see another. In 1978, when the International Society of Women Airline Pilots was founded, it boasted only twenty-one members.[31]

Women and men attracted to the excitement of air travel have pursued their dreams largely through two very different avenues. Men have become pilots and women have become flight attendants. Today, 73 percent of flight attendants are female and 94 percent of pilots are male.[32] This is **gendered job**

segregation, the practice of filling occupations with mostly male or mostly female workers. Just as we gender all kinds of things, we gender jobs. Collectively, we understand certain jobs as somehow for women (like nursing and teaching) and others as for men (construction work and computer programming).

Gendered job segregation doesn't reflect inherent masculine or feminine qualities of a job; instead, occupations are socially constructed to suggest they're best suited for stereotypical women or men, while features that would undermine the idea are ignored.[33] For example, male insurance agents describe successful colleagues as men who love competition and possess a "killer instinct."[34] In reality, an insurance salesperson also needs to be able to communicate trustworthiness, quickly forge bonds with strangers, and read emotions. If the job were gendered female, we would probably see more emphasis on interpersonal skills.

Because jobs are not naturally gendered, we find great variation across cultures. Medicine is a female job in Russia and Finland, as is dentistry in Latvia and Lithuania.[35] In Iran, Uzbekistan, Azerbaijan, and Saudi Arabia, women earn the majority of science degrees.[36] In Armenia, half of computer science college professors are women.[37] Women dominate computer science in Malaysia, too, where abstract thinking and office work are seen as feminine compared to more "physical" labor.[38] Likewise, Malaysians see chemical engineering as feminine

A female laborer in the Indian state of Gujarat carries bricks needed for a construction site. Construction is gendered female in India and male in the United States.

because it involves working in a lab, but civil engineering as masculine because it involves going to worksites and overseeing construction. In contrast, in India, women make up a large share of the construction industry; it makes sense to them because Indian society holds women responsible for the home.[39] We make work meaningful in gendered ways and slot men and women into occupations accordingly.

How Much Job Segregation Is There?

Figure 12.2 presents data for some of the most gender-segregated occupations in the United States. Overall, about four in ten American women work in jobs that are at least 75 percent female and men work in even more gender-segregated environments.[40] To achieve perfect integration in the United States, 34 percent of workers would have to switch to a differently gendered job. Internationally, the amount of gender segregation in jobs varies; the United States is in the middle of the pack.[41] Among developed countries, the percentage of people who would have to switch jobs varies from 23 percent in Japan to 45 percent in Luxembourg.

We see gender segregation not just between occupations—between nursing and car repair, for example—but within them. Consider that there are lots of both waitresses and waiters, but servers at very expensive restaurants tend to be both male and female, while lower-priced restaurants tend to employ women.[42] Among doctors, gender correlates with specialty: Women make up 62 percent of pediatricians but only 5 percent of orthopedic surgeons.[43] The skills and responsibilities of barbers and hairdressers, for instance, are more alike than different, but men and women tend to get different job titles and work in different establishments serving different customers.

Gender intersects with other characteristics to stratify the workforce. Depending on what part of the United States we're in, the (likely female) housekeeper at our local motel will be white, Latina, or African American.[44] The janitor or maintenance worker will probably be the same race but the other gender. African American women make up only 6 percent of the general population but represent nearly a third of active-duty enlisted women in the military.[45] Fully 99 percent of New York City's nearly 40,000 taxi drivers are male and 96 percent are immigrants; 24 percent are from Bangladesh alone.[46] Jobs are segregated by sexual orientation, too. Lesbian and bisexual women are ten times more likely than heterosexual women to work as police officers.[47] And, while not all male flight attendants are gay, gay and bisexual men are overrepresented compared to the overall population.[48]

What causes this divvying up of men and women into different kinds of jobs?

FIGURE 12.2 | SOME OF THE MOST GENDER-SEGREGATED OCCUPATIONS

Female-dominated occupations	How female is it?
Speech-language pathologist	98%
Preschool and kindergarten teacher	98%
Dental hygienist	95%
Secretary and administrative assistant	95%
Dietician and nutritionist	94%
Childcare worker	94%
Hairdresser, hairstylist, and cosmetologist	93%
Medical record and health information technician	92%
Medical assistant	92%
Receptionist and information clerk	91%
Registered nurse	90%
Nursing, psychiatric, and home-health aide	89%

Male-dominated occupations	How male is it?
Roofer	99%
Automotive service technician and mechanic	98%
Carpenter	98%
Firefighter	97%
Construction laborer	97%
Crane/tower operator	96%
Maintenance and repair worker	96%
Welder	96%
Truck driver	94%
Grounds maintenance worker	94%
Pest control worker	94%
Mechanical engineer	91%

Source: Bureau of Labor Statistics, "Labor Force Statistics from the Current Population Survey: Table 11; Employed Persons by Detailed Occupation, Sex, Race, and Hispanic or Latino Ethnicity." Retrieved from www.bls.gov/cps/cpsaat11.pdf.

Causes of Job Segregation

Men and women usually end up in gender-stereotypical jobs through a compli-cated congruence of socialization, employer selection, and selective exit. The **socialization hypothesis** suggests that men and women respond to gender ste-reotypes when planning, training, and applying for jobs.[49] We are socialized to be interested in and prepare for different kinds of jobs, while also reading the signals sent by occupations and the people in them. In one study, for example, psycholo-gists invited students into a classroom and asked them to fill out a questionnaire regarding their interest and perceived ability in computer science.[50] One set of people entered a room covered in "computer geeky" things: a *Star Trek* poster, comic books, video game boxes, empty soda cans and junk food, and technical magazines. The other group entered a room without these objects. Men were unfazed by the geekery, but women who encountered the geeked-up room were significantly less likely to say they were considering a computer science major. Whether it's the "macho" image of the construction worker or the "bro" image of the tech guy, the message to women is "no girls allowed."[51]

The **employer selection hypothesis** proposes that employers tend to prefer men for masculine jobs and women for feminine jobs, slotting applicants into gender-consistent roles during hiring and promotion. Certain kinds of factory work, for example, are heavily female because employers prefer to hire women. As one manager at a high-tech manufacturing company told a researcher: "Just three things I look for in hiring: small, foreign, and female."[52] Hiring in Silicon Valley in the 1960s and 1970s, by contrast, was driven by employers' belief that nerdy male misfits made the best computer programmers.[53] Once a job is dominated by men or women, employers assume that it's for a good reason and select new employees accordingly.[54]

The **selective exit hypothesis** highlights workers' abandonment of counterstereotypical occupations. One study found that 61 percent of women in male-dominated occupations leave their job within ten years, compared with less than 30 percent of their male colleagues; half of these women switched to a female-dominated occupation.[55] In engineering, for example, 35 percent of women, but only 10 percent of men, either never enter the field after getting their degree, or leave it sometime after they do.[56] Among those female engineers who leave, a majority blamed its hypermasculine work culture.[57] Sometimes women enter male-dominated occupations but have negative experiences that push them to leave.

All three of these factors—socialization, employer selection, and selective exit—are sources of job segregation, with socialization and selective exit likely the most substantial contributors. Gendered job segregation in itself, however, isn't sufficient to explain the pay gap. It's only the start.

Different and Unequal

A Floridian Cuban named Celio Diaz was the first man to use the Civil Rights Act to sue for gender discrimination.[58] In the 1960s, only 4 percent of flight attendants were men and most airlines refused to hire them. Pan Am, for example, who rejected Diaz's application, argued that men simply couldn't "convey the charm, the tact, the grace, the liveliness that young girls can."[59] Or, if they could, Pan Am claimed, it might "arouse feelings" in a male passenger "that he would rather not have aroused."[60]

Pan Am appealed all the way to the U.S. Supreme Court, but they lost. Beginning in 1971, airlines were forced to begin hiring men alongside women. The media had a field day. The *Miami Herald* ran a story with a picture of a stocky, hairy-legged man in a miniskirt and knee-high socks, a purse hanging from his cocked arm. It read: "Here's the worst thing that could happen to commercial airlines."[61]

It's funny that the American media thought the idea of a "he-stewardess" was absurd because the word "stewardess" is a feminized version of the word "steward." In fact, early stewardesses *were* stewards and the job was almost exclusively male for some time.[62] Pan Am, the airline Diaz sued, had itself maintained an all-male steward workforce for sixteen years. It integrated in 1944, as did many other airlines, because of the shortage of men on the home front during World War II. By 1958, Pan Am had entirely reversed its policy. Soon American flight attendants were almost all female. One advertising executive in 1967 explained: "When a tired businessman gets on an airplane, we think he ought to be allowed to look at a pretty girl."[63]

The occupation's "sex change" is a great example of the gendered social construction of jobs; it also reveals how prestige and pay tend to follow sex. Early airlines hired white male flight attendants in order to assure passengers that they would be safe.[64] Ocean liners and train cars, the models on which airlines built their businesses, largely employed black men, but airlines believed their overwhelmingly white passengers wouldn't feel comfortable placing their lives in the hands of a black person. So they hired white men to ensure that the occupation carried a degree of gravitas. Stewards embodied professionalism and dignity, wearing military-inspired uniforms and changing into white sport coats and gloves to serve dinner. They were chaperones of the sky but also capable crew.

When the aisle was turned over to women, the role was reimagined. As the occupation was feminized, the seriousness of the job was downplayed and the subordinate role of supportive and sometimes sexually playful service was emphasized. As one flight attendant described it, the job

Think of her as your mother.

She only wants what's best for you.
A cool drink. A good dinner. A soft pillow and a warm blanket.
This is not just maternal instinct. It's the result of the longest
Stewardess training in the industry.
Training in service, not just a beauty course.
Service, after all, is what makes professional travellers prefer American.
And makes new travellers want to keep on flying with us.
So we see that every passenger gets the same professional treatment.
That's the American Way.

Fly the American Way
American Airlines

Although the text of this ad for American Airlines presents its flight attendants as both motherly and professional, the picture tells a very different story of women's service work.

became "part mother, part servant, and part tart."[65] Just like with cheerleading, there was a decline in status.

We have seen such changes in response to the feminization or masculinization of many different occupations. Clerical work in the United States, for example, was almost exclusively male until the late 1800s. Typing was considered "too strenuous for women."[66] Later, as it became associated with women, the necessary qualification would be shifted from "arduous labor" to "dexterity."[67] Today most people don't think much of "secretaries," but they were respected enough at one time that we still use the term to refer to high-level government positions like secretary of state.

During World War II, women's support roles as typists funneled them into early computer programming.[68] The government employed women in top secret positions as "compute-ers," workers who operated and supervised computing machines.[69] They were preferred because it was believed that the work required patience, something women supposedly had thanks to "maternal instinct." "It's just like planning a dinner," explained the pioneering programmer Grace Hopper to *Cosmopolitan* in 1967; it "requires patience and the ability to handle detail. Women are 'naturals' at computer programming."[70] As late as the mid-1980s, computer science was more gender-integrated than other science, technology, and engineering fields. Women made lots of important contributions to computer science during this time, but as the value of computing rose and women were pushed out, their contributions were made invisible. Reimagined as a nerd's playground, computer science today is among the least sex-integrated occupations and, not coincidentally, highest in prestige and pay.

Other occupations have also changed gender and, when they do, we see a similar shift in value.[71] Since 1970, for example, enrollment in veterinary college has gone from 11 percent to over 80 percent female.[72] Wages have correspondingly stagnated compared to similar professions like medicine and law, which have seen less overall feminization. Generally, the rule is clear: As women enter an occupation, status goes down; as men enter it, status goes up. It's as if men's social status rubs off on the work they do.[73] In one study, for example, ten- and eleven-year-olds were asked to rate the status of fake jobs like "cilpster" and "heigist."[74] The children who were told that these jobs were performed mostly by men gave them higher status rankings than the children who were told they were done primarily by women. In other studies, college students asked to rank the prestige of jobs will rank them lower if they are told that the occupation is feminizing and higher if they're told it's masculinizing.[75]

We call this the **androcentric pay scale**, a strong correlation between wages and the gender composition of the job.[76] Even when we hold things like education, skill, and experience constant, the gender composition of a job plays an important role in determining wages. In fact, according to a study by the Bureau of Labor

These IBM computers look unusual and outdated for modern eyes, but the female technicians may also seem surprising, given our myth of progress on all fronts for women. The rising status of computer sciences is associated with a falling share of women in this field.

Statistics, the gender composition of a job is the *single largest contributor* to the gender wage gap.[77] It is more important than level of unionization, industry, supply and demand, the safety or comfort of the work, and workers' education, marital status, and experience. Even controlling for all these things, "women's work" pays, on average, anywhere between 5 and 21 percent less than "men's work."[78] The effect grows larger as occupations become increasingly male or female dominated.

If there is an androcentric pay scale, then we should expect male-dominated jobs to be among the highest paying. They are. Consider Figure 12.3, which lists all American occupations (with reliable demographic data) that pay over $100,000 a year.[79] In the rightmost columns, we include the gender and race composition of these high-paying jobs. Since men make up 53 percent of the workforce, any job that is more than 53 percent male is disproportionately so, or more male than we would expect by chance alone. Likewise, since 63 percent of the workforce identifies as non-Hispanic white, any job that is more than 63 percent white is disproportionately so.

Figure 12.3 shows that sixteen of the twenty-five highest-paying occupations are more than 53 percent male and six are more than 75 percent male. All but two of these occupations—computer hardware engineer and software developer—are disproportionately white.

FIGURE 12.3 | GENDER AND RACE COMPOSITION OF THE HIGHEST-PAYING JOBS IN THE UNITED STATES

Occupation	Avg. Annual Wage	% Male	% White
Physicians and surgeons	$214,700	60%	66%
Chief executives	$196,050	72%	86%
Dentists	$180,010	64%	77%
Computer and information systems managers	$149,730	71%	72%
Architectural and engineering managers	$146,290	91%	74%
Financial managers	$143,530	44%	73%
Lawyers	$141,890	63%	84%
Marketing and sales managers	$140,600	55%	77%
Aircraft pilots and flight engineers	$138,690	94%	88%
Public relations and fundraising managers	$127,690	37%	85%
Personal financial advisors	$124,140	68%	80%
Advertising and promotions managers	$123,880	47%	78%
Human resources managers	$123,510	29%	75%
General and operations managers	$123,460	66%	75%
Purchasing managers	$121,810	48%	76%
Pharmacists	$121,710	43%	64%
Judges, magistrates, and other judicial workers	$121,050	72%	81%
Computer hardware engineers	$119,650	83%	48%
Optometrists	$119,100	50%	89%
Training and development managers	$117,690	40%	81%
Aerospace engineers	$115,300	91%	74%
Chemical engineers	$112,430	83%	87%
Software developers	$111,780	81%	54%
Medical and health services managers	$111,680	30%	70%
Industrial production managers	$110,580	74%	81%

Sources: Bureau of Labor Statistics, 2018, "Labor Force Statistics from the Current Population Survey," Employed Persons by Detailed Occupation, Sex, Race, and Hispanic or Latino Ethnicity." Retrieved from www.bls.gov/cps/cpsaat11.htm; Bureau of Labor Statistics, 2018, "May 2017 National Occupational Employment and Wage Estimates." Retrieved from www.bls.gov/oes/current/oes_nat.htm.

In the last chapter we introduced the idea of the feminization of poverty; we might call the concentration of men in high-earning occupations, and their resulting ability to accumulate savings, investments, and assets, a **masculinization of wealth**.[80] Believe it or not, this accumulation of money starts when men are boys. Sons are 15 percent more likely than daughters to get an allowance in exchange for doing chores; even when daughters get paid, sons get paid more.[81] In other words, boys spend fewer hours on chores than girls, enjoy more leisure time, and *still* end up with more money in their piggybanks.

The Value of Gendered Work

In 2013, an Asiana flight crash-landed at San Francisco International Airport. While the survival of all but two of the 307 passengers was called a "miracle," it was in no small part thanks to the flight attendants on board. They successfully enacted the protocol for a ninety-second evacuation, despite two slides that didn't correctly deploy. As passengers were fleeing the wreckage, some flight attendants fought the rising flames while others hacked trapped passengers out of their seatbelts with knives. They carried injured passengers out on their backs. "I wasn't really thinking, but my body started carrying out the steps needed for an evacuation," explained Lee Yoon Hye, one of the flight attendants. "I was only thinking about rescuing the next passenger."[82] Later she learned that she'd sustained a broken tailbone.

The top five news stories at the time used passive language that made the work of the flight attendants invisible: "slides had deployed" and passengers "managed to get off."[83] Instead of being described as the first responders they were, flight attendants were portrayed as just a special kind of passenger. The crash forced "frightened passengers and crew to scamper," read one article; another reported that "passengers and crew were being treated" at local hospitals. Only one of the five stories acknowledged that the sixteen flight attendants *worked* through the crash and its aftermath.

Which leads us to ask: Do flight attendants have skills?

They do. Flight attendants learn hundreds of regulations and the safety features of multiple types of airplanes. They know how to evacuate a plane on land or sea within ninety seconds; fight fires 35,000 feet in the air; keep a heart attack or stroke victim alive; calm or restrain an anxious, aggressive, or mentally ill passenger; respond to hijackings and terrorist attacks; communicate effectively with people who are frozen in fear; and survive in the case of a crash landing in the jungle, sea, desert, or Arctic. As one flight attendant said: "I don't think of myself as a sex symbol or a servant. I think of myself as somebody who knows how to open the door of a 747 in the dark, upside down, and in the water."[84]

Flight attendants are doing a job that's supposed to remain invisible unless needed. "I have an outer appearance of calm and reserve," explained one flight attendant.[85] But she is alert and prepared. "You always have to be ready for an emergency—something with another crew member, passenger has an epileptic attack, emergency landing. I could go on and on." Even when survival is unlikely, many flight attendants take their job gravely seriously. As one flight attendant said:

> If we were going to make a ditching in water, the chances of our surviving are slim, even though we know exactly what to do. But I think I would probably—and I think I can say this for most of my fellow flight attendants—be able to keep [the passengers] from being too worried about it. I mean my voice might quiver a little during the announcements, but somehow I feel we could get them to believe ... the best.[86]

Many lives have been saved, and many final moments have been less filled with sheer terror, thanks to well-trained and effective flight attendants who are committed to doing their job well—if necessary, until the bitter end.

Airlines, though, are loath to reveal the intense and ongoing emergency, security, first-aid, combat, and survival training that flight attendants receive. Talking about the "live fire pit" and "ditching pool" used for training might remind passengers of the potential dangers of air travel.[87] It's much better for airlines if we think flight attendants are just "sky waitresses" and, if we're lucky, we'll never be in a situation in which their skills and knowledge become suddenly and terrifyingly apparent.

So, many of the skills flight attendants have are invisible to most of us most of the time, both by circumstance and design. Meanwhile, we tend to dismiss the work we see as unskilled. Early airlines hired women for their extraordinary beauty, grace, and charm. They were to have a "modest but friendly smile," be "alert, attentive, not overly aggressive, but not reticent either," "outgoing but not effusive," "enthusiastic with calm and poise," and "vivacious but not effervescent."[88] No problem, right? All women *don't* naturally have these skills; that's why flight attendants were valorized as the perfect women.

This part of the job is referred to as **emotion work**, the act of controlling one's own emotions and managing the emotions of others. Flight attendants are tasked with seamlessly performing the proper emotions in interaction with an impossibly wide range of people who bring their own, often negative emotions to the moment. And, thousands of feet up in the air, there is no manager to ask for help or call for backup. Trying to summarize the job, one flight attendant said:

> *[It] requires judgment, ingenuity, skill, and independence in an area of the most difficult sort—not handling inanimate and usually predictable machinery—but large numbers of human beings of all ages, walks of life, varied national and racial backgrounds, under panic conditions.*[89]

And one has to be nice about it. One stewardess working in the 1960s described having to "force a drunk passenger in the back of the cabin to sit down and stop throwing cigarette butts on the floor *with gentleness*."[90] In 2001, another explained how she managed the problem of sexual harassment without offending her customer: "If someone puts their hand on your bottom, you should say, 'Excuse me, sir, but my bottom accidentally fell into your hand.'"[91]

These are impressive interpersonal talents. "Even when people are paid to be nice," wrote one scholar studying this kind of emotion work, "it is hard for them to be nice at all times, and when their efforts succeed, it is a remarkable accomplishment."[92] Or, as one flight attendant put it: "We, basically, are the best actors and actresses in the world."[93]

Undeniably, these skills are also *valuable* resources for the airlines. Yet airlines have historically framed their flight attendants' performances as "natural." As historian Kathleen Barry explains:

[A]irlines' favorite metaphor for stewardesses' work was that they were playing gracious hostess to guests in one's own home, which suggested their efforts were a natural, voluntary expression of female domesticity and of social rather than economic value.[94]

The work of flight attendants, in other words, was defined as *outside the realm of work*. If being nice just comes naturally, then the flight attendants are just being themselves. Being oneself is not a *skill* and, therefore, it shouldn't be compensated as one. The benevolently sexist idea that women are naturally gracious causes us to dismiss the work of female flight attendants as nothing special.

In fact, lots of the work women disproportionately do is framed as natural to the female sex. In contrast, "men's work" is usually considered skilled almost by definition. Stereotypes of men include being good with their hands, talented at understanding how things work, and steadfast behind the wheel. If we were inclined to devalue these skills, we could argue that it was only natural that men would become surgeons, engineers, and truck drivers. Given the opportunity, the logic would go, they would do these things anyway because that's just how they *are*; we'll pay them for their time, but it's ridiculous to argue that these are *skills*. That is, in fact, exactly how "women's work" is frequently understood.

Traditional women's work—like soothing an autistic child, organizing twenty kindergarteners, making middle school kids care about literature, ensuring a boss's day runs smoothly, or carefully monitoring the health of an elderly patient—all require knowledge, concentration, effort, creativity, problem solving, practice, and emotion work.

So does responding to sexual harassment in ways that are effective but not explosive. In a 2017 article about sexism in the tech industry, entrepreneur and investor Susan Wu discusses

the countless times I've had to move a man's hand from my thigh (or back or shoulder or hair or arm) during a meeting (or networking event or professional lunch or brainstorming session or pitch meeting) without seeming confrontational (or bitchy or rejecting or demanding or aggressive). . . . [It's] a pretty important skill that I would bet most successful women in our industry have.[95]

Women are still apologizing for their bottoms falling into men's hands, and we continue to devalue women's work as unskilled and unworthy of the compensation awarded to men's work.

If jobs filled by women are devalued, then we should expect these jobs to pay less than jobs filled by men. They do. Consider Figure 12.4, which lists all American occupations (with reliable data) that pay under $25,000 a year.[96] In

FIGURE 12.4 | GENDER AND RACE COMPOSITION OF THE LOWEST-PAYING JOBS IN THE UNITED STATES

Occupation	Avg. Yearly Wage	% Female	% Minority
Cashier	$22,130	73%	47%
Dishwasher	$22,210	20%	57%
Host and hostess	$22,290	86%	41%
Counter attendant	$22,530	62%	47%
Dining room cafeteria attendant and bartender helper	$23,050	46%	49%
Entertainment attendant	$23,480	43%	41%
Lifeguard/ski patrol	$23,570	50%	20%
Childcare worker	$23,760	94%	43%
Laundry and dry-cleaning worker	$23,770	68%	69%
Food preparation worker	$23,900	59%	52%
Gaming services worker	$23,950	47%	64%
Home health aide	$24,280	89%	59%
Personal care aide	$24,100	84%	57%
Food server, non-restaurant	$24,150	70%	50%
Hotel, motel, and resort desk clerk	$24,250	61%	51%
Parking lot attendant	$24,330	17%	67%
Grader and sorter, agricultural products	$24,620	67%	64%
Maid/housekeeper	$24,630	88%	70%

Sources: Bureau of Labor Statistics, 2018, "Labor Force Statistics from the Current Population Survey," Employed Persons by Detailed Occupation, Sex, Race, and Hispanic or Latino Ethnicity." Retrieved from www.bls.gov/cps/cpsaat11.htm; Bureau of Labor Statistics, 2018, "May 2017 National Occupational Employment and Wage Estimates." Retrieved from www.bls.gov/oes/current/oes_nat.htm.

the rightmost columns, we include the gender and race composition of these low-paying jobs. Since women make up 47 percent of the workforce, any job that is more than 47 percent female is disproportionately so. Likewise, since 63 percent of the workforce identifies as non-Hispanic white, any job that is more than 37 percent minority is more so than we would expect by chance alone.

More than two-thirds of the lowest-paying occupations (thirteen of eighteen) are disproportionately female; five are more than three-fourths female. The remainder of the jobs—the ones not disproportionately held by women—are filled by men, but not white men. Black men are twice as likely as white men to work in feminized industries and Latino and Asian men are one and a half times as likely.[97] This is partly because racial discrimination gives men of color fewer options than white men, but also possibly because men of color are more likely to adopt feminized qualities like care and kindness as valued personal characteristics.[98] With few exceptions, the lowest-paying jobs in America are disproportionately staffed by racial minority women (in twelve occupations) or, barring that, mostly women or racial minorities (in one and five occupations, respectively).

The devaluation of feminized occupations is especially acute for **care work**, work that involves face-to-face caretaking of the physical, emotional, and educational needs of others: children, the elderly, the sick, and the disabled. These jobs are paid *even less* than other feminized jobs, holding education and training constant.[99] Consider the job of childcare worker. In 2017, the average yearly income for childcare workers was $23,760.[100] You know who's paid more than the people who are taking care of children? People who take care of coats in the coat check, parked cars, broken bicycles, dry cleaning, motel reservations, and roadkill.

Job segregation contributes to the gender pay gap because we attribute more value to "men's work" than "women's work." An occupation disproportionately filled by women is seen as *legitimately* lower paid than an occupation dominated by men. Because of this, job segregation doesn't just create a differentiated workforce; it creates an unequal one. This means that both men and women can lose prestige and income when they enter a feminine occupation. Women working in predominantly female occupations earn 26 percent less than women working in mostly male ones; men pay a similar price.[101] It also explains the pay gaps between heterosexual and homosexual women and men.[102] Openly gay and bisexual men are more likely to go into feminized occupations and openly gay and bisexual women into masculinized ones. Gay and bisexual men earn about 30 percent less than heterosexual men, whereas gay and bisexual women earn about 20 percent more than their heterosexual counterparts.

Job segregation, then, explains a large part of the pay gap. But it doesn't explain all of it. Women are not just paid less than men overall; they are also paid less than men *in the same occupations*. What is going on?

DISCRIMINATION AND PREFERENTIAL TREATMENT

Thanks to the Civil Rights Act of 1964, it's no longer legal to discriminate based on gender, but discrimination didn't simply vanish. Enforcing the new law meant going to court, proving the existence of discrimination and the intent to discriminate, and creating consequences. It took decades for the hundreds of cases filed by flight attendants, for example, to make their way through the courts. The last marriage ban was struck down in 1970; routine weigh-ins for female (but not male) members of the cabin crew were standard as late as the 1990s.[103]

Today, flight attendants still deal with sexual objectification from coworkers and passengers as well as bosses who police their bodies.[104] Sexual harassment from passengers is just a "hazard of the job," according to one flight attendant.[105] Some pilots also continue to see flight attendants as a source of sexual titillation

FIGURE 12.5 | WOMEN'S EARNINGS FOR EVERY DOLLAR OF MEN'S IN THE
20 MOST COMMON OCCUPATIONS FOR WOMEN AND MEN*

Occupation	Cents/Men's Dollar
Registered nurse	$0.91
Cook	$0.91
Customer service representative	$0.90
Elementary and middle school teacher	$0.87
Secretary and administrative assistant	$0.86
Cashier	$0.86
Nursing, psychiatric, and home health aide	$0.85
Laborers and freight, stock, and material mover	$0.84
Janitor and building cleaner	$0.84
First-line supervisor of office/administrative support workers	$0.83
Software developer	$0.83
Chief executive	$0.80
Sales representative	$0.78
Manager, all other	$0.77
Accountant and auditor	$0.77
Retail salesperson	$0.74
Driver/sales worker and truck driver	$0.73
First-line supervisor of retail sales workers	$0.72

*Some of the most common occupations for men are also the most common for women, so the total number of occupations is less than 20.
Source: Institute for Women's Policy Research, "The Gender Wage Gap by Occupation 2017 and by Race and Ethnicity," April 2018.
Retrieved from https://iwpr.org/publications/gender-wage-gap-occupation-2017-race-ethnicity/.

and pleasure to which they're entitled. In 2011 a pilot hoping to "get lucky" on his layover was caught on tape complaining to his copilot that the flight attendants assigned to his flight were "eleven f****** over-the-top f******, ass-f****** homosexuals and a granny."[106]

And, yes, there is a pay gap in this profession today: Female flight attendants make $0.82 for every dollar made by their male counterparts.[107] The gendered pay gap isn't just true overall, it's true for almost every occupation in the United States. Figure 12.5 shows the wage gap in the most common occupations for men and women, ranked from smallest difference in pay (among registered nurses and cooks) to the largest (among retail salesperson supervisors).

Gender discrimination accounts for some of the wage gap within occupations: Men are seen as better workers and supervisors no matter what qualities are considered ideal for the job. In one study, participants rated two hypothetical candidates for the job of police chief: one named Michael and the other Michelle.[108] When Michael was described as "streetwise" and Michelle as "formally educated," participants recommended hiring Michael on the basis that he was tough, a risk taker, and physically fit. When Michelle was the one described as streetwise, however, they *still* recommended Michael, this time on the basis that he was well educated, able to communicate with the media, and politically connected. In other words, participants moved the goalposts in order to ensure that, whatever the qualifications, Michael was seen as more qualified than Michelle. Both men and women exhibited this bias, but men more than women.

If this sounds implausible, consider the stories of people who have been both a man and a woman in the workplace. In a study of twenty-nine trans men, two-thirds reported that they received a post-transition advantage at work. This was especially true if they were white and tall. Crispin, for example, worked at Home Depot; he said customers had often dismissed his expertise when they perceived him as a woman, but now heartily welcomed his advice. Henry said he was suddenly "right a lot more" than he had been before.[109] Trans men said they got more credit for less work and, if they wanted, they could be less nice and suffer no consequences. Keith said that behavior perceived as overly "assertive" when he was seen as a woman was now "take charge."[110] Preston explained that before his transition, his bosses and coworkers were rarely helpful, but things changed after: "I swear it was like from one day to the next of me transitioning, I need this, this is what I want and [snaps his fingers]. I have not had to fight about anything."[111] Thomas, who previously went by Susan, told a story that sums it up: After his transition, a client commended his boss for firing "Susan" and hiring the "new guy" who was "just delightful!"[112]

Because of discrimination of this sort, women and men continue to turn to the courts for justice. Many American companies and public service sectors have lost or settled gender-based class action lawsuits in the last fifteen years, including Abercrombie & Fitch, Albertson's, Bank of America, Best Buy, Boeing, Coca-Cola, Costco, the FBI, Goodyear, Heald College, Hewlett-Packard, Home Depot, the International Longshoremen's Union, LexisNexis, Los Alamos National Laboratory, Merrill Lynch, Metropolitan Life Insurance Company, Mitsubishi Motors, Morgan Stanley, Novartis Pharmaceuticals, Outback Steakhouse, Publix Supermarkets, Qualcomm, Smith Barney/Citigroup, State Farm Insurance, Tony Roma's, Uber, Union Pacific Railroad, United Airlines, the U.S. Mint, Wachovia, Walmart, and Wells Fargo.

Clearly, sexism is still prevalent in the workplace. Scholars have identified three forms it takes: men's hostile and benevolent sexism, women's double binds, and employers' preferences for men.

Hostile and Benevolent Sexism

Most men do not exhibit sexist behavior at work and, even among those who do, some are more aggressive or persistent than others, but it only takes one or two sexist people in a workplace to create a hostile environment. Recent high-profile cases—like those against the actor Kevin Spacey, the mega movie producer Harvey Weinstein, the comedian and producer Louis C.K., and the television hosts Bill O'Reilly and Matt Lauer (all credibly accused of patterns of sexual harassment of multiple women)—reveal that just one person can do a lot of damage. Even in less lofty and visible workplaces, a few particularly sexist superiors can do significant harm, even if the employees targeted are generally surrounded by supportive colleagues of all sexes. On average, traditionalist men with homemaker wives are more likely to be discriminatory; unfortunately, it is exactly these kinds of men who are disproportionately bosses, officers, and managers.[113]

When asked, 22 percent of men and 42 percent of women reported being the victim of gender discrimination at work, with women in male-dominated workplaces most likely to say so.[114] The discrimination includes being treated as incompetent; passed over for good assignments or promotions; and silenced, slighted, or isolated; as well as receiving less support from superiors. Some of this discrimination takes the form of overtly hostile sexism, including sexual harassment and violence, and some of it comes in the form of benevolent sexism.

Benevolent sexism is discrimination in the form of chivalry. In this case, men attempt to protect women from unpleasant, dirty, confrontational, dangerous, or otherwise unfeminine activities and, in doing so, end up undermining women's career trajectories. Cynthia, a construction worker, described how her coworker behaved toward her at work and what she did about it:

> One journeyman treated me more like his wife because he pampers his wife. [He would say:] "Don't carry this and don't carry that." I started getting in this rut of standing at the bottom of the ladder handing him tools. So one day, I said this is such crap, I've got to do something. I just started doing everything before he had a chance. I'd grab the ladder and make him do the light work. I said, "Let me do some work, I'm an electrician."[115]

In another occupational context entirely, researchers found that tech industry managers give women less concrete negative feedback than men because they don't want to hurt their female employees' feelings.[116] Without straightforward critique and clear ideas for improvement, women are at a disadvantage compared to men, who are better positioned to know how to improve their performance. Benevolent sexists may be trying to be "nice," but they hurt female employees when "protection" prevents them from learning their job, demonstrating their skills, or becoming better and more effective employees.

Discrimination against women also comes in the form of hostile sexism. Especially in some occupations, some men feel strongly that women should stay in the home or shouldn't be doing men's work, so they isolate women or put them in dangerous situations. Female construction workers, for example, report being forced to do "two-man" jobs all by themselves just to prove they can.[117] Such women are in lose-lose situations: If they try to prove they can "work like a man," they end up doing the dirtiest work or getting hurt. If they refuse to do that kind of work, they get accused of demanding "special treatment."

Sometimes hostile sexism is also sexual. In Chicago, for example, the city's Fire Department is currently facing a lawsuit brought by five female paramedics.[118] They allege sexual comments and texts from several male coworkers and superiors (e.g., "What kind of panties do you wear at work?"), requests for sexual favors (e.g., asked for sex in exchange for a schedule change), sexual threats (e.g., cornered in a private sleeping space by a superior), and physical violations (e.g., kissed and licked against their will and having their hands placed on men's genitals). At least one woman was retaliated against for reporting the harassment to the city's Equal Employment Opportunity Commission.

Sexual harassment is sometimes argued to be a harmless show of attraction, but these are not clumsy attempts at flirting. They're reassertions of dominance in response to the entrance of women into jobs to which men feel entitled.[119] In these instances, women are a **symbolic threat**; their presence potentially degrades the identity of the dominant group. Female construction workers, tech workers, firefighters, and other women in masculinized occupations present a symbolic threat to men in their trades insofar as the men's self-esteem comes, in part, from being a man doing men's work. As long as men's esteem rests on being different from and better than women, men will likely resist women's entry into male-dominated jobs.

Interrupting the idea that some kinds of work are for "manly men" can be good for both men and women. In 1997, Rick Fox, a man in charge of the operation of the then-deepest offshore oil well ever dug, embarked on an unusual experiment.[120] Working on an oil rig ranks among the ten most dangerous jobs, and Fox figured that men's concern with showing weakness, fear, or ignorance—violations of core tenants of masculinity—was part of why. If men were averse to asking questions when they didn't know something, admit nervousness when something seemed dangerous, or show weakness if they couldn't handle a task, accidents were going to happen.

So, Fox collected his men and brought in a facilitator to get them thinking about, and sharing, their fears and insecurities. In front of their coworkers, men confessed to losing loved ones, drowning their sorrows in alcohol, worrying about being a good husband and father, and more. In the end, they felt much more comfortable asking for help, listening, and cooperating—core tenets of femininity—and this transformed the workplace. Over the next fifteen years, Fox's company implemented this training across all its oil platforms. The accident rate declined by 84 percent and productivity increased.[121]

When men embrace elements of femininity as job skills, they become more accepting of women, trans men and women, and less masculine men as coworkers. Anthropologist Jessica Smith, for example, studied the expansion

Women of color are disproportionately well represented in male-dominated physical jobs.

of a Wyoming coal mine as it began incorporating female miners to meet labor demand.[122] Instead of reacting to the symbolic threat to their individual interest, the miners were encouraged to think of their crew as a family. "A good miner was someone who cared for their coworkers," wrote Smith.[123] They were responsible not just for themselves but for their whole crew-family. Because care was considered a female strength, it was easy for men to imagine that their new female coworkers would be excellent coal miners.

Men's workplace discrimination against women and other men isn't inevitable. It can be interrupted, especially when employment opportunities are expanding and men aren't worried about losing their jobs.[124] When it is, hegemonic masculinity, compulsive heterosexuality, and the gender binary may lose, but most everyone else wins. And when women are successfully integrated into workplaces, their mere presence further appears to reduce sexist beliefs and behavior.[125] The presence of high-status female managers also makes a difference, decreasing the pay gap between men and women in their companies.[126]

Hostile and benevolent sexism limit career choices, create hostile and dangerous workplaces, and harm career trajectories. Women pay more of these costs. In male-dominated occupations, though, women not only have to deal with sexism; they also have to contend with the idea that women aren't as suited as men for these occupations, a sentiment often shared by men and women alike.

The Double Bind

Women in masculine occupations often suffer from the perception that they're not quite right for the job. Some attorneys, for example, will describe litigators in gendered terms. Being a lawyer is a "male thing," they say; it's "men beating each other up."[127] Ineffective attorneys are described as "impotent" or needing to "man up." Women in these jobs, then, experience a tension between being a worker and being a woman. This is the double bind discussed in the "Women and Femininities" chapter: To be successful at her job, a woman needs to do masculinity, but to be accepted by her boss, colleagues, and clients, she needs to do femininity.[128] Each undermines the other. Feminine women are seen as likeable but incompetent, while women who do masculinity are seen as competent but not likeable.

Many women workers experience this kind of impossible balancing act. "I'd rather act feminine and friendly and cute than get harassed, ignored, or treated worse," said one lesbian-identified woman in this position.[129] She worked in construction and understood quite well that performing a feminine apologetic was required to avoid being the target of hostile sexism. She also understood, though, that being too feminine would undermine her credibility as a worker. "It's like I have to be careful that I don't act overly feminine," she continued, "because they'll think I can't work." Her male coworkers didn't believe that women—feminine women, anyway—could do the job, but they also didn't tolerate women who weren't feminine. She was stuck.

Because both men and women tend to dislike women who act "like men" at work, those who act confident in their abilities, ask for raises and promotions, and negotiate with their bosses are evaluated less positively than women who don't and men who do. It doesn't matter if they demand or ask nicely.[130] One study, for example, examined how people responded to hypothetical men and women who expressed anger or sadness after losing a client because a colleague was late to a meeting.[131] The angry male was evaluated most favorably, followed by the sad female, the sad male and, lastly and least, the angry female. They saw the angry woman as "out of control" but considered the angry man to be legitimately upset. Asked to attribute a salary to each, participants offered the angry woman $0.62 on the angry man's dollar.

All too often, in all too many spaces, women are damned if they do and damned if they don't.

Invisible Obstructions and Opportunities

WOMEN IN MALE-DOMINATED OCCUPATIONS Together, these findings—the costs of hostile and benevolent sexism and the double bind—are behind the idea of the **glass ceiling**, an invisible barrier between women and top positions in masculine occupations. Most women simply don't get the training, mentorship, or promotions received by many men.[132] Men, on average, enter the workforce at a higher rank with a better salary and then advance and see their pay rise more quickly. These findings are true even when researchers account for the number of years in the workforce, the industry, geographical location, parenthood status, women's level of ambition, and the strategies they use for advancement. Even very successful businesswomen feel the strain: nearly three-quarters of successful female executives at Fortune 1000 companies agree that gender stereotypes are a barrier to women's success.[133]

For black women and Latinas, the proper metaphor may not be glass but concrete.[134] Such women are even less likely than white and Asian women to hold jobs in the top ranks of professions.[135] Stereotypes such as the "angry black woman" and the "hot-blooded Latina" doubly penalize women of color for not living up to expectations for white femininity. This requires them to put even more energy into their feminine apologetic.

When women do break through a ceiling, they often encounter a **glass cliff**, a heightened risk of failing, compared with similar men.[136] This is not because women are unsuited for leadership; rather, it's because women tend to be promoted during times of crisis and given jobs with a higher risk of failure. This phenomenon is found in contexts as wide-ranging as funeral homes, music festivals, political elections, and law. Because of the glass cliff, the average tenure of female CEOs is just half that of male CEOs.[137]

If women are seen as less capable than men, why would companies promote them in times of crisis? The answer has less to do with how managers feel about women than it does with how they feel about their male coworkers. When decision makers are predominantly male, they may make efforts to ensure that men with whom they feel chummy get the better positions. The bad jobs are then given to whomever is left over: typically women and racial minorities of both sexes.[138] This was the experience of one female Marine Corps officer: "It's the good old boys network. The guys helping each other out and we don't have the women helping each other out because there are not enough of us around. The good old boys network put the guys they want to get promoted in certain jobs to make them stand out, look good."[139]

When women succeed in precarious positions, and they often do, their reward is often to be put in charge of yet another fragile project. Many women, faced with a revolving door of failing assignments, eventually do fail. Or they burn out from stress. In fact, while we often hear the claim that women "opt out" of high-pressure jobs because they want to spend more time with their families, in real life women cite this as the reason for leaving their jobs only 2 to 3 percent of the time (that is, no more often than men). Dissatisfaction, feelings of underappreciation, blocked opportunities, discrimination, and harassment are much more significant factors.[140] If women seem to be less ambitious than men, then, this can be at least partly explained by the fact that they face barriers at work that men, all things being equal, do not.

This resonates with research on work more generally: People in jobs with a **sticky floor**, ones with no or low opportunity for promotion, tend to limit their aspirations.[141] Women, more often than men, find themselves in a position where it doesn't make sense to be ambitious, and this is even more true for women of color and immigrant women. In contrast, both women and men in high-mobility positions with a significant chance of promotion tend to be correspondingly motivated.

MEN IN FEMALE-DOMINATED OCCUPATIONS Do men in female-dominated occupations face the same struggles as women in male-dominated ones? It turns out, no. Men in female-dominated occupations are disadvantaged relative to men in male-dominated occupations, but they aren't disadvantaged relative to their female coworkers. Instead of facing glass ceilings or cliffs, they often are presented with a **glass escalator**: an invisible ride to the top offered to men in female-dominated occupations.[142]

A series of studies have found that men in female-dominated occupations are advantaged in terms of pay, promotions, and support from colleagues and supervisors.[143] In a two-year study of 5,734 secondary and elementary school teachers, for example, all else being equal, men were three times more likely than women to be promoted to administrative positions.[144] Likewise, though women are overrepresented in fashion design, men are more likely to win accolades and awards on the assumption that their work is more inspired and artistic.[145] This is true especially if they're white and, in some cases, heterosexual.[146] Some sexual minorities report being forced to stay in a **glass closet**, an invisible place in which sexual minorities hide their identities in order to avoid stigma, suspicion, or censure at work.[147]

Not all men, though, view the glass escalator as a blessing. Sociologist Christine Williams, who coined the phrase, described how a male librarian, six months after starting his first job, was criticized by his supervisors for "not shooting high enough."[148] "Seriously," he said, "they assumed that because I was a male—and they told me this . . . that somehow I wasn't doing the kind of management-oriented work that they thought I should be doing." He worked in the children's collection for ten years and had to fight the whole time to avoid being promoted; he enjoyed the job he had. Male nurses, likewise, often find themselves steered to emergency medicine, where salaries are higher.[149] Gender stereotypes are at work here—and not just positive ones like the idea that men are better leaders, but also negative ones like the idea that men aren't suited to working with children.

Men who pursue feminized occupations, then, may face policing from their peers and bring home lower salaries than they would if they were in male-dominated occupations but, relative to their female colleagues, they will be promoted more quickly and earn more money.[150] This isn't necessarily what all men want, but it does translate into advantages at work and the persistence of the pay gap.

Glass and concrete ceilings, alongside glass cliffs, closets, and escalators, conspire with sticky floors to keep (white, heterosexual) men at the top of many workplaces. Expectations surrounding parenthood contribute as well.

PARENTHOOD: THE FACTS AND THE FICTION

Today one can't read a mommy blog without encountering the problem of so-called work-life balance. Almost always considered a "women's issue," the conflict rests on the incompatibility of two hegemonic cultural ideologies: intensive motherhood, which we discussed in the last chapter, and the **ideal worker norm**, the idea that an employee should commit their energies to their job without the distraction of family responsibilities.[151] Echoing the norm, one senior manager interviewed for a study about workplace culture explained:

> *The members of the Management Committee of this company aren't the smartest. . . . We're the hardest working. We work like dogs. We out-work the others. We out-practice them. We out-train them. . . . What counts is work and commitment. . . . I don't think we can get commitment with less than fifty or sixty hours a week. . . . To be competitive, that's what we need to do.*[152]

The ideal worker norm is especially strong in the United States.[153] It frames employees as less than ideal if they sometimes need time off to do family-related tasks (attend parent-teacher meetings, care for sick children or ailing parents, step in when daycare arrangements fall through) or can't always go above and beyond stated job responsibilities (work overtime and on weekends, on short notice, or relocate for the company). In Northern California's Silicon Valley, ideal workers are described as ones with "zero drag," meaning that absolutely nothing about their lives interferes with their ability to work. Po Bronson, a journalist who investigated this hypercompetitive workplace culture, wrote that

> *new applicants would jokingly be asked about their "drag coefficient." Since the job is a full hour's commute from San Francisco, an apartment in the city was a full unit of drag. A spouse? Drag coefficient of one. Kids? A half point per.*[154]

Employees who do "just" a good job are penalized; great workers go "above and beyond," creating a cycle in which workers have to outwork each other just to stay in the game.

The ideal worker norm assumes that workers have homemaker partners or paid help to take care of any family- or house-related demands. All individuals with family responsibilities (and many without) often find themselves straining to live up to this norm, but women with children bear the brunt.[155] Research finds that they often suffer a **motherhood penalty**, a loss in wages per hour on the job associated with becoming a mother. U.S. mothers experience, on average, a 7 percent decline in their wages for each child.[156] Women married to men, poor women, highly educated women, and white women face the largest penalties. Mothers married to women are an exception; they see their wages go up.[157]

Dads, for their part, receive a **fatherhood premium**, a wage increase that accrues to married men who become fathers.[158] Married fathers earn 4 to 7 percent *more* than married men without children. Stepfathers, fathers without custody of their kids, racial minorities, and less educated men see a smaller fatherhood premium or none at all. If we put the penalty and premium together, the numbers are stark: Among all full-time workers, women make 82 percent of what men do; but among parents working full time, women's relative earnings drop to 71 percent.[159]

The motherhood penalty and fatherhood premium are a result of both *actual* time and effort spent on work and, even more so, employers' *beliefs* about time and effort.

Working on the Mommy Track

More than nine times out of ten, if a parent takes time off work after a child is born, it's a woman.[160] If that woman has two children three years apart and takes a break from work that lasts until the second child enters preschool, she'll have been out of the workforce for seven years. Those are unpaid years, and when she returns to work, she'll have less work experience than a person who didn't take time off. Most women do not take this much time out of the workforce, but they are still substantially more likely than men to take at least some, and that time makes them less competitive at work.

When women do go back to work, what happens at home matters, too. Recall that married mothers and fathers have a tendency to specialize: men do about two-thirds of the paid work and women do about two-thirds of the housework and childcare.[161] Struggling with work-life balance, mothers may allow themselves to be put on a **mommy track**, a workplace euphemism that refers to expecting less intense commitment from mothers, with the understanding that they're sacrificing the right to expect equal pay, regular raises, or promotions.

The mommy track sends a message: we'll let you stay, but we don't think you're an ideal worker.

In contrast, fathers often increase their effort at work. This choice likely resonates with their employers' gender ideology. Employers sometimes accept that a woman needs to respond to her children's schedule and take care of emergencies, even if they begrudge them this flexibility. Those same employers often do not accept that men have to do the same. Since there is rarely a daddy track, new fathers likely face fewer options than new mothers: be an ideal worker or get fired.

Time out of the workforce to care for children and reduced overall work hours are plausible causes of mothers' economic disadvantage. But there are reasons to question whether it's the whole story. Studies actually find that many mothers *do* put in great amounts of effort at work; some evidence even suggests they're *more* productive than non-mothers.[162] This is consistent with the finding that the bigger contributor to the motherhood penalty and the fatherhood premium isn't how mothers and fathers actually perform at work, it's employers' and coworkers' *beliefs* about how they perform.[163]

Beliefs about Moms and Dads

Research shows that many employers see mothers as less-than-ideal employees and fathers as especially ideal ones regardless of how much talent and effort men and women display at work.[164] Mothers may find themselves put on the mommy track based purely on stereotypes: sent home when others are asked to stay late, excused from important work-related travel, kept off intensive projects that require long hours. In a striking example from one study, for instance, a new mom started getting sent home at 5:30 sharp while her husband, who worked for the same person, was given extra work designed to boost his career.[165]

As law professor Joan C. Williams describes it: "Managers and coworkers may mentally cloak pregnant women and new mothers in a haze of femininity, assuming they will be empathetic, emotional, gentle, nonaggressive—that is, not very good at business."[166] In fact, mothers' value at work is ranked as about equivalent to other stigmatized workers: elderly persons and people receiving welfare. Single mothers and black mothers are often judged even more harshly.[167] And the more motherly they are, the less we value them. One study, for instance, found that respondents judge breastfeeding mothers to be less competent workers than mothers who bottle-feed.[168]

But, Williams continues, "If these women shine through the haze and remain tough, cool, emphatic, and committed to their jobs, colleagues may indict them for being insufficiently maternal."[169] What would we think, after all, of a new mother who *didn't* want to go home early? Mothers face a double bind: Their supervisors and coworkers don't take them seriously as employees; if they shine as employees, their coworkers might conclude that the mothers shouldn't be rewarded for what is perceived to be neglectful parenting.

The belief that mothers are bad workers sits alongside the belief that fathers are the best workers. Sociologist Shelley Correll and her colleagues studied whether individuals reviewing applications for a marketing job would evaluate female and male parents and non-parents differently.[170] They did. Mothers were considered to be the least hirable: Only 47 percent of the mothers were recommended for hire, compared to 84 percent of the non-mothers. And if hired, mothers were offered starting salaries that were $13,477 less per year than those of non-mothers. Mothers were rated as the least competent, committed, promotable, and suited for management training. In contrast, fathers were rated *more* favorably than non-fathers: 73 percent of fathers were recommended for hire, compared to 62 percent of non-fathers. Fathers were seen as more committed and more likely to be promoted. They were also considered to be worth $7,351 more a year than non-fathers and $15,927 more than mothers.

These findings hold up in the real world. Following up, Correll and her colleagues sent 1,276 fake résumés, carefully constructed to give hints as to parental status, to 638 actual employers. Mothers received fewer than half as many callbacks as non-mothers. Fathers were called back at a slightly higher rate than non-fathers. Non-mothers actually received the most callbacks. Employers generally seem to like hiring women, then, maybe even more than they like hiring men; they just don't like moms.

THE CHANGING WORKPLACE, REVISITED

If being a flight attendant in 1945 was almost as glamorous as being a movie star, it certainly isn't anymore. Commercial air travel today is an unpleasant form of mass transportation: more like riding a city bus than being escorted through the sky by a white-jacketed steward.[171] While once airlines offered plenty of space, free full-course meals, and blankets and pillows, today they offer little more than the opportunity to get from one place to another safely, with a beverage and snack service sufficient to ensure that passengers literally don't pass out from thirst or hunger.

In the United States, this shift from elite to "economy class" was spurred by the federal government's decision to set fewer standards on air travel.[172] Deregulation, complete by 1985, left airlines to set their own fares and routes. Without a regulatory floor, capitalist competition sent airlines into a downward spiral as they slashed costs to try to offer the cheapest fares. It was a battle for survival and many airlines at the time went bankrupt, while others saw their debt soar.

The need to reduce cost is why most airlines today offer only the most basic of amenities for non–first class passengers; it's also meant squeezing as much work out of the fewest employees for as little pay and benefits as possible.[173] Flight attendants had a strong history of labor unionization and were organized to protect their rights and interests as coworkers, but legal and illegal efforts by airlines to "bust" unions hindered their ability to collectively bargain.

Consequently, the working conditions, security, and pay of flight attendants were devastated. Flight attendants suffered huge layoffs, heightened work demands, and more unpredictable and erratic schedules. In the 1980s, their income fell by a third.[174] In the meantime, passengers are now even more likely to be tired, frustrated, and uncomfortable, so flight attendants have to work harder than ever to soothe them.[175] "Ask any flight attendant," said a veteran stewardess in 2003, "when we all took this job, it was for the lifestyle, the freedom. But it's changed so much, with mergers and layoffs and concessions and service reductions and waiting for pay cuts. The thrill is gone."[176]

Indeed, the thrill is gone for many workers throughout the Western world, but especially in the United States.[177] Compared to the mid-twentieth century, most employees today work harder for less. As Figure 12.6 shows, starting in the early 1970s, employers stopped sharing profits with their employees, keeping more and more for themselves. Today's workers enjoy less pay, flexibility, and security, and fewer benefits, even as their productivity has risen.[178] As the gap between the rich and poor has widened, a middle-class lifestyle has become increasingly elusive. The top 1 percent of Americans now brings home 22 percent of all income and holds 39 percent of all wealth, more than all the income and wealth enjoyed by the bottom 90 percent combined.[179]

Like with the flight attendants, these outcomes are largely the result of a combination of governmental policies and workplace practices. Our economy is now characterized by a commitment to the "free market" at the expense of protecting workers, producing low regulation and suppression of union activity. Teachers' work conditions and pay have declined so markedly, for example, that many must take second jobs to make ends meet; companies like Uber are even actively recruiting them ("Teachers: Driving Our Future" was an actual tagline).[180] More than half of American workers today work "by the hour" and 6.4 million of them are working part time when they'd rather have a full-time job.[181] The service industry now generally prefers to hire workers part time to avoid having to offer employees benefits. Part-time workers can also be denied regular work hours; they're often given shifts that vary from week to week with little to no notice, so they can't count on a steady income, even a low one.

For many other kinds of workers, too, the absence of "good jobs" has pushed them into the "gig economy," a romanticized form of self-employment that, in practice, typically means patching together a variety of dead-end jobs like driving, delivering, and walking dogs.[182] But surviving on an assemblage of odd jobs

FIGURE 12.6 | THE GROWING GAP BETWEEN PRODUCTIVITY AND WORKERS' COMPENSATION

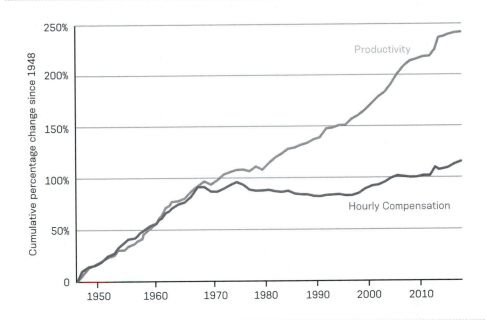

Note: *Data are for compensation (wages and benefits) of production/nonsupervisory workers in the private sector and net productivity of the total economy. "Net productivity" is the growth of output of goods and services less depreciation per hour worked.*
Source: Economic Policy Institute, "The Productivity-Pay Gap," October 2017, Retrieved https://www.epi.org/productivity-pay-gap/

brings no benefits and offers no security. This is not the kind of work that allows either women or men to support their families. Nevertheless, this is a new normal: since 2007, involuntary part-time work has increased five times faster than voluntary part-time work and eighteen times faster than all work.[183]

With the decline of labor unions, employers get to choose whether to be generous with pay and benefits. Some of the highest-paying occupations treat employees quite well—the corporate giants of the tech industry, for example, famously offer benefits like egg freezing to delay motherhood and free chef-prepared meals—but most jobs are not like this. Nearly half of U.S. workers make under $15 an hour.[184] Because women, especially women of color, are clustered in industries that pay at or near the minimum wage (or, in the case of tipped workers and home health aides, even less), their financial situation is especially precarious. Poverty and homelessness for families headed by women earners are rising, even as more families are depending on women's wages. Experts estimate that over a million children experience homelessness each year.[185]

Men, though, as well as women and children, have been harmed by growing inequality in the economy. We noted earlier, for example, that a quarter of the decline in the wage gap is due to men's declining wages. The absence of

a breadwinner wage—one that is sufficient to support a family—has contributed to demoralization and family fragility in African American communities for decades. Now that white men's jobs, families, and communities are
being affected, it's becoming recognized as a serious flaw in how the economy
is organized.[186]

As women of color have noted in the past, closing the gender pay gap will
be a bittersweet victory if men's wages are depressed and few jobs offer secure
work that pays the bills. Indeed, even if all forms of discrimination were elim-
inated tomorrow, life-threatening inequalities in income would persist. This is
something that many Americans, including ones who identify as feminist, have
been working on, and is part of the larger topic of political activism that we
tackle next.

Revisiting the Question

 **If women now have equal rights in the workplace, why
aren't they as successful as men at work?**

Women are less successful for a complex set of reasons: About 10 percent of
the pay gap is explained by differences in job experience due to time spent in
and out of the workforce, largely for the purposes of caregiving.[187] Almost half
(49 percent) is explained by job segregation and the devaluation of women's
work. The remaining 41 percent is likely due to discrimination against women
and mothers.

Not all these factors are present to the same degree in every workplace. Discrimination against women is a larger factor in blue-collar occupations than
discrimination against mothers, while the opposite appears to be true in white-
collar workplaces.[188] Many supervisors, both male and female, go out of their
way to ensure women can compete on equal footing with men. Many women are
talented and dedicated enough to overcome at least some of the gendered disadvantages. Still, despite many individual and organizational examples to the
contrary, women as a group still face barriers to success at work that men do not.

As a result, women who work full time earn $0.82 for every dollar earned by
comparable men. For the typical woman working fifty weeks a year, that means
earning $8,550 less each year.[189] This isn't just problematic *in principle*. For poor
women and their families, economic disadvantage translates into *real* deprivation: an inability to pay rent, keep food on the table, or buy their children back-
to-school clothes. For more financially secure women, it translates into fewer
opportunities and pleasures. With an extra $8,550 a year, a woman could pay
the majority of the tuition and fees at her local state college, get a massage every
two and a half days for a year, or learn how to fly an airplane.[190] If she invested it,
experts predict it'd be worth $46,405 twenty-five years later. If she saved for ten

years, $85,500 would be enough to start a business or put a hefty down payment on a house. Maybe she's not interested in buying a home and settling down. She could use that money to take an entire year off work, maybe three. It's easy to think about the wage gap in purely theoretical terms, but money buys everything but happiness. It matters.

Next . . .

The last few chapters have established that gender inequality is not just a theoretical exercise but a lived experience. Sexism, androcentrism, and subordination play a role in how we understand and express our sexualities, organize and experience our home lives, and earn a living and pursue our careers. Gendered ideas, interactions, and institutions structure our lives at every turn, creating both difference and inequality. Gender inequality is clearly not good for women, but it's not ideal for most men either. This is what motivates many people to get involved in changing or conserving the social constructions, interpersonal interactions, and institutions that organize our societies. In the next chapter, we'll ask:

How do we change societies?

This is politics.

FOR FURTHER READING

American Association of University Women. "The Simple Truth about the Gender Pay Gap." Spring 2018. Retrieved from www.aauw.org/resource/the-simple-truth-about-the-gender-pay-gap/.

Chang, Emily. *Brotopia: Breaking up the Boys' Club of Silicon Valley*. New York: Penguin Random House, 2018.

Connell, Catherine. *School's Out: Gay and Lesbian Teachers in the Classroom*. Berkeley: University of California Press, 2015.

Goldin, Claudia. *Understanding the Gender Gap: An Economic History of American Women*. New York: Oxford University Press, 1990.

Harrington Meyer, Madonna, and Pamela Herd. *Market Friendly or Family Friendly: The State and Gender Equality in Old Age*. New York: Russell Sage Foundation, 2007.

Kessler-Harris, Alice. "The Wage Conceived: Value and Need as Measures of a Woman's Worth." In *A Woman's Wage: Historical Meanings and Social Consequences*. Lexington: University of Kentucky Press, 1990, 6–32.

Rohm, Robin (ed.). *Double Bind: Women on Ambition*. New York: W. W. Norton, 2017.

Thomas, Gillian. *Because of Sex: One Law, Ten Cases, and Fifty Years That Changed American Women's Lives at Work*. New York: St Martin's Press, 2016.

NEVERTHELESS,
SHE PERSISTED.

—SEN. MITCH McCONNELL[1]

13

Politics

For most of modern history, governments did not allow women the right to vote. Nor did they grant women the other rights and responsibilities of citizenship: to serve on juries, give legal testimony, or hold public office. This meant that women had no formal right to choose who represented them to state and federal governments, weigh in on laws and policies, be elected to represent others, be judged by a jury of their peers, or testify at a trial, even in their own defense.

American women were no exception. So, in 1848, at the first-ever women's rights convention in the United States, a small group made the first recorded decision to change this. They resolved that women should act to "secure to themselves their sacred right to the elective franchise." And with that they began a movement for women's **suffrage**, the right to vote.

Opponents of women's suffrage began organizing in response. They thought the idea was dangerous. In their minds, women were wives and, if wives could vote, it would mean that their husbands weren't voting *for* them. Would husbands no longer be the representatives of the family? Clergymen worried aloud that husbands and wives would hold different political positions, threatening family unity with disagreements over the dinner table. It was much better, they surmised, if women didn't have political opinions at all.

Votes for Women

We demand the vote.

An Advocate for Women's Rights.

This pro-suffrage cat from around 1908 may look cute, but don't be fooled—it was used to suggest that giving women the vote would be as absurd as extending the vote to felines.

They also thought it was laughable. Women belonged in the home, they argued, apart from public life. They compared wives to another domesticated animal: the housecat.[2] "I want my vote!" meowed a black and white kitten on an anti-suffrage poster. The message was clear: respecting women's capacity to make a reasoned decision was about as sensible as respecting the preferences of a pet.

Proponents of the female vote, called suffragists, fought back. In a time-honored tradition, they embraced the insult intended to mock them. A pro-suffrage Christmas card issued in 1908 featured a tabby standing on its hind legs holding a sign that read, "Votes for Women." The accompanying poem was a pledge:

> *I'm a catty suffragette.*
> *I scratch and fight the P'lice.*
> *So long as they withhold the vote*
> *my warfare will not cease.*[3]

It was a long war. Suffrage was not won quickly or easily, and many suffragists died of old age before they could see their efforts realized. In addition to criticism and ridicule, suffragists faced government repression and violence. Over 1,000 suffragists would be imprisoned in the United Kingdom and United States. There they endured brutal force-feeding after initiating hunger strikes.[4] Most suffragists were peaceful, but some weren't above aggression themselves. One group in the United Kingdom set buildings on fire and learned jujitsu to defend themselves from the police; they made that catty pledge a reality.[5]

The fight for suffrage involved both inspiring coalitions and ugly divides. Many suffragists were **abolitionists** first, activists in the fight against human slavery. White and black men and women worked side by side for this hard-won victory. After slavery was abolished in 1865 and black men were granted suffrage in 1869, black women continued to fight valiantly for their own vote. As the abolitionist Sojourner Truth observed: "If colored men get their rights, and colored women not theirs, the colored men will be masters over the women, and it will be just as bad as it was before."[6]

White suffragists often disagreed as to whether their efforts should benefit all women or only white women.[7] Anti-suffrage activists tapped into widespread animosity toward black people, reminding a racist public that women's suffrage would not only put women into the voting booth, it would double the black vote. Some suffragist groups were themselves racist, excluding black women from their organizations, activities, or platforms. Consequently, some black women leaders like Ida B. Wells Barnett started suffrage organizations of their own.

Suffragists around the world started to work together in the 1880s and, by the early 1900s, this international women's organizing had begun to shift public opinion. New Zealand was the first to grant women the right to vote, in 1893. The U.S. federal government came around just about one hundred years ago, in 1920, giving suffrage to both black and white women together; Native American women and men would have to wait four more years.

By then the movement was rolling across the globe. In less than thirty years, women's suffrage became a global norm.[8] There were a few holdouts, but the last nation to allow women to vote, Saudi Arabia, did so in 2015.[9] Today **universal suffrage**, the right of all citizens to vote, is the very definition of democracy. In the 1800s, however, it was a wholly **radical claim**, or an idea that doesn't (yet) resonate with most members of a population.[10]

Ida B. Wells Barnett was a founder of the National Association of Colored Women's Clubs, created to address both black civil rights and women's suffrage. After a friend was lynched, she became a passionate crusader against white mob violence.

That universal suffrage is now almost universally supported is evidence that change—even radical change—is possible. In fact, as the timeline in Table 13.1 illustrates, feminists and other activists have turned plenty of radical ideas into the status quo. They continue to do so. Some of the most exciting feminist activism in world history may even be happening right now. We don't know what will come next. Many things that seem radical today may become part of the taken-for-granted way societies operate a hundred years from now.

Our final question, then, is:

Q+A   How do we change societies?

We change them with politics.

Politics is the word we use to describe the various activities involved in determining public policies, and electing people to guide this process. The word is often used derisively, like when politicians are described as corrupt or dishonest, but politicking isn't inherently this way. Instead, politics is how we make decisions. It isn't always pretty, and we don't always get along, but it's the only way we have to get together and figure out the best way to be a society.

This chapter is about the **politics of gender**: how people change and resist change to the gender order. **Feminist politics** are those involving efforts to make society's gender order less hierarchical and more supportive of the full development of human capacities for everyone. **Anti-feminist politics** is committed to the value of gender difference and hierarchy and aims to prevent feminist change. This isn't necessarily about going "back" to how things used to be; it could be an invention of a future kind of techno-patriarchal society. Patriarchy changed radically at least once, with industrialization, and it could be modified again as we move into a new, differently shaped future.

In doing this work, feminists don't just wrestle with often stubborn governments and dedicated anti-feminists, but with one another. They have always disagreed, and continue to do so, about what a **feminist utopia**—or a perfectly gender-egalitarian society—might look like. Because feminists come in all shapes and sizes, are differently positioned in society, and have different needs, feminist politics are necessarily and inevitably intersectional. This leads to sometimes tough negotiations, but it's undoubtedly strengthened feminism by making it more responsive to people of all genders and all intersectional identities.

Gaining rights has always been an incremental process reflecting the slow dismantling of many different social hierarchies. As the timeline in Table 13.1 shows, rights have often been granted unevenly by race, sexuality, family status, and more. Wealthy white women are usually the ones to break glass ceilings because they generally carry more privilege and have more opportunity than poor women, women of color, and women disadvantaged in other ways. The first woman to serve in Congress, for example, was Jeannette Rankin, a white woman from Montana. She was elected in 1916, before the federal government granted women the vote but after Montana had. It would be another eighty-three years before the first openly gay woman was elected. Likewise, in 1981 Sandra Day O'Connor, a white woman, became the first woman appointed to the Supreme Court. The first woman of color was appointed in 2009.

Nothing about politics is simple. It's a thorny, often heated enterprise with lots of moving parts. It can be both exciting and intimidating, as there are no predetermined endings or guarantees. What comes next is uncertain, but one thing is for sure: politics will be involved.

TABLE 13.1 | MOMENTS IN U.S. GENDER POLITICS SINCE SUFFRAGE

1920	Most American women win the right to vote.
1922	The Supreme Court decides that U.S. women who marry noncitizen men are able to retain their own citizenship.
1923	The Equal Rights Amendment is introduced into Congress.
1924	Native American men and women win suffrage.
1928	Puerto Rican women win suffrage.
1933	Frances Perkins becomes the first woman member of a presidential cabinet.
1963	The Equal Pay Act makes it illegal to pay men and women different wages for exactly the same job.
1964	The Civil Rights Act outlaws discrimination on the basis of racial, ethnic, or national origin, religion, and sex.
1965	The Supreme Court decriminalizes the use of birth control by married people.
1968	The Equal Employment Opportunity Commission rules that gender segregation of "Help Wanted" ads is illegal.
1970	The last "marriage ban" barring women from paid employment is struck down.
1972	The Supreme Court extends to single people the right to use contraceptives.
	Title IX bans sex discrimination in schools receiving federal funding.
	The Equal Rights Amendment is passed by Congress. Thirty-five states would ratify the amendment, falling short of the thirty-eight needed.
1973	The Supreme Court grants women the right to abortion in the first and second trimesters.
1974	The Equal Credit Opportunity Act establishes married women's right to have a credit card in their own name and, thus, have a credit history and score.
	The Supreme Court rules that mandatory dismissals of public school teachers who become pregnant are unconstitutional.
1975	The Supreme Court grants women equal rights and responsibilities for jury duty.
1976	Military academies are ordered to admit women.
	Nebraska becomes the first state to make marital rape illegal.
1978	The Pregnancy Discrimination Act requires employers treat pregnancy like any other temporary disability.
1981	Women are allowed to enlist in all military branches.
1992	The "Year of the Woman" sees an unprecedented number of women elected to Congress.
1993	Don't Ask, Don't Tell is introduced, requiring sexual minorities to remain closeted if they want to serve in the military, but protecting them if they do.
1996	President Bill Clinton signs the Defense of Marriage Act, defining marriage as only between a man and a woman.
	The Supreme Court declares that states cannot deny gays and lesbians protection from discrimination.

(continued)

TABLE 13.1 | *continued*

1999	Tammy Baldwin becomes the first openly gay person to serve in Congress.
2004	Massachusetts becomes the first state to legalize same-sex marriage.
2009	The Lily Ledbetter Fair Pay Restoration Act overturns a Supreme Court decision that prevented women from challenging past pay discrimination.
	Sonia Sotomayor becomes the first woman of color confirmed to the Supreme Court.
2010	The Navy ban on women serving on submarines is overturned.
	Don't Ask, Don't Tell is repealed.
2012	The Affordable Care Act requires health insurance to cover contraception.
2015	The Supreme Court declares same-sex marriage a legal right in all fifty states.
	The military begins allowing women to serve in front-line combat roles and lifts the ban on military service by trans people.
2016	Hillary Rodham Clinton becomes the first woman nominated by a major political party for president of the United States.
2017	Americans march for women's rights in the largest protest in U.S. history.
	Danica Roem becomes the first openly trans state legislator (Virginia).
2018	Tammy Duckworth becomes the first senator to give birth while in office.

To begin, let's go over some basics: what is "the state" and why should we care?

THE STATE

States are institutions entrusted with the power to regulate everyday life on behalf of the group. They are what we, in more ordinary language, refer to as countries or nations. States are important because they wield a greater power than almost any other social entity on earth, second only, perhaps, to global alliances like the United Nations and transnational corporations like Google. States have vast resources and the exclusive right to pass laws, collect taxes, and detain and imprison citizens. States can even legally wage war according to a set of international rules.

Today, states are the dominant way of promoting group welfare. This is called **governance**: the process of making decisions for the nation, enforcing the laws of the land, and—if the state is a democracy—ensuring the state's accountability to its citizens. There are two ways to think about gender and governance.[11] The first involves the **governance of gender**: how the gender of residents shapes the way they are regulated. The second is the **gender of governance**: who holds political office and whether it matters. In this section, we talk about both as well as consider what feminists think the governance of gender should look like.

The Governance of Gender

Though the state can seem abstract and distant, its policies affect all aspects of our daily lives, from what we're paid for our work, to the health of our environments, to the content of our education, and more. State policies are also gendered, sometimes explicitly and intentionally and sometimes in their unintended consequences.

GENDER AND POLICY At the most basic level, states enforce gender ideologies in deciding how many and which gender categories to recognize. In the United States, birth certificates, drivers' licenses, and passports reflect the gender binary, requiring that everyone identify as male or female, not neither, both, or other. This is required by the federal government and nearly all states, with the notable exceptions of California, Oregon, and Washington.[12]

Other states formalize different gender categories. In some cases, these categories are specific: in India and Bangladesh, a person can formally identify as hijra. In other states, third gender categories are broadly defined to capture individuals who don't identify with the binary for any reason, as in Australia, Canada, and Germany. Whether this is allowed for adults, children, or both, and what documents it applies to, varies by country.

States also decide whether to require gender binary spaces (like public restrooms, prisons, and military barracks); enforce gendered roles in marriage; and allow trans men and women to modify their names, bodies, or documents. If German parents do identify a sex for their babies, for instance, the law requires that the child be given a clearly masculine or feminine name.[13] In the United States, if the Transportation Security Administration decides to pat down a passenger being screened at the airport, they must use a same-sex attendant. In large and small ways, states send messages and enforce rules that both challenge and affirm gender ideologies.

Policies do more than just shape our identities, though; they also shape our lives. Gender is governed with policies influencing how we work and whether we marry and have children. Since the number of births and participation in the workforce influence whether a country can feed and educate its citizens, fill its jobs, support its elderly, or fight a war, this is very serious business for states. In Japan, for example, the fertility rate has fallen to 1.4 children per woman, far below the number required to maintain the population. Scholars point to a failure to protect working mothers (70 percent of women quit their job when they become pregnant) and the prohibitive cost of childrearing (2.5 times more expensive than in the United States).[14] There are so few babies that, as one commentator put it, "Sales of adult diapers will soon surpass those of baby diapers."[15]

In response, Japan, like the United States, has begun offering tax credits for every child in the household. This is a **pro-natal policy**, one that encourages childbearing, whether intentionally or not. Japan might also consider giving new mothers a "baby box," like they do in Finland, filled with diapers, baby clothes, crib sheets, and other goods worth several hundred dollars. Or providing day care at virtually no cost, like they do in France. Each of these policies encourages childbearing by making it a little more affordable and convenient.

States also make **anti-natal policy** discouraging childbearing. Worried about overpopulation, China, for instance, imposed a "one-child policy" in 1979, revising it to a "two-child policy" in 2015. India distributes educational material encouraging couples to have just one child and offers money in return for undergoing sterilization. Both pro- and anti-natal policies can have unintended consequences that states have to address in turn. Because of preferences for boys over girls, and illegal but widely employed sex-selective abortion, China and India now have a different problem: 107 million more men than women and a marriage crisis.[16]

Work-related policies can also be pro- and anti-natal. More support for balancing work and family encourages childbearing, while less support discourages it. Parental leave policies are an example. In most states featured in Figure 13.1, either the employer or government subsidizes new parents' wages so that they lose little or no income (though not all states extend these benefits to all parents). The United States offers no paid leave at all. It guarantees only twelve weeks of unpaid leave, and only if parents can afford to take them without pay, and only to the third of Americans who work a minimum number of hours at the right kind of company. Other countries, including most in Europe, offer months or even a full year of paid leave. Some of these even set aside some time specifically for the father, ensuring that men get used to being active participants in childrearing early.

Some U.S. states have "family caps" on their support for poor parents, hoping to discourage them from having more babies, revealing that family and work policy is not only gendered, but intersectionally so.[17] In contrast to the tax policies that encourage high income earners to specialize and leave one spouse at home, policy aimed toward poor women pushes them into the workforce by requiring mothers to hold a job to remain eligible for benefits like low-income housing, childcare waivers, and "food stamps." Regardless of whether we think mothers of young kids should hold paid jobs, it might be surprising that state policy encourages one kind of mothering for poor kids and another for wealthier ones.

States govern, then, in gendered ways. Today they typically do so with a balance of incentives and disincentives that don't specifically apply to men and

FIGURE 13.1 | STATE VARIATION IN PAID MATERNITY LEAVE

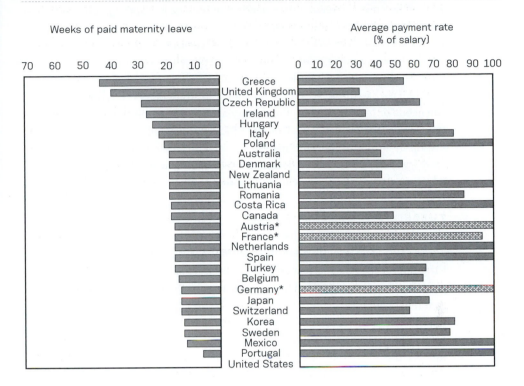

*Cross-hatching indicates payment rates based on net earnings.

Source: OECD Family Database, "PF2.1 Key Characteristics of Parental Leave Systems," Oct. 26, 2017, Retrieved from http://www.oecd .org/els/family/database.htm.

women differently, but have gendered effects because we live in a gendered society. Moreover, these policies support some visions of the gender order but not others, and they often do so in intersectional ways. Because gendered policy effects are often unintended, thinking about gender when making policy is important.

Accordingly, some feminists want politicians to commit to **gender-aware policymaking**, a practice of carefully considering the likely effects of a policy on both men and women, as well as different kinds of men and women. The European Union instituted gender-aware policymaking almost twenty-five years ago and the programs of the United Nations—from peacekeeping operations to refugee support—now give attention to gender as a matter of official policy.[18]

Consider the buses, trams, trains, and subways of Vienna, Austria. During a recent reorganization of their public transit system, city planners discovered that it was designed around the needs of men commuting to work.[19] The typical woman had more diverse transit needs that included shopping, taking children to school and doctor appointments, and getting to work and back again at more irregular times. To make the transit system friendlier to the typical woman, the city instituted zoning rules to minimize distances among housing, stores, and medical clinics, and scheduled more trains and busses during the day.

Changes like these reduce the isolation and stress of mothers, but also address the needs of "atypical" men: single, stay-at-home, or primary-caretaker dads, or men who are retired, disabled, or unemployed. They help men because systems are rarely organized around men to begin with; they're organized around the *stereotype* of a man. In fact, decisions made to help women often also make life a little easier for all people who don't meet hegemonic expectations.

THEORIZING GENDER EQUALITY Even gender-aware policymaking, though, doesn't necessarily help us know what to do. Feminists themselves disagree as to what exactly a feminist utopia might look like. There are roughly three approaches that correspond to the three types of inequality: sexism, androcentrism, and subordination. Most countries incorporate at least some policies that reflect each.

The United States is a good example of a society that emphasizes **equal access**, an approach to ending sexism focused on dismantling legal barriers and reducing sex discrimination. Examples of this include laws that make it illegal to discriminate in the workplace, guarantee equal access to education, and allow women to enlist in the military.

Such policies significantly reduce sexism but can exist quite comfortably alongside androcentrism and subordination. They don't do anything to encourage people to value femininity, nor do they ensure that women will be able, in practice, to enter the masculine arenas to which these policies promise access. Equal access works well, then, for women who aim to be in the same places that men already are, whether in a coal mine or a boardroom, but it doesn't do anything to widen men's opportunities and may not appeal to women who prefer the feminized spheres of life.

An **equal value** model is designed to tackle the problem of androcentrism by raising the value of the feminine to match the value of the masculine. This strategy is compatible with gendered divisions of labor but resists the idea that different is unequal. A society characterized by equal value, for example, would reward reproductive labor (pregnancy, breastfeeding, and childcare responsibilities) so that this didn't result in economic insecurity for women, as many states in Figure 13.1 do.

For women and men who embrace femininity, equal value is a more promising model than equal access. It would destigmatize the feminine side of the binary, giving men the opportunity to balance femininity and masculinity, much as women already do. It would also raise the prestige and pay of both women and men who work in feminized jobs or specialize in the domestic sphere.

Some countries put more emphasis on equal value than equal access. Compared to the United States, for instance, Germany has weak gender discrimination laws but generous social services for parents. If a new mother takes all of her federally guaranteed maternity leave, she can stay home with her child for thirteen and a half months and be paid 73 percent of her salary.[20] As a result, German mothers often work quite a bit less than American mothers, but they enjoy greater emotional and financial well-being.[21] American women have more opportunities to compete in the workplace, but the state support available to them if they become mothers is relatively meager.

Some feminists are enthusiastic about the potential of the equal value model. In their view, gender difference is a significant source of pleasure, and could be even more so.[22] If gender was no longer a metaphor for power, men wouldn't feel the need to be masculine to feel powerful, and neither would women. New femininities and masculinities might emerge. Meanwhile, if the binary was no longer an ideological infrastructure for inequality, its importance might fade, making more room for people who don't identify as male or female.

Many feminists, however, are concerned that equal value strategies will lead to coercive enforcement of gendered roles. Both the Vatican and the Arab states of the Middle East use the idea of equal value to resist equal access. They believe that the gender binary is God-given and challenges by women, sexual minorities, trans, and nonbinary folks are inherently wrong. In this scenario, women and men would enjoy status contingent on their conformity to their expected social roles, and women's positions would remain subordinate to male authority. So challenging the devaluation of androcentrism without also tackling sexism and subordination is a risky strategy.

If equal access tackles sexism and equal value speaks to androcentrism, then the **equal sharing** approach targets subordination by attempting to ensure that men and women participate equally in positions conventionally understood as masculine and feminine. Unlike the equal access approach, this model presses for dramatic shifts in how men spend their time. It does so by providing incentives for men and women to take more proportionate responsibility for the less valued parts of life.[23] In Iceland, for instance, parents get nine months of paid leave but, for couples in other-sex marriages, three months of these can only be used by the father. If he doesn't take them, the family forfeits the paid time off.

The sharing approach appeals greatly to those who believe that we should be working to establish societies in which gender all but disappears as a meaningful category.[24] If everyone is doing the same work, it may no longer matter who is who at all. In this model, one's genitals would be about as significant as whether one is right- or left-handed, making the gender binary, heteronormativity, and the concept of a fixed sexual orientation a thing of the past.

Those of us who are strongly invested in our gender identities—including some trans men and women, many of whom have had to fight hard personal, interpersonal, and political battles for recognition—may not be pleased to see something important to them disappear. Others argue that the trans experience would be substantially less stressful in a society without a gender binary to begin with. Like so many of the issues feminists wrestle with, there is rarely an easy answer that satisfies everyone and has no undesirable consequences.

Even beyond the ideas of equal access, value, and sharing, there are different ways of thinking about what a feminist utopia looks like.[25] There are socialist feminists who worry most about the intersection of gender with class; libertarian and anarchist feminists who focus on freeing women and men from state control; ecofeminists who draw connections between men's treatment of women and their treatment of nature; postcolonial feminists who oppose the imposition of Western feminisms around the world; and black, Chicana, indigenous, Muslim feminisms, and more. There are feminists who think that women and men are essentially the same and ones who think we are inherently different. There are separatist feminists who want nothing to do with men, feminists who are men, and feminists who make understanding masculinity their primary concern. There are also feminist reformers who try to achieve incremental gains and radical feminists who specialize in asking societies for things that seem impossible.

As this list suggests, people who call themselves "feminist" often have very different ideas about how to solve the problem of gender inequality. This can cause disagreement, but it can also spark productive conversations about what feminist activism should look like. This is part of why it's helpful to think of feminism as a *conversation* instead of a set of *positions*.

This conversation, alongside the work of imagining and implementing policies that govern gender, is why early American women wanted the right to vote, and it continues to motivate people of all genders to get involved in politics.

The Gender of Governance

In modern history, it is overwhelmingly men who have been granted the power to govern nations: to theorize our political systems, write our national constitutions, develop and vote on our laws, guide our economies, and determine our foreign affairs. This was true in societies that operated as classic patriarchies, in which men were lawfully in charge, but it's also the case in the types of modified patriarchies we live in now. To give American women the right to vote and run for political office was to give women **standing** alongside men: the right to represent herself and others in decisions being made.

By changing who had standing in American politics, universal suffrage was a massively important step toward dismantling political systems that recognized some people as full citizens but not others. Though its effects were slow and cumulative, and have not been fully realized, giving women standing disrupted all three types of inequality: the classic patriarchal rule that women cannot hold power (sexism), the modified patriarchal belief that power is inherently masculine (androcentrism), and men's prerogative to make decisions on behalf of women (subordination).

GENDER IN THE LEGISLATURE Table 13.2 shows the global rise in the number of female politicians over time. Across the world, the percentage of women in **legislatures**—groups of individuals elected to represent their constituents in regulating the affairs of the country—ranges from 0 to 56 percent. The countries most inclusive of women are those with highly egalitarian approaches to gender (such as in Scandinavia) and states where wars have discredited men's leadership while giving women peace activists special standing (as in Rwanda and Sierra Leone). In these types of countries, women represent 40 percent or more of members of legislatures.[26]

The United States has not been a leader in this regard.[27] As of 2018, U.S. women hold 22 percent of states' elective executive offices, 25 percent of seats in state legislatures, and 20 percent of seats in Congress.[28] Internationally, this level of representation is the middle of the pack.[29] Still, the rapid rise of women in American politics is remarkable; of all the women who have *ever* been elected to Congress in its more than 225-year history, about a third (107 of 322) are holding seats at

TABLE 13.2 | HISTORICAL COMPARISON OF THE PERCENTAGE OF WOMEN IN POLITICS ACROSS REGIONS

Region	Percent of Women in Legislatures						
	1955	1965	1975	1985	1995	2005	2018
United States	3%	2%	4%	5%	11%	15%	20%
Scandinavia	10%	9%	16%	28%	34%	38%	41%
Western Industrial*	4%	4%	6%	9%	13%	23%	29%
Latin America	3%	3%	5%	8%	10%	17%	26%
Africa	1%	3%	5%	8%	10%	16%	22%
Eastern Europe	17%	18%	25%	27%	8%	16%	22%
Asia	5%	5%	3%	6%	9%	15%	17%
Middle East	1%	1%	3%	4%	4%	8%	15%

*Includes the United States.

Source: Table adapted from Pamela Paxton, Sheri Kunovich, and Melanie M. Hughes, "Gender in Politics," *Annual Review of Sociology* 33 (2007): 263–284. Additional calculations by the authors with data from the Inter-Parliamentary Union, "Women in National Parliaments," May 1, 2018, Retrieved from http://archive.ipu.org/wmn-e/classif.htm.

the time we are writing this book.[30] Thirty-eight of these, or 7 percent of all seats in Congress, are held by women of color.

Feminists might support shared governance in principle, but does it matter in practice? Does **symbolic representation**—women's presence in government—translate into **substantive representation**—policies important and helpful to women? Yes and no.

On many issues—such as the economy, religion, and the highly partisan issue of abortion—gender has made little difference.[31] Male and female politicians in the same party tend to vote largely similarly. Meanwhile, diversity among women means that any individual woman may have something in common with other women, but other, sometimes more important things, in common with their fellow male legislators. So, women don't often vote as a bloc.

On other issues, though, such as support for peace and environmental causes, women's opinions have long differed on average from men's.[32] Women legislators in the United States are more supportive of measures to reduce climate change, for example, even after controlling for partisanship.[33] In countries with more elected women making decisions, levels of greenhouse gases are lower.[34] Female politicians also tend to vote differently than men on issues that obviously affect female constituents.[35] They show strong support for social welfare, women's health, and family-friendly workplaces, and for reducing inequality of all kinds.[36] Some of this difference has to do with shifts in what male politicians support, not long-standing differences between men and women. Health, welfare, and environmental issues used to have widespread bipartisan support from both sexes, but male politicians have shifted away from supporting these issues, especially since the 1990s.[37]

Female politicians are also more likely than male ones to introduce bills that address women's needs.[38] So, the presence of female politicians changes what legislators of both sexes are voting *on*. Many male politicians support these initiatives, reminding us that it's not just that women vote "like men." Men also vote "like women" when they have the opportunity to do so.

There may be something to the principle of it, too. Getting women elected is one step toward ensuring that politicians remember that women are part of the population they are governing. When they are there, it's harder for the men who've historically had power to ignore issues that impact women's lives. In other words, just having women in office may make policymakers more gender-aware, and having more kinds of women in office can make them even more so.

This is why what Tammy Duckworth did in 2018 was so remarkable. Injured while serving in the Army, in 2017 she became the first disabled woman elected to Congress. She is also the first member of Congress born in Thailand. And, in 2018, she became the first sitting senator to give birth. Ten days later, Duckworth rolled into the Senate chamber to take a vote with her baby in her lap.

There had been weeks of debate in Congress.[39] Senator Orrin Hatch worried about inviting a baby boom: "But what if there are ten babies on the floor of the Senate?" Eventually the senators voted unanimously to allow Duckworth to bring the baby, though some were reluctant. Responding to their concerns, she promised no diaper changes or breastfeeding. And they made exceptions to the dress code. "The baby will not be required to wear pants or a skirt or a tie," reported one of the senators. The baby was also not required to abide by the rules for hat wearing and proper footwear. It could even go barefoot. Would the baby be required to wear the Senate pin? No.

Of course, Duckworth isn't the first parent of an infant to serve in the Senate. She is just the first *woman* to do so. The fact that no baby had ever before been brought to the Senate floor reveals that both parenting and working remain strongly gendered. So, when she came to work that day with baby in tow, she served as a real reminder not just that women exist, but that mothers exist—*working* mothers even—and that makes the struggles faced by working parents of all genders just a little harder for all those men to ignore.

Senator Tammy Duckworth beams as she arrives at the U.S. Capitol Building with her ten-day-old child. "It feels great," she told reporters. "It is about time, huh?"

In the aftermath of the Trump election, Emily's List, an organization aimed at supporting Democratic women's aspirations for political office, saw a tremendous twelve-fold increase in potential candidates.[40] Record numbers of women have filed as candidates for the House of Representatives, the Senate, and governor's races.[41] This group is also more diverse than any previous group of aspiring female politicians: there are more women of color and immigrants, many are young and single, and two candidates have run campaign ads in which they discuss their political positions while breastfeeding their babies.

This is significant because when women run for political office, they raise just as much money as men, get as many votes, and are equally likely to win.[42] The average man in the United States seems rather indifferent toward a candidate's sex, whereas the average woman tends to prefer female candidates.[43] Things can change, radically, and fast.

But as the Trump election demonstrated to all, the "highest hardest glass ceiling" in the United States remains intact. What did we learn about gender and the American presidency in 2016?

GENDER AND THE AMERICAN PRESIDENCY The United States still has yet to elect a woman president. Many other countries have. In 1960, Sirimavo Bandaranaike of Sri Lanka became the first women elected to lead a modern country. Since then, more than fifty women have served as head of state. Female leaders have been found disproportionately in Europe, but every region on earth has seen at least one.

Who has the standing to lead the United States? If our nation is "the homeland," and our internal politics are "domestic," then the president is the metaphorical "head of the household": a leader taking care of a national family, setting the house rules, disciplining the disobedient and, above all, protecting its members from the outside world.[44] Family is the dominant metaphor for the state, and it's a gendered one. As presidential historian Forrest McDonald put it: "Whether as a warrior-leader, father of his people, or protector, the president is during his tenure the living embodiment of the nation."[45]

Scholars argue, in fact, that the U.S. presidency is possibly the most masculine job in the nation.[46] This has long made candidates' masculinity a central feature of political campaigns. Throughout the twentieth century, manliness explicitly came into political debates about wars (from the Spanish-American to Iraq), and many presidential candidates tried to show they had masculine hobbies (like brush-clearing, ranching, or football), used masculinized talk (seeming brash, risk-embracing, and adventurous), and discussed policy in terms of power (by being "tough on crime" and "strong on national security").

In this way, the battle for the Republican presidential nomination in 2016 was relatively routine: It was a battle among men over manliness. Rick Perry challenged Donald Trump to a pull-up contest. Trump and Ted Cruz competed over the attractiveness of their respective wives. The Cruz campaign made fun of Marco Rubio's fashionable boots, calling them "high-heeled booties." Trump attempted to emasculate his rivals, calling Ben Carson "super low energy," Jeb Bush "really weak," and Rubio a "frightened little puppy." Rubio responded by suggesting that Trump had a small penis. Trump retorted: "I guarantee you there is no problem."

Trump in particular performed an "unapologetic masculinity," one that, at its core, was about dominating others: "winning" in business, with women, in politics, and over other men.[47] He had a signature violent handshake, promised to "bomb the shit" out of enemies, claimed immigrants were rapists, and boasted of kissing and grabbing women without their permission. When these revelations threatened his campaign, he invoked exculpatory chauvinism—that idea that men are naturally "bad boys" and that being bad is part of what makes them great—calling it "locker room talk." *I'm a bad boy*, Trump seemed to say unapologetically, *but a bad boy is exactly what America needs right now.* All of this, including the dozen alleged sexual assaults, likely both helped and hurt his election chances.

After the primaries, during the face-off between Donald Trump and Hillary Clinton, both used coded language invoking masculinity.[48] Trump repeatedly questioned Clinton's strength, stating at one rally: "Hillary's not strong. Hillary's weak, frankly. She's got no stamina." In a campaign ad for Trump, the voiceover said: "Hillary Clinton doesn't have the fortitude, strength, or stamina to lead in our world." He also claimed that Clinton didn't have a "presidential look" and suggested that she was unattractive.

In response, Clinton questioned what *kind* of man Trump was. "A man you can bait with a tweet," she warned, "is not a man we can trust with nuclear weapons." In her convention speech, she followed that statement by quoting former First Lady Jackie Kennedy, who once said that wars were started not by "big men with self-control and restraint, but by little men—the ones moved by fear and pride." In her own way, Clinton was asserting that Trump was not man enough to be president. Whether the candidate was male or female, Republican or Democrat, then, the masculinity of all these presidential candidates was on trial.

Ultimately, Trump did become president. We know that gender was a part of the campaign rhetoric, but did it also factor into the decisions of voters? And did it change how men and women orient themselves toward politics? We know a few things already.

First, while Americans have become increasingly approving of female politicians, there are some holdouts and some exceptions, increasingly structured on partisan lines.[49] While most report that they would be "comfortable" with a female president, only 28 percent of Americans are enthusiastic about one, and 26 percent of American voters are hostile to the idea.[50] Half of Americans say women's family responsibilities don't leave them enough time for politics and a quarter believe they aren't "tough enough."[51] Two studies have found that Americans are more comfortable with women in lower-level political offices than in higher-level ones.[52]

In practice, the average American also appears to be more comfortable with women *in* office than with women *running for* office. For decades, Clinton's popularity among Americans was tied to whether she was in office (during which time between 20 and 40 percent saw her unfavorably) or running for office (during which her unfavorability scores would rise to 45 to 55 percent).[53] In her final week as secretary of state in 2013, for instance, her favorability rating was at an all-time high of 67 percent, but during her runs for Senate and the 2008 and 2016 presidential nomination, that number was below 50.

It's Crunch Time, America!

No more nuts in the White House

2016 OR BUST!

HILLARY NUTCRACKER

Gendered messaging was pervasive during the 2016 presidential campaign.

Second, sexism, hostile sexism, and precarious masculinity were all at work in the 2016 presidential election. Compared to people who didn't vote for Trump, Trump voters scored higher on measures of hostile sexism and were more likely to report dislike and distrust of working women.[54] Stoking anger—something Trump did expertly on the campaign trail—intersected with sexism among men, increasing support for the Republican candidate.[55] In one study, men who were exposed to a threat to their masculinity changed their voting preferences; like the men who chose boxing over a puzzle after being asked to braid hair, men who were primed to think about how women now outearn their husbands in a growing number of households were less likely to support Clinton over Trump.[56]

Among women, internalized sexism predicted support for Trump, too.[57] Some are attracted to a breadwinner/homemaker model and are eager to see men's economic strength enhanced, even relative to women's.[58] For women whose own economic options are quite limited, a patriarchal bargain that gives men more ability to support them makes good sense; meanwhile, they don't see the more feminist-inclined Democratic Party as doing much for women like them, and they may not be wrong. Other women may be pro-life or anti-"big" government and put those concerns before any they had about Trump. And, of course, some women, like some men, were motivated by racist, anti-immigrant, or Islamophobic sentiment. Sexism was predictive of voting decisions in 2016, but racism was even more so.[59]

Third, this election was striking in how starkly it separated the sexes. Women voted for Clinton over Trump by about 12 percentage points, and men voted for Trump over Clinton by about the same margin. This in itself is not surprising—as gendered issues like climate change and concern about inequality have become more partisan, women have leaned Democratic and men more Republican (Figure 13.2)—but the gender difference in the 2016 election was bigger than any seen in the last twelve presidential elections.[60]

The numbers are even more striking when we consider them intersectionally.[61] Young voters—ages eighteen to twenty-nine—were least likely to vote for Trump, but gender still mattered: Sixty-three percent of young women voted for Clinton compared to 47 percent of men. Seventy percent of young Latinas and 64 percent of Latinos voted for Clinton, alongside a whopping 94 percent of black women and 75 percent of black men, compared to 50 percent of white women and 35 percent of white men. All told, no demographic intersection under thirty voted for Trump in the majority except white men (at 52 percent). This group, further, was especially motivated to get out and vote: about a million more young white men came out to vote in 2016 than is typical.[62]

Finally, Hillary Clinton wasn't just *any* woman; she had endured sexist portrayals in the media for decades. In 1978, when her husband was first elected governor of Arkansas, the *New York Times* referred to her as an "ardent feminist"

FIGURE 13.2 | GENDER GAP IN PRESIDENTIAL VOTING

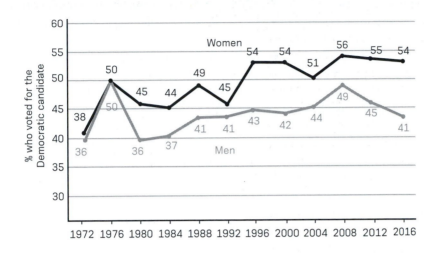

Source: Richa Chaturvedi, "A closer look at the gender gap in presidential voting," *Pew Research Center*, July 28, 2016, Retrieved from http://www.pewresearch.org/fact-tank/2016/07/28/a-closer-look-at-the-gender-gap-in-presidential -voting/; Alec Tyson and Shiva Maniam, "Behind Trump's victory: Divisions by race, gender, education," *Pew Research Center*, Nov. 9, 2016, Retrieved from http://www.pewresearch.org/fact-tank/2016/11/09/behind-trumps-victory-divisions -by-race-gender-education/.

because she had chosen to keep her own last name: Rodham. This launched four decades of jokes about her being a dumb blonde, a bitch, and a witch.[63] In 1992, when her husband was running for president, twelve years after she'd caved and changed her name to his, she finally replied to relentless questions from the media about whether she would quit her job: "I suppose I could have stayed home and baked cookies and had teas, but what I decided to do was to fulfill my profession." That year she got more attention than Madonna.[64] By 2016, when she ran against Trump, it was easy to cast her as a pariah.

There is no doubt that 2016 was a gendered election. A man and a woman faced off for the presidency for the first time in American history, gendered messaging was pervasive, and men and women voted differently, even more differently than in previous elections. Men and women also responded differently to Trump's victory. After the election, women's confidence in the future of the United States dropped: 43 percent of women said they had "quite a lot" of confidence in the future of the country before the election, compared to 29 percent after.[65] In contrast, men's confidence rose, from 47 percent to 53 percent. Among people born in the 1980s and after, 44 percent of men, but only 32 percent of women, agreed with the statement "Trump is my president."[66] Nine months into Trump's term, men were substantially more likely to approve of his job as president (44 percent of men compared to 31 percent of women).[67] Gender differences are not new to American politics, but the Trump-Clinton race, the Trump victory, and the ensuing Trump presidency have exacerbated gender difference, pushing men and women further apart politically.

Hillary Clinton did not become the first female president in 2016, and her loss was a window into the persistence of sexism in America, but there are silver linings. She was the first woman in this country's 239-year history to be nominated for president by one of its two major parties, and she won the popular vote (48 percent of voters cast their ballot for Clinton, compared to 46 percent for Trump). These are meaningful "firsts" that reflect a hundred years of increasing female representation in our legislatures. Women have fought to be recognized and most men have changed how they think about women.[68] Undoubtedly, women will keep fighting and the face of politics will continue to change. In the meantime, many of those battles—just like ones first fought by suffragists— won't happen on the inside of politics; they'll happen on the outside.

SOCIAL MOVEMENTS

The suffragist Elizabeth Cady Stanton understood that the vote was the first step toward women's full emancipation. "The grant of this right," she declared, "will secure all the others." In fact, founding documents of many countries around the world were amended in the latter half of the 1900s to grant equal political rights to women, but the U.S. Constitution was not one of them. Instead, the Supreme Court first held that women were a "new class of citizens" who could vote but did not automatically have other rights.

To change the U.S. Constitution to ensure women's rights, American feminists have introduced an Equal Rights Amendment every year since 1923. If adopted, the Constitution would include the statement, "Equality of rights under the law shall not be denied or abridged by the United States or by any state on account of sex." Feminists are still waiting to see it passed and ratified.

Congress *can* pass gender-equality laws, then, but it doesn't have to, nor does it have to renew the ones now on the books. Women's right to credit cards, jury duty, and equal education—*all* women's rights—are contingent on the whims of legislators and the will of their constituents. It might sound impossible that such rights could disappear, but there's no rule that radical changes can't involve a return to somewhere we've already been, or a place we think is even worse.

In the meantime, feminists have had to fight for each right individually. They have done this like through "regular" politics like voting, supporting legislation, and lobbying, and also "irregular" politics like protest campaigns, public marches, and demonstrations. This latter type of politics is part of what we call **social movements**: collective, nongovernmental efforts to change societies. The remainder of this chapter is about how women and their allies have used social movement tactics to secure rights for women, and continue to do so.

Feminist Politics across the Generations

The visibility and viability of feminist politics have waxed and waned over the decades, leading observers to make references to feminist "waves." The metaphor is a little too neat: It suggests clear beginnings and ends and oversimplifies what feminists wanted at any given time.[69] But it does capture the ebb and flow of feminist politics in American history.

As we noted earlier, the first feminist campaigns began in the mid-1800s. This first wave won many women suffrage, family rights, and the right to higher education. First wave feminists also campaigned against drunkenness (which often led to domestic violence and poverty for women) and for maternal and child welfare, public education, and world peace. They also drafted the Equal Rights Amendment and began to challenge Congress to pass it.

Many women-led organizations were born in this first wave, including parent-teacher organizations, the League of Women Voters, the National Association of Colored Women, and Women's International League for Peace and Freedom.[70] Because they did not have the vote in most states until the 1920s, these women also organized to pressure male legislators, arguably becoming the first political lobbyists in the United States.[71] They campaigned on many political issues in which they believed women had special interests but followed a policy of being absolutely nonpartisan.

In the 1960s and 1970s, the second wave of feminism aimed to end gender segregation in higher education, challenge job and wage discrimination, make marriage and family law gender neutral, and give women control over their own bodies in sex and reproduction (by organizing around sexual assault and harassment, access to contraception, coerced sterilization, and abortion). The first national women's advocacy organization, the National Organization for Women, was founded in 1966.[72] Second wave feminists echoed the first wave in building **women's movements**, social movements organized by women for women. By definition, women's movements are **autonomous** in that they can function independently of men's participation and approval.[73]

Feminists in the second wave shared the first wave's global perspective and willingness to challenge political bodies in which they had no standing, like the United Nations. The United Nations responded by initiating conferences organized around an International Women's Year in 1975, described as "the world's largest consciousness-raising session."[74] In 1977, when the United States had its own International Women's Year Conference in Houston, it became the first battleground for struggles between feminists and anti-feminists, those who saw themselves as "defending the family" from single mothers, homosexuality, easy divorce, and career women. This resonated with media portrayals of second wave feminists as humorless, hostile to sexual pleasure, and anti-man. This was exactly the environment that Hillary Clinton stepped into when she entered public life and, decades later, a surprising number of people still believe that feminists are ugly, uptight, angry, aggressive, dogmatic, and demanding.[75]

The backlash stalled the process of state ratification of the Equal Rights Amendment, which had sailed through Congress in 1972 after forty-nine years of feminist organizing. And when the United Nations released a statement in support of gender equality in 1979, the Convention on the Elimination of All Forms of Discrimination Against Women, the United States did not sign on. Sixteen years later, the United States did join 182 other countries in agreeing to a global "Platform for Action" driven by the belief that "women's rights are human rights."[76] These statements have helped to legitimize an international norm of gender equality, but the United States has only ambivalently committed itself to it.

Many of the changes in patriarchal relations we have traced in this book are thanks to the mobilization of the second wave, not only in new women's rights lobbying organizations, but also in a proliferation of new knowledge about women, initially in women's bookstores and now institutionalized in higher education as women's, gender, and sexuality studies programs. Gender awareness took the form of consciousness-raising for women, rediscovery of lesbian and gay history, and challenges to sexual objectification.[77] Increasingly, their feminism focused on intersectional issues like racial justice, labor rights, queer politics, and human rights.

The backlash also drew partisan lines, pushing feminists into one political camp and anti-feminists into the other. Men and women began to vote more differently than before, with women, including non-activists, increasingly likely to identify as Democrats. Ironically, this undid an earlier association between feminism and the Republican Party, which supported the Equal Rights Amendment and abortion rights until 1980.

The third wave started in the mid-1990s, after an African American law professor's testimony splashed across the screens of televisions across the country. Anita Hill had been called before the Senate Judiciary Committee to testify that Clarence Thomas, a nominee for the Supreme Court, had sexually harassed her. This was a scandalous accusation, then even more than now. Transfixed, the public watched as an all-white, all-male panel of fourteen senators delivered an "aggressive, gloves-off" attack on Hill's character.[78] Many women saw this as a sign that men did not understand women's experiences and they brought their frustration to the ballot box.[79] In the next election, twenty-four women were elected to the House, the largest single group of women ever. And the number of women in the Senate tripled, from two to six.

In 1991 Anita Hill testified before an all-white, all-male panel of senators that Supreme Court nominee Clarence Thomas sexually harassed her.

The third wave took an even broader view of what was needed to end patriarchy: attacking gendered norms, including the gender binary and heteronormativity, and reaffirming its concern with peace, environmental protection, child health, and public education.[80] Responding to the stereotypes applied to second wavers, third wavers also embraced femininity and sex positivity. By this time, most feminist activists also saw their issues as aligned with the Democratic Party.

Third wavers addressed some of the earlier problems with transnational feminist activism. Western feminists had sometimes exhibited a troublesome tendency to think they were more *advanced* than women in other countries, leading them to try to export their own version of women's liberation around the globe. Third wave feminists got better at understanding that there are feminisms, not a feminism, and began working with women and their allies in other countries more collaboratively.

Likewise, they continued efforts by earlier feminists to build a more inclusive feminism, advocating for an **intersectional feminist activism**, one that attends to the lived experiences of different kinds of women and men.[81] Today the phrase "it's not feminism if it's not intersectional" has become a common rallying cry. Young feminists of color are among the leading innovators of "hashtag movements" that are decentralized, less hierarchical, and more intersectionally inclusive, including #BlackLivesMatter and #SayHerName, against

This cartoon by Malcolm Evans draws attention to the fact that definitions of women's oppression and liberation can vary tremendously.

police violence suffered by African Americans, and #NeverAgain, the gun control movement started by the victims of the mass shooting at Marjory Stoneman Douglas High.

These hashtags bring us into the present, and some argue that the third wave has evolved into a fourth wave that is happening right now.

Feminist Politics Today

A substantial majority of people today believe men and women are inherently equal and should be treated as such.[82] Americans coming of age in the 2000s and later show the strongest support for gender equality.[83] Today's young feminists are also more diverse than those in previous generations: they are more likely to identify as queer, nonwhite, or multiracial, and are more politicized around disability, immigration, and more. Thanks to the work of previous generations, these feminists are well poised to take advantage of the international norms of gender equality, prebuilt feminist movement organizations, and some hard work toward making feminism more inclusive.[84] Truly, it's an exciting time to be a feminist.

So, what's up for the fourth wave? In some ways, today's feminists are up against the same old forces that American feminists have fought for nearly two hundred years: anti-feminists, stubborn government bureaucracy, ugly stereotypes, negative press, lack of inclusivity and equality in feminist circles, and the sheer effort of organizing over decades, even lifetimes. But in other ways they're facing new forces, both helpful and troubling.[85] The remainder of this chapter discusses some of the novel context for contemporary feminist organizing.

NEW COMMUNICATION TECHNOLOGIES Before the mid-1990s, media gatekeepers tightly controlled what could be mass produced and disseminated through print, radio, and television. Today, the Internet gives a much wider proportion of the population the ability to produce media content. These technologies are also less costly, more efficient, and wider reaching than the mimeographs and newsprint used by women's groups of the 1970s.[86] This has particularly helped members of groups who've historically been excluded from and misrepresented by the mass media. Especially since the mid-2000s, anyone with access to the Internet can contribute to the international conversation, making an amazing array of feminists just a search away.

Regardless of whether this vast global network brings activists into the streets, it supports a sense of community built around norms of gender equality. The hashtag #metoo is a powerful example. Coined in 2006 by African American activist Tarana Burke, it catapulted into awareness after movie producer Harvey Weinstein's decades of abuse of women became public. When actress Alyssa Milano invited people on Twitter to say #metoo, half a million people responded within twenty-four hours.[87] In that same time period on Facebook, twelve million posts and comments were uploaded.[88] A millennial version of the second wave slogan "the personal is political," #metoo was a new way to "come out" and make what feels personal a very public and political issue.

The hashtag was more than just an easy click on a computer; it drew attention to the pervasiveness of the problem of sexual harassment and assault. Soon it became a chorus of #allwomen, including those in middle- and low-status and pay occupations.[89] It was used by sexual minorities, trans women, and cisgender men to draw attention to their abuse, too.[90] Both domestically and internationally, #metoo resonated with already-organized feminist efforts, spurring mobilization around gendered violence globally.[91]

Online organizing, around hashtags and otherwise, has been an incredible tool in the new millennium.[92] But anti-feminists have taken advantage of this as well.[93] Sometimes misleadingly called "men's rights advocates," anti-feminists have used the Internet to nurture and strategize around their anger at women, make life uncomfortable for women's advocates online, and potentially radicalize violent misogynists. In online spaces, aggrieved men define themselves as incels (involuntary celibates), MGTOWs (male separatists), and Red Pillers (who share tips for how to dominate women), and sometimes applaud mass murderers.[94]

Even as a daily experience, online harassment makes for a hostile environment. Women are twice as likely as men to report being sexually harassed online and are more likely than men to state that harassment online is a "major problem" (70 and 54 percent, respectively).[95] Men are more invested than women in defining it as free speech (56 and 36 percent, respectively), with 64 percent of men saying that online harassment is "taken too seriously." As law professor Mary Anne Franks argues, it is exactly because it is seen as so normal—described, often, as *merely* trolling—that makes it "both so effective and so harmful, especially as a form of discrimination."[96]

Governments and corporations have been caught unawares by these developments and both have been slow to take them seriously.[97] In addition to creating opportunities, then, the Internet has created new problems and threats for feminists, as well as new areas of law and practice that feminists need to press companies and governments to address meaningfully.

There are other things to watch out for in this brave new world.

INDIVIDUALISM AND "YOU GO GIRL" CAPITALISM Ever since men were encouraged to be competitive in the workforce and women were encouraged to practice selflessness in the home, putting oneself first has been considered masculine. As women have been offered increasing opportunities to enter masculine spheres of work and play, they've become increasingly like men in this regard. Accordingly, we've seen a rise in **individualism** in the United States, a focus on the individual over the group, and a decline in **civic awareness**, a focus on the well-being of groups and societies as wholes.[98]

Individualism can lead people to assume that gender inequality is an individual problem that requires only individual solutions. A recent study on the gender politics of young adults found that almost all believe that people have the right to live their lives however they like, gender notwithstanding, but had a difficult time thinking of what they might do to change the world, over and above designing innovative lifestyles.[99] This is partly because capitalist forces encourage us to think about ourselves in individual terms and use consumption as a way to express our identities. In a **corporate co-optation of feminism**, companies today often encourage this, using feminist-sounding language and imagery for marketing purposes.[100] Both the makeup company CoverGirl (#GirlsCan) and the feminine hygiene product brand Always (#LikeaGirl) have recently taken this approach.

Most of this marketing reduces feminism to individual empowerment and ties that empowerment to a product the company has for sale. Dove, for example, launched a highly successful viral ad campaign titled Real Beauty Sketches.[101] In the ad, a sketch artist draws women both as they describe themselves and as another describes them, then reveals both sketches to the participants. The women inevitably look more beautiful in the second sketch than the first, sending the message that others see their beauty more clearly than they do. One participant responded: "I should be more grateful of my natural beauty. It impacts the choices and friends we make, the jobs we apply for, how we treat our children. It impacts everything. It couldn't be more critical to our happiness." In other words, it's empowering just to *feel* more beautiful.

Fair enough. At best, though, the message is that each individual woman can choose to feel better about how she looks. Dove's #realbeauty and #redefiningbeauty campaigns never suggest looks are irrelevant to a woman's value. The company doesn't go that far, because challenging the social power of appearance norms in actual interactions would disrupt their profits: women would spend a lot less money on fashion and beauty products if they were less worried about being judged on their looks.

Marketing with feminist content is, first and foremost, intended to entice people to buy things, which makes some people wealthy at the expense of others. Meanwhile, the same companies also often exploit female workers. The developer and distributor of Ivanka Trump's clothing and accessories line, for instance, is aimed specifically at working mothers and branded with the hashtag #womenwhowork.[102] Ironically, at a factory in Indonesia where her clothes are manufactured, the employees—three-quarters of whom are women—receive only the government-mandated parental leave, are paid no more than the mandated minimum wage, and are allegedly forced to work overtime for no pay. Many are so poor that they can't afford basic necessities like baby formula or school books.[103]

Elsewhere, in Sri Lanka, girls as young as ten years old work sixty hours a week in uncomfortable "sweatshop"-like conditions.[104] It would take them a month to earn enough money to buy a single pair of leggings from the clothing line they work for: Beyoncé's Ivy Park. About the brand, Beyoncé says: "I know that when I feel physically strong, I am mentally strong, and I wanted to create a brand that made other women feel the same way."[105] Feminist advertising, no matter how "woke," doesn't usually translate into feminist practices.

The frequency with which pseudo-feminist themes appear in advertising has made "girl power" a cliché and the preponderance of such rhetoric makes it conceptually difficult to distinguish between feminism and individualism. Often, it's simply self-promotional egotism, telling girls and women they're awesome just by virtue of being female and so they deserve to be and have anything they want. But having a diva complex doesn't make a person a feminist. Likewise, advertising that tells girls and women they should be self-centered does not empower women to work for gender justice for anyone but themselves.

NATIONALISM AND THE RISE OF AUTHORITARIANISM Before the 2016 U.S. presidential election, no one would have imagined that a candidate like Trump—one who'd insulted women's faces, bodies, and temperaments on record; who'd said "putting a wife to work is a very dangerous thing" and pregnancy is "an inconvenience for a business"; who advocated treating women "like shit" and called his own daughter "a piece of ass"; who'd bragged about grabbing women and had been accused of sexual assault—could *win*. Prior to Trump, neither Republican nor Democratic candidates spoke in this way. Even relatively minor gaffes, like Mitt Romney's clumsy comment that he had "binders full of women" to consider for jobs, were considered damaging to a campaign.[106] Trump's election revealed that Americans aren't as opposed to his version of masculinity as politicians thought. And the continued support of his presidency by voters and fellow politicians alike—even as he bears the brunt of new sex scandals and successfully enacts anti-feminist policies—shows that he is the representative of a set of values in American society, not just an unlikely presidential candidate.

Politics can change, radically, and not always in ways that feminists want. Here, Americans' rights to birth control and reproductive freedom are illustrative. Long before Trump chose as his vice president a politician strongly hostile to women's rights to abortion and contraceptive use, a movement had been growing to limit access to both. In the five years before Trump announced his candidacy, states adopted 288 new laws aimed at restricting women's access to abortion, including mandatory counseling and waiting periods, required parental consent or notification, and new regulations on abortion clinics, many of which were forced to close.[107] Today, 90 percent of counties in the United States do not have a single abortion provider.[108]

In 2014, the Obama administration granted religious nonprofit organizations—like schools and hospitals—an exemption to the law requiring businesses to provide contraceptive health care coverage to their employees. In 2017, the Trump administration extended this right to *any* employers who object to their employees using birth control. Bills have also been introduced into Congress to make some forms of birth control illegal and stop anyone on public health care programs (including the forty million women on Medicaid) from receiving birth control or prenatal care from Planned Parenthood.[109] The Trump administration also reinstated the Bush-era "global gag rule," forbidding all domestic and foreign health care providers who receive funding from the United States even to mention abortion. And Trump has pledged to nominate only pro-life judges to the Supreme Court in the hopes of overturning *Roe v. Wade*, which guarantees women a limited right to abortion.

Reproductive politics that override women's choices are often found in countries experiencing a rise in **nationalism**, a belief in the superiority of one's own country, its rightful dominance over others, and exclusionary policies that restrict citizenship by race, ethnicity, or religion. Nationalists see some kinds of people as the rightful residents of nations and use group membership as grounds for exclusion. Nationalists see women as responsible for reproducing the nation that nationalists want.[110] Nationalist thinking, then, justifies aiming pro-natal policies (like restrictions on abortion) at women seen as legitimate citizens and anti-natal policies (like forced sterilization) toward other women.

Nationalist sentiment offers men the opportunity to dominate other men and gain control of women, and it's on the rise today in the United States and elsewhere.[111] Across Europe, there is a turn toward harsh treatment of immigrants and ethnic minorities as well as restrictions of the rights of sexual minorities, limitations on women's reproductive decision making, and attacks on gender-aware politics. In the United States, President Trump has assembled the most male-dominated staff in decades, appointed known white nationalists to senior positions, and undermined freedoms and protections previously thought safe.

In fact, Trump's election is part of a global retreat from states transparently sharing governance with legislators and citizens.[112] Since 2006, *The Economist* has published a regular report on the state of democracies around the world. High scores reflect "full" democracies, measured by scores on sixty indicators, including strong voting rights, high inclusion and participation, a healthy political culture, and the protection of civil liberties.[113] Low scores indicate an authoritarian regime, one controlled by an authority with near total power and little accountability. Between 2016 and 2017, more than half of the 167 countries measured fell away from democracy and toward **authoritarianism**, a leadership style that celebrates patriarchal power and masculine aggression as national values. The United States' own score has been consistently falling since 2006 and we are now what *The Economist* calls a "flawed" democracy. We are nowhere near being labeled an authoritarian regime, but Trump's election suggests that there is plenty of support among Americans for authoritarian-style leadership.

The authoritarianism we observe is also closely tied to a global politics of masculinity. In India, some Hindus are celebrating the assassination of Gandhi as a defeat of pacifism, which they see as weak and feminine. In the Philippines, strongman Rodrigo Duarte ordered his soldiers to shoot female rebels "in the vagina." And Vladimir Putin, in Russia, uses his control over state media to release staged photographs of him lifting weights, riding horseback bare-chested, and hunting a Siberian tiger, while making it illegal to distribute any material related to rights for sexual minorities, in the name of "traditional values."

Today's feminists are up against a rising tide of nationalism and the anti-immigrant mobilization and repression of gender freedoms that come with it. A substantial proportion of the American public is attracted to authoritarian leadership and support rolling back many of the rights feminists and others have fought for in the century in which they've had the right to vote. If the nationalist and authoritarian turn has alarmed feminists, though, it has also mobilized them.

NEW POLITICAL OPPORTUNITIES In the aftermath of Trump's election, many Americans who'd believed that feminist progress was secure and inevitable suddenly realized that it was neither, while longtime feminists found themselves reinvigorated. The 2017 Women's March on Washington was one sign of this gain in momentum.

The Women's March was scheduled for January 21, the day after Trump's inauguration, as a protest against all his election suggested. First envisioned by a white woman and man, it was criticized in its early planning stages for centering the perspective of white women.[114] Responding to this criticism, the organizers diversified their team to include an organizing group of about twenty individuals with a wide array of backgrounds.[115] This made the march more inclusive and resulted in a platform that emphasized traditional feminist concerns like reproductive rights and violence against women, but also the problems of violence in policing; workers', disability, immigrant, and indigenous rights; equality for sexual and religious minorities; and civil rights and environmental justice for all.[116]

Even with such a broad platform, no one anticipated the incredible turnout. Crowd estimates ranged from three to five million across the United States, making it the largest protest in American history.[117] Marchers included men as well as women, nonbinary and trans individuals, the young and the old, and people of all colors and religions. A third of attendees reported that this was their very first protest; more than half said they hadn't been to a protest in the last five years.[118] Trump's election had newly politicized people, inspiring them to get out into the streets, be seen, and stand up.

Clever handmade protest signs revealed this new energy, engagement with electoral politics, and feminism's decades-long trend toward inclusiveness. "So outraged," said one sign, "I'm running for office."[119] "Gun violence is a woman's issue" and "Destroy the patriarchy, not the planet," said two more.[120] A white-haired woman held a sign declaring, "Ninety, nasty, and not giving up!"[121] And a young woman's sign pledged: "I have only begun to fight."[122]

The marchers' messages crystallized under the symbolism of the now famous "pussy hats": pink knitted caps, some with cat ears, worn to convey resistance to the way that Trump spoke about women. Many of the handmade signs also took up the theme of "pussy grabs back." Its resonance with the "catty suffragettes" who promised to "scratch and fight" until they won the vote is probably just coincidence, but it draws an evocative line, across 169 years, from the first wave of feminism to the fourth.

Protesters in pussy hats invoke the full weight of history during the 2017 Women's March on Washington.

Revisiting the Question

 How do we change societies?

We do it with passion, commitment, and cooperation. In every society there is tension between the gender order—its entrenched and often unquestioned ideas about gender, interactions that reproduce it, and gendered institutions— and the power of individuals to resist and transform it. Every individual has at least a little bit of power and, when individuals join together, that power accumulates. In other words, the system is bigger than any one of us, but *we're in it together*. If enough of us decide we want to change it, we can.

The best strategies are to get women and feminist-friendly politicians on the "inside" and an intersectional group of feminists and their allies on the "outside" building support for feminist policies through movement activism.[123] Using that strategy, feminists have changed states dramatically in the last hundred years. They have changed each other as well, adding texture and depth to feminist politics by widening the scope of their attention to many of the inequalities with which women live and setting up a new generation of activists to imagine an even more radical future.

Next . . .

A farewell and some advice!

FOR FURTHER READING

Crossley, Alison Dahl. *Finding Feminism: Millennial Activists and the Unfinished Gender Revolution*. New York: New York University Press, 2017.

Dahlerup, Drude. *Has Democracy Failed Women?* Malden, MA: Polity, 2018.

Goss, Kristen. *The Paradox of Gender Equality: How American Women's Groups Gained and Lost Their Public Voice*. Ann Arbor: University of Michigan Press, 2013.

Hogan, Kristen. *The Feminist Bookstore Movement: Lesbian Antiracism and Feminist Accountability*. Durham: Duke University Press, 2016.

Htun, Mala, and S. Laurel Weldon. *The Logics of Gender Justice: State Action on Women's Rights Around the World*. New York: Cambridge University Press, 2018.

Mohanty, Chandra. "Under Western Eyes: Feminist Scholarship and Colonial Discourses." *Feminist Review* no. 30 (1988): 65–88.

Olcutt, Jocelyn. *International Women's Year: The Greatest Consciousness-Raising Event in History*. New York: Oxford University Press, 2017.

Weiss, Penny A. (ed.), *Feminist Manifestos: A Global Documentary Reader*. New York: New York University Press, 2018.

IN MANY WAYS IT IS A TERRIBLE
LESSON; IN MANY WAYS A
MAGNIFICENT ONE.

—C. WRIGHT MILLS[1]

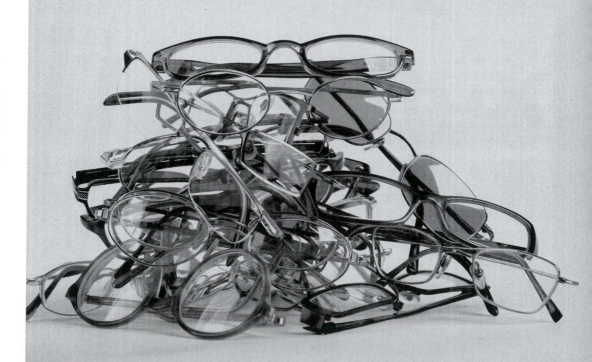

Conclusion

Gender is a powerful idea that shapes our experience of ourselves, each other, and the institutions with which we interact. It's pervasive and unavoidable. And while it's fun
sometimes—more for some of us than others—it's also unfair. Our
ideas about gender support a hierarchical system, one that intersects with other hierarchies in ways that ensure some men have more
power than other men, most women, and people who are neither.

Everyone pays a price.

We all contend with forces that narrow the options for the type of
person we're allowed to be. It may not feel like oppression—men are
told that masculinity is better than femininity and many have internalized an aversion to the feminine that has come to feel natural—
but masculinity, even for men who take to it easily, is not the same
thing as freedom. It's a set of rules that threatens to undermine
men's value in their own eyes and those of others. Still, many men
embrace the gender order because it offers a psychological wage:
the idea that they're superior to women and at least some other men.

Some women, in turn, might feel like gender isn't the oppressive force it used to be. Their daily lives may feel freer than those of
the men around them, and they may be right. But the cultural permission to perform masculinity isn't liberation; it's an "homage to

patriarchy."[2] It affirms the superiority of men and masculinity, just as men's avoidance of femininity is a sign that they think less of it. Women are allowed a taste of the privileges that come with being male (and if they are otherwise advantaged in society, they may enjoy other privileges as well), but ultimately the requirement to do femininity translates into a social system in which women as a group will be seen as less valuable than men and will do a disproportionate amount of the least rewarded work. If they do defy these expectations—if they demand or enact equality with men in sex, family life, at work, or in politics—they risk being a pariah.

For young people in college, this might sound absurd. The average woman outperforms her male peers throughout school: She gets better grades, runs the clubs, dominates student government, and outnumbers men in higher education. But that's exactly why what happens after college is unfair. Privilege is, by definition, unearned. So, men as a group will still be advantaged. This will become more acutely noticeable in heterosexual interaction (where women enjoy fewer orgasms and face greater danger) and more obvious in the workplace (where the average male college graduate earns more than his female counterpart from day one), in families (where the responsibility for unpaid housework and childcare falls disproportionately on women), and in the power centers of our societies (where men overwhelmingly are positioned to make the big decisions).

Those are the facts. The gender binary isn't real, it isn't fair, and we can't pretend it doesn't affect us. For 4,000 years, its purpose has been to differentiate us and place us in a hierarchy. And the good and bad things in life are still distributed along that hierarchy in unequal ways. That's the world we live in and there's no guarantee that it will be better, or even as good as it is now, in the future.

This is an unpleasant reality, which is why we began this chapter with C. Wright Mills's observation that the attainment of new knowledge can be, in many ways, terrible. Truly, this book has given you plenty of good reasons to be angry, sad, scared, or frustrated. But Mills also points out that knowledge, even of terrible things, can be *magnificent*. This is because understanding the system in which we live is the first step toward changing it. Knowledge helps us make more informed decisions for ourselves, treat others with more empathy, and get to work making a better world. So, before we end, here are some suggestions for how to put its lessons to work in your daily life.

Consider tossing your gender binary glasses

With your glasses off, you can now see the gender binary for what it really is—a social construction—but you'll still encounter the idea that men and women are "opposite" sexes every day. Try to be skeptical. Don't forget the basics: All differences are average differences with a great deal of overlap; men are not all alike and neither are all women; differences and similarities are caused by the intersection of nature and nurture, not one or the other; and science shows that we are more alike than different, and probably for good evolutionary reasons.

That the gender binary is a social construction applies to *you*, too, of course. If you're a person who sometimes worries about whether you fit into the binary, know that it's perfectly normal to wonder. The binary isn't real, so, to a greater or lesser degree, we're all square pegs being hammered into round holes. Don't blame yourself for how uncomfortable it is. And even if you personally feel quite comfortable, try to be understanding toward people who aren't and give them space for finding their own comfort zone.

Think about how you want to interact with others

You already break gender rules all the time, but now you probably do so more consciously. When you're policed, remember there are three options: obey and refrain from breaking the rule, break the rule but offer an account that affirms it, or renounce the rule as arbitrary and unnecessary. The last option has the most potential for destabilizing the rules and the gender binary they protect. Think about if and when you might want to do this. It would be exhausting to do it all the time and, in some cases, the price you could pay might be too high. Sometimes, though, the rewards outweigh the costs.

You can also choose to police the policers by pointing out other people's efforts to enforce gender rules. Challenging the entitlement of others to demand obedience to gender rules can provoke both mild and severe negative reactions: irritated parents, alienated friends, angry bosses, or retaliation from peers. Pay attention to when other people are likely to get your point and then balance the harm of their policing with the penalties you might face. Sometimes it will feel like the right thing to do.

Another possibility is to personally opt out of gender policing. This will take practice, since most of us police gender out of habit. Don't forget that policing people away from gender stereotypes (like pushing a little sister to be less concerned with her appearance) is not the *opposite* of policing; it's just enforcing a different set of gender rules. Opting out means not reacting to gender performances *at all*, refraining from making comments aimed at endorsing, questioning, or attacking someone's choices. This isn't the final answer to the problem—there will still be people who defend the gender binary, marketers with products to sell, and policy makers who pass gendered laws—but you will be making a real difference by quietly contributing to a freer and less judgmental space for your friends, family, and coworkers.

Reflect on your relationship with the institutions around you

Gendered institutions push us to make gendered decisions while also making these choices seem natural and inevitable. Now you can see these forces for what they are. Use this knowledge to wrest some autonomy from the institutions that bear down on you.

You may want to do this in order to satisfy your individual preferences; resisting institutional pressures can mean living a life more in tune with who you are. Or, you may choose to resist these pressures because of the way institutions place you into unequal relationships with others. Because institutions reflect not only gender inequality but all social inequities, our participation in them typically means being advantaged by virtue of someone else's disadvantage. We hope you keep sight of this fact and make it a practice to ask how institutions are tying you to both visible and invisible others in ways you may not like.

Some institutions are in real flux, making it easier to get around them. At this point in history, for example, the way we institutionalize family life is undergoing rapid and dramatic change. When so many people are making unconventional choices, it becomes easier for others to do so. Neither marriage, nor heterosexuality, nor parenthood is mandatory anymore. Consider all your options. And think about how your career choices might help or hurt your ability to live the life you want. You might have to make some hard sacrifices. They might just be worth it.

Do your best and be creative, but be flexible, too. One of the most striking findings in the study of gender, work, and marriage is that young people's plans for their future families have almost no relationship to their lives a decade or more later.[3] Our ideals have to compete with other realities, like unexpected fertility or infertility, whether we end up with a well-paying job that we enjoy, surprising reactions to the practice of parenting, and the unpredictable qualities of the person we fall in love with, as well as the not-unlikely possibility that we'll pass through our childbearing years without meeting someone at all. Happiness isn't about getting what we want; it's about finding a way to find joy in what we get.

While the institution of the family is in flux, other institutions are much more deeply entrenched. Even in these cases, though, there are some things we can do. The institutions that function to produce, transport, and sell the vast majority of goods and services we consume are incredibly hard to avoid, for instance, but there are some choices you can make. Buying clothes second hand is a way to avoid supporting a garment industry that exploits mostly female labor. Buying gender-neutral products over gendered ones—from deodorant, to exercise equipment, to cell phone covers—can discourage companies from exploiting gender stereotypes to get your money. Paying feminized labor a living wage can help, too, whether in the tips you leave for your waitress or the wages you pay to a housekeeper. Think about how you can opt out, even in small ways, of institutions you feel have harmful effects on people's lives.

Some of you may have more freedom than others to make choices that oppose institutionalized norms; it depends on your particular mix of advantages and disadvantages. If you *can* make counterinstitutional choices, and you choose to do so, know that you'll slowly be helping to dismantle ideologies and practices that others have less freedom to resist. You'll be using your privilege, in other words, to help others with less of it.

Remember that the mechanisms that produce inequality aren't simple

Compared to the average person, you have a much more sophisticated understanding of how gender inequality is maintained. Most people are familiar with the idea of sexism and object to the idea that one sex should receive preferential treatment, but androcentrism and subordination are less well understood and less obviously problematic. *You*, though, understand. You're tuned into the hierarchy of men and the way that gender inequality places men in competition for the rewards that accrue to masculinity; you are also aware that not all men benefit equally from gender inequality.

You see that intersectionality complicates the notion that anyone is subordinated or elevated by virtue of their sex alone. You're more likely to notice how women, too, enjoy certain privileges and enter into relationships of exploitation. You are aware of how much is going on when individual men or women make patriarchal bargains, and you can be both more critical of *and* sympathetic to these choices. Relatedly, you have a more nuanced sense of the attitude, behavior, and policy changes required to challenge gender inequality, as well as a healthy appreciation for just how intensely feminists debate their utopias.

Use this knowledge to resist the common misperceptions about feminist progress, like the idea that equality is simply a matter of ensuring equal access and that we can proclaim "mission accomplished" once we get a few privileged women into corner offices. Or the notion that men have nothing to gain from reducing gender inequality, as if they aren't in many ways constrained by the gender binary and its masculine hierarchy. Question the suggestion that feminists are driven by anger instead of empathy; feminists are in it not because they hate men, but because they care about both men and women and the struggles they face. Recognize, too, that because most feminists are concerned with racism, poverty, and other -isms and injustices, their goal is not to point fingers; since there is always some dimension on which any given person has some privilege, it would be self-destructive to think about activism as a matter of assigning guilt and claiming innocence. Finally, be suspicious of anyone who tells you liberation can be found in the right purchase, a good slogan, or sheer narcissism.

All this may leave you with more questions than answers, which is a really good place to be. Keep asking those questions, trying out answers, listening to others' perspectives, and forming your own theory of how the world works. No one has the last word on truth. So, continue to puzzle over the ideas shared here, add them to the bank of information you've learned from others, see if they explain your own experiences, and let your understanding of the world evolve.

Know that change is always possible

Sometimes problems seem overwhelmingly large and entrenched, but now you know that gender relations change, sometimes dramatically and surprisingly quickly, and in unpredictable ways. At the core of these changes are people. Social change is about power and everybody has some. Individuals work—alone or together—to imagine, enact, and share new ways of doing things.

Some of you may be passionate about reducing gender inequality and may decide to make activism a central part of your life. There are lots of ways to do this. You can write and speak about injustice, donate time or money to feminist organizations, or be an activist in your workplace, your church, or a political campaign. Others of you may not be interested in activism, but that doesn't mean your choices aren't political ones. We're all political whether we like it or not: We either accept the status quo or try to change things. Doing nothing *is* doing something. That's OK, but be aware that this is a political choice, too.

Even if you're not a passionate activist, there are probably *some* things you'd like to see change. Go ahead and pick a battle or two. That's how most of us do it.[4] Maybe you decide to be the person in your social circle who tries out a gender-neutral pronoun just to see what it's like; you might give relief to a nonbinary friend you didn't know you had. Or maybe you're a woman who decides to quit wearing makeup every day; suddenly you're an inspiration for a friend who isn't as brave or deeply motivated. Or maybe you're the man who commits to calling himself a feminist; now you're pushing back against the idea that feminism has nothing to offer men, as well as the idea that men don't care about women's rights.

If you're a student, you can question the gender order in your immediate environment. Maybe you'll be the one to start an organization on campus dedicated to exploring what it means to be a man, the one who ensures that the college provides unisex bathrooms for genderqueer and trans students, or the one who does the research to find out whether your school's sexual assault policy is in compliance with federal law.[5] It might be intimidating, and it's impossible to know if you'll succeed, but these are all things you could do *today*. Think about what inspires you.

Once you leave school, you'll have even more opportunities to remake the world. As a police officer, parent, teacher, or religious leader you will be a part of the institutions that maintain order, raise and educate young people, nurture spirituality, and promote social responsibility. You may be an employee of a corporation with a hand in making key decisions about how its goods are designed, produced, or marketed; its profits allocated; or its impact on the environment managed. You might see ways to improve these institutions from the inside or you might take your critique outside and try to press for change from there. Make like-minded friends and see what you can do. As the anthropologist Margaret Mead famously said: "Never doubt that a small group of thoughtful, committed citizens can change the world; indeed, it's the only thing that ever has."[6]

Ultimately, no matter how passionate you are, aim for balance. As legal scholar Joan Williams reminds us, "Equality is not everything, even for feminists themselves."[7] Maybe another political issue is more important to you: immigration reform, climate change, or the opioid epidemic. All these issues are important and, as you already likely suspect, gendered. It's also OK to want peace at the holiday dinner table, even if your grandfather still thinks it's strange that men today wear earrings and women get tattoos. It's OK to want to look beautiful in an evening gown or dashing in a tuxedo. That craft beer with the sexist ad campaign is *delicious*; we get it. Even the most dedicated feminists make trade-offs. They balance a desire for social justice with the need for happy, productive, meaningful lives. Feminist principles win out some times and not others. And that's life.

Enjoy the vertigo

For better or worse, the gender binary offers us a clear path; it helps us make decisions, from the minor to the momentous. Without gender to push some options off to the side and place others in front of us, we are left to make these decisions with fewer guidelines. This can be incredibly disorienting. The sociologist Barbara Risman calls it "vertigo," capturing how dizzying letting go of gendered logic can be.[8] Standing at a precipice, looking at a vast expanse of possibility, you are no longer protected by familiar boundaries. It's both exhilarating and frightening. Enjoy the magnificent lessons you've learned: the way that understanding how gender is a social construction makes life a little more fun, a little more interesting, and a little freer.

It's pretty great, actually.

But know, also, that the terrible part never fully goes away. At times it will be upsetting. Feel free to be annoyed and share your frustrations. This might make people a little annoyed with *you*, but there are worse things. Sometimes the terrible part will be deeply personal, as you struggle with your own challenges. Other times you will be angry with what you see around you and feel small and powerless to change things. We all do from time to time. And, of course, sometimes you can only laugh.

In the mix of frustration, disorientation, and hope, though, is the magic. It's what frees our minds and gives us the motivation to think up alternate realities. Remember that "radical" ideas are only ideas that haven't been accepted *yet*. So go ahead and imagine the unimaginable. The future is yet unwritten.

GLOSSARY

ableism individual and institutional bias against people with differently abled bodies

abolitionists activists in the fight against human slavery

account an explanation for why a person broke a gender rule that works to excuse his or her behavior

accountability an obligation to explain why we don't follow social rules that other people think we should know and obey

action effect within biological limits, our bodies react to use by developing the capacities we ask of them

ageism an institutionalized preference for the young and the cultural association of aging with decreased social value

aggrieved entitlement a kind of anger felt by some men based in the idea that something they rightfully own or deserve is being unjustly taken or withheld from them

agrarian a type of society in which the invention of agriculture—the cultivation of domesticated crops—allows groups to put down roots

androcentric pay scale a strong correlation between wages and the gender composition of a job

androcentrism the granting of higher status, respect, value, reward, and power to the masculine compared to the feminine

androgyny the blending of masculinity and femininity or absence of gender cues

anti-feminist politics activities of those committed to the value of gender difference and hierarchy and aiming to prevent feminist change

anti-natal policies those policies that discourage childbearing, whether intentionally or not

associative memory a phenomenon in which cells in our brains that process and transmit information make literal connections between concepts, such that some ideas are associated with other ideas

authoritarianism a leadership style that celebrates patriarchal power and masculine aggression as national values

autonomous functioning independently of men's participation and approval

benevolent sexism the attribution of positive traits to women that, nonetheless, justify women's subordination to men

binary a system with two and only two separate and distinct parts, like binary code (the 1s and 0s used in computing) or a binary star system (in which two stars orbit around each other)

biocultural interaction how our bodies respond to our cultural environment and vice versa

brain organization theory the idea that male and female brains may have different strengths and weaknesses

breadwinner/housewife marriage a model of marriage that did not legally subordinate wives to husbands but continued to define the rights and responsibilities of husbands and wives differently; women owed men domestic services and men were legally required to support their wives financially

care chain a series of nurturing relationships in which the care of children, the disabled, or the elderly is displaced onto increasingly disadvantaged paid or unpaid caregivers

care work such work that involves face-to-face caretaking of the physical, emotional, and educational needs of others

cisgender a term to describe male-bodied people who comfortably identify as men and female-bodied people who comfortably identify as women

civic awareness a focus on the well-being of groups and societies as wholes

coital imperative the idea that any fully sexually active couple must be having penile-vaginal intercourse (also known as "coitus") and any fully completed sexual activity will include it

colorism a racist preference for light over dark skin

commodification the process by which goods transition from something a family provided for itself into something bought with a wage

commodity a thing that can be bought and sold

compensatory masculinity acts undertaken to reassert one's manliness in the face of a threat

compulsory heterosexuality a rule that all men be attracted to women and all women to men

concerted cultivation an active and organized effort to develop in children a wide range of skills and talents

corporate co-optation of feminism the use of feminist-sounding language and imagery for marketing purposes

cult of domesticity the notion that women could and should wholeheartedly embrace the work of making a loving home

cultural competence a familiarity and facility with how the members of a society typically think and behave

cultural traveling moving from one cultural or subcultural context to another and sometimes back

culturalism the idea that we are "blank slates" that become who we are purely through learning and socialization

culturally unintelligible to be so outside the symbolic meaning system that people will not know how to interact with you

culture a group's shared beliefs and the practices and material things that reflect them

deceptive differences those differences that, by being embodied and observed, can make it seem as if men and women are more sexually dimorphic than they naturally need to be

democratic brotherhood the distribution of citizenship rights to certain classes of men

disability prejudice bias against people with disabilities

distinction efforts to distinguish one's own group from others

doing gender a phrase used to describe the ways in which we actively obey and break gender rules

domestic outsourcing paying non-family members to do family-related tasks

double bind a situation in which cultural expectations are contradictory

drag queens and kings conventionally gendered and often heterosexual men and women who dress up and behave like members of the opposite sex, usually for fun or pay

dual-nurturers families in which individuals disinvest in work together and turn their energy toward the home

egalitarians people who prefer relationships in which both partners do their fair share of breadwinning, housekeeping, and child rearing

emasculation a loss of masculinity

emotion work the act of controlling one's own emotions and managing the emotions of others

emphasized femininity an exaggerated form of femininity "oriented to accommodating the interests and desires of men"

emphatic sameness a strategy by which women try to be "just one of the guys"

employer selection hypothesis a theory that proposes that employers tend to prefer men for masculine jobs and women for feminine jobs, slotting applicants into gender-consistent roles during hiring and promotion

equal access a model of creating egalitarianism by dismantling legal barriers and reducing sex discrimination

equal sharing a model of creating egalitarianism that targets subordination by attempting to ensure that men and women participate equally in masculine and feminine spheres

equal value a model of creating egalitarianism designed to tackle the problem of androcentrism by raising the value of the feminine to match the value of the masculine

erotic marketplace the ways in which people are organized and ordered according to their perceived sexual desirability

exculpatory chauvinism a phenomenon in which negative characteristics ascribed to men are presented as "natural" and offered as acceptable justifications of men's dominance over women

family wage an income paid to one male earner that was large enough to support a home, a wife, and children

fatherhood premium a wage increase that accrues to married men who become fathers

female a type of sex

female-bodied used to specify that sex refers to the body and may not extend to how a person feels or acts

feminine apologetic a requirement that women balance their appropriation of masculine interests, traits, and activities with feminine performance

feminine things we associate with women

feminism the belief that all men and women should have equal rights and opportunities

feminist politics activities of those involved in efforts to make society's gender order less hierarchical and more supportive of the full development of human capacities for everyone

feminist utopia a perfectly gender-egalitarian society

feminization of poverty a trend in which the poor are increasingly female

forager societies ones that migrate seasonally, following crops and game across the landscape

formal gender equality the legal requirement that men and women be treated more or less the same

fragile masculinity an exaggerated aversion some men have to doing femininity that, ironically, imbues femininity with the power to damage or destroy manliness

gender the symbolism of masculinity and femininity that we connect to being male-bodied or female-bodied

gender-aware policymaking a type of policymaking in which consideration of the effects on both men and women—and different kinds of men and women—is a required part of the policymaking process

gender binary the idea that there are only two types of people—male-bodied people who are masculine and female-bodied people who are feminine

gender binary glasses a pair of lenses that separate everything we see into masculine and feminine categories

gender binary subdivision the practice by which we divide and redivide by gender again and again, adding finer and finer *degrees* of masculinity and femininity to the world

gender dysphoria a term used to describe the discomfort some people experience with the relationship between their bodies' assigned sex and their gender identity

gender equivocation the use of both emphasized femininity and emphatic sameness when they're useful and culturally expected

gender expression a way of expressing one's gender identity through appearance, dress, and behavior

gender fluid without a fixed gender identity

gender identity a sense of oneself as male or female

gender ideologies widely shared beliefs about how men and women are and should be

gender of governance who holds political office and whether it matters

gender order the social organization of gender relations in a society

gender pay gap the difference between the incomes of the average man and woman who work full time

gender policing a response to the violation of gender rules that is aimed at exacting conformity

gender rules instructions for how to appear and behave as a man or a woman

gender salience the relevance of gender across contexts, activities, and spaces

gender strategy finding a way of doing gender that works for us as unique individuals who are also shaped by other parts of our identity and the material realities of our lives

genderqueer identifying as outside of or between the binary between male and female (see also nonbinary)

gendered institution a social institution in which gender is used as an organizing principle

gendered job segregation the practice of filling occupations with mostly male or mostly female workers

gendered love/sex binary a projection of the gender binary onto the ideas of love and sex

genes a set of instructions for building and maintaining our bodies

genotype a unique set of genes

glass ceiling the idea that there is an invisible barrier between women and top positions in masculine occupations

glass cliff a heightened risk of failing faced by women who break through the glass ceiling

glass closet an invisible place in which sexual minorities hide their identities in order to avoid stigma, suspicion, or censure at work

glass escalator an invisible ride to the top offered to men in female-dominated occupations

going steady the practice of an often short-lived, but still exclusive, public pairing off

good girl/bad girl dichotomy the idea that women who behave themselves sexually are worthy of respect and women who don't are not

governance of gender how the gender of a country's residents shapes the way they are regulated

governance the process of making decisions for the nation, ensuring the state's accountability to its citizens and enforcing the laws of the land

greedy institutions those institutions, such as work and family, that take up an incredible amount of time and energy

hegemonic masculinity pertaining to a type of man, idealized by men and women alike, who functions to justify and naturalize gender inequality

hegemony a state of collective consent to inequality that is secured by the idea that it is inevitable, natural, or desirable

hegemonic masculinity a type of masculine performance, idealized by men and women alike, that functions to justify and naturalize gender inequality, assuring widespread consent to the social disadvantage of most women and some men

heteronormative designed on the assumption that everyone is heterosexual, with individuals pre-

suming so unless there are culturally recognizable signs indicating otherwise

heterosexism individual and institutional bias against sexual minorities

heterosexual male gaze a way of looking at society from the perspective of a hypothetical heterosexual man

hierarchy of masculinity a rough ranking of men from most to least masculine, with the assumption that more is always better

homonormativity a practice of obeying every gender rule except the ones that say we must sexually desire and partner with someone of the other sex

hookup culture a new norm on college campuses in which casual sexual contact in the absence of romantic intentions is held up by many as an ideal

hookups one-time nonromantic sexual encounters

hormones messengers in a chemical communication system

hostile sexism the use of harassment, threats, and violence to enforce women's subservience to men

hybrid masculinities a collection of gender strategies that selectively incorporate symbols, performances, and identities that society associates with women or low-status men

hypermasculinity extreme conformity to the more aggressive rules of masculinity

ideal worker norm the idea that an employee should have the ability to devote themselves to their job without the distraction of family responsibilities

ideology a set of ideas widely shared by members of a society that guides identities, behaviors, and institutions

ideology of intensive motherhood see *intensive motherhood*

individualism an attitude that reflects a focus on the individual over the group

institutions persistent patterns of social interaction aimed at meeting the needs of a society that can't easily be met by individuals alone

integrated motherhood an ideology of motherhood that includes work outside the home, financial self-sufficiency, and a network of support

intensive motherhood the idea that (1) mothers should be the primary caretaker of their children, (2) child rearing should include "copious amounts of time, energy, and material resources," and (3) giving children these things takes priority over all other interests, desires, and demands

intersectional feminist activism feminist activism that attends to the lived experiences of different kinds of women and men

intersectionality the fact that gender is not an isolated social fact about us but instead intersects with all the other distinctions among people made important by our society

intersex bodies that are not clearly male or female

kin groups collections of individuals considered family

learned differences those differences that are a result of our familial or sociocultural environment

learning model of socialization a model that suggests that socialization is a lifelong process of learning and relearning gendered expectations and how to negotiate them

legislatures groups of individuals elected to represent their constituents in regulating the affairs of the country

male a type of sex

male flight a phenomenon in which men abandon feminizing arenas of life

male-bodied used to specify that sex refers to the body and may not extend to how a person feels or acts

marriage bans policies against employing married women

mascing advertising one's masculine traits and concealing one's feminine ones in an effort to appease others' preferences for masculine men

masculine things we associate with men

masculinities different ways of doing masculinity, arrayed in a hierarchy, that are more or less available to people with different social positions, intersectional identities, and contexts of interaction

masculinization of wealth the concentration of men in high-earning occupations

matrix of domination a structure in which multiple hierarchies intersect to create a pyramid of privilege, leaving on top only those people who are advantaged in every hierarchy

mental rotation the ability to imagine an object rotating in your mind

misogyny fear and hatred of women with power

misogynistic murder the killing of women by men who are motivated to punish them for attempting to exercise that power

modified patriarchies societies in which women have been granted formal gender equality but the patriarchal conflation of power with men and masculinity remains a central part of daily life

mommy tax a term for the lost wages, benefits, and Social Security contributions that come with taking time out of the workforce to raise small children and then re-entering it with less momentum

mommy track a workplace euphemism that refers to expecting less from mothers, with the understanding that they are sacrificing the right to expect equal pay, regular raises, or promotions

monogamy the open practice and encouragement of long-term intimate relationships with only one person

mononormativity the normalizing of monogamy

motherhood penalty a loss in wages associated with becoming a mother

nationalism a belief in the superiority of one's own country, its rightful dominance over others, and exclusionary policies that restrict citizenship by race, ethnicity, or religion

naturalism the idea that biology affects our behavior independently of our environment

nature/nurture debate argument between people who believe that observed differences between men and women are biological and those who believe that these differences are acquired through socialization

neo-traditionalists people who embrace a modified version of traditionalism: They think that a woman should be able to work if she desires, but only if it doesn't interfere with her "real" duty to take care of her husband and children

nonbinary identifying as outside of or between the binary between male and female (see also *genderqueer*)

norms beliefs and practices that are well known, widely followed, and culturally approved

nuclear family a monogamous mother and father with children who live together without extended kin

observed differences findings from surveys, experiments, and other types of studies that detect differences between men and women

open relationships relationships in which comitted partners agree that each can have sexual encounters outside the relationship

orgasm gap a phenomenon in which women involved in heterosexual relationships report fewer orgasms than men

otherfathers men in the neighborhood who act as substitute fathers out of inclination or kindness

othermothers women in the neighborhood who act as substitute mothers out of inclination or kindness

pariah femininities ways of being a woman that, by virtue of directly challenging male dominance, are widely and aggressively policed

partnership marriage a model of marriage based on love and companionship between two equals who negotiate a division of labor unique to their relationship

patriarch/property marriage a model of marriage in which a woman was entered into a marriage by her father, who owned her until he "gave her away" at the wedding

patriarchal bargain a deal in which an individual or group accepts or even legitimates some of the costs of patriarchy in exchange for receiving some of its rewards

patriarchy literally, "the rule of the father"; it refers to the control of female and younger male family members by select adult men, or patriarchs

phenotype an observable set of physical and behavioral traits

policies explicit and codified expectations, often with stated consequences for deviance

politics the activities involved in determining national policies and electing people to guide this process

politics of gender how people change and resist change to the gender order

politics of respectability a form of resistance to negative racial stereotypes that involves being "good" and following conservative norms of appearance and behavior

polyamory the open practice and encouragement of long-term intimate relationships with more than one partner at a time

precarious masculinity the idea that manhood is more difficult to earn and easier to lose than femininity

priming a trick in which study subjects are reminded of a stereotype right before a test

privilege unearned social and economic advantage based on our location in a social hierarchy

production the making of goods for sale

pro-natal policies those policies that encourage childbearing, whether intentionally or not

protective legislation policies designed to protect women from exploitation by restricting their workplace participation

push-and-resist dynamic a situation in which it is normal for men to press sexual activity consistently in the direction of increasing intimacy (whether he wants to or not) and for women to stop or slow down the accelerating intimacy when he's going "too far" (whether she wants to or not)

racial prejudice attitudes and behaviors that are biased against some races and in favor of others

racism social arrangements systematically designed to advantage one race over others

radical claim an idea that doesn't (yet) resonate with most members of a population

rape culture an environment that justifies, naturalizes, and even glorifies sexual pressure, coercion, and violence

reproduction the making and nurturing of human beings

second shift work that greets us when we come home from work

selective exit hypothesis an explanation for job segregation that emphasizes workers' abandonment of counterstereotypical occupations

self-objectify the process by which people internalize the idea that their value is heavily dependent on their physical attractiveness

separate spheres the idea of a masculinized work world and a feminized home life

service and information economy an economy dependent on jobs focused on providing services for others or working with ideas

sex physical differences in primary sexual characteristics (the presence of organs directly involved in reproduction) and secondary sexual characteristics (such as patterns of hair growth, the amount of breast tissue, and distribution of body fat)

sexism the favoring of one sex over the other, both ideologically and in practice

sexual dimorphism degrees of difference in appearance and behavior between males and females of a species

sexual double standard different rules for the sexual behavior of men and women

sexual minorities gays, lesbians, bisexuals, and others who identify as nonheterosexual

sexual objectification the reduction of a person to his or her sex appeal

sexual orientation whether one prefers male-bodied or female-bodied people as sexual partners, or both or neither.

sexual script the rules that guide sexual interaction

sexual subjectification the process by which people are told what their internal thoughts and feelings should be

sharing doing more or less symmetrical amounts of paid and unpaid work

smashing a term used to describe having a same-sex crush

social construct an arbitrary but influential shared interpretation of reality

social construction a process by which we make reality meaningful through shared interpretation

social identity a culturally available and socially constructed category of people in which we place ourselves or are placed by others

social movements collective, nongovernmental efforts to change societies

social structure the entire set of interlocked institutions within which we live our lives

socialization hypothesis a theory that suggests that men and women respond to gender stereotypes when planning, training, and applying for jobs

specialization splitting unpaid and paid work so that each partner does more of one than the other

spectating watching one's sexual performance from the outside

stalled revolution a sweeping change in gender relations that is stuck halfway through

standing the right to represent oneself and others in decisions being made

states institutions entrusted with the power to regulate everyday life on behalf of the group

stereotypes fixed, oversimplified, and distorted ideas about what people are like

sticky floor a metaphorical barrier to advancement describing jobs with no or low opportunity for promotion

subjectivity internal thoughts and feelings

subordination the placing of women into positions that make them subservient to or dependent on men

substantive representation policies important and helpful to women

suffrage the right to vote

symbolic representation women's presence in government

symbolic threat a presence that potentially degrades the identity of the dominant group

toxic masculinity strategic enactments of masculinities that are harmful both to the men who enact them and to the people around them

traditionalists people who ascribe to the values of the breadwinner/housewife marriage that emerged with industrialization and came to be seen as "traditional" and who believe that men should be responsible for earning income and women should be responsible for housework and childcare

trans (or transgender) a diverse group of people who experience some form of discomfort with the relationship between their bodies' assigned sex and their gender identity, or otherwise reject the gender binary for themselves

transnational feminist activism a type of activism that involves efforts by feminists to change gender relations outside their own states and collaboration between and among feminists in different countries

treating a practice in which a man funds a woman's night on the town

universal suffrage the right of all citizens to vote

unmarked category the identity that is assumed for a role or context without qualification

victim blaming identifying something done by a victim as a cause their victimization

wage money gained from working in places like factories, mines, and shops that belong to others

women's movements social movements organized by women for women

working poor individuals who work but still live in poverty

xenophobia individual and institutional bias against people seen as foreign

NOTES

Chapter 1: Introduction

1. Elizabeth Semmelhack, *Heights of Fashion: A History of the Elevated Shoe* (Penzanze, UK: Periscope, 2008).

2. Nancy E. Rexford, *Women's Shoes in America, 1795–1930* (Kent, OH: Kent State University Press, 2000).

3. Shari Benstock and Suzanne Ferriss, eds., "Introduction," in *Footnotes: On Shoes* (New Brunswick, NJ: Rutgers University Press, 1993).

Chapter 2: Ideas

1. Carol Martin and Diane Ruble, "Children's Search for Gender Cues," *Current Directions in Psychological Science* 13, no. 2 (2004): 67.

2. Thomas Laqueur, *Making Sex: Body and Gender from the Greeks to Freud* (Cambridge: Harvard University Press, 1990).

3. Quoted in Laqueur, note 11, p. 4.

4. Georgiann Davis, *Contesting Intersex: The Dubious Diagnosis* (New York: New York University Press, 2015).

5. Leuan A. Hughes, John D. Davies, Trevor I Bunch, Bickie Pasteriski, Kiki Mastroyannopoulou, and Jane MacDougall, "Androgren Insensitivity Syndrome," *The Lancet* 380, no 9851 (2012): 1419–28.

6. Sarah S. Richardson, *Sex Itself: The Search for Male and Female in the Human Genome* (Chicago: University of Chicago Press, 2013).

7. Melanie Blackless, Anthony Charuvastra, Amanda Derryck, Anne Fausto-Sterling, Karl Lauzanne, and Ellen Lee, "How Sexually Dimorphic Are We? Review and Synthesis," *American Journal of Human Biology* 12, no. 2 (2000): 151–66; Gary Gates, "How Many People Are Lesbian, Gay, Bisexual, and Transgender?" The Williams Institute, 2011. Retrieved from http://williamsinstitute.law.ucla.edu/wp-content/uploads/Gates-How-Many-People-LGBT-Apr-2011.pdf.

8. National Institutes of Health, "What Is Klinefelter Syndrome?" 2007. Retrieved from https://rarediseases.info.nih.gov/diseases/8705/klinefelter-syndrome/cases/22820.

9. Mayo Clinic Staff, "Triple X Syndrome," Mayo Clinic, November 8, 2012. Retrieved from www.mayoclinic.com/health/triple-x-syndrome/DS01090.

10. Medline Plus, "Turner Syndrome," *National Institutes of Health*, January 4, 2014. Retrieved from www.nlm.nih.gov/medlineplus/turnersyndrome.html.

11. Georgiann Davis, *Contesting Intersex: The Dubious Diagnosis* (New York: New York University Press, 2015).

12. Margaret McDowell, Cheryl D. Fryar, Cynthia L. Ogden, and Katherine M. Flegal, "Anthropometric Reference Data for Children and Adults: United States, 2003–2006," *National Health Statistics Reports* 10 (October 22, 2008): 1–48.

13. Melissa Whitworth, "Victoria's Secret Show: What Does It Take to Be a Victoria's Secret Angel?" *Telegraph*, November 7, 2011. Retrieved from http://fashion.telegraph.co.uk/news-features/TMG8872623/Victorias-Secret-show-What-does-it-take-to-be-a-Victorias-Secret-Angel.html.

14. Katherine DM Clover, "5 Unexpected Gender Differences in Children's Clothing," Parent Co., January 27, 2017. Retrieved from www.parent.com/5-unexpected-gender-differences-in-childrens-clothing/.

15. American Society of Plastic Surgeons, "2016 Plastic Surgery Statistics Report." Retrieved from www.plasticsurgery.org/documents/News/Statistics/2016/plastic-surgery-statistics-full-report-2016.pdf; Alex Kuczynski, "A Sense of Anxiety a Shirt Won't Cover," *New York Times*, June 14, 2007. Retrieved from www.nytimes.com/2007/06/14/fashion/14reduction.html.

16. Gilbert Herdt, *Same Sex, Different Cultures: Exploring Gay and Lesbian Lives* (Boulder, CO: Westview Press, 1997).

17. Quoted in Jorge Rivas, "Native Americans Talk Gender at 'Two-Spirit' Powwow," *Fusion*, February 9, 2015. Retrieved from www.fusion.kinja.com/native-americans-talk-gender-identity-at-a-two-spirit-1793845144.

18. Quoted in "The Beautiful Way Hawaiian Culture Embraces a Particular Kind of Transgender Identity," *Huffington Post*, April 28, 2015. Retrieved from www.huffingtonpost.com/2015/04/28/hawaiian-culture-transgender_n_7158130.html.

19. Niko Besnier, "Polynesian Gender Liminality through Time and Space," in *Third Sex, Third Gender: Beyond Sexual Dimorphism in Culture and History*, ed. Gilbert Herdt (New York: Zone Books [distributed by Massachusetts Institute of Technology Press], 1994), 285–328; Serena Nanda, *Gender Diversity: Cross-Cultural Variations* (Long Grove, IL: Waveland Press Inc., 2000).

20. Marc Lacey, "A Lifestyle Distinct: The Muxe of Mexico," *New York Times*, December 6, 2008. Retrieved from www.nytimes.com/2008/12/07/weekinreview/07lacey.html.

21. Shanoor Seervai, "Laxmi Narayan Tripathi: India's Third Gender," *Guernica*, March 16, 2015.

22. Ivan Olita, *Muxes*, 2016, www.shortoftheweek.com/2017/01/03/muxes/.

23. Ibid.

24. Ibid.

25. PBS, "A Map of Gender-Diverse Cultures," August 11, 2015. Retrieved from www.pbs.org/independentlens/content/two-spirits_map-html.

26. Christine Helliwell, "'It's Only a Penis': Rape, Feminism, and Difference," *Signs* 25, no. 3 (2000): 806–7.

27. Susan Chira, "When Japan Had a Third Gender," *New York Times*, March 10, 2017. Retrieved from www.nytimes.com/2017/03/10/arts/design/when-japan-had-a-third-gender.html.

28. Christine Gailey, "Evolutionary Perspectives on Gender Hierarchy," in *Analyzing Gender: A Handbook of Social Science Research*, ed. Beth Hess and Myra Marx Ferree (Thousand Oaks, CA: Sage Publishing, 1987).

29. Ifi Amadiume, *Male Daughters, Female Husbands: Gender and Sex in an African Society* (London: Zed Books, 1987).

30. Nelly Oudshoorn, *Beyond the Natural Body: An Archeology of Sex Hormones* (New York: Routledge, 1994).

31. Ross Nehm and Rebecca Young, "'Sex Hormones' in Secondary School Biology Textbooks," *Science and Education* 17 (2008): 1175–90.

32. Jenny Nordberg, "Afghan Boys Are Prized, So Girls Live the Part," *New York Times*, September 20, 2010. Retrieved from www.nytimes.com/2010/09/21/world/asia/21gender.html.

33. René Grémaux, "Woman Becomes Man in the Balkans," in *Third Sex, Third Gender: Beyond Sexual Dimorphism in Culture and History*, ed. Gilbert Herdt (New York: Zone Books [distributed by Massachusetts Institute of Technology Press], 1996); Antonia Young, *Women Who Become Men: Albanian Sworn Virgins* (New York: Berg, 2000); and Serena Nanda, *Gender Diversity: Cross-Cultural Variations* (Long Grove, IL: Waveland Press Inc., 2000).

34. Stanley B. Alpern, *Amazons of Black Sparta: The Women Warriors of Dahomey* (New York: New York University Press, 1998).

35. *The Sworn Virgins of Albania*, RT Documentary, December 18, 2016. Retrieved from www.youtube.com/watch?v=3UUikqpotiE.

36. Nicola Smith, "Sworn Virgins Dying Out as Albanian Girls Reject Manly Role," *Times of London*, January 6, 2008. Retrieved from www.thetimes.co.uk/article/sworn-virgins-dying-out-as-albanian-girls-reject-manly-role-v2ft3x82lz5.

37. Peter Berger and Thomas Luckmann, *The Social Construction of Reality: A Treatise in the Sociology of Knowledge* (New York: Doubleday, 1966).

38. P. W. Hammond, *Food & Feast in Medieval England* (Gloucestershire, UK: Alan Sutton, 1993).

39. Malia Wollan, "Rise and Shine: What Kids Around the World Eat for Breakfast," *New York Times Magazine*, August 10, 2014. Retrieved from www .nytimes.com/interactive/2014/10/08/magazine /eaters-all-over.html; Pamela Goyan Kittler, Kathryn P. Sucher, and Marcia Nahikian-Nelms, "Chapter 13: People of the Balkans and the Middle East" in *Food and Culture*, 6th ed. (Belmont, CA: Wadsworth, Cengage Learning, 2012).

40. Douglas S. Massey, "A Brief History of Human Society: The Origin and Role of Emotion in Social Life," *American Sociological Review* 67 (2002): 1–29.

41. Discussed on p. 229 of Cordelia Fine, *Delusions of Gender: How Our Minds, Society, and Neurosexism Create Difference* (New York: W. W. Norton and Company, 2010).

42. Daniel Schacter and Elaine Scarry, *Memory Brain and Belief* (Cambridge: Harvard University Press, 2001); Steven B. Most, Anne Verbeck Sorber, and Joseph G. Cunningham, "Auditory Stroop Reveals Implicit Gender Associations in Adults and Children," *Journal of Experimental Social Psychology* 43, no. 2 (2007): 287–94.

43. Sandra Lipsitz Bem, "Androgyny and Gender Schema Theory: A Conceptual and Empirical Integration," in *Nebraska Symposium on Motivation 1984: Psychology and Gender*, ed. T. B. Sonderegger (Lincoln: University of Nebraska Press, 1985).

44. Daniel Schacter and Elaine Scarry, *Memory Brain and Belief* (Cambridge: Harvard University Press, 2001); Steven B. Most, Anne Verbeck Sorber, and Joseph G. Cunningham, "Auditory Stroop Reveals Implicit Gender Associations in Adults and Children," *Journal of Experimental Social Psychology* 43, no. 2 (2007): 287–94.

45. Sandra Lipsitz Bem, "Gender Schema Theory: A Cognitive Account of Sex Typing," *Psychological Review* 88, no. 4 (1981): 354–64.

46. Cecilia L. Ridgeway, "Framed by Gender: How Inequality Persists in the Modern World," *European Sociological Review* 29, no. 2 (2013): 408–10.

47. Alison P. Lenton, Irene V. Blair, and Reid Hastie, "Illusions of Gender: Stereotypes Evoke False Memories," *Journal of Experimental Social Psychology* 37, no. 1 (2001): 3–14; L. S. Liben and M. L. Signorella, "Gender-Related Schemata and Constructive Memory in Children," *Child Development* 51, no. 1 (1980): 11–18.

48. Carol Martin and Diane Ruble, "Children's Search for Gender Cues," *Current Directions in Psychological Science* 13, no. 2 (2004): 67–70; Timothy J. Frawley, "Gender Schema and Prejudicial Recall: How Children Misremember, Fabricate, and Distort Gendered Picture Book Information," *Journal of Research in Childhood Education* 22, no. 3 (2008): 291–303; J. Susskind, "Children's Perception of Gender-Based Illusory Correlations: Enhancing Preexisting Relationships between Gender and Behavior," *Sex Roles* 48, no. 11 (2003): 483–94; Lea Conkright, Dorothy Flannagan, and James Dykes, "Effects of Pronoun Type and Gender Role Consistency on Children's Recall and Interpretation of Stories," *Sex Roles* 43, no. 7/8 (2000): 481–97; L. Conkright, D. Flannagan, and J. Dykes, "Effects of Pronoun Type and Gender Role Consistency on Children's Recall and Interpretations of Stories," *Sex Roles* 43, no. 7/8 (2000): 481–98; A. P. Lenton, I. V. Blair, and R. Hastie, "Illusions of Gender: Stereotypes Evoke False Memories," *Journal of Experimental Social Psychology* 37, no. 1 (2001): 3–14; J. E. Susskind, "Children's Perceptions of Gender Based Illusory Correlations: Enhancing Preexisting Relationships between Gender and Behavior," *Sex Roles* 48, no. 11–12 (2003): 483–94; Eileen Wood, Alison Groves, Shirliana Bruce, Teena Willoughby, and Serge Desmarais, "Can Gender Stereotypes Facilitate Memory When Elaborative Strategies Are Used?" *Educational Psychology* 23, no. 2 (2003): 169–80.

49. Mahzarin Banaji and R. Bhaskar, "Implicit Stereotypes and Memory: The Bounded Rationality of Social Beliefs," in *Memory, Brain, and Belief*, ed. Daniel L. Schacter and Elaine Scarry (Cambridge: Harvard University Press, 2000); Heather M. Kleider, Kathy Pezdek, Stephen D. Goldinger, and Alice Kirk, "Schema-Driven Source Misattribution Errors: Remembering the Expected from a Witnessed Event," *Applied Cognitive Psychology* 22, no. 1 (2008):1–20; Kimberly A. Quinn, C. Neil Macrae, and Galen V. Bodenhausen, "Stereotyping and Impression Formation: How Categorical Thinking Shapes Person Perceptions," in *The SAGE Handbook of Social Psychology: Concise Student Edition*, ed. Michael A. Hogg and Joel Cooper (London: Sage Publications, 2007).

50. Lauren R. Shapiro, "Eyewitness Testimony for a Simulated Juvenile Crime by Male and Female

Criminals with Consistent or Inconsistent Gender-Role Characteristics," *Journal of Applied Developmental Psychology* 30, no. 6 (2009): 649–66.

51. Ibid., 651.

52. Armand Chatard, Serge Guimond, and Leila Selimbegovic. "'How Good Are You in Math?' The Effect of Gender Stereotypes on Students' Recollection of Their School Marks," *Journal of Experimental Social Psychology* 43, no. 6 (2007): 1017–24.

Chapter 3: Bodies

1. Kathryn Dindia, "Men Are from North Dakota, Women Are from South Dakota," in *Sex Differences and Similarities in Communication*, 2nd ed., ed. Kathryn Dindia and Daniel J. Canary (Mahwah, NJ: Erlbaum, 2006), 3–18.

2. Dorothy Sayers, "The Human-Not-Quite-Human," in *On the Contrary: Essays by Men and Women*, ed. Martha Rainbolt and Janet Fleetwood (New York: SUNY Press, 1983), 10.

3. Kim Parker, Juliana Menasce Horowitz, and Renee Stepler, "On Gender Differences, No Consensus on Nature vs. Nurture," *Pew Research Center*, December 5, 2017. Retrieved from www.pewsocialtrends.org/2017/12/05/on-gender-differences-no-consensus-on-nature-vs-nurture/.

4. Ethan Zell, Zlatan Krizan, and Sabrina Teeter, "Evaluating Gender Similarities and Differences Using Metasynthesis," *American Psychologist* 70, no. 1 (2015): 10–20.

5. Mary Beth Oliver and Janet S. Hyde, "Gender Differences in Sexuality: A Meta-Analysis," *Psychological Bulletin* 114 (1993): 29–51.

6. Reviewed in Janet Hyde, "The Gender Similarities Hypothesis," *American Psychologist* 60, no. 6 (2005): 581–92.

7. Richard Joiner, Caroline Stewart, Chelsey Beaney, Amy Moon, Pam Maras, Jane Guiller, Helen Gregory, Jeff Gavin, John Cromby, and Mark Brosnan, "Publically Different, Privately the Same: Gender Differences and Similarities in Response to Facebook Status Updates," *Computers in Human Behavior* 39: 165–69.

8. M. H. Davies and L. A. Kraus, "Personality and Empathic Accuracy," in *Empathic Accuracy*, ed. William J. Ickes (New York: The Guilford Press, 1997), 144–68; Nancy Briton and Judith Hall, "Beliefs about Female and Male Non-Verbal Communication," *Sex Roles* 32 (1995): 79–90.

9. D. M. Marx and D. A. Stapel, "It Depends on Your Perspective: The Role of Self-Relevance in Stereotype-Based Underperformance," *Journal of Experimental Social Psychology* 42 (2006): 768–75.

10. K. J. K. Klein and S. D. Hodges, "Gender Differences, Motivation, and Empathic Accuracy: When It Pays to Understand," *Personality and Social Psychology Bulletin* 27, no. 6 (2001): 720–30; Michael J. Clarke, Anthony D. G. Marks, and Amy D. Lykins, "Bridging the Gap: The Effect of Gender Normativity on Differences in Empathy and Emotional Intelligence," *Journal of Gender Studies* 25, no. 5 (2016): 522–39.

11. G. Thomas and G. R. Maio, "Man, I Feel Like a Woman: When and How Gender-Role Motivation Helps Mind-Reading," *Journal of Personality and Social Psychology* 95, no. 5 (2008): 1165–79.

12. Anne Fausto-Sterling, Cynthia Garcia Coll, and Meghan Lamarre, "Sexing the Baby: Part 1—What Do We Really Know about Sex Differentiation in the First Three Years of Life?" *Social Science & Medicine* 74, no. 11 (2012): 1684–92; Anne Fausto-Sterling, Cynthia Garcia Coll, and Meghan Lamarre, "Sexing the Baby: Part 2—Applying Dynamic Systems Theory to the Emergences of Sex-Related Differences in Infants and Toddlers," *Social Science & Medicine* 74, no. 11 (2012): 1693–17.

13. Joseph Henrich, Steven J. Heine, and Ara Norenzayan, "The Weirdest People in the World," *Behavioral and Brain Sciences* 33 (2010): 61–135.

14. Joan Chrisler and Donald McCreary, eds., *Handbook of Gender Research in Psychology* (New York: Springer, 2010).

15. Brian Nosek, Mahzarin Banaji, and Anthony Greenwald, "Math = Male, Me = Female, Therefore Math ≠ Me," *Journal of Personality and Social Psychology* 83, no. 1 (2002): 44–59.

16. Natalie Angier and Kenneth Chang, "Gray Matter and Sexes: A Gray Area Scientifically," *New York Times*, January 24, 2005. Retrieved from www.nytimes.com/2005/01/24/science/24women.html?_r=1.

17. Janet S. Hyde, Sara M. Lindberg, Marcia C. Linn, Amy B. Ellis, and Caroline C. Williams, "Gender Similarities Characterize Math Performance," *Science* 321 (2008): 494–95; Sara M. Lindberg, Janet Shibley Hyde, Jennifer L. Petersen, and Marcia C. Linn, "New Trends in Gender and Mathematics Performance: A Meta-Analysis," *Psychological Bulletin* 136, no. 6 (November 2010): 1123–35; David I. Miller and Diane F. Halpern, "The New Science of Cogni-

tive Sex Differences," *Trends in Cognitive Science* 18, no. 1 (2014): 37–45.

18. Natalie Angier and Kenneth Chang, "Gray Matter and Sexes: A Gray Area Scientifically," *New York Times*, January 24, 2005. Retrieved from, www.nytimes.com/2005/01/24/science/24women.html?_r=1.

19. Ibid.

20. D. Reilly, D. L. Neumann, and G. Andrews, "Sex Differences in Mathematics and Science Achievement: A Meta-Analysis of National Assessment of Educational Progress Assessments," *Journal of Educational Psychology* 107, no. 3 (2015): 645–62.

21. Natalie Angier and Kenneth Chang, "Gray Matter and Sexes: A Gray Area Scientifically," *New York Times*, January 24, 2005. Retrieved from www.nytimes.com/2005/01/24/science/24women.html?_r=1.

22. Janet S. Hyde, Sara M. Lindberg, Marcia C. Linn, Amy B. Ellis, and Caroline C. Williams, "Gender Similarities Characterize Math Performance," *Science* 321 (2008): 494–95; Sara M. Lindberg, Janet Shibley Hyde, Jennifer L. Petersen, and Marcia C. Linn, "New Trends in Gender and Mathematics Performance: A Meta-Analysis," *Psychological Bulletin* 136, no. 6 (November 2010): 1123–35.

23. Jonathan Wai, Megan Cacchio, Martha Putallaz, and Matthew C. Makel, "Sex Differences in the Right Tail of Cognitive Abilities: A 30 Year Examination," *Intelligence* 38, no. 4 (2010): 412–23.

24. Elizabeth Spelke, "Sex Differences in Intrinsic Aptitude for Mathematics and Science? A Critical Review," *American Psychologist* 60, no. 9 (2005): 950–58.

25. Joan Burrelli, *Thirty-Three Years of Women in S&E Faculty Positions*, InfoBrief. Science Resources Statistics, NSF 08-308, National Science Foundation Directorate for Social, Behavioral, and Economic Sciences, 2008. Retrieved from www.nsf.gov/statistics/infbrief/nsf08308/nsf08308.pdf; see also Robert J. Daverman (AMS Secretary), "Statistics on Women Mathematicians Compiled by the AMS," *Notices of the AMS* 58 (2011): 1310; National Science Foundation, National Center for Science and Engineering Statistics. 2017. Women, Minorities, and Persons with Disabilities in Science and Engineering: 2017. Special Report NSF 17-310. Arlington, VA. Retrieved from www.nsf.gov/statistics/wmpd/.

26. Brian A. Nosek et al., "National Differences in Gender–Science Stereotypes Predict National Sex Differences in Science and Math Achievement," *Proceedings of the National Academy of Sciences* 106, no. 26 (June 30, 2009):10593–97.

27. Luigi Guiso, Ferdinando Monte, Paola Sapienza, and Luigi Zingales, "Culture, Gender, and Math." *Science* 320, no. 5880 (May 30, 2008): 1164–65; Nicole Else-Quest, Janet Hyde, and Marcia Linn, "Cross-National Patterns of Gender Differences in Mathematics: A Meta-Analysis," *Psychological Bulletin* 136, no. 1 (2010): 103–27.

28. Diane Halpern, Camilla Benbow, David Geary, Ruben Gur, Janet Hyde, and Morton Gernsbacher, "The Science of Sex Differences in Science and Mathematics," *Psychological Science in the Public Interest* 8, no. 1 (2007): 1–51.

29. Jonathan Wai, Megan Cacchio, Martha Putallaz, and Matthew C. Makel, "Sex Differences in the Right Tail of Cognitive Abilities: A 30 Year Examination," *Intelligence* 38, no. 4 (2010): 412–23.

30. Catherine P. Cross, Cyrenne M. De-Laine, and Gillian R. Brown. "Sex Differences in Sensation-Seeking: A Meta-Analysis," *Scientific Reports* 3 (2013): 2486.

31. Ian Craig, Emma Harper, and Caroline Loat, "The Genetic Basis for Sex Differences in Human Behaviour: Role of the Sex Chromosomes," *Annals of Human Genetics* 68 (2004): 269–84.

32. Ibid.

33. R. Scott Hawley, and Catherine A. Mori, *The Human Genome: A User's Guide* (San Diego: Academic Press, 1999).

34. E. Turkheimer and D. F. Halpern, "Sex Differences in Variability for Cognitive Measures: Do the Ends Justify the Genes?" *Perspectives on Psychological Science* 4 (2009): 612–14.

35. Angela Book, Katherine Starzyk, and Vernon Quinsey, "The Relationship between Testosterone and Aggression: A Meta-Analysis," *Aggression and Violent Behavior* 6 (2001): 579–99; Allan Mazur and Alan Booth, "Testosterone and Dominance in Men," *Behavioral and Brain Sciences* 21 (1998): 353–97; Melissa Hines, *Brain Gender* (New York: Oxford University Press, 2004); Brenda K. Todd, Rico A. Fischer, Steven Di Costa, Amanda Roestorf, Kate Harbour, Paul Hardiman, and John A. Barry, "Sex Differences in Children's Toy Preferences: A Systematic Review, Meta-Regression, and Meta-Analysis," *Infant and Child Development* (2017) [in press]. Retrieved from https://onlinelibrary.wiley.com/doi/full/10.1002/icd.2064.

36. Roy Baumeister, Kathleen Catanese, and Kathleen Vohs, "Is There a Gender Difference in Strength

of Sex Drive? Theoretical Views, Conceptual Distinctions, and a Review of Relevant Evidence," *Personality and Social Psychology Review* 5, no. 3 (2001): 242–73.

37. Diane Halpern, *Sex Differences in Cognitive Abilities*, 4th ed. (New York: Psychology Press, 2012).

38. Diane Halpern, *Sex Differences in Cognitive Abilities*; E. G. Oinonen, Kirsten Mazmanian, and Dwight Mazmanian, "Effects of Oral Contraceptives on Daily Self-Ratings of Positive and Negative Affect," *Journal of Psychosomatic Research* 51 (2001): 647–58.

39. Annette L. Stanton, Marci Lobel, Sharon Sears, and Robyn Stein DeLuca, "Psychosocial Aspects of Selected Issues in Women's Reproductive Health: Current Status and Future Directions," *Journal of Consulting and Clinical Psychology* 70, no. 3 (July 2002): 751–70; Sharon Golub, *Periods: From Menarche to Menopause* (Thousand Oaks, CA: Sage Publishing, 1992).

40. Jessica McFarlane, Carol Martin, and Tannis Williams, "Mood Fluctuations: Women versus Men and Menstrual versus Other Cycles," *Psychology of Women Quarterly* 12 (1988): 201–24; Jessica McFarlane and Tannis Williams, "Placing Premenstrual Syndrome in Perspective," *Psychology of Women Quarterly* 18 (1994): 339–74.

41. Robert Sapolsky, *The Trouble with Testosterone and Other Essays on the Biology of the Human Predicament* (New York: Simon and Schuster, 1997), 154; W. R. Yates, P. J. Perry, J. MacIndoe, T. Holman, and V. Ellingrod, "Psychosexual Effects of Three Doses of Testosterone Cycling in Normal Men," *Biological Psychiatry* 45, no. 3 (February 1, 1999): 254–60; B. Sherwin, "A Comparative Analysis of the Role of Androgen in Human Male and Female Sexual Behavior: Behavioral Specificity, Critical Thresholds, and Sensitivity," *Psychobiology* 16 (1988): 416–25.

42. Anne Fausto-Sterling, *Myths of Gender: Biological Theories about Women and Men* (New York: Basic Books, 1992).

43. Anthony Esgate and David Groome, *An Introduction to Applied Cognitive Psychology* (Hove: Psychology Press, 2004).

44. Melissa Hines, "Sex-Related Variation in Human Behavior and the Brain," *Trends in Cognitive Science* 14, no. 10 (2010): 448–56; YS Zhu and LQ Cai, "Effects of Male Sex Hormones on Gender Identity, Sexual Behavior, and Cognitive Function," *Zhong Nan Da Xue Xue Bao Yi Xue Ban* 31 no. 2 (2006): 149–61; A. N. V. Ruigrok, G. Salimi-Khorshidi, M.-C.

Lai, S. Baron-Cohen, M. V. Lombardo, R. J. Tait, and J. Suckling, "A Meta-Analysis of Sex Differences in Human Brain Structure," *Neuroscience and Biobehavioral Reviews* 3 (2014): 34–50.

45. Diane Halpern, *Sex Differences in Cognitive Abilities*.

46. Ibid.

47. Daphna Joel, Zohar Berman, Ido Tavor, Nadav Wexler, Olga Gaber, Yaniv Stein, Nisan Shefi, Jared Pool, Sebastian Urchs, Daniel S. Margulies, Franziskus Liem, Jürgen Hänggi, Lutz Jäncke, Yaniv Assaf, "Sex Beyond the Genitalia: The Human Brain Mosaic," *Proceedings of the National Academy of Sciences* 112, no. 50 (2015): 15468–73.

48. Ibid.

49. Diane Halpern, *Sex Differences in Cognitive Abilities*; Melissa Hines, *Brain Gender* (New York: Oxford University Press, 2004).

50. Geert J. De Vries, "Sex Differences in Adult and Developing Brains: Compensation, Compensation, Compensation," *Endocrinology* 145, no. 3 (2004): 1063–68; C. Moore, "Maternal Contributions to Mammalian Reproductive Development and the Divergence of Males and Females," *Advances in the Study of Behavior* 24 (1995): 47–118; N. Jaušovec and K. Jaušovec, "Sex Differences in Mental Rotation and Cortical Activation Patterns: Can Training Change Them?" *Intelligence* 40 (2012): 151–62; R. K. Lenroot and J. N. Giedd, "Sex Differences in the Adolescent Brain," *Brain and Cognition* 72, no. 1 (2010): 48–55.

51. Brenda K. Todd, Rico A. Fischer, Steven Di Costa, Amanda Roestorf, Kate Harbour, Paul Hardiman, and John A. Barry, "Sex Differences in Children's Toy Preferences: A Systematic Review, Meta-Regression, and Meta-Analysis," *Infant and Child Development* 27, no. 2 (2018): e2064.

52. Jacques Balthazart, "Minireview: Hormones and Human Sexual Orientation," *Endocrinology* 152, no. 8 (2011): 2937–47; Elke Stefanie Smith, Jessica Junger, Birgit Derntl, and Ute Habel, "The Transsexual Brain—A Review of Findings on the Neural Basis of Transsexualism," *Neuroscience & Biobehavioral Reviews* 59 (2015): 251–66; Baudewijntje P. C. Kreukels and Peggy T Cohen-Kettenis, "Male Gender Identity and Masculine Behavior: The Role of Sex Hormones in Brain Development," in *Hormonal Therapy for Male Sexual Dysfunction*, ed. Mario Maggi (Oxford: John Wiley & Sons, 2012); Ai-Min Bao and Dick F. Swaab, "Sexual Differentiation of the Human Brain: Relation to Gender Identity, Sexual Orienta-

tion and Neuropsychiatric Disorders," *Frontiers in Neuroendocrinology* 32, no. 2 (2011): 214–26; Jacque Balthazart, "Brain Development and Sexual Orientation," *Colloquium Series on the Developing Brain* 3, no. 2 (2012): 1–134; Alicia Garcia-Flagueras and Dick F. Swaab, "Sexual Hormones and the Brain: An Essential Alliance for Sexual Identity and Sexual Orientation," in *Pediatric Neuroendocrinology*, ed. Sandro Loche, Marco Cappa, Lucia Ghizzoni, Mohamad Maghnie, Martin O. Savage (Basel, Switzerland: Karger, 2010), 22–35; Simon LeVay, *Gay, Straight, and the Reason Why: The Science of Sexual Orientation* (New York: Oxford University Press, 2011, 2017); Annelou L. C. de Vries, Baudewijntje P.C. Kreukels, Thomas D. Steensma, and Jenifer K. McGuire, "Gender Identity Development: A Biopsychosocial Perspective," in *Gender Dysphoria and Disorders of Sex Development: Progress in Care and Knowledge*, ed. Baudewijntje P. C. Kreukels, Thomas D. Steensma, and Annelou L. C. de Vries (New York: Springer, 2014).

53. David H. Uttal, Nathaniel G. Meadow, Elizabeth Tipton, Linda L. Hand, Alison R. Alden, and Christopher Warren, "The Malleability of Spatial Skills: A Meta-Analysis of Training Studies," *Psychological Bulletin* 139, no. 2 (2013): 352–402.

54. Melissa S. Terlecki, Nora S. Newcombe, and Michelle Little, "Durable and Generalized Effects of Spatial Experience on Mental Rotation: Gender Differences in Growth Patterns," *Applied Cognitive Psychology* 22 (2007): 996–1013.

55. Jing Feng, Ian Spence, and Jay Pratt, "Playing an Action Video Game Reduces Gender Differences in Spatial Cognition," *Psychological Science* 18 (2007): 850–55.

56. Richard De Lisi and Jennifer Wolford, "Improving Children's Mental Rotation Accuracy with Computer Game Playing," *The Journal of Genetic Psychology* 163, no. 3 (2002): 272–82.

57. Isabelle D. Cherney, Kavita Jagarlamudi, Erika Lawrence, and Nicole Shimabuku, "Experiential Factors on Sex Differences in Mental Rotation," *Perceptual and Motor Skills* 96 (July 2003): 1062–70.

58. For a summary, see Isabelle D. Cherney, "Mom, Let Me Play More Computer Games: They Improve My Mental Rotation Skills," *Sex Roles* 59 (2008): 776–86.

59. Nora Newcombe, "Science Seriously: Straight Thinking about Spatial Sex Differences," in *Why Aren't More Women in Science? Top Researchers Debate the Evidence*, ed. Stephen Ceci and Wendy Williams (Washington, DC: American Psychological Association, 2007).

60. Lise Eliot, *Pink Brain, Blue Brain* (New York: Houghton Mifflin Harcourt Publishing Company, 2009); I. D. Cherney and K. L. London, "Gender-Linked Differences in the Toys, Television Shows, Computer Games, and Outdoor Activities of 5- to 13-Year-Old Children," *Sex Roles* 54 (2006): 717–26; Joanne Kersh, Beth M. Casey, and Jessica Mercer Young, "Research on Spatial Skills and Block Building in Girls and Boys: The Relationship to Later Mathematics Learning," in *Mathematics, Science and Technology in Early Childhood Education: Contemporary Perspectives on Mathematics in Early Childhood Education*, ed. B. Spodak and O. N. Saracho (Charlotte, NC: Information Age, 2008), 233–53.

61. S. C. Levine, M. Vasilyeva, S. F. Lourenco, N. S. Newcombe, and J. Huttenlocher, "Socioeconomic Status Modifies the Sex Difference in Spatial Skill," *Psychological Science* 16, no. 11 (November 2005): 841–45; K. G. Noble, M. F. Norman, and M. J. Farah, "Neurocognitive Correlates of Socioeconomic Status in Kindergarten Children." *Developmental Science* 8 (2005): 74–87.

62. Maryann Baenninger and Nora Newcombe, "Environmental Input to the Development of Sex-Related Differences in Spatial and Mathematical Ability," *Learning and Individual Differences* 7, no. 4 (1995): 363–79.

63. Lise Eliot, *Pink Brain, Blue Brain* (New York: Houghton Mifflin Harcourt Publishing Company, 2009).

64. Mark Pagel, *Wired for Culture: Originas of the Human Social Mind* (New York: W. W. Norton and Company, 2012); Joseph Henrich and Rich McElreath, "The Evolution of Cultural Evolution," *Evolutionary Anthropology* 12, no. 3 (2003): 123–35.

65. "About, Book Reviews, News Mentions and Foreign Editions," Retrieved from www.cordeliafine.com /general-information.html.

66. Frank Browning, *The Fate of Gender: Nature, Nurture and the Human Future* (New York: Bloomsbury Publishing, 2016); Anne Fausto-Sterling, Cynthia Garcia Coll, and Meghan Lamarre, "Sexing the Baby: Part 2—Applying Dynamic Systems Theory to the Emergences of Sex-Related Differences in Infants and Toddlers," *Social Science & Medicine* 74, no. 11 (2012): 1693–17; Anne Fausto-Sterling, "The Bare Bones of Sex: Part I—Sex and Gender," *Signs* 30, no. 2 (2005): 1510.

67. Described in Michael J. Meaney, "The Nature of Nurture: Maternal Effects and Chromatin Remodelling," in *Essays in Social Neuroscience*, ed. John T. Cacioppo and Gary G. Berntson (Cambridge: Massachusetts Institute of Technology Press, 2004).

68. Judith Lorber, *Paradoxes of Gender* (New Haven: Yale University Press, 1993), x.

69. Charlie Lovett, *Olympic Marathon: A Centennial History of the Games' Most Storied Race* (Westport, CT: Praeger Publishers, 1997).

70. Diane Halpern, *Sex Differences in Cognitive Abilities*, 4th ed. (New York: Psychology Press, 2012); Rebecca Jordan-Young, *Brain Storm: The Flaws in the Science of Sex Differences* (Cambridge: Harvard University Press, 2010).

71. Richard J. Haier, Sherif Karama, Leonard Leyba, and Rex E Jung, "MRI Assessment of Cortical Thickness and Functional Activity Changes in Adolescent Girls Following Three Months of Practice on a Visual-Spatial Task," *BioMed Central Research Notes* 2 (2009): 174.

72. Norbert Jaušovec and Ksenija Jaušovec, "Sex Differences in Mental Rotation and Cortical Activation Patterns: Can Training Change Them?" *Intelligence* 40, no. 2 (2012): 151–62.

73. M. Taubert, B. Draganski, A. Anwander, K. Müller, A. Horstmann, A. Villringer, and P. Ragert, "Dynamic Properties of Human Brain Structure: Learning-Related Changes in Cortical Areas and Associated Fiber Connections," *The Journal of Neuroscience* 30, no. 35 (September 1, 2010): 11670–77.

74. Sari M. van Anders and Neil V. Watson, "Social Neuroendocrinology: Effects of Social Contexts and Behaviors on Sex Steroids in Humans," *Human Nature* 17, no. 2 (2006): 212–37; Rui F. Oliveira, "Social Behavior in Context: Hormonal Modulation of Behavioral Plasticity and Social Competence," *Integrative and Comparative Biology*, 49, no. 4 (2009): 423–40.

75. David Edwards, "Competition and Testosterone," *Hormones and Behavior* 50 (2006): 682; L. van der Meij, A. P. Buunk, J. P. van de Sande, and A. Salvador, "The Presence of a Woman Increases Testosterone in Aggressive Dominant Men," *Hormones and Behavior* 54, no. 5 (November 2008): 640–44; Alicia Salvador, "Coping with Competitive Situations in Humans," *Neuroscience and Biobehavioral Reviews* 29, no.1 (2005): 195–205.

76. Allan Mazur, Elizabeth Susman, and Sandy Edelbrock, "Sex Difference in Testosterone Response to a Video Game Contest," *Evolution and Human Behavior* 18, no. 5 (1997): 317–26; Richard E. Nisbett and Dov Cohen, *Culture of Honor: The Psychology of Violence in the South* (Boulder, CO: Westview, 1996); A. Booth, G. Shelley, A. Mazur, g. Tharp, and R. Kittok, "Testosterone, and Winning and Losing in Human Competition," *Hormones and Behavior* 23, no. 4 (December 1989): 556–71; A. Booth, D. R. Johnson, and D. A. Granger, "Testosterone and Men's Depression: The Role of Social Behavior," *Journal of Health and Social Behavior* 40 (1999): 130–40; Robert Sapolsky, *The Trouble with Testosterone and Other Essays on the Biology of the Human Predicament* (New York: Simon and Schuster, 1997).

77. Allan Mazur, Alan Booth, and James Dabbs, Jr., "Testosterone and Chess Competition," *Social Psychology Quarterly* 55, no. 1 (1992): 70–77.

78. P. C. Bernhardt, J. M. Dabbs Jr., J. A. Fielden, and C. D. Lutter, "Testosterone Changes during Vicarious Experiences of Winning and Losing among Fans at Sporting Events," *Physiology and Behavior* 65, no. 1 (1998): 59–62.

79. Gad Saad and John Vongas, "The Effect of Conspicuous Consumption on Men's Testosterone Levels," *Organizational Behavior and Human Decision Processes* 110, no. 2 (2009): 80–92.

80. Steven J. Stanton, Jacinta C. Beehner, Ekjyot K. Saini, Cynthia M. Kuhn, and Kevin S. LaBar, "Dominance, Politics, and Physiology: Voters' Testosterone Changes on the Night of the 2008 United States Presidential Election," *PLoS ONE* 4, no. 10 (2009): 7543.

81. Cordelia Fine, *Testosterone Rex: Myths of Sex, Science, and Society* (New York: W. W. Norton and Company, 2017).

82. Sari M. van Anders, Jeffrey Steiger, and Katherine L. Goldey, "Effects of Gendered Behavior on Testosterone in Women and Men," *PNAS* 112, no. 45 (2015): 13805–10.

83. National Science Foundation, "Men Also Wired for Childcare," *National Science Foundation*, September 13, 2011. Retrieved from www.nsf.gov/news/news_summ.jsp?cntn_id=121658; Allan Mazur and Joel Michalek, "Marriage, Divorce, and Male Testosterone," *Social Forces* 77, no. 1 (1998): 315–30; Lee T. Gettler, Thomas W. McDade, Alan B. Feranil, and Christopher W. Kuzawa, "Longitudinal Evidence that Fatherhood Decreases Testosterone in Human Males," *Proceedings of the National Academy of Sciences* 108, no. 39 (2011): 16194–99.

84. C. W. Kuzawa, L. T. Gettler, M. N. Muller, T. W. McDade, and A. B. Feranil, "Fatherhood, Pairbond-

ing, and Testosterone in the Philippines," *Hormones and Behavior* 56, no. 4 (October 2009): 429–35; Lee T. Gettler, Thomas W. McDade, Alan B. Feranil, and Christopher W. Kuzawa, "Longitudinal Evidence that Fatherhood Decreases Testosterone in Human Males," *Proceedings of the National Academy of Sciences* 108, no. 39 (2011): 16194–99; S. M. van Anders, R. M. Tolman, and B. L. Volling, "Baby Cries and Nurturance Affect Testosterone in Men," *Hormonal Behavior* 61, no. 1 (2012): 31–36.

85. Martin N. Muller, Frank W. Marlowe, Revocatus Bugumba, and Peter T. Ellison, "Testosterone and Paternal Care in East African Foragers and Pastoralists," *Proceedings of the Royal Society B: Biological Sciences* 276, no. 1655 (January 22, 2009): 347–54.

86. Rebecca Jordan-Young, *Brain Storm: The Flaws in the Science of Sex Differences* (Cambridge: Harvard University Press, 2010), 271; Michael Meaney, "Nature, Nurture, and the Disunity of Knowledge," *Annals New York Academy of Sciences* 935 (2001): 50–61; Alissa J. Mrazek, Joan Y. Chiao, Katherine D. Blizinksy, Janetta Lun, and Michele J. Gelfand, "The Role of Culture–Gene Coevolution in Morality Judgment: Examining the Interplay between Tightness–Looseness and Allelic Variation of the Serotonin Transporter Gene, *Culture and Brain* 1, no. 2–4 (2013): 100–117; Helga Nowotny and Giuseppe Testa, *Naked Genes: Reinventing the Human in the Molecular Age*, (Cambridge, Massachusetts Institute of Technology Press: 2010).

87. Genetic Science Learning Center, "Insights from Identical Twins," *Learn.Genetics*, January 5, 2014. Retrieved from http://learn.genetics.utah.edu/content/epigenetics/twins/.

88. Kristen Jacobson, "Considering Interactions between Genes, Environments, Biology, and Social Context," *Science Briefs*, American Psychological Association, April 2009. Retrieved from www.apa.org/science/about/psa/2009/04/sci-brief.aspx.

89. R. J. Cadoret, W. R. Yates, and E. Troughton, "Genetic-Environmental Interaction in the Genesis of Aggressivity and Conduct Disorders," *Archives of General Psychiatry* 52 (1995): 916–24.

90. Cynthia Fuchs Epstein, *Deceptive Distinctions: Sex, Gender, and the Social Order* (New Haven: Yale University Press, 1988).

91. Gilbert Herdt, ed., *Third Sex, Third Gender: Beyond Sexual Dimorphism in Culture and History* (New York: Zone Books [distributed by Massachusetts Institute of Technology Press], 1994).

92. Phys.org., "Annual Bone Fracture Rate Almost 4 Percent and Double Previous Estimates," *Phys.org*, January 17, 2008. Retrieved from http://phys.org/news119786629.html.

93. Rebecca Jordan-Young, *Brain Storm: The Flaws in the Science of Sex Differences* (Cambridge: Harvard University Press, 2010), 285.

94. Anne Fausto-Sterling, "The Bare Bones of Sex: Part I—Sex and Gender," *Signs* 30, no. 2 (2005).

95. Gloria Anzaldua, *Borderlands/La Frontera: The New Mestiza* (San Francisco: Aunt Lute Books, 1987); Kimberlé W. Crenshaw, "Mapping the Margins: Intersectionality, Identity Politics, and Violence against Women of Color," *Stanford Law Review* 43, no. 6 (1991): 1241–99; Patricia Hill Collins, *Black Feminist Thought: Knowledge, Consciousness, and the Politics of Empowerment* (New York: Routledge, 1991).

96. David Riches, "Hunting and Gathering Societies," in *Encyclopedia of Social and Cultural Anthropology*, 2nd ed., ed. Alan Barnard and Jonathan Spencer (New York: Routledge, 2009).

97. Cara M. Wall-Scheffler, "Energetics, Locomotion, and Female Reproduction: Implications for Human Evolution," *Annual Review of Anthropology* 41, no. 1 (2012): 71–85.

98. V. Spike Peterson, "Sex Matters: A Queer History of Hierarchies," *International Feminist Journal of Politics* 16, no. 3–3 (2014): 389–409. Scholars also think that Christians of the fourth and fifth century shared this view of women as more carnal and sexually insatiable, but viewed this as diabolic. See Sheila Briggs, "Women and Religion," in Beth H. Hess and Myra Marx Ferree, *Analyzing Gender* (Thousand Oaks, CA: Sage Publishing, 1987), 408–41.

99. R. C. Kirkpatrick, "The Evolution of Human Homosexual Behavior," *Current Anthropology* 41, no. 3 (2000): 385–413.

100. Gilbert Herdt, ed., *Third Sex, Third Gender: Beyond Sexual Dimorphism in Culture and History* (New York: Zone Books [distributed by Massachusetts Institute of Technology Press], 1994).

101. R. C. Kirkpatrick, "The Evolution of Human Homosexual Behavior," *Current Anthropology* 41, no. 3 (2000): 385–413; Frans de Waal, *Chimpanzee Politics: Power and Sex among Apes* (New York: Harper and Row, 2007).

102. Cordelia Fine, *Testosterone Rex: Myths of Sex, Science, and Society* (New York: W. W. Norton and Company, 2017).

103. Ibid.

104. Oyeronke Oyewumi, *What Gender Is Motherhood? Changing Yoruba Ideals of Power, Procreation, and Identity in the Age of Modernity* (New York, Palgrave Macmillan: 2016).

105. Peterson, 392, refers to these as "heterarchies" rather than hierarchies. See also J. E. Levy, "Gender, Heterarchy, and Hierarchy," in *Handbook of Gender in Archaeology*, ed. S. M. Nelson (Lanham, MD: AltaMira, 2006), 219–46.

106. Christine W. Gailey, "Evolutionary Perspectives on Gender Hierarchy," in *Analyzing Gender*, ed. Beth H. Hess and Myra Marx Ferree (Thousand Oaks, CA: Sage Publishing, 1987), 32–67; and Peterson op cit.

107. H. L. Mencken, "The Divine Afflatus," *New York Evening Mail*, November 16, 1917.

108. Edward O. Wilson, "On Human Nature," in. *The Biology and Psychology of Moral Agency*, ed. William Andrew Rottschaefer (Cambridge: Cambridge University Press, 1998), 58.

Chapter 4: Performances

1. U.S. Department of Education, National Center for Education Statistics, "Digest of Education Statistics: Table 318.30: Bachelor's, master's, and doctor's degrees conferred by postsecondary institutions, by sex of student and discipline division: 2014–15," January 2017. Retrieved from https://nces.ed.gov/programs/digest/d16/tables/dt16_318.30.asp?current=yes.

2. Rose A. Woods, "Spotlight on Statistics: Sports and Exercise," U.S. Bureau of Labor Statistics, May 2017. Retrieved from www.bls.gov/spotlight/2017/sports-and-exercise/pdf/sports-and-exercise.pdf.

3. Pew Research Center, "The Gender Gap in Religion Around the World," March 22, 2016. Retrieved from www.pewforum.org/2016/03/22/the-gender-gap-in-religion-around-the-world/.

4. Michael Kimmel, *The Gendered Society* (New York: Oxford University Press, 2004), 94.

5. Sandra L. Bem, *The Lenses of Gender: Transforming the Debate on Sexual Inequality* (New Haven: Yale University Press, 1993), 149.

6. Jessica Rose, Susan Mackey-Kallis, Len Shyles, Kelly Barry, Danielle Biagini, Colleen Hart, and Lauren Jack, "Face It: The Impact of Gender on Social Media Images," *Communication Quarterly* 60, no. 5 (2012): 588–607; Mike Thelwall and Farida Vis, "Gender and Image Sharing on Facebook, Twitter, Instagram, Snapchat and WhatsApp in the UK: Hobbying Alone or Filtering for Friends?" *Aslib Journal of Information Management* 69 no. 6 (2017): 702–20; Richard Joiner, Caroline Stewart, Chelsey Beaney, Amy Moon, Pam Maras, Jane Guiller, Helen Gregory, Jeff Gavin, John Cromby, and Mark Brosnan, "Publically Different, Privately the Same: Gender Differences and Similarities in Response to Facebook Status Updates," *Computers in Human Behavior* 39: 165–69; Sigal Tiffert and Iris Vilnai-Yavetz, "Gender Differences in Facebook Self-Presentation: An International Randomized Study," *Computers in Human Behavior* 35 (2014): 388–99; F. Rangel, I. Hernandez, P. Rosso, and A. Reyes, "Emotions and Irony per Gender in Facebook," in *Proceedings of the Workshop on Emotion, Social Signals, Sentiment & Linked Open Data*, 68–73. Reykjavik, Iceland, May 26–31, 2014; P. Lauren, H. Kuo, Y. Chiu, and S. Chang, "Social Support on Facebook: The Influence of Tie Strength and Gender Differences, *International Journal of Electronic Commerce Studies* 6, no.1 (2015): 37–50.

7. L. Susan Williams, "Trying on Gender, Gender Regimes, and the Process of Becoming Women," *Gender & Society* 16, no. 1 (2002): 29–52.

8. Miki Nakai, "Social Stratification and Consumption Patterns: Cultural Practices and Lifestyles in Japan," in *New Perspectives in Statistical Modeling and Data Analysis: Studies in Classification, Data Analysis, and Knowledge Organization*, ed. S. Ingrassia, R. Rocci, and M. Vichi (Berlin, Heidelberg: Springer, 2011), 211–18

9. Margo DeMello, *Encyclopedia of Body Adornment* (Westport, CT: Greenwood Press, 2007).

10. Amy Wilkins, *Wannabes, Goths, and Christians: The Boundaries of Sex, Style, and Status* (Chicago: University of Chicago Press, 2008), 35.

11. Carla Pfeffer, *Queering Families: The Postmodern Partnerships of Cisgender Women and Transgender Men* (New York: Oxford University Press, 2017), 55.

12. For a review, see Carol Martin and Diane Ruble, "Children's Search for Gender Cues," *Current Directions in Psychological Science* 13, no. 2 (2004): 69.

13. Joan Roughgarden, *Evolution's Rainbow: Diversity, Gender and Sexuality in Nature and People* (Berkeley: University of California Press, 2004), 27.

14. Emily Kane, *The Gender Trap* (New York: New York University Press, 2012).

15. Elizabeth Sweet, "Toys Are More Divided by Gender Now than They Were 50 Years Ago," *The Atlantic*, December 9, 2014. Retrieved from www.theatlantic.com/business/archive/2014/12/toys

-are-more-divided-by-gender-now-than-they-were
-50-years-ago/383556/; Carol J. Auster and Claire S. Mansbach, "The Gender Marketing of Toys: An Analysis of Color and Type of Toy on the Disney Store Website," *Sex Roles* 67, no. 7–8 (2012): 375–88.

16. Michael Messner, "Barbie Girls versus Sea Monsters: Children Constructing Gender," *Gender and Society* 14, no. 6 (2000): 765–84; Barrie Thorne, *Gender Play* (New Brunswick, NJ: Rutgers, 1995).

17. Melanie Koss, "Diversity in Contemporary Picturebooks: A Content Analysis," *Journal of Children's Literature* 41, no. 1 (2015): 32–42; Isabella Steyer, "Gender Representations in Children's Media and Their Influence," *Campus-Wide Information Systems* 31, no. 2/3 (2014): 171–80; Sarah K. Murnen, Claire Greenfield, Abigail Younger, Hope Boyd, "Boys Act and Girls Appear: A Content Analysis of Gender Stereotypes Associated with Characters in Children's Popular Culture," *Sex Roles* 74 (2016): 78–91.

18. Carol Martin and Diane Ruble, "Children's Search for Gender Cues." *Current Directions in Psychological Science* 13, no. 2 (4002): 67.

19. Ibid., 67.

20. David F. Bjorklund, *Children's Thinking: Developmental Function and Individual Differences* (Belmont, CA: Wadsworth, 2000); B. Martin, *Children at Play: Learning Gender in the Early Years* (Stoke-on-Trent Sterling, VA: Trentham Books, 2011).

21. Carol Martin and Diane Ruble, "Children's Search for Gender Cues." *Current Directions in Psychological Science* 13, no. 2 (4002): 67–70.

22. Hanns M. Trautner, Diane N. Ruble, Lisa Cyphers, Barbara Kirsten, Regina Behrendt, and Petra Hartmann, "Rigidity and Flexibility of Gender Stereotypes in Childhood: Developmental or Differential?" *Infant and Child Development* 14, no. 4 (October 26, 2005): 365–81.

23. Emily Kane, *The Gender Trap* (New York: New York University Press, 2012).

24. Ibid, 2.

25. Lauren Spinner, Lindsey Cameron, and Rachel Calogero, "Peer Toy Play as a Gateway to Children's Gender Flexibility: The Effect of (Counter)Stereotypic Portrayals of Peers in Children's Magazines," *Sex Roles* (2018). Retrieved from https://link.springer.com/article/10.1007/s11199-017-0883-3.

26. Cecilia L. Ridgeway, *Framed by Gender: How Gender Inequality Persists in the Modern World* (New York: Oxford University Press, 2011).

27. Evan Urquhart, "Why I'm Still a Butch Lesbian," *Slate*, July 25, 2014. Retrieved from www.slate.com/blogs/outward/2014/07/25/a_butch_lesbian_rejects_a_non_binary_identity.html.

28. Martin Weinberg and Colin Williams, "Fecal Matters: Habitus, Embodiments, and Deviance," *Social Problems* 52, no. 3 (2005): 315–36.

29. Kate Handley, "The Unbearable Daintiness of Women Who Eat with Men," *Sociological Images*, December 27, 2015. Retrieved from www.thesocietypages.org/socimages/2015/12/27/the-unbearable-daintiness-of-women-who-eat-with-men/.

30. U.S. Department of Justice, Federal Bureau of Investigation, "Hate Crime Statistics, 2016," Table 1: Incidents, Offenses, Victims, and Known Offenders. Retrieved from https://ucr.fbi.gov/hate-crime/2016/tables/table-1.

31. Laurel Westbrook and Kristin Schilt, "Doing Gender, Determining Gender: Transgender People, Gender Panics, and the Maintenance of the Sex/Gender/Sexuality System," *Gender & Society* 28 no. 1, (2014): 32–57; Kristen Schilt and Laurel Westbrook, "Doing Gender, Doing Heteronormativity: 'Gender Normals,' Transgender People, and the Social Maintenance of Heterosexuality, " *Gender & Society* 23, no. 4 (2009): 440–64; Betsy Lucal, "What It Means to Be Gendered Me: Life on the Boundaries of a Dichotomous Gender System," *Gender & Society* 13, no. 6 (1999): 781–97.

32. Cecilia L. Ridgeway, *Framed by Gender: How Gender Inequality Persists in the Modern World* (New York: Oxford University Press, 2011).

33. Betsy Lucal, "What It Means to Be Gendered Me: Life on the Boundaries of a Dichotomous Gender System," *Gender & Society* 13, no. 6 (1999): 781–97.

Chapter 5: Intersections

1. Fem Korsten, "Grappling with My Sexuality Now That I'm in a Wheelchair," *xoJane UK* (blog), September 19, 2012. Retrieved from www.xojane.co.uk/issues/disability-sexuality-street-harassment.

2. Henri Tajfel, *Human Groups and Social Categories: Studies in Social Psychology* (Cambridge: Cambridge University Press, 1981); Peggy A. Thoits and Lauren K. Virshup, "Me's and We's: Forms and Functions of Social Identities," in *Self and Identity: Fundamental Issues*, ed. R. D. Ashmore and L. Jussim (New York: Oxford University Press, 1997), 106–33.

3. Gloria Anzaldua, *Borderlands/La Frontera: The New Mestiza* (San Francisco: Aunt Lute Books, 1987); Kimberlé W. Crenshaw, "Mapping the Margins: Intersectionality, Identity Politics, and Violence against Women of Color," *Stanford Law Review* 43, no. 6

(1991): 1241–99; Patricia Hill Collins, *Black Feminist Thought: Knowledge, Consciousness, and the Politics of Empowerment* (New York: Routledge, 1991).

4. Arlie Hochschild, *The Second Shift* (New York: Viking, 1989).

5. Arlie Hochschild, "Giving at the Office," in *Men and Masculinity: A Text-Reader*, ed. Theodore Cohen (Belmont, CA: Wadsworth, 2001).

6. Ibid.

7. Arlie Hochschild, *The Second Shift* (New York: Viking, 1989); Kathleen Gerson, *No Man's Land: Men's Changing Commitments to Family and Work* (New York: Basic Books, 1993); Theodore Cohen and John Durst, "Leaving Work and Staying Home: The Impact on Men of Terminating the Male Economic-Provider Role," in *Men and Masculinity: A Text-Reader*, ed. Theodore Cohen (Belmont, CA: Wadsworth, 2001), 302–19; Kathleen Gerson, *The Unfinished Revolution: Coming of Age in a New Era of Gender, Work, and Family* (New York: Oxford University Press, 2010); Kathleen Gerson, *Hard Choices: How Women Decide About Work, Career and Motherhood* (Berkeley: University of California Press, 1986).

8. Jane Collins and Victoria Mayer, *With Both Hands Tied: Welfare Reform and the Race to the Bottom in the Low-Wage Labor Market* (Chicago: University of Chicago Press, 2010).

9. Scott Coltrane, *Family Man: Fatherhood, Housework, and Gender Equity* (New York: Oxford University Press, 1996).

10. Ibid., 140.

11. Carla Shows and Naomi Gerstel, "Fathering, Class, and Gender: A Comparison of Physicians and EMTs," *Gender & Society* 23, no. 2 (2009): 161–87.

12. Ibid., 179.

13. Karen D. Pyke, "Class-Based Masculinities: The Interdependence of Gender, Class, and Interpersonal Power," *Gender & Society* 10, no. 5 (1996): 531.

14. Kris Paap, *Working Construction: Why White Working-Class Men Put Themselves—and the Labor Movement—in Harm's Way* (Ithaca and London: IRL Press, 2006),

15. Ibid., 137.

16. Jo Little, *Gender and Rural Geography: Identity, Sexuality and Power in the Countryside* (London: Pearson, 2002); Jo Little and Ruth Panelli, "Gender Research in Rural Geography," *Gender, Place, and Culture* 10, no. 3 (2003): 281–89; Emily Kazyak, "Midwest or Lesbian? Gender, Rurality, and Sexuality," *Gender & Society* 26, no. 6 (2012): 825–48; Barbara Pini, "Farm Women: Driving Tractors and Negotiating Gender," *International Journal of Sociology of Agriculture and Food* 13, no. 1 (2005) 1–18.

17. Emily Kazyak, "Midwest or Lesbian? Gender, Rurality, and Sexuality," *Gender & Society* 26, no. 6 (2012): 837.

18. Ibid., 837.

19. Tara Bahrampour, "They Considered Themselves White, but DNA Tests Told a More Complex Story," *Washington Post*, Feb. 6, 2018. Retrieved from www.washingtonpost.com/local/social-issues/they-considered-themselves-white-but-dna-tests-told-a-more-complex-story/2018/02/06/16215d1a-e181-11e7-8679-a9728984779c_story.html?utm_term=.40290f873f57; Ryan Brown and George Armelagos, "Apportionment of Racial Diversity: A Review," *Evolutionary Anthropology* 10 (2001): 34–40; Luigi Cavalli-Sforza, Paolo Menozzi, and Alberto Piazza, *The History and Geography of Human Genes* (Princeton: Princeton University Press, 2004); Lynn Jorde, "Genetic Variation and Human Evolution," 2003, Retrieved February 21, 2017, from www.ashg.org/education/pdf/geneticvariation.pdf; L. B. Jorde, W. S. Watkins, M. J. Bamshad, M. E. Dixon, C. E. Ricker, M. T. Seielstad, and M. A. Batzer, "The Distribution of Human Genetic Diversity: A Comparison of Mitochondrial, Autosomal, and Y-Chromosome Data," *American Journal of Human Genetics* 66 (2000): 979–88; Richard Lewontin, "Race and Genomics," 2006, Retrieved January 29, 2017, from http://raceandgenomics.ssrc.org/Lewontin/; David Serre and Svante Pääbo, "Evidence for Gradients of Human Genetic Diversity Within and Among Continents," *Genome Research* 14, no. 9 (2004): 1679–85; Dalton Conley and Jason Fletcher, *The Genome Factor: What the Social Genomics Revolution Reveals about Ourselves, Our History, and the Future* (Princeton: Princeton University Press, 2017).

20. Joane Nagel, *Race, Ethnicity, and Sexuality: Intimate Intersections, Forbidden Frontiers* (New York: Oxford University Press, 2003).

21. Ibid.

22. Yolanda F. Niemann, Leilani Jennings, Richard M. Rozelle, James C. Baxter, and Elroy Sullivan, "Use of Free Responses and Cluster Analysis to Determine Stereotypes of Eight Groups," *Personality and Social Psychology Bulletin* 20 (1994): 379–90; John Wilson, Kurt Hugenberg, and Nicholas Rule, "Racial Bias in Judgments of Physical Size and Formidability: From Size to Threat," *Journal of Personality and Social Psychology*, published online March 13, 2017.

23. Adam D. Galinsky, Erika V. Hall, and Amy J. C. Cuddy. "Gendered Races: Implications for Interracial Marriage, Leadership Selection, and Athletic Participation." *Psychological Science*, 24, no. 4 (2013): 498–506.

24. Ann Ferguson, *Bad Boys: Public Schools in the Making of Black Masculinity* (Ann Arbor: University of Michigan Press, 2001).

25. Ibid.

26. U.S. Department of Education Office for Civil Rights, "Civil Rights Data Collection: Data Snapshot (School Discipline)," Issue Brief #1, March 21, 2014. Retrieved from https://ocrdata.ed.gov/Downloads /CRDC-School-Discipline-Snapshot.pdf.

27. Dawn Dow, "The Deadly Challenges of Raising African American Boys: Navigating the Controlling Image of the 'Thug,'" *Gender & Society*, 30, no. 2 (2016): 161–88.

28. Ibid., 180.

29. Ibid., 87; Joe R. Feagin, "The Continuing Significance of Race: Antiblack Discrimination in Public Places," in *Rethinking the Color Line: Readings in Race and Ethnicity*, ed. Charles A. Gallagher (New York: McGraw Hill, 1999).

30. Rashawn Ray, "Black People Don't Exercise in My Neighborhood: Perceived Racial Composition and Leisure-Time Physical Activity among Middle Class Blacks and Whites," *Social Science Research* 66 (2017): 42–57.

31. Brent Staples, "Just Walk on By: A Black Man Ponders His Power to Alter Public Space," in *Reconstructing Gender: A Multicultural Anthology*, ed. Estelle Disch (New York: McGraw Hill, 1997), 168.

32. Odis Johnson, Jr., Keon Gilbert, and Habiba Ibrahim, "Race, Gender, and the Contexts of Unarmed Fatal Interactions with Police," Fatal Interactions with Police (FIPS) research project. Retrieved from https://cpb-us-west-2-juc1ugur1qwqqqo4.stackpath dns.com/sites.wustl.edu/dist/b/1205/files/2018/02 /Race-Gender-and-Unarmed-1y6zo9a.pdf; Ryan Gabrielson, Eric Sagara, and Ryan Grochowski Jones, "Deadly Force, in Black and White: A ProPublica Analysis of Killings by Police Shows Outsize Rise for Young Black Males," *ProPublica*, October 10, 2014. Retrieved from www.propublica.org/article/deadly -force-in-black-and-white; Dara Lind, "The FBI Is Trying to Get Better Data on Police Killings. Here's What We Know Now," *Vox*, April 10, 2015. Retrieved from www.vox.com/2014/8/21/6051043/how-many -people-killed-police-statistics-homicide-official-black; Todd Beer, "Police Killing of Blacks: Data for 2015,

2016, 2017," *Sociology Toolbox*, January 30, 2016. Retrieved from https://thesocietypages.org/toolbox /police-killing-of-blacks/; E. Ashby Plant, Joanna Goplen, and Jonathan W. Kunstman, "Selective Responses to Threat: The Roles of Race and Gender in Decisions to Shoot," *Personality and Social Psychology Bulletin* 37, no. 9 (2011): 1274–81; Lance Hannon, "Race, Victim Precipitated Homicide, and the Subculture of Violence Thesis," *The Social Science Journal* 41, no. 1 (2004): 115–21.

33. German Lopez, "This Chart Explains Why Black People Fear Being Killed by the Police," *Vox*, July 29, 2015. Retrieved from www.vox.com/2015/4 /10/8382457/police-shootings-racism.

34. Evelynn M. Hammonds, "Toward a Genealogy of Black Female Sexuality: The Problematic of Silence," in *Feminist Genealogies, Colonial Legacies, Democratic Futures*, ed. M. Jacqui Alexander and Chandra Talpade Mohanty (New York: Routledge, 1997), 170–82; Siobhan Somerville, *Queering the Color Line: Race and the Invention of Homosexuality in American Culture* (Durham: Duke University Press, 2000); Patricia Hill Collins, *Black Sexual Politics: African Americans, Gender, and the New Racism* (New York: Routledge, 2004); Deborah Gray White, *Ar'n't I a Woman? Female Slaves in the Plantation South* (New York: W. W. Norton and Company, 1985); Robert Fogel, *Without Consent or Contract: The Rise and Fall of American Slavery* (New York: W. W. Norton and Company, 1989); Evelyn Brooks Higginbotham, "African American Women's History and the Metalanguage of Race" *Signs* 17, no. 2 (1992): 251–74.

35. Evelyn Brooks Higginbotham, "African American Women's History and the Metalanguage of Race" *Signs* 17, no. 2 (1992): 251–74.

36. Drucilla Cornell, "Las Grenudas: Recollections on Consciousness-Raising," *Signs* 25, no. 4 (2000): 1033–39; Patricia Hill Collins, *Black Sexual Politics: African Americans, Gender, and the New Racism* (New York: Routledge, 2004); Charisse Jones and Kumea Shorter-Gooden, *Shifting: The Double Lives of Black Women in America* (New York: HarperCollins Publishers, Inc., 2003).

37. Tamara Beauboeuf-Lafontant, *Behind the Mask of the Strong Black Woman: Voice and the Embodiment of a Costly Performance* (Philadelphia: Temple University Press, 2009); Patricia Hill Collins, *Black Sexual Politics: African Americans, Gender, and the New Racism* (New York: Routledge, 2004); bell hooks, *Ain't I a Woman: Black Women and Feminism* (New York: Routledge, 2015).

38. Bonnie Thornton Dill, "The Dialectics of Black Womanhood," *Signs* 4, no. 3 (1979): 543–55; Gregory S. Parks, Shayne E. Jones, Rashawn Ray, Matthew W. Hughey, and Jonathan M. Cox, "White Boys Drink, Black Girls Yell? A Racialized and Gendered Analysis of Violent Hazing and the Law," *The Journal of Gender, Race, and Justice* 18 (2015): 97–168.

39. John F. Dovidio, "Under the Radar: How Unexamined Biases in Decision-Making Processes in Clinical Interactions Can Contribute to Health Care Disparities," *American Journal of Public Health* 102, no. 5 (2012): 945–52; Elizabeth N. Chapman, Anna Kaatz, and Molly Carnes, "Physicians and Implicit Bias: How Doctors May Unwittingly Perpetuate Health Care Disparities," *Journal of General Internal Medicine* 28, no. 11 (2013): 1504–10; Joe Feagin and Zinobia Bennefield, "Systemic Racism and U.S. Health Care," *Social Science & Medicine* 103 (2014): 7–14.

40. Julilly Kohler-Hausmann, "The Crime of Survival": Fraud Prosecutions, Community Surveillance, and the Original 'Welfare Queen,'" *Journal of Social History* 41, no. 2 (2007).

41. Lily D. McNair and Helen Neville, "African American Women Survivors of Sexual Assault: The Intersection of Race and Class," *Women & Therapy* 18, no. 3–4 (1996): 107–18.

42. Odis Johnson, Jr., Keon Gilbert, and Habiba Ibrahim, "Race, Gender, and the Contexts of Unarmed Fatal Interactions with Police," Fatal Interactions with Police (FIPS) research project. Retrieved from https://cpb-us-west-2-juc1ugur1qwqqqo4.stackpath dns.com/sites.wustl.edu/dist/b/1205/files/2018/02 /Race-Gender-and-Unarmed-1y6zo9a.pdf; Monique W. Morris, *Pushout: The Criminalization of Black Girls in Schools* (New York: The New Press, 2016).

43. Kimberlé Williams Crenshaw and Andrea J. Ritchie, "Say Her Name: Resisting Police Brutality against Black Women" (New York: African American Policy Forum, 2015); Human Rights Campaign, "Violence against the Transgender Community," 2018. Retrieved from www.hrc.org/resources/violence -against-the-transgender-community-in-2017.

44. Kim Parker, Juliana Menasce Horowitz, and Renee Stepler, "On Gender Differences, No Consensus on Nature vs. Nurture," *Pew Research Center,* December 5, 2017. Retrieved from www.pewsocial trends.org/2017/12/05/americans-see-society-placing -more-of-a-premium-on-masculinity-than-on-femi ninity/; Elizabeth R. Cole and Alyssa N. Zuckerman, "Black and White Women's Perspectives on Femininity," *Cultural Diversity and Ethnic Minority Psychology* 13, no. 1 (2007): 1–9; Roxanne Angela Donovan and Michelle Williams, "Living at the Intersection: The Effects of Racism and Sexism on Black Rape Survivors," *Women & Therapy* 25, no. 3–4 (2002): 95–105.

45. Hannah Eko, "As a Black Woman, I'm Tired of Having to Prove My Womanhood," *Buzzfeed News,* February 27, 2018. Retrieved from https://www.buzz feed.com/hannaheko/aint-i-a-woman.

46. Ibid.

47. Yolanda F. Niemman, Leilani Jennings, Richard M. Rozelle, James C. Baxter, and Elroy Sullivan, "Use of Free Responses and Cluster Analysis to Determine Stereotypes of Eight Groups," *Personality and Social Psychology Bulletin* 20 (1994): 379–90; Adam D. Galinsky, Erika V. Hall, and Amy J. C. Cuddy. "Gendered Races: Implications for Interracial Marriage, Leadership Selection, and Athletic Participation," *Psychological Science* 24, no. 4 (2013): 498–506.

48. Robert Lee, *Orientals: Asian Americans in Popular Culture* (Philadelphia: Temple University Press, 1999).

49. Anthony Chen, "Lives at the Center of the Periphery, Lives at the Periphery of the Center: Chinese American Masculinities and Bargaining with Hegemony," *Gender & Society* 13, no. 5 (1999): 584–607.

50. Ronald Takaki, *Strangers from a Different Shore* (New York: Little, Brown and Company, 1998).

51. Yen L. Espiritu, *Asian American Women and Men* (Thousand Oaks, CA: Sage, 1997); Renee E. Tajima, "Lotus Blossoms Don't Bleed: Images of Asian Women," in *Making Waves,* ed. Asian Women United of California (Boston: Beacon Press, 1989), 308–17.

52. Karen Eng, "The Yellow Fever Pages," *Bitch* 12 (Summer 2000): 69.

53. Ibid., 70.

54. Karen D. Pyke and Denise L. Johnson, "Asian American Women and Racialized Femininities: 'Doing' Gender across Cultural Worlds," *Gender & Society* 17, no. 1 (2003): 46.

55. Ibid., 45.

56. Amy Wilkins, *Wannabes, Goths, and Christians: The Boundaries of Sex, Style, and Status* (Chicago: University of Chicago Press, 2008), 52.

57. Ibid.

58. Ibid., 151.

59. Ibid., 198.

60. Gerard Wright, "Gay Grief in Cowboy Country," *Guardian*, March 27, 1999. Retrieved from www .guardian.co.uk/books/1999/mar/27/books.guard ianreview7?INTCMP=SRCH; Tony Silva, "Bud Sex: Constructing Normative Masculinity among Rural Straight Men That Have Sex with Men," *Gender & Society* 31, no. 1 (2016): 51–73; Tony Silva, "'Helpin' a Buddy Out": Perceptions of Identity and Behavior among Rural Straight Men That Have Sex with Each Other," *Sexualities* 21, no. 1–2 (2017): 68–89.

61. Michelle A. Marzullo and Alyn J. Libman, "Hate Crimes and Violence Against LGBTQ People," (Washington, D.C.: Human Rights Campaign Foundation: 2009); Ilan H. Meyer, "Gender Nonconformity as a Target of Prejudice, Discrimination, and Violence Against LGB Individuals," *Journal of LGBT Health Research* 3, no. 3 (2007): 55–71.

62. Laura Hamilton, "Trading on Heterosexuality: College Women's Gender Strategies and Homophobia," *Gender & Society* 21, no. 2 (2007): 156.

63. Anthony Ocampo, "Making Masculinity: Negotiations of Gender Presentation among Latino Gay Men," *Latino Studies*, 10, no. 4 (2012) 448–72.

64. Kirsten Dellinger and Christine Williams, "Makeup at Work: Negotiating Appearance Rules in the Workplace," *Gender & Society* 11, no. 2 (1997): 162.

65. Michael Price, "Rugby as a Gay Men's Game" (Ph.D. diss., University of Warwick, Coventry, UK, 2000).

66. Jennifer Taub, "Bisexual Women and Beauty Norms: A Qualitative Examination," in *Lesbians, Levis and Lipstick: The Meaning of Beauty in Our Lives*, ed. Joanie Erickson and Jeanine Cogan, Haworth Gay and Lesbian Studies (New York: Routledge, 1999), 27–36.

67. Lisa Duggan, *The Twilight of Equality? Neoliberalism, Cultural Politics, and the Attack on Democracy* (Boston: Beacon Press, 2003); Mignon R. Moore, "Lipstick or Timberlands? Meanings of Gender Presentation in Black Lesbian Communities," *Signs* 32, no. 1 (2006): 113–39.

68. Jennifer Taub, "Bisexual Women and Beauty Norms: A Qualitative Examination," in *Lesbians, Levis and Lipstick: The Meaning of Beauty in Our Lives*, ed. Joanie Erickson and Jeanine Cogan, Haworth Gay and Lesbian Studies (New York: Routledge, 1999), 31.

69. Mignon R. Moore, "'Black and Gay in L.A.': The Relationships Black Lesbians and Gay Men have with their Racial and Religious Communities," in *Black Los Angeles: American Dreams and Racial Realities*, ed. Darnell Hunt and Ana-Christina Ramon (New York: New York University Press, 2010), 188–212.

70. Kerry GerMalone, "Two-Spirit: The Journey of Indigenous Gender Identity," *Snap Judgment*. Retrieved from http://snapjudgment.org/two-spirit -journey-indigenous-gender-identity.

71. Mignon Moore, *Invisible Families: Gay Identities, Relationships, and Motherhood among Black Women* (Berkeley: University of California Press, 2011).

72. JeeYeun Lee, "Why Suzie Wong Is Not a Lesbian: Asian and Asian American Lesbian and Bisexual Women and Femme/Butch/Gender Identities," in *Queer Studies: A Lesbian, Gay, Bisexual and Transgender Anthology*, ed. Brett Beemyn and Mickey Eliason (New York: New York University Press, 1996), 123.

73. Patricia Hill Collins, *Black Feminist Thought: Knowledge, Consciousness, and the Politics of Empowerment* (New York: Routledge, 1991).

74. Mignon R. Moore, "Lipstick or Timberlands? Meanings of Gender Presentation in Black Lesbian Communities," *Signs* 32, no. 1 (2006): 113–39.

75. Michael Stambolis-Ruhstorfer, "Labels of Love: How Migrants Negotiate (or Not) the Culture of Sexual Identity," *American Journal of Cultural Sociology* 1, no. 3 (2013): 321–45.

76. Lesley Doyal, Sara Paparini, and Jane Anderson, "'Elvis Died and I Was Born': Black African Men Negotiating Same-Sex Desire in London," *Sexualities* 11, no. 1–2 (2008): 171–92.

77. Ibid., 179–80.

78. For a review of this phenomenon among Asian immigrants, see Yen Le Espiritu, "Asian American Panethnicity: Bridging Institutions and Identities," in *Rethinking the Color Line: Readings in Race and Ethnicity*, ed. Charles A. Gallagher (New York: McGraw Hill, 1999).

79. Cecilia Menjivar, "The Intersection of Work and Gender: Central American Immigrant Women and Employment in California," *American Behavioral Scientist* 42, no. 4 (1999); Pierrette Hondagneu-Sotelo, "Overcoming Patriarchial Constraints: The Reconstruction of Gender Relations among Mexican Immigrant Women and Men," *Gender & Society* 6, no. 3 (1992): 393–415; Leah Schmalzbauer, "'Doing Gender,' Ensuring Survival: Mexican Migration and

Economic Crisis in the Rural Mountain West," *Rural Sociology* 76, no. 4 (2011): 441–60; Lan Anh Hoang and Brenda Yeoh, "Breadwinning Wives and 'Left-Behind' Husbands: Men and Masculinities in the Vietnamese Transnational Family," *Gender & Society* 25, no. 6 (2011): 717–39; Deborah A. Boehm, "Intimate Migrations: Gender, Family, and Illegality among Transnational Mexicans," (New York: New York University Press: 2012); Jason Pribilsky, *La Chulla Vida: Gender, Migration, and the Family in Andean Ecuador and New York City* (Syracuse: Syracuse University Press, 2007); Thai, Hung Cam, *For Better or for Worse: Vietnamese International Marriages in the New Global Economy* (New Brunswick: Rutgers University Press, 2008); Jennifer S. Hirsch, *A Courtship After Marriage: Sexuality and Love in Mexican Transnational Families* (Berkeley: University of California Press, 2003); Peggy Levitt, *The Transnational Villagers* (Berkeley: University of California Press, 2001).

80. Rhacel Salazar Parrenas, *Servants of Globalization: Women, Migration, and Domestic Work* (Stanford: Stanford University Press, 2001); Majella Kilkey, Diane Perrons, Ania Plomien, *Gender, Migration and Domestic Work: Masculinities, Male Labour and Fathering in the UK and USA* (New York: Palgrave Macmillan, 2013); Barbara Ehrenreich and Arlie Russell Hochschild, *Global Woman: Nannies, Maids, and Sex Workers in the New Economy* (New York: Henry Holt and Company, 2002); Denise A. Segura and Patricia Zavella, *Women and Migration in the U.S.-Mexico Borderlands: A Reader* (Durham: Duke University Press, 2007); Ingrid Palmary, Erica Burman, Khatigja Chantler, Peace Kiguwa, *Gender and Migration: Feminist Interventions* (New York: Zed Books, 2010); Robert Courtney Smith, *Mexican New York* (Berkeley: University of California Press, 2006).

81. Leisy Abrego and Ralph LaRossa, "Economic Well-Being in Salvadoran Transnational Families: How Gender Affects Remittance Practices," *Journal of Marriage and Family* 71, no. 4 (2009): 1070–85; Anju Mary Paul, "Negotiating Migration, Performing Gender," *Social Forces* 94, no. 1 (2015): 271–93.

82. Deborah A. Boehm, "'Now I Am a Man *and a* Woman!' Gendered Moves and Migrations in a Transnational Mexican Community," *Latin American Perspectives* 35, no. 1 (2008): 16–30, p. 16.

83. Pierrette Hondagneu-Sotelo, "Overcoming Patriarchial Constraints: The Reconstruction of Gender Relations among Mexican Immigrant Women and Men," *Gender & Society* 6, no. 3 (1992): 393–415, p. 408.

84. Leah Schmalzbauer, "'Doing Gender,' Ensuring Survival: Mexican Migration and Economic Crisis in the Rural Mountain West," *Rural Sociology* 76, no. 4 (2011): 441–60, p. 450.

85. Cecilia Menjivar, "The Intersection of Work and Gender: Central American Immigrant Women and Employment in California," *American Behavioral Scientist* 42, no. 4 (1999).

86. Ibid., 609.

87. Ibid., 616.

88. Ibid., 611.

89. Thomas J. Gerschick, "Toward a Theory of Disability and Gender," *Signs* 25, no. 4 (2000): 1264.

90. Thomas Gerschick and Adam Miller, "Coming to Terms: Masculinity and Physical Disability," in *Men's Health and Illness: Gender, Power, and the Body*, ed. Donald Sabo and David Frederick Gordon (Thousand Oaks, CA: Sage Publications, 1995), 192.

91. Ibid.

92. Ibid.

93. R. Noam Ostrander, "When Identities Collide: Masculinity, Disability, and Race," *Disability & Society* 23, no. 6 (2008): 585–97.

94. Ibid., 594.

95. Ingunn Moser, "Sociotechnical Practices and Difference: On the Interferences between Disability, Gender, and Class," *Science, Technology, and Human Values* 31, no. 5 (2006): 537–64.

96. Ibid., 538.

97. Ibid., 548.

98. Tom Shakespeare, Kath Gillespie-Sells, and Dominic Davies, *The Sexual Politics of Disability: Untold Desires* (London, UK: Cassell, 1996).

99. Ibid., 10.

100. Michelle Fine and Adrienne Asch, *Women with Disabilities: Essays in Psychology, Culture and Politics* (Philadelphia: Temple University Press, 1988), 29.

101. Harilyn Rousso, "Daughters with Disabilities: Defective Women or Minority Women?" in *Women with Disabilities: Essays in Psychology, Culture and Politics*, ed. Michelle Fine and Adrienne Asch (Philadelphia: Temple University Press, 1988), 139–71.

102. Nasa Begum, "Disabled Women and the Feminist Agenda," *Feminist Review* 40 (1992): 70–84.

103. Deborah Lisi, "Found Voices: Women, Disability and Cultural Transformation," *Women & Therapy* 14, no. 3/4 (1994): 195–209.

104. Ibid.

105. Ingunn Moser, "Sociotechnical Practices and Difference: On the Interferences between Disability, Gender, and Class," *Science, Technology, and Human Values* 31, no. 5 (2006): 553.

106. Ibid., 554.

107. Cheryl Laz, "Act Your Age," *Sociological Forum* 13, no. 1 (1998): 85–113.

108. Ibid., 86.

109. Barbro Johanssen, "Doing Age and Gender through Fashion," in *INTER: A European Cultural Studies Conference in Sweden, 11–13 June 2007*, ed. Johan Fornäs, Martin Fredriksson, Conference Proceedings (2007): 285. Retrieved from www.ep.liu.se/ecp/025/029/ecp072529 .pdf.

110. R. N. Butler, "Ageism: Another Form of Bigotry," *Gerontologist* 9 (1969): 243–46.

111. Susan Sontag, "The Double Standard of Aging," *The Saturday Review*, September 23, 1972, 29–38.

112. Ibid.

113. Ibid.

114. Duncan Kennedy, *Sexy Dressing, Etc.: Essays on the Power and Politics of Cultural Identity* (Cambridge: Harvard University Press, 1993), 164.

115. Gina Marie Longo, "Keeping it in 'the Family': Using Gender Norms to Shape U.S. Marriage Migration Politics," *Gender & Society* 32, no. 4 (2018): 469–92.

116. NiCole R. Keith, Kimberly A. Hemmerlein, and Daniel O. Clark, "Weight Loss Attitudes and Social Forces in Urban Poor Black and White Women," *American Journal of Health Behavior* 39, no. 1 (2015): 34.

117. Elizabeth A. Pascoe and Laura Smart Richman, "Perceived Discrimination and Health: A Meta-Analytic Review," *Psychological Bulletin* 135, no. 4 (2009): 531–54.

Chapter 6: Inequality: Men and Masculinities

1. Andrea Waling, "'We Are So Pumped Full of Shit by the Media': Masculinity, Magazines, and the Lack of Self-Identification," *Men and Masculinities* 20, no. 4 (2016): 427–52, p. 444.

2. John Gamlich, "10 Things We Learned about Gender Issues in the U.S. in 2017," *Pew Research Center*, December 28, 2017. Retrieved from www.pewresearch.org/fact-tank/2017/12/28/10-things-we-learned-about-gender-issues-in-the-u-s-in-2017/.

3. Quoted in Natalie Adams and Pamela Bettis, "Commanding the Room in Short Skirts: Cheering as the Embodiment of Ideal Girlhood," *Gender & Society* 17, no. 1 (2003): 76.

4. Rebecca Boyce, "Cheerleading in the Context of Title IX and Gendering in Sport," *The Sports Journal* 11, no. 3: (2008).

5. Quoted in Mary Ellen Hanson, *Go! Fight! Win! Cheerleading in American Culture* (Bowling Green, OH: Bowling Green State University Popular Press), 13.

6. Ibid., 2.

7. Ibid., 17.

8. Quoted in Laurel Davis, "A Postmodern Paradox? Cheerleaders at Women's Sporting Events," in *Women, Sport, and Culture*, ed. Susan Birrell and Cheryl Cole (Champaign: Human Kinetics Press, 1994), 153.

9. Quoted in Mary Ellen Hanson, *Go! Fight! Win! Cheerleading in American Culture* (Bowling Green: Bowling Green State University Popular Press), 16.

10. James McElroy, *We've Got Spirit: The Life and Times of America's Greatest Cheerleading Team* (New York: Simon & Schuster, 1999), 15.

11. Ibid., 2–3.

12. Pamela Paxton, Sheri Kunovich, and Melanie Hughes, "Gender in Politics," *Annual Review of Sociology* 33 (2007): 263–84; Law Library of Congress, State Suffrage Laws, http://memory.loc.gov/ammem/awhhtml/awlaw3/suffrage.html.

13. J. R. Lambdin, K. M. Greer, K. S. Jibotian, K. R. Wood, and M. C. Hamilton, "The Animal = Male Hypothesis: Children's and Adults' Beliefs about the Sex of Non-Sex-Specific Stuffed Animals," *Sex Roles* 48 (2003): 471–82.

14. Mykol Hamilton, "Masculine Bias in the Attribution of Personhood: People = Male, Male = People," *Psychology of Women Quarterly* 15, no. 3 (1991): 393–402; Sik Hung Ng, "Androcentric Coding of Man and His in Memory by Language Users," *Journal of Experimental Social Psychology* 26, no. 5 (1990): 455–64; J. Gastil, "Generic Pronouns and Sexist Language: The Oxymoronic Character of Masculine Generics," *Sex Roles* 23 (1990): 629–43.

15. R. Moyer, "Covering Gender on Memory's Front Page: Men's Prominence and Women's Prospects," *Sex Roles* 37 (1997): 595–618; D. Stahlberg, S. Sczesny, and F. Braun, "Name Your Favourite Musician: Effects of Masculine Generics and Their Alternatives in

German," *Journal of Language and Social Psychology* 20 (2001): 464–69.

16. Geena Davis Institute on Gender in Media, "The Reel Truth: Women Aren't Seen or Heard," Retrieved from https://seejane.org/wp-content/uploads/gdiq-reel-truth-women-arent-seen-or-heard-automated-analysis.pdf.

17. BBC, "100 Women: How Hollywood Fails Women on Screen," BBC, March 2, 2018. Retrieved from www.bbc.com/news/world-43197774.

18. Carolyn Cocca, *Superwomen: Gender, Power, and Representation* (New York: Bloomsbury, 2016); Mykol C. Hamilton, David Anderson, Michelle Broaddus, and Kate Young, "Gender Stereotyping and Under-Representation of Female Characters in 200 Popular Children's Books: A Twenty-First Century Update," *Sex Roles* 55, no. 11–12 (2006): 757–65; Dennis J. Ganahl, Thomas J. Prinsen, and Sara Baker Netzley, "A Content Analysis of Prime Time Commercials: A Contextual Framework of Gender Representation," *Sex Roles* 49, no. 9–10 (2003): 545–51; Dmitri Williams, Nicole Martins, Mia Consalvo, and James D. Ivory, "The Virtual Census: Representations of Gender, Race and Age in Video Games," *New Media & Society* 11, no. 5 (2009): 815–34; Edward Downs and Stacy L. Smith, "Keeping Abreast of Hypersexuality: A Video Game Character Content Analysis," *Sex Roles* 62, no .11–12 (2010): 721–33; Rebecca L. Collins, "Content Analysis of Gender Roles in Media: Where Are We Now and Where Should We Go?," *Sex Roles* 64, no. 3–4 (2011): 290–98; Beth Hentges and Kim Case, "Gender Representations on Disney Channel, Cartoon Network, and Nickelodeon Broadcasts in the United States," *Journal of Children and Media* 7, no. 3 (2013) 319–33.

19. Mary Beard, *Women and Power: A Manifesto* (New York: W. W. Norton and Company, 2017).

20. *Thesaurus.com* s.v. "power." Retrieved from www.thesaurus.com/browse/power?s=t.

21. *Thesaurus.com* s.v. "femininity." Retrieved from www.thesaurus.com/browse/femininity?s=t.

22. Joan Wallace Scott, *Gender and the Politics of History* (New York: Columbia University Press, 1999), 44.

23. Karen Ross, *Gendered Media: Women, Men, and Identity Politics* (Lanham, MD: Rowman & Littlefield, 2010); Rosalind Gill, *Gender and the Media* (Malden, MA: Polity Press, 2007).

24. Amanda Shendruk, "Analyzing the Gender Representation of 34,476 Comic Book Characters," *The Pudding*. Retrieved from https://pudding.cool/2017/07/comics/.

25. Janet Swim et al., "Joan McKay versus John McKay: Do Gender Stereotypes Bias Evaluations?" *Psychological Bulletin* 105, no. 3 (1989): 409–29; Pamela Paxton, Sheri Kunovich, and Melanie Hughes, "Gender in Politics," *Annual Review of Sociology* 33 (2007): 263–84.

26. Corinne Moss-Racusin et al., "Science Faculty's Subtle Gender Biases Favor Male Students," *Proceedings of the National Academy of Sciences* 109, no. 41 (2012): 16474–79.

27. Janet Swim et al., "Joan McKay versus John McKay: Do Gender Stereotypes Bias Evaluations?" *Psychological Bulletin* 105, no. 3 (1989): 409–29.

28. S. Lieberson, S. Dumais, and S. Baumann, "The Instability of Androgynous Names: The Symbolic Maintenance of Gender Boundaries," *American Journal of Sociology* 105, no. 5 (2000): 1249–87.

29. NameTrends.net, "Leslie." Retrieved from https://nametrends.net/name.php?name=Leslie.

30. U.S. Bureau of Labor Statistics, "Labor Force Statistics from the Current Population Survey: Employed Persons by Detailed Occupation and Sex, and Hispanic or Latino Ethnicity," January 19, 2018. Retrieved from www.bls.gov/cps/cpsaat11.htm.

31. U.S. Bureau of Labor Statistics, "Employed Persons by Detailed Occupation and Sex, 2007 Annual Averages, 2008. Retrieved from www.bls.gov/cps/wlf-table11-2008.pdf.

32. U.S. Bureau of Labor Statistics, "Labor Force Statistics from the Current Population Survey: Employed Persons by Detailed Occupation and Sex, and Hispanic or Latino Ethnicity," January 19, 2018. Retrieved from www.bls.gov/cps/cpsaat11.htm.

33. Patricia Yancey Martin, "'Said and Done' versus 'Saying and Doing'—Gendering Practices, Practicing Gender at Work," *Gender & Society* 17, no. 3 (2003): 342–66; Rosabeth Moss Kanter, *Men and Women of the Corporation* (New York: Basic Books, 1993); Joan C. Williams, Rachel Dempsey, Anne-Marie Slaughter, *What Works for Women at Work: Four Patterns Working Women Need to Know* (New York: New York University Press, 2014); Deborah L. Kidder, "The Influence of Gender on the Performance of Organizational Citizenship Behaviors," *Journal of Management* 28, no. 5 (2002): 629–48.

34. Patricia Yancey Martin, "'Said and Done' versus 'Saying and Doing'—Gendering Practices, Practicing Gender at Work," *Gender & Society* 17, no. 3 (2003): 342–66.

35. Emily Kane, "'No Way My Boys Are Going to be Like That!' Parents' Responses to Children's Gender Nonconformity," *Gender & Society* 20, no. 2 (2006): 149–76.

36. Ibid., 159.

37. Ibid., 159.

38. Julia Menasce Horowitz, "Most Americans See Value in Steering Children toward Toys, Activities Associated with Opposite Gender," *Pew Research Center*, December 19, 2017. Retrieved from www.pew research.org/fact-tank/2017/12/19/most-americans -see-value-in-steering-children-toward-toys-activities -associated-with-opposite-gender/.

39. C. J. Pascoe, *Dude, You're a Fag* (Berkeley: University of California Press, 2011); E. Anderson, "'Being Masculine Is Not about Who You Sleep with . . .:' Heterosexual Athletes Contesting Masculinity and the One-Time Rule of Homosexuality," *Sex Roles: A Journal of Research*, 58, no 1–2 (2008): 104–15; Tristan Bridges, "A Very 'Gay' Straight?: Hybrid Masculinities, Sexual Aesthetics, and the Changing Relationship between Masculinity and Homophobia." *Gender & Society* 28, no. 1 (2014): 58–82.

40. Eric Anderson, "Open Gay Athletes: Contesting Hegemonic Masculinity in a Homophobic Environment," *Gender & Society* 16, no. 6 (2002): 872.

41. Ibid., 872.

42. Kim Parker, Juliana Menasce Horowitz, and Renee Stepler, "On Gender Differences, No Consensus on Nature vs. Nurture," *Pew Research Center*, December 5, 2017. Retrieved from www.pewsocial trends.org/2017/12/05/on-gender-differences-no-con sensus-on-nature-vs-nurture/.

43. Ibid.

44. "Top 10: Drinks Real Men Don't Order," *AskMen*. Retrieved from www.askmen.com/top_10/entertain ment/top-10-drinks-real-men-dont-order_10.html; "Girl Drinks—A List of Drinks Men Should Never Order," *CampusSqueeze*.

45. Paula England and Su Li, "Desegregation Stalled: The Changing Gender Composition of College Majors, 1971–2002," *Gender & Society* 20, no. 5 (2006): 657–77.

46. Anne Lincoln, "The Shifting Supply of Men and Women to Occupation: Feminization in Veterinary Education," *Social Forces* 88, no. 5 (2010): 1969–98.

47. R. Stillwell and J. Sable, Public School Graduates and Dropouts from the Common Core of Data: School Year 2009–10: First Look (Provisional Data) (NCES 2013-309rev). U.S. Department of Education. Washington, DC: National Center for Education Statistics, 2013. Retrieved from https://nces .ed.gov/pubs2013/2013309rev.pdf; Office for Civil Rights. Gender Equity in Education: A Data Snapshot. Office for Civil Rights, 2012. Retrieved from https://www2.ed.gov/about/offices/list/ocr/docs/gen der-equity-in-education.pdf.

48. College Board, "2016 College-Bound Seniors: Total Group Profile Report," Retrieved from https:// reports.collegeboard.org/pdf/total-group-2016.pdf.

49. U.S. Department of Education, National Center for Education Statistics, Bachelor's, Master's, and Doctor's Degrees Conferred by Postsecondary Institutions, by Sex of Student and Discipline Division: 2014–15. Retrieved from https://nces.ed.gov/prog rams/digest/d16/tables/dt16_318.30.asp?current=yes; U.S. Department of Education, National Center for Education Statistics, Associate's Degrees Conferred by Postsecondary Institutions, by Sex of Student and Discipline Division: 2003–04 through 2013–14. Retrieved from https://nces.ed.gov/programs/digest /d15/tables/dt15_321.10.asp.

50. Jack Kahn, Benjamin Brett, and Jessica Holmes, "Concerns with Men's Academic Motivation in Higher Education: An Exploratory Investigation of the Role of Masculinity," *Journal of Men's Studies* 19, no. 1 (2011): 65–82; Paul Willis, *Learning to Labor: How Working Class Kids Get Working Class Jobs* (New York: Columbia University Press, 1977); D. Epstein, "Real Boys Don't Work: 'Underachievement,' Masculinity, and the Harassment of 'Sissies,'" in *Failing Boys? Issues in Gender and Achievement*, ed. D. Epstein et al. (Buckingham: Open University Press, 1998), 96–108.

51. Jack Kahn, Benjamin Brett, and Jessica Holmes, "Concerns with Men's Academic Motivation in Higher Education: An Exploratory Investigation of the Role of Masculinity," *Journal of Men's Studies* 19, no. 1 (2011): 65–82.

52. R. W. Connell, *Gender and Power: Society, the Person, and Sexual Politics* (Stanford: Stanford University Press, 1987); R. W. Connell and James Messerschmidt, "Hegemonic Masculinity: Rethinking the Concept," *Gender & Society* 19, no. 6 (2005): 829–59.

53. Peter Glick, Maria Lameiras, Susan T. Fiske, Thomas Eckes, Barbara Masser, Chiara Volpato, Anna Maria Manganelli, Jolynn C. X. Pek, Li-li Huang, Nuray Sakalli-Ugurlu, Yolanda Rodriguez Castro, Maria Luiza D'Avila Pereira, Tineke M. Willemsen, Annetje Brunner, Iris Six-Materna, and

Robin Wells, "Bad but Bold: Ambivalent Attitudes Toward Men Predict Gender Inequality in 16 Nations," *Journal of Personality and Social Psychology* 86, no. 5 (2004): 713–28.

54. MetaFilter, "Men Will Never . . . Clean without Being Asked 'because It Sucks,'" *MetaFilter*, May 16, 2013. Retrieved from www.metafilter.com/128141/Men-will-neverclean-without-being-asked-because-it-sucks.

55. Ibid.

56. Katherine S. Newman, *Falling from Grace: Downward Mobility in the Age of Affluence* (Berkeley: University of California Press, 1999).

57. Elliot Liebow, *Tally's Corner: A Study of Negro Streetcorner Men* (Lanham, MD: Rowman & Littlefield, 2003).

58. Lisa Wade crowdsourced this phrase on social media. Thanks to the whole team, especially Scott Knickelbine and Damian Tatum, who dropped "exculpatory" and "chauvinism," respectively, and Jay Livingston, who recommended Elliot Liebow's "Theory of Manly Flaws."

59. Peter Glick, Maria Lameiras, Susan T. Fiske, Thomas Eckes, Barbara Masser, Chiara Volpato, Anna Maria Manganelli, Jolynn C. X. Pek, Li-li Huang, Nuray Sakalli-Ugurlu, Yolanda Rodriguez Castro, Maria Luiza D'Avila Pereira, Tineke M. Willemsen, Annetje Brunner, Iris Six-Materna, and Robin Wells, "Bad but Bold: Ambivalent Attitudes Toward Men Predict Gender Inequality in 16 Nations," *Journal of Personality and Social Psychology* 86, no. 5 (2004): 713–28.

60. Sarah Grogan and Helen Richards, "Body Image: Focus Groups with Boys and Men," *Men and Masculinities* 4, no. 3 (2002): 219–32; Marissa E. Wagner Oehlhof, Dara R. Musher-Eizenman, Jennie M. Neufeld, Jessica C. Hauser, "Self-Objectification and Ideal Body Shape for Men and Women," *Body Image* 6, no. 4 (2009): 308–10; John F. Morgan, "Body Image in Gay and Straight Men: A Qualitative Study," *European Eating Disorders Review* 17, no. 6 (2009): 435–43; M. Tiggemann, "Sociocultural Perspectives on Human Appearance and Body Image," in *Body Image: A Handbook of Science, Practice, and Prevention*, ed. T. F. Cash and L. Smolak (New York: Guilford Press, 2011), 12–19; Sarah Grogan, *Body Image: Understanding Body Dissatisfaction in Men, Women and Children* (New York: Routledge, 2016).

61. Shamus Rahman Khan, *Privilege: The Making of an Adolescent Elite at St. Paul's School* (Princeton: Princeton University Press, 2012); M. Tiggemann,

"Sociocultural Perspectives on Human Appearance and Body Image," in *Body Image: A Handbook of Science, Practice, and Prevention*, ed. T. F. Cash and L. Smolak (New York: Guilford Press, 2011), 12–19.

62. Melanie A. Morrison, Todd G. Morrison, and Cheryl-Lee Sager, "Does Body Satisfaction Differ between Gay Men and Lesbian Women and Heterosexual Men and Women?: A Meta-Analytic Review," *Body Image* 1, no. 2 (2004): 127–38.

63. Andrea Waling, "'We Are So Pumped Full of Shit by the Media': Masculinity, Magazines, and the Lack of Self-Identification," *Men and Masculinities* 20, no. 4 (2016): 427–52, p. 444.

64. Erving Goffman, *Stigma* (Englewood Cliffs, NJ: Prentice Hall, 1963).

65. Michael Kaufman, "Men, Feminism, and Men's Contradictory Experiences of Power," in *Theorizing Masculinities*, ed. Harry Brod and Michael Kaufman, Sage Series on Men and Masculinity (Newbury Park: Sage Publications, 1994), 142–65.

66. Ibid., 148.

67. Gwen Sharp, "Policing Masculinity in Slim Jim's 'Spice Loss' Ads," *Sociological Images* (blog), August 21, 2012. Retrieved from http://thesocietypages.org/socimages/2012/08/21/policing-masculinity-in-slim-jims-spice-loss-ads/.

68. David Gal and James Wilkie, "Real Men Don't Eat Quiche: Regulation of Gender-Expressive Choices by Men, *Social Psychological and Personality Science* 1, no. 4 (2010): 291–301.

69. Joseph A. Vandello and Jennifer K. Bosson, "Hard Won and Easily Lost: A Review and Synthesis of Theory and Research on Precarious Manhood," *Psychology of Men & Masculinity* 14, no. 2 (2013): 101–13.

70. J. Weaver, J. A. Vandello, J. K. Bosson, and R. Burnaford, "The Proof Is in the Punch: Gender Differences in Perceptions of Action and Aggression as Components of Manhood," *Sex Roles* 62 (2010): 241–51.

71. J. K. Bosson, J. A. Vandello, R. Burnaford, J. Weaver, and A. Wasti, "The Links between Precarious Manhood and Physical Aggression," *Personality and Social Psychology Bulletin* 35 (2009): 623–34.

72. Deborah Bach, "Manning Up: Men May Overcompensate When Their Masculinity Is Threatened," *UW News*, June 22, 2015, Retrieved from www.washington.edu/news/2015/06/22/manning-up-men-may-overcompensate-when-their-masculinity-is-threatened/; Robb Willer, Christabel L. Rogalin,

Bridget Conlon, and Michael T. Wojnowicz, "Overdoing Gender: A Test of the Masculine Overcompensation Thesis," *American Journal of Sociology* 118, no. 4 (2013): 980–1022; Phillip Atiba Goff, Brooke Allison Lewis Di Leone, and Kimberly Barsamian Kahn, "Racism Leads to Pushups: How Racial Discrimination Threatens Subordinate Men's Masculinity," *Journal of Experimental Social Psychology* 48, no. 5 (2012): 1111–16; Sherilyn MacGregor, *Routledge Handbook of Gender and Environment* (New York: Routledge, 2017).

73. N. Kosakowska-Berezecka, T. Besta, K. Adamska, M. Jaśkiewicz, P. Jurek, and J. A. Vandello, "If My Masculinity Is Threatened I Won't Support Gender Equality? The Role of Agentic Self-Stereotyping in Restoration of Manhood and Perception of Gender Relations. *Psychology of Men & Masculinity* 17, no. 3 (2016): 274–84; Robb Willer, Christabel L. Rogalin, Bridget Conlon, and Michael T. Wojnowicz, "Overdoing Gender: A Test of the Masculine Overcompensation Thesis." *American Journal of Sociology* 118, no. 4 (2013): 980–1022; Christin L. Munsch and Robb Willer, "The Role of Gender Identity Threat in Perceptions of Date Rape and Sexual Coercion," *Violence Against Women* 18, no. 10 (2012): 1125–46; Michael Schwalbe, *Manhood Acts: Gender and the Practices of Domination* (New York: Routledge, 2014); Christin L. Munsch, "Her Support, His Support: Money, Masculinity, and Marital Infidelity," *American Sociological Review* 80, no. 3 (2015): 469–95.

74. Carl A. Kallgren, Raymond R. Reno, and Robert B. Cialdini, "A Focus Theory of Normative Conduct: When Norms Do and Do Not Affect Behavior," *Personality and Social Psychology Bulletin* 26, no. 8 (2000): 1002–12; Lynnette C. Zelezny, Poh-Pheng Chua, and Christina Aldrich, "New Ways of Thinking about Environmentalism: Elaborating on Gender Differences in Environmentalism," *Journal of Social Issues* 56, no. 3 (2002): 443–57; R. Raty and A. Carlsson-Kanyama, "Energy Consumption by Gender in Some European Countries," *Energy Policy* 38, no 1 (2010): 646–49; Jessica Greenebaum and Brandon Dexter, "Vegan Men and Hybrid Masculinity," *Journal of Gender Studies* (2017); Aaron R. Brough, James E. B. Wilkie, Jingjing Ma, Mathew S. Isaac, and David Gal, "Is Eco-Friendly Unmanly? The Green-Feminine Stereotype and Its Effect on Sustainable Consumption," *Journal of Consumer Research*, 43, no. 4, (2016): 567–82.

75. Keith Edwards and Susan Jones, "'Putting My Man Face On': A Grounded Theory of College Men's Gender Identity Development," *Journal of College Student Development* 50 (2009): 216.

76. Ibid., 219.

77. Ibid., 218.

78. Michael Kaufman, "Men, Feminism, and Men's Contradictory Experiences of Power," in *Theorizing Masculinities*, ed. Harry Brod and Michael Kaufman, Sage Series on Men and Masculinity (Newbury Park: Sage Publications, 1994), 142–165.

79. Douglas Schrock and Michael Schwalbe, "Men, Masculinity, and Manhood Acts," *Annual Review of Sociology* 35 (2009): 277–95.

80. Judith Kegan Gardiner, "Masculinity, the Teening of America, and Empathic Targeting," *Signs* 25, no. 4 (2000): 1257–61.

81. Beverly Fehr, *Friendship Processes*, SAGE series on close relationships (Newbury Park, Sage Publications, 1996); Jeffrey Hall, "Sex Differences in Friendship Expectations: A Meta-Analysis," *Journal of Social and Personal Relationships* 28, no. 6 (2011): 723–47; Geoffrey Greif, *Buddy System: Understanding Male Friendships*, (New York, Oxford University Press, 2008).

82. Niobe Way, *Deep Secrets* (Cambridge: Harvard University Press, 2011), 2.

83. Miller McPherson, Lynn Smith-Lovin, and Matthew Brashears, "Social Isolation in America: Changes in Core Discussion Networks over Two Decades," *American Sociological Review* 71, no. 3 (2006): 353–75.

84. Lillian Rubin, *Just Friends: The Role of Friendship in Our Lives* (New York: Harper & Row, 1985); Gale Berkowitz, "UCLA Study On Friendship among Women: An Alternative to Fight or Flight," *Melissa Kaplan's Chronic Neuroimmune Diseases*, 2002. Retrieved from www.anapsid.org/cnd/gender/tendfend.html; Natasha Raymond, "The Hug Drug," *Psychology Today*, November 1, 1999. Retrieved from www.psychologytoday.com/articles/199911/the-hug-drug; Tara Parker-Pope, "What Are Friends For? A Longer Life," *New York Times*, April 20, 2009. Retrieved from www.nytimes.com/2009/04/21/health/21well.html?_r=4&.

85. Douglas Schrock and Michael Schwalbe, "Men, Masculinity, and Manhood Acts," *Annual Review of Sociology* 35 (2009): 277–95; Jen'nan Ghazal Read and Bridget K. Gorman, "Gender and Health Inequality." *Annual Review of Sociology* 36 (2010): 371–86; U.S. Federal Bureau of Investigation, Crime in the

United States, 2012. Retrieved from www.fbi.gov /about-us/cjis/ucr/crime-in-the-u.s/2012/crime-in-the -u.s.-2012; James Byrnes, David Miller, and William Schafer, "Gender Differences in Risk Taking: A Meta-Analysis," *Psychological Bulletin* 125, no. 3 (1999): 367–83; Bryan Denham, "Masculinities in Hardcore Bodybuilding," *Men and Masculinities* 11, no. 2 (2008): 234–42.

86. World Health Organization, "Gender and Road Traffic Injuries," *Gender and Health* (2002), http:// whqlibdoc.who.int/gender/2002/a85576.pdf.

87. U.S. Bureau of Labor Statistics. (2017). "Census of Fatal Occupational Injuries Charts, 1992–2016." Retrieved from www.bls.gov/iif/oshwc/cfoi/cfch00 15.pdf.

88. Deborah B. Reed, Steven R. Browning, Susan C. Westneat, and Pamela S. Kidd, "Personal Protective Equipment Use and Safety Behaviors among Farm Adolescents: Gender Differences and Predictors of Work Practices," *Journal of Rural Health* 22, no. 4 (2006): 314–20.

89. Will Courtenay, "Constructions of Masculinity and their Influence on Men's Well-Being: A Theory of Gender and Health," *Social Science & Medicine* 50 (2000): 1385–401.

90. For a review, see Will Courtenay, "Constructions of Masculinity and Their Influence on Men's Well-Being: A Theory of Gender and Health," *Social Science & Medicine* 50 (2000): 1385–401.

91. Ibid.; American Cancer Society, "Cancer Facts & Figures 2017," Retrieved from www.cancer.org/con tent/dam/cancer-org/research/cancer-facts-and -statistics/annual-cancer-facts-and-figures/2017/can cer-facts-and-figures-2017.pdf.

92. Zed Nelson, *Love Me* (Rome: Contrasto, 2009). Retrieved from www.zednelson.com/?LoveMe:31.

93. Douglas Schrock and Michael Schwalbe, "Men, Masculinity, and Manhood Acts," *Annual Review of Sociology* 35 (2009): 289.

94. American Foundation for Suicide Prevention, "Suicide Statistics." Retrieved from https://afsp.org /about-suicide/suicide-statistics/; Michael E. Addis, "Gender and Depression in Men," *Clinical Psychology: Science and Practice* 15, no. 3 (2008): 153–68; John L. Oliffe and Melanie J. Phillips, "Men, Depression and Masculinities: A Review and Recommendations," *Journal of Men's Health* 5, no. 3 (2008): 194–202.

95. Federal Bureau of Investigation, "Crime in the U.S., 2015." Retrieved from https://ucr.fbi.gov/crime -in-the-u.s/2015/crime-in-the-u.s.-2015/tables/table-35.

96. Tristan Bridges and Tara Leigh Tober, "Mass Shootings in the U.S. Are on the Rise. What Makes American Men So Dangerous?" *Sociological* Images, December 31, 2015. Retrieved from https://theso cietypages.org/socimages/2015/12/31/mass-shoot ings-in-the-u-s-what-makes-so-many-american-men -dangerous/.

97. Michael Kimmel, *Healing from Hate: How Young Men Get Into—and Out of—Violent Extremism* (Berkeley: University of California Press, 2018).

98. Ibid., 10.

99. Ibid.

100. Michael Ian Black, "The Boys Are Not All Right," *The New York Times*, February 21, 2018. Retrieved from www.nytimes.com/2018/02/21/opinion/boys -violence-shootings-guns.html.

101. Deniz Kandiyoti, "Bargaining with Patriarchy," *Gender & Society* 2, no. 3 (1988): 274–90.

102. Michael Messner, "Becoming 100 Percent Straight," in *Privilege*, ed. Michael Kimmel and Abby Ferber (Boulder: Westview Press, 2003), 184.

103. Stacy Jones, "White Men Account for 72% of Corporate Leadership at 16 of the Fortune 500 Companies," *Fortune*, June 9, 2017. Retrieved from http:// fortune.com/2017/06/09/white-men-senior-execu tives-fortune-500-companies-diversity-data/; Rosabeth Moss Kanter, *Men and Women of the Corporation* (New York: Basic Books, 1993); Joan C. Williams, Rachel Dempsey, Anne-Marie Slaughter, *What Works for Women at Work: Four Patterns Working Women Need to Know* (New York: New York University Press, 2014); Deborah L. Kidder, "The Influence of Gender on the Performance of Organizational Citizenship Behaviors," *Journal of Management* 28, no. 5 (2002): 629–48.

104. Patricia Yancey Martin, "'Mobilizing Masculinities': Women's Experiences of Men at Work," *Organization* 8, no. 4 (2001): 587–618.

105. Patricia Yancey Martin, "'Said and Done' versus 'Saying and Doing'—Gendering Practices, Practicing Gender at Work," *Gender & Society* 17, no. 3 (2003): 342–66.

106. Yeung King-To, Mindy Stombler, and Renee Wharton, "Making Men in Gay Fraternities: Resisting and Reproducing Multiple Dimensions of Hegemonic Masculinity," *Gender & Society* 20, no. 1 (2006): 5–31.

107. Ibid., 22.

108. Lori Kendall, "'Oh No! I'm a Nerd!': Hegemonic Masculinity on an Online Forum," *Gender &*

Society, 14, no. 2 (2000): 256–74; James S. Martin, Christian A. Vaccaro, D. Alex Heckert, and Robert Heasley, "Epic Glory and Manhood Acts in Fantasy Role-Playing Dagorhir as a Case Study," *The Journal of Men's Studies* 23, no. 3 (2015): 293–314.

109. Jesse Fox and Wai Yen Tang, "Sexism in Online Video Games: The Role of Conformity to Masculine Norms and Social Dominance Orientation," *Computers in Human Behavior* 33 (2014): 314–20; Jesse Fox and Wai Yen Tang, "Women's Experiences with General and Sexual Harassment in Online Video Games: Rumination, Organizational Responsiveness, Withdrawal, and Coping Strategies," *New Media & Society* 19, no. 8 (2016): 1290–307; Wai Yen Tang and Jesse Fox, "Men's Harassment Behavior in Online Video Games: Personality Traits and Game Factors," *Aggressive Behavior* 42, no. 6 (2016): 513–21; Teresa Lynch, Jessica E. Tompkins, Irene I. van Driel, and Niki Fritz, "Sexy, Strong, and Secondary: A Content Analysis of Female Characters in Video Games across 31 Years," *Journal of Communication* 66, no. 4 (2016): 564–84; Nicholas Johnson, "Misogyny in Virtual Space: Representations of Women in Popular Video Games," A Thesis Submitted in Partial Fulfillment of the Requirements for the Degree of. Master of Arts in Sociology, Middle Tennessee State University, May 2015; Alicia Summers and Monica K. Miller, "From Damsels in Distress to Sexy Superheroes: How the Portrayal of Sexism in Video Game Magazines Has Changed in the Last Twenty Years," *Feminist Media Studies* 14, no. 6 (2014): 1028–40.

110. Jackson Katz, "8 Reasons Why Eminem's Popularity is a Disaster for Women," 2002. Retrieved from www.jacksonkatz.com/pub-eminem2/.

111. Michael M. Kasumovic, Jeffrey H. Kuznekoff, "Insights into Sexism: Male Status and Performance Moderates Female-Directed Hostile and Amicable Behaviour," *PLoS ONE* 10, no. 7 (2015): 1–14; Michael Kimmel, *Angry White Men: American Masculinity at the End of an Era* (New York: Nation Books, 2013).

112. Demetrakis Demetriou, "Connell's Concept of Hegemonic Masculinity: A Critique," *Theory and Society* 30 (2001): 337–61; Tristan Bridges and C. J. Pascoe, "Hybrid Masculinities: New Directions in the Sociology of Men and Masculinities," *Sociology Compass* 8, no. 3 (2014): 246–58.

113. Eric Anderson, *Inclusive Masculinity* (New York: Routledge, 2009).

114. Michael Messner, "Changing Men' and Feminist Politics in the United States,' *Theory and Society* 22, no. 5 (1993): 723–37.

115. N. Tatiana Masters, "'My Strength Is Not for Hurting': Men's Anti-Rape Websites and Their Construction of Masculinity and Male Sexuality," *Sexualities* 13, no. 1 (2010): 33–46; Michael Murphy, "Can 'Men' Stop Rape? Visualizing Gender in the 'My Strength Is Not for Hurting' Rape Prevention Campaign," *Men and Masculinities* 12, no. 1 (2009): 113–30.

116. Melanie Heath, "Soft-Boiled Masculinity," *Gender & Society* 17, no. 3 (2003): 423–44.

117. Jocelyn Hollander, "The Roots of Resistance to Women's Self-Defense." *Violence Against Women* 15, no. 5 (2009): 574–94.

118. Jessica Pfaffendorf, "Sensitive Cowboys: Privileged Young Men and the Mobilization of Hybrid Masculinities in a Therapeutic Boarding School," *Gender & Society*, April 2017.

119. Ibid., 215.

120. Lisa Wade, *The Big Picture: Confronting Manhood after Trump*, Public Books, January 1, 2018. Retrieved from www.publicbooks.org/pb-staff-favorites-2017-big-picture-confronting-manhood-trump/.

121. Eric Anderson, *Inclusive Masculinity: the Changing Nature of Masculinities* (New York: Routledge, 2009); Robert Jensen, *The End of Patriarchy: Radical Feminism for Men* (Victoria, Australia: Spinifix Press, 2017); Jackson Katz, *The Macho Paradox: Why Some Men Hurt Women and How All Men Can Help* (Naperville, IL: Sourcebooks, Inc., 2006); Michael Kimmel, *Healing from Hate: How Young Men Get Into—and Out of—Violent Extremism* (Berkeley,: University of California Press, 2018); John Stoltenberg, *Refusing to Be a Man: Essays on Sex and Justice* (Abingdon, Oxon, UK: Routledge, 2000); Allan G. Johnson, *The Gender Knot: Unraveling Our Patriarchal Legacy* (Philadelphia: Temple University Press, 2014).

Chapter 7: Inequality: Women and Femininities

1. Natalie Adams and Pamela Bettis, "Commanding the Room in Short Skirts: Cheering as the Embodiment of Ideal Girlhood," *Gender & Society* 17, no. 1 (2003): 73–91.

2. Nada Naiyer, Thiphalak Chounthirath, and Gary A. Smith, "Pediatric Cheerleading Injuries Treated in Emergency Departments in the United States," *Clinical Pediatrics* 56, no. 11 (2017): 985–92.

3. Eric Anderson, "'I Used to Think Women Were Weak': Orthodox Masculinity, Gender Segregation, and Sport," *Sociological Forum* 23, no. 2 (2008): 270.

4. Ibid.

5. Laura Grindstaff and Emily West, "Cheerleading and the Gendered Politics of Sport." *Social Problems* 53, no. 4 (2006): 500.

6. Ibid., 509–10.

7. Ibid., 510.

8. Elisabeth Sherman, "Why Don't More People Consider Competitive Cheerleading a Sport?" *The Atlantic*, May 2, 2017. Retrieved from www.theatlantic.com/entertainment/archive/2017/05/why-dont-more-people-consider-competitive-cheerleading-a-sport/524940/.

9. Kristen L. Kucera and Leah Cox Thomas, "Catastrophic Sports Injury Research: Thirty-Fourth Annual Report: Fall 1982–Spring 2016," National Center for Catastrophic Sport Injury Research at the university of North Caroline at Chapel Hill. Retrieved from https://nccsir.unc.edu/files/2013/10/NCCSIR-34th-Annual-All-Sport-Report-1982_2016_FINAL.pdf; Fitness CoSMa Policy Statement: "Cheerleading Injuries: Epidemiology and Recommendations for Prevention," *Pediatrics* 130, no. 5 (2012): 966–71; Bill Pennington, "Pompoms, Pyramids and Peril," *New York Times*, March 30, 2007.

10. Frederick Mueller, "Cheerleading Injuries and Safety," *Journal of Athletic Training* 44, no. 6 (2009): 565–66.

11. Claire Cain Miller, "Americans Might No Longer Prefer Sons Over Daughters," *New York Times*, March 5, 2018. Retrieved from www.nytimes.com/2018/03/05/upshot/americans-might-no-longer-prefer-sons-over-daughters.html.

12. Emily Kane, "'No Way My Boys Are Going to Be Like That!' Parents' Responses to Children's Gender Nonconformity," *Gender & Society* 20, no. 2 (2006): 149–76.

13. Ibid., 156–57.

14. Tom Vanden Brook, "Pentagon Opening Front-Line Combat Roles to Women." *USA Today*, June 18, 2013.

15. Kim Parker, Juliana Menasce Horowitz, and Renee Stepler, "On Gender Differences, No Consensus on Nature vs. Nurture," *Pew Research Center*, December 5, 2017. Retrieved from www.pewsocialtrends.org/2017/12/05/on-gender-differences-no-consensus-on-nature-vs-nurture/.

16. Ibid.

17. Ibid.

18. YouTube, "NASCAR's First Female Pit Crew Member." Retrieved from www.youtube.com/watch?v=doZmQaJDkCc.

19. Elizabeth Narins, "In Defense of Female Cross-Fit Competitors: Strong Women Aren't Just Meatheads," *Cosmopolitan*, August 13, 2015. Retrieved from www.cosmopolitan.com/health-fitness/a44819/christmas-abbott-crossfit-body-image/.

20. *Inked*, "Christmas Abbott," December 19, 2013. Retrieved from www.inkedmag.com/articles/christmas-abbott/.

21. Mignon R. Moore, *Invisible Families: Gay Identities, Relationships and Motherhood among Black Women* (Berkeley: University of California Press, 2011), 26; see also Mignon Moore, "Intersectionality and the Study of Black, Sexual Minority Women," *Gender & Society* 26, no. 1 (2012): 33–39; Mignon R. Moore, "Lipstick or Timberlands? Meanings of Gender Presentation in Black Lesbian Communities," *Signs: Journal of Women in Culture and Society* 32, no. 1 (Autumn 2006): 113–39.

22. Ingrid Banks, *Hair Matters: Beauty, Power, and Black Women's Consciousness* (New York: New York University Press, 2000); Rose Weitz, *Rapunzel's Daughters: What Women's Hair Tells Us about Women's Lives* (New York: Farrar, Straus and Giroux, 2004); Nadia Brown, "'It's More than Hair . . . That's Why You Should Care': The Politics of Appearance for Black Women State Legislators," *Politics, Groups, and Identities* 2, no. 3 (2014): 295–312; Germine H. Awad, Carolette Norwood, Desire S. Taylor, Mercedes Martinez, Shannon McClain, Bianca Jones, Andrea Holman, and Collette Chapman-Hilliard, "Beauty and Body Image Concerns among African American College Women," *Journal of Black Psychology* 41, no. 6 (2014): 540–64; Althea Prince, *The Politics of Black Women's Hair* (London, Ontario, Canada: Insomnia Press, 2009); Ayana Byrd and Lori Tharps, *Hair Story: Untangling the Roots of Black Hair in America* (New York: St. Martin's Press, 2001).

23. Rose Weitz, *Rapunzel's Daughters: What Women's Hair Tells Us about Women's Lives* (New York: Farrar, Straus and Giroux, 2004), 125.

24. Paulette M. Caldwell, "A Hair Piece: Perspectives on the Intersection of Race and Gender," *Duke Law Review* 1991, no. 2 (1991): 365–976.

25. Maya Rhodan, "U.S. Military Rolls Back Restrictions on Black Hairstyles," *Time*, August 13, 2014. Retrieved from http://time.com/3107647/military-black-hairstyles/.

26. Taryn Finley, "Appeals Court Rules Employers Can Ban Dreadlocks at Work," *Huffington Post*, September 20, 2016. Retrieved from www.huffingtonpost

.com/entry/appeals-court-rules-dreadlocks-work_us
_57e0252ae4b0071a6e08a7c3.

27. Cindy Boren, "'There's No Wrong Way to Be a Woman': Serena Williams Drops a Powerful Message in Nike Ad," *Washington Post*, March 5, 2018. Retrieved from www.washingtonpost.com/news/early-lead/wp/2018/03/05/theres-no-wrong-way-to-be-a-woman-serena-williams-drops-a-powerful-message-in-nike-ad/?utm_term=.1948a9dba615.

28. Mimi Schippers, "Recovering the Feminine Other: Masculinity, Femininity, and Gender Hegemony," *Theory and Society* 36 (2007): 85–102.

29. Ryan Noonan, Office of the Chief Economist, Economics and Statistics Administration, U.S. Department of Commerce (November 13, 2017), Women in STEM: 2017 Update (ESA Issue Brief #06-17). Retrieved from www.esa.gov/reports/women-stem-2017-update; Statistic Brain, "Youth Sports Statistics." Retrieved from www.statisticbrain.com/youth-sports-statistics/; Merran Toerien, Sue Wilkinson, and Precilla Y. L. Choi, "Body Hair Removal: The 'Mundane' Production of Normative Femininity," *Sex Roles* 52, no. 5–6 (2005): 399–406; Marika Tiggemann and Suzanna Hodgson, "The Hairlessness Norm Extended: Reasons for and Predictors of Women's Body Hair Removal at Different Body Sites," *Sex Roles* 59, no. 11–12 (2008): 889–97; Michael S. Boroughs, "Body Depilation among Women and Men: The Association of Body Hair Reduction or Removal with Body Satisfaction, Appearance Comparison, Body Image Disturbance, and Body Dysmorphic Disorder Symptomatology," Dissertation, 2012, scholarcommons.usf.edu.

30. Susan A. Basow and Joanna Willis, "Perceptions of Body Hair on White Women: Effects of Labeling," *Psychological Reports* 89 (2001): 571–76; Breanne Fahs, "Dreaded 'Otherness': Heteronormative Patrolling in Women's Body Hair Rebellions," *Gender & Society* 25, no. 4 (2011): 451–72; Breanne Fahs, "Shaving It All off: Examining Social Norms of Body Hair among College Men in a Women's Studies Course," *Women's Studies: An Inter-disciplinary Journal* 42 (2013): 559–77; Breanne Fahs, "Perilous Patches and Pitstaches: Imagined versus Lived Experiences of Women's Body Hair Growth," *Psychology of Women Quarterly* 38, no. 2 (2014): 167–80; Breanne Fahs and Denise A. Delgado, "The Specter of Excess: Race, Class, and Gender in Women's Body Hair Narratives." In *Embodied Resistance: Breaking the Rules, Challenging the Norms*, ed. Chris Bobel and Samantha Kwan (Nashville: Vanderbilt University Press, 2011), 13–25; Rebecca M. Herzig, *Plucked:*

A History of Hair Removal (New York: New York University Press, 2015).

31. Claudia Goldin and Cecilia Rouse, "Orchestrating Impartiality: The Impact of 'Blind Auditions' on Female Musicians," *The American Economic Review* 90, no. 4 (September 2000): 715–41.

32. Deborah Rhode, *Speaking of Sex: The Denial of Gender Inequality* (Cambridge: Harvard University Press, 1997), 15; Sandra Lee Bartky, "Foucault, Femininity, and the Modernization of Patriarchal Power." In *Writing on the Body: Female Embodiment and Feminist Theory*, ed. Katie Conboy, Nadia Medina, and Sarah Stanbury (New York: Columbia University Press, 1997).

33. Peter Glick et al., "Beyond Prejudice as Simple Antipathy: Hostile and Benevolent Sexism across Cultures," *Journal of Personality and Social Psychology* 79, no. 5 (2000): 765.

34. Sandra Lee Bartky, "Foucault, Femininity, and the Modernization of Patriarchal Power." In *Writing on the Body: Female Embodiment and Feminist Theory*, ed. Katie Conboy, Nadia Medina, and Sarah Stanbury (New York: Columbia University Press, 1997).

35. Dana Berkowitz, *Botox Nation: The Changing Face of America* (New York: New York University Press, 2017).

36. Karin Martin, "Giving Birth Like a Girl," *Gender and Society* 17, no. 1 (2003): 54–72.

37. Ibid, 62.

38. Ibid.

39. Nathan Ferguson, "Is This Assistant Bothering You?" *Cyborgology*, March 28, 2018. Retrieved from https://thesocietypages.org/cyborgology/2018/03/28/is-this-assistant-bothering-you/.

40. Sandra Lee Bartky, "Foucault, Femininity, and the Modernization of Patriarchal Power." In *Writing on the Body: Female Embodiment and Feminist Theory*, ed. Katie Conboy, Nadia Medina, and Sarah Stanbury (New York: Columbia University Press, 1997).

41. Ibid.

42. William M. O'Barr and Bowman K. Atkins, "'Women's Language' or 'Powerless Language'?" In *Language and Gender: A Reader*, 2nd ed., ed. Jennifer Coates (Malden, MA: Wiley-Blackwell, 2011).

43. Michael Kimmel, *Angry White Men: American Masculinity at the End of an Era* (New York, Nation Books, 2013).

44. Peter Glick et al., "Beyond Prejudice as Simple Antipathy: Hostile and Benevolent Sexism across

Cultures," *Journal of Personality and Social Psychology* 79, no. 5 (2000): 765.

45. Amanda LeCouteur and Melissa Oxlad, "Managing Accountability for Domestic Violence: Identities, Membership Categories and Morality in Perpetrators' Talk" *Feminism & Psychology* 21, no. 1 (2011): 5–28.

46. Kelly Dedel, "Sexual Assault of Women by Strangers," *Problem-Oriented Guides for Police: Problem-Specific Guides Series* 62 (2011). Retrieved from www.popcenter.org/problems/pdfs/sex_assault _women.pdf.

47. Michael M. Kasumovi and Jeffrey H. Kuzekoff, "Insights into Sexism: Male Status and Performance Moderates Female-Directed Hostile and Amicable Behaviour," *PLOS ONE* 10, no. 7 (2015): e0131613.

48. Megan Garvey, "Transcript of the Disturbing Video 'Elliot Rodger's Retribution,'" *Los Angeles Times*, May 24, 2014. Retrieved from www.latimes .com/local/lanow/la-me-ln-transcript-ucsb-shootings -video-20140524-story.html.

49. Valerie Jenness, "Engendering Hate Crime Police: Gender, the 'Dilemma' of Difference, and the Creation of Legal Subjects," *Journal of Hate Studies* 2, no. 1 (2003): 74.

50. ABC News, "George Sodini's Blog: Full Text by Alleged Gym Shooter," August 5, 2009. Retrieved from http://abcnews.go.com/US/story?id=8258001 &page=1&singlePage=true.

51. Jody Allard, M. L. Lyke, and Amy Wang, "Washington Mall Shooting Suspect Confesses to Killings, *Washington Post*, September 26, 2016. Retrieved from www.washingtonpost.com/news/post-nation /wp/2016/09/25/after-day-long-manhunt-police -arrest-20-year-old-in-washington-state-mall-killings/.

52. Nicole Chavez, "Toronto Van Attack Suspect's Facebook Post Linked to Anti-Women Ideology," *CNN*, April 25, 2018. Retrieved from www.cnn.com /2018/04/25/americas/toronto-van-attack/index. html; Kelley Weill, Taylor Lorenz, Samantha Allen, and Kate Briquelet, "White Supremacists Claim Nikolas Cruz Trained with Them; Students Say He Wore Trump Hat in School," *Daily Beast*, February 15, 2018. Retrieved from www.thedailybeast.com/nikolas-cruz -trained-with-florida-white-supremacist-group-leader- says.

53. Centers for Disease Control and Prevention, "The National Intimate Partner and Sexual Violence Survey," September 25, 2017. Retrieved from www .cdc.gov/violenceprevention/nisvs/index.html.

54. Susan B. Sorenson and Rebecca A. Schut, "Nonfatal Gun Use in Intimate Partner Violence: A Systematic Review of the Literature," *Trauma, Violence, and Abuse*, September 14, 2016.

55. Shannan Catalano, "Intimate Partner Violence; Attributes of Victimization, 1993–2011," Bureau of Justice Statistics, November 2013. Retrieved from www.bjs.gov/content/pub/pdf/ipvav9311.pdf.

56. Centers for Disease Control and Prevention, "The National Intimate Partner and Sexual Violence Survey," September 25, 2017. Retrieved from www .cdc.gov/violenceprevention/nisvs/index.html.

57. Everytown for Gun Safety, "Mass Shootings in the United States: 2009–2016, March 2017. Retrieved from https://everytownresearch.org/wp-content/up loads/2017/03/Analysis_of_Mass_Shooting_033 117.pdf.

58. Human Rights Campaign Foundation and Trans People of Color Coalition, "A Time to Act: Fatal Violence against Transgender People in America 2017," November 2017. Retrieved from http://assets2.hrc .org/files/assets/resources/A_Time_To_Act_2017 _REV3.pdf; Federal Bureau of Investigation, "Hate Crime Statistics: 2016," Fall 2017. Retrieved from https://ucr.fbi.gov/hate-crime/2016/topic-pages/vic tims.pdf.

59. Human Rights Campaign Foundation and Trans People of Color Coalition, "A Time to Act: Fatal Violence against Transgender People in America 2017," November 2017. Retrieved from http://assets2.hrc .org/files/assets/resources/A_Time_To_Act_2017 _REV3.pdf.

60. Emily Waters, Larissa Pham, and Chelsea Convery, "A Crisis of Hate: A Report on Homicides against Lesbian, Gay, Bisexual and Transgender People," National Coalition of AntiViolence Programs (NCAVP), 2018. Retrieved from http://avp .org/wp-content/uploads/2018/01/a-crisis-of-hate -january-release-12218.pdf.

61. George Yancy, "James Bond Is a Wimp," *New York Times*, February 26, 2018. Retrieved from www .nytimes.com/2018/02/26/opinion/drucilla-cornell -misogyny-sex-gender.html.

62. Suruchi Thapar-Bjoerkert and, Karen J. Morgan, "'But Sometimes I Think . . . They Put Themselves in the Situation': Exploring Blame and Responsibility in Interpersonal Violence," *Violence against Women* 16, no. 1 (2010): 32–59.

63. Laurie Penny, "Who Does She Think She Is?" *Longreads*, March 2018. Retrieved from https://

longreads.com/2018/03/28/who-does-she-think-she-is/.

64. Susan Bordo, *The Male Body: A New Look at Men in Public and Private* (New York: Farrar Straus Giroux, 1999); Josep Armengol (ed.), *Embodying Masculinities: Towards a History of the Male Body in U.S. Culture and Literature* (New York: Peter Lang, 2013); Robert Rushing, *Descended from Hercules: Biopolitics and the Muscled Male Body on Screen* (Bloomington: Indiana University Press, 2016); Iris Marion Young, *On Female Body Experience: "Throwing Like a Girl" and Other Essays* (New York: Oxford University Press, 2005); Jocelyn Hollander, "Vulnerability and Dangerousness: The Construction of Gender through Conversations about Violence," *Gender & Society* 15, no. 1 (2001): 83–109; Sandra Bartky, "Foucault, Femininity, and the Modernization of Patriarchal Power." In *Feminism and Foucault: Reflections on Resistance*, ed. Irene Diamond and Lee Quinby (Boston: Northeastern University Press, 1988), 93–111; Susan Bordo, "Reading the Slender Body." In *Body Politics: Women and the Discourses of Science*, ed. Mary Jacobus, Evelyn Fox Keller, and Sally Shuttleworth (New York: Routledge, 1990), 83–112.

65. Jill E. Yavorsky and Liana Sayer, "'Doing Fear': The Influence of Hetero-Femininity on (Trans)women's Fears of Victimization," *Sociological Quarterly* 54, no. 4 (2013): 511–33.

66. Ibid., 511–33.

67. J. Clay Warner, "Avoiding Rape: The Effects of Protective Actions and Situational Factors on Rape Outcome," *Violence and Victims* 17 (2002): 691–705; S. E. Ullman, "Does Offender Violence Escalate When Women Fight Back?" *Journal of Interpersonal Violence* 13 (1998): 179–92; S. E. Ullman, "A 10-Year Update of 'Review and Critique of Empirical Studies of Rape Avoidance,'" *Criminal Justice and Behavior* 34 (2007): 1–19.

68. Jocelyn Hollander, "The Roots of Resistance to Women's Self-Defense," *Violence against Women* 15, no. 5 (2009): 574–94.

69. Ellen Barry, "In Sweden's Preschools, Boys Learn to Dance and Girls Learn to Yell," *New York Times*, March 24, 2018. Retrieved from www.nytimes.com/2018/03/24/world/europe/sweden-gender-neutral-preschools.html.

70. R. W. Connell, *Gender and Power: Society, the Person, and Sexual Politics* (Stanford: Stanford University Press, 1987), 183.

71. Ashley Mears, "Girls as Elite Distinction: The Appropriation of Bodily Capital," *Poetics* 53 (2015): 22–37; Kimberly Kay Hoang, *Dealing in Desire: Asian Ascendancy, Western Decline, and the Hidden Currencies of Global Sex Work* (Berkeley: University of California Press, 2015).

72. Kimberly Kay Hoang, *Dealing in Desire: Asian Ascendancy, Western Decline, and the Hidden Currencies of Global Sex Work* (Berkeley: University of California Press, 2015).

73. Michael Kimmel, "Saving the Males: The Sociological Implications of the Virginia Military Institute and the Citadel," *Gender & Society* 14, no. 4 (2000): 494–516.

74. Nikki Jones, "Working 'the Code': On Girls, Gender, and Inner-City Violence," *Australian & New Zealand Journal of Criminology* 41, no. 1 (2008): 63–83.

75. Nikki Jones, "'I Was Aggressive for the Streets, Pretty for the Pictures': Gender, Difference, and the Inner-City Girl," *Gender & Society* 23, no. 1 (2009): 89–93, p. 89.

76. Center for American Women and Politics, "Finding Gender in Election 2016: Lessons from Presidential Gender Watch." Retrieved from http://presidentialgenderwatch.org/wp-content/uploads/2017/05/Finding-Gender-in-Election-2016_Highlights.pdf.

77. Ju-Min Park, "Is South Korea Ready for 'Madame President'?" *Chicago Tribune*, December 11, 2012.

78. Ermine Saner, "Top 10 Sexist Moments in Politics: Julia Gillard, Hillary Clinton and More," *Guardian*, June 14, 2013.

79. Gina Serignese Woodall and Kim L. Fridkin, "Shaping Women's Chances: Stereotypes and the Media." In *Rethinking Madam President: Are We Ready for a Woman in the White House?* ed. Lori Cox Han and Caroline Heldman (Boulder, CO: Lynne Rienner Publishers, 2007), 1–16.

80. Nathan Heflick and Jamie Goldenberg, "Sarah Palin, a Nation Object(ifie)s," *Sex Roles* 65 (2011): 156–64; Jennier L. Pozner, "Hot and Bothering: Media Treatment of Sarah Palin," *NPR*, July 8, 2009. Retrieved from www.npr.org/templates/story/story.php?storyId=106384060.

81. Patricia Hill Collins, *Black Feminist Thought: Knowledge, Consciousness, and the Politics of Empowerment* (Boston: Unwin Hyman, 1990); bell hooks, *Feminist Theory: From Margin to Center* (Cambridge, MA: South End Press, 1984); Gloria Anzaldúa, *Borderlands/La Frontera: The New Mestiza* (San Francisco: Aunt Lute Books, 1987); Trinh T. Minh-Ha, *Woman, Native, Other: Writing Postcoloniality and*

Feminism (Bloomington: Indiana University Press, 1989).

82. Patricia Hill Collins, *Black Feminist Thought: Knowledge, Consciousness, and the Politics of Empowerment* (New York: Routledge, 1990).

83. Collins and Bilge, *Intersectionality* (Cambridge, UK: Polity, 2017).

84. Feminist.com, "Pro-Feminist Men's Groups Links," Feminist.com. Retrieved from www.feminist.com /resources/links/links_men.html.

85. *White Ribbon*, www.whiteribbon.ca/; Michael Kaufman, "White Ribbon Campaign: 20 Years Working to End Violence against Women," *Michael Kaufman* (blog), November 24, 2011. Retrieved from www .michaelkaufman.com/2011/white-ribbon-campaign -20-years-working-to-end-violence-against-women/.

86. *National Organization for Men against Sexism*, http://nomas.org/principles/.

87. Men Can Stop Rape, "Our Mission & History." Retrieved from www.mencanstoprape.org/Our-Mission-History/.

88. Floyd Dell, "Feminism for Men." In *Against the Tide: Profeminist Men in the United States, 1776–1990, a Documentary History*, ed. Michael Kimmel and Thomas Mosmiller (Boston: Beacon Press, 1992 [1917]).

89. Jean Twenge, "Status and Gender: The Paradox of Progress in an Age of Narcissism," *Sex Roles* 61 (2009): 338–40.

90. Philip Cohen, "How Can We Jump-Start the Struggle for Gender Equality?" *New York Times*, November 23, 2013; Paula England, "The Gender Revolution: Uneven and Stalled," *Gender & Society* 24, no. 2 (2010): 149–66; Scott Jaschik, "Women Lead in Doctorates," *Inside Higher Ed*, September 14, 2010. Retrieved from www.insidehighered.com/news /2010/09/14/doctorates; David Cotter, Joan H. Hermsen, and Reeve Vanneman, "The End of the Gender Revolution? Gender Role Attitudes from 1977 to 2008," *American Journal of Sociology* 117, no. 1 (2011): 259–89; Sarah Friedman, "Still a 'Stalled Revolution'? Work/Family Experiences, Hegemonic Masculinity, and Moving toward Gender Equality," *Sociology Compass* 9, no. 2 (2015): 140–55.

91. Bureau of Labor Statistics, "Women in the Labor Force: A Databook," November 2017. Retrieved from www.bls.gov/opub/reports/womens-databook/2017 /home.htm.

92. U.S. Department of Education, National Center for Education Statistics, "Digest of Education Statistics," Table 318.10: Degrees Conferred by Postsecondary Institutions, by Level of Degree and Sex of Student: Selected Years, 1869–70 through 2026–27. Retrieved from https://nces.ed.gov/programs/digest /d16/tables/dt16_318.10.asp?current=yes.

93. Arlie Russell Hochschild, with Anne Machung, *The Second Shift: Working Parents and the Revolution at Home* (New York: Penguin Books, 1989).

Chapter 8: Institutions

1. Strobe Talbott, "Monnet's Brandy and Europe's Fate," The Brookings Essay, February 11, 2014. Retrieved from http://csweb.brookings.edu/content /research/essays/2014/monnets-brandy-and-europes -fate.html.

2. Juliet Lapidos, "Do Kids Need a Summer Vacation?" *Slate*, July 11, 2007. Retrieved from www.slate .com/articles/news_and_politics/explainer/2007 /07/do_kids_need_a_summer_vacation.html.

3. Barrie Thorne, *Gender Play: Girls and Boy in School* (New Brunswick: Rutgers University Press, 1993), 44.

4. Ibid., 44.

5. Ibid., 84.

6. See http://riceinstitute.org/wordpress/2014/07/01 /new-maps-which-country-has-the-most-open-defe cation-in-the-world/.

7. Terry Kogan, "Sex Separation: The Cure-All for Victorian Social Anxiety," in *Toilet: Public Restrooms and the Politics of Sharing*, ed. Harvey Molotch and Laura Norén (New York: New York University Press, 2010), quoted on p. 157.

8. Ibid., quoted on p. 157.

9. Ibid., 145–64.

10. Harvey Molotch and Laura Norén, *Toilet: Public Restrooms and the Politics of Sharing* (New York: New York University Press, 2010).

11. Betsy Lucal, "What It Means to Be Gendered Me: Life on the Boundaries of a Dichotomous Gender System," *Gender & Society* 13, no. 6 (1999): 787.

12. Ibid., 787.

13. U.S. Equal Employment Opportunity Commission, "Bathroom/Facility Access and Transgender Employees." Retrieved from www.eeoc.gov/eeoc /publications/fs-bathroom-access-transgender.cfm; Jeremy W. Peters, Jo Becker, and Julie Hirschfeld Davis, "Trump Rescinds Rules on Bathrooms for Transgender Students," *New York Times*, Febru-

ary 22, 2017. Retrieved from www.nytimes.com/2017/02/22/us/politics/devos-sessions-transgender-students-rights.html.

14. Emanuella Grinberg and Dani Stewart, "3 Myths That Shape the Transgender Bathroom Debate," *CNN*, March 7, 2017. Retrieved from www.cnn.com/2017/03/07/health/transgender-bathroom-law-facts-myths/.

15. Eileen Boris, "'You Wouldn't Want One of 'Em Dancing with Your Wife': Racialized Bodies on the Job in World War II," *American Quarterly* 50, no. 1 (1998): 77–108.

16. Statista, "Wholesale Sales of U.S. Sports Product Industry in the U.S. 2008–2016," Statista, March 2017. Retrieved from www.statista.com/statistics/240946/sports-products-industry-wholesale-sales-in-the-us/.

17. Maury Brown, "MLB Sets Record for Revenues in 2017, Increasing More than $500 Million since 2015," *Forbes*, November 22, 2017. Retrieved from www.forbes.com/sites/maurybrown/2017/11/22/mlb-sets-record-for-revenues-in-2017-increasing-more-than-500-million-since-2015/#69051b4a7880; Eben Novy-Williams, "NFL Teams Split Record $7.8 Billion in 2016, Up 10 Percent," *Bloomberg*, July 12, 2017. Retrieved from www.bloomberg.com/news/articles/2017-07-12/nfl-teams-split-record-7-8-billion-in-2016-up-10-percent.

18. Sue Macy, *Wheels of Change: How Women Rode the Bicycle to Freedom (with a Few Flat Tires along the Way)* (National Geographic Society, 2011).

19. Nellie Bly, "'Let Me Tell You What I Think of Bicycling': Nellie Bly Interviews Susan B. Anthony, 1896," *The Hairpin*, April 28, 2014. Retrieved from https://thehairpin.com/let-me-tell-you-what-i-think-of-bicycling-nellie-bly-interviews-susan-b-anthony-1896-c2b15900a5a8.

20. Joseph Stromberg, "'Bicycle Face': A 19th-Century Health Problem Made Up to Scare Women Away from Biking," *Vox*, March 24, 2015. Retrieved from www.vox.com/2014/7/8/5880931/the-19th-century-health-scare-that-told-women-to-worry-about-bicycle.

21. Statistic Brain, "Youth Sports Statistics." Retrieved from www.statisticbrain.com/youth-sports-statistics/.

22. Jean Twenge, "Mapping Gender: The Multifactorial Approach and the Organization of Gender-Related Attributes," *Psychology of Women Quarterly* 23, no. 3 (1999): 485–502.

23. Rosalind Miles, *The Rites of Man: Love, Sex, and Death in the Making of the Male* (Hammersmith, UK: Paladin, 1992); Michael Messner, *Power at Play: Sports and the Problem of Masculinity* (Boston: Beacon Press, 1992), 24.

24. Michael Messner, *Power at Play: Sports and the Problem of Masculinity* (Boston: Beacon Press, 1992), 61.

25. R. W. Connell, *Which Way Is Up?* (North Sydney: George Unwin and Allen, 1983), 18.

26. Michael Messner, "Becoming 100% Straight," in *Privilege: A Reader*, ed. Michael Kimmel and Abby Ferber (Philadelphia: Westview Press, 2010), 87.

27. Michael Messner, *Power at Play: Sports and the Problem of Masculinity* (Boston: Beacon Press, 1992), 33.

28. Messner quoted in Jennifer Hargreaves, *Sporting Females: Critical Issues in the History and Sociology of Women's Sports* (New York: Routledge, 1994), 38.

29. Todd W. Crosset, *Outsiders in the Clubhouse: The World of Women's Professional Golf* (Albany: State University of New York Press, 1995), 223–24.

30. Michael Messner, "Boys and Girls Together: The Promise and Limitations of Equal Opportunity in Sports," in *Sex, Violence, and Power in Sports: Rethinking Masculinity*, ed. Michael Messner and Donald Sabo (Freedom, CA: The Crossing Press, 1994), 200.

31. Jane English, "Sex Equality in Sports," in *Femininity, Masculinity, and Androgyny*, ed. Mary Vetterling-Braggin (Boston: Littlefield, Adams, 1982).

32. Michael Messner, "Sports and Male Domination: The Female Athlete as Contested Ideological Terrain," in *Women, Sport and Culture*, ed. Susan Birrell and Cheryl L. Cole (Champaign, IL: Human Kinetics, 1994), 65–80.

33. Ibid., 71.

34. Ibid., 71.

35. Olympic Games, "BMX Course Ready to Roll for Rio 2016," September 9, 2015. Retrieved from www.olympic.org/news/bmx-course-ready-to-roll-for-rio-2016; Ella Koeze, "What If Men and Women Skied against Each Other in the Olympics?" Five ThirtyEight, February 14, 2018. Retrieved from https://fivethirtyeight.com/features/what-if-men-and-women-skied-against-each-other-in-the-olympics/?src=ob bottom=ar_5.

36. Abigail Feder, "'A Radiant Smile from the Lovely Lady': Overdetermined Femininity in 'Ladies' Figure Skating," in *Women on Ice*, ed. Cynthia Baughman (New York: Routledge, 1995), 24.

37. Lex Boyle, "Flexing the Tensions of Female Muscularity: How Female Bodybuilders Negotiate Normative

Femininity in Competitive Bodybuilding," *Women's Studies Quarterly* 33, no. 1/2 (2005): 134–49; see also Anne Bolin, "Vandalized Vanity: Feminine Physiques Betrayed and Portrayed," in *Tattoo, Torture, Mutilation, and Adornment: The Denaturalization of the Body in Culture and Text*, ed. Frances Mascia-Lees and Patricia Sharpe (Albany: State University of New York Press, 1992), 79–99.

38. International Federation of Bodybuilding, "IFBB Rules for Bodybuilding and Fitness: 2017 Edition." Retrieved from www.ifbb.com/wp-content/uploads/2017/07/IFBB-General-Rules-2017-Julio.pdf.

39. Susan Mitchell and Ken Dyer, *Winning Women: Challenging the Norms in Australian Sport* (Ringwood, Victoria: Penguin, 1985).

40. Michael Messner, *Power at Play: Sports and the Problem of Masculinity* (Boston: Beacon Press, 1992), 1.

41. Jonathan Wall, "Girl Football Player Sits Out Game after Foe Threatens Forfeit," *Yahoo! Sports*, October 13, 2011. Retrieved from https://ca.sports.yahoo.com/blogs/highschool-prep-rally/girl-football-player-sits-game-foe-threatens-forfeit-130942497.html.

42. Boston Globe, "Lunenburg Girl Won a Boys' Golf Tournament But Was Denied the Trophy, *Boston Globe*, October 26, 2017. Retrieved from www.bostonglobe.com/sports/high-schools/2017/10/25/lunenburg-emily-nash-won-boys-golf-tournament-but-was-denied-winner-trophy-because-she-girl/WtZDRnhPDe8rd7Bv5vMJ5J/story.html.

43. Colleen O'Connor, "Girls Going to the Mat," *Denver Post*, December 23, 2007.

44. Eileen McDonagh and Laura Pappano, *Playing with the Boys: Why Separate Is Not Equal in Sports* (New York: Oxford University Press, 2008).

45. Staff, "Vision Quest: Alaskan Girl Wins State H.S. Wrestling Title Over Boys," *Sports Illustrated*, February 6, 2006.

46. Ella Koeze, "What If Men and Women Skied against Each Other in the Olympics?" FiveThirtyEight, February 14, 2018. Retrieved from https://fivethirtyeight.com/features/what-if-men-and-women-skied-against-each-other-in-the-olympics/?src=ob bottom=ar_5.

47. Jessica Dickler, "This WNBA Superstar Earns Just 20% of an NBA Player's Salary," *CNBC*, October 3, 2017. Retrieved from www.cnbc.com/2017/10/03/this-wnba-superstar-earns-just-20-percent-of-an-nba-players-salary.html.

48. *Forbes*, "The World's Highest-Paid Athletes," *Forbes*, June 2017. Retrieved from www.forbes.com/athletes/list/.

49. Todd W. Crosset, *Outsiders in the Clubhouse: The World of Women's Professional Golf* (Albany: State University of New York Press, 1995), 224.

50. Laura La Bella, *Women in Sports* (New York: The Rosen Publishing Group, 2013).

51. Todd W. Crosset, *Outsiders in the Clubhouse: The World of Women's Professional Golf* (Albany: State University of New York Press, 1995), 225.

52. Harvey Molotch, "On Not Making History: What NYU Did with the Toilet and What It Means for the World," in *Toilet: Public Restrooms and the Politics of Sharing*, ed. Harvey Molotch and Laura Norén (New York: New York University Press, 2010), 255–72.

53. Ibid., 258.

54. Ibid., 261.

55. U.S. Code Title 20, Chapter 38, Section 1681: Sex, *Legal Information Institute*. Retrieved from www.law.cornell.edu/uscode/20/1681.html.

56. NCAA, "45 Years of Title IX: The Status of Women in Intercollegiate Athletics," NCAA, June 2017. Retrieved from www.ncaa.org/sites/default/files/TitleIX45-295-FINAL_WEB.pdf.

57. Ibid.

58. Liz Roscher, "MLB Announces New Girls Baseball Camp, Plus the Return of the All-Girls Trailblazer Series," *Yahoo! Sports*, April 2, 2018. Retrieved from https://sports.yahoo.com/mlb-announces-new-girls-baseball-camp-plus-return-girls-trailblazer-series-162654801.html.

59. Raewyn Connell, *Gender and Power: Society, the Person, and Sexual Politics* (Stanford: Stanford University Press, 1987), 139.

Chapter 9: Change

1. Jaclyn Geller, *Here Comes the Bride: Women, Weddings, and the Marriage Mystique* (New York: Four Walls Eight Windows, 2001).

2. John D'Emilio and Estelle Freedman, *Intimate Matters: A History of Sexuality in America* (Chicago: University of Chicago Press, 1997), 28.

3. Ibid.

4. Quoted in Claude Levi-Strauss, *The Elementary Structures of Kinship* (Boston: Beacon Press, [1949], 1969), 481.

5. Francis J. Bremer and Tom Webster, *Puritans and Puritanism in Europe and America: A Comprehensive Encyclopedia*, vol. 2 (Santa Barbara: ABC-CLIO, Inc., 2006), 152.

6. Alan Taylor, *American Colonies* (New York: Viking, 2001).

7. Robert Fogel, *Without Consent or Contract: The Rise and Fall of American Slavery* (New York: W. W. Norton and Company, 1989); Shirley Hill, "Class, Race, and Gender Dimensions of Child Rearing in African American Families," *Journal of Black Studies* 31, no. 4 (2001): 494–508.

8. Quoted in Robert Fogel, *Without Consent or Contract: The Rise and Fall of American Slavery* (New York: W. W. Norton and Company, 1989), 163.

9. Estelle Freeman, "Sexuality in Nineteenth-Century America: Behavior, Ideology, and Politics," *Reviews in American History* 10, no. 4 (1982): 196–215.

10. Ibid; see also Robert Woods, *The Demography of Victorian England and Wales* (Cambridge: Cambridge University Press, 2000).

11. Estelle Freeman, "Sexuality in Nineteenth-Century America: Behavior, Ideology, and Politics," *Reviews in American History* 10, no. 4 (1982): 196–215.

12. Ibid.; see also Steven Seidman, "The Power of Desire and the Danger of Pleasure: Victorian Sexuality Reconsidered," *Journal of Social History* 24, no. 1 (1990): 47–67.

13. Francesca Cancian, "The Feminization of Love," *Signs* 11, no. 4 (1986): 692–709; Steven Seidman, "The Power of Desire and the Danger of Pleasure: Victorian Sexuality Reconsidered," *Journal of Social History* 24, no. 1 (1990): 47–67.

14. Steven Seidman, "The Power of Desire and the Danger of Pleasure: Victorian Sexuality Reconsidered," *Journal of Social History* 24, no. 1 (1990): 47–67; Estelle Freeman, "Sexuality in Nineteenth-Century America: Behavior, Ideology, and Politics," *Reviews in American History* 10, no. 4 (1982): 196–215.

15. Ibid.

16. Robert Long, "Sexuality in the Victorian Era." Lecture Presented to Innominate Society. Retrieved from www.innominatesociety.com/Articles/Sexuality%20In%20The%20Victorian%20Era.htm.

17. Ibid.

18. William Acton, *Prostitution, Considered in Its Moral, Social, and Sanitary Aspects* (1870). Retrieved from http://archive.org/details/prostitutioncons00

acto; Stephanie Coontz, "Blame Affairs on Evolution of Sex Roles," *CNN Opinion*, November 18, 2012. Retrieved from www.cnn.com/2012/11/17/opinion/coontz-powerful-men-affairs/index.html.

19. Estelle Freeman, "Sexuality in Nineteenth-Century America: Behavior, Ideology, and Politics," *Reviews in American History* 10, no. 4 (1982): 196–215; Joane Nagel, *Race, Ethnicity, and Sexuality: Intimate Intersections, Forbidden Frontiers* (New York: Oxford University Press, 2003).

20. Joy Hakim, *War, Peace, and All That Jazz* (New York: Oxford University Press, 1995).

21. Douglas Harper, *Online Etymology Dictionary*, 2014. Retrieved from www.etymonline.com/index.php?allowed_in_frame=0&search=sexy&searchmode=none.

22. John D'Emilio and Estelle Freedman, *Intimate Matters: A History of Sexuality in America* (Chicago: University of Chicago Press, 1997), 279.

23. Beth Bailey, *From Front Porch to Back Seat* (Baltimore: Johns Hopkins University, 1988).

24. Ibid., 20.

25. Ibid., 20.

26. Kathy Peiss, "'Charity Girls' and City Pleasures: Historical Notes on Working-Class Sexuality, 1880–1920," in *Passion and Power: Sexuality in History*, ed. Kathy Peiss and Christina Simmons, with Robert A. Padgug (Philadelphia: Temple University Press, 1989), 63.

27. Ibid., 61.

28. Lynn Peril, *College Girls: Bluestockings, Sex Kittens, and Coeds, Then and Now* (New York: W. W. Norton and Company, 2006).

29. John M. Murrin, Paul E. Jonson, and James M. McPherson, *Liberty, Equality, Power: A History of the American People* (Boston: Thomson Wadsworth, 2008).

30. John D'Emilio and Estelle Freedman, *Intimate Matters: A History of Sexuality in America* (Chicago: University of Chicago Press, 1997), 279.

31. Ibid., 199.

32. National Abortion Federation, "History of Abortion." Retrieved from https://prochoice.org/education-and-advocacy/about-abortion/history-of-abortion/.

33. Amin Ghaziani, *Sex Cultures* (Malden, MA: Polity Press, 2017); Colin Spencer, *Homosexuality in*

History (New York: Harcourt Brace & Company, 1995); George Chauncey, *Gay New York: Gender, Urban Culture, and the Making of the Gay Male World, 1890–1940* (New York: Basic Books, 1994).

34. Quoted in D'Emilio and Freedman, *Intimate Matters: A History of Sexuality in America* (Chicago: University of Chicago Press, 1997), 226–27.

35. John D'Emilio, "Capitalism and Gay Identity," in *Powers of Desire: The Politics of Sexuality*, ed. A. Snitow, C. Stansell, and S. Thompson (New York: Monthly Review Press, 1983), 100–113.

36. B. E. Wells and J. M. Twenge, "Changes in Young People's Sexual Behavior and Attitudes, 1943–1999: A Cross-Temporal Meta-Analysis," *Review of General Psychology* 9 (2005): 249–61; Jennifer L. Petersen and Janet Shilbey Hyde, "A Meta-Analytic Review of Research on Gender Differences in Sexuality, 1993–2007," *Psychological Bulletin* 136, no. 1 (2010): 21–38.

37. Stephanie Coontz, "The World Historical Transformation of Marriage," *Journal of Marriage and Family* 66, no. 4 (2004): 974–79, 977.

38. Ibid.

39. Linda Gordon, *Social Insurance and Public Assistance: The Influence of Gender in Welfare Thought in the United States, 1890–1935* (Madison: University of Wisconsin Press, 1992).

40. Stephanie Coontz, *The Way We Never Were: American Families and the Nostalgia Trap* (New York: Basic Books, 1992), 58.

41. Estelle Freeman, "Sexuality in Nineteenth-Century America: Behavior, Ideology, and Politics," *Reviews in American History* 10, no. 4 (1982): 196–215; Stephanie Coontz, *The Way We Never Were: American Families and the Nostalgia Trap* (New York: Basic Books, 1992).

42. Stephanie Coontz, *The Way We Never Were: American Families and the Nostalgia Trap* (New York: Basic Books, 1992), 25, 27.

43. John D'Emilio and Estelle Freedman, *Intimate Matters: A History of Sexuality in America* (Chicago: University of Chicago Press, 1997), 283.

44. Carroll Smith-Rosenberg, *Disorderly Conduct: Visions of Gender in Victorian America* (New York: Oxford University Press, 1985), 55–56.

45. Beth Bailey, *From Front Porch to Back Seat* (Baltimore: Johns Hopkins University, 1988); Lynn Peril, *College Girls: Bluestockings, Sex Kittens, and Coeds,*

Then and Now (New York: W. W. Norton and Company, 2006).

46. John D'Emilio and Estelle Freedman, *Intimate Matters: A History of Sexuality in America* (Chicago: University of Chicago Press, 1997), citing a study by Katharine Davis, p. 193.

47. K. A. Cuordileone, "'Politics in an Age of Anxiety': Cold War Political Culture and the Crisis in American Masculinity, 1949–1960," *The Journal of American History* 87, no. 2 (2000): 515–45.

48. Francis J. Bremer and Tom Webster, *Puritans and Puritanism in Europe and America: A Comprehensive Encyclopedia*, vol. 2 (Santa Barbara: ABC-CLIO, Inc., 2006).

49. U.S. Selective Service and Victory (Washington, D.C.: Government Printing Office, 1948), 91.

50. John D'Emilio and Estelle Freedman, *Intimate Matters: A History of Sexuality in America* (Chicago: University of Chicago Press, 1997), 290.

51. Ibid., 289.

52. For historical context, see the documentary *Before Stonewall*, dir. Greta Schiller and Robert Rosenberg (1984). Retrieved from www.imdb.com/title/tt0088782/.

53. K. A. Cuordileone, "'Politics in an Age of Anxiety': Cold War Political Culture and the Crisis in American Masculinity, 1949–1960," *The Journal of American History* 87, no. 2 (2000): 515–45.

54. Gwendolyn Mink, *The Wages of Motherhood: Inequality in the Welfare State 1917–1943* (Ithaca: Cornell University Press, 1996).

55. Fred Fejes, "Murder, Perversion, and Moral Panic: The 1954 Media Campaign against Miami's Homosexuals and the Discourse of Civic Betterment," *Journal of the History of Sexuality* 9, no. 3 (2000): 305–47.

56. K. A. Cuordileone, "'Politics in an Age of Anxiety': Cold War Political Culture and the Crisis in American Masculinity, 1949–1960," *The Journal of American History* 87, no. 2 (2000): 532.

57. Ibid., 515–45.

58. Beth Bailey, *From Front Porch to Back Seat* (Baltimore: Johns Hopkins University Press, 1988).

59. Ibid., 53.

60. John D'Emilio and Estelle Freedman, *Intimate Matters: A History of Sexuality in America* (Chicago: University of Chicago Press, 1997), 261.

61. Cited in Beth Bailey, *From Front Porch to Back Seat* (Baltimore: Johns Hopkins University Press, 1988), 81.

62. Stephanie Coontz, *The Way We Never Were: American Families and the Nostalgia Trap* (New York: Basic Books, 2002), 202.

63. United States Census Bureau, "Historical Marital Status Tables," *Estimated Median Age of First Marriage, by Sex: 1890 to Present*, November 2017. Retrieved from www.census.gov/data/tables/time-series/demo/families/marital.html.

64. Alfred Kinsey, *Sexual Behavior of the Human Male* (Bloomington: Indiana University Press, 1948).

65. Betty Friedan, *The Feminine Mystique* (New York: W. W. Norton and Company, 1963), 15.

66. Louis Menand, "Books as Bombs: Why the Women's Movement Needed *The Feminine Mystique*," *New Yorker*, January 24, 2011. Retrieved from www.newyorker.com/arts/critics/books/2011/01/24/110124crbo_books_menand.

67. Stephanie Coontz, *A Strange Stirring: The Feminine Mystique and American Women at the Dawn of the 1960s* (Philadelphia: Basic Books, 2011).

68. Stephanie Coontz, *The Way We Never Were: American Families and the Nostalgia Trap* (New York: Basic Books, 1992).

69. Ibid., 31.

70. Carol Warren, *Madwives: Schizophrenic Women in the 1950s* (New Brunswick: Rutgers University Press, 1987).

71. Stephanie Coontz, *The Way We Never Were: American Families and the Nostalgia Trap* (New York: Basic Books, 1992), 37.

72. Quoted in ibid., 37.

73. Jennifer L. Reimer, "Psychiatric Drugs: A History in Ads," *Practical Madness*, March 2010. Retrieved from www.practiceofmadness.com/2010/03/psychiatric-drugs-a-history-in-ads/.

74. Stephanie Coontz, *The Way We Never Were: American Families and the Nostalgia Trap* (New York: Basic Books, 1992), 36.

75. S. Straussner and P. Attia, "Women's Addiction and Treatment through a Historical Lens," in *The Handbook of Addiction Treatment for Women*, ed. S. Straussner and S. Brown (San Francisco: Jossey-Bass, 2002), 3–25.

76. Betty Friedan, *The Feminine Mystique* (New York: W. W. Norton and Company, 1963), 15.

77. Barbara Ehrenreich, *The Hearts of Men: American Dreams and the Flight from Commitment* (New York: Anchor Books, 1987).

78. Ibid., 50.

79. Ibid., 50.

80. Claudia Goldin, *Understanding the Gender Gap: An Economic History of American Women* (New York: Oxford University Press, 1990).

81. Judith Warner, *Perfect Madness: Motherhood in the Age of Anxiety* (New York: Riverhead Books, 2005), 138; D. A. Cotter, J. M. Hermsen, and P. England, "Moms and Jobs: Trends in Mothers' Employment and which Mothers Stay Home," in *American Families: A Multicultural Reader*, ed. S. Coontz, M. Parson, and G. Raley, 2nd. ed. (New York: Routledge, 2008), 379–86.

82. C. Wright Mills, *White Collar: The American Middle Classes* (New York: Oxford University Press, 1951).

83. Claudia Goldin, *Understanding the Gender Gap: An Economic History of American Women* (New York: Oxford University Press, 1990); Stephanie Coontz, *The Way We Never Were: American Families and the Nostalgia Trap* (New York: Basic Books, 1992).

84. Beth Bailey, *From Front Porch to Back Seat* (Baltimore: Johns Hopkins University Press, 1988).

85. Claudia Goldin, *Understanding the Gender Gap: An Economic History of American Women* (New York: Oxford University Press, 1990).

86. Ibid.

87. Ibid.

88. Susan Lehrer, *Origins of Protective Labor Legislation for Women* (Albany: State University of New York Press, 1987).

89. Ibid.

90. Ibid.

91. Cynthia Deitch, "Gender, Race, and Class Politics and the Inclusion of Women in the Title VII of the 1964 Civil Rights Act," *Gender & Society* 7, no. 2 (1993): 183–203.

92. Jo Freeman, *We Will Be Heard: Women's Struggles for Political Power in the United States* (New York: Rowman & Littlefield Publishers, 2008).

93. Myra Marx Ferree, "Beyond Separate Spheres: Feminism and Family Research," *Journal of Marriage and Family* 52, no. 4 (1990): 866–84.

94. Lynn Weiner, *From Working Girl to Working Mother: The Female Labor Force in the United States*

1820–1980 (Chapel Hill: University of Carolina Press, 2016).

95. James Dobson, "Dr. James Dobson's Newsletter: Marriage on the Ropes?" *Focus on the Family Newsletter*, September 2003. Retrieved from www.catholicfamilycatalog.com/dr-james-dobson-on-marriage.htm.

96. Heidi I. Hartmann, "The Family as the Locus of Gender, Class, and Political Struggle: The Example of Housework," *Signs* 6, no. 3 (1981): 366–94.

97. Lenore Weitzman, *The Divorce Revolution: The Unexpected Social and Economic Consequences for Women and Children in America* (New York: The Free Press, 1985).

98. P. J. Smock, W. D. Manning, and S. Gupta, "The Effect of Marriage and Divorce on Women's Economic Well-Being," *American Sociological Review* 64, no. 6 (1999): 794–812.

99. Reprints of her more incendiary speeches from the 1970s are collected in Phyllis Schlafly, *Feminist Fantasies*, ed. Ann Coulter (Dallas: Spence Publishers, 2003).

100. Leslie Steiner, *Mommy Wars: Stay-at-Home and Career Moms Face Off about Their Choices, Their Lives, Their Families* (New York: Random House, 2006); Miriam Peskowitz, *The Truth Behind the Mommy Wars* (Boston: DaCapo Press, 2005).

101. Myra Marx Ferree, "The View from Below: Women's Employment and Gender Equality in Working Class Families," *Marriage and Family Review* 7, no. 3/4 (1984): 57–75; Myra Marx Ferree, "Class, Housework, and Happiness," *Sex Roles* 11, no. 11/12 (1984): 1057–74.

102. Stephanie Coontz, "The World Historical Transformation of Marriage," *Journal of Marriage and Family* 66, no. 4 (2004): 974.

103. Ye Luo, Tracey A. LaPierre, Mary Elizabeth Hughes, and Linda J. Waite, "Grandparents Providing Care to Grandchildren: A Population-Based Study of Continuity and Change," *Journal of Family Issues* 33, no. 9 (2012): 1143–67.

104. Charles Q. Strohm, Judith A. Seltzer, Susan D. Cochran, and Vickie Mays, "Living Apart Together: Relationships in the United States," *Demographic Research* 21 (2009): 177–214.

105. Pew Research Social & Demographic Trends Project, "The Decline of Marriage and Rise of New Families," *Pew Research Center*, November 18, 2010. Retrieved from www.pewsocialtrends.org/2010/11/18/the-decline-of-marriage-and-rise-of-new-families/.

106. Kim Parker and Renee Stepler, "As U.S. Marriage Rate Hovers at 50%, Education Gap in Marital Status Widens," *Pew Research Center*, September 14, 2017, Retrieved from www.pewresearch.org/fact-tank/2017/09/14/as-u-s-marriage-rate-hovers-at-50-education-gap-in-marital-status-widens/; U.S. Census Bureau, "Historical Living Arrangements of Adults," Table AD-3: Living Arrangements of Adults 18 and Over, 1967 to Present." Retrieved from www.census.gov/data/tables/time-series/demo/families/adults.html.

107. Pew Research Social & Demographic Trends Project, "The Decline of Marriage and Rise of New Families," *Pew Research Center*, November 18, 2010. Retrieved from www.pewsocialtrends.org/2010/11/18/the-decline-of-marriage-and-rise-of-new-families/; Sharon Sassler, *Cohabitation Nation: Gender, Class, and the Remaking of Relationships* (Berkeley: University of California Press, 2017).

108. Kim Parker and Renee Stepler, "As U.S. Marriage Rate Hovers at 50%, Education Gap in Marital Status Widens," *Pew Research Center*, September 14, 2017. Retrieved from www.pewresearch.org/fact-tank/2017/09/14/as-u-s-marriage-rate-hovers-at-50-education-gap-in-marital-status-widens/.

109. J. A. Martin, B. E. Hamilton, M. J. K. Osterman, A. K. Driscoll, and P. Drake, "Births: Final Data for 2016," *National Vital Statistics Reports* 67, no 1 (Hyattsville, MD: National Center for Health Statistics, 2018). Retrieved from www.cdc.gov/nchs/data/nvsr/nvsr67/nvsr67_01.pdf.

110. Stephanie Coontz, "The World Historical Transformation of Marriage," *Journal of Marriage and Family* 66, no. 4 (2004): 978.

111. Pew Research Social & Demographic Trends Project, "A Portrait of Stepfamilies," *Pew Research Center*, January 13, 2011. Retrieved from www.pewsocialtrends.org/2011/01/13/a-portrait-of-stepfamilies/.

112. Myra Marx Ferree, "The Gay Wedding Backlash," *Newsday*, May 23, 2004.

113. Gallup, "Gay and Lesbian Rights." Retrieved from http://news.gallup.com/poll/1651/gay-lesbian-rights.aspx.

Chapter 10: Sexualities

1. Leonore Tiefer, *Sex Is Not a Natural Act & Other Essays* (San Francisco: Westview Press, 1995).

2. Lisa Wade, *American Hookup: The New Culture of Sex on Campus* (New York: W. W. Norton and Company, 2017).

3. Jess Butler, *Sexual Subjects: Hooking Up in the Age of Postfeminism* (PhD diss, University of Southern California, 2013), 74.

4. Jessie Ford, Paula England, and Jonathan Bearak, "The American College Hookup Scene: Findings from the Online College Social Life Survey." (presentation, American Sociological Association Annual Meeting, Chicago, IL, August 2015).

5. Lisa Wade and Joseph Padgett, "Hookup Culture and Higher Education," in *Handbook of Contemporary Feminism*, ed. Andrea Press and Tasha Oren (New York: Routledge, forthcoming); Janelle M. Pham, "Beyond Hookup Culture: Current Trends in the Study of College Student Sex and Where to Next." *Sociology Compass* 11, no. 8 (2017):e12499; C. Wood and D. Perlman, "Hooking Up in the United States," in *The Wiley Blackwell Encyclopedia of Family Studies*, ed. Constance Shehan (Hoboken: Wiley, 2016).

6. Zhana Vrangalova and Anthony Ong, "Who Benefits from Casual Sex? The Moderating Role of Sociosexuality," *Social Psychological and Personality Science* 5, no. 8 (2014): 883–91; Lisa Wade, *American Hookup: The New Culture of Sex on Campus* (New York: W. W. Norton and Company, 2017).

7. Michel Foucault, *The History of Sexuality: An Introduction* (New York: Vintage Books, 1978); J. Weeks, *Sexuality and Its Discontents: Meaning, Myths and Modern Sexualities* (New York: Routledge, 1985); Adrienne Rich, "Compulsory Heterosexuality and Lesbian Existence," *Signs*, 5 (1980): 631–60; Leonore Tiefer, *Sex is Not a Natural Act & Other Essays* (San Francisco: Westview Press, 1995).

8. U.S. Census Bureau, "Live Births, Deaths, Infant Deaths, and Maternal Deaths: 1900 to 2001" (2003). Retrieved from www2.census.gov/library/publications/2004/compendia/statab/123ed/hist/hs-13.pdf.

9. Angus McLaren, *Twentieth Century Sexuality: A History* (Oxford: Blackwell Publishers Ltd., 1999).

10. Tom Smith, "A Report: The Sexual Revolution?" *Public Opinion Quarterly* 54, no. 3 (1990): 415–35; Elina Haavio-Mannila, J. P. Roos, and Osmo Kontula. "Repression, Revolution and Ambivalence: The Sexual Life of Three Generations," *Acta Sociologica* 39, no. 4 (1996): 409–30; Gerbert Kraaykamp, "Trends and Countertrends in Sexual Permissiveness: Three Decades of Attitude Change in The Netherlands 1965–1995," *Journal of Marriage and Family* 64 (2002): 225–39; George H. Gallup, Jr., "Current Views on Premarital, Extramarital Sex," June 24, 2003. Retrieved from http://www.gallup.com/poll/8704/current-views-premarital-extramarital-sex.aspx.

11. Brooke Wells and Jean Twenge, "Changes in Young People's Sexual Behavior and Attitudes, 1943–1999: A Cross-Temporal Meta-Analysis," *Review of General Psychology*, 9 (2005): 249–261; Jennifer L. Petersen and Janet Shilbey Hyde, "A Meta-Analytic Review of Research on Gender Differences in Sexuality, 1993–2007," *Psychological Bulletin* 136, no. 1 (2010): 21–38; for a great overview, see M.C. Willetts, S. Sprecher, & F. D. Beck, "Overview of Sexual Practices and Attitudes within Relational Contexts," In J.H. Harvey, A. Wenzel, & S. Specher (eds.) *The Handbook of Sexuality in Close Relationships* (pp. 57–85). Mahwah, NJ: Erlbaum, 2004.

12. Nancy L. Cohen, "How the Sexual Revolution Changed America Forever," *Alternet*, February 5, 2012. Retrieved from www.alternet.org/story/153969/how_the_sexual_revolution_changed_america_forever.

13. Lucian Truscott IV, "View from Outside," *Village Voice*, July 2, 1969; Howard Smith, "View from Inside," *Village Voice*, July 2, 1969.

14. Angus McLaren, *Twentieth Century Sexuality: A History* (Oxford: Blackwell Publishers Ltd., 1999).

15. Randy Shilts, *And the Band Played On: Politics, People, and the AIDS Epidemic, 20th Anniversary Ed.* (New York: St. Martin's Griffin, 2007).

16. J. Chin, "Global Estimates of AIDS Cases and HIV Infections," *AIDS* 4, Suppl 1:S (1990): 277–83.

17. D. W. Haffner, "What's Wrong With Abstinence-Only Sex Education Programs," *SIECUS Report* 25, no. 4 (1997): 9–14; Kaiser Family Foundation, "Sex Education in America: A Series of National Surveys of Students, Parents, Teachers, and Principals," Menlo Park, California: 2000; J. Levine, *Harmful to Minors: The Perils of Protecting Children from Sex.* Minneapolis: University of Minnesota Press, 2002; Leslie M. Kantor, John S. Santelli, Julien Teitler, and Randall Balmer, "Abstinence-Only Policies and Programs: An Overview," *Sexuality Research and Social Policy*, 5, no.3 (2008): 6–17; Douglas Kirby, "Emerging Answers 2007: Research Findings on Programs to Reduce Teen Pregnancy and Sexually Transmitted Diseases," Washington, D.C.: National Campaign to Prevent Teen and Unplanned Pregnancy, 2007. Retrieved from https://powertodecide.org/sites/default/files/resources/primary-download/emerging-answers.pdf; Douglas Kirby, "The Impact of Abstinence and Comprehensive Sex and STD/

HIV Education Programs on Adolescent Sexual Behavior," *Sexuality Research and Social Policy* 5, no. 3 (2008), 18–27.

18. M. Kempner, "A Controversial Decade: 10 Years of Tracking Debates Around Sex Education," *SIECUS Report* 31, no. 6 (2003): 33–48.

19. See note 17 above.

20. The Museum of Broadcast Communications, "Encyclopedia of Television—United States: Cable Television," 2018. Retrieved from http://www.museum.tv/eotv/unitedstatesc.htm, and U.S. Census Bureau, "Historical National Population Estimates: July 1, 1900 to July 1, 1999," June 28, 2000. Retrieved from https://www.census.gov/population/estimates/nation/popclockest.txt

21. D. Cosper, "Shock value," *Print*, 51 (1997): 38–40; A. Vagnoni, "Something About this Advertising, *Advertising Age* February 8, 1999: 30; M. L. Wald, "Shock to Replace Dummies in TV Ads on Seat Belt Use. *New York Times*, January 27, 1999: 12; Media Education Foundation: Documentary Films. Challenging Media. Retrieved from www.mediaed.org/assets/products/101/transcript_101.pdf.

22. A. Levy, *Female Chauvinist Pigs: Women and the Rise of Raunch Culture* (Melbourne: Schwartz Publishing, 2005); K. Nikunen, S. Paasonen, and L. Saarenmaa, *Pornification: Sex and Sexuality in Media Culture* (New York: Berg Publishers, 2007); P. Paul, *Pornified: How Pornography Is Transforming our Lives, our Relationships, and our Families* (New York: Henry Holt and Company, 2005); C. Sarracino and K. M. Scott, *The Porning of America: The Rise of Porn Culture, What It Means, and Where We Go from Here* (Boston: Beacon Press, 2008).

23. J. K. Swim, L. L. Hyers, L. L. Cohen, and M. J. Ferguson, "Everyday Sexism: Evidence for Its Incidence, Nature, and Psychological Impact from Three Daily Diary Studies," *Journal of Social Issues* 57 (2001): 31–53; M. J. Thompson, "Gender in Magazine Advertising: Skin Sells Best," *Clothing and Textiles Research Journal* 18 (2000): 178–81; Erin Hatton and Mary Nell Trautner, "Equal Opportunity Objectification? The Sexualization of Men and Women on the Cover of *Rolling Stone*," *Sexuality & Culture* 15, no. 3 (2011): 256–78.

24. R. Jensen, *Getting off: Pornography and the End of Masculinity* (Cambridge: South End Press, 2007); K. Nikunen, K., S. Paasonen, and L. Saarenmaa, *Pornification: Sex and Sexuality in Media Culture* (New York: Berg Publishers, 2007); Ana J. Bridges, Robert Wosnitzer, Erica Scharrer, Chyng Sun, and Rachael Liberman, "Aggression and Sexual Behav-ior in Best-Selling Pornography Videos: A Content Analysis Update," *Violence Against Women* 16, no. 10 (2010): 1065–85; Robert Jensen, "Pornography Is What the End of the World Looks Like," in *Everyday Pornography*, ed. Karen Boyle (New York: Routledge, 2010), 105–13; M. Barron, and M.S. Kimmel, "Sexual Violence in Three Pornographic Media," *Journal of Sex Research* 37 (2010): 161–69; Chyng Sun, Robert Wosnitzer, Ana J. Bridges, Erica Scharrer and Rachael Liberman, "Harder and Harder: The Content of Popular Pornographic Movies," in *Victims of Sexual Assault and Abuse: Resources and Responses for Individuals and Families*, ed. Michele A. Paludi and Florence L. Denmark (Santa Barbara, CA: Praeger Publishers, 2010).

25. Jeffrey M. Jones, "Americans Hold Record Liberal Views on Most Moral Issues," *Gallup*, May 11, 2017. Retrieved from http://news.gallup.com/poll/210542/americans-hold-record-liberal-views-moral-issues.aspx.

26. Pornhub, "2017 Year in Review," Jan. 9, 2018. Retrieved from https://www.pornhub.com/insights/2017-year-in-review

27. A. Levy, *Female Chauvinist Pigs: Women and the Rise of Raunch Culture* (Melbourne: Schwartz Publishing, 2005); C. Snyder, "What Is Third-Wave Feminism? A New Directions Essay," *Signs* 34 (2008): 175–96; J. Scanlon, "Sexy from the Start: Anticipatory Elements of Second Wave Feminism," *Women's Studies* 38 (2009): 127–50.

28. Laura M. Carpenter, *Virginity Lost: An Intimate Portrait of First Sexual Experiences* (New York: New York University Press, 2005).

29. Joyce C. Abma, Gladys M. Martinez, and Casey E. Copen, "Teenagers in the United States: Sexual Activity, Contraceptive Use, and Childbearing, National Survey of Family Growth 2006–2008," *Vital and Health Statistics* Series 23, no. 30 (June 2010); Lawrence Finer, "Trends in Premarital Sex in the United States, 1954–2003," *Public Health Reports* 122, no. 1 (2007): 73–78. Retrieved from www.ncbi.nlm.nih.gov/pubmed/17236611; Kaiser Family Foundation, "National Survey of Adolescents and Young Adults: Sexual Health Knowledge, Attitudes and Experiences," Menlo Park, California: 2003. Retrieved from http://kff.org/hivaids/report/national-survey-of-adolescents-and-young-adults/.

30. Lisa Wade, *American Hookup: The New Culture of Sex on Campus* (New York: W. W. Norton and Company, 2017).

31. Justin Garcia and Chris Reiber, "Hook-up Behavior: A Biopsychosocial Perspective," *Journal of

Social, Evolutionary, and Cultural Psychology 2, no. 4 (2008): 192–208; Lisa Wade, *American Hookup: The New Culture of Sex on Campus* (New York: W. W. Norton and Company, 2017); Peggy Orenstein, *Girls and Sex: Navigating the Complicated New Landscape* (New York: Harper, 2016).

32. Lawrence Finer, "Trends in Premarital Sex in the United States, 1954–2003," *Public Health Reports* 122, no. 1 (2007): 73–78. Retrieved from www.ncbi .nlm.nih.gov/pubmed/17236611; Kaiser Family Foundation, "National Survey of Adolescents and Young Adults: Sexual Health Knowledge, Attitudes and Experiences," Menlo Park, California: 2003. Retrieved from http://kff.org/hivaids/report/national-survey -of-adolescents-and-young-adults/.

33. Angus McLaren, *Twentieth Century Sexuality: A History* (Oxford: Blackwell Publishers Ltd., 1999).

34. Lisa Wade, *American Hookup: The New Culture of Sex on Campus* (New York: W. W. Norton and Company, 2017), 67.

35. Brooke Wells and Jean Twenge, "Changes in Young People's Sexual Behavior and Attitudes, 1943– 1999: A Cross-Temporal Meta-Analysis," *Review of General Psychology*, 9 (2005): 249–61; Jennifer L. Petersen and Janet Shilbey Hyde, "A Meta-Analytic Review of Research on Gender Differences in Sexuality, 1993–2007." *Psychological Bulletin* 136, no. 1 (2010): 21–38; M.C. Willetts, S. Sprecher, & F. D. Beck, "Overview of Sexual Practices and Attitudes within Relational Contexts," In J.H. Harvey, A. Wenzel, & S. Specher (eds.) *The Handbook of Sexuality in Close Relationships* (Mahwah, NJ: Erlbaum, 2004): 57–85; A. Chandra, W.D. Mosher, C. Copen, and C. Sionean, "Sexual Behavior, Sexual Attraction, and Sexual Identity in the United States: Data From the 2006–2008," National Health Statistics Reports, no. 36, March 3, 2011, Retrieved from https://www .cdc.gov/nchs/data/nhsr/nhsr036.pdf.

36. Shabana Mir, *Muslim American Women on Campus: Undergraduate Social Life and Identity* (Chapel Hill: University of North Carolina Press, 2014); Lisa Wade. *American Hookup: The New Culture of Sex on Campus* (New York: W. W. Norton and Company, 2017).

37. Lisa Wade, *American Hookup: The New Culture of Sex on Campus* (New York: W. W. Norton and Company, 2017), 120.

38. Angus McLaren, *Twentieth Century Sexuality: A History* (Oxford: Blackwell Publishers Ltd., 1999).

39. Lisa Rofel, "Qualities of Desire: Imagining Gay Identities in China," *GLQ* 5, no. 4 (1999): 451–74;

Raymond Hibbins, "Sexuality and Constructions of Gender Identity among Chinese Male Migrants in Australia," *Asian Studies Review* 30 (2006): 289– 303.

40. Jane Ward, *Not Gay: Sex Between Straight White Men* (New York: New York University Press, 2015); E. Anderson, "'Being Masculine is not about who you Sleep with. . . .': Heterosexual Athletes Contesting Masculinity and the One-Time Rule of Homosexuality," *Sex Roles: A Journal of Research* 58 (2008): 104–15; Brandon Robinson and Salvador Vidal-Ortiz, 2013. "Displacing the Dominant 'Down Low' Discourse: Deviance, Same-Sex Sesire, and Craigslist.org," *Deviant Behavior* 34, no.3 (2013): 224–41.

41. Eliza Brown and Paula England, "Sexual Orientation Versus Behavior—Different for Men and Women?" *Contexts* (blog), February 29, 2016. Retrieved from https://contexts.org/blog/sexual -orientation-versus-behavior-different-for-men-and -women/.

42. Steven Seidman, Chet Meeks, and Francie Traschen, "Beyond the Closet? The Changing Social Meaning of Homosexuality in the United States," in *Sexuality and Gender*, ed. Christine L. Williams and Arlene Stein (Malden: Blackwell Publishers, 2002), 427–45.

43. K. McPhillips, V. Braun, and N. Gavey, "Defining Heterosex: How Imperative Is the 'Coital imperative'?" *Women's Studies International Forum* 24 (2001): 229–40.

44. Jason D. Hans, Martie Gillen and Katrina Akande, "Sex Redefined: The Reclassification of Oral-Genital Contact," *Guttmacher Institute*, March 30, 2010. Retrieved from https://doi.org/10.1363/420 7410; Lisa Remez, "Oral Sex among Adolescents: Is It Sex or Is It Abstinence?" *Family Planning Perspectives* 32, no.6 (2000): 298–304; Stephanie A. Sanders and June Machover Reinisch, "Would You Say You "Had Sex" If . . .?" *JAMA* 281, no. 3 (1999): 257–77. Retrieved from https://jamanetwork.com /journals/jama/fullarticle/188367; Melina M. Bersamin, Deborah A. Fisher, Samantha Walker, Douglas L. Hill and Joel W. Grube, "Defining Virginity and Abstinence: Adolescents' Interpretations of Sexual Behaviors," *Journal of Adolescent Health* 41, no. 2 (2007): 182–88. Retrieved from www.ncbi.nlm .nih.gov/pmc/articles/PMC1941649/.

45. Stephanie A. Sanders and June Machover Reinisch, "Would You Say You "Had Sex" If . . .?" *JAMA* 281, no. 3 (1999): 257–77. Retrieved from https:// jamanetwork.com/journals/jama/fullarticle/188367;

Melina M. Bersamin, Deborah A. Fisher, Samantha Walker, Douglas L. Hill and Joel W. Grube, "Defining Virginity and Abstinence: Adolescents' Interpretations of Sexual Behaviors," *Journal of Adolescent Health* 41, no. 2 (2007): 182–88. Retrieved from www.ncbi.nlm.nih.gov/pmc/articles/PMC1941649/.

46. Kelsey K. Sewell, Larissa A. McGarrity and Donald S. Strassberg, "Sexual Behavior, Definitions of Sex and the Role of Self-Partner Context Among Lesbian, Gay, and Bisexual Adults," *The Journal of Sex Research* 54, no. 7 (2017): 825–31. Retrieved from www.tandfonline.com/doi/abs/10.1080/00224 499.2016.1249331; Ava D. Horowitz and Edward Bedford, "Graded Structure in Sexual Definitions: Categorizations of Having 'Had Sex' and Virginity Loss Among Homosexual and Heterosexual Men and Women," *Archives of Sexual Behavior* 46, no. 5 (2017): 1653–65. Retrieved from https://link .springer.com/article/10.1007/s10508-016-0905-1.

47. Leonore Tiefer, *Sex is Not a Natural Act & Other Essays*, 2nd ed. (Boulder, CO: Westview Press, 2004).

48. Elisabeth Anne Lloyd, *The Case of the Female Orgasm: Bias in the Science of Evolution* (Boston: Harvard University Press, 2005); Shere Hite, *The Hite Report: A Nationwide Study of Female Sexuality* (New York: Seven Stories Press, 1977).

49. Peggy Orenstein, *Girls and Sex: Navigating the Complicated New Landscape* (New York: Harper, 2016); Ruth Lewis and Cicely Marston, "Give and Take? Reciprocity in Young People's Accounts of Oral Heterosex" (presentation, American Sociological Association Annual Meeting, San Francisco, August 2014); Laina Bay-Cheng, Adjoa Robinson, and Alyssa Zucker, "Behavioral and Relational Contexts of Adolescent Desire, Wanting, and Pleasure: Undergraduate Women's Retrospective Accounts," *Journal of Sex Research* 46, no. 6 (2009): 511–24; Jessie Ford, Paula England, and Jonathan Bearak, "The American College Hookup Scene: Findings from the Online College Social Life Survey" (presentation, American Sociological Association Annual Meeting, Chicago, August 2015); Laura Backstrom, Elizabeth Armstrong, and Jennifer Puentes, "Women's Negotiation of Cunnilingus in College Hookups and Relationships," *Journal of Sex Research* 49, 1 (2012): 1–12.

50. E. O. Laumann, John H. Gagnon, Robert T. Michael, and Stuart Michaels, *The Social Organization of Sexuality: Sexual Practices in the United States* (Chicago: University of Chicago Press, 1994); Debby Herbenick, Michael Reece, Vanessa Schick, Stephanie Sanders, Brian Dodge, and J. Dennis Fortenberry, "An Event-Level Analysis of the Sexual Characteristics and Composition among Adults Ages 18 to 59: Results from a National Probability Sample in the United States," *Journal of Sexual Medicine* 7, no. 5 (2010): 346–61; Alfred Kinsey, Wardell Pomeroy, Clyde Martin, and Paul Gebhard, *Sexual Behavior in the Human Female* (Philadelphia: Saunders, 1953).

51. Jess Butler, "Sexual Subjects: Hooking Up in the Age of Postfeminism" (PhD diss., University of Southern California, 2013).

52. Zach Beauchamp, "6 Maps and Charts that Explain Sex around the World," *Vox*, May 26, 2015.

53. Emily Coleman, Peter Hoon, and Emily Hoon, "Arousability and Sexual Satisfaction in Lesbian and Heterosexual Women," *Journal of Sex Research* 19, no. 1 (1983): 58–73; John Harvey, Amy Wenzel, and Susan Sprecher, *The Handbook of Sexuality in Close Relationships* (New York: Routledge, 2004); Shere Hite, *The Hite Report: A Nationwide Study of Female Sexuality* (New York: Seven Stories Press, 1977); David A. Frederick, H. Kate St. John, Justin R. Garcia, and Elisabeth Anne Lloyd, "Differences in Orgasm Frequency Among Gay, Lesbian, Bisexual, and Heterosexual Men and Women in a U.S. National Sample," *Archives of Sexual Behavior* 47, no.1 (2018): 273–88; Heather Armstrong and Elke Reissing, "Women Who Have Sex with Women: A Comprehensive Review of the Literature and Conceptual Model of Sexual Function," *Sexual and Relationship Therapy* 28, no. 4 (2013): 364–99; Marcia Douglass and Lisa Douglass, *Are We Having Fun Yet?* (New York: Hyperion, 1997); Alfred Kinsey, Wardell Pomeroy, Clyde Martin, and Paul Gebhard, *Sexual Behavior in the Human Female* (Philadelphia: Saunders, 1953); Elisabeth Lloyd, *The Case of the Female Orgasm: Bias in the Science of Evolution* (Cambridge: Harvard University Press, 2005); Sharon Thompson, "Search for Tomorrow: On Feminism and the Reconstruction of Teen Romance," in *Pleasure and Danger: Exploring Female Sexuality*, ed. Carole Vance (London: Pandora, 1989); Justin Garcia, Elisabeth Lloyd, Kim Wallen, and Helen Fisher, "Variation in Orgasm Occurrence by Sexual Orientation in a Sample of U.S. Singles," *International Society for Sexual Medicine* 11, no. 11 (2014): 2645–52; B. J. Tilos, Misha Wilks, Jenna Alley, Chantal Avakain-Fisher, and David Frederick, "The Orgasm Gaps: Differences in Reported Orgasm Frequency by Gender and Sexual Orientation" (poster presentation, Gender Development Research Conference, San Francisco, CA, 2014).

54. E. Armstrong, P. England, and Alison Fogarty, "Orgasm in College Hookups and Relationships," in *Families as They Really Are*, ed. Barbara Risman (New York: W. W. Norton and Company, 2009).

55. M. Douglass and L. Douglass, *Are We Having Fun Yet?* (New York: Hyperion, 1997); Alfred Kinsey, Wardell Pomeroy, Clyde Martin, and Paul Gebhard, *Sexual Behavior in the Human Female* (Philadelphia: Saunders, 1953); see also S. Thompson, "Search for Tomorrow: On Feminism and the Reconstruction of Teen Romance," in *Pleasure and Danger: Exploring Female Sexuality*, ed. C. S. Vance (London: Pandora, 1989); John Harvey, Amy Wenzel, and Susan Sprecher, *The Handbook of Sexuality in Close Relationships* (Mahwah, NJ.: Lawrence Erlbaum Associates, 2004).

56. Lisa Wade, Emily Kremer, and Jessica Brown. "The Incidental Orgasm: The Presence of Clitoral Knowledge and the Absence of Orgasm for Women," *Women and Health* 42, 1 (2005): 117–38.

57. J. Holland, C. Ramazanoglu, S. Sharpe, and R. Thomson, *The Male in the Head: Young People, Heterosexuality and Power* (London: The Tufnell, 1998); J. Levine, *Harmful to Minors: The Perils of Protecting Children from Sex* (Minneapolis: University of Minnesota Press, 2002); I. Vanwesenbeeck, "The Context of Women's Power(lessness) in Heterosexual Interactions," in *New Sexual Agendas*, ed. L. Segal (New York: New York University Press, 1997).

58. Lisa Wade and Gwen Sharp, "Selling Sex," in *Images that Injure: Pictorial Stereotypes in the Media*, ed. Lester Paul and Susan Ross (Westport, CT: Praeger, 2011), 165.

59. J. Holland, C. Ramazanoglu, S. Sharpe, and R. Thomson, *The Male in the Head: Young People, Heterosexuality and Power* (London: The Tufnell Press, 1998).

60. J. Levine, *Harmful to Minors: The Perils of Protecting Children from Sex* (Minneapolis: University of Minnesota Press, 2002); Michelle Fine, "Sexuality, Schooling, and Adolescent Females," *Harvard Educational Review* 58, no. 1 (1988): 29–54.

61. Sinikka Elliot, *Not My Kid: What Parents Believe about the Sex Lives of Their Teenagers* (New York: New York University Press, 2012).

62. Carole S. Vance, ed., *Pleasure and Danger: Exploring Female Sexuality* (London: Pandora, 1984); Lorena Garcia, *Respect Yourself, Protect Yourself: Latina Girls and Sexual Identity* (New York: New York University Press, 2012); Peggy Orenstein, *Girls and Sex: Navigating the Complicated New Landscape* (New York: Harper, 2016); Christine E. Beyer, Roberta J. Ogletree, Dale O. Ritzel, Judy C. Drolet, Sharon L. Gilbert and Dale Brown, "Gender Representation in Illustrations, Text, and Topic Areas in Sexuality Education Curricula," *Journal of School Health* 66, no. 10 (1996).

63. Laura Mulvey, "Visual Pleasure and Narrative Cinema," *Screen* 16, no. 3 (1975): 6–18.

64. Marika Tiggemann and Julia K. Kuring, "The Role of Body Objectification in Disordered Eating and Depressed Mood," *British Journal of Clinical Psychology* 43, no. 3 (2004): 299–311; N. M. McKinley, "Gender Differences in Undergraduates' Body Esteem: The Mediating Effect of Objectified Body Consciousness and Actual/Ideal Weight Discrepancy," *Sex Roles* 39 (1998): 113–23; N. M. McKinley, "Longitudinal Gender Differences in Objectified Body Consciousness and Weight-Related Attitudes and Behaviors: Cultural and Developmental Contexts in the Transition from College," *Sex Roles* 54 (2006): 159–73; S. M. Lindberg, J. S. Hyde, and N. M. McKinley, "A Measure of Objectified Body Consciousness for Preadolescent and Adolescent Youth," *Psychology of Women Quarterly* 30 (2006): 65–76; M. R. Hebl, E. B. King, and J. Lin, "The Swimsuit Becomes Us All: Ethnicity, Gender, and Vulnerability to Self-Objectification," *Personality and Social Psychology Bulletin* 30 (2004): 1322–31; Sarah E. Lowery, Sharon E. Robinson Kurpius, Christie Befort, Elva Hull Blanks, Sonja Sollenberger, Megan Foley Nicpon, and Laura Huser, "Body Image, Self-Esteem, and Health-Related Behaviors among Male and Female First Year College Students," *Journal of College Student Development* 46 (2005): 612–23; Shelly Grabe and Janet Shibley Hyde, "Body Objectification, MTV, and Psychological Outcomes Among Female Adolescents," *Journal of Applied Psychology*, 39, no. 12 (2009): 2840–58; Shelly Grabe, Janet Shibley Hyde, and Sara M. Lindberg, "Body Objectification and Depression in Adolescents: The Role of Gender, Shame, and Rumination," *Psychology of Women Quarterly* 31, no. 2 (2007): 164–75.

65. Kim Parker, Juliana Menasce Horowitz, and Renee Stepler, "On Gender Differences, No Consensus on Nature vs. Nurture," *Pew Research Center*, December 5, 2017. Retrieved from www.pewsocialtrends.org/2017/12/05/on-gender-differences-no-consensus-on-nature-vs-nurture/.

66. Michael D. Siever, "Sexual Orientation and Gender as Factors in Socioculturally Acquired Vulnerability to Body Dissatisfaction and Eating Disorders," *Journal of Consulting and Clinical Psychology* 62,

no. 2 (1994): 252–60; Melanie S. Hill, "Examining Objectification Theory: Lesbian and Heterosexual Women's Experiences With Sexual-and Self-Objectification," *The Counseling Psychologist* 36, no. 5 (2008): 745–76. Retrieved from www.research gate.net/profile/Melanie_Hill/publication/354871 56_Examining_objectification_theory_sexual_objec tification's_link_with_self-objectification_and_mod eration_by_sexual_orientation_and_age_in_white _women/links/55cb625308aeca747d6c1146.pdf.

67. Christian Rudder, "Your Looks and Your Inbox," *OkTrends* (blog), November 17, 2009. Retrieved from https://web.archive.org/web/20100725135317 /http://blog.okcupid.com/index.php/your-looks -and-online-dating.

68. B. L. Fredrickson and T. A. Roberts, "Objectification Theory: Toward Understanding Women's Lived Experiences and Mental Health Risks," *Psychology of Women Quarterly* 21, no. 2 (1997): 173–206.

69. Rachel M. Calogero and J. Kevin Thompson, "Potential Implications of the Objectification of Women's Bodies and Sexual Satisfaction," *Body Image* 6, no. 2 (2009): 145–48; Amy Steer and Marika Tiggemann, "The Role of Self-Objectification in Women's Sexual Functioning," *Journal of Social and Clinical Psychology* 27, no. 3 (2008): 205–25.

70. Y. Martins, M. Tiggemann, and A. Kirkbride, "Those Speedos Become Them: The Role of Self-Objectification in Gay and Heterosexual Men's Body Image," *Personality and Social Psychology Bulletin* 33 (2007): 634–47; Megan Kozak, Heidi Franken-hauser, and Tomi-Ann Roberts, "Objects of Desire: Objectification as a Function of Male Sexual Orientation," *Psychology of Men & Masculinity* 10, no. 3 (2009): 225–30; Michael D. Siever, "Sexual Orientation and Gender as Factors in Socioculturally Acquired Vulnerability to Body Dissatisfaction and Eating Disorders," *Journal of Consulting and Clinical Psychology* 62, no. 2 (1994): 252–60; Francisco J. Sanchez, Stefanie T. Greenberg, William Ming Liu and Eric Vilain, "Reported Effects of Masculine Ideals on Gay Men," *Psychology of Men & Masculinity* 10, no. 1 (2009): 73–87; Matthew S. Michaels, Mike C. Parent and Bonnie Moradi, "Does Exposure to Muscularity-Idealizing Images of Self-Objection Have Consequences for Heterosexual and Sexual Minority Men?" *Psychology of Men & Masculinity* 14, no. 2 (2013): 175–83. Retrieved from www.research gate.net/profile/Mike_Parent/publication/2326057 30_Does_Exposure_to_Muscularity-Idealizing _Images_Have_Self-Objectification_Consequences

_for_Heterosexual_and_Sexual_Minority_Men /links/5588616e08ae347f9bda9bad.pdf.

71. David Whittier and Rita Melendez, "Intersubjectivity in the Intrapsychic Sexual Scripting of Gay Men," *Culture, Health & Society* 6, no. 2 (2004): 131–43.

72. Audre Lorde, *Sister Outsider: Essays and Speeches* (New York: Crossing Press, 2007). Retrieved from www.cds.hawaii.edu/sites/default/files/downloads /resources/diversity/SisterOutside.pdf.

73. Catherine Hakim, "Erotic Capital," *European Sociological Review*, 26, no. 5 (October 2010): 499–518; Adam Green, "The Social Organization of Desire: The Sexual Fields Approach," *Sociological Theory* 26, no. 1 (2008): 25–50.

74. Kerri L. Johnson, Jonathan B. Freeman, and Kristin Pauker, "Race Is Gendered: How Covarying Phenotypes and Stereotypes Bias Sex Categorization," *Journal of Personality and Social Psychology*, 102, no. 1 (January 2012): 116–31.

75. N. K. Denzin, "Selling Images of Inequality: Hollywood Cinema and the Reproduction of Racial and Gender Stereotypes," in *The Blackwell Companion to Social Inequalities*, ed. M. Romero and E. Margolis (Malden, MA: Blackwell Publishing, 2005), 469–501; Charles Ramirez Berg, *Latino Images in Film: Stereotypes, Subversion and Resistance* (Austin: University of Texas Press, 2002); Stephanie Greco Larson, *Media & Minorities: The Politics of Race in News and Entertainment* (Lanham, MA: Rowman and Littlefield Publishers, Inc., 2006); Scott Poulson-Bryant, *Hung: A Meditation on the Measure of Black Men in America* (New York: Harlem Moon, 2005).

76. Adam Green, "The Social Organization of Desire: The Sexual Fields Approach," *Sociological Theory* 26, no. 1 (2008): 25–50.

77. Ida B. Wells-Barnett, *Southern Horrors: Lynch Law in All Its Phases* (New York: New York Age Print, 1892); Angela Y. Davis, "Rape, Racism, and the Myth of the Black Rapist," in *Women, Race, and Class* (New York: Random House, 1983), 172–201; C. B. Feimster, *Southern Horrors: Women and the Politics of Rape and Lynching* (Cambridge: Harvard University Press, 2011); M. Mahan, "The Racial Origins of U.S. Domestic Violence Law" (PhD diss., University of California, Berkeley, 2017).

78. Michael Kimmel, *Guyland: The Perilous World Where Boys Become Men* (New York: HarperCollins, 2008).

79. Evelyn Brooks Higginbotham, *Righteous Discontent: The Women's Movement in the Black Baptist Church, 1880–1920* (Cambridge: Harvard University Press, 1993); Rashawn Ray and Jason A. Rosow, "Getting Off and Getting Intimate: How Normative Institutional Arrangements Structure Black and White Fraternity Men's Approaches toward Women," *Men and Masculinities* 12, no. 5 (2010): 523–46.

80. Michael Kimmel, *Guyland: The Perilous World Where Boys Become Men* (New York: HarperCollins, 2008).

81. Ibid; Robert G. Lee, *Orientals: Asian Americans in Popular Culture* (Philadelphia: Temple University Press, 1999); Anthony Chen, "Lives at the Center of the Periphery, Lives at the Periphery of the Center: Chinese American Masculinities and Bargaining with Hegemony," *Gender & Society* 13, no. 5 (1999): 584–607; Yen L. Espiritu, *Asian American Women and Men* (Thousand Oaks: Sage, 1997); Y. Joel Wong, Jesse Owen, Kimberly K. Tran, Dana L. Collins, and Claire E. Higgins, "Asian American Male College Students' Perceptions of People's Stereotypes About Asian American Men," *Psychology of Men & Masculinity*, 13, no. 1 (2012): 75–88.

82. Yen Lee Espiritu, *Asian American Women and Men: Labor, Laws, and Love* (Lanham: Rowman & Littlefield Publishers, Inc., 2008), 110.

83. Geoffrey Hunt, Kristin Evans, Eileen Wu, and Alicia Reyes, "Asian American Youth, the Dance Scene, and Club Drugs," *Journal of Drug Issues* 35, no. 4 (2005): 695–732.

84. Christian Rudder, "How Your Race Affects the Messages You Get," *OkTrends* (blog), October 5, 2009. Retrieved from https://web.archive.org/web/20111008215612/http://blog.okcupid.com/index.php/your-race-affects-whether-people-write-you-back/.

85. Ken-Hou Lin and Jennifer Lundquist, "Mate Selection in Cyberspace: The Intersection of Race, Gender, and Education," *American Journal of Sociology* 119, no. 1 (2013): 183–215.

86. Courtney Weaver, "Tiny, Flat-chested, and Hairless!," *Salon*, May 6, 1998. Retrieved from www.salon.com/1998/05/06/weav_22/.

87. Kevin K. Kumashiro, "Supplementing Normalcy and Otherness: Queer Asian American Men Reflect on Stereotypes, Identity, and Oppression," International Journal of Qualitative Studies in Education 12, no. 5 (1999): 491–508; 503.

88. Ken-Hou Lin and Jennifer Lundquist, "Mate Selection in Cyberspace: The Intersection of Race, Gender, and Education," *American Journal of Sociology* 119, no. 1 (2013): 183–215.

89. Jerry A. Jacobs and Teresa G. Labov, "Gender Differentials in Intermarriage among Sixteen Race and Ethnic Groups," *Sociological Forum* 17 (2002): 621–46; U.S. Census Bureau, America's Families and Living Arrangements. Table FG-4, 2010. Retrieved from http://www.census.gov/population/www/socdemo/hh-fam/cps2010.html.

90. Zhenchao Qian and Daniel T. Lichter, "Social Boundaries and Marital Assimilation: Interpreting Trends in Racial and Ethnic Intermarriage," *American Sociological Review* 72, no. 1 (2007): 68–94; Zhenchao Qian and Daniel T. Lichter. "Changing Patterns of Interracial Marriage in a Multiracial Society," *Journal of Marriage and Family* 73, no. 5 (2011): 1065–84.

91. Zhenchao Qian, "Breaking the Last Taboo: Interracial Marriage in America," *Contexts* 4, no. 4 (2005): 33–37.

92. Jane R. Conway, Nyala Noe, Gert Stulp, and Thomas V. Pollet, "Finding your Soulmate: Homosexual and Heterosexual Age Preferences in Online Dating," Personal Relationships, *Journal of the International Association for Relationship Research*, 2015, DOI: 10.1111/pere.12102, Retrieved from www.gertstulp.com/pdf/2015_Conway_et_al_PR_Preferences.pdf; Matthew H. Rafalow, Cynthia Feliciano, Belinda Robnett, "Racialized Femininity and Masculinity in the Preferences of Online Same-Sex Daters," *Social Currents* 4, no. 4 (2017): 306–21, https://doi.org/10.1177/2329496516686621.

93. Christian Rudder, "Your Looks and Your Inbox," *OkTrends* (blog) November 17, 2009. Retrieved from https://web.archive.org/web/20100725135317/http://blog.okcupid.com/index.php/your-looks-and-online-dating.

94. Ibid.

95. Leonardo Bursztyn, Thomas Fujiwara, and Amanda Pallais, "'Acting Wife': Marriage Market Incentives and Labor Market Investments," *American Economic Review* 107, no. 11 (2017): 3288–3319. Retrieved from https://scholar.harvard.edu/files/pallais/files/actingwife.pdf.

96. Marianne Bertrand, Jessica Pan, and Emir Kamenica, "Gender Identity and Relative Income within Households," *Quarterly Journal of Economics*, Oxford University Press, 130, no. 2, (2015): 571–614; Yasemin Besen-Cassino and Dan Cassino, "Division of House Chores and the Curious Case of Cooking:

The Effects of Earning Inequality on House Chores among Dual-Earner Couples," *AboutGender*, 3, no. 6 (2014). Retrieved from www.aboutgender.unige.it /index.php/generis/article/view/176.

97. Christine A. Smith and Shannon Stillman, "Butch/ Femme in the Personal Advertisements of Lesbians," *Journal of Lesbian Studies* 6, no. 1 (2002): 45–51; Michael J. Bailey, Peggy Y. Kim, Alex Hills, Joan A. W. Linsenmeier, "Butch, Femme, or Straight Acting? Partner Preferences of Gay Men and Lesbians," *Journal of Personality and Social Psychology* 73, no. 5 (November 1997): 960–73.

98. Nathan S. Rodriguez, Jennifer Huemmer, and Lindsey E. Blumell, "Mobile Masculinities: An Investigation of Networked Masculinities in Gay Dating Apps," *Masculinities & Social Change* 5, no. 3 (2016): 241–67; Peter Nardi, "Anything For a Sis, Mary: An Introduction to Gay Masculinities," *Gay Masculinities* 12, no. 1 (2000): 1–11; Francisco J. Sanchez, Stefanie T. Greenberg, William Ming Liu, and Eric Vilain, "Reported Effects of Masculine Ideals on Gay Men," *Psychology of Men & Masculinity*, 10, no. 1 (2009): 73–87. DOI: 10.1037/a0013513; Martin Holt, "Gay Men and Ambivalence About 'Gay Community': From Gay Community Attachment to Personal Communities." *Culture, Health & Sexuality* 13, no. 8 (2011), 857–71; Chelsea Reynolds, "'I Am Super Straight and I Prefer You Be Too': Constructions of Heterosexual Masculinity in Online Personal Ads For 'Straight' Men Seeking Sex With Men," *Journal of Communication Inquiry* 39, no. 3 (2015): 213–31; Shinsuke Eguchi, Shinsuke, "Negotiating Hegemonic Masculinity: The Rhetorical Strategy of 'Straight-Acting' Among Gay Men.,' *Journal of Intercultural Communication Research* 38 (2009): 193–209; Jay Clarkson, "'Everyday Joe' Versus 'Pissy, Bitchy, Queens': Gay Masculinity on StraightActing .com," *Journal of Men's Studies* 14, no. 2 (2006): 191–207.

99. Nathan S. Rodriguez, Jennifer Huemmer and Lindsey E. Blumell, "Mobile Masculinities: An Investigation of Networked Masculinities in Gay Dating Apps," *Masculinities & Social Change* 5, no. 3 (2016): 241–67.

100. Tony Silva, "Bud-Sex: Constructing Normative Masculinity among Rural Straight Men that Have Sex with Men," *Gender & Society*, 31 no. 1 (2016): 51–73; 64.

101. Ibid., 63.

102. See also: Ken-Hou Lin and Jennifer Lundquist, "Mate Selection in Cyberspace: The Intersection of Race, Gender, and Education," *American Journal of Sociology* 119, no. 1 (2013): 183–215; Michael Rosenfeld and Reuben Thomas, "Searching for a Mate: The Rise of the Internet as Social Intermediary," *American Sociological Review* 77, no. 4 (2012): 523–47.

103. John Gagnon and William Simon, *Sexual Conduct: The Social Sources of Human Sexuality* (Chicago: Aldine, 1973); Michael W. Wiederman, "Sexual Script Theory: Past, Present, and Future," *Handbook of the Sociology of Sexualities,* (Cham: Springer, 2015).

104. Lisa Wade, Emily Kremer, and Jessica Brown, "The Incidental Orgasm: The Presence of Clitoral Knowledge and the Absence of Orgasm for Women," *Women and Health* 42, no. 1 (2005): 117–38; Diana Sanchez, Jennifer Crocker, and Karlee Boike, "Doing Gender in the Bedroom: Investing in Gender Norms and the Sexual Experience," *Personality and Social Psychology Bulletin* 31, no. 10 (2005): 1445–55.

105. N. Gavey, *Just Sex? The Cultural Scaffolding of Rape* (London: Routledge, 2005).

106. Elizabeth A. Armstrong, Miriam Gleckman-Krut, and Lanora Johnson, "Silence, Power, and Inequality: An Intersectional Approach to Sexual Violence," *Annual Review of Sociology* 44 (2018); The National Intimate Partner and Sexual Violence Survey, "NISVS: An Overview of 2010 Findings on Victimization by Sexual Orientation." Retrieved from www.cdc.gov/violenceprevention/pdf/cdc_nisvs _victimization_final-a.pdf; U.S. Department of Justice, "Crime Against People with Disabilities, 2007," National Crime Victimization Survey, 2009. Retrieved from www.bjs.gov/content/pub/pdf/cap d07.pdf; Centers for Disease Control and Prevention, "Sexual Violence Prevention," 2018. Retrieved from www.cdc.gov/features/sexualviolence/index .html; M. L. Walters, J. Chen, and M. J. Breiding, "The National Intimate Partner and Sexual Violence Survey (NISVS): 2010 Findings on Victimization by Sexual Orientation," Atlanta, GA: National Center for Injury Prevention and Control, Centers for Disease Control and Prevention, 2013. Retrieved from www.cdc.gov/ViolencePrevention/pdf/NISVS _SOfindings.pdf; A. M. Messinger, *LGBTQ Intimate Partner Violence: Lessons for Policy, Practice, and Research* (Berkeley: University of California Press, 2017); B. Richie, *Arrested Justice: Black Women, Violence, and America's Prison Nation* (New York: New York University Press, 2012); P. Tjaden and N. Thoennes, "Extent, Nature, and Consequences of Intimate Partner Violence: Findings from the National Violence Against Women Survey." National Insti-

tute of Justice, July 2000. Retrieved from https://www.ncjrs.gov/pdffiles1/nij/181867.pdf; S. Wahab and L. Olson, "Intimate Partner Violence and Sexual Assault in Native American Communities," *Trauma Violence Abuse* 5, no. 4 (2004): 353–66; D. Finkelhor, A. Shattuck, H. Turner, and S. Hamby, "The Lifetime Prevalence of Child Sexual Abuse and Sexual Assault in Late Adolescence," *Journal of Adolescent Health* 55, no. 3 (2014): 329–33; M. Planty, L. Langton, C. Krebs, M. Berzofsky, and H. Smiley-McDonald, "Female Victims of Sexual Violence, 1994–2010," Washington, D.C.: Bureau of Justice Statistics, 2013; Z. D. Peterson, E. K. Voller, M. A. Polusny, M. Murdoch, "Prevalence and Consequences of Adult Sexual Assault of Men: Review of Empirical Findings and State of the Literature," *Clinical Psychology Review* 31, no. 1 (2011)):1–24; W. G. Axinn, M. E. Bardos, B. T. West, "General Population Estimates of the Association between College Experience and the Odds of Forced Intercourse," *Social Science Research* 70 (2017): 131–43; J. Barber, Y. Kusunoki, and J. Budnick, "Women Not Enrolled in Four-Year Universities and Colleges Have Higher Risk of Sexual Assault," Brief Reports, Council on Contemporary Families, University of Texas at Austin, April 20, 2015. Retrieved from https://contemporaryfamilies.org/not-enrolled-brief-report/; C. A. Mellins, K. Walsh, A. L. Sarvet, M. Wall, L. Gilbert, et al., "Sexual Assault Incidents among College Undergraduates: Prevalence and Factors Associated with Risk," *PLOS ONE* 13, no. 1 (2008): e0192129.

107. Federal Bureau of Investigation, Crime in the U.S., 2015. Retrieved from https://ucr.fbi.gov/crime-in-the-u.s/2015/crime-in-the-u.s.-2015/tables/table-35.

108. M. P. Koss, C. A. Gidycz, and N. Wisniewski, "The Scope of Rape: Incidence and Prevalence of Sexual Aggression and Victimization in a National Sample of Higher Education Students. *Journal of Consulting and Clinical Psychology* 55, no. 2 (1987): 162–70; D. Scully and J. Marolla, "Convicted Rapists' Vocabulary of Motive: Excuses and Justifications," *Social Problems* 31, no. 5 (1984): 530–44.

109. A. T. Tharp, S. DeGue, L. A. Valle, K. A. Brookmeyer, G. M. Massetti, and J. L. Matjasko, "A Systematic Qualitative Review of Risk and Protective Factors for Sexual Violence Perpetration," *Trauma Violence Abuse* 14, no. 2 (2012):133–67.

110. P. H. Collins, *Black Sexual Politics: African Americans, Gender, and the New Racism* (New York: Routledge, 2004); E. B. Freedman, *Redefining Rape: Sexual Violence in the Era of Suffrage and Segregation* (Cambridge: Harvard University Press, 2013).

111. S. Block, *Rape and Sexual Power in Early America* (Chapel Hill: University of North Carolina Press, 2006); E. Fox-Genovese, *Within the Plantation Household: Black and White Women of the Old South* (Chapel Hill: University of North Carolina Press, 1988); D. E. Russell, *Rape in Marriage* (Bloomington: Indiana University Press, 1990); T. A. Foster, "The Sexual Abuse of Black Men under American Slavery," *Journal of the History of Sexuality* 20, no. 3 (2011): 445–64; M. A. McLaurin, *Celia, A Slave: A True Story* (New York: Avon Books, 1991).

112. A. I. Castaneda, "Sexual Violence in the Politics and Policies of Conquest: Amerindian Women and the Spanish Conquest of Alta California," in *Building with Our Hands: New Directions in Chicana Studies*, ed. A. de la Torre, B. M. Pesquera (Berkeley: University of California Press, 1993), 15–33.

113. Catharine MacKinnon, *Sexual Harassment of Working Women: A Case of Sex Discrimination* (New Haven: Yale University Press, 1979); Kathrin Zippel, *The Politics of Sexual Harassment: A Comparative Study of the United States, the European Union and Germany* (Cambridge, Cambridge University Press, 2006); Abigail Saguy, *Sexual Harassment in France: From Capitol Hill to the Sorbonne* (Los Angeles: University of California Press, 2003).

114. U.S. Department of Justice, "Crime in the United States 2013," Uniform Crime Reporting, Federal Bureau of Investigation, 2014, Washington, D.C. Retrieved from https://ucr.fbi.gov/crime-in-the-u.s/2013/crime-in-the-u.s.-2013/violent-crime/rape.

115. Susan Estrich, *Real Rape* (Cambridge: Harvard University Press, 1987); Susan Brownmiller, *Against Our Will: Men, Women, and Rape* (New York: Simon & Schuster, 1975); C. Spohn and J. Horney, *Rape Law Reform: A Grassroots Revolution and Its Impact* (New York: Plenum Press, 1992); D. E. Russell, *Rape in Marriage* (Bloomington: Indiana University Press, 1990); K. Bumiller, *The Civil Rights Society: The Social Construction of Victims* (Baltimore: Johns Hopkins University Press, 1988).

116. Amy Elman, "Gender Violence," in *The Oxford Handbook of Gender and Politics*, ed. Georgina Waylen, Karen Celis, Johanna Kantola, and S. Laurel Weldon (New York: Oxford University Press, 2013); Laurel Weldon, *Protest, Policy, and the Problem of Violence against Women: A Cross-National Comparison* (Pittsburgh: University of Pittsburgh Press, 2002).

117. J. Wheeler, "A Review of National Crime Victim Victimization Findings on Rape and Sexual Assault," Brief Report, Council on Contemporary Families,

University of Texas at Austin, 2015. Retrieved from https://contemporaryfamilies.org/crime-victimization-brief-report/; M. Planty, L. Langton, C. Krebs, M. Berzofsky, and H. Smiley-McDonald, "Female Victims of Sexual Violence, 1994–2010," Washington, D.C.: Bureau of Justice Statistics, 2013.

118. K. Bumiller, *The Civil Rights Society: The Social Construction of Victims* (Baltimore: Johns Hopkins University Press, 1988); C. Cleere and S. J. Lynn, "Acknowledged Versus Unacknowledged Sexual Assault among College Women," *Journal of Interpersonal Violence* 28, no. 12 (2013): 2593–611; C. E. Ahrens, "Being Silenced: The Impact of Negative Social Reactions on the Disclosure of Rape," *American Journal of Community Psychology* 38, no. 3–4 (2006): 263–74; M. P. Koss, C. A. Gidycz, N. Wisniewski, "The Scope of Rape: Incidence and Prevalence of Sexual Aggression and Victimization in a National Sample of Higher Education Students," *Journal of Consulting Clinical Psychology* 55, no. 2 (1987): 162–70; L. M. Phillips, *Flirting with Danger: Young Women's Reflections on Sexuality and Domination* (New York: New York University Press, 2000).

119. R. M. Hayes, R. L. Abbott, and S. Cook, "It's Her Fault: Student Acceptance of Rape Myths on Two College Campuses," *Violence Against Women* 22, no. 13 (2016): 1540–55.

120. RAINN, "The Criminal Justice System: Statistics," 2018. Retrieved from www.rainn.org/statistics/criminal-justice-system; Rachel E. Morgan and Grace Kena, "Criminal Victimization, 2016," December 2017. Retrievedfromwww.bjs.gov/content/pub/pdf/cv16.pdf; R. A. Donovan and M. Williams, "Living at the Intersection: The Effects of Racism and Sexism on Black Rape Survivors," *Women & Therapy* 25, no. 3–4 (2002): 95–105; B. Fisher, L.E. Diagle, F. T. Cullen and M. G. Turner, "Acknowledging Sexual Victimization as Rape: Results from a National-Level Survey," *Justice Quarterly* 20, no. 3 (2003): 535–74.

121. National Sexual Violence Resource Center, "False Reporting," 2012. Retrieved from www.nsvrc.org/sites/default/files/Publications_NSVRC_Overview_False-Reporting.pdf; J. Shaw, R. Campbell, D. Cain, and H. Feeney, "Beyond Surveys and Scales: How Rape Myths Manifest in Sexual Assault Police Records," *Psychology of Violence* 7, no. 4 (2017): 602–14; K. A. Lonsway, J. Archambault, and D. Lisak, "False Reports: Moving beyond the Issue to Successfully Investigate and Prosecute Non-Stranger Sexual Assault," *The Voice* 3, no. 1 (2009), 1–11. National District Attorneys Association. Retrieved from www.ndaa.org/pdf/the_voice_vol_3_no_1_2009.pdf;

S. Dinos, N. Burrowes, K. Hammond, C. Cunliffe, "A Systematic Review of Juries' Assessment of Rape Victims: Do Rape Myths Impact on Juror Decision-Making?" *International Journal of Law, Crime, and Justice* 43, no. 1 (2015): 36–49; D. Lisak, L. Gardinier, S. C. Nicksa, and A. M. Cote, "False Allegations of Sexual Assault: An Analysis of Ten Years of Reported Cases," *Violence Against Women* 16 (2010): 1318–34; J. R. Krakauer, *Missoula: Rape and the Justice System in a College Town* (New York: Doubleday, 2015); J. E. Williams and K. A. Holmes, *The Second Assault: Rape and Public Attitudes* (Westport, CT: Greenwood Press, 1981); P. Y. Martin, *Rape Work: Victims, Gender, and Emotions in Organization and Community Context* (New York: Routledge, 2005); S. Mulla, *The Violence of Care: Rape Victims, Forensic Nurses, and Sexual Assault Intervention* (New York: New York University Press, 2014).

122. Michelle Davies, "Male Sexual Assault Victims: A Selective Review of the Literature and Implications for Support Services," *Aggression and Violent Behavior* 7 (2002): 203–14. Retrieved from www.researchgate.net/profile/Michelle_Lowe7/publication/222607725_Male_Sexual_Assault_Victims_A_Selective_Review_of_the_Literature_and_Implications_for_Support_Services/links/59f0792a4585_15bfd07bf3a9/Male-Sexual-Assault-Victims-A-Selective-Review-of-the-Literature-and-Implications-for-Support-Services.pdf; Michelle Davies and Paul Rogers, "Perceptions of Male Victims in Depicted Sexual Assaults: A Review of the Literature," *Aggression and Violent Behavior* 11 (2006): 367–77. Retrieved from www.researchgate.net/profile/Michelle_Lowe7/publication/222600153_Perceptions_of_male_victims_in_depicted_sexual_assaults_A_review_of_the_literature/links/59f07929458515bfd07bf3a8/Perceptions-of-male-victims-in-depicted-sexual-assaults-A-review-of-the-literature.pdf; J. L. Small, "Trying Male Rape: Legal Renderings of Masculinity, Vulnerability, and Sexual Violence," (PhD diss., University of Michigan, Ann Arbor, 2015); J. M. Owen, 1995. "Women-Talk and Men-Talk: Defining and Resisting Victim Statuses," in *Gender and Crime*, ed. R. E. Dobash, R. Dobash, and L. Noaks (Cardiff, UK: University of Wales Press, 1995), 46–68; R. Corrigan, *Up Against a Wall: Rape Reform and the Failure of Success* (New York: New York University Press, 2013); D. Lisak, L. Gardinier, S. C. Nicksa, and A. M. Cote, "False Allegations of Sexual Assault: An Analysis of Ten Years of Reported Cases," *Violence Against Women* 16 (2010): 1318–34; X. L. Guadalupe-Diaz and J. Jasinski,"'I Wasn't a Priority, I Wasn't a Victim': Challenges in Help

Seeking for Transgender Survivors of Intimate Partner Violence," *Violence Against Women* 23, no. 6 (2016)):772–92; M. R. Greeson, R. Campbell, and G. Fehler-Cabral, "'Nobody Deserves This': Adolescent Sexual Assault Victims' Perceptions of Disbelief and Victim Blame from Police," *Journal of Community Psychology* 44, no. 1 (2016): 90–110; P. H. Collins, *Black Sexual Politics: African Americans, Gender, and the New Racism* (New York: Routledge, 2004); J. C. Nash, "Black Women and Rape: A Review of the Literature." Brandeis University, Feminist Sexual Ethics Project June 12, 2009; H. A. Neville, E. Oh, L. B. Spanierman, M. J. Heppner, and M. Clark, "General and Culturally Specific Factors Influencing Black and White Rape Survivors' Self-Esteem," *Psychology of Women Quarterly* 28, no. 1 (2004): 83–94; S. R. Gross, M. Possley, and K. Stephens, 2017. "Race and Wrongful Convictions in the United States," Report, National Registry of Exonerations, Newkirk Center for Science and Society, University of California at Irvine, Irvine, CA: March 7, 2017. Retrieved from http://www.law.umich.edu/special/exoneration/Documents/Race_and_Wrongful_Convictions.pdf.

123. Christopher Maxwell, Amanda Robinson, and Lori Post, "The Impact of Race on the Adjudication of Sexual Assault and Other Violent Crimes," *Journal of Criminal Justice* 31 (2003): 523–38; Patricia Hill Collins, *Black Sexual Politics: African Americans, Gender, and the New Racism* (New York: Routledge, 2005); Angela Davis, *Women, Race, and Class* (New York: Vintage Books, 1983); Pierrette Hondagneu-Sotelo and Michael A. Messner, "Gender Displays and Men's Power: The "New Man" and the Mexican Immigrant Man," in *Theorizing Masculinities*, ed. Harry Brod and Michael Kaufman (New York: Sage, 1994); Susan Estrich, *Real Rape* (Cambridge: Harvard University Press, 1987); K. W. Crenshaw, "Mapping the Margins: Intersectionality, Identity Politics, and Violence against Women of Color," *Stanford Law Review* 43, no. 6 (1991): 1241–99; B. Richie, *Arrested Justice: Black Women, Violence, and America's Prison Nation* (New York: New York University Press, 2012); K. Weis and S. S. Borges, "Victimology and Rape: The Case of the Legitimate Victim," *Issues in Criminology* 8, no. 2 (1973): 71–115; M. J. Brown and J. Groscup, "Perceptions of Same-Sex Domestic Violence among Crisis Center Staff," *Journal of Family Violence* 24, no. 2 (2009): 87–93; M. Heenan and S. Murray, "Study of Reported Rapes in Victoria 2000–2003: Summary Research Report. The State of Victoria (Australia), Department of Human Services, 2006.

Retrieved from http://mams.rmit.edu.au/igzdo8ddxtpwz.pdf.

124. S. R. Gross, M. Possley, and K. Stephens, 2017. "Race and Wrongful Convictions in the United States," Report, National Registry of Exonerations, Newkirk Center for Science and Society, University of California at Irvine, Irvine, CA: March 7, 2017. Retrieved from http://www.law.umich.edu/special/exoneration/Documents/Race_and_Wrongful_Convictions.pdf.

125. Elizabeth A. Armstrong, Miriam Gleckman-Krut, and Lanora Johnson, "Silence, Power, and Inequality: An Intersectional Approach to Sexual Violence," *Annual Review of Sociology*, 44 (2018).

126. Peggy Reeves Sanday, "The Socio-Cultural Context of Rape: A Cross-Cultural Study," *Journal of Social Issues*, 37, no. 4 (1981). Retrieved from https://doi.org/10.1111/j.1540-4560.1981.tb01068.x; Christine Helliwell, "'It's Only a Penis': Rape, Feminism, and Difference." *Signs* 25, no. 3 (2000):789–816; Maria Barbara Watson-Franke, "A World in which Women Move Freely without Fear of Men: An Anthropological Perspective on Rape," 25, no. 6 (2002): 599–606.

127. Catharine MacKinnon, *Toward a Feminist Theory of the State* (Boston: Harvard University Press, 1989); Sharon Marcus, "Fighting Bodies, Fighting Words: A Theory and Politics of Rape Prevention," in *Feminists Theorize the Political*, ed. Judith Butler and Joan W. Scott (New York: Routledge, 1992), 385–403; V. Jenness and S. Fenstermaker, "Forty Years after Brownmiller: Prisons for Men, Transgender Inmates, and the Rape of the Feminine," *Gender & Society* 30, no. 1 (2016): 14–29; C. J. Pascoe and J. A. Hollander, "Good Guys Don't Rape: Gender, Domination, and Mobilizing Rape," *Gender & Society* 3, no. 1 (2016): 67–79; J. L. Small, "Trying Male Rape: Legal Renderings of Masculinity, Vulnerability, and Sexual Violence," (PhD diss., University of Michigan, Ann Arbor, 2015).

128. Virginia Braun and Sue Wilkinson, "Sociocultural Representations of the Vagina." *Journal of Reproductive and Infant Psychology* 19, no. 1 (2001): 17–32; Anna Chave, "O'Keefe and the Masculine Gaze," in *Reading American Art*, ed. Marianne Doezema and Elizabeth Milroy (New Haven: Yale University Press, 1998), 350–70.

129. Scott Poulson-Bryant, *Hung: A Meditation on the Measure of Black Men in America* (New York: Random House, 2005); Leonore Tiefer, *Sex is Not a Natural Act, & Other Essays*, 2nd ed. (Boulder, CO: Westview Press, 2004); David Friedman, *A Mind of*

Its Own: A Cultural History of the Penis (New York: Penguin Books, 2001).

130. Christine Halliwell, "'It's Only a Penis': Rape, Feminism, and Difference." *Signs* 25, no. 3 (2000): 789–816; Elwin Verrier, "The Vagina Dentata Legend," *British Journal of Medical Psychology*, 19, no. 3–4 (1943): 439–53. Retrieved from https://doi.org/10.1111/j.2044-8341.1943.tb00338.x; Benjamin Beit-Hallahmi, "Dangers of the Vagina," *British Journal of Medical Psychology*, 58, no. 4 (1985): 351–56.

131. Kate Harding, *Asking for It: The Alarming Rise of Rape Culture—and What We Can Do about It* (Boston, MA: Da Capo Press, 2015).

132. Tanya Serisier, "Sex Crimes and the Media," *Oxford Research Encyclopedia of Criminology*, 2017. Retrieved from http://criminology.oxfordre.com/view/10.1093/acrefore/9780190264079.001.0001/acrefore-9780190264079-e-118.

133. N. Stein, "Locating a Secret Problem: Sexual Violence in Elementary and Secondary Schools," in eds. Laura O'Toole, Jessica R. Schiffman, and Margie L. Kiter Edwards, *Gender Violence: Interdisciplinary Perspectives*, 2nd edition (New York: New York University Press, 2007): 323–332. Faye Mishna, Kaitlin J. Schwan, Arija Birze, Melissa Van Wert, Ashley Lacombe-Duncan, Lauren McInroy, and Shalhevet Attar-Schwartz, "Gendered and Sexualized Bullying and Cyber Bullying: Spotlighting Girls and Making Boys Invisible," *Youth & Society*, February 19, 2018. Retrieved from https://doi.org/10.1177/0044118X18757150

134. Robert Jensen, "Rape, Rape Culture and the Problem of Patriarchy," *Waging Nonviolence*, April 29, 2014. Retrieved from https://wagingnonviolence.org/feature/rape-rape-culture-problem-patriarchy/; see also Philip Kavanaugh, "The Continuum of Sexual Violence: Women's Accounts of Victimization in Urban Nightlife," *Feminist Criminology* 8, no. 1 (2013): 20–39.

135. Katie Way, "I Went on a Date with Aziz Ansari. It Turned into the Worst Night of My Life," *babe*. Retrieved from https://babe.net/2018/01/13/aziz-ansari-28355.

136. Natalie Jarvey, "Sexual Assault Movement #MeToo Reaches Nearly 500,000 Tweets," *Hollywood Reporter*, October 16, 2017. Retrieved from https://www.hollywoodreporter.com/news/metoo-sexual-assault-movement-reaches-500000-tweets-1049235; CBS/AP, "More than 12M 'Me Too' Facebook posts, comments, reactions in 24 hours," *CBS*, October 17, 2017. Retrieved from https://www.cbsnews.com/news/metoo-more-than-12-million-facebook-posts-comments-reactions-24-hours/; J. R. Thorpe, "This Is How Many People Have Posted 'Me Too' Since October, According to New Data," *Bustle*, December 1, 2017. Retrieved from www.bustle.com/p/this-is-how-many-people-have-posted-me-too-since-october-according-to-new-data-6753697.

137. Thomas Vander Ven, *Getting Wasted: Why College Students Drink Too Much and Party Too Hard* (New York: New York University Press, 2011), 2.

138. Thomas Vander Ven, *Getting Wasted: Why College Students Drink Too Much and Party Too Hard* (New York: New York University Press, 2011), 75.

139. Nicholas Syrett, *The Company He Keeps: A History of White College Fraternities* (Chapel Hill: University of North Carolina Press, 2009).

140. Lynn Peril, *College Girls: Bluestockings, Sex Kittens, and Coeds, Then and Now* (New York: W. W. Norton and Company, 2006); B. J. Willoughby et al., "The Decline of in loco parentis and the Shift to Coed Housing on College Campuses," *Journal of Adolescent Research* 24, no. 1 (2009): 21–36.

141. Michael Moffett, *Coming of Age in New Jersey: College and American Culture* (New Brunswick: Rutgers University Press, 1898).

142. Murray Sperber, *Beer and Circus: How Big-Time College Sport is Crippling Undergraduate Education* (New York: Henry Holt, 2000); Henry Wechsler and Bernice Wuethrich, *Dying to Drink: Confronting Binge Drinking on College Campuses* (Emmaus, PA: Rodale Books, 2002).

143. Elizabeth Armstrong and Laura Hamilton, *Paying for the Party: How College Maintains Inequality* (Cambridge: Harvard University Press, 2013); Jill Russett, "Women's Perceptions of High-Risk Drinking: Understanding Binge Drinking in a Gender Biased Setting," (PhD diss., The College of William and Mary, 2008); Lisa Wade, 2 *American Hookup: The New Culture of Sex on Campus* (New York: W. W. Norton and Company, 2017).

144. K. A. Bogle, *Hooking up: Sex, Dating, and Relationships on Campus* (New York: New York University Press, 2008); Donna Freitas, *Sex and the Soul: Juggling Sexuality, Spirituality, Romance, and Religion on America's College Campuses* (New York: Oxford University Press, 2008); J. J.Owen, Galena K. Rhoades, Scott M. Stanley, and Frank D. Fincham, "'Hooking Up' among College Students: Demographic and Psychosocial Correlates," *Archives of Sexual Behavior* 39, no. 3 (2010): 653–63; Laura Ham-

ilton, "Trading on Heterosexuality: College Women's Gender Strategies and Homophobia," *Gender & Society* 21, no. 2 (2007): 145–72; Rashawn Ray and Jason A. Rosow, "Getting Off and Getting Intimate: How Normative Institutional Arrangements Structure Black and White Fraternity Men's Approaches toward Women," *Men and Masculinities* 12, no. 5 (2010): 523–46; Personal communication: Paula England; Rachel Allison and Barbara Risman, "'It Goes Hand in Hand with the Parties': Race, Class, and Residence in College Negotiations of Hooking Up," *Sociological Perspectives* 57, no. 1 (2014): 102–23; L. Hamilton and E. A. Armstrong, "Gendered Sexuality in Young Adulthood: Double Binds and Flawed Options," *Gender & Society* 23, no. 5 (2009): 589–616; Elizabeth Armstrong and Laura Hamilton, *Paying for the Party: How College Maintains Inequality* (Boston: Harvard University Press, 2013); Lisa Wade, *American Hookup: The New Culture of Sex on Campus* (New York: W. W. Norton and Company, 2017).

145. Sarah K. Murnen and Marla H. Kohlman, "Athletic Participation, Fraternity Membership, and Sexual Aggression Among College Men: A Meta-analytic Review," *Sex Roles* 57, no. 1-2 (July 2007): 145–57. Retrieved from https://link.springer.com/article/10.1007/s11199-007-9225-1; Kaitlin Boyle, "Social Psychological Processes that Facilitate Sexual Assault within the Fraternity Party Subculture," *Sociology Compass* 9, no. 5 (2015): 386–99.

146. Clare Hollowell, "The Subject of Fun: Young Women, Freedom and Feminism," (PhD diss., Centre for Gender and Women's Studies, Lancaster University, 2010).

147. John Conklin, *Campus Life in the Movies: A Critical Survey from the Silent Era to the Present* (Jefferson, NC: McFarland, 2008); Justin R. Garcia, Chris Reiber, Sean G. Massey, and Ann M. Merriwether, "Sexual Hookup Culture: A Review," *Review of General Psychology* 16, no. 2(2012):161–76; Matthew Hartley and Christopher Morphew, "What's Being Sold and To What End? A Content Analysis of College Viewbooks," *Journal of Higher Education* 79, no. 6 (2008): 671–91; Pauline Reynolds, "Representing 'U': Popular Culture, Media, and Higher Education," *ASHE Higher Education Report* 41, 4 (2014): 1–145.

148. American College Health Association, "American College Health Association–National College Health Assessment II: Reference Group Executive Summary Spring 2013," Hanover, MD: American College Health Association, 2013. Retrieved from http://www.acha-ncha.org/docs/acha-ncha-ii_referencegroup_executivesummary_spring2013.pdf

149. Jessie Ford, Paula England, and Jonathan Bearak, "The American College Hookup Scene: Findings from the Online College Social Life Survey," (presentation, American Sociological Association Annual Meeting, Chicago, August 2015); Jeremy Uecker, Lisa Pearce, and Brita Andercheck, "The Four U's: Latent Classes of Hookup Motivations among College Students," *Social Currents* 2, no. 2 (2015): 163–81; Rachel Kalish, "Sexual Decision Making in the Context of Hookup Culture: A Mixed-Method Examination," (Ph.D. diss., Stony Brook University, 2014); Justin R. Garcia, Chris Reiber, Sean G. Massey, and Ann M. Merriwether, "Sexual Hookup Culture: A Review," *Review of General Psychology* 16, no. 2 (2012): 161–76; Arielle Kuperberg, and Joseph E. Padgett, "The Role of Culture in Explaining College Students' Selection into Hookups, Dates, and Long-Term Romantic Relationships," *Journal of Social and Personal Relationships*, 33, no. 8 (2016): 1070–96.

150. K. A. Bogle, *Hooking Up: Sex, Dating, and Relationships on Campus* (New York: New York University Press, 2008); E. Paul, "Beer Goggles, Catching Feelings, and the Walk of Shame: Myths and Realities of the Hookup Experience," in *Relating Difficulty: The Processes of Constructing and Managing Difficult Interaction*, ed. D. C. Kirkpatrick, S. Duck, and M. K. Foley (Mahwah, NJ: Lawrence Erlbaum, 2006), 141-60; T. A. Lambert, A. S. Kahn, and K. J. Applie, "Pluralistic Ignorance and Hooking Up," *Journal of Sex Research* 40 (2003): 129–33.

151. Jessie Ford, Paula England, and Jonathan Bearak, "The American College Hookup Scene: Findings from the Online College Social Life Survey," (presentation, American Sociological Association Annual Meeting, Chicago, August, 2015).

152. P. England, E. F. Shafer, and A. C. K. Fogerty, "Hooking Up and Forming Relationships on Today's College Campuses," in *The Gendered Society Reader*, ed. Michael Kimmel (New York: Oxford University Press, 2008), 531–93; Lisa Wade and Caroline Heldman, "Hooking Up and Opting Out: What Students Learn about Sex in their First Year of College," in *Sex for Life: From Virginity to Viagra, How Sexuality Changes Throughout our Lives*, ed. Laura Carpenter and John DeLamater (New York: New York University Press, 2012), 128–145; Jessie Ford, Paula England, and Jonathan Bearak, "The American College Hookup Scene: Findings from the Online College Social Life Survey," (presentation, American

Sociological Association Annual Meeting, Chicago, August, 2015).

153. Jessie Ford, Paula England, and Jonathan Bearak, "The American College Hookup Scene: Findings from the Online College Social Life Survey," (presentation, American Sociological Association Annual Meeting, Chicago, August, 2015).

154. Rachel Allison and Barbara J. Risman, "'It Goes Hand in Hand with the Parties': Race, Class, and Residence in College Student Negotiations of Hooking Up." *Sociological Perspectives* 57, no. 1 (2014): 102–23; Elizabeth Armstrong and Laura Hamilton, *Paying for the Party: How College Maintains Inequality* (Cambridge: Harvard University Press, 2013); Kathleen A. Bogle, *Hooking Up: Sex, Dating, and Relationships on Campus* (New York: New York University Press, 2008); Ted Brimeyer and William Smith, "Religion, Race, Social Class, and Gender Differences in Dating and Hooking Up among College Students," *Sociological Spectrum* 32, no. 5 (2014): 462–73; Donna Freitas, *Sex and the Soul: Juggling Sexuality, Spirituality, Romance, and Religion on America's College Campuses* (Oxford: Oxford University Press, 2008); Arielle Kuperberg and Joseph E. Padgett, "Dating and Hooking Up in College: Meeting Contexts, Sex, and Variation by Gender, Partner's Gender, and Class Standing," *Journal of Sex Research*, 52, no. 5 (2015): 517–31; Arielle Kuperberg and Joseph E. Padgett, "The Role of Culture in Explaining College Students' Selection into Hookups, Dates, and Long-Term Romantic Relationships," *Journal of Social and Personal Relationships* 33, no. 8 (2016): 1070–96; Jesse Owen, Frank Fincham, and Jon Moore, "Short-term Prospective Study of Hooking Up among College Students," *Archives of Sexual Behavior* 40 (2011): 331–41; Leila Rupp and Verta Taylor, "Queer Girls on Campus: New Intimacies and Sexual Identities," in *Intimacies: A New World of Relational Life*, ed. Alan Frank, Patricia Clough, and Steven Seidman (New York: Routledge, 2013), 82–97; Leila Rupp, Verta Taylor, Shiri Regev-Messalem, Alison C. K. Fogarty, and Paula England, "Queer Women in the Hookup Scene: Beyond the Closet?" *Gender & Society*, 28, no. 2 (2014):212–35; Sarah Spell, "Not Just Black and White: How Race/Ethnicity and Gender Intersect in Hookup Culture," *Sociology of Race and Ethnicity* 3, no. 2 (2016): 172–87; Lisa Wade and Joseph Padgett, "Hookup Culture and Higher Education," in *Handbook of Contemporary Feminism*, ed. Andrea Press and Tasha Oren (New York: Routledge, forthcoming).

155. Laura Hamilton, "Trading on Heterosexuality: College Women's Gender Strategies and Homopho-

bia," *Gender & Society* 21, no. 2 (2007): 145–72; Leila Rupp, Shiri Regev-Messalem, Alison C. K. Fogarty, and Paula England, "Queer Women in the Hookup Scene: Beyond the Closet?" *Gender & Society* 28, no. 2 (2014): 212–35.

156. Laura Hamilton, "Trading on Heterosexuality: College Women's Gender Strategies and Homophobia," *Gender & Society* 21, no. 2 (2007): 145–72.

157. Arielle Kuperberg and Joseph E. Padgett, "The Role of Culture in Explaining College Students' Selection into Hookups, Dates, and Long-Term Romantic Relationships," *Journal of Social and Personal Relationships* 33, no. 8 (2016): 1070–96.

158. Personal communication: Paula England; Rachel Allison and Barbara Risman, "'It Goes Hand in Hand with the Parties': Race, Class, and Residence in College Negotiations of Hooking Up," *Sociological Perspectives* 57, no. 1 (2014): 102–23.

159. Jess Butler, "Sexual Subjects: Hooking Up in the Age of Postfeminism," (PhD diss., University of Southern California, 2013); Michael Kimmel, *Guyland: The Perilous World Where Boys Become Men* (New York: HarperCollins, 2008); Kristine J. Ajrouch, "Gender, Race, and Symbolic Boundaries: Contested Spaces of Identity Among Arab American Adolescents," *Sociological Perspectives*, 47, no. 4 (2004): 371–91, DOI: 10.1525/sop.2004.47.4.371.

160. Yen Le Espiritu, "'We Don't Sleep around like White Girls Do': Family, Culture, and Gender in Filipina American Lives," *Journal of Women in Culture and Society*, 26, no. 2 (Winter, 2001): 415–40; 415. Retrieved from https://doi.org/10.1086/495599.

161. Michael Kimmel, *Guyland: The Perilous World Where Boys Become Men* (New York: HarperCollins, 2008), 204.

162. Ibid.

163. Personal communication: Paula England; Rachel Allison and Barbara Risman, "'It Goes Hand in Hand with the Parties': Race, Class, and Residence in College Negotiations of Hooking Up," *Sociological Perspectives* 57, no. 1 (2014): 102–23; L. Hamilton and E. A. Armstrong, "Gendered Sexuality in Young Adulthood: Double Binds and Flawed Options," *Gender & Society* 23, no. 5 (2009): 589–616; Laura Hamilton, "Trading on Heterosexuality: College Women's Gender Strategies and Homophobia," *Gender & Society* 21, no. 2 (2007): 145–72; Elizabeth Armstrong and Laura Hamilton, *Paying for the Party: How College Maintains Inequality* (Boston: Harvard University Press, 2013).

164. Elizabeth A. Armstrong, Laura T. Hamilton, Elizabeth M. Armstrong, J. Lotus Seeley, "'Good Girls': Gender, Social Class, and Slut Discourse on Campus," *Social Psychology Quarterly*, 77, no. 2, (2014): 100–22.

165. L. Hamilton and E. A. Armstrong, "Gendered Sexuality in Young Adulthood: Double Binds and Flawed Options," *Gender & Society* 23, no. 5 (2009): 589–616.

166. Rachel Allison and Barbara Risman, "'It Goes Hand in Hand with the Parties': Race, Class, and Residence in College Negotiations of Hooking Up," *Sociological Perspectives* 57, no. 1 (2014): 102–23.

167. Lisa Wade. Unpublished data.

168. M. M. Bersamin, B. L. Zamboanga, S. J. Schwartz, M. B. Donnellan, M. Hudson, R. S. Weisskirch, and S. J. Caraway, "Risky Business: Is There an Association between Casual Sex and Mental Health among Emerging Adults?" *Journal of Sex Research* 51, no. 1 (2013): 43–51; K. Eagan, J. B. Lozano, S. Hurtado, and M. H. Case, "The American Freshman: National Norms Fall 2013," Los Angeles: Higher Education Research Institute, UCLA, 2013; E. M. Eshbaugh, G. Gute, "Hookups and Sexual Regret among College Women," *Journal of Social Psychology* 148 (2008): 77–90; M. L. Fisher, K. Worth, J. R. Garcia, and T. Meredith, "Feelings of Regret Following Uncommitted Sexual Encounters in Canadian University Students," *Culture, Health & Sexuality* 14 (2012): 45–57; W. F. Flack, K. A. Daubman, M. L. Caron, J. A. Asadorian, N. R. D'Aureli, S. N. Gigliotti, and E. R. Stine, "Risk Factors and Consequences of Unwanted Sex among University Students: Hooking Up, Alcohol, and Stress Response," *Journal of Interpersonal Violence* 22 (2007): 139–57; Donna Freitas, *The End of Sex: How Hookup Culture is Leaving a Generation Unhappy, Sexually Unfulfilled, and Confused About Intimacy* (New York: Basic Books, 2013); M. A. Lewis, D. C. Atkins, J. A. Blayney, D. V. Dent, and D. L. Kaysen, "What Is Hooking Up? Examining Definitions of Hooking Up in Relation to Behavior and Normative Perceptions," *Journal of Sex Research* 50, no. 8 (2012): 757–66; M. A. Lewis, H. Granato, J. A. Blayney, T. W. Lostutter, and J. R Kilmer, "Predictors of Hooking Up Sexual Behaviors and Emotional Reactions among U.S. College Students," *Archives of Sexual Behavior* 41 (2012): 1219–29; J. Owen, F. D. Fincham, J. Moore, "Short-Term Prospective Study of Hooking Up among College Students," *Archives of Sexual Behavior* 40 (2011): 331–41; E. L. Paul, K. A. Hayes, "The Casualties of 'Casual' Sex: A Qualitative Exploration of the Phenomenology of College Students' Hookups," *Journal of Social and Personal Relationships* 19 (2002): 639–61; Christian Smith with Kari Kristofferson, Hillary Davidson, and Patricia Snell Herzog, "Lost in Transition: The Dark Side of Emerging Adulthood," (New York: Oxford University Press, 2011); L. S. Stepp, *Unhooked: How Young Women Pursue Sex, Delay Love, and Lose at Both* (New York: Riverhead Books; 2007).

169. Jessie Ford, Paula England, and Jonathan Bearak "The American College Hookup Scene: Findings from the Online College Social Life Survey," (presentation, American Sociological Association Annual Meeting, Chicago, August 2015); Jeremy Uecker, Lisa Pearce, and Brita Andercheck "The Four U's: Latent Classes of Hookup Motivations among College Students," *Social Currents* 2, no. 2 (2015): 163–81; Justin R. Garcia, Chris Reiber, Sean G. Massey, and Ann M. Merriwether, "Sexual Hookup Culture: A Review," *Review of General Psychology*, 16, no. 2 (2012): 161–76.

170. Lisa Wade. *American Hookup: The New Culture of Sex on Campus* (New York: W. W. Norton and Company, 2017).

171. Rachel Kalish, "Sexual Decision Making in the Context of Hookup Culture: A Mixed-Method Examination," (PhD diss., Stony Brook University, 2014); Arielle Kuperberg and Joseph E. Padgett, "Dating and Hooking Up in College: Meeting Contexts, Sex, and Variation by Gender, Partner's Gender, and Class Standing," *Journal of Sex Research* 52, no. 5 (2015): 517–31; Martin A. Monto and Anna G. Carey, "A New Standard of Sexual Behavior? Are Claims Associated with The 'Hookup Culture' Supported by General Social Survey Data?" *Journal of Sex Research* 51, no. 6 (2014): 605–15; Jessie Ford, Paula England, and Jonathan Bearak, "The American College Hookup Scene: Findings from the Online College Social Life Survey," (presentation, American Sociological Association Annual Meeting, Chicago, August 2015).

172. Lisa Wade, *American Hookup: The New Culture of Sex on Campus* (New York: W. W. Norton and Company, 2017), 141.

173. Jessie Ford, Paula England, and Jonathan Bearak, "The American College Hookup Scene: Findings from the Online College Social Life Survey," (presentation, American Sociological Association Annual Meeting, Chicago, August 2015).

174. Mimi Schippers, n.d. "Mononormativity and Gender Inequality in Hookup Culture," Unpublished manuscript.

175. Jessie Ford, Paula England, and Jonathan Bearak, "The American College Hookup Scene: Findings from the Online College Social Life Survey," (presentation, American Sociological Association Annual Meeting, Chicago, August 2015). See also E. Armstrong, P. England, and A. Fogarty, "Accounting for Women's Orgasm and Sexual Enjoyment in College Hook-ups and Relationships," *American Sociological Review* 77, no. 3 (2012): 435–62.

176. J. J. Owen, Galena K. Rhoades, Scott M. Stanley, and Frank D. Fincham, "'Hooking Up' among College Students: Demographic and Psychosocial Correlates," *Archives of Sexual Behavior* 39, no. 3 (2010): 653–63.

177. E. A. Armstrong, P. England, and A. C. K. Fogarty, "Orgasm in College Hook-ups and Relationships," in *Families as They Really Are*, ed. Barbara Risman (New York: W. W. Norton and Company, 2009).

178. E. Armstrong, P. England, and A. Fogarty, "Accounting for Women's Orgasm and Sexual Enjoyment in College Hook-ups and Relationships," *American Sociological Review* 77, no. 3 (2012): 435–62.

179. Lisa Wade, *American Hookup: The New Culture of Sex on Campus* (New York: W. W. Norton and Company, 2017).

180. Jessie Ford, Paula England, and Jonathan Bearak, "The American College Hookup Scene: Findings from the Online College Social Life Survey," (presentation, American Sociological Association Annual Meeting, Chicago, August 2015). See also Bonnie Fisher, Francis Cullen, and Michael Turner, "The Sexual Victimization of College Women," Washington, D.C.: National Institute of Justice and Bureau of Justice Statistics, 2000; David Cantor, Bonnie Fisher, Susan Chibnall, Reanne Townsend, Hyunshik Lee, Carol Bruce, and Gail Thomas, "Report on the AAU Campus Climate Survey on Sexual Assault and Sexual Misconduct," *Association of American Universities*, 2015. Retrieved from https://www.aau.edu/key-issues/aau-climate-survey-sexual-assault-and-sexual-misconduct-2015; Dean Kilpatrick, Heidi Resnick, Kenneth Ruggiero, Lauren Conoscenti, and Janna McCauley, *Drug-Facilitated, Incapacitated, and Forcible Rape: A National Study*. National Crime Victims Research and Treatment Center, 2007. Retrieved from www.ncjrs.gov/pdffiles1/nij/grants/219181.pdf; Christopher Krebs, Christine Lindquist, Tara Warner, Bonnie Fischer, and Sandra Martin, "The Campus Sexual Assault Study," National Institute of Justice, 2007. Retrieved from www.ncjrs.gov/pdffiles1/nij/grants/221153.pdf; Sofi

Sinozich and Lynn Langton, "Rape and Sexual Assault Victimization Among College-Age Females, 1995–2013," U.S. Department of Justice, 2014. Retrieved from www.bjs.gov/content/pub/pdf/rsavcaf9513.pdf; White House Task Force to Protect Students from Sexual Assault, *Not Alone: The First Report of the White House Task Force to Protect Students from Sexual Assault*, 2014. Retrieved from https://www.justice.gov/ovw/page/file/905942/download.

181. Lexie Bean, ed., *Written on the Body: Letters from Trans and Non-Binary Survivors of Sexual Assault and Domestic Violence* (London: Jessica Kinsley Publishers, 2018).

182. K. M. Swartout, M. P. Koss, J. W. White, M. P. Thompson, A. Abbey, A. L. Bellis, "Trajectory Analysis of the Campus Serial Rapist Assumption," *JAMA Pediatrics*, 169, no. 12 (2015): 1148–54, DOI: 10.1001/jamapediatrics.2015.0707. See also C. A. Mellins, K. Walsh, A. L. Sarvet, M. Wall, and L. Gilbert et al., "Sexual Assault Incidents among College Undergraduates: Prevalence and Factors Associated with Risk," *PLOS ONE* 13, no. 1 (2008): e0192129.

183. Elizabeth Armstrong and Jamie Budnick, "Sexual Assault on Campus," Brief Reports, *Council on Contemporary Families*, April 20, 2015. Retrieved from https://contemporaryfamilies.org/assault-on-campus-brief-report/; Elizabeth Armstrong, Laura Hamilton, and Brian Sweeney, "Sexual Assault on Campus: A Multilevel, Integrative Approach to Party Rape" *Social Problems* 53, no. 4 (2006): 483–99; Heather Littleton, Holly Tabernik, Erika J. Canales, and Tamika Backstrom, "Risky Situation or Harmless Fun? A Qualitative Examination of College Women's Bad Hook-Up and Rape Scripts," *Sex Roles* 60, no. 11/12 (2009): 793–804; E. Paul, "Beer Goggles, Catching Feelings, and the Walk of Shame: Myths and Realities of the Hookup Experience," in *Relating Difficulty: The Processes of Constructing and Managing Difficult Interaction*, ed. D. C. Kirkpatrick, S. Duck, and M. K. Foley (Mahwah, NJ: Lawrence Erlbaum, 2006), 141–60.

184. K. M. Swartout, M. P. Koss, J. W. White, M. P. Thompson, A. Abbey, and A. L. Bellis, "Trajectory Analysis of the Campus Serial Rapist Assumption," *JAMA Pediatrics*, 169, no. 12 (2015): 1148:54, DOI: 10.1001/jamapediatrics.2015.0707.

185. Department of Education, "Dear Colleague Letter: Office of the Assistant Secretary," October 16, 2015. Retrieved from www2.ed.gov/about/offices/list/ocr/letters/colleague-201104.html.

186. A. E. Clark and A. L. Pino, eds., *We Believe You: Survivors of Campus Sexual Assault Speak Out* (New York: Holt, 2016).

187. White House Task Force to Protect Students from Sexual Assault, *Not Alone: The First Report of the White House Task Force to Protect Students from Sexual Assault*, 2014. Retrieved from https://www.justice.gov/ovw/page/file/905942/download.

188. Katie J. M. Baker, "Here Is The Powerful Letter The Stanford Victim Read Aloud To Her Attacker," *Buzzfeed*, June 3, 2016. Retrieved from https://www.buzzfeed.com/katiejmbaker/heres-the-powerful-letter-the-stanford-victim-read-to-her-ra?utm_term=.meX4KNYXE#.cbxNqy2dg.

189. Victoria Banyard, Elizabethe Plante, and Mary Moynihan, "Bystander Education: Bringing a Broader Community Perspective to Sexual Violence Prevention," *Journal of Community Psychology* 32, no. 1 (2004): 61–79; Victoria Banyard, Mary Moynihan, and Elizabethe Plante, "Sexual Violence Prevention through Bystander Education: An Experimental Evaluation," *Journal of Community Psychology* 35, no. 4 (2007): 463–81; Ann Coker et al., "Evaluation of Green Dot: An Active Bystander Intervention to Reduce Sexual Violence on College Campuses," *Violence Against Women* 17, no. 6 (2011): 777–96; Charlene, Y. Senn, Misha Eliasziw, Paula C. Barata, Wilfreda E. Thurston, Ian R. Newby-Clark, Lorraine Radtke, and Karen L. Hobden, "Efficacy of Sexual Assault Resistance Program for University Women," *New England Journal of Medicine*, 372 (2015): 2326–35, DOI: 10.1056/NEJMsa1411131; Charlene Y. Senn, Misha Eliasziw, Karen L. Hobden, Ian R. Newby-Clark, Paula C. Barata, H. Lorraine Radtke, Wilfreda E. Thurston, "Secondary and 2-Year Outcomes of a Sexual Assault Resistance Program for University Women," *Psychology of Women* 41, no. 2 (2017): 147–62. Retrieved from https://doi.org/10.1177/0361684317690119; Social Programs That Work, "Enhanced Assess, Acknowledge, Act (EAAA) Sexual Assault Resistance Program," November 2017. Retrieved from http://evidencebasedprograms.org/programs/enhanced-assess-acknowledge-act-eaaa-sexual-assault-resistance-program/.

190. Richard Fry, "The Reversal of the College Marriage Gap," *Pew Research: Social & Demographic Trends*, October 7, 2010. Retrieved from http://www.pewsocialtrends.org/2010/10/07/the-reversal-of-the-college-marriage-gap/.

191. Betsey Stevenson and Justin Wolfers, "The Paradox of Declining Female Happiness, 2009." Retrieved from http://clalit2oplus.co.il/NR/rdonlyres/08586B39-9E87-4A86-ACDA-BB50CD52F1EB/0/The_Paradox_of_Declining_Female_Happiness.pdf; Sampson Lee Blair and Michael P. Johnson, "Wives' Perceptions of the Fairness of the Division of Household Labor: The Intersection of Housework and Ideology," *Journal of Marriage and the Family* 54, no. 3 (1992): 570–81; Theodore N. Greenstein, "Gender Ideology and the Perceptions of the Fairness of the Division of Household Labor: Effects on Marital Quality," *Social Forces* 74, no. 3 (1996): 1029–42; Arlie Hochschild, *The Second Shift* (New York: Penguin Group, 1989); Michelle Frisco and Kristi Williams, "Perceived Housework Equity, Marital Happiness, and Divorce in Dual-Earner Households," *Journal of Family Issues* 24, no. 1 (2003): 51–73; Mamadi Corra et al., "Trends in Marital Happiness by Gender and Race, 1973 to 2006," *Journal of Family Issues* 30, no. 10 (2009): 1379–1404; P. R. Amato, David R. Johnson, Alan Booth, and Stacy J. Rogers, "Continuity and Change in Marital Quality between 1980 and 2000," *Journal of Marriage and Family* 65, no. 1 (2003): 1–22; R. A. Faulkner, M. Davey, and A. Davey, "Gender-Related Predictors of Change in Marital Satisfaction and Marital Conflict," *American Journal of Family Therapy* 33, no. 1 (2005): 61–83; R. G. Henry, R. B. Miller, and R. Giarrusso, "Difficulties, Disagreements, and Disappointments in Late-Life Marriages." *International Journal of Aging & Human Development* 61, no. 3 (2005): 243–65; G. Kaufman and H. Taniguchi, "Gender and Marital Happiness in Later Life," *Journal of Family Issues* 27, no. 6 (2006): 735–57; L. L. W. Tsang et al., "The Effects of Children, Dual Earner Status, Sex Role Traditionalism, and Marital Structure on Marital Happiness over Time," *Journal of Family and Economic Issues* 24, no. 1 (2003): 5–26.

Chapter 11: Families

1. Arlie Hochschild, *The Second Shift* (New York: Penguin Group, 1989), 7.

2. Michelle Frisco and Kristi Williams, "Perceived Housework Equity, Marital Happiness, and Divorce in Dual-Earner Households," *Journal of Family Issues* 24, no. 1 (2003): 51–73; Mamadi Corra, Shannon K. Carter, J. Scott Carter, and David Knox, "Trends in Marital Happiness by Gender and Race, 1973–2006," *Journal of Family Issues* 30, no. 10 (2009): 1379–404; Paul R. Amato, David R. Johnson, Alan Booth, and Stacy J. Rogers, "Continuity and Change in Marital Quality between 1980 and 2000,"

Journal of Marriage and Family 65 (2003): 1–22; R. A. Faulkner, M. Davey, and A. Davey, "Gender-Related Predictors of Change in Marital Satisfaction and Marital Conflict," *American Journal of Family Therapy* 33 (2005): 61–83; R. G. Henry, R. B. Miller, and R. Giarrusso, "Difficulties, Disagreements, and Disappointments in Late-Life Marriages," *International Journal of Aging & Human Development* 61 (2005): 243–65; G. Kaufman and H. Taniguchi, "Gender and Marital Happiness in Later Life," *Journal of Family Issues* 27 (2006): 735–57; Laura Lo Wa Tsang, Carol D. H. Harvey, Karen A. Duncan, and Reena Sommer, "The Effects of Children, Dual Earner Status, Sex Role Traditionalism, and Marital Structure on Marital Happiness Over Time," *Journal of Family and Economic Issues* 24, no. 1 (2003): 5–26; Betsey Stevenson and Justin Wolfers, "The Paradox of Declining Female Happiness," Bonn, Germany: IZA, May 2009. Retrieved from http://clalit2oplus.co.il/NR/rdonlyres/08586B39-9E87-4A86-ACDA-BB50CD52F1EB/0/The_Paradox_of_Declining_Female_Happiness.pdf; Belinda Hewitt, Mark Western, and Janeen Baxter, "Who Decides? The Social Characteristics of Who Initiates Divorce?" *Journal of Marriage and Family* 68, no. 5 (2006): 1165–77; Matthijs Kalmijn and Anne-Rigt Poortman, "His or Her Divorce? The Gendered Nature of Divorce and Its Determinants," *European Sociological Review* 22, no. 2 (2006): 201–14; Paula England, Paul D. Allison, and Liana C. Sayer, "When One Spouse Has an Affair, Who Is More Likely to Leave?" *Demographic Research* 30 (2014): 535–46; Mamadi Corra, Shannon K. Carter, J. Scott Carter, and David Knox, "Trends in Marital Happiness by Gender and Race, 1973–2006," *Journal of Family Issues* 30, no. 10 (2009): 1379–404; Michael S. Rendall, Margaret M. Weden, Melissa M. Favreault, and Hilary Waldron, "The Protective Effect of Marriage for Survival: A Review and Update," *Demography* 48, no. 2 (2011): 481–506; Kain Kolves, Naoko Ide, and Diego De Leo, "Suicidal Ideation and Behavior in the Aftermath of Marital Separation: Gender Differences," *Journal of Affective Disorders* 120, no. 1–3 (2010): 48–53; Richard Lampard and Kay Peggs, "Repartnering: The Relevance of Parenthood and Gender to Cohabitation and Remarriage among the Formerly Married," *British Journal of Sociology* 50, no. 3 (1999): 443–65; L. Davidson, "Late Life Widowhood, Selfishness and New Partnership Choices: A Gendered Perspective," *Ageing and Society* 2, no. 3 (2001): 297–317.

3. Kimberly F. Balsam, Theodore P. Beauchaine, Esther D. Rothblum, and Sondra E. Soloman, "Three-Year Follow-Up of Same-Sex Couples Who Had Civil Unions in Vermont, Same-Sex Couples Not in Civil Unions, and Heterosexual Married Couples," *Developmental Psychology* 44, no. 1 (2008): 102–16; Robert-Jay Green, interview by Lourdes Garcia-Navarro, "Same-Sex Couples May Have More Egalitarian Relationships," *All Things Considered.* American University, Washington, D.C., December 9, 2014; J. M. Gottman, R. W. Levenson, J. Gross, B. L. Frederickson, K. McCoy, L. Rosenthal, and D. Yoshimoto, "Correlates of Gay and Lesbian Couples Relationship Satisfaction and Relationship Dissolution," *Journal of Homosexuality* 45, no. 1 (2003): 22–43; John Mordechai Gottman, Robert Wayne Levenon, Catherine Swanson, Kristin Swanson, Rebecca Tyson, and Dan Yoshimoto, "Observing Gay, Lesbian, and Heterosexual Couples' Relationships: Mathematical Modeling of Conflict Interaction," *Journal of Homosexuality* 45, no. 1 (2003): 65–91; Francisco Perales and Janeen Baxter, "Sexual Identity and Relationship Quality in Australia and the United Kingdom," *Family Relations: Interdisciplinary Journal of Applied Family Science* 67, no. 1 (2018): 55–69; Lawrence A. Kurdek. "Relationship Outcomes and Their Predictors: Longitudinal Evidence from Heterosexual Married, Gay Cohabiting, and Lesbian Cohabiting Couples," *Journal of Marriage and Family* 60, no. 3 (August 1998): 553–68.

4. D'Vera Cohn, Gretchen Livingston, and Wendy Wang, "After Decades of Decline, A Rise in Stay-at-Home Mothers," *Pew Research Center,* April 8, 2014. Retrieved from www.pewsocialtrends.org/2014/04/08/after-decades-of-decline-a-rise-in-stay-at-home-mothers/.

5. Bureau of Labor Statistics, "Employment Characteristics of Families Summary: 2017," April 19, 2018. Retrieved from www.bls.gov/news.release/famee.nr0.htm.

6. Arlie Hochschild, *The Second Shift* (New York: Penguin Group, 1989).

7. Suzanne Bianchi, John Robinson, and Melissa Milkie, *Changing Rhythms of American Family Life* (New York: Russell Sage Foundation, 2007).

8. Janet C. Gornick and Marcia K. Meyers, *Families That Work: Policies for Reconciling Parenthood and Employment* (New York: Russell Sage Foundation, 2003); Suzanne Bianchi, John Robinson, and Melissa Milkie, eds., *Changing Rhythms of American Family Life* (New York: Russell Sage Foundation, 2007).

9. Kimberley Fisher, Muriel Egerton, Jonathan I. Gershuny, and John P. Robinson, "Gender Conver-

gence in the American Heritage Time Use Study," *Social Indicators Research* 82 (2006): 1–33; David Cotter, Paula England, and Joan Hermsen, "Moms and Jobs: Trends in Mothers' Employment and Which Mothers Stay Home," in *American Families: A Multicultural Reader*, ed. Stephanie Coontz (New York: Routledge, 2008); Nicholas Townsend, *The Package Deal: Marriage, Work, and Fatherhood in Men's Lives* (Philadelphia: Temple University Press, 2002); United States Department of Labor, "Women in the Labor Force in 2010." Retrieved from www.dol.gov/wb/factsheets/Qf-laborforce-10.htm#.UNzcVuQ72Ag.

10. CDC, "Marriage and Cohabitation in the United States: A Statistical Portrait Based on Cycle 6 (2002) of the National Survey of Family Growth," *Vital and Health Statistics* 23, no. 28 (2010); A. E. Goldberg and A. Sayer, "Lesbian Couples' Relationship Quality across the Transition to Parenthood," *Journal of Marriage and Family* 68 (2006): 87–100; B. D. Doss, G. K. Rhoades, S. M. Stanley, and H. J. Markman, "Marital Therapy, Retreats, and Books: The Who, What, When and Why of Relationship Help-Seeking Behaviors," *Journal of Marital and Family Therapy* 35, 18–29 (2009); Claire Kimberly and Amanda Williams, "Decade Review of Research on Lesbian Romantic Relationship Satisfaction," *Journal of LGBT Issues in Counseling* 11, no. 2 (2017): 119–35; S. K. Nelson, K. Kushlev, and S. Lyubomirsky, "The Pains and Pleasures of Parenting: When, Why, and How Is Parenthood Associated with More or Less Well-Being?" *Psychological Bulletin* 140, no. 3 (2014): 846–95; Kei M. Nomaguchi and Melissa A. Milkie, "Costs and Rewards of Children: The Effects of Becoming a Parent on Adults' Lives," *Journal of Marriage and Family* 65, no. 2 (2004): 356–74; Debra Umberson, Tetyana Pudrovska, and Corinne Reczek, "Parenthood, Childlessness, and Well-Being: A Life Course Perspective," *Journal of Marriage and Family* 72 (2010): 612–29.

11. Thomas Weisner and Ronald Gallimore, "My Brother's Keeper: Child and Sibling Caretaking," *Current Anthropology* 18 (1977): 169–89; Elinor Ochs and Carolina Izquierdo, "Responsibility in Childhood: Three Developmental Trajectories," *Ethos* 37, no. 4 (2009): 394.

12. Peter Stearns, *Anxious Parents: A History of Modern Childrearing in America* (New York: New York University Press, 2004), 3.

13. Sharon Hays, *The Cultural Contradictions of Motherhood* (New Haven: Yale University Press, 1996), 159.

14. Ibid., 8.

15. Annette Lareau, "Invisible Inequality: Social Class and Childrearing in Black Families and White Families," *American Sociological Review* 67, no. 5 (2002): 747–76.

16. J. Sunderland, "Baby Entertainer, Bumbling Assistant and Line Manager: Discourses of Fatherhood in Parent Craft Texts," *Discourse and Society* 11, no. 2 (2000): 249–74; J. Sunderland, "'Parenting' or 'Mothering'? The Case of Modern Child Care Magazines," *Discourse and Society* 17, no. 4 (2006): 503–27; Glenda Wall and Stephanie Arnold, "How Involved Is Involved Fathering?: An Exploration of the Contemporary Culture of Fatherhood," *Gender & Society* 21, no. 4 (2007): 508–27; Jennifer Krafchick, Toni Schindler Zimmerman, Shelley A. Haddock, and James H. Banning, "Best Selling Books Advising Parents about Gender: A Feminist Analysis," *Family Relations* 54 (2005): 84–100.

17. J. Sunderland, "'Parenting' or 'Mothering'? The Case of Modern Child Care Magazines," *Discourse and Society* 17, no. 4 (2006): 512.

18. Lisa Rashley, "'Work It Out with Your Wife': Gendered Expectations and Parenting Rhetoric Online," *Feminist Formations* 17, no. 1 (2005): 58–92.

19. Gayle Kaufman, "The Portrayal of Men's Family Roles in Television Commercials," *Sex Roles* 41, no. 5/6 (1999): 439–58.

20. Kristin Natalier, "'I'm Not His Wife': Doing Gender and Doing Housework in the Absence of Women," *Journal of Sociology* 39, no. 3 (2003): 253–69.

21. Ibid.

22. Carla Pfeffer, "'Women's Work'? Women Partners of Transgender Men Doing Housework and Emotion Work." *Journal of Marriage and Family* 72 (2010): 165–83.

23. Ibid., 172.

24. Ibid., 173.

25. D. Berkowitz, "Maternal Instincts, Biological Clocks, and Soccer Moms: Gay Men's Parenting and Family Narratives," *Symbolic Interaction* 34, no. 4 (2011): 514–35.

26. Ibid., 518.

27. B. Harrington, F. Van Deusen, and I. Mazar, "The New Dad: Right at Home," Boston College Center for Work & Family, 2012. Retrieved from www.bc.edu/content/dam/files/centers/cwf/research/publications/researchreports/The%20New%20Dad%202012_Right%20at%20Home; Catherine Solomon, "'I

Feel Like a Rock Star': Fatherhood for Stay-at-Home Fathers," *Fathering* 12, 1 (2014): 52–70.

28. B. Harrington, F. Van Deusen, and I. Mazar, "The New Dad: Right at Home," Boston College Center for Work & Family, 2012. Retrieved from www.bc .edu/content/dam/files/centers/cwf/research/pub lications/researchreports/The%20New%20Dad%20 2012_Right%20at%20Home

29. Kim Parker and Wendy Wang, "Modern Parenthood: Roles of Moms and Dads Converge as They Balance Work and Family," *Pew Research: Social & Demographic Trends*, March 14, 2013. Retrieved from www.pewsocialtrends.org/2013/03/14/modern -parenthood-roles-of-moms-and-dads-converge-as -they-balance-work-and-family/?src=rss_main; Kimberley Fisher, Muriel Egerton, Jonathan I. Gershuny, and John P. Robinson, "Gender Convergence in the American Heritage Time Use Study," *Social Indicators Research* 82 (2006): 1–33.

30. Bureau of Labor Statistics, "American Time Use Survey—2016 Results," June 27, 2017. Retrieved from www.bls.gov/tus/home.htm#data.

31. Jane Riblett Wilkie, Myra Marx Ferree, and Kathryn Ratliff, "Gender and Fairness: Marital Satisfaction in Two-Earner Couples," *Journal of Marriage and the Family* 60 (1998): 577–94; J. Baxter, B. Hewitt, and M. Haynes, "Life Course Transitions and Housework: Marriage, Parenthood, and Time on Housework," *Journal of Marriage and Family* 70 (2008): 259–72; Suzanne Bianchi, John Robinson, and Melissa Milkie, eds., *Changing Rhythms of American Family Life*, (New York: Russell Sage Foundation, 2007).

32. Arlie Hochschild, *The Second Shift* (New York: Penguin Group, 1989), 62, 68.

33. Ibid., 62, 68.

34. David Cotter, Paula England, and Joan Hermsen. "Moms and Jobs: Trends in Mothers' Employment and Which Mothers Stay Home," in *American Families: A Multicultural Reader*, ed. Stephanie Coontz (New York: Routledge, 2008).

35. Ibid.

36. Brigid Schulte and Alieza Durana, "The New America Care Report," *New America*, September 28, 2016. Retrieved from www.newamerica.org/better -life-lab/policy-papers/new-america-care-report/.

37. Ibid.

38. Percent of stay-at-home parents calculated using percent of at-home mothers and fathers and percent saying that they are there primarily for child care. Retrieved from www.pewsocialtrends.org/2014/06

/05/chapter-1-the-likelihood-of-being-a-stay-at-home -father/; Gretchen Livingston, "Growing Number of Dads Home with the Kids," Pew Research Center, June 5, 2014. Retrieved from www.pewsocialtrends .org/2014/06/05/growing-number-of-dads-home -with-the-kids/; Karen Z. Kramer, "At-Home Father Families in the United States: Gender Ideology, Human Capital, and Unemployment," *Journal of Marriage and Family* 78, no. 5 (2016): 1315–31; Caryn E. Medved, "Stay-at-Home Fathering as a Feminist Opportunity: Perpetuating, Resisting and Transforming Gender Relations of Caring and Earning," *Journal of Family Communication* 16, no. 1 (2016): 16–31.

39. Noelle Chesley and Sarah Flood, "Signs of Change? At-Home and Breadwinner Parents' Housework and Child-Care Time," *Journal of Marriage and Family* 79, no. 2 (2017): 511–34.

40. Kathleen Gerson, *The Unfinished Revolution: Coming of Age in a New Era of Gender, Work, and Family* (New York: Oxford University Press, 2010), 176.

41. Bureau of Labor Statistics, "American Time Use Survey—2016 Results," June 27, 2017. Retrieved from www.bls.gov/tus/home.htm#data.

42. Pew Research Center, "Modern Parenthood: Roles of Moms and Dads Converge as They Balance Work and Family," March 14, 2013. Retrieved from http://assets.pewresearch.org/wp-content/uploads /sites/3/2013/03/FINAL_modern_parenthood _03-2013.pdf; Shira Offer and Barbara Schneider, "Revisiting the Gender Gap in Time-Use Patterns: Multitasking and Well-Being among Mothers and Fathers in Dual-Earner Families," *American Sociological Review* 76, no. 6: 809–33; John Robinson and Geoffrey Godbey, *Time for Life: The Surprising Ways Americans Use Their Time*, 2nd ed. (University Park: Pennsylvania State University Press, 1999); Kimberley Fisher, Muriel Egerton, Jonathan I. Gershuny, and John P. Robinson, "Gender Convergence in the American Heritage Time Use Study," *Social Indicators Research* 82 (2006): 1–33; OECD, "Key Findings on Chapter 1: Unpaid Work," Society at a Glance, December 4, 2011. Retrieved from www.oecd.org /social/soc/47573400.pdf; Mary Dorinda Allard, Suzanne Bianchi, Jay Stewart, and Vanessa R. Wight, "Comparing Child Care Measures in the ATUS and Earlier Time-Diary Studies," *Monthly Labor Review* 130, no. 5 (2007): 27–36.

43. J. Sunderland, "'Parenting' or 'Mothering'? The Case of Modern Child Care Magazines," *Discourse and Society* 17, no. 4 (2006): 521.

44. Carla Pfeffer, "'Women's Work'? Women Partners of Transgender Men Doing Housework and Emotion Work," *Journal of Marriage and Family* 72 (2010): 165–83, p. 174.

45. Susan Walzer, "Thinking about the Baby: Gender and the Division of Infant Care," *Social Problems* 43, no. 2 (1996): 219–34. p. 200.

46. Christopher Carrington, *No Place Like Home: Relationships and Family Life among Lesbians and Gay Men* (Chicago: University of Chicago Press, 1999), 79.

47. Ibid., 79–80.

48. Susan Walzer, "Thinking about the Baby: Gender and the Division of Infant Care," *Social Problems* 43, no. 2 (1996): 219–34.

49. Ann Crittenden, *The Price of Motherhood: Why the Most Important Job in the World Is Still the Least Valued* (New York: Henry Holt and Company, 2002), 12.

50. Ibid., 236–37.

51. Kathleen Gerson, *The Unfinished Revolution: Coming of Age in a New Era of Gender, Work, and Family* (New York: Oxford University Press, 2010).

52. Christopher Carrington, *No Place Like Home: Relationships and Family Life among Lesbians and Gay Men* (Chicago: University of Chicago Press, 1999), 54.

53. Judith Warner, "The Opt-Out Generation Wants Back In," *New York Times*, August 7, 2013: MM25. Retrieved from www.nytimes.com/2013/08/11/magazine/the-opt-out-generation-wants-back-in.html?pagewanted=all.

54. Susan Walzer, "Thinking about the Baby: Gender and the Division of Infant Care," *Social Problems* 43, no. 2 (1996): 200–201.

55. B. Harrington, F. Van Deusen, and I. Mazar, "The New Dad: Right at Home," Boston College Center for Work & Family, 2012. Retrieved from www.bc.edu/content/dam/files/centers/cwf/research/publications/researchreports/The%20New%20Dad%202012_Right%20at%20Home.

56. Susan Dalton and Denise Bielby, "'That's Our Kind of Constellation': Lesbian Mothers Negotiate Institutionalized Understandings of Gender within the Family," *Gender & Society* 14, no. 1 (2000): 36–61; Maureen Sullivan, "Rozzie and Harriet? Gender and Family Patterns of Lesbian Coparents," *Gender & Society* 10 (1996): 747–67; Elizabeth Sheff, *Gender, Family, and Sexuality: Exploring Polyamorous Community* (PhD diss, University of Colorado, 2005); Anisa Zvonkovic, Kathleen M. Greaves, Cynthia J. Schmiege, and Leslie D. Hall, "The Marital Construction of Gender through Work and Family Decisions: A Qualitative Analysis," *Journal of Marriage and the Family* 58, no. 1 (1996): 91–100.

57. Adjusted for inflation.

58. Sylvia Ann Hewlett, *Off-Ramps and On-Ramps* (Cambridge: Harvard Business School Press, 2007), 46; Jennifer Glass, "Blessing or Curse? Work-Family Policies and Mothers' Wage Growth over Time," *Work and Occupations* 31 (2004): 367–94.

59. Ann Crittenden, *The Price of Motherhood: Why the Most Important Job in the World Is Still the Least Valued* (New York: Henry Holt and Company, 2002).

60. Rhacel S. Parreñas, *Servants of Globalization: Women, Migration and Domestic Work* (Stanford: Stanford University Press, 2001); Arlie Hochschild, "The Nanny Chain," *The American Prospect*, December 19, 2001. Retrieved from http://prospect.org/article/nanny-chain; Cameron MacDonald, *Shadow Mothers: Nannies, Au Pairs, and the Micropolitics of Mothering* (Berkeley: University of California Press, 2010).

61. Linda Burnham and Nik Theodore, "Home Economics: The Invisible and Unregulated World of Domestic Work," National Domestic Workers Alliance: Center for Urban Economic Development, University of Illinois at Chicago Data Center, 2012.

62. Linda Burnham and Nik Theodore, "Home Economics: The Invisible and Unregulated World of Domestic Work," National Domestic Workers Alliance: Center for Urban Economic Development, University of Illinois at Chicago Data Center, 2012.

63. Rhacel S. Parreñas, *Servants of Globalization: Women, Migration and Domestic Work* (Stanford: Stanford University Press, 2001).

64. Arlie Hochschild, "The Nanny Chain," *The American Prospect*, December 19, 2001. Retrieved from http://prospect.org/article/nanny-chain.

65. Cameron MacDonald, *Shadow Mothers: Nannies, Au Pairs, and the Micropolitics of Mothering* (Berkeley: University of California Press, 2010).

66. Daniel Schneider and Orestes P. Hastings, "Income Inequality and Household Labor," *Social Forces* 96, no. 2 (2017): 481–505.

67. Kathleen Gerson, *The Unfinished Revolution: Coming of Age in a New Era of Gender, Work, and Family* (New York: Oxford University Press, 2010).

68. Ibid., 105–107.

69. Council on Contemporary Families, "CCF Press Advisory: Gender and Millennials Online Symposium," March 30, 2017, Retrieved from https://contemporaryfamilies.org/ccf-gender-and-millennials-online-symposium/; Barbara Risman, *Where the Millennials Will Take Us* (New York: Oxford University Press, 2018).

70. Lewis A. Coser, *Greedy Institutions: Patterns of Undivided Commitment* (New York: Free Press, 1974).

71. Mary Blair-Loy, *Competing Devotions: Career and Family among Women Executives* (Cambridge: Harvard University Press, 2005).

72. This doesn't apply to the *highest* income earners because social security taxation is capped.

73. Julie Brines, "Economic Dependency, Gender and the Division of Labor at Home," *AJS* 100, no. 3 (1994): 652–58; Shannon Davis and Jeremiah Wills, "Theoretical Explanations amid Social Change: A Content Analysis of Housework Research (1975–2012)," *Journal of Family Issues* 35, no. 6 (2014): 808–24.

74. Shelly Lundberg and Elaina Rose, "Parenthood and the Earnings of Married Men and Women," *Labour Economics* 7, no. 6 (2000): 689–710.

75. Suzanne Bianchi, John Robinson, and Melissa Milkie, eds., *Changing Rhythms of American Family Life* (New York: Russell Sage Foundation, 2007).

76. Mary Blair-Loy, *Competing Devotions: Career and Family among Women Executives* (Cambridge: Harvard University Press, 2003).

77. Christopher Carrington, *No Place Like Home: Relationships and Family Life among Lesbians and Gay Men* (Chicago: University of Chicago Press, 1999); Mignon Moore, "Gendered Power Relations among Women: A Study of Household Decision Making in Black, Lesbian Stepfamilies," *American Sociological Review* 73, no. 2 (2008): 335–56.

78. Christopher Carrington, *No Place Like Home: Relationships and Family Life among Lesbians and Gay Men* (Chicago: University of Chicago Press, 1999); Mignon Moore, "Gendered Power Relations among Women: A Study of Household Decision Making in Black, Lesbian Stepfamilies," *American Sociological Review* 73, no. 2 (2008): 335–56; Claire Cain Miller, "How Same-Sex Couples Divide Chores, and What It Reveals about Modern Parenting," *New York Times*, May 16, 2018. Retrieved from www.nytimes.com/2018/05/16/upshot/same-sex-couples-divide-chores-much-more-evenly-until-they-become-parents.html; Samantha L. Tornello, Bettina N. Sonnenberg, and Charlotte J. Patterson, "Division of Labor among Gay Fathers: Associations with Parent, Couple, and Child Adjustment," *Psychology of Sexual Orientation and Gender Diversity* 2, no. 4 (2015): 365–75; Charlotte J. Patterson, Erin L. Sutfin, and Megan Fulcher, "Division of Labor among Lesbian and Heterosexual Parenting Couples: Correlates of Specialized versus Shared Patterns," *Journal of Adult Development* 11, no. 3 (2004): 179–89; Sondra E. Solomon, Esther D. Rothblum, and Kimberly F. Balsam, "Money, Housework, Sex, and Conflict: Same-Sex Couples in Civil Unions, Those Not in Civil Unions, and Heterosexual Married Siblings," *Sex Roles* 52, no. 9–10 (2005): 561–75; Melanie E. Brewster, "Lesbian Women and Household Labor Division: A Systematic Review of Scholarly Research from 2000 to 2015," *Journal of Lesbian Studies* 21, no. 1 (2017): 47–69; Alyssa Schneebaum, "The Economics of Same-Sex Couple Households: Essays on Work, Wages, and Poverty," Open Access Dissertations, 2013, 818. Retrieved from https://scholarworks.umass.edu/open_access_dissertations/818; Gabrielle Gotta, Robert-Jay Green, Esther Rothblum, Sondra Solomon, Kimberly Balsam, and Pepper Schwartz, "Heterosexual, Lesbian, and Gay Male Relationships: A Comparison of Couples in 1975 and 2000," *Family Process* 50, no. 3 (2011): 353–76.

79. Kathleen Gerson, *The Unfinished Revolution: Coming of Age in a New Era of Gender, Work, and Family* (New York: Oxford University Press, 2010).

80. Ibid., 162.

81. Ibid., 167.

82. D. Feder, "Feminists to Women: Shut Up and Do as You're Told," *Human Events* (March 2006): 15.

83. Susan Walzer, "Thinking about the Baby: Gender and the Division of Infant Care." *Social Problems* 43, no. 2 (1996): 219–34.

84. Garey Ramey and Valerie A. Ramey, "The Rug Rat Race," *Brookings Papers on Economic Activity* 41, no. 1 (Spring 2010): 129–99. Economic Studies Program, The Brookings Institution.

85. Eileen Patten and Kim Parker, "A Gender Reversal on Career Aspirations: Young Women Now Top Young Men in Valuing a High-Paying Career," *Pew Research: Social & Demographic Trends*, April 19, 2012. Retrieved from www.pewsocialtrends.org/2012/04/19/a-gender-reversal-on-career-aspirations/?src=prc-headline.

86. David M. Blau and Wilbert H. van der Klaauw, "A Demographic Analysis of the Family Structure Experiences of Children in the United States," Bonn, Germany: IZA, August 2007. Retrieved from http://ideas.repec.org/p/iza/izadps/dp3001.html; Timothy S. Grall, "Custodial Mothers and Fathers and Their Child Support: 2015," U.S. Census Bureau, January 2018. Retrieved from www.census.gov/content/dam/Census/library/publications/2018/demo/P60-262.pdf.

87. Kathleen Gerson, *No Man's Land: Men's Changing Commitments to Family and Work* (New York: Basic Books, 1993); Kathleen Gerson, *Hard Choices: How Women Decide about Work, Career, and Motherhood* (Berkeley: University of California Press, 1986); Barbara Risman, *Gender Vertigo: American Families in Transition* (New Haven: Yale University Press, 1999).

88. Kathryn Edin and Maria Kefalas, *Why Poor Women Put Motherhood before Marriage* (Berkeley: University of California Press, 2011).

89. Kathryn Edin and Maria Kefalas, "Unmarried with Children," *Contexts* 4, no. 2 (2005): 16–22; Liana C. Landivar, "How the Timing of Children Affects Earnings in 20 Occupations," *SocArXiv*, April 10, 2018. doi:10.17605/OSF.IO/VN7ZT.

90. Amanda Riley-Jones, "Mothers without Men," *Guardian*, June 9, 2000. Retrieved from www.guardian.co.uk/theguardian/2000/jun/10/weekend7.weekend2.

91. Sally C. Curtin, Stephanie J. Ventura, and Gladys M. Martinez, "Recent Declines in Nonmarital Childbearing in the United States," *NCHS Data Brief*, no 162 (2014). Hyattsville, MD: National Center for Health Statistics; The Hamilton Project, "Percent of Births to Unmarried Mothers by Education, 1970–2012," June 19, 2014. Retrieved from www.hamiltonproject.org/charts/percent_of_births_to_unmarried_mothers_by_education_1970-2012; Gretchen Livingston, "They're Waiting Longer, but U.S. Women Today More Likely to Have Children than a Decade Ago," Pew Research Center, January 18, 2018. Retrieved from www.pewsocialtrends.org/2018/01/18/theyre-waiting-longer-but-u-s-women-today-more-likely-to-have-children-than-a-decade-ago/.

92. Casey Stockstill and Katie Fallon, "The Condensed Courtship Clock: How Elite Women Manage Self-Development and Marriage Ideals," ASA Presentation, 2017.

93. Susanna Graham, "Choosing Single Motherhood? Single Women Negotiating the Nuclear Family Ideal," in *Families—Beyond the Nuclear Ideal*, ed. Daniela Cutas and Sarah Chan (New York: Bloomsbury Academic, 2012).

94. Gretchen Livingston, "The Rise of Single Fathers," Pew Research Center, July 2, 2013. Retrieved from www.pewsocialtrends.org/2013/07/02/the-rise-of-single-fathers/.

95. Single Mother Guide, "Single Mother Statistics," January, 10, 2018. Retrieved from https://singlemotherguide.com/single-mother-statistics/.

96. Karen Schulman and Helen Blank, "Persistent Gaps: State Child Care Assistance Policies 2017," National Women's Law Center, October 2017, Retrieved from https://nwlc-ciw49tixgw5lbab.stackpathdns.com/wp-content/uploads/2017/10/NWLC-State-Child-Care-Assistance-Policies-2017-1.pdf.

97. Bureau of Labor Statistics, "Employment Characteristics of Families Summary: 2017," April 19. 2018. Retrieved from www.bls.gov/news.release/famee.nr0.htm.

98. Jessica L. Semega, Kayla R. Fontenot, and Melissa A. Kollar, "Income and Poverty in the United States: 2016," U.S. Census Bureau, Current Population Reports, September 2017. Retrieved from www.census.gov/content/dam/Census/library/publications/2017/demo/P60-259.pdf.

99. Bureau of Labor Statistics, "A Profile of the Working Poor, 2015," April 2017. Retrieved from www.bls.gov/opub/reports/working-poor/2015/home.htm.

100. Ann Crittenden, *The Price of Motherhood: Why the Most Important Job in the World Is Still the Least Valued* (New York: Henry Holt and Company, 2002); Elizabeth Warren and Amelia Tyagi, *The Two-Income Trap: Why Middle-Class Parents Are Going Broke* (New York: Basic Books, 2003).

101. Daniel L. Carlson, Amanda J. Miller, Sharon Sassler, and Sarah Hanson, "The Gendered Division of Housework and Couples' Sexual Relationships: A Reexamination," *Journal of Marriage and Family* 78, no. 4 (2016): 975–95; American Sociological Association, "Couples that Split Childcare Duties Have Higher-Quality Relationships and Sex Lives," August 23, 2015. Retrieved from www.asanet.org/press-center/press-releases/couples-split-childcare-duties-have-higher-quality-relationships-and-sex-lives; Neil Chethik, *VoiceMale: What Husbands Really Think about Their Marriages, Their Wives, Sex, Housework, and Commitment* (New York: Simon &

Schuster, 2006); M. L. Frisco, and K. Williams, "Perceived Housework Equity, Marital Happiness, and Divorce in Dual-Earner Households," *Journal of Family Issues* 24 (2003): 51–73; J. R. Wilkie, M. M. Ferree, and K. S. Ratcliff, "Gender and Fairness: Marital Satisfaction in Two-Earner Couples," *Journal of Marriage and Family* 60 (1998): 577–94; P. Schwartz, *What Sexual Scientists Know about . . . Sexual Satisfaction in Committed Relationships* (Allentown, PA: The Society for the Scientific Study of Sexuality, 2007).

102. Lynn Cooke, "'Traditional' Marriages Now Less Stable than Ones Where Couples Share Work and Household Chores," in *Families as They Really Are*, ed. Barbara Risman (New York: W. W. Norton and Company, 2010).

103. Barbara Risman, *Gender Vertigo: American Families in Transition* (New Haven: Yale University Press, 1999).

104. Naomi Gerstel and Daniel Clawson, "Class Advantage and the Gender Divide: Flexibility on the Job and at Home," *AJS* 120, no. 2 (2014): 395–431.

105. Barbara Risman, *Gender Vertigo: American Families in Transition* (New Haven: Yale University Press, 1999).

106. Francisco Perales and Janeen Baxter, "Sexual Identity and Relationship Quality in Australia and the United Kingdom," *Family Relations: Interdisciplinary Journal of Applied Family Science* 67, no. 1 (2018): 55–69; John Mordechai Gottman, Robert Wayne Levenson, Catherine Swanson, Kristin Swanson, Rebecca Tyson, and Dan Yoshimoto, "Observing Gay, Lesbian, and Heterosexual Couples' Relationships: Mathematical Modeling of Conflict Interaction," *Journal of Homosexuality* 45, no. 1 (2003): 65–91. Retrieved from www.johngottman.net/wp-content/uploads/2011/05/Observing-Gay-Lesbian-and-heterosexual-Couples-Relationships-Mathematical-modeling-of-conflict-interactions.pdf.

107. Lynn Cooke, "'Traditional' Marriages Now Less Stable than Ones Where Couples Share Work and Household Chores," in *Families as They Really Are*, ed. Barbara Risman (New York: W. W. Norton and Company, 2010).

108. Brady E. Hamilton, Joyce A. Martin, and Stephanie J. Ventura, "Births: Preliminary Data for 2012," *National Vital Statistics Report* 62, no. 3 (September 6, 2013). U.S. Department of Health and Human Services. Retrieved from www.cdc.gov/nchs/data/nvsr/nvsr62/nvsr62_03.pdf.

109. Brady E. Hamilton, Joyce A. Martin, Michelle J. K. Osterman, Anne K. Driscoll, and Lauren M. Rossen, "Births: Provisional Data for 2017," *Vital Statistics Rapid Release*, no. 4 (May 2018). Hyattsville, MD: National Center for Health Statistics. Retrieved from www.cdc.gov/nchs/data/vsrr/report004.pdf.

110. R. Gillespie, "Childfree and Feminine: Understanding the Gender Identity of Voluntarily Childless Women," *Gender & Society* 17, no. 1 (2003): 131.

111. S. K. Nelson, K. Kushlev, and S. Lyubomirsky, "The Pains and Pleasures of Parenting: When, Why, and How Is Parenthood Associated with More or Less Well-Being?" *Psychological Bulletin* (February 3, 2014). Advance online publication. Retrieved from http://dx.doi.org/10.1037/a0035444; Thomas Hansen, "Parenthood and Happiness: A Review of Folk Theories versus Empirical Evidence," *Social Indicators Research* 108, no. 1 (2012): 1–36; Jean M. Twenge, W. Keither Campbell, and Craig A. Foster, "Parenthood and Marital Satisfaction: A Meta-Analytic Review," *Journal of Marriage and Family* 65, no. 3 (2004): 574–83; Dei Nomaguchi and Melissa Milke, "Costs and Rewards of Children: The Effects of Becoming a Parent on Adults' Lives," *Journal of Marriage and the Family* 66 (2003): 413–30; Ranae Evenson and Robin W. Simon, "Clarifying the Relationship between Parenthood and Depression," *Journal of Health and Social Behavior* 46 (2005): 341–58; Hyeyoung Woo and R. Kelly Raley, "A Small Extension to 'Costs and Rewards of Children: The Effects of Becoming a Parent on Adults' Lives.'" *Journal of Marriage and Family* 67 (2005): 216–21; Debra Umberson, Tetyana Pudrovska, and Corinne Reczek, "Parenthood, Childlessness, and Well-Being: A Life Course Perspective," *Journal of Marriage and Family* 72 (2010): 612–29; Daniel Gilbert, *Stumbling on Happiness* (New York: Random House, 2007).

112. B. Harrington, F. Van Deusen, and I. Mazar, "The New Dad: Right at Home," Boston College Center for Work & Family, 2012. Retrieved from www.bc.edu/content/dam/files/centers/cwf/research/publications/researchreports/The%20New%20Dad%202012_Right%20at%20Home.

113. Tanya Koropeckyj-Cox, "Beyond Parental Status: Psychological Well-Being in Middle and Older Age," *Journal of Marriage and Family* 64 (2002): 957–71; Melissa A. Milke, Alex Bierman, and Scott Schieman, "How Adult Children Influence Older Parents' Mental Health: Integrating Stress-Process and Life-Course Perspectives," *Social Psychology Quarterly* 71 (2008): 86–105; Kei M. Nomaguchi and

Melissa A. Milkie, "Costs and Rewards of Children: The Effects of Becoming a Parent on Adults' Lives," *Journal of Marriage and Family* 65, no. 2 (2004): 356–74; Tetyana Pudrovska, "Psychological Implications of Motherhood and Fatherhood in Mid Life: Evidence from Siblings Models," *Journal of Marriage and the Family* 70 (2008): 168–81.

114. Lisa Wade, Interview. Personal records.

115. Rachel Margolis and Mikko Myrskylä, "A Global Perspective on Happiness and Fertility," *Population and Development Review* 37, no. 1 (2011): 29–56; Hiroshi Ono and Kristen Schultz Lee, "Welfare States and the Redistribution of Happiness," *Social Forces* 92 (2013): 789–814; Luca Stanca, "Suffer the Little Children: Measuring the Effects of Parenthood on Well-Being Worldwide," *Journal of Economic Behavior and Organization* 81 (2012): 742–50; Jennifer Glass, Robin W. Simon, and Matthew A. Andersson, "Parenthood and Happiness: Effects of Work-Family Reconciliation Policies in 22 OECD Countries," *American Journal of Sociology* 122, no. 3 (2016): 886–929.

116. Jennifer Glass, Robin W. Simon, and Matthew A. Anderson, "Parenthood and Happiness: Effects of Work-Family Reconciliation Policies in 22 OECD Countries," *American Journal of Sociology* 122, no. 3 (November 2016): 886–929; Hiroshi Ono and Kristen Schultz Lee, "Welfare States and the Redistribution of Happiness," *Social Forces* 92 (2013): 789–814.

117. Ranae Evenson and Robin W. Simon, "Clarifying the Relationship between Parenthood and Depression," *Journal of Health and Social Behavior* 46 (2005): 341–58; Jennifer Glass, Robin W. Simon, and Matthew A. Anderson, "Parenthood and Happiness: Effects of Work-Family Reconciliation Policies in 22 OECD Countries," *American Journal of Sociology* 122, no. 3 (November 2016): 886–929. Retrieved from https://doi.org/10.1086/688892.

118. From www.mosuoproject.org/walking.htm.

119. Child Trends, *World Family Map 2015: Mapping Family Change and Child Well-Being Outcomes.* Retrieved from http://worldfamilymap.ifstudies.org /2015/articles/world-family-indicators/family -structure.

120. Rachael Gelfman Schultz, "Modern Israel: The Kibbutz Movement," *My Jewish Learning.* Retrieved from www.myjewishlearning.com/article/the-kibbutz -movement/; A. Ebenstein, M. Hazan, and A. Simhon, "Changing the Cost of Children and Fertility: Evidence from the Israeli Kibbutz," *Econ J* 126 (2016): 2038–63.

121. Sidney W. Mintz and Eric R. Wolf, "An Analysis of Ritual Co-Parenthood (Compadrazgo)," *Southwestern Journal of Anthropology* 6, no. 4 (1950): 341–68.

122. Naomi Gerstel and Dan Clawson, "Low Wage Care Workers: Extended Family as a Strategy for Survival," in *Caring on the Clock,* ed. Mignon Duffy, Amy Armenia, and Clare Stacey (New Brunswick: Rutgers University Press, 2014).

123. Stanlie M. James, "Mothering: A Possible Black Feminist Link to Social Transformation," in *Theorizing Black Feminisms: The Visionary Pragmatism of Black Women,* ed. Stanlie M. James and Abena P. A. Busia (London: Routledge, 1993), 45; Linda M. Chatters, Robert Joseph Taylor, and Rukmailie Jayakody, "Fictive Kinship Relations in Black Extended Families," *Journal of Comparative Family Studies* 25, no. 3 (Autumn 1994): 297–312.

124. Lynne Haney and Miranda March, "Married Fathers and Caring Daddies: Welfare Reform and the Discursive Politics of Paternity," *Social Problems* 50, no. 4 (2003): 478; K. Roy and J. Smith, "Nonresident Fathers and Intergenerational Parenting in Kin Networks," in *Handbook of Father Involvement: Multidisciplinary Perspectives,* 2nd ed., ed. N. Cabrera and C. Tamis-LeMonda (New York: Routledge, 2012), 320–37; S. Madhavan, and K. Roy, "Securing Fatherhood through Kin Work: A Comparison of Black Low Income Fathers and Families in South Africa and the U.S.," *Journal of Family Issues* 33 (2012): 801–22.

125. Christopher Carrington, *No Place Like Home: Relationships and Family Life among Lesbians and Gay Men* (Chicago: University of Chicago Press, 1999).

126. Elisabeth Sheff, *The Polyamorists Next Door: Inside Multiple-Partner Relationships and Families* (Lanham, MD: Rowman & Littlefield, 2014).

127. Elisabeth Sheff, "Children in Polyamorous Families Part 1," *Psychology Today,* April 2, 2017. Retrieved from www.psychologytoday.com/us/blog/the-poly amorists-next-door/201704/children-in-polyamorous -families-part-1.

128. Laura Hamilton, Claudia Geist, and Brian Powell, "Marital Name Change as a Window into Gender Attitudes," *Gender & Society* 25, no. 2 (2011): 145–75; Rachael D. Robnett and Campbell Leaper, "'Girls Don't Propose! Ew': A Mixed-Methods Examination of Marriage Tradition Preferences and Benevolent Sexism in Emerging Adults," *Journal of Adolescent Research* 28, no. 1 (2013): 96–121; Michael Slade,

"Who Wears the Pants? The Difficulties Men Face When Trying to Take Their Spouse's Surname after Marriage," *Family Court Review* 53, no. 2 (2015): 336–51.

129. Bureau of Labor Statistics, "Women in the Labor Force: A Databook," November 2017. Retrieved from www.bls.gov/opub/reports/womens-databook/2017/home.htm.

Chapter 12: Work

1. Drew Whitelegg, *Working the Skies: The Fast-Paced, Disorienting World of the Flight Attendant* (New York: New York University Press, 2007), 1.

2. Eileen Patten and Kim Parker, "A Gender Reversal on Career Aspirations: Young Women Now Top Young Men in Valuing a High-Paying Career," *Pew Research: Social & Demographic Trends*, April 19, 2012. Retrieved from www.pewsocialtrends.org/2012/04/19/a-gender-reversal-on-career-aspirations/?src=prc-headline.

3. Bureau of Labor Statistics, "Usual Weekly Earnings of Wage and Salary Workers; First Quarter 2018," Table 5, April 13, 2018. Retrieved from www.bls.gov/news.release/pdf/wkyeng.pdf.

4. Julie Zauzmer, "Where We Stand: The Class of 2013 Senior Survey," *Harvard Crimson*, May 28, 2013. Retrieved from www.thecrimson.com/article/2013/5/28/senior-survey-2013/?page=single.

5. Kevin Miller, *The Simple Truth about the Gender Pay Gap*, AAUW, Spring 2018. Retrieved from www.aauw.org/resource/the-simple-truth-about-the-gender-pay-gap/.

6. Kathleen Barry, "'Too Glamorous to Be Considered Workers': Flight Attendants and Pink-Collar Activism in Mid-Twentieth-Century America," *Labor: Studies in Working-Class History of the Americas* 3, no. 3 (2006): 119.

7. Kathleen Barry, *Femininity in Flight: A History of Flight Attendants* (Durham: Duke University Press, 2007), 98.

8. Ibid., 62.

9. Linda Mizejewski, *Ziegfeld Girl: Image and Icon in Culture and Cinema* (Durham: Duke University Press, 1999), 12.

10. Kathleen Barry, *Femininity in Flight: A History of Flight Attendants* (Durham: Duke University Press, 2007).

11. Kathleen Barry, "'Too Glamorous to Be Considered Workers': Flight Attendants and Pink-Collar Activism in Mid-Twentieth-Century America," *Labor: Studies in Working-Class History of the Americas* 3, no. 3: 135; Drew Whitelegg, *Working the Skies: The Fast-Paced, Disorienting World of the Flight Attendant* (New York: New York University Press, 2007), 47, 133.

12. Kathleen Barry, *Femininity in Flight: A History of Flight Attendants* (Durham: Duke University Press, 2007); Arlie Hochschild, *The Managed Heart: Commercialization of Human Feeling* (Berkeley: University of California Press, 1983); Melissa Tyler and Pamela Abbott, "Chocs Away: Weight Watching in the Contemporary Airline Industry," *Sociology* 32, no. 3 (1998): 433–50.

13. Victoria Vantoch, *The Jet Sex: Airline Stewardesses and the Making of an American Icon* (Philadelphia: University of Pennsylvania Press, 2013).

14. Drew Whitelegg, *Working the Skies: The Fast-Paced, Disorienting World of the Flight Attendant* (New York: New York University Press, 2007). 58.

15. Kathleen Barry, *Femininity in Flight: A History of Flight Attendants* (Durham: Duke University Press, 2007), 26.

16. Claire Williams, "Sky Service: The Demands of Emotional Labour in the Airline Industry," *Gender, Work and Organization* 10, no. 5 (2003): 513–50.

17. Kathleen Barry, *Femininity in Flight: A History of Flight Attendants* (Durham and London: Duke University Press, 2007), 119.

18. Ibid.

19. Catalyst, "Pyramid: Women in S&P 500 Companies," March 1, 2017. Retrieved from www.catalyst.org/knowledge/women-sp-500-companies.

20. Claire Cain Miller, Kevin Quealy, and Margot Sanger-Katz, "The Top Jobs Where Women are Outnumbered by Men Named John," *New York Times*, April 24, 2018. Retrieved from www.nytimes.com/interactive/2018/04/24/upshot/women-and-men-named-john.html.

21. Ariane Hegewisch and Emma Williams-Baron, *The Gender Wage Gap by Occupation 2017 and by Race and Ethnicity*, Institute for Women's Policy Research, April 2018. Retrieved from https://iwpr.org/wp-content/uploads/2018/04/C467_2018-Occupational-Wage-Gap.pdf.

22. Heidi Shierholz, "The Wrong Route to Equality: Men's Declining Wages," Council for Contemporary Families, Equal Pay Symposium 2013. Retrieved

from https://contemporaryfamilies.org/equal-pay-symposium-50-years-since-equal-pay-act-1963/.

23. L. Cooke, "Pathology of Patriarchy and Family Inequalities," in *Family Inequalities in Europe and the Americas: Causes and Consequences,* ed. Naomi Cahn, June Carbone, W. Bradford Wilcox, and Laurie DeRose (Cambridge: Cambridge University Press, 2017).

24. Janet Adamy and Paul Overberg, "Women in Elite Jobs Face Stubborn Pay Gap," *Wall Street Journal,* May 17, 2016. Retrieved from www.wsj.com/articles/women-in-elite-jobs-face-stubborn-pay-gap-1463502938?tesla=y.

25. Marianne Bertrand, Claudia Goldin, and Lawrence F. Katz, "Dynamics of the Gender Gap for Young Professionals in the Financial and Corporate Sectors," *American Economic Journal: Applied Economics* 2 (July 2010): 228–55.

26. National Women's Law Center, *Women and the Lifetime Wage Gap: How Many Woman Years Does It Take to Equal 40 Man Years?* March 2017. Retrieved from https://nwlc-ciw49tixgw5lbab.stackpathdns.com/wp-content/uploads/2017/03/Women-and-the-Lifetime-Wage-Gap-2017-1.pdf. Amounts converted from 2015 to 2018 numbers.

27. U.S. Social Security Administration, "Annual Statistical Supplement to the Social Security Bulletin, 2017: 6B: OASDI Benefits Awarded: Retired Workers." Retrieved from www.ssa.gov/policy/docs/statcomps/supplement/2017/supplement17.pdf.

28. Juliette Cubanski, Kendal Orgera, Anthony Damico, and Tricia Neuman, "How Many Seniors Are Living in Poverty? National and State Estimates Under the Official and Supplemental Poverty Measures in 2016," Kaiser Family Foundation, March 2, 2018. Retrieved from www.kff.org/medicare/issue-brief/how-many-seniors-are-living-in-poverty-national-and-state-estimates-under-the-official-and-supplemental-poverty-measures-in-2016/.

29. Kathleen Barry, *Femininity in Flight: A History of Flight Attendants* (Durham: Duke University Press, 2007).

30. Henry Holden, "Women in Aviation—A Legacy of Success," *Airport Journals,* March 2003, Retrieved from http://www.census.gov/cps/data/cpstablecreator.html.

31. Albert Mills, "Cockpits, Hangars, Boys and Galleys: Corporate Masculinities and the Development of British Airways," *Gender, Work and Organization* 5, no. 3 (1998): 172–88.

32. Bureau of Labor Statistics, "Labor Force Statistics from the Current Population Survey: Table 11: Employed Persons by Detailed Occupation, Sex, Race, and Hispanic or Latino Ethnicity." Retrieved from www.bls.gov/cps/cpsaat11.htm.

33. Robin Leidner, "Selling Hamburgers and Selling Insurance: Gender, Work, and Identity in Interactive Service Jobs," *Gender & Society* 5 (1991): 174.

34. Ibid., 174; Robin Leidner, *Fast Food, Fast Talk: Service Work and the Routinization of Everyday Life* (Berkeley: University of California Press, 1993).

35. Lynn Carlisle, "The Gender Shift, the Demographics of Women in Dentistry. What Impact Will It Have?" *In a Spirit of Caring,* n.d. Retrieved from www.spiritofcaring.com/public/488.cfm.

36. Maria Charles, "What Gender is Science?" *Contexts* 10, no. 2 (2011). Retrieved from http://contexts.org/articles/spring-2011/what-gender-is-science/.

37. H. Gharibyan and S. Gunsaulus, "Gender Gap in Computer Science Does not Exist in One Former Soviet Republic: Results of a Study," Annual Joint Conference Integrating Technology into Computer Science Education. Proceedings of the 11th Annual SIGCSE Conference on Innovation and Technology in Computer Science Education. Bologna, Italy, 2006.

38. Vivian Anette Lagesen, "Extreme Make-Over? The Making of Gender and Computer Science" (PhD diss., STS report 71, Trondeim: NTNU, Department of Interdisciplinary Studies of Culture, 2005).

39. "Women in India's Construction Industry," Women in Informal Employment: Globalizing and Organizing. Retrieved from http://www.wiego.org/informal-economy/women-india%E2%80%99s-construction-industry.

40. Ariane Hegewisch and Emma Williams-Baron, *The Gender Wage Gap by Occupation 2017 and by Race and Ethnicity,* Institute for Women's Policy Research, April 2018. Retrieved from https://iwpr.org/publications/gender-wage-gap-occupation-2017-race-ethnicity/.

41. Joyce Jacobsen, *The Economics of Gender* (Malden, MA: Wiley-Blackwell, 2007), data from International Labour Organization, *Yearbook of Labour Statistics* (1985–2004), 2007.

42. Sara Rab, "Sex Discrimination in Restaurant Hiring," (MA thesis, University of Pennsylvania, 2001).

43. Association of American Medical College, "2016 Physicians Specialty Data Book," 2016. Retrieved from www.aamc.org/download/313228/data/2012 physicianspecialtydatabook.pdf.

44. Bureau of Labor Statistics, "Labor Force Statistics from the Current Population Survey: Table 11: Employed Persons by Detailed Occupation, Sex, Race, and Hispanic or Latino Ethnicity." Retrieved from www.bls.gov/cps/cpsaat11.htm.

45. Eileen Patten and Kim Parker, "Women in the U.S. Military: Growing Share, Distinctive Profile," *Pew Research: Social & Demographic Trends*. Retrieved from www.pewsocialtrends.org/files/2011/12/women -in-the-military.pdf.

46. New York City Taxi and Limousine Commission, "2016 TLC Factbook." Retrieved from www .nyc.gov/html/tlc/downloads/pdf/2016_tlc_fact book.pdf.

47. John Blandford, "The Nexus of Sexual Orientation and Gender in the Determination of Earnings," *Industrial and Labor Relations Review* 56, no. 4 (2003): 622–42.

48. Phil Tiemeyer, *Plane Queer: Labor, Sexuality, and AIDS in the History of Male Flight Attendants* (Berkeley: University of California Press, 2013).

49. Maria Charles, "A World of Difference: International Trends in Women's Economic Status," *Annual Review of Sociology* 37 (2011): 355–71; Robin Ely, "Effects of Organizational Demographics and Social Identity on Relationships among Professional Women," *Administrative Science Quarterly* 39, no. 2 (1994): 203–38.

50. Sapna Cheryan, Victoria C. Plaut, Paul G. Davies, and Claude M. Steele, "Ambient Belonging: How Stereotypical Cues Impact Gender Participation in Computer Science," *Journal of Personality and Social Psychology* 97, no. 6 (2009): 1045–60.

51. Emily Chang, *Brotopia: Breaking Up the Boys' Club of Silicon Valley* (New York: Portfolio, 2018); Amy M. Denissen, "The Right Tools for the Job: Constructing Gender Meanings and Identities in the Male-Dominated Building Trades," *Human Relations* 63, no. 7 (2010): 1051–69.

52. Karen Hossfield, "Hiring Immigrant Women: Silicon Valley's Simple Formula," in *Women of Color in U.S. Society*, ed. Maxine Baca Zinn and Bonnie Thornton Dill, (Philadelphia: Temple University Press, 1994), 65.

53. Emily Chang, "Women Once Ruled the Computer World. When Did Silicon Valley Become Brotopia?" *Bloomberg*, February 1, 2018. Retrieved from www.bloomberg.com/news/features/2018-02 -01/women-once-ruled-computers-when-did-the-val ley-become-brotopia.

54. Stefanie K. Johnson, David R. Hekman, and Elsa T. Chan, "If There's Only One Woman in Your Candidate Pool, There's Statistically No Chance She'll Be Hired," *Harvard Business Review*, April 26, 2016. Retrieved from https://hbr.org/2016/04/if -theres-only-one-woman-in-your-candidate-pool -theres-statistically-no-chance-shell-be-hired.

55. David J. Maume, "Occupational Segregation and the Career Mobility of White Men and Women," *Social Forces* 77, no. 4 (1999): 1449. See also *PBS News Hour*, "Why Engineering, Science Gender Gap Persists," April 25, 2012. Retrieved from www .pbs.org/newshour/rundown/science-engineering -and-the-gender-gap/.

56. Molly Connell, "Lack of Female Role Models Undermining STEM Career Paths," *Business Women Media*, April 15, 2017. Retrieved from www.the businesswomanmedia.com/female-undermining -career-paths/.

57. Susan Chira, "The 'Manly' Jobs Problem," *New York Times*, February 8, 2018. Retrieved from www .nytimes.com/2018/02/08/sunday-review/sexual -harassment-masculine-jobs.html.

58. Phil Tiemeyer, *Plane Queer: Labor, Sexuality, and AIDS in the History of Male Flight Attendants* (Berkeley: University of California Press, 2013), 93.

59. Ibid., 91.

60. Ibid., 102.

61. Ibid., 113.

62. Ibid.

63. Kathleen Barry, *Femininity in Flight: A History of Flight Attendants* (Durham: Duke University Press, 2007), 97.

64. Ibid.

65. Melissa Tyler and Pamela Abbott, "Chocs Away: Weight Watching in the Contemporary Airline Industry," *Sociology* 32, no. 3 (1998): 440.

66. Claudia Goldin, *Understanding the Gender Gap: An Economic History of American Women* (New York: Oxford University Press, 1990), 204.

67. Margery Davies, *Woman's Place is at the Typewriter: Office Work and Office Workers, 1870–1930* (Philadelphia: Temple University Press, 1984); Claudia Goldin, *Understanding the Gender Gap: An*

Economic History of American Women (New York: Oxford University Press, 1990).

68. Thomas Misa, ed., *Gender Codes: Why Women are Leaving Computing* (Hoboken, NJ: John Wiley and Sons, Inc., 2010).

69. *Top Secret Rosies: The Female Computers of World War II*. Documentary, dir. LeAnn Erickson (2010), http://www.topsecretrosies.com/.

70. Anna Lewis, "Girls Go Geek . . . Again!" *Fog Creek Software* (blog), July 26, 2011. Retrieved from http://blog.fogcreek.com/girls-go-geek-again/.

71. For reviews, see Philip Cohen and Matt L. Huffman, "Individuals, Jobs, and Labor Markets: The Devaluation of Women's Work," *American Sociological Review* 68, no. 3 (2007): 443–63; and Asaf Levanon, Paula England, and Paul Allison, "Occupational Feminization and Pay: Assessing Causal Dynamics Using 1950-2000 U.S. Census Data," *Social Forces*, 88, Issue 2 (December 2009): 865–91.

72. Katie Burns, "At Veterinary Colleges, Male Students Are in the Minority," JAVMA, February 1, 2010. Retrieved from www.avma.org/News/JAVMA News/Pages/100215g.aspx; Greg Kelly, "Veterinary Medicine Is a Woman's World," *Veterinarian's Money Digest*, May 7, 2017. Retrieved from www.vmdtoday.com/news/veterinary-medicine-is-a-womans-world.

73. Harry Parker, Fong Chan, and Bernard Saper, "Occupational Representativeness and Prestige Rating: Some Observations," *Journal of Employment Counseling* 26, no. 3 (1989): 117–31; Karen Beyard-Tyler and Marilyn Haring, "Gender-Related Aspects of Occupational Prestige," *Vocational Behavior* 24, no. 2 (1984): 194–203.

74. L. S. Liben, R. S. Bigler, and H. K. Krogh, "Pink and Blue Collar Jobs: Children's Judgments of Job Status and Job Aspirations in Relation to Sex of Worker," *Journal of Experimental Child Psychology*, 79 (2001): 346–63.

75. John Touhey, "Effects of Additional Men on Prestige and Desirability of Occupations Typically Performed by Women," *Journal of Applied Social Psychology* 4, no. 4 (1974): 330–35; John Touhey, "Effects of Additional Women Professionals on Ratings of Occupational Prestige and Desirability," *Journal of Personality and Social Psychology* 29, no. 1 (1974): 86–89.

76. For a review, see Philip Cohen and Matt L. Huffman, "Individuals, Jobs, and Labor Markets: The Devaluation of Women's Work," *American Sociological Review* 68, no. 3 (2007): 443–63.

77. Stephanie Boraas and William M. Rodgers III, "How Does Gender Play a Role in the Earnings Gap? An Update," *Monthly Labor Review* (March 2003). Retrieved from www.bls.gov/opub/mlr/2003/03/art 2full.pdf; Trond Peterson and Laurie A. Morgan, "Separate and Unequal: Occupation-Establishment Sex Segregation and the Gender Wage Gap," *American Journal of Sociology* 101 (1995): 329–65; Donald J. Treiman and Heidi I. Hartman, eds., *Women, Work, and Wages: Equal Pay for Jobs of Equal Value* (Washington, D.C.: National Academy Press, 1981); see also: Paula England, "Gender Inequality in Labor Markets: The Role of Motherhood and Segregation," *Social Politics: International Studies in Gender, State and Society* 12, no. 2 (2005): 264–88; Philip Cohen and Matt L. Huffman, "Individuals, Jobs, and Labor Markets: The Devaluation of Women's Work," *American Sociological Review* 68, no. 3 (2007): 443–63.

78. For a review, see Philip Cohen and Matt L. Huffman, "Individuals, Jobs, and Labor Markets: The Devaluation of Women's Work," *American Sociological Review* 68, no. 3 (2007): 443–63; Stephanie Boraas and William M. Rodgers III, "How Does Gender Play a Role in the Earnings Gap? An Update," *Monthly Labor Review* (March 2003). Retrieved from www.bls.gov/opub/mlr/2003/03/art 2full.pdf.

79. Occupations with average wages over $100,000 a year for which there are not reliable demographic data include nurse anesthetist, nuclear engineer, podiatrist, natural science manager, petroleum engineer, air traffic controller, astronomer/physicist, optometrist, geological engineer, actuary, compensation/benefits manager, training/development manager, and computer/information scientist.

80. Michael S. Kimmel, "Why Men Should Support Gender Equity," *Women's Studies Review* (Fall 2005). Retrieved from www.lehman.edu/academics/inter /women-studies/documents/why-men.pdf.

81. Soraya Chemaly, "What's Your Kids' Wage Gap? Boys Paid More, More Profitably," *Huffington Post*, Jan. 22, 2015. Retrieved from www.huffingtonpost .com/soraya-chemaly/whats-your-kids-wage-gap _b_6518772.html.

82. Nadine Kalinauskas, "Heroic Asiana Flight Attendant Carried Passengers to Safety on Her Back," *Yahoo! News Canada*, July 13, 2013. Retrieved from http://ca.news.yahoo.com/blogs/good-news /heroic-asiana-flight-attendant-carried-passengers -safety-her-183216700.html.

83. Lisa Wade, "The Unsung Heroes of the Crash Landing in San Francisco," *Sociological Images*, December 26, 2013. Retrieved from https://the societypages.org/socimages/2013/12/26/working -through-the-crash-landing-in-san-francisco/.

84. Quoted in Kathleen Barry, "'Too Glamorous to Be Considered Workers': Flight Attendants and Pink-Collar Activism in Mid-Twentieth-Century America," *Labor: Studies in Working-Class History of the Americas* 3, no. 3 (2006): 135.

85. Drew Whitelegg, *Working the Skies: The Fast-Paced, Disorienting World of the Flight Attendant* (New York: New York University Press, 2007), 98.

86. Arlie Hochschild, *The Managed Heart: Commercialization of Human Feeling* (Berkeley: University of California Press, 1983), 107.

87. Delta, "Flight Attendant Training." Retrieved from https://www.delta.com/content/www/en_US /about-delta/business-programs/training-and-con sulting-services/flight-attendant-training/in-flight -training-facilities.html; Drew Whitelegg, *Working the Skies: The Fast-Paced, Disorienting World of the Flight Attendant* (New York: New York University Press, 2007).

88. Arlie Hochschild, *The Managed Heart: Commercialization of Human Feeling* (Berkeley: University of California Press, 1983), 96.

89. Kathleen Barry, *Femininity in Flight: A History of Flight Attendants* (Durham: Duke University Press, 2007), 78.

90. Ibid., 108–109.

91. T. J. Ballard, L. Corradi, L. Lauria, C. Mazzanti, G. Zcaravelli, F. Sgorbissa, P. Romito, and A. Verdecchia, "Integrating Qualitative Methods into Occupational Health Research: A Study of Women Flight Attendants," *Occupational and Environmental Medicine*, 61 (2004): 163–66.

92. Arlie Hochschild, *The Managed Heart: Commercialization of Human Feeling* (Berkeley: University of California Press, 1983), 118.

93. Drew Whitelegg, *Working the Skies: The Fast-Paced, Disorienting World of the Flight Attendant* (New York: New York University Press, 2007).

94. Kathleen Barry, Femininity in Flight: A History of Flight Attendants (Durham: Duke University Press, 2007), 27.

95. Liza Mundy, "Why Is Silicon Valley So Awful to Women?" *Atlantic*, April 2017. Retrieved from www.theatlantic.com/magazine/archive/2017/04 /why-is-silicon-valley-so-awful-to-women/517788/.

96. Occupations with average wages under $25,000 a year for which there are not reliable demographic data include shampooer; usher, lobby attendant, ticket taker; coatroom attendant; and motion-picture projectionist. Minorities include Black/African American, Asian, and Hispanic/Latino. The U.S. Census does not report statistics for American Indians because their population numbers are so low. Arab and Middle Eastern Americans are considered White by the U.S. government.

97. Jill E. Yavorsky, Philip N. Cohen, and Yue Qian, "MAN UP, MAN DOWN: Race–Ethnicity and the Hierarchy of Men in Female-Dominated Work," *The Sociological Quarterly* 57 (2016): 733–58.

98. Michele Lamont, *The Dignity of Working Men: Morality and the Boundaries of Race, Class, and Immigration* (New York: Russell Sage Foundation, 2000).

99. Paula England, "Gender Inequality in Labor Markets: The Role of Motherhood and Segregation," *Social Politics: International Studies in Gender, State and Society* 12, no. 2 (2005): 264–88; Paula England, Lori L. Reid, and Barbara S. Kilbourne, "The Effect of Sex Composition on the Starting Wages in an Organization: Findings from the NLSY," *Demography* 33, no. 4 (1996): 511–22.

100. Bureau of Labor Statistics, "Occupational Employment Statistics: May 2017 National Occupational Employment and Wage Estimates: United States," May 1, 2018. Retrieved from www.bls.gov /oes/current/oes399011.htm.

101. Stephanie Boraas and William M. Rodgers III, "How Does Gender Play a Role in the Earnings Gap? An Update," Monthly Labor Review (March 2003). Retrieved from www.bls.gov/opub/mlr/2003/03/art 2full.pdf.

102. John Blandford, "The Nexus of Sexual Orientation and Gender in the Determination of Earnings," *Industrial and Labor Relations Review* 56, no. 4 (2003): 622–42.

103. Melissa Tyler and Pamela Abbott, "Chocs Away: Weight Watching in the Contemporary Airline Industry," *Sociology* 32, no. 3 (1998): 433–50; Claudia Goldin, *Understanding the Gender Gap: An Economic History of American Women* (New York: Oxford University Press, 1990).

104. Melissa Tyler and Steve Taylor, "The Exchange of Aesthetics: Women's Work and 'The Gift,'" *Gender, Work and Organization* 5, no. 3 (1998): 165–71; Melissa Tyler and Pamela Abbott, "Chocs Away:

Weight Watching in the Contemporary Airline Industry." *Sociology* 32, no. 3 (1998): 433–50.

105. Claire Williams, "Sky Service: The Demands of Emotional Labour in the Airline Industry," *Gender, Work and Organization* 10, no. 5 (2003): 538.

106. Stephen T. Wilson, "Fly the Unfriendly Skies," SteveWilsonBlog, June 23, 2011. Retrieved from https://thesocietypages.org/socimages/2011/06/24/fly-the-unfriendly-skies/.

107. Paul Overberg and Janet Adamy, "What's Your Pay Gap?" *Wall Street Journal*, May 17, 2016. Retrieved from http://graphics.wsj.com/gender-pay-gap/.

108. Eric Uhlmann and Geoffrey Cohen, "Constructed Criteria: Redefining Merit to Justify Discrimination," *Psychological Science* 16, no. 6 (2005): 474–80.

109. Kristen Schilt, "Just One of the Guys? How Transmen Make Gender Visible at Work," *Gender & Society* 20, no. 4 (2006): 483.

110. Ibid., 477.

111. Ibid., 478.

112. Ibid., 476.

113. Arlie Hochschild, *The Time Bind: When Work Becomes Home and Home Becomes Work* (New York: Henry Holt and Company, 2001), 108–109; Sreedhari Desai, Dolly Chugh, and Arthur Brief, "Marriage Structure and Resistance to the Gender Revolution in the Workplace," Working Paper. Social Science Research Network, 2012. Retrieved from http://papers.ssrn.com/sol3/papers.cfm?abstract_id=2018259; M. E. Inesi and D. Cable, "When Accomplishments Come Back to Haunt You: The Negative Effect of Competence Signals on Women's Performance Evaluations," *Personnel Psychology*, 68 (2015): 615–57.

114. Kim Parker, "Women in Majority-Male Workplaces Report Higher Rates of Gender Discrimination," Pew Research Center, March 7, 2018. Retrieved from www.pewresearch.org/fact-tank/2018/03/07/women-in-majority-male-workplaces-report-higher-rates-of-gender-discrimination/; Kim Parker and Cary Funk, "Gender Discrimination Comes in Many Forms for Today's Working Women," Pew Research Center, December 14, 2017. Retrieved from www.pewresearch.org/fact-tank/2017/12/14/gender-discrimination-comes-in-many-forms-for-todays-working-women/; see also Chai R. Feldblum and Victoria A. Lipnic, *Select Task Force on the Study of Harassment in the Workplace*, U.S. Equal Employment Opportunity Commission, June

2016. Retrieved from www.eeoc.gov/eeoc/task_force/harassment/report.cfm; Rachel Thomas, Marianne Cooper, Ellen Konar, Megan Rooney, Ashley Finc, Lareina Yee, Alexis Krivkovich, Irina Starikova, Kelsey Robinson, and Rachel Valentino, *Women in the Workplace, 2017*, LeanIn.Org and McKinsey & Company, 2017. Retrieved from https://womenintheworkplace.com/.

115. Amy M. Denissen, "The Right Tools for the Job: Constructing Gender Meanings and Identities in the Male-Dominated Building Trades," Human Relations 63, no. 7 (2010): 1061–62.

116. Shelley Correll and Caroline Simard, "Research: Vague Feedback Is Holding Women Back," *Harvard Business Review*, April 29, 2016. Retrieved from https://hbr.org/2016/04/research-vague-feedback-is-holding-women-back.

117. Amy M. Denissen, "The Right Tools for the Job: Constructing Gender Meanings and Identities in the Male-Dominated Building Trades," Human Relations 63, no. 7 (2010): 1051–69.

118. Annie Sweeney and Jason Meisner, "Five Female Paramedics Sue, Alleging Pervasive Sexual Harassment at Chicago Fire Department," *Chicago Tribune*, May 2, 2018. Retrieved from www.chicagotribune.com/news/local/breaking/ct-met-sex-harassment-lawsuit-chicago-fire-department-2018-0501-story.html.

119. J. Berdahl, "The Sexual Harassment of Uppity Women," *Journal of Applied Psychology* 92 (2007): 425–37.

120. Angus Chen, "Invisibilia: How Learning To Be Vulnerable Can Make Life Safer," NPR, June 17, 2016. Retrieved from www.npr.org/sections/health-shots/2016/06/17/482203447/invisibilia-how-learning-to-be-vulnerable-can-make-life-safer.

121. Robin J. Ely and Debra Meyerson, "Unmasking Manly Men," *Harvard Business Review*, 2008. Retrieved from https://hbr.org/2008/07/unmasking-manly-men.

122. Jessica Smith Rolston, *Mining Coal and Undermining Gender: Rhythms of Work and Family in the American West*, (New Brunswick, NJ: Rutgers University Press, 2014).

123. Susan Chira, "The 'Manly' Jobs Problem," *The New York Times*, February 8, 2018, Retrieved from https://www.nytimes.com/2018/02/08/sunday-review/sexual-harassment-masculine-jobs.html; Angus Chen, "Invisibilia: How Learning To Be Vulnerable Can Make Life Safer," *NPR*, June 17, 2016, Retrieved from https://www.npr.org/sections/health

-shots/2016/06/17/482203447/invisibilia-how-learning-to-be-vulnerable-can-make-life-safer.

124. Jessica Smith Rolston, *Mining Coal and Undermining Gender: Rhythms of Work and Family in the American West*, (New Brunswick, NJ: Rutgers University Press, 2014).

125. Robin J. Ely, "The Power in Demography: Women's Social Constructions of Gender Identity at Work," *Academy of Management Journal* 38 (1995): 589–634.

126. Philip Cohen and Matt Huffman, "Working for the Woman? Female Managers and the Gender Wage Gap," *American Sociological Review* 72, no. 5 (2007): 681–704.

127. Jennifer L. Pierce, *Gender Trials: Emotional Lives in Contemporary Law Firms* (Berkeley: University of California Press, 1995), 68.

128. Alice H. Eagly and Linda L. Carli, "Women and the Labyrinth of Leadership," *Harvard Business Review*, September 2007. Retrieved from http://hbr.org/2007/09/women-and-the-labyrinth-of-leadership/ar/1; L. A. Rudman and P. Glick, "Feminized Management and Backlash toward Agentic Women: The Hidden Costs to Women of a Kinder, Gentler Image of Middle Managers," *Journal of Personality and Social Psychology*, 77 (1999): 1004–10; A. H. Eagly, M. G. Makhijani, and B. G. Klonsky, "Gender and the Evaluation of Leaders: A Meta-Analysis," *Psychological Bulletin* 111 (1992): 3–22.

129. Amy M. Denissen and Abigail C. Saguy, "Gendered Homophobia and the Contradictions of Workplace Discrimination for Women in the Building Trades," *Gender & Society*, 28, no. 3 (December 5, 2013): 381–403.

130. Hannah Bowles, Linda Babcock, and Lei Lai, "Social Incentives for Gender Differences in the Propensity to Initiate Negotiations: Sometimes it Does Hurt to Ask," *Organizational Behavior and Human Decision Processes* 103 (2007): 84–103.

131. Victoria Brescoll and Eric Uhlmann, "Can an Angry Woman Get Ahead? Status Conferral, Gender, and Expression of Emotion in the Workplace," *Psychological Science* 19, no. 3 (2008): 268–75.

132. Nancy M. Carter and Christine Silva, *Pipeline's Broken Promise* (Catalyst, 2010).

133. S. Wellington, M. Kropf, and P. Gerkovich, "What's Holding Women Back?" *Harvard Business Review* 81, no. 6 (2003): 18–19.

134. D. K. King, "Multiple Jeopardy, Multiple Consciousness: The Context of Black Feminist Ideology," *Signs* 14, no. 1 (1988): 42–72; A. Mitra, "Breaking the Glass Ceiling: African-American Women in Management Positions," *Equal Opportunities International* 22, no. 2 (2003): 67–79.

135. Marlese Durr and Adia M. Harvey Wingfield, "Keep Your 'N' in Check: African American Women and the Interactive Effects of Etiquette and Emotional Labor," *Critical Sociology*, 37, no. 5, (March 28, 2011): 557–71.

136. M. K. Ryan and S. A. Haslam, "The Glass Cliff: Evidence that Women are Over-Represented in Precarious Leadership Positions," *British Journal of Management*, 16 (2005), 81–90; Michelle Ryan and Alexander Haslam, "The Glass Cliff: Exploring the Dynamics Surrounding the Appointment of Women to Precarious Leadership Positions," *Academy of Management Review* 32, no. 2 (2007): 549–72.

137. K. Blanton, "Above Glass Ceiling Footing is Fragile: Factors Appear to Work Against Longer Tenures for Women CEOs," *Boston Globe*, February 18, 2005: D1.

138. Alison Cook and Christy Glass. "Glass Cliffs and Organizational Saviors: Barriers to Minority Leadership in Work Organizations," *Social Problems* 60, no. 2 (2013): 168–87.

139. Amy Nesbitt, "The Glass Ceiling Effect and Its Impact on Mid-Level Female Officer Career Progression in the United States Marine Corps and Air Force" (MA thesis, Naval Postgraduate School, 2004), 78. Retrieved from http://calhoun.nps.edu/public/handle/10945/1711.

140. S. A. Hewlett and C. B. Luce, "Off-Ramps and On-Ramps: Keeping Talented Women on the Road to Success," *Harvard Business Review* 83, no. 3 (2005): 43–54; Nancy M. Carter and Christine Silva, *Pipeline's Broken Promise* (Catalyst, 2010); L. K. Stroh, J. M. Brett, and A. H. Reilly, "Family Structure, Glass Ceiling, and Traditional Explanations for the Differential Rate of Turnover of Female and Male Managers," *Journal of Vocational Behavior* 49 (1996): 99–118; Lauren Noel and Christie Hunter Arscott, "Millennial Women: What Executives Need to Know about Millennial Women," The International Consortium for Executive Development Research, April 2016. Retrieved from www.icedr.org/research/documents/15_millennial_women.pdf.

141. Rosabeth Moss Kanter, "The Impact of Hierarchical Structures on the Work Behavior of Women and Men," *Social Problems* 23, no. 4 (1976): 415–30.

142. Christine Williams, "The Glass Escalator: Hidden Advantages for Men in the 'Female' Professions," *Social Problems* 39, no. 3 (1992): 253–67.

143. Christine Williams, *Still a Man's World: Men Who Do Women's Work* (Berkeley: University of California Press, 1995); Matt Huffman, "Gender Inequality Across Wage Hierarchies," *Work and Occupations* 31, no. 3 (2004): 323–44; Mia Hultin, "Some Take the Glass Escalator, Some Hit the Glass Ceiling: Career Consequences of Occupational Sex Segregation," *Work and Occupations* 30 (2003): 30–61; David J. Maume, "Glass Ceilings and Glass Escalators: Occupational Segregation and Race and Sex Differences in Managerial Promotions," *Work and Occupations* 26, no. 4 (1999): 483–509; David J. Maume, "Is the Glass Ceiling a Unique Form of Inequality? Evidence from a Random Effects Model of Managerial Attainment," *Work and Occupations* 31, no. 2 (2004): 250–74; Janice Yoder, "Rethinking Tokenism: Looking beyond Numbers," *Gender & Society* 5, no. 2 (1991): 178–92; Deborah A. Harris and Patti Giuffre, *Taking the Heat: Women Chefs and Gender Inequality in the Professional Kitchen* (New Brunswick: Rutgers University Press, 2015).

144. Andrew Cognard-Black, "Will They Stay, or Will They Go? Sex-Atypical Work among Token Men Who Teach," *Sociological Quarterly* 45, no. 1 (2004): 113–39.

145. Allyson Stokes, "The Glass Runway: How Gender and Sexuality Shape the Spotlight in Fashion Design," *Gender & Society*, 29, no. 2 (March 16, 2015): 219–43.

146. Adia Wingfield, "Racializing the Glass Escalator: Reconsidering Men's Experiences with Women's Work," *Gender & Society* 23, no. 1 (2009): 5–26; Ryan Smith, "Money, Benefits, and Power: A Test of the Glass Ceiling and Glass Escalator Hypotheses," *The Annals of the American Academy of Political and Social Science* 639, no. 1 (2012): 149–72; Catherine Connell, "Dangerous Disclosures," *Sexuality Research and Social Policy* 9 (2012): 168–77; Kristen Schilt, *Just One of the Guys?* (Chicago: University of Chicago Press, 2011); Michelle Budig, "Male Advantage and the Gender Composition of Jobs: Who Rides the Glass Escalator?" *Social Problems* 49, no. 2 (2002): 258–77.

147. Catherine Connell, *School's Out: Gay and Lesbian Teachers in the Classroom*, (Oakland: University of California Press, 2015).

148. Christine Williams, *Still a Man's World: Men Who Do Women's Work* (Berkeley: University of California Press, 1995), 88.

149. Laura Stokowski, "Just Call Us Nurses: Men in Nursing," *MedScape*, August 16, 2012.

150. Mia Hultin, "Some Take the Glass Escalator, Some Hit the Glass Ceiling: Career Consequences of Occupational Sex Segregation," *Work and Occupations* 30 (2003): 30–61; Christine Williams, "The Glass Escalator: Hidden Advantages for Men in the 'Female' Professions," *Social Problems* 39, no. 3 (1992): 253–67.

151. Joan Acker, "Hierarchies, Jobs, Bodies: A Theory of Gendered Organizations," *Gender & Society* 4, no. 2 (1990); Barbara Risman, *Gender Vertigo: American Families in Transition* (New Haven: Yale University Press, 1999); Phyllis Moen and Patricia Roehling, *The Career Mystique: Cracks in the American Dream* (Lanham, MD: Rowan and Littlefield, 2005).

152. Arlie Hochschild, *The Time Bind: When Work Becomes Home and Home Becomes Work* (New York: Henry Holt and Company, 2001), 56.

153. OECD, *OECD Employment Outlook* 2017, OECD Publishing, 2017. Retrieved from https://read.oecd-ilibrary.org/employment/oecd-employment-outlook-2017_empl_outlook-2017-en#page211.

154. Quoted in Arlie Hochschild, *The Time Bind: When Work Becomes Home and Home Becomes Work* (New York: Henry Holt and Company, 2001), xix.

155. Arlie Hochschild, *The Second Shift* (New York: Penguin Group, 1989).

156. Michelle Budig, "The Fatherhood Bonus and the Motherhood Penalty: Parenthood and the Gender Gap in Pay," *Third Way*, September 2, 2017; Michelle Budig and Paula England., "The Wage Penalty for Motherhood," *American Sociological Review* 66, no. 2 (2001): 204–25; Deborah J. Anderson, Melissa Binder, and Kate Krause, "The Motherhood Wage Penalty Revisited: Experience, Heterogeneity, Work Effort and Work-Schedule Flexibility," *Industrial and Labor Relations Review* 56 (2003): 273–94; Margaret Gough and Mary Noonan, "A Review of the Motherhood Wage Penalty in the United States," *Sociology Compass*, 7, no. 4 (March 21, 2013).

157. Amanda Baumle, "The Cost of Parenthood: Unraveling the Effects of Sexual Orientation and Gender on Income," *Social Science Quarterly* 90, no. 4 (2009): 983–1002.

158. Alexandra Killewald, "A Reconsideration of the Fatherhood Premium: Marriage, Coresidence, Biology, and Fathers' Wages," *American Sociological Review* 78, no. 1 (2013): 96–116; Rebecca Glauber,

"Race and Gender in Families at Work: The Fatherhood Wage Premium," *Gender & Society* 22, no. 1 (2008): 8–30; Melissa Hodges and Michelle Budig, "Who Gets the Daddy Bonus?: Organizational Hegemonic Masculinity and the Impact of Fatherhood on Earnings," *Gender & Society* 24, no. 6 (2010): 717–45; Renske Keizer, Pearl Dykstra, and Anne-Rigt Poortman, "Life Outcomes of Childless Men and Fathers," *European Sociological Review* 26, no. 1 (2010): 1–15; Institute for Public Policy Research, "Mothers Earn Just 71 Percent of What Fathers Earn," May 23, 2017. Retrieved from https://iwpr.org/publications/mothers-earn-just-71-percent-fathers-earn/.

159. Emma Williams-Baron, Julie Anderson, and Ariane Hegewisch, "Mothers Earn Just 71 Percent of What Fathers Earn," Institute for Women's Policy Research, May 2017. Retrieved from https://iwpr.org/wp-content/uploads/2017/05/Q062-Mothers-Earn-71-Percent-of-Fathers.pdf.

160. Kevin Miller, *The Simple Truth about the Gender Pay Gap*, AAUW, Spring 2018. Retrieved from www.aauw.org/resource/the-simple-truth-about-the-gender-pay-gap/.

161. Bureau of Labor Statistics, "American Time Use Survey—2016 Results," June 27, 2017. Retrieved from www.bls.gov/tus/home.htm#data.; Kim Parker and Wendy Wang, "Modern Parenthood: Roles of Moms and Dads Converge as They Balance Work and Family," *Pew Research: Social & Demographic Trends*, March 14, 2013. Retrieved from www.pewsocialtrends.org/2013/03/14/modern-parenthood-roles-of-moms-and-dads-converge-as-they-balance-work-and-family/?src=rss_main; Kimberley Fisher et al., "Gender Convergence in the American Heritage Time Use Study," *Social Indicators Research* 82 (2006): 1–33.

162. Denise D. Bielby and William T. Bielby, "She Works Hard for the Money: Household Responsibilities and the Allocation of Work Effort," *American Journal of Sociology* 93, no. 5 (1998): 1031–59; Peter Marsden, Arne Kalleberg, and Cynthia Cook, "Gender Differences in Organizational Commitment: Influences of Work Positions and Family Roles," *Work and Occupations* 20, no. 3 (1993): 368–90; William T. Bielby and Denise D. Bielby, "Family Ties: Balancing Commitments to Work and Family in Dual Earner Households," *American Sociological Review* 5, no. 4 (1989): 776–89; William T. Bielby and Denise D. Bielby, "Telling Stories about Gender and Effort: Social Science Narratives about Who Works Hard for the Money," in *The New Economic Sociology*, ed. Mauro F. Guillen, Randall Collins, Paula

England, and Marshall Meyer (New York: Russell Sage, 2002), 193–217; Denise D. Bielby and William T. Bielby, "Work Commitment, Sex-Role Attitudes, and Women's Employment," *American Sociological Review* 49 (1984): 234–47; Jenny Anderson, "The Ultimate Efficiency Hack: Have Kids," *Quartz*, October 11, 2016; Ylan Q. Mui, "Study: Women With More Children are More Productive at Work," *Washington Post*, October 30, 2014; Julie Kmec, "Are Motherhood Penalties and Fatherhood Bonuses Warranted? Comparing Pro-Work Behaviors and Conditions of Mothers, Fathers, and Non-Parents," *Social Science Research* 40, 2 (2010).

163. Kevin Leicht, "Broken Down by Race and Gender? Sociological Explanations of New Sources of Earnings Inequality," *Annual Review of Sociology* 34 (2008): 237–55.

164. Michelle Budig, "The Fatherhood Bonus and the Motherhood Penalty: Parenthood and the Gender Gap in Pay," *Third Way*, September 2, 2017; Michelle Budig and Paula England, "The Wage Penalty for Motherhood," *American Sociological Review* 66, no. 2 (2001): 204–25; Shelley Correll, Stephen Benard, and In Paik, "Getting a Job: Is There a Motherhood Penalty?" *American Journal of Sociology* 112, no. 5 (2007): 1297–339; Amy Cuddy, Susan Fiske, and Peter Glick, "When Professionals Become Mothers, Warmth Doesn't Cut the Ice," *Journal of Social Issues* 60, no. 4 (2004): 701–18; Jane A. Halpert, Midge L. Wilson, and Julia Hickman, "Pregnancy as a Source of Bias in Performance Appraisals," *Journal of Organizational Behavior* 14 (1993): 649–63; Kathleen Fuegen, Monica Biernat, Elizabeth Haines, and Kay Deaux, "Mothers and Fathers in the Workplace: How Gender and Parental Status Influence Judgments of Job-Related Competence," *Journal of Social Issues* 60, no. 4 (2004): 737–54; Susan T. Fiske et al., "A model of (Often Mixed) Stereotype Content: Competence and Warmth Respectively Follow from Perceived sSatus and Competence," *Journal of Personality and Social Psychology* 82 (2002): 878–902; Jessi Smith, Kristin Hawkinson, and Kelli Paull, "Spoiled Milk: An Experimental Examination of Bias Against Mothers who Breastfeed," *Personality and Social Psychology Bulletin* 37, no. 7 (2011): 867–78; Kathleen Fuegen, Monica Biernat, Elizabeth Haines, and Kay Deaux, "Mothers and Fathers in the Workplace: How Gender and Parental Status Influence Judgments of Job-Related Competence," *Journal of Social Issues* 60, no. 4 (2004): 737–54; Madeline E. Heilman and Tyler G. Okimoto, "Motherhood: A Potential Source of Bias in Employment

Decisions," *Journal of Applied Psychology* 93, no.1 (2008): 189–98.

165. Joan C. Williams, "The Maternal Wall," *Harvard Business Review*, October 2004. Retrieved from https://hbr.org/2004/10/the-maternal-wall.

166. Ibid.

167. Ivy Kennelly, "'That Single Mother Element': How White Employers Typify Black Women," *Gender & Society* 13, no. 2 (1999):168-92.

168. Jessi Smith, Kristin Hawkinson, and Kelli Paull, "Spoiled Milk: An Experimental Examination of Bias Against Mothers who Breastfeed," *Personality and Social Psychology Bulletin* 37, no. 7 (2011): 867-78.

169. Joan C. Williams, "The Maternal Wall," *Harvard Business Review*, October 2004. Retrieved from https://hbr.org/2004/10/the-maternal-wall.

170. Shelley Correll, Stephen Benard, and In Paik, "Getting a Job: Is There a Motherhood Penalty?" *American Journal of Sociology* 112, no. 5 (2007): 1297–339; dollars converted from 2007 to 2018 dollars.

171. Ann Bergman and Gunnar Gillberg, "The Cabin Crew Blues: Middle-Aged Cabin Attendants and Their Working Conditions," *Nordic Journal of Working Life Studies*, 5, no. 4 (December 2015): 23–39.

172. Kathleen Barry, *Femininity in Flight: A History of Flight Attendants* (Durham: Duke University Press, 2007).

173. F. Dobruszkes, "An Analysis of European Low-Cost Airlines and their Networks." *Journal of Transport Geography* 14, no. 4 (2006): 249–64; Ann Bergman and Gunnar Gillberg, "The Cabin Crew Blues: Middle-Aged Cabin Attendants and Their Working Conditions," *Nordic Journal of Working Life Studies*, 5, no. 4 (December 2015): 23–39.

174. Cited in Kathleen Barry, *Femininity in Flight: A History of Flight Attendants* (Durham: Duke University Press, 2007).

175. E. Heuven, and A. Bakker, "Emotional Dissonance and Burnout among Cabin Attendants," *European Journal of Work and Organizational Psychology*, 12, no. 1 (2003): 81–100; Christine Williams, "Sky Service: The Demands of Emotional Labour in the Airline Industry," *Gender, Work & Organization* 10, no. 5 (2003): 513–50; Arlie Hochschild, *The Managed Heart: Commercialization of Human Feeling* (Berkeley: University of California Press, 1983).

176. Micheline Maynard, "Coffee, Tea or Job? For Airline Workers, an Uncertain Future," *New York Times*, September 3, 2004. Retrieved from www.nytimes.com/2004/09/03/business/coffee-tea-or-job-for-airline-workers-an-uncertain-future.html; See also P. Taylor, and S. Moore, "Cabin Crew Collectivism: Labour Process and the Roots of Mobilization," *Work Employment & Society*, 29, no. 1 (2015): 79–98.

177. Thomas Piketty, *Capital in the Twenty-First Century* (Cambridge: Harvard University Press, 2014).

178. Anna Louie Sussman, "Inside the Fight Over Productivity and Wages," *Wall Street Journal*, September 8, 2015. Retrieved from https://blogs.wsj.com/economics/2015/09/08/inside-the-fight-over-productivity-and-wages/; Michael D. Giandrea and Shawn A. Sprague, "Estimating the U.S. Labor Share," *Monthly Labor Review*, U.S. Labor Statistics, February 2017. Retrieved from www.bls.gov/opub/mlr/2017/article/estimating-the-us-labor-share.htm.

179. Jesse Bricker, Lisa J. Dettling, Alice Henriques, Joanne W. Hsu, Lindsay Jacobs, Kevin B. Moore, Sarah Pack, John Sabelhaus, Jeffrey Thompson, and Richard A. Windle, "Changes in the U.S. Family Finances from 2013 to 2016: Evidence from the Survey of Consumer Finances," *Federal Reserve Bulletin* 103, no. 3 (September 2017): 1-42; Emmanuel Saez, "Striking it Richer: The Evolution of Top Incomes in the United States," June 30, 2016, Retrieved from https://eml.berkeley.edu/~saez/saez-UStopincomes-2015.pdf; Emmanuel Saez and Gabriel Zucman, "Wealth Inequality in the United States Since 1913: Evidence from Capitalized Income Tax Data," *Quarterly Journal of Economics*, 131, no. 2, (May 2016): 519–78.

180. Alissa Quart, "Teachers Are Working for Uber Just to Keep a Foothold in the Middle Class," *Nation*, September 7, 2016. Retrieved from www.thenation.com/article/teachers-are-working-for-uber-just-to-keep-a-foothold-in-the-middle-class/; Sylvia Allegretto and Ilan Tojerow, "Teacher Staffing and Pay Differences: Public and Private Schools," *Monthly Labor Review*, U.S. Bureau of Labor Statistics, September 2014. Retrieved from www.bls.gov/opub/mlr/2014/article/teacher-staffing-and-pay-differences.htm.

181. U.S. Bureau of Labor Statistics, *Characteristics of Minimum Wage Workers, 2016*, Report 1067, April 2017. Retrieved from www.bls.gov/opub/reports/minimum-wage/2016/home.htm; Lonnie Golden, "Still Falling Short on Hours and Pay: Part-Time Work Becoming New Normal," Economic Policy

Institute, December 5, 2016. Retrieved from www .epi.org/publication/still-falling-short-on-hours -and-pay-part-time-work-becoming-new-normal/.

182. Guy Standing, *The Precariat: The New Dangerous Class*, (London: Bloomsbury, Reprint ed., 2016); Gerald Friedman, "Workers without Employers: Shadow Corporations and the Rise of the Gig Economy," *Review of Keynesian Economics*, 2, no. 2 (2014): 171–88. Retrieved from www.researchgate.net/pro file/Gerald_Friedman/publication/276191257_Work ers_without_employers_Shadow_corporations_and _the_rise_of_the_gig_economy/links/5731c7bf 08ae6cca19a3081f.pdf; Angie Beeman, "Gig Economy or Odd Jobs: What May Seem Trendy to Privileged City Dwellers and Suburbanites is as Old as Poverty," *Counterpunch*, May 22, 2017. Retrieved from www.counterpunch.org/2017/05/22/gig-eco nomy-or-odd-jobs-what-may-seem-trendy-to-privi leged-city-dwellers-and-suburbanites-is-as-old-as -poverty/.

183. Lonnie Golden, *Still Falling Short on Hours and Pay: Part-Time Work Becoming New Normal*, Economic Policy Institute, December 5, 2016. Retrieved from www.epi.org/publication/still-falling-short-on -hours-and-pay-part-time-work-becoming-new-normal/.

184. Oxfam America and Economic Policy Institute, *Few Rewards: An Agenda to Give America's Working Poor a Raise*, 2016. Retrieved from www .oxfamamerica.org/static/media/files/Few_Rewards _Report_2016_web.pdf.

185. National Law Center on Homelessness & Poverty, U.S. Human Rights Network, and UPR Housing Working Group, *Housing and Homelessness in the United States of America*, September 15, 2014. Retrieved from https://nlchp.org/documents/UPR _Housing_Report_2014.

186. Monique Morrissey, *The State of American Retirement: How 401(k)s Have Failed Most American Workers*, Economic Policy Institute, March 3, 2016. Retrieved from www.epi.org/publication/retire ment-in-america/.

187. Francine Blau and Lawrence Kahn, "The Gender Pay Gap: Have Women Gone as Far as They Can?" *Academy of Management Perspectives* 21 (2007): 7–23.

188. Gönkçe Güngör and Monica Biernat, "Gender Bias or Motherhood Disadvantage? Judgements of Blue Collar Mothers and Fathers in the Workplace," *Sex Roles* 60 (2008): 232–46.

189. Bureau of Labor Statistics, "Usual Weekly Earnings of Wage and Salary Workers; First Quarter 2018," Table 5, April 13, 2018. Retrieved from www .bls.gov/news.release/pdf/wkyeng.pdf.

190. "Average Published Undergraduate Charges by Sector, 2017–18," *College Board Advocacy & Policy Center*. Retrieved from https://trends.college board.org/college-pricing/figures-tables/average -published-undergraduate-charges-sector-2017 -18; "Cost of Living in Amsterdam, Netherlands," *Numbeo*. Retrieved from www.numbeo.com/cost-of -living/city_result.jsp?country=Netherlands&city =Amsterdam.

Chapter 13: Politics

1. U.S. Congress. (2017). Congressional Record. 115th Congress, 1st session, February 7, 163(20), pt 2. Retrieved from www.congress.gov/crec/2017 /02/06/CREC-2017-02-06-bk2.pdf.

2. Corey Wrenn, "Woman-as-Cat in Anti-Suffrage Propaganda," *Sociological Images* (December 4, 2013). Retrieved from https://thesocietypages.org/socim ages/2013/12/04/the-feminization-of-the-cat-in-anti -suffrage-propaganda/.

3. Quoted in Hilda Kean, *Animal Rights: Political and Social Change in Britain since 1800* (London: Reaktion Books, 1998).

4. June Purvis, "The Prison Experiences of the Euffragists in Edwardian Britain," *Women's History Review* 4, no. 1 (1995): 103.

5. Janice Tyrwhitt, "Why the Lady Horsewhipped Winston Churchill," *Montreal Gazette*, October 16, 1965, 6–9. Retrieved from http://news.google.com /newspapers?id=C5QtAAAAIBAJ&sjid=Yp8FAAA AIBAJ&pg=6699,4358424&dq=suffragist+mrs+pan khurst+bodyguards&hl=en%20%20; John S. Nash, "The Martial Chronicles: Fighting Like a Girl 2," *Bloody Elbow* (blog), February 23, 2013 (11:14 a.m.). Retrieved from www.bloodyelbow.com/2013/2/23 /4007176/the-martial-chronicles-fighting-like-a-girl -2-the-ju-jutsuffragists.

6. Address to the First Annual Meeting of the American Equal Rights Association, New York City, May 9, 1867.

7. Paula Giddings, *When and Where I Enter: The Impact of Black Women on Race and Sex in America* (New York: Bantam, 1984).

8. Francisco Ramirez, Yasmin Soysal, and S. Shanahan, "The Changing Logic of Political Citizenship: Cross-National Acquisition of Women's Suffrage Rights, 1890 to 1990," *American Sociological Review* 62, no. 5 (1997): 735–45.

9. Asma Alsharif, "Update 2-Saudi King Gives Women Right to Vote," *Reuters*, September 25, 2011. Retrieved from www.reuters.com/article/2011/09/25/saudi-king-women-idUSL5E7KP0IB20110925.

10. Myra Marx Ferree, "Resonance and Radicalism: Feminist Framing in the Abortion Debates of the United States and Germany," *The American Journal of Sociology* 109, no. 2 (2003): 304–44.

11. Lisa Brush, *Gender and Governance* (Walnut Creek: Rowman Altamira, 2003); Louise Chappell, "The State and Governance," in *The Oxford Handbook of Gender and Politics*, ed. Georgina Waylen, Karen Celis, Johanna Kantola, and S. Laurel Weldon (New York: Oxford University Press, 2013).

12. Curtis M. Wong, "Washington State to Offer Non-Binary Option on Birth Certificates." *Huffington Post*, January 5, 2018. Retrieved from www.huffingtonpost.com/entry/washington-nonbinary-sex-gender-option_us_5a4fa70fe4b089e14dba7d48.

13. Jacinta Nandi, "Germany Got It Right by Offering a Third Gender Option on Birth Certificates." *Guardian*. November 10, 2013. Retrieved from www.theguardian.com/commentisfree/2013/nov/10/germany-third-gender-birth-certificate.

14. Staff, "Gender Issues Key to Low Birth Rate." *BBC News*, November 20, 2007. Retrieved from http://news.bbc.co.uk/2/hi/asia-pacific/7096092.stm.

15. Alexandra Harney, "Without Babies, Can Japan Survive?" *New York Times*, December 15, 2012. Retrieved from www.nytimes.com/2012/12/16/opinion/.../without-babies-can-japan-survive.html.

16. Simon Denyer and Annie Gowen, "Too Many Men." *Washington Post*, April 18, 2018. Retrieved from www.washingtonpost.com/graphics/2018/world/too-many-men/?utm_term=.7a0a0c72fbf9.

17. Joe Soss, Richard C. Fording, and Sanford Schram, *Disciplining the Poor: Neoliberal Paternalism and the Persistent Power of Race* (Chicago: University of Chicago Press, 2011).

18. Kristy Kelly, *Learning to Mainstream Gender in Vietnam: Where "Equity" Means "Locality" in Development Policy* (PhD diss., University of Wisconsin, 2010); Elizabeth Schmidt, James H Mittelman, Fantu Cheru, Aili Mari Tripp, "Development in Africa: What Is the Cutting Edge in Thinking and Policy?" *Review of African Political Economy* 36, no. 120 (2009): 273–82.

19. Clare Foran, "How to Design a City for Women," *City Lab, The Atlantic*, September 16, 2013.

20. Organisation for Economic Co-operation and Development (OECD). 2017. "PF2.1: Key Characteristics of Parental Leave Systems." OECD Family Database, Organisation for Economic Co-Operation and Development, Paris, France.

21. Myra Marx Ferree, *Varieties of Feminism: German Gender Politics in Global Perspective* (Stanford: Stanford University Press, 2012).

22. Cecilia Ridgeway, *Framed by Gender: How Gender Inequality Persists in the Modern World* (New York: Oxford University Press, 2011); Michael Kimmel, *Misframing Men: The Contemporary Politics of Masculinity* (New Brunswick: Rutgers University Press, 2010); Raewyn Connell, *Gender: Short Introductions* (Stafford BC, Australia: Polity Press, 2009).

23. Andreas Kotsadam and Henning Finseraas, "The State Intervenes in the Battle of the Sexes: Causal Effects of Paternity Leave," *Social Science Research* 40, no. 6 (2011): 1611–22.

24. Judith Lorber, "Gender Equality: Utopian and Realistic," (plenary address, American Sociological Association Annual Meetings, Denver, CO, August 16, 2012); Barbara Risman, Judith Lorber, and Jessica Sherwood, "Toward a World Beyond Gender: A Utopian Vision" (revised version of remarks presented at American Sociological Association Annual Meetings, Denver, CO., August 16, 2012); Michael Kimmel, "Comments on Risman, Lorber, and Sherwood," (American Sociological Association Annual Meetings, Denver, CO, August 16, 2012).

25. Judith Lorber, *Gender Inequality* (New York: Oxford University Press, 2010).

26. Sarah Childs, "Political Representation," in *The Oxford Handbook of Gender and Politics*, ed. Georgina Waylen, Karen Celis, Johanna Kantola, and S. Laurel Weldon (New York: Oxford University Press, 2013); Aili Tripp, "Political Systems and Gender," in *The Oxford Handbook of Gender and Politics*, ed. Georgina Waylen, Karen Celis, Johanna Kantola, and S. Laurel Weldon (New York: Oxford University Press, 2013); Aili Tripp and Alice Kang, "The Global Impact of Quotas: On the Fast Track to Increased Female Legislative Representation," *Comparative Political Studies* 41, no. 3 (2008): 338–61; Mona Tajali, "Gender Quota Adoption in Postconflict Contexts: An Analysis of Actors and Factors Involved," *Journal of Women, Politics & Policy* 34, no.3 (2013): 261–85; Mona Krook, "Women's Representation in Parliament: A Qualitative Comparative Analysis," *Political Studies* 58, no. 5 (2010): 886–908; Aili Mari

Tripp, *Women and Power in Postconflict Africa* (New York: Cambridge University Press, 2015).

27. Farida Jalalzai, "Women Political Leaders: Past and Present," *Women & Politics* 26, no. 3/4 (2004): 85–108.

28. "Women in Elective Office 2018," *Center for American Women and Politics*. Retrieved from www.cawp.rutgers.edu/women-elective-office-2018.

29. Calculated from "Women in National Parliaments," *Inter-Parliamentary Union*, April 1, 2018. Retrieved from www.ipu.org/wmn-e/classif.htm.

30. The statistics in this paragraph are from the Center for Women in American Politics, Rutgers University. Retrieved from www.cawp.rutgers.edu/fast_facts/levels_of_office/documents/cong.pdf.

31. Caroline Tolbert and Gertrude Steuernagel, "Women Lawmakers, State Mandates and Women's Health," *Women & Politics* 22, no. 1 (2001): 1–39; Pippa Norris and Jovi Lovenduski, "Westminster Women: The Politics of Presence," *Political Studies* 51, no. 1 (2003): 84–102.

32. T. J. Blocker, D. L. Eckberg, "Gender and Environmentalism: Results from the 1993 General Social Survey," *Social Science Quarterly* 78 (1997); 841–58; Kari Norgaard and Richard York, "Gender Equality and State Environmentalism," *Gender & Society* 19, no. 4 (August 2005): 506–22.

33. Debra Dodson, *The Impact of Women in Congress* (New York: Oxford University Press, 2006); Pippa Norris and Jovi Lovenduski, "Westminster Women: The Politics of Presence," *Political Studies* 51, no. 1 (2003): 84–102; Presidential Gender Watch 2016, "Finding Gender in Election 2016: Lessons from Presidential Gender Watch" (2017). Retrieved from http://presidentialgenderwatch.org/wp-content/uploads/2017/05/Finding-Gender-in-Election-2016_Highlights.pdf; Per G. Fredriksson and Le Wang, "Sex and Environmental Policy in the U.S. House of Representatives," *Economics Letters* 113 (2011): 228–30.

34. Christina Ergas and Richard York, "Women's Status and Carbon Dioxide Emissions: A Quantitative Cross-National Analysis," *Social Science Research* 41 (2012): 965–76.

35. Pippa Norris and Jovi Lovenduski, "Westminster Women: The Politics of Presence," *Political Studies* 51, no. 1 (2003): 84–102; Kathleen Bratton and Kerry Haynie, "Agenda Setting and Legislative Success in State Legislatures: The Effects of Gender and Race," *The Journal of Politics* 61, no. 3 (1999): 658–79; Edith Barrett, "The Policy Priorities of African American Women in State Legislatures," *Legislative Studies Quarterly* 20, no. 2 (1995): 223–47; Sarah Gershon, "Communicating Female and Minority Interests Online: A Study of Web Site Issue Discussion among Female, Latino, and African American Members of Congress," *The International Journal of Press/Politics* 13, no. 2 (2008): 120–40; Karen Kaufmann and John Petrocik, "The Changing Politics of American Men: Understanding the Sources of the Gender Gap," *American Journal of Political Science* 43, no. 3 (1999): 864–87.

36. Sarah Poggione, "Exploring Gender Differences in State Legislators' Policy Preferences," *Political Research Quarterly* 57 (2004): 305–14; Barbara Burrell, *A Woman's Place is in the House: Campaigning for Congress in the Feminist Era* (Ann Arbor: University of Michigan Press, 1996); Michele Swers, "Are Congresswomen More Likely to Vote for Women's Issue Bills than Their Male Colleagues?" *Legislative Studies Quarterly* 23 (1998): 435–48; Lyn Kathlene, "Alternative Views of Crime: Legislative Policymaking in Gendered Terms," *Journal of Politics* 57, no. 3 (1995): 696–723; Noelle Norton, "Uncovering the Dimensionality of Gender Voting in Congress," *Legislative Studies Quarterly* 24, no. 1 (1999): 65–86.

37. Karen Kaufmann and John Petrocik, "The Changing Politics of American Men: Understanding the Sources of the Gender Gap," *American Journal of Political Science* 43, no. 3 (1999): 864–87; Laurel Elder, "Contrasting Party Dynamics: A Three-Decade Analysis of the Representation of Democratic Versus Republican Women State legislators," *Social Science Journal* 51, no. 3 (2014): 377–85.

38. Dorothy McBride and Amy Mazur, "Women's Policy Agencies and State Feminism," in *The Oxford Handbook of Gender and Politics*, ed. Georgina Wayne, Karen Celis, Johanna Kantola, and S. Laurel Weldon (New York: Oxford University Press, 2013); Michele Swers, *The Difference Women Make: The Policy Impact of Women in Congress* (Chicago: University of Chicago Press, 2002); Sue Thomas, "The Impact of Women on State Legislative Policies." *The Journal of Politics* 53, no. 4 (1991): 958–76; Thomas Little, Dana Dunn, and Rebecca Deen, "A View from the Top: Gender Differences in Legislative Priorities among State Legislative Leaders." *Women & Politics* 22, no. 4 (2001): 29–50; Leslie Schwindt-Bayer, "Still Supermadres? Gender and the Policy Priorities of Latin American Legislators," *American Journal of Political Science* 50, no. 3 (2006): 570–85; Lena Wängnerud, "Testing the Politics of Presence: Women's Representation in the Swedish Riksdag," *Scandinavian Political Studies* 23, no. 1

(2000): 67–91; Kathleen Bratton and Kerry Haynie, "Agenda Setting and Legislative Success in State Legislatures: The Effects of Gender and Race," *Journal of Politics* 61, no. 3 (1999): 658–79; Kathleen Bratton, "Critical Mass Theory Revisited: The Behavior and Success of Token Women in State Legislatures," *Politics & Gender* 1, no. 1 (2005): 97–125; Jessica Gerrity, Tracy Osborn, and Jeanette Mendez, "Women and Representation: A Different View of the District?" *Politics & Gender* 3 (2007): 179–200; Beth Reingold, *Representing Women: Sex, Gender, and Legislative Behavior in Arizona and California* (Chapel Hill: University of North Carolina Press, 2000); Christina Wolbrecht, *The Politics of Women's Rights: Parties, Positions and Change* (Princeton: Princeton University Press, 2000); Debra Dodson, "Representing Women's Interests in the U.S. House of Representatives," in *Women and Elective Office: Past, Present, and Future*, ed. Sue Thomas and Clyde Wilcox (New York: Oxford University Press, 1998); Laurel Weldon, *When Protest Makes Policy: How Social Movements Represent Disadvantaged Groups* (Ann Arbor: University of Michigan Press, 2014).

39. Sheryl Gay Stolberg, "'It's About Time': A Baby Comes to the Senate Floor," *New York Times*, April 19, 2018. Retrieved from www.nytimes.com/2018/04/19/us/politics/baby-duckworth-senate-floor.html; Laurie Kellman, "Senate Allows Babies in Chamber despite Concerns from Older, Male Senators," *Chicago Tribune*, April 18, 2018. Retrieved from www.chicagotribune.com/news/nationworld/ct-senate-babies-chamber-duckworth-20180418-story.html.

40. Emma-Kate Symons, "Surge of Women Clamoring to Run for Public Office in Wake of 2016 Election," *Women in the World*, May 5, 2017. Retrieved from https://womenintheworld.com/2017/05/05/surge-of-women-clamoring-to-run-for-public-office-in-wake-of-2016-election-outcome/; Emily's List, "Emily's List: More Than 11000 Democratic Women Are Interested in Running for Office So Far This Year." April 23, 2017. Retrieved from www.emilyslist.org/news/entry/11000-women-interested-in-running-for-office-glamour.

41. Margaret Talbot, "The Women Running in the Midterms during the Trump Era," *The New Yorker*, April 18, 2018. Retrieved from www.newyorker.com/news/news-desk/2018-midterm-elections-women-candidates-trump.

42. Kathleen Dolan, *Voting for Women: How the Public Evaluates Women Candidates* (Boulder: Westview Press, 2004); Pamela Paxton, Sheri Kunovich, and Melanie Hughes, "Gender and Politics," *The Annual Review of Sociology* 33 (2007): 263–84; Richard L. Fox, "Congressional Elections: Women's Candidacies and the Road to Gender Parity," in *Gender and Elections*, 2nd ed., ed. S. Carroll and R. Fox (New York: Cambridge University Press, 2010); Jennifer L. Lawless and Kathryn Pearson, "The Primary Reason for Women's Under-Representation: Re-Evaluating the Conventional Wisdom," *Journal of Politics* 70, no. 1 (2008): 67–82; Sarah Anzia and Christopher Berry, "The Jackie (and Jill) Robinson Effect: Why Do Congresswomen Out-Perform Congressmen?" *American Journal of Political Science* 55, no. 3 (2011): 478–93; Richard Selzer, Jody Newman, and Melissa Leighton, *Sex as a Political Variable: Women as Candidates and Voters in U.S. Elections* (Boulder, CO: Lynne Rienner, 1997).

43. Robert Darcy, Janet Clark, and Susan Welch, *Women, Elections, and Representation* (Lincoln: University of Nebraska Press, 1994); Eric Smith and Richard Fox, "The Electoral Fortunes of Women Candidates for Congress," *Political Research Quarterly* 54, no. 1 (2001): 205–21.

44. K. Ahrens (ed.), *Politics, Gender and Conceptual Metaphors* (New York: Palgrave, 2009); Maureen Molloy, "Imagining (the) Difference: Gender, Ethnicity and Metaphors of Nation," *Feminist Review* 51 (Autumn 1995): 94–112; Julie Mostov and Rada Ivekovic (eds.), *From Gender to Nation* (New Delhi: Zubaan Books, 2006); Joane Nagel, *Race, Ethnicity, and Sexuality* (New York: Oxford University Press, 2003).

45. Quoted in Jackson Katz. *Leading Men: Presidential Campaigns and the Politics of Manhood* (Northampton, MA: Interlink Books, 2013).

46. Jackson Katz, *Leading Men: Presidential Campaigns and the Politics of Manhood* (Northampton, MA: Interlink Books, 2013); Meredith Conroy, *Masculinity, Media, and the American Presidency* (New York: Palgrave Macmillan, 2015); Kristin L. Hoganson, *Fighting for American Manhood: How Gender Politics Provoked the Spanish-American and Philippine-American Wars* (New Haven, Yale University Press: 1998); Wendy M. Christensen and Myra Marx Ferree, "Cowboy of the World? Gender Discourse and the Iraq War Debate," *Qualitative Sociology* 31, no. 3 (2008): 287–306.

47. C. J. Pascoe, "Homophobia Linked to Definition of Masculinity," *The Register-Guard*, May 23, 2017. Retrieved from http://registerguard.com/rg/opinion/35604020-78/homophobia-linked-to-definition-of-masculinity.html.csp; C. J. Pascoe, "Who is a Real Man? The Gender of Trumpism," *Masculinities and Social Change*, 6, no. 2 (2017).

48. C. J. Pascoe, "Who is a Real Man? The Gender of Trumpism," *Masculinities and Social Change*, 6, no. 2 (2017).

49. Juliana Menasce Horowitz, Kim Parker, and Renee Stepler, "Wide Partisan Gaps in U.S. Over How Far the Country Has Come on Gender Equality," *Pew Research Center*, October 18, 2017. Retrieved from www.pewsocialtrends.org/2017/10/18/wide-partisan -gaps-in-u-s-over-how-far-the-country-has-come-on -gender-equality/; Pew Research Center, "The Partisan Divide on Political Values Grows Even Wider," October 5, 2017. Retrieved from www.people-press .org/2017/10/05/the-partisan-divide-on-political -values-grows-even-wider/.

50. Matthew J. Streb, Barbara Burrell, Brian Frederick, and Michael A. Genovese, "Social Desirability Effects and Support for a Female American President." *Public Opinion Quarterly* 72, no. 1 (2008): 76–89; Clare Malone, "From 1937 to Hillary Clinton, How Americans Have Felt about a Woman President," *FiveThirtyEight*, June 9, 2016; see also: Myra Marx Ferree, "A Woman for President? Changing Responses 1958–1972," *Public Opinion Quarterly* 38, no. 3 (1974): 390–99; Presidential Gender Watch, "Finding Gender in Election 2016: Lessons from Presidential Gender Watch" (2017). Retrieved from http://oe9e345wags3x5 qikp6dg012.wpengine.netdna-cdn.com/wp-content /uploads/PGW-Finding-Gender_Report_May2017 .pdf; "Madame President: Changing Attitudes about a Woman President," *Roper Center for Public Opinion Research, Cornell University*. Retrieved from https:// ropercenter.cornell.edu/changing-attitudes-about -a-woman-president/.

51. Pew Research Center, "Women and Leadership," January 14, 2015. Retrieved from www.pewsocial trends.org/2015/01/14/chapter-3-obstacles-to -female-leadership/.

52. Leonie Huddy and Nayda Terkildsen, "The Consequences of Gender Stereotypes for Women Candidates at Different Levels and Types of Offices." *Political Research Quarterly* 46, no. 3 (1993): 503–25; David Lublin and Sarah E. Brewer, "The Continuing Dominance of Traditional Gender Roles in Southern Elections." *Social Science Quarterly* 84, no. 2 (2003): 380–96.

53. Greg Sargent, "What Hillary Clinton's Sinking Poll Numbers Really Mean, In One Chart," *Washington Post*, September 2, 2015. Retrieved from https://www.washingtonpost.com/blogs/plum -line/wp/2015/09/02/what-hillarys-sinking-poll -numbers-really-mean-in-one-chart/.

54. Angie Maxwell and Todd Shields, "The Impact of 'Modern Sexism' on the 2016 Presidential Election," 2016 Blair Center Poll. Retrieved from https:// blaircenter.uark.edu/the-impact-of-modern-sexism/; Jarrod Bock, Jennifer Byrd-Craven, Melissa Burkley, "The Role of Sexism in Voting in the 2016 Presidential Election," *Personality and Individual Differences* 119 (December 2017): 189–93; Brain F. Schaffner, Matthew MacWilliams, and Tatishe Nteta, "Explaining White Polarization in the 2016 Vote for President: The Sobering Role of Racism and Sexism," *Political Science Quarterly* 133, no. 1 (2018): 9–34.

55. Carly Wayne, Nicholas Valentino, and Marzia Oceno, "How Sexism Drives Support for Donald Trump," *Washington Post*, October 23, 2016. Retrieved from www.washingtonpost.com/news/monkey-cage /wp/2016/10/23/how-sexism-drives-support-for -donald-trump/?utm_term=.26bf74b843b1.

56. Dan Cassino, "Some Men Feel the Need to Compensate for Relative Loss of Income to Women. How They Do so Varies," *Council on Contemporary Families*, March 30, 2017. Retrieved from https://contem poraryfamilies.org/3-cassino-men-compensate-for -income-to-women/.

57. Carl Bialik, "How Unconscious Sexism Could Help Explain Trump's Win," *FiveThirtyEight*, January 21, 2017. Retrieved from https://fivethirtyeight .com/features/how-unconscious-sexism-could-help -explain-trumps-win/.

58. Daniel Denvir, "Why Women Are Still Voting for Trump, despite his Misogyny," *Vox*, October 25, 2016. Retrieved from www.vox.com/conversations /2016/10/25/13384528/donald-trump-women-steph anie-coontz.

59. Brian F. Schaffner, Matthew MacWilliams, and Tatishe Nteta, "Explaining White Polarization in the 2016 Vote for President: The Sobering Role of Racism and Sexism," *Political Science Quarterly* 133, no. 1 (2018): 9–34.

60. Alec Tyson and Shiva Maniam, "Behind Trump's Victory: Divisions by Race, Gender, Education," *Pew Research Center*, November 9, 2016. Retrieved from www.pewresearch.org/fact-tank/2016/11/09/be hind-trumps-victory-divisions-by-race-gender-edu cation/; Richa Chaturvedi, "A Closer Look at the Gender Gap in Presidential Voting," *Pew Research Center*, July 28, 2016. Retrieved from www.pewre search.org/fact-tank/2016/07/28/a-closer-look-at-the -gender-gap-in-presidential-voting/; Kei Kawashima-Ginsberg, "How Gender Mattered to Millennials in the 2016 Election and Beyond," *The Society Pages*,

paper presented at the Council on Contemporary Families Online Symposium on Gender and Millennials, March 31, 2017. Retrieved from https://thesocietypages.org/ccf/2017/05/23/how-gender-mattered-to-millennials-in-the-2016-election-and-beyond/.

61. Kei Kawashima-Ginsberg, "How Gender Mattered to Millennials in the 2016 Election and Beyond," *The Society Pages*, paper presented at the Council on Contemporary Families Online Symposium on Gender and Millennials, March 31, 2017. Retrieved from https://thesocietypages.org/ccf/2017/05/23/how-gender-mattered-to-millennials-in-the-2016-election-and-beyond/.

62. Ibid.

63. Jeannie B. Thomas, "Dumb Blondes, Dan Quayle, and Hillary Clinton: Gender, Sexuality, and Stupidity in Jokes," *The Journal of American Folklore*, 110, no. 437 (1997): 277–313.

64. Chase Purdy, "The Blatantly Sexist Cookie Bake-Off that Has Haunted Hillary Clinton for Two Decades Is Back," *Quartz Media*, August 21, 2016. Retrieved from https://qz.com/762881/the-blatantly-sexist-cookie-bake-off-that-has-haunted-hillary-clinton-for-two-decades-is-back/; Susan Jeanne Douglas, *Where the Girls Are: Growing Up Female With the Mass Media* (New York: Three Rivers Press, 1994).

65. Samantha Smith, "In Trump Era, Women's Views of Nation's Prospects Take a Negative Turn," Pew Research Center, May 15, 2017. Retrieved from www.pewresearch.org/fact-tank/2017/05/15/in-trump-era-womens-views-of-nations-prospects-take-a-negative-turn/.

66. Kei Kawashima-Ginsberg, "How Gender Mattered to Millennials in the 2016 Election and Beyond," *The Society Pages*, paper presented at the Council on Contemporary Families Online Symposium on Gender and Millennials, March 31, 2017. Retrieved from https://thesocietypages.org/ccf/2017/05/23/how-gender-mattered-to-millennials-in-the-2016-election-and-beyond/.

67. Daniel Cox and Robert P. Jones, "Support for Impeachment Grows; Half of Americans Believe Russia Interfered with Election," Public Religion Research Institute, August 17, 2017. Retrieved from www.prri.org/research/poll-trump-russia-investigation-impeachment-republican-party/.

68. Raewyn Connell, "Change among the Gatekeepers: Men, Masculinities, and Gender Equality in the Global Arena," *Signs* 30, no. 3 (2005): 1801–25.

69. Constance Grady, "The Waves of Feminism, and Why People Keep Fighting over Them, Explained," *Vox*, March 20, 2018. Retrieved from www.vox.com/2018/3/20/16955588/feminism-waves-explained-first-second-third-fourth.

70. Kristen Goss, *The Paradox of Gender Equality: How American Women's Groups Gained and Lost their Public Voice* (Ann Arbor: University of Michigan Press, 2013); Nancy Cott, *The Grounding of Modern Feminism* (New Haven: Yale University Press, 1989).

71. Elisabeth Clemons, *The People's Lobby* (Chicago: University of Chicago Press, 1997); Kristen Goss, *The Paradox of Gender Equality: How American Women's Groups Gained and Lost their Public Voice* (Ann Arbor: University of Michigan Press, 2013).

72. Jo Freeman, *The Politics of Women's Liberation* (Chicago: University of Chicago Press, 1976).

73. Harry Boyte and Sara Evans, *Free Spaces: The Sources of Democratic Change in America* (Chicago: Chicago University Press, 1986); Jane J. Mansbridge and Aldon Morris, eds., *Oppositional Consciousness: The Subjective Roots of Social Problems* (Chicago: Chicago University Press, 2001).

74. Jocelyn Olcutt, *International Women's Year: The Greatest Consciousness-Raising Event in History* (New York: Oxford University Press, 2017).

75. Miriam Liss, Carolyn Hoffner, and Mary Crawford, "What Do Feminists Believe?" *Psychology of Women Quarterly* 24 (2000): 279–84; C. Cockburn, "Equal Opportunities: The Short and Long Agenda," *Industrial Relations Journal* 20, no. 3 (1989): 213–25; M. Callaghan, C. Cranmer, M. Rowan, G. Siann, and F. Wilson, "'Feminism in Scotland: Self Identification and Stereotypes', *Gender & Education* 11, no. 2 (1999): 161–77; A. Thomas, "The Significance of Gender Politics in Men's Accounts of Their 'Gender Identity,'" in *Men, Masculinities and Social Theory*, ed. J. Hearn and D. Morgan (London: Unwin Hyman, 1990), 143–59; Susan Faludi, *Backlash: The Undeclared War against American Women* (New York: Crown, 1990); Myra Ferree and Beth B. Hess. *Controversy and Coalition: The New Feminist Movement across Four Decades of Change*, 3rd ed. (New York: Routledge, 1995).

76. "The United Nations Fourth World Conference on Women: Platform for Action," *United Nations Entity for Gender Equality and the Empowerment of Women*, September 1995. Retrieved from www.un.org/womenwatch/daw/beijing/platform/plat1.htm.

77. Myra Marx Ferree and Beth B. Hess, *Controversy and Coalition: The New Feminist Movement across Four Decades of Change*, 3rd ed., (New York: Routledge, 2000).

78. Douglas Frantz and Sam Fulwood III, "Senators' Private Deal Kept '2nd Woman' Off TV: Thomas: Democrats Feared Republican Attacks on Angela Wright's Public Testimony. Biden's Handling of the Hearing is Criticized," *Los Angeles Times*, October 17, 1991. Retrieved from http://articles.latimes.com/1991-10-17/news/mn-911_1_angela-wright.

79. Susan Hansen, "Talking About Politics: Gender and Contextual Effects on Political Proselytizing," *Journal of Politics* 59, no. 1 (1997): 73–103.

80. Constance Grady, "The Waves of Feminism, and Why People Keep Fighting over Them, Explained," *Vox*, March 20, 2018. Retrieved from www.vox.com/2018/3/20/16955588/feminism-waves-explained-first-second-third-fourth.

81. Jo Reger, *Everywhere and Nowhere: Contemporary Feminism in the United States* (New York: Oxford University Press, 2012).

82. Jennifer Baumgardner and Amy Richards, *Manifesta: Young Women, Feminism and the Future* (New York: Farrar, Straus and Giroux, 2000); Astrid Henry, *Not My Mother's Sister: Generational Conflict and Third Wave Feminism* (Bloomington: Indiana University Press, 2004); Leslie Heywood and Jennifer Drake, *Third Wave Agenda: Being Feminist, Doing Feminism* (Minneapolis: University of Minnesota Press, 1997).

83. Christina Ewig and Myra Marx Ferree, "Feminist Organizing: What's Old, What's New? History, Trends, and Issues," in *The Oxford Handbook of Gender and Politics*, ed. Georgina Waylen, Karen Celis, Johanna Kantola, and S. Laurel Weldon (New York: Oxford University Press, 2013), 437–61; Jo Reger, *Everywhere and Nowhere: Contemporary Feminism in the United States* (New York: Oxford University Press, 2012); Barbara Risman, *Where the Millennials Will Take Us* (New York: Oxford University Press, 2018); Rebecca Walker, ed., *To Be Real: Telling the Truth and Changing the Face of Feminism* (New York: Anchor, 1995); Leslie Heywood and Jennifer Drake, *Third Wave Agenda: Being Feminist, Doing Feminism* (Minneapolis: University of Minnesota Press, 1997); Clare Snyder, "What Is Third-Wave Feminism? A New Directions Essay," *Signs* 34, no. 1 (2008): 175–96; Jean M. Twenge, *Generation Me: Why Today's Young Americans Are More Confident, Assertive, Entitled–And More Miserable than Ever Before* (New York: Simon & Schuster, 2006); Charlotte Kro-løkke and Anne Scott Sørensen, "Three Waves of Feminism: From Suffragettes to Grrls," in *Gender Communication Theories & Analyses: From Silence to Performance* (Thousand Oaks: SAGE Publications, 2006), 1–25.

84. Myra Marx Ferree and Patricia Yancey Martin (eds.), *Feminist Organizations: Harvest of the New Women's Movement* (Philadelphia: Temple University Press, 1995).

85. Christina Ewig and Myra Marx Ferree, "Feminist Organizing: What's Old, What's New? History, Trends, and Issues," in *The Oxford Handbook of Gender and Politics*, ed. Georgina Waylen, Karen Celis, Johanna Kantola, and S. Laurel Weldon (New York: Oxford University Press, 2013); Jennifer Baumgardner and Amy Richards, *Manifesta: Young Women, Feminism and the Future* (New York: Farrar, Straus and Giroux, 2000).

86. Jo Reger, *Everywhere and Nowhere: Contemporary Feminism in the United States* (New York: Oxford University Press, 2012).

87. Natalie Jarvey, "Sexual Assault Movement #MeToo Reaches Nearly 500,000 Tweets," *Hollywood Reporter*, October 16, 2017. Retrieved from www.hollywoodreporter.com/news/metoo-sexual-assault-movement-reaches-500000-tweets-1049235.

88. *CBS/Associated Press*, "More than 12M 'Me Too' Facebook Posts, Comments Reactions in 24 Hours," *CBS*, October 17, 2017. Retrieved from www.cbsnews.com/news/metoo-more-than-12-million-facebook-posts-comments-reactions-24-hours/.

89. *The New York Times* Editorial Board, "For Women, It's Not Just the O'Reilly Problem," April 22, 2017. Retrieved from www.nytimes.com/2017/04/22/opinion/sunday/for-women-its-not-just-the-oreilly-problem.html; Kathryn Casteel, "Sexual Harassment Isn't Just a Silicon Valley Problem," *FiveThirtyEight*, July 13, 2017. Retrieved from https://fivethirtyeight.com/features/sexual-harassment-isnt-just-a-silicon-valley-problem/.

90. Human Rights Campaign, "Sexual Assault and the LGBTQ Community," *Human Rights Campaign*, 2018. Retrieved from www.hrc.org/resources/sexual-assault-and-the-lgbt-community.

91. J. R. Thorpe, "This Is How Many People Have Posted 'Me Too' since October, According to New Data," *Bustle*, December 1, 2017. Retrieved from www.bustle.com/p/this-is-how-many-people-have-posted-me-too-since-october-according-to-new-data-6753697; *The Conversation*, "#MeToo Is Riding a

New Wave of Feminism in India," *The Conversation*, February 1, 2018. Retrieved from http://theconversation.com/metoo-is-riding-a-new-wave-of-feminism-in-india-89842; Pardis Mahdavi, "How #MeToo Became a Global Movement," *Foreign Affairs*, March 6, 2018. Retrieved from www.foreignaffairs.com/articles/2018-03-06/how-metoo-became-global-movement.

92. Nancy Whittier, "Activism against Sexual Violence Is Central to a New Women's Movement: Resistance to Trump, Campus Sexual Assault, and #MeToo," *Gender & Society*, February 7, 2018. Retrieved from https://gendersociety.wordpress.com/2018/02/07/activism-against-sexual-violence-is-central-to-a-new-womens-movement-resistance-to-trump-campus-sexual-assault-and-metoo/.

93. Tamara Shepherd, Alison Harvey, Tim Jordan, Sam Srauy, and Kate Miltner, "Histories of Hating," *Social Media + Society* 1, no. 2 (2015): 1–10; Emma A. Jane, *Misogyny Online: A Short (and Brutish) History* (London: SAGE Swifts, 2017); Becky Gardiner, Mahana Mansfield, Ian Anderson, Josh Holder, Daan Louter, and Monica Ulmanu, "The Dark Side of Guardian Comments," *Guardian*, April 12, 2016. Retrieved from https://www.theguardian.com/technology/2016/apr/12/the-dark-side-of-guardian-comments.

94. David Futrelle, "When a Mass Murderer Has a Cult Following," *The Cut*, April 27, 2018. Retrieved from www.thecut.com/2018/04/incel-meaning-rebellion-alex-minassian-elliot-rodger-reddit.html; Hailey Branson-Potts and Richard Winton, "How Elliot Rodger Went from Misfit Mass Murderer to 'Saint' for Group of Misogynists—and Suspected Toronto Killer," *Los Angeles Times*, April 26, 2018. Retrieved from www.latimes.com/local/lanow/la-me-ln-elliot-rodger-incel-20180426-story.html.

95. Maeve Duggan, "Online Harassment 2017," *Pew Research Center*, July 11, 2017. Retrieved from www.pewinternet.org/2017/07/11/online-harassment-2017/.

96. Quoted in Amanda Hess, "Why Women Aren't Welcome on the Internet," *Pacific Standard*, January 6, 2014. Retrieved from https://psmag.com/social-justice/women-arent-welcome-internet-72170#.Usq9QZi5wZA.twitter.

97. Amanda Hess, "Why Women Aren't Welcome on the Internet," *Pacific Standard*, January 6, 2014. Retrieved from https://psmag.com/social-justice/women-arent-welcome-internet-72170#.Usq9QZi5wZA.twitter; Adrienne Massanari, "#Gamergate and the Fappening: How Reddit's Algorithm, Governance, and Culture Support Toxic Technocultures," *New Media & Society*, 19, no. 3 (2017): 329–46.

98. Jean M. Twenge, *Generation Me: Why Today's Young Americans Are More Confident, Assertive, Entitled–And More Miserable than Ever Before* (New York: Simon & Schuster, 2006); Jo Reger, *Everywhere and Nowhere: Contemporary Feminism in the United States* (New York: Oxford University Press, 2012).

99. Barbara Risman, *Where the Millennials Will Take Us* (New York: Oxford University Press, 2018); See also Kei Kawashima-Ginsberg, "How Gender Mattered to Millennials in the 2016 Election and Beyond," Council on Contemporary Families, May 23, 2017. Retrieved from https://thesocietypages.org/ccf/2017/05/23/how-gender-mattered-to-millennials-in-the-2016-election-and-beyond/.

100. Andi Zeisler, *We Were Feminists Once: From Riot Grrrl to Cover Girl, the Buying and Selling of a Political Movement* (New York: Public Affairs, 2016).

101. Samantha Murphy Kelly, "Viral Dove Campaign Becomes Most Watched Ad Ever," *Mashable*, May 20, 2013. Retrieved from http://mashable.com/2013/05/20/dove-ad-most-watche/.

102. Emily Jane Fox, "Ivanka Trump Has Her Own 'Woman' Problem Now," *Vanity Fair*, August 8, 2016. Retrieved from www.vanityfair.com/news/2016/08/ivanka-trump-maternity-leave.

103. Krithika Varagur, "Revealed: Reality of Life Working in an Ivanka Trump Clothing Factory," *Guardian*, June 13, 2017. Retrieved from www.theguardian.com/us-news/2017/jun/13/revealed-reality-of-a-life-working-in-an-ivanka-trump-clothing-factory?CMP=share_btn_tw.

104. James Mills, "Exposed: Sweatshop 'Slaves' Earning Just 44p an Hour Making 'Empowering' Beyonce Clobber," *Sun*, May 7, 2016. Retrieved from www.thesun.co.uk/archives/news/1176905/exposed-sweatshop-slaves-earning-just-44p-an-hour-making-empowering-beyonce-clobber/.

105. Jess Cartner-Morley, "Beyoncé Stamps Her Unmistakable Brand on Sportswear Fashion," *Guardian*, April 1, 2016. Retrieved from www.theguardian.com/fashion/2016/apr/01/beyonce-stamps-her-unmistakable-brand-on-sportswear-fashion.

106. Carrie Rentschler, "Doing Feminism in the Network: Networked Laughter and the 'Binders Full of Women' Meme," *Feminist Theory* 16, no. 3 (2015): 329–59.

107. The Guttmacher Institute, May 11, 2017. Retrieved from www.guttmacher.org/united-states/abortion/state-policies-abortion.

108. Rachel K. Jones and Jenna Jerman, "Abortion Incidence and Service Availability in the United States, 2014," *Perspectives on Sexual and Reproductive Health* 49, no. 1 (2017): doi: 10.1363/psrh.12015.

109. Hannah Katch, Jessica Schubel, and Matt Broaddus, "Medicaid Works for Women—But Proposed Cuts Would Have Harsh, Disproportionate Impact," Center on Budget and Policy Priorities, May 11, 2017. Retrieved from www.cbpp.org/research/health/medicaid-works-for-women-but-proposed-cuts-would-have-harsh-disproportionate-impact.

110. Sikata Banerjee, "Gender and Nationalism: the Masculinization of Hinduism and Female Political Participation in India," *Women's Studies International Forum* 26 no. 2 (2003): 167–79; Nira Yuval-Davis, *Gender & Nation* (Thousand Oaks: SAGE Publications, 1997); Mieke Verloo, ed., *Varieties of Opposition to Gender Equality in Europe* (New York: Routledge, 2018).

111. Nira Yuval-Davis, *Gender & Nation* (Thousand Oaks: SAGE Publications, 1997); Mieke Verloo, ed., *Varieties of Opposition to Gender Equality in Europe* (New York: Routledge, 2018); Pankaj Mishra, "The Crisis in Modern Masculinity," *Guardian*, March 17, 2018. Retrieved from www.theguardian.com/books/2018/mar/17/the-crisis-in-modern-masculinity.

112. Joshau Kurlantzick, *Democracy in Retreat: The Revolt of the Middle Class and the Worldwide Decline of Representative Government* (New Haven: Yale University Press, 2013).

113. "Democracy Continues Its Disturbing Retreat," *The Economist*, January 31, 2018. Retrieved from www.economist.com/blogs/graphicdetail/2018/01/daily-chart-21.

114. Erica Chenoweth and Jeremy Pressman, "This Is What We Learned by Counting the Women's Marches," *Washington Post*, February 7, 2017. Retrieved from www.washingtonpost.com/news/monkey-cage/wp/2017/02/07/this-is-what-we-learned-by-counting-the-womens-marches/; Farah Stockman, "Women's March on Washington Opens Contentious Dialogues about Race," *New York Times*, January 9, 2017. Retrieved from www.nytimes.com/2017/01/09/us/womens-march-on-washington-opens-contentious-dialogues-about-race.html.

115. Banu Gökarıksel and Sara Smith, "Intersectional Feminism beyond U.S. Flag Hijab and Pussy Hats in Trump's America," *Gender, Place & Culture* 24, no. 5 (2017): 628–44.

116. Women's March, "Principles," May 11, 2017. Retrieved from www.womensmarch.com/.

117. Conor Friedersdorf, "The Significance of Millions in the Streets," *The Atlantic*, January 23, 2017. Retrieved from www.theatlantic.com/politics/archive/2017/01/the-significance-of-millions-in-the-streets/514091/.

118. Dawn M. Dow, Dana R. Fisher, and Rashawn Roy, "This Is What Democracy Looks Like!" *The Society Pages*, February 6, 2017. Retrieved from https://thesocietypages.org/socimages/2017/02/06/this-is-what-democracy-looks-like/.

119. Julia Reinstein, "45 Clever Signs from the 2018 Women's March," *Buzzfeed*, January 20, 2018. Retrieved from www.buzzfeed.com/juliareinstein/womens-march-2018-signs?utm_term=.ldGleL81R#.paOjXzlA2.

120. Alanna Vagianos and Damon Dahlen, "89 Badass Feminist Signs from the Women's March on Washington," *Huffington Post*, January 21, 2017. Retrieved from www.huffingtonpost.com/entry/89-badass-feminist-signs-from-the-womens-march-on-washington_us_5883ea28e4b070d8cad310cd; Sebastian Murdock, "Signs for the 2018 Women's March Prove the Movement Is Here to Stay," *Huffington Post*, January 20, 2018. Retrieved from www.huffingtonpost.com/entry/signs-2018-womens-march-movement_us_5a6371d9e4b0e56300701d7c.

121. Greta J., "10+ Nasty Grandmas Who Can't Believe They Still Have to March for Women's Rights," *Bored Panda*. Retrieved from www.boredpanda.com/grandmas-still-fighting-women-rights-marching-donald-trump/.

122. *Los Angeles Times*, "Signposts from the Women's March—Angry, Ironic and Sometimes Really Funny," January 20, 2018, Retrieved from http://www.latimes.com/nation/la-na-womens-march-signs-20180120-story.html

123. Debra Dodson, *The Impact of Women in Congress* (New York: Oxford University Press, 2006); Laurel Weldon, *When Protest Makes Policy: How Social Movements Represent Disadvantaged Groups* (Ann Arbor: University of Michigan Press, 2014); Laurel Weldon, *Protest, Policy, and the Problem of Violence against Women: A Cross-National Comparison* (Pittsburgh: University of Pittsburgh Press, 2002).

Chapter 14: Conclusion

1. C. Wright Mills, *The Sociological Imagination* (New York: Oxford University Press, 1959).

2. Scott Richardson, "Blurred Lines of a Different Kind: Sexism, Sex, Media and Kids," in *Gender and Pop Culture: A Text-Reader*, ed. Adrienne Trier-Bieniek and Patricia Leavy (Rotterdam, the Netherlands: Sense Publishers, 2014), 27–52.

3. Kathleen Gerson, *Hard Choices: How Women Decide about Work, Career, and Motherhood* (Berkeley: University of California Press, 1986); Barbara Risman, *Gender Vertigo: American Families in Transition* (New Haven: Yale University Press, 1998); Christopher Carrington, *No Place like Home: Relationships and Family Life among Lesbians and Gay Men* (Chicago: University of Chicago Press, 1999), 32.

4. Gloria Steinem, *Outrageous Acts and Everyday Rebellions* (New York: Henry Holt and Company, 1995).

5. Heather Karjane, Bonnie Fisher, and Francis Cullen, *Sexual Assault on Campus: What Colleges and Universities Are Doing about It* (Washington, D.C.: U.S. Department of Justice, 2005). Retrieved from www.ncjrs.gov/pdffiles1/nij/205521.pdf.

6. Quoted in Frank Sommers and Tana Dineen, *Curing Nuclear Madness: A New Age Prescription for Personal Action* (United Kingdom: Methuen, 1984), 158.

7. Joan Williams, *Unbending Gender: Why Family and Work Conflict and What To Do About It* (New York: Oxford University Press, 2000), 242.

8. Barbara Risman, *Gender Vertigo: American Families in Transition* (New Haven: Yale University Press, 1999).

CREDITS

INDEX